Study Guide

Cornelius Rea
Douglas College and
Simon Fraser University

Study Guide

to accompany

FIFTH EDITION
PSYCHOLOGY

Don H. Hockenbury
Sandra E. Hockenbury

WORTH PUBLISHERS

Study Guide
by Cornelius Rea
to accompany
Hockenbury and Hockenbury: **Psychology**, Fifth Edition

Printed in the United States of America

ISBN 10: 1-4292-3060-6
ISBN 13: 978-1-4292-3060-5

First printing

Worth Publishers
41 Madison Avenue
New York, NY 10010

Contents

To the Student

This Study Guide is designed to help you to study effectively and to learn the important concepts in *Psychology*, Fifth Edition, by Don and Sandy Hockenbury. Use this study guide in an active manner and as a complement to the textbook, not as a substitute for it. By actively interacting with the text material and this study guide, you will be able to master the chapter concepts in a straightforward and enjoyable manner. Our goal is to create independent, motivated students who enjoy learning for its own sake, who can think critically, and who have a deep conceptual understanding of the information presented in the text.

Your first course in psychology is very exciting but it is also challenging. Besides the volume of new information you will be asked to learn, you are faced with learning new terminology, novel concepts, unfamiliar theories, and, most important, the scientific way of thinking. "How to Use This Guide" explains how best to use the study guide to learn all the new material. "Study Tips" (p. ix) provides some practical suggestions for improving your ability to learn, understand, and remember.

HOW TO USE THIS GUIDE

Scanning

Scanning is a useful strategy that can facilitate learning. When you scan a chapter, you get a better idea of what lies ahead. So survey the text chapter first. Spend some time looking at the graphics, and examine the special features, boxed inserts, and concept reviews; note the parts that look interesting to you. Pay attention to the diagrams, graphs, photographs, cartoons, and tables. This preview will give you a clearer impression of what is going to be covered in the chapter. Don't worry about the details at this point; just try to get the big picture.

Next read the chapter overview (Chapter . . . At a Glance) in the study guide. This will give you a general, but more detailed, summary of what you are about to encounter in the chapter. This type of previewing activity will help you to develop a conceptual framework (or cognitive map) that will allow you to more readily understand the details of what you are about to read and will make learning the material easier. For example, imagine trying to put together a large jigsaw puzzle without knowing what the finished picture looked like. Do you think it would be easier if you could see the finished picture? Of course it would! Likewise, when you scan the chapter and read the preview, you will have some idea of the big picture and of how the various pieces of the chapter fit together.

Advance Organizers and Preview Questions

The text authors have provided advance organizers at the beginning of each major section of a chapter in the form of key questions/key themes. These will help you to start thinking about the material and will give you an overview of what lies ahead. The preview questions at the beginning of each main section in the study guide are derived from these advance organizers. Read these preview questions before you read each section of the text chapter and before you start the exercises in the study guide. Both the advance organizers and the preview questions are directly linked to the concept checks, true/false tests, matching exercises, progress tests, and graphic organizers in the study guide. Successful completion of these activities will prepare you for tests, quizzes, exams, and other evaluation procedures.

Structured Note Taking

Good note taking is very important to learning. So we encourage you to take notes. The study guide structures your note taking by prompting you to write definitions, to paraphrase information, and to integrate concepts. Simply highlighting sentences in the textbook is not sufficient. Highlighting does not involve active cognitive processing of the information, whereas writing, especially using your own words, does.

Graphic Organizers

An important aid to better understanding text material is the use of visualization. Completing the graphs, charts, and flow diagrams will provide a visual synopsis that will help you understand and remember the material. So be sure to complete all these exercises, and practice making up your own graphic organizers.

Corrective Feedback: Concept Checks, Matching Exercises, True/False Tests, and Progress Tests

At the end of each major section in the study guide are learning checks in the form of conceptual questions, matching exercises, and true/false tests. These exercises provide you with feedback as you progress through the chapter. Be sure to complete each of these before going on to the next section. Three progress tests containing multiple-choice questions conclude each chapter. These are designed to help you assess your mastery of the material. If you don't know the answers to these questions, go back and study the parts of the text that you didn't understand.

If your instructor gives a quiz or test after each chapter, complete all three progress tests before the exam. Testing, and the corrective feedback it provides, will give you a more realistic idea of how well prepared you actually are and thus reduces the tendency for "overconfidence."

If your exam covers a number of chapters, it is a good idea to complete progress tests 1 and 2 after you have studied each chapter, then create a "comprehensive pretest" from progress test 3 in all the relevant chapters. Taking this larger test will give you a better idea of what the exam is going to be like. Also, be sure to ask your instructor if material other than that covered in the textbook (e.g., material from lectures, videos, lab demonstrations, and tutorials) will be on the exam.

One additional point: It is important not to confuse your recognition ability with your ability to recall and write about a topic. Multiple-choice questions tap your ability to recognize the correct answer, but do not assess your ability to express your ideas logically and coherently. You need to develop both types of skills.

Something to Think About

Each study guide chapter concludes with a special feature called Something to Think About, which contains thought-provoking questions about the material. We encourage you to think actively about what you have read in the chapter. Discuss these topics with friends and family members. This will help you remember the concepts and make learning more enjoyable.

You can also use the ideas from these sections as a guide for writing short essays or papers or for preparing for a presentation.

Answers   The answers to all the questions are included at the end of each chapter. Check your answers as you work your way through the material: Getting immediate corrective feedback facilitates the learning process.

STUDY TIPS   What are the five or ten most effective ways to improve your ability to learn, comprehend, and remember the material in this course? The truth is that there is probably no single list of techniques, no matter who develops it, that will work for all learners all the time. Everyone has a different way or style of learning; becoming familiar with your own unique learning style is the first step in becoming a successful student. However, we can all improve our ability to learn and to remember what we have learned. On that optimistic note, here are some general strategies that can be of value and can benefit almost anyone who makes the effort to use them. So, when faced with the challenge of mastering a large amount of new material try some, or all, of the following (For additional information about how your memory works and how to improve it, look ahead to text Chapter 6; in particular, read the Application "Superpower Memory in Minutes Per Day."

Use Distributed Practice   You know that you should not cram. Cramming, or what psychologists called massed practice, is not good for long-term retention of material. Spacing out your studying, or distributed practice, on the other hand, enhances your ability to remember. This is one of the most well-established principles in psychology—the spacing effect. Instead of studying for five straight hours at one time, you would be much better off studying one hour a day over five days. This technique also works at shorter intervals. For example, if you have to memorize a formula, you will probably repeat it over and over (say, ten times) until you feel confident you have it memorized. This, of course, is massed practice, and the sense of confidence that typically accompanies it is often misleading. A better way to maximize the benefits of those ten rehearsals is to space them over time, allowing a longer interval after each rehearsal than the one before.

Reduce Interference   One reason we tend to forget new information is that other information (either previously learned or learned later) can interfere with the material we are trying to master. So, if you are studying for a number of courses at the same time, try to study subjects that are different from each other. The more similar they are, the greater the interference. Another source of interference comes from social activities, such as watching TV or interacting with friends. When you engage in these activities after studying, you increase the risk of interference. In addition, playing loud music, having the TV on, or listening to other people's conversations while you are studying can cause distraction and interfere with learning. The best advice? Go to sleep after studying. A good sleep is the best way to cut down on interference and it helps consolidate memories. The worst thing to do? Stay up all night cramming for an exam that is being given the next day.

Try Overlearning   Overlearning is another very effective, and relatively simple, technique for preventing forgetting. When you feel you have mastered the material in a chapter, and you have just answered all the progress test questions correctly, you usually feel relieved and put away the books. It is at this point, however, that overlearning is useful. If you had spent, say, an hour and a half getting to this level, what you need to do now is spend another 10 to 15 minutes reviewing the material one more time. These few extra minutes of studying are the most beneficial minutes you can spend in terms of consolidating your memory and preventing the forgetting of material you have just learned. Hermann Ebbinghaus showed, over a hundred years ago, that most of the information is lost very soon after it is learned. He was the first to demonstrate the powerful effect of overlearning as a way of dealing with this problem.

Get Corrective Feedback

If you studied hard and felt you really knew the material, it is a bit of a shock to find that you did poorly on the test. What could have happened? One possibility is that you only thought you knew the material and you were suffering from "the overconfidence effect." A simple way of preventing this is to get corrective feedback on what you know before taking the exam. For example, using the True/False tests and the Matching Tests, completing the Graphic Organizers, and, of course, taking the Progress Tests will give you the feedback you need.

Be aware, however, that this is not necessarily a perfect gauge of how you will do on the real exam. When you are testing yourself, you tend to be in a much more relaxed state: You have just studied the material and you are in no particular rush. If you make a mistake, it is no big deal; you can simply look up the answers at the end of the chapter (this is not something that you can do in the exam!). These factors often lead students to the false conclusion that the questions on the real exam were much harder than the ones in the progress tests, sample exams, and so forth. Try to make your self-testing as real as possible (get a little anxious); that way you will benefit most from corrective feedback.

Use Mnemonics

Use of memory aids, called mnemonics, can help in memorizing new material and in preventing forgetting. Visual imagery, in particular, is very effective with some material. Try to vividly imagine what it is you are attempting to memorize. A picture is worth a thousand words and is much more memorable. For other material, try making up a story that links elements together. Create acronyms for lists of terms or complex concept names, for example (it is easier to remember SCUBA than self-contained underwater breathing apparatus).

Develop Good Study Habits

Most top students get good grades because of effective study habits (not sheer brilliance). Evaluate your current study habits. Manage your time effectively. Remember, we are usually poor judges about how long things take to do (late papers are a typical example that is the result of our poor judgment). So, after you have made your plans, allow yourself some extra time.

Make studying a priority and firmly commit to doing well in school. Don't let other people interfere with your goal of mastering the material and getting good grades. Study by yourself (too much socializing takes place in study groups). Reward yourself with social activities, if that's what is important to you, AFTER you have successfully completed your study and have achieved an A+ on the progress tests. If you like music, play soft instrumental music. Take a short break after an hour or so of studying—walk around for a few minutes. Do some exercise. Don't study when you are sleep deprived, very tired, or stressed out. If you are getting nowhere and can't concentrate on the material, do something else for a while (a breath of fresh air, a brief nap, a little walk, a chat with a friend, a little meditation or exercise, can all be helpful).

Try Exercise Exercising before you study will help relieve stress and will induce a more relaxed state. This is because exercise causes the brain to release pain-killing chemicals called endorphins (you have your own little drug-producing factory). It is also a good idea to exercise before a major exam for the same reasons. If aerobic exercise is not your thing (if it makes you tired and unable to concentrate), try something less strenuous, like walking. Anxiety interferes with performance, so anything you can do to effectively control and reduce your anxiety will help. Have fun, good luck, and enjoy your introductory psychology course.

Comments are welcome at StudyGuide@DiscoveringPsychology.com.

Study Guide

CHAPTER 1

Introduction and Research Methods

<table>
<tr>
<td>PREVIEW</td>
<td>Reading the section below first will give you a general sense of the chapter's contents and an initial introduction to some of the major concepts and terms. This will prime you for what you are about to read and help you to develop a "cognitive map" that will guide your study of the material in this chapter. Likewise, reading the preview questions at the beginning of each major section will improve your ability to understand, learn, and retain the information.</td>
</tr>
</table>

CHAPTER 1 . . . AT A GLANCE   Chapter 1 first defines psychology, then gives a brief history of the people and events that influenced its development. Beginning with the contributions of philosophy and physiology, the chapter discusses the two early schools, structuralism and functionalism, as well as psychoanalysis, behaviorism, and humanistic psychology; the emergence of the major perspectives in contemporary psychology; and the major specialty areas.

The four goals of psychology are used to introduce the scientific method. The descriptive research methods are outlined, and some advantages are discussed. Important issues such as the need for representative sampling and random selection are raised. The section concludes with a discussion of the uses and limitations of correlational studies. The concepts of correlation, the correlation coefficient, and negative and positive correlations are described and explained.

The experimental method is explained in detail, using specific studies to illustrate important concepts such as dependent and independent variables, experimental and control groups, extraneous variables, the placebo effect, experimental and control groups, demand characteristics, practice effects, main effects, and random assignment. Also presented are variations in experimental design and a discussion of the main brain imaging techniques (PET, MRI, and fMRI) and their limitations.

The chapter concludes with an important discussion of the ethical guidelines that regulate psychological research and the role played by the American Psychological Association. The Application provides important guidelines for evaluating information about psychology and psychological topics reported in the mass media.

Introduction: The Origins of Psychology

Preview Questions

Consider the following questions as you study this section of the chapter.

- How is psychology defined today?
- Which two disciplines influenced the emergence of psychology as a science?
- Who established psychology as a distinct scientific discipline?
- What were the first two schools of psychology called, who is associated with their founding, and how do they differ?
- Which four students were influenced by William James, and what were their accomplishments?
- Who founded psychoanalysis, and what was its main focus?
- What are the goals of behaviorism, and who were the three main proponents of this perspective?
- What is the emphasis of humanistic psychology, and what are the names of its two major advocates?

*Read the section "Introduction: The Origins of Psychology" and **write** your answers to the following:*

1. Psychology is defined as _____
   _____

2. The two disciplines that influenced the emergence of psychology were _____
   _____

3. The person who established psychology as a distinct scientific discipline was _____
   _____

4. The first two schools of psychology were
   _____ ,
   and the people associated with their beginnings were _____

5. Structuralism emphasized _____
   _____
   _____
   Functionalism stressed the importance of
   _____
   _____

6. Four students (and their accomplishments) who were influenced by William James were
   _____
   _____
   _____
   _____

7. Psychoanalysis was founded by
   _____ .
   This theory focused on _____
   _____
   _____

8. Behaviorism focused on _____
   _____
   _____
   and rejected _____
   _____
   _____

9. The main proponents of behaviorism were
   _____

10. Humanistic psychology emphasized _____
    _____
    Its two major advocates were
    _____

After you have carefully studied the preceding section, complete the following exercises.

Concept Check 1

Read the following and write the correct term in the space provided.

1. A psychologist who stresses the importance of how behavior enables organisms to adapt to their environment would be classified as belonging to the _____ school of psychology.

2. Dr. Levine adheres to the theory that emphasizes the role of unconscious conflicts in determining behavior and personality. This viewpoint is most consistent with the _____ school of psychology.

3. Environmental influences and overt measurable behavior are to _____ as conscious experience, psychological growth, and self-direction are to _____ .

4. While researching a paper on the history of psychology, John discovered that René Descartes, a seventeenth-century philosopher, promoted the idea that the mind and body are separate entities that interact to produce sensations, emotions, and other conscious experiences. Descartes's view is called _____ .

5. Dr. Brunac's research focuses on the question of the degree to which heredity and environment influence the development of human abilities such as intelligence and personality characteristics. Dr. Brunac is interested in the _____ issue.

6. Alvira believes that our most complex conscious experiences can be broken down into elemental structures, or basic components, of sensations and feelings through the research method of introspection. Alvira's view is most consistent with the school of thought in psychology called _____ .

Review of Terms, Concepts, and Names 1

Use the terms in this list to complete the Matching Test, then to help you answer the True/False items correctly.

psychology
interactive dualism
nature–nurture issue
  (heredity versus
  environment)
physiology
Wilhelm Wundt
Edward B. Titchener
structuralism
introspection
stimulus
William James
Charles Darwin
functionalism
G. Stanley Hall

Mary Whiton Calkins
Margaret Floy
  Washburn
Francis C. Sumner
Sigmund Freud
psychoanalysis
behaviorism
overt behavior
Ivan Pavlov
John B. Watson
learning
B. F. Skinner
humanistic psychology
Carl Rogers
Abraham Maslow

Matching Exercise

Match the appropriate term/name with its definition or description.

1. _____ American psychologist who established the first psychology research laboratory in the United States and founded the American Psychological Association.

2. _____ Looking inward in an attempt to reconstruct feelings and sensations experienced immediately after viewing a stimulus object.

3. _____ School of psychology and theoretical viewpoint that emphasizes each person's unique potential for psychological growth and self-direction.

4. _____ American psychologist who founded behaviorism, emphasizing the study of observable behavior and rejecting the study of mental processes.

5. _____ Early school of psychology that emphasized studying the purpose, or function, of behavior and mental experiences.

6. _____ The scientific study of behavior and mental processes.

7. _____ The idea that the mind and body are separate entities that interact to produce sensations, emotions, and other conscious experiences.

8. _____ German physiologist who established psychology as a formal science and opened the first psychology research laboratory in 1879.

9. _____ British-born American psychologist who founded structuralism, the first school of psychology.

10. _____ School of psychology and theoretical viewpoint that emphasizes the study of observable behaviors, especially as they pertain to the process of learning.

11. _____ American psychologist who was largely responsible for founding the school of humanistic psychology.

12. _____ Anything perceptible to the senses, such as a sight, sound, smell, touch, or taste.

13. _____ The acquisition and modification of behavior in response to environmental influences.

14. _____ American psychologist who was the first African American to receive a doctorate in psychology in the United States.

True/False Test

Indicate whether each statement is true or false by placing T or F in the blank space next to each item.

1. ____ Margaret Floy Washburn was the American psychologist who conducted research on memory, personality, and dreams and was the first woman president of the American Psychological Association.

2. ____ Structuralism was an early school of psychology that emphasized studying the most basic components, or structures, of conscious experience.

3. ____ Physiology is a branch of biology that studies the functions and parts of living organisms, including human beings.

4. ____ William James was an American philosopher and psychologist who was instrumental in establishing psychology in the United States and whose ideas became the basis for the psychological school called functionalism.

5. ____ The issue of heredity versus environment is the same as the nature–nurture issue and refers to the debate over which is more important, the inborn characteristics of the individual or the impact of the environment.

6. ____ Mary Whiton Calkins was an American psychologist who published research on mental processes in animals and was the first woman in the United States to earn a doctorate in psychology.

7. ____ Ivan Pavlov was an Austrian physician whose work focused on the unconscious causes of behavior and personality formation and who founded psychoanalysis.

8. ____ B. F. Skinner was the American psychologist and leading proponent of behaviorism who developed a model of learning called operant conditioning and emphasized studying the relationship between environmental factors and observable behavior.

9. ____ Abraham Maslow was an American humanistic psychologist who developed a theory of motivation that emphasized psychological growth.

10. ____ Psychoanalysis is a personality theory and form of psychotherapy that emphasizes the role of unconscious factors in personality and behavior.

11. ____ Sigmund Freud was a Russian physiologist whose pioneering research on learning contributed to the development of behaviorism and who discovered the basic learning process that is now called classical conditioning.

12. ____ Observable behavior that can be objectively measured and verified is called overt behavior.

13. ____ Charles Darwin was the English naturalist and scientist whose theory of evolution through natural selection was first published in *On the Origin of Species* in 1859.

Check your answers and review any areas of weakness before going on to the next section.

Contemporary Psychology

Preview Questions

Consider the following questions as you study this section of the chapter.

- What are the eight major perspectives in contemporary psychology, and how do they differ?

- What are fifteen important specialty areas in contemporary psychology?

- How do clinical psychologists and psychiatrists differ?

*Read the section "Contemporary Psychology" and **write** your answers to the following:*

1. The eight major perspectives in psychology are

_____

_____

_____

2. Fifteen important specialty areas in contemporary psychology are _____

_____

_____

_____

_____

_____

3. The difference between a clinical psychologist and a psychiatrist is _____

_____

_____

_____

_____

_____

After you have carefully studied the preceding section, complete the following exercises.

Concept Check 2

Which specialty area is represented by each of the following?

1. Dr. Matthews studies the relationship between psychological processes and the body's physical systems and has a particular interest in the structure and activity of the intact brain. She would most likely be classified as a(n) _____ psychologist.

2. Michele wants to study physical, social, and psychological changes that occur over the lifespan when she attends graduate school. Michele is planning to be a(n) _____ psychologist.

3. Dr. Bowman studies the causes, treatment, and prevention of different types of behavioral and emotional disorders. Dr. Bowman is most likely a(n) _____ psychologist.

4. Dr. Ying explores how individuals are affected by their social environments, how people think about and influence others, and the factors that influence conformity and obedience. Dr. Ying is a(n) _____ psychologist.

5. Dr. Steinberg examines individual differences and the characteristics that make each person unique. He is most likely a(n) _____ psychologist.

6. Ingrid is interested in investigating mental processes such as reasoning, thinking, memory, perception, and problem solving. Ingrid is probably planning a career as a(n) _____ psychologist.

7. Dr. Whinney develops instructional methods and materials used to train people in both educational and work settings; she also studies how people of all ages learn. She is a(n) _____ psychologist.

8. Dr. Barton is concerned with stress and coping, the relationship between psychological factors and physical health, and ways of promoting health-enhancing behaviors. Dr. Barton is probably a(n) _____ psychologist.

9. Pitor, who just completed his Ph.D., applied for a job concerned with the relationship between people and work, including the study of job satisfaction, worker productivity, personnel selection and training, leadership, and group behavior within organizations. Pitor has applied for a job as a(n) _____ psychologist.

10. Dr. Manhas has a medical degree plus years of specialized training in the treatment of psychological disorders. He typically prescribes medication for his patients' psychological problems. Dr. Manhas is a _____ .

11. Prosecutors used a psychologist who specializes in applying psychological principles and techniques to legal issues to determine the mental competency of the accused to stand trial. This specialist is most likely a _____ psychologist.

12. To improve the swim team's performance the coach sought the advice of Dr. Cox, who uses psychological theory and knowledge to enhance athletic motivation, performance, and consistency. Dr. Cox is a _____ psychologist.

13. While recovering from a stroke, Maurice was treated by a psychologist who applies psychological knowledge to help people with chronic and disabling health conditions adapt to their situation and attain optimal psychological, interpersonal, and physical functioning, a specialty area called _____ psychology.

14. Dr. Telleman's interests are sensory and perceptual processes, principles of learning, emotion and motivation, and most of her time is spent conducting and supervising basic research projects. Her specialty area is _____ psychology.

Graphic Organizer 1

The statements in the table below represent some of the major perspectives and specialty areas in contemporary psychology. Which perspective is reflected by each statement, and which specialty area is being described? Write your answers in the spaces provided.

Statement	Perspective	Specialty
1. I'm interested in how different parenting styles and techniques influence each child's individual potential for growth and self-determination.		
2. I study the relationship between people and work and, more specifically, how to increase productivity. I believe that by changing environmental factors, increasing the use of rewards and praise for correct behavior, and providing corrective feedback, workers' overt behavior can be changed.		
3. I study how people of all ages learn, and I develop instructional methods and materials to help the learning process. In particular, I stress the roles played by thinking, problem solving, memory, and mental imagery.		
4. Technological advances such as PET scans, MRIs, and functional MRIs have allowed me and my colleagues to study the relationship between psychological processes and the body's physical systems, in particular, the structure and activity of the brain. I am particularly interested in applying this knowledge to enhance athletic motivation and performance.		
5. I often travel to different countries to research people's attitudes and group relations. My research tends to show that many behavioral patterns—for instance, the amount of personal space people require to feel comfortable—vary from one country to another.		
6. I believe that unconscious conflicts, early childhood experiences, and repressed sexual and aggressive feelings make us who we are, and I use this point of view in my work on individual differences and in trying to determine which characteristics make each of us unique.		
7. I focus on the relationship between psychological factors and health, in particular on how people cope with stress in their lives. It is not what happens to us that is important; rather, how we perceive and think about potentially stressful events determines our well-being.		
8. When I went to graduate school, I conducted research in a relatively new area of psychology, which focuses on the conditions and processes that contribute to optimal functioning of people, groups, and institutions. My main task is to help people with disabling health conditions adapt to their situation and obtain optimal psychological, interpersonal, and physical functioning.		
9. Psychological processes that have helped individuals adapt to their environment have also helped them to survive, reproduce, and pass those abilities on to their offspring. I adopt this point of view in my investigations of interpersonal attraction, prejudice, and aggression.		

Graphic Organizer 2

Origins of Psychology, First Schools, and Key Figures

Flow diagram exercise: To help you develop the technique of creating your own graphic organizers, we encourage you to try making a flow diagram/timeline, using boxes, lines, and arrows, that contains the following information. Using a separate sheet of paper, generate your own graphic organizer, then compare it to the sample in the answer section. To help you in this early stage of your study, we've filled in portions of the first two boxes.

Philosophy (list key figures)	Physiology (list key figures)

1. Two areas that influenced the beginnings of psychology and the key figures in each.
2. The founder of psychology and the year the first psychology research lab was established.
3. First school in psychology and key figure.
4. First American school in psychology and key figures.
5. Two approaches (and key figures in each) that challenged the first two schools in psychology.
6. New school that emerged in the 1950s and key figures.

Review of Terms, Concepts, and Names 2

Use the terms in this list to complete the Matching Test, then to help you answer the True/False items correctly.

perspective
specialty area
biological perspective
  (biological psychology)
neuroscientists
psychodynamic
  perspective
behavioral perspective
humanistic perspective
positive psychology
  perspective (positive
  psychology)
cognitive perspective
  (cognitive psychology)
cross-cultural
  perspective (cross-
  cultural psychology)
social loafing
evolutionary perspective
  (evolutionary
  psychology)
natural selection
culture
ethnocentrism
individualistic cultures
collectivistic cultures
clinical psychology
counseling psychology

educational psychology
experimental psychology
developmental
  psychology
forensic psychology
health psychology
industrial/organizational
  psychology
personality psychology
rehabilitation
  psychology
social psychology
sports psychology
school psychology
clinical psychologist
psychiatry and
  psychiatrist

Matching Exercise

Match the appropriate term/name with its definition or description.

1. _____ Psychologist who has a doctorate in psychology and extensive training in the causes, diagnosis, treatment, and prevention of different types of behavioral and emotional disorders.

2. _____ Specialty area that studies the physical, social, and psychological changes that occur at different ages and stages of the lifespan, from conception to old age.

3. _____ Specialty area in psychology that studies how people of all ages learn and is concerned with developing instructional methods and material used to train people.

4. _____ Specialty area that investigates such basic psychological topics as sensory and perceptual processes, learning, emotion, and motivation.

5. _____ Point of view or general framework that reflects a psychologist's emphasis in investigating psychological topics.

6. _____ Specific area in psychology in which psychologists are trained and in which they work or practice.

7. _____ Broad term that refers to the attitudes, values, beliefs, and behaviors shared by a group of people and communicated from one generation to another.

8. _____ Perspective and specialty area that investigates mental processes, including reasoning, thinking, problem solving, language, perception, mental imagery, and memory.

9. _____ Specialty area in psychology that examines individual differences and the characteristics that make each person unique,

including how those characteristics originated and developed.

10. _____ Perspective in psychology that studies how behavior is acquired or modified by environmental consequences and whose focus is on observable behavior and the fundamental laws of learning.

11. _____ The tendency to use your own culture as the standard for judging other cultures.

12. _____ Perspective and specialty area in psychology that studies the relationship between psychological processes and the body's physical systems including the brain and the rest of the nervous system, the endocrine system, the immune system, and genetics.

13. _____ Perspective and branch of psychology that studies the effects of culture on behavior and mental processes.

14. _____ Biological psychologists who specialize in the study of the brain and the rest of the nervous system.

15. _____ Principle that organisms that inherit characteristics that increase their chances of survival in their particular habitat are more likely to survive, reproduce, and pass on their characteristics to their offspring.

16. _____ Specialty area in psychology that provides a variety of psychological services to children, adolescents, families, and administrators in public and private schools.

True/False Test

Indicate whether each statement is true or false by placing T or F in the blank space next to each item.

1. ____ Psychiatrists work in a medical specialty area that focuses on the diagnosis, treatment, causes, and prevention of mental and behavioral disorders, and can prescribe medications and other biomedical therapies.

2. ____ The evolutionary perspective (evolutionary psychology) uses the principles of evolution, including natural selection, to explain psychological processes and phenomena.

3. ____ Counseling psychology is concerned with the relationship between people and work, and it includes the study of job satisfaction, worker productivity, leadership, personnel selection and training, and group behavior within organizations.

4. ____ Forensic psychology applies psychological principles and techniques to legal issues, such as the assessment and treatment of offenders, mental competency to stand trial, child custody, jury selection, and eyewitness testimony.

5. ____ The specialty area that applies psychological knowledge to helping people with chronic and disabling health conditions adapt to their situation and attain optimal psychological, interpersonal, and physical functioning is called health psychology

6. ____ Psychologists who explore how people are affected by their social environments and what factors influence conformity, obedience, persuasion, interpersonal attraction, helping behavior, aggression, prejudice, social beliefs, and other related phenomena work in a specialty area called social psychology.

7. ____ Individualistic cultures emphasize the needs and goals of the group over the needs and goals of the individual.

8. ____ Rehabilitation psychology focuses on the role of psychological factors in the development, prevention, and treatment of illness and includes such areas as stress and coping, the relationship between psychological factors and physical health, and ways of promoting health-enhancing behaviors.

9. ____ Industrial/organizational psychology helps people of all ages adjust, adapt, and cope with personal and interpersonal problems in such diverse areas as relationships, work, education, marriage, child-rearing, and aging.

10. ____ Psychologists who take the humanistic perspective emphasize the importance of unconscious influences, early life experiences, and interpersonal relationships in explaining the underlying dynamics of behavior or treating people with psychological problems.

11. ____ Collectivistic cultures emphasize the needs and goals of the individual over the needs and goals of the group.

12. ____ The psychodynamic perspective focuses on the motivation of people to grow psychologically, the influence of interpersonal relationships on a person's self-concept, and the importance of choice and self-direction in striving to reach one's potential.

13. ____ Sports psychology uses psychological theory and knowledge to enhance athletic motivation, performance, and consistency.

14. ___ The study of positive emotions and psychological states, positive individual traits, and the social institutions that foster positive qualities in individuals and communities is called positive psychology (the positive psychology perspective).

15. ___ Social loafing refers to a psychological finding that people in American and European cultures exert more effort on a task when working alone than when working as part of a group.

16. ___ Clinical psychology studies the causes, diagnosis, treatment, and prevention of different types of behavioral and emotional disorders, such as anxiety, mood, or eating disorders

Check your answers and review any areas of weakness before going on to the next section.

The Scientific Method

Preview Questions

Consider the following questions as you study this section of the chapter.

- What are the four basic goals of psychology?
- What is the scientific method?
- What assumptions and attitudes guide psychologists?
- What is meant by empirical evidence, and what are the four basic steps of the scientific method?
- What are theories, how do they differ from hypotheses, and what principle do they reflect?

*Read the section "The Scientific Method" and **write** your answers to the following:*

1. The four basic goals of psychology are to _____

2. The scientific method refers to _____

3. Psychologists are guided by the basic assumptions that _____

4. Psychologists share a set of attitudes, including _____

5. Empirical evidence refers to _____

The four basic steps of the scientific method are _____

6. A theory is _____

A hypothesis is _____

It is different from a theory in that _____

7. The role of statistics in psychological research is to _____

8. Theories can evolve and change because they reflect the _____

After you have carefully studied the preceding section, complete the following exercises.

Concept Check 3

Read the following and write the correct term in the space provided.

1. Dr. Marlow is interested in drinking and driving behavior and wants to know the frequency with which people will drive after receiving feedback from a Breathalyzer test. In one condition, she sets up her equipment in a bar and administers the test to patrons who are leaving and planning to drive and then observes whether feedback on their level of intoxication influences their decision to drive. Dr. Marlow is using _____ research.

2. In the previous example, Dr. Marlow makes this prediction: The majority of people who are told that they are over the legal limit will still drive; the higher the level on the Breathalyzer test, the more likely it is that they will drive. Dr. Marlow has formulated a _____ .

3. After collecting data over many weeks, Dr. Marlow performs calculations and mathematical tests to see if her prediction was correct. Dr. Marlow is using _____ to analyze her data.

4. Dr. Marlow next writes a report describing the background of this research and details her research design, data collection methods, results, analyses, and conclusions. She submits her report to a respected psychology journal for peer review and publication. She is following step _____ of producing scientific evidence by _____ .

5. In order to examine the overall trends in this particular area of research, Dr. Marlow pools the results of a number of similar studies with her own data and does a single analysis of the collective data. She has used a statistical technique called _____ .

Review of Terms and Concepts 3

Use the terms in this list to complete the Matching Test, then to help you answer the True/False items correctly.

scientific method
empirical evidence
hypothesis
variable
operational definition
critical thinking
descriptive methods

experimental method
statistics
statistically significant
meta-analysis
replicate
theory (model)
pseudoscience

Matching Exercise

Match the appropriate term/name with its definition or description.

1. _____ Statistical technique that involves combining and analyzing the results of many research studies on a specific topic in order to identify overall trends.

2. _____ To repeat or duplicate a scientific study in order to increase confidence in the validity of the original findings.

3. _____ A set of assumptions, attitudes, and procedures that guide researchers in creating questions to investigate, in generating evidence, and in drawing conclusions.

4. _____ Tentative statement about the relationship between two or more variables.

5. _____ Precise description of how the variables in a study will be manipulated or measured.

6. _____ Method of investigation used to demonstrate cause-and-effect relationships by purposely manipulating a factor thought to produce change in a second factor.

7. _____ Mathematical methods used to summarize, analyze, and draw conclusions about data.

True/False Test

Indicate whether each statement is true or false by placing T or F in the blank space next to each item.

1. ____ A statistically significant finding is one that is likely to have occurred by chance.

2. ____ Empirical evidence is evidence that is the result of observation, measurement, and experimentation.

3. ____ A theory (or model) is a tentative explanation that tries to integrate and account for the relationships of various findings and observations.

4. ____ Descriptive methods are research strategies for observing and describing behavior and include naturalistic observation, surveys, case studies, and correlational studies.

5. ____ A pseudoscience is a fake or false science that makes claims based on little or no scientific evidence.

6. ____ Critical thinking is the active process of minimizing preconceptions and biases while evaluating evidence, determining what conclusions can reasonably be drawn from the evidence, and considering alternative explanations for research findings or other phenomena.

7. ____ A variable is any factor that can vary, or change, in ways that can be observed, measured, and verified.

Descriptive Research Methods

Preview Questions

Consider the following questions as you study this section of the chapter.

- What are descriptive research methods?
- How is naturalistic observation typically conducted?
- What are case studies, and when are they normally used?
- What is a survey, and how do researchers ensure that their sample closely parallels the larger group on relevant characteristics?
- What is random selection, and why is it important for obtaining accurate results?
- What does a correlational study involve, and what are its limitations?
- What is the correlation coefficient, and how does a negative correlation differ from a positive correlation?

Read the section "Descriptive Research Methods" and **write** *your answers to the following:*

1. Descriptive research methods are _____

   _____

   _____

2. Naturalistic observation involves the _____

   _____

   _____

3. A case study is _____

   _____

   Case studies are typically used to _____

   _____

   _____

4. In a survey, the researcher _____

   _____

   _____

   _____

5. Researchers ensure that their sample closely parallels the population of interest by

   _____

   _____

   _____

6. Random selection refers to _____

   _____

   It is important because _____

   _____

   _____

   _____

7. Correlational studies show _____

   _____

   _____

   _____

   They are limited because _____

   _____

   _____

8. The correlation coefficient is _____

   _____

   _____

   The correlation coefficient has two parts:

   _____

   _____

   _____

9. A positive correlation is one in which _____

   _____

   A negative correlation is one in which _____

   _____

   _____

Concept Check 4

Read the following and decide which term applies in each case.

1. If a researcher found a correlation coefficient of −0.85 between amount of exercise and weight, this would indicate that the _____ (more/less) people exercise, the _____ (more/less) they weigh.

2. If an organization wants to find out about the spending habits of high-income people, they would be advised to conduct a _____ , using a representative _____ that would be _____ selected from this population.

3. Dr. Klatz is interested in whether there is a difference in the way males and females carry objects such as textbooks, bags, and other large items, so she sets up a hidden camera on the main quad of a large university and videotapes people at various times throughout the day. Dr. Klatz is using

   _____ .

4. A psychologist discovers that the more control people feel they have over what happens in their work environments, the more productive they are. The psychologist has discovered a _____ correlation between perceived control and productivity.

5. A psychologist who is interested in finding out about the lives and experiences of people who claim to have been abducted by aliens and who wants to know how these people are viewed by their families, friends, and coworkers would be advised to use the _____ method of research.

6. In his correlational research, Dr. Hamashima discovered that university graduates earn significantly more money than high school graduates. He also found that the more education people had, the less likely they were to be diagnosed with psychological problems. In this research, it appears that there is a

   _____ correlation between education and income and a _____ correlation between education and psychological health.

Graphic Organizer 3
Positive and Negative Correlations

The following box shows both positive and negative correlations between variables. In cells A through D the arrows indicate a relationship between the amount students study (variable X) and their grade point average (GPA) (variable Y). Fill in the appropriate term in each space provided.

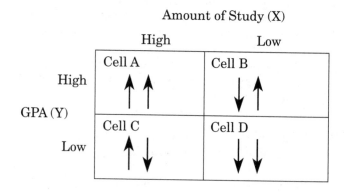

1. Cell A indicates a _____ correlation, and cell D indicates a _____ correlation.

2. Cell C indicates a _____ correlation, and cell B indicates a _____ correlation.

3. Cell A: _____ amounts of X are associated with _____ levels of Y.

   Cell D: _____ amounts of X are associated with _____ levels of Y.

4. Cell C: _____ amounts of X are associated with _____ levels of Y.

   Cell B: _____ amounts of X are associated with _____ levels of Y.

Review of Terms and Concepts 4

Use the terms in this list to complete the Matching Test, then to help you answer the True/False items correctly.

descriptive research
   methods
naturalistic observation
case study
survey
sample

representative sample
random selection
correlational study
correlation coefficient
positive correlation
negative correlation

Matching Exercise

Match the appropriate term with its definition or description.

1. _____ A questionnaire or interview designed to investigate the opinions, behaviors, or characteristics of a particular group.

2. _____ General term for scientific procedures that involve systematically observing behavior in order to describe the relationships among behaviors and events.

3. _____ Selected segment of the population under study.

4. _____ Selected segment that very closely parallels the larger population being studied on relevant characteristics.

5. _____ Research strategy that allows the precise calculation of how strongly related two factors are to each other.

6. _____ Process in which participants are selected from the larger group such that every member has an equal chance of being included in the study.

True/False Test

Indicate whether each statement is true or false by placing T or F in the blank space next to each item.

1. ____ A case study is an intensive, in-depth investigation of a single individual or small group of individuals.

2. ____ A negative correlation between two variables means that the two factors are totally unrelated.

3. ____ Naturalistic observation is the systematic observation and recording of behaviors as they occur in their natural setting.

4. ____ A correlation coefficient is a numerical indication of the magnitude and direction of the relationship between two variables.

5. ____ A positive correlation is one in which the two variables move in opposite directions; as one factor increases, the other decreases.

Check your answers and review any areas of weakness before going on to the next section.

The Experimental Method and Ethics in Psychological Research

Preview Questions

Consider the following questions as you study these sections of the chapter.

- What is the experimental method, and what is its main purpose?

- What are independent and dependent variables, and what are extraneous variables?

- What is the experimental group, the placebo control group, the placebo, the placebo effect, and why do researchers use random assignment?

- What is the double-blind technique, why do researchers use this technique, and what is meant by demand characteristics, the practice effect, and the main effect?

- What is the control group (control condition) and what purpose does it serve?

- What is a natural experiment?

- What are the major imaging techniques used to study the brain and what are the limitations of this technology?

- What is comparative psychology?

*Read the sections "The Experimental Method" and "Ethics in Psychological Research" and **write** your answers to the following:*

1. The experimental method of investigation is used to _____

   _____

   _____

2. The independent variable is the _____

   _____

   The dependent variable is the _____

   _____

   Extraneous variables are _____

   _____

3. The experimental group (experimental condition) is _____
_____

The placebo control group is _____
_____
_____

4. A placebo is _____
_____

The placebo effect is _____
_____
_____

5. Random assignment means that _____
_____
_____

It helps ensure that _____
_____
_____

6. The double-blind technique is _____
_____
_____

It is used to _____
_____
_____

Demand characteristics are _____
_____
_____

Practice effects are _____
_____
_____

Main effects are _____
_____
_____

7. The control group (or control condition) is _____
_____
_____

8. A natural experiment is a study _____
_____
_____

9. (Focus on Neuroscience) The major imaging techniques used to study the brain are
_____
_____
_____

10. (Focus on Neuroscience) Limitations of this technology are as follows: _____
_____
_____
_____
_____

11. Comparative psychology is _____
_____
_____

12. Five key provisions of the APA ethical guidelines regulating research with human participants are

(a) _____

(b) _____

(c) _____

(d) _____

(e) _____

After you have carefully studied the preceding section, complete the following exercises.

Concept Check 5

Read the following and decide which term applies in each case.

Dr. Denton studies the effects of marijuana on memory. He designs an ethically approved experiment that consists of two groups: Group A are given a pill containing the active ingredient in cannabis, THC, and group B are given a harmless inert substance. Neither the researcher nor the participants know who is getting the drug and who is not. Participants are assigned to each group by chance, and all participants are told to learn a long list of word pairs and later take a memory test.

1. The independent variable in this study is _____ and the fake independent variable is _____.

2. The dependent variable is the _____
_____.

3. Group A is the _____ group, and group B is the _____ group.

4. Dr. Denton has used a _____ technique in designing the experiment; along with the control procedure used, this should help guard against _____ and

_____ .

5. Subjects ended up in group A or group B on the basis of _____ .

6. Researchers were interested in determining whether changing a person's belief about the exercise benefits of a particular activity would result in health benefits. They recruited 84 female housekeeping staff from seven hotels and randomly assigned them to the informed group (told their work was good exercise) or the uninformed group (not told that their work was good exercise). At the end of the month-long study (during which all other conditions were held constant) health questionnaires were completed and measures of physical health were obtained.

(a) The hypothesis in this study was _____

_____

_____

(b) The independent variable in this study was

_____

The dependent variables were _____

_____

_____

Review of Terms and Concepts 5

Use the terms in this list to complete the Matching Test, then to help you answer the True/False items correctly.

experimental method
independent variable
  (treatment variable)
extraneous variable
  (confounding variable)
experimental controls
dependent variable
random assignment
experimental group
  (experimental
  condition)
placebo control group

placebo
placebo effects
  (expectancy effects)
double-blind technique
single-blind study
demand characteristics
practice effect
main effect
control group (control
  condition)
natural experiment

positron emission
  tomography (PET)
magnetic resonance
  imaging (MRI)

functional MRI (fMRI)
comparative psychology

Matching Exercise

Match the appropriate term with its definition or description.

1. _____ Experimental technique in which the researchers, but not the participants, are aware of the critical information about the experiment.

2. _____ Method of investigation used to demonstrate cause-and-effect relationships by purposely manipulating one factor thought to produce change in another factor.

3. _____ In an experiment, the factor that is observed and measured for change and is thought to be influenced by the independent variable.

4. _____ Branch of psychology that studies the behavior of different animal species.

5. _____ Any change attributed to a person's beliefs and expectations rather than an actual drug, treatment, or procedure.

6. _____ In an experiment, the group of participants who are exposed to all experimental conditions, except the independent variable or treatment variable, and against which changes in the experimental group are compared.

7. _____ In a research study, subtle cues or signals expressed by the researcher that communicate the kind of response or behavior that is expected from the participant.

8. _____ A noninvasive technique that produces computer generated detailed images of the brain using electromagnetic signals generated by the brain in response to magnetic fields.

9. _____ Specific strategies and procedures that help minimize the possibility that extraneous variables or some other uncontrolled factor will influence the outcome of the experiment.

10. _____ An invasive imaging technique that provides computer generated color-coded images of brain activity by tracking the brain's use of a radioactively tagged compound, such as glucose, oxygen, or other substances.

11. _____ A study investigating the effects of a naturally occurring event on the research participants.

True/False Test

Indicate whether each item is true or false by placing T or F in the blank space next to each item.

1. ____ Random assignment means that all participants have an equal chance of being assigned to any of the conditions or groups in the study.

2. ____ The placebo control group is the group of participants who receive a fake substance, treatment, or procedure that has no known direct effects.

3. ____ The experimental group (or experimental condition) is the group of participants who are exposed to all experimental conditions, including the independent variable or treatment variable.

4. ____ The independent variable (treatment variable) in an experiment is purposely manipulated in order to cause a change in another variable.

5. ____ A double-blind technique is one in which neither the participants nor the researcher interacting with the participants is aware of the group or condition to which participants have been assigned.

6. ____ A placebo is a fake substance, or procedure, that has no known direct effects.

7. ____ An extraneous, or confounding, variable is a factor or variable other than the ones being studied that, if not controlled, could affect the outcome of the experiment.

8. ____ Any change that can be directly attributed to the independent or treatment variable after controlling for other possible influences is called a main effect.

9. ____ Any change in performance that results from mere repetition of a task is called a practice effect.

10. ____ Functional magnetic resonance imaging (fMRI) is a noninvasive technique that produces detailed images of the brain using electromagnetic signals that track changes in metabolic activity, such as increased blood flow to particular areas of the brain, providing a series of scans that show moment-by-moment "movies" of the brain's changing activities.

Check your answers and review any areas of weakness before going on to the next section.

Something to Think About

1. When family and friends find out you are taking a psychology course, someone typically makes some comment about "headshrinking" and "psychoanalyzing," or notes that "psychology is just plain common sense." To prepare yourself for these remarks, think about how you would explain what psychology really is and how you might "educate" your family and friends about the difference between psychiatry, clinical psychology, and psychoanalysis.

2. If you are like most introductory psychology students, you were probably motivated to take this course, at least in part, because of questions about human behavior and mental processes. For example, students often wonder if hypnosis can really help recover repressed memories and memories of past lives; if a lie detector really can detect lies; if "satanic messages" embedded in the lyrics of rock music can cause people to commit suicide; if ESP really exists; or whether subliminal tapes can really improve memory, clear up acne, or improve self-esteem. Now that you know more about the science of psychology, take one of your questions and think about how a psychologist would try to answer it.

Check your answers and review any areas of weakness before doing the following progress tests.

Progress Test 1

Review the complete chapter (including all boxed inserts), review all your study notes, and then test yourself on the following progress test. Check your answers. If you make a mistake, review your notes, check the relevant section in the study guide, and, if necessary, go back and read the appropriate part of your textbook.

1. Two disciplines influenced the founding of psychology. The discipline that concerns itself with questions such as mind–body dualism and the nature–nurture issue is _____; the discipline that is a branch of biology and

studies functions and structures of living organisms is _____ .

(a) chemistry; physics
(b) neurology; sociology
(c) physics; neurology
(d) philosophy; physiology

2. A Japanese psychologist investigating the relationship between worker satisfaction and productivity was surprised to find that North American workers were less productive when working as part of a group than when working alone. In some Asian countries, he had found the opposite to be true. This researcher probably has a _____ perspective, and his specialty area is _____ psychology.

(a) cross-cultural; developmental
(b) behavioral; health
(c) behavioral; developmental
(d) cross-cultural; industrial/organizational

3. Dr. Hammersly focuses on the role of unconscious factors in his patients' behaviors and spends time analyzing their dreams and delving into their early childhood experiences. Dr. Finkleman is more concerned with the way her patients think and reason, and her psychotherapy involves teaching her patients how to recognize irrational thinking and to find different ways of thinking about their situation. Dr. Hammersly's perspective is _____ , and Dr. Finkleman's perspective is

_____ .

(a) cognitive; behavioral
(b) psychodynamic; cognitive
(c) humanistic; biological
(d) cognitive; psychodynamic

4. In a double-blind experiment testing the effects of memory-enhancing subliminal tapes, both the experimental and control groups were given a number of cognitive tests at the beginning (pretest) and end (posttest) of the three-month-long study. On the posttest, both groups showed improvement, but there was no difference in the level of improvement between the two groups. The researchers can conclude that

(a) the improvement in both groups was probably due to demand characteristics.
(b) the double-blind technique failed to eliminate extraneous variables.

(c) the improvement in both groups was probably due to a practice effect.
(d) memory-enhancing subliminal tapes work.

5. Dr. Lebel investigates how people differ on such characteristics as shyness, assertiveness, and self-esteem. It is most likely that she is a _____ psychologist.

(a) clinical   (c) developmental
(b) biological   (d) personality

6. To ensure that differences among participants are evenly distributed across all conditions in the experiment and that there is no bias in how participants are assigned to their respective groups, a researcher studying the behavioral effects of playing violent video games should

(a) operationally define each participant's role and assign participants on the basis of how closely they fit the definition.
(b) make sure that the most aggressive people are assigned to the experimental condition.
(c) make sure that the most aggressive people are assigned to the control group.
(d) randomly assign the participants to each condition in the experiment.

7. A researcher is interested in how sleep deprivation affects performance and cognitive abilities. She proposes that there is a relationship between the amount of sleep deprivation and the ability to solve complex mental tasks; the more sleep-deprived people are, the more mistakes they are likely to make. She has

(a) developed a theory.
(b) formulated a hypothesis.
(c) produced empirical evidence.
(d) merely stated the obvious.

8. In a study investigating emotional arousal and memory, Dr. Alves discovers a statistically significant difference in recall ability between the high-arousal group and the low-arousal group. This finding indicates that

(a) the participants were not randomly assigned to the two groups.
(b) the difference between the two groups is likely to have occurred by chance.
(c) extraneous variables were responsible for the difference in recall ability between the two groups.
(d) the difference between the two groups is not likely to have occurred by chance.

9. Dr. Barbone and his colleagues decide to repeat the essence of an earlier study using different participants. They are
   (a) replicating the previous study.
   (b) wasting their time.
   (c) doing a meta-analysis.
   (d) violating one of the ethical codes of the American Psychological Association.

10. In an experiment designed to test the effects of alcohol on motor coordination, group 1 participants are given a precise amount of alcohol in a mixed drink and group 2 participants are given a drink that smells and tastes exactly like the alcoholic drink but contains no alcohol. Which of the following is true?
    (a) Group 1 is the placebo control group.
    (b) Group 2 is the experimental group.
    (c) Group 2 is the placebo control group.
    (d) Group 1 will have much more fun than group 2.

11. A researcher is interested in whether people talk when they are riding in elevators, so she and her research assistants spend many hours riding in elevators and unobtrusively noting when they hear a conversation. This researcher is using
    (a) naturalistic observation.
    (b) experimental research.
    (c) correlational research.
    (d) case study research.

12. In an attempt to understand how traumatic brain injuries affect behavior, Dr. Nicolai extensively and carefully observes and questions three accident victims who had suffered brain injuries. Which research method is Dr. Nicolai utilizing?
    (a) naturalistic observation
    (b) experimental method
    (c) correlational research
    (d) case study

13. In her research, Dr. Cranshaw focuses on the application of principles of natural selection to explain psychological processes and phenomena. Dr. Cranshaw is most likely a(n) _____ psychologist.
    (a) evolutionary   (c) behavioral
    (b) biological   (d) psychodynamic

14. Petra was injected with a small amount of radioactively tagged glucose. Then, while lying in a scanner, she tried to recall a list of words she had memorized earlier. The scanner tracked the glucose as her brain was using it. A computer then analyzed this data and produced color-coded images of her brain activity. Petra was participating in an experiment using
    (a) positron-emission tomography (PET).
    (b) magnetic resonance imaging (MRI).
    (c) the double-blind technique.
    (d) functional magnetic resonance imaging (fMRI).

15. According to Science Versus Pseudoscience, which of the following is true of pseudoscience?
    (a) It is a legitimate science that uses both established and unorthodox methods in the search for the truth.
    (b) It is a fake or false science that makes claims based on little or no scientific evidence.
    (c) It is not accepted by most of the scientific establishment because pseudoscientists have discovered truths that threaten all the fundamental laws and principles of science.
    (d) It does not use sophisticated jargon, impressive-looking statistical graphs, or elaborate theories, and virtually no pseudoscientist has impressive-sounding credentials.

Progress Test 2

After you have checked your understanding of the material in Progress Test 1 and have done a complete chapter review with special focus on any areas of weakness, you are ready to assess your knowledge on Progress Test 2. Check your answers. If you make a mistake, review your notes and the relevant section of the study guide and, if necessary, review the appropriate part of your textbook.

1. In an experiment, children were randomly assigned to a group that watched a violent video or to a group that watched a nonviolent video; later, researchers measured the level of aggression in both groups under controlled laboratory conditions. In this example, the measure of the children's aggression was the
   (a) dependent variable.
   (b) independent variable.
   (c) extraneous variable.
   (d) naturalistic variable.

2. Dr. Ames researches changes in people's intellectual abilities as they grow older. Dr. Ames's specialty area is _____ psychology.

   (a) social
   (b) educational
   (c) developmental
   (d) clinical

3. While researching a paper for her history of psychology course, Sangeeta noted that behaviorism and psychoanalysis dominated psychology for many decades early in the twentieth century. However, in the 1950s a new school of thought emerged that emphasized conscious experience and each person's unique potential for psychological growth, self-determination, and free will. This school of psychology is called

   (a) structuralism.
   (b) functionalism.
   (c) humanistic psychology.
   (d) cross-cultural psychology.

4. Dr. Sandman investigates the relationship between sleep deprivation and cognitive abilities. He decides to test research participants in his sleep research lab under varying conditions. First, he allows all his participants to get a number of uninterrupted nights' sleep and records how long each participant sleeps on average. Next, he decides that sleep deprivation would be either two, three, or four hours fewer than the average for each participant. Dr. Sandman

   (a) has operationally defined one of his variables.
   (b) is using cruel and unusual punishment.
   (c) is conducting correlational research.
   (d) has proposed a theory.

5. An educational psychologist is interested in whether having students evaluate instructors' performance is actually a good measure of teaching ability. A review of the literature showed some inconsistent findings across hundreds of different studies. To get a sense of the overall trends in this body of research, the investigator would be advised to use a technique called

   (a) the correlation coefficient.
   (b) meta-analysis.
   (c) the case study.
   (d) replication.

6. Compared to clinical psychologists, psychiatrists are more likely to

   (a) prescribe drugs and other medical procedures for their clients.
   (b) assume that psychological disorders result from unconscious conflicts.
   (c) use a cognitively based therapy rather than a biologically based therapy.
   (d) favor a humanistic perspective rather than a psychoanalytic perspective.

7. In order to test the claim that listening to classical music improves cognitive functioning, researchers divided participants into three groups. Group A listened to classical music, group B listened to instrumental jazz, and group C spent the same amount of time in silence. All participants were given a standard cognitive reasoning test before and after being exposed to the treatment of interest. In this experiment, the independent variable was _____ and the dependent variable was _____ .

   (a) group C; groups A and B
   (b) the music and silent conditions; scores on the pretest and posttest
   (c) Groups A and B; group C
   (d) scores on the pretest and posttest; the music and silent conditions

8. In an experiment, participants were randomly assigned to one of three conditions. The purpose of random assignment is to

   (a) increase the probability that the same number of participants end up in each condition.
   (b) increase the likelihood that the participants are representative of people in general.
   (c) decrease the probability of expectancy effects.
   (d) reduce the possibility of bias and ensure that differences among participants are spread out across all experimental conditions.

9. Neither the researchers nor the participants in a study examining the effects of alcohol on inhibitions are aware of who actually received the active ingredient (the alcohol) and who were given a placebo. This study involves the use of

   (a) replication.
   (b) the single-blind procedure.
   (c) the double-blind technique.
   (d) correlational techniques.

10. Researchers using a form of descriptive research have found that the larger a person's line of credit, the more money he or she is likely to owe. The researchers have found a(n) _____ between the size of a credit line and the amount of debt.
    (a) positive correlation
    (b) negative correlation
    (c) a cause-and-effect relationship
    (d) zero correlation

11. Mary is interviewed in depth, and her friends, family, and coworkers are contacted for further information. She also takes a number of psychological tests, and her behavior in various situations is observed. This is an example of
    (a) a survey.
    (b) correlational research.
    (c) a case study.
    (d) experimental research.

12. In an attempt to predict the winner in the next election, The Kneed to Know Kompany contacts a randomly selected representative sample of the voting population and questions them about their voting plans. This is an example of
    (a) correlational research.
    (b) a survey.
    (c) a case study.
    (d) experimental research.

13. When Drew goes to graduate school, he intends to pursue research in an area called positive psychology. Drew is most likely to
    (a) focus on the diagnosis, treatment, causes, and prevention of mental and behavior disorders.
    (b) study positive emotions and psychological states, positive individual traits, and the social institutions that foster positive qualities in individuals and communities.
    (c) apply the principles of evolution, including natural selection, to explain psychological processes and phenomena.
    (d) investigate the physical, social, and psychological changes that occur at different ages and stages of the lifespan, from conception to old age.

14. According to Culture and Human Behavior, ethnocentrism is
    (a) the tendency to use one's own culture as the standard for judging other cultures.
    (b) introspective, self-centered analysis.
    (c) much more common in individualistic cultures than in collectivistic cultures.
    (d) much more common in collectivistic cultures than in individualistic cultures.

15. When evaluating claims made in the media about psychology-related topics, the Application makes the point that
    (a) anecdotal evidence is not scientific evidence.
    (b) there is no way to sort out true claims from false claims.
    (c) testimonials are the most reliable source of information.
    (d) correlational research is the most valid type of research because it can clearly establish cause-and-effect relationships between two variables.

Progress Test 3

After you have checked your understanding of the material in Progress Tests 1 and 2 and have done a complete chapter review with special focus on any areas of weakness, you are ready to assess your knowledge with Progress Test 3. Check your answers. If you make a mistake, review your notes and the relevant section of the study guide and, if necessary, review the appropriate part of your textbook.

1. An emphasis on the physical bases of behavior is to the _____ perspective as an emphasis on the influence of culture on behavior is to the _____ perspective.
   (a) biological; evolutionary
   (b) behavioral; humanistic
   (c) biological; cross-cultural
   (d) behavioral; cognitive

2. The evolutionary perspective focuses on _____ , whereas the cognitive perspective emphasizes _____ .
   (a) the physical bases of behavior; environmental influences on behavior
   (b) unconscious influences on behavior and personality; psychological growth and personal potential
   (c) mental processes, information processing, problem solving, and thinking; the influence of culture on behavior
   (d) the application of principles of natural selection to explain psychological processes and phenomena; information processing, problem solving, and thinking

3. Dr. Creedon believes in each person's unique potential for psychological growth, self-direction, and self-determination, and in the importance of free will in making choices about one's life. He also emphasizes the conscious experiences of his clients. His approach is most similar to one taken by

   (a) John B. Watson and behaviorism.
   (b) Sigmund Freud and psychoanalysis.
   (c) Carl Rogers and humanistic psychology.
   (d) Charles Darwin and evolutionary psychology.

4. In a memory experiment, half the participants were given the title of a passage before being asked to memorize it and the other half were simply told to memorize the passage but were not given the title. Later, all participants were given a memory test in which they were asked to recall as much of the passage as they could, and the overall results of both groups were compared. In this example the independent variable was _____ and the dependent variable was _____ .

   (a) the scores on the memory test; the title/no title manipulation
   (b) the group given the title; the group not given the title
   (c) the title/no title manipulation; the scores on the memory test
   (d) the group not given the title; the group given the title
   (e) the overall scores of the two groups; the time it took the two groups to memorize the passage

5. In conducting research on the effects of a new memory-enhancing drug, Dr. Simpleton used the double-blind technique. The purpose of doing so was to guard against the possibility that the researcher will inadvertently display

   (a) expectancy effects.
   (b) demand characteristics.
   (c) placebo effects.
   (d) ethnocentrism.

6. In order to learn students' opinions about the recent cutbacks at her university, Gira sent a questionnaire to every twentieth person on the list of currently enrolled students. Gira used the technique of

   (a) replication.   (c) random sampling.
   (b) meta-analysis.   (d) interviewing.

7. Research showing that students with the highest GPAs study approximately twice as many hours per week as those with the lowest GPAs would indicate that

   (a) there is a positive correlation between study behavior and GPA.
   (b) there is a negative correlation between study behavior and GPA.
   (c) high GPA causes good study behavior.
   (d) the correlation coefficient would probably exceed +1.50.

8. Ethical principles developed by the American Psychological Association require psychologists to

   (a) always tell the participants the exact nature of the experiment and inform them of the hypothesis that will be tested.
   (b) never, under any circumstances, use deception with potential participants.
   (c) withhold all information about the nature, results, and conclusions of the study because of the confidentiality principle.
   (d) obtain informed consent and voluntary participation of potential participants.

9. Dr. Joyce supports the view that the goal of psychology should be to discover the fundamental principles of learning and that psychologists should focus exclusively on overt behavior rather than on mental processes. Dr. Joyce favors the _____ perspective in psychology.

   (a) behavioral   (c) psychodynamic
   (b) cognitive   (d) humanistic

10. An experimenter found that variable A and variable B had a correlation coefficient of +.55, and variable C and variable D had a correlation coefficient of −.75. She can conclude that

    (a) variables A and B have a stronger correlation than variables C and D.
    (b) variable A causes variable B, but C and D are unrelated.
    (c) variables A and B have a weaker correlation than variables C and D.
    (d) variables A and B are strongly correlated, but C and D have no relationship.

11. If researchers wanted to discover the extent to which education level can be used to predict political preferences, they would most likely use
    (a) correlational research.
    (b) naturalistic observation.
    (c) experimental research.
    (d) a type of research called comparative psychology.

12. Dr. Angellino stated, "Psychology should study the purpose of behavior and mental processes and how they function to allow organisms to adapt to their environment." It is most likely that Dr. Angellino belonged to the _____ school of psychology.
    (a) functionalist
    (b) structuralist
    (c) behaviorist
    (d) psychoanalytic

13. When all the data were collected and analyzed, the researchers were confident that the observed change was not caused by placebo effects, practice effects, confounding variables, or other influences. Rather, the change could be directly attributed to the treatment variable, or independent variable, and this change is called the
    (a) practice effect.
    (b) main effect.
    (c) extraneous variable.
    (d) expectancy effect.

14. According to In Focus, animal research is condoned by the American Psychological Association as long as the research
    (a) has an acceptable scientific purpose.
    (b) will likely increase knowledge about behavior.
    (c) will likely increase understanding of the species under study.
    (d) produces results that benefit the health and welfare of humans or other animals.
    (e) has all of these characteristics.

15. According to Critical Thinking, critical thinking involves
    (a) minimizing the influence of preconceptions and biases while rationally evaluating evidence.
    (b) determining the conclusions that can be drawn from the evidence.
    (c) considering alternative explanations.
    (d) all of these characteristics.

Answers

Introduction: The Origins of Psychology

1. *Psychology is defined as* the scientific study of behavior and mental processes.

2. *The two disciplines that influenced the emergence of psychology were* philosophy and physiology.

3. *The person who established psychology as a distinct scientific discipline was* Wilhelm Wundt.

4. *The first two schools of psychology were* structuralism and functionalism, *and the people associated with their beginnings were* Edward B. Titchener and William James.

5. *Structuralism emphasized* studying the most basic components, or structures, of conscious experience using a procedure called introspection. *Functionalism stressed the importance of* how behavior functions to allow people and animals to adapt to their environments.

6. *Four students (and their accomplishments), who were influenced by William James were* G. Stanley Hall (awarded the first Ph.D. in psychology in the United States), Mary Whiton Calkins (first female president of the American Psychological Association), Margaret Floy Washburn (first female to be awarded a Ph.D. in psychology and second female president of the American Psychological Association), and Francis C. Sumner (first African American to receive a Ph.D. in psychology and chaired the psychology department at Howard University).

7. *Psychoanalysis was founded by* Sigmund Freud. *This theory focused on* the role of unconscious conflicts in determining personality and behavior.

8. *Behaviorism focused on* the scientific study of overt behavior that could be objectively measured and verified *and rejected* the emphasis on consciousness promoted by structuralism and functionalism, as well as Freudian notions of unconscious influences.

9. *The main proponents of behaviorism were* Ivan Pavlov, John B. Watson, and B. F. Skinner.

10. *Humanistic psychology emphasized* each person's unique potential for psychological growth and self-direction. *Its two major advocates were* Carl Rogers and Abraham Maslow.

Concept Check 1

1. functionalist

2. psychoanalytic

3. behaviorism; humanistic psychology

4. interactive dualism

5. nature–nurture

6. structuralism

Matching Exercise 1

1. G. Stanley Hall

2. introspection

3. humanistic psychology

4. John B. Watson

5. functionalism

6. psychology

7. interactive dualism

8. Wilhelm Wundt

9. Edward B. Titchener

10. behaviorism

11. Carl Rogers

12. stimulus

13. learning

14. Frances C. Sumner

True/False Test 1

1. F	7. F	13. T
2. T	8. T	
3. T	9. T	
4. T	10. T	
5. T	11. F	
6. F	12. T	

Contemporary Psychology

1. *The eight major perspectives in psychology are* biological, psychodynamic, behavioral, humanistic, positive psychology, cognitive, cross-cultural, and evolutionary.

2. *The fifteen important specialty areas in contemporary psychology are* biological, clinical, cognitive, counseling, educational, experimental, developmental, forensic, health, industrial/organizational, personality, rehabilitation, school, social, and sports psychology.

3. *The difference between a clinical psychologist and a psychiatrist is* that a clinical psychologist typically has a doctorate in clinical psychology, which includes extensive training in the different types of psychotherapy, and a psychiatrist has a medical degree plus additional specialized training in the treatment of mental disorders. A psychiatrist also can prescribe medications and other biomedical treatments.

Concept Check 2

1. biological

2. developmental

3. clinical

4. social

5. personality

6. cognitive

7. educational

8. health

9. industrial/organizational

10. psychiatrist

11. forensic

12. sports

13. rehabilitation

14. experimental

Graphic Organizer 1

PERSPECTIVE	SPECIALTY
1. humanistic	developmental
2. behavioral	industrial/organizational
3. cognitive	educational
4. biological	sports
5. cross-cultural	social
6. psychodynamic	personality
7. cognitive	health
8. positive psychology	rehabilitation
9. evolutionary	social

Graphic Organizer 2

Origins of Psychology, First Schools, and Key Figures

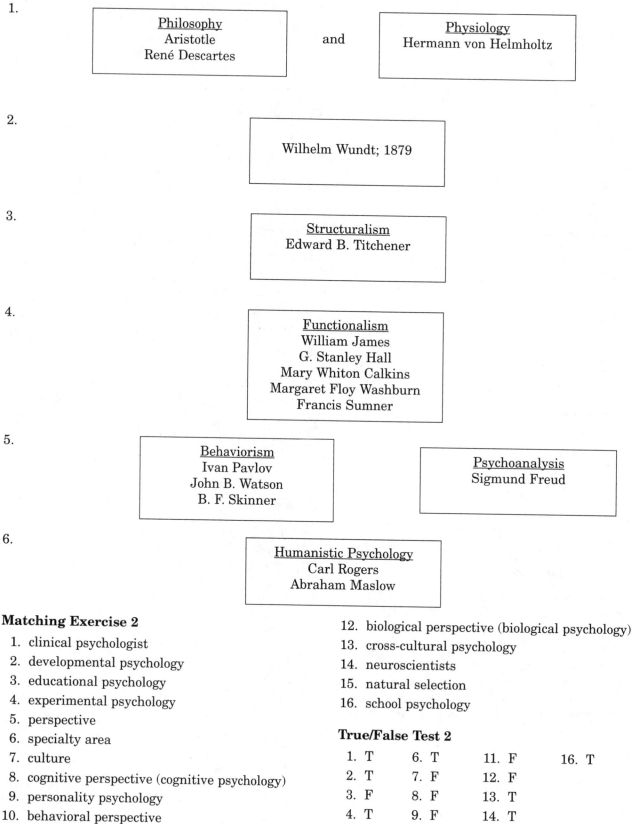

1.

> **Philosophy**
> Aristotle
> René Descartes

and

> **Physiology**
> Hermann von Helmholtz

2.

> Wilhelm Wundt; 1879

3.

> **Structuralism**
> Edward B. Titchener

4.

> **Functionalism**
> William James
> G. Stanley Hall
> Mary Whiton Calkins
> Margaret Floy Washburn
> Francis Sumner

5.

> **Behaviorism**
> Ivan Pavlov
> John B. Watson
> B. F. Skinner

> **Psychoanalysis**
> Sigmund Freud

6.

> **Humanistic Psychology**
> Carl Rogers
> Abraham Maslow

Matching Exercise 2

1. clinical psychologist
2. developmental psychology
3. educational psychology
4. experimental psychology
5. perspective
6. specialty area
7. culture
8. cognitive perspective (cognitive psychology)
9. personality psychology
10. behavioral perspective
11. ethnocentrism
12. biological perspective (biological psychology)
13. cross-cultural psychology
14. neuroscientists
15. natural selection
16. school psychology

True/False Test 2

1. T	6. T	11. F	16. T
2. T	7. F	12. F	
3. F	8. F	13. T	
4. T	9. F	14. T	
5. F	10. F	15. T	

The Scientific Method

1. *The four basic goals of psychology are to* describe, explain, predict, and control or influence behavior and mental processes.

2. *The scientific method refers to* a set of assumptions, attitudes, and procedures that guide researchers in creating questions to investigate, in generating evidence, and in drawing conclusions.

3. *Psychologists are guided by the basic assumptions that* all events are lawful, which means that behavior and mental processes follow consistent patterns, and that events are explainable, which means that behavior and mental processes have a cause or causes that can be understood through careful, systematic study.

4. *Psychologists share a set of attitudes, including* open-mindedness, scientific skepticism, caution in making claims, and a willingness to critically evaluate the evidence for new findings.

5. *Empirical evidence refers to* evidence that is the result of objective observation, measurement, and experimentation. *The four basic steps of the scientific method are* formulate a specific question that can be tested empirically, design a study to collect relevant data, analyze the data to arrive at conclusions, and, finally, report the results.

6. *A theory is* a tentative explanation that tries to account for diverse findings on the same topic. *A hypothesis is* a specific question or prediction about the relationship between two or more variables that is to be tested. *It is different from a theory in that* a theory integrates and summarizes a large number of findings and observations and often generates predictions and new hypotheses that can be tested by further research.

7. *The role of statistics in psychological research is to* enable researchers to summarize, analyze, and draw conclusions about the data they have collected.

8. *Theories can evolve and change because they reflect the* self-correcting nature of the scientific enterprise; when new research findings challenge established ways of thinking about a phenomenon, theories are expanded, modified, and even replaced.

Concept Check 3

1. experimental (in a natural setting)
2. hypothesis
3. statistics

4. 4; reporting her findings
5. meta-analysis

Matching Exercise 3

1. meta-analysis
2. replicate
3. scientific method
4. hypothesis
5. operational definition
6. experimental method
7. statistics

True/False Test 3

1. F	4. T	7. T
2. T	5. T	
3. T	6. T	

Descriptive Research Methods

1. *Descriptive research methods are* scientific procedures that involve systematically observing behavior in order to describe the relationship among behaviors and events.

2. *Naturalistic observation involves the* systematic observation and recording of behaviors as they occur in their natural settings.

3. *A case study is* an intensive, in-depth investigation of a single individual or small group of individuals. *Case studies are typically used to* develop a complete profile of a psychotherapy client and to investigate rare, unusual, or extreme conditions.

4. *In a survey, the researcher* develops a questionnaire or conducts an interview designed to investigate the opinions, behaviors, or characteristics of a particular group. Computer-based or Internet-based surveys have become increasingly more common.

5. *Researchers ensure that their sample closely parallels the population of interest by* selecting a representative sample that matches the larger group on relevant characteristics, such as age, sex, race, marital status, and educational level.

6. *Random selection refers to* the process in which subjects are selected randomly from a larger group such that every member has an equal chance of being included in the study. *It is important because* it ensures that the sample is representative, on relevant characteristics, of the larger population being studied.

7. *Correlational studies show* how strongly two factors, or variables, are related to each other and can sometimes be used for making meaningful predictions. *They are limited because* they cannot be used to demonstrate cause-and-effect relationships (experimental research is used to do that).

8. *The correlation coefficient is* a numerical indication of the magnitude and direction of the relationship between two variables; it always falls in the range from −1.00 to +1.00. *The correlation coefficient has two parts:* the number indicates the strength of the relationship (the bigger the number, the stronger the relationship) and the sign (+ or −) indicates the direction of the relationship between the two variables.

9. *A positive correlation is one in which* the two factors vary in the same direction, increasing together or decreasing together. *A negative correlation is one in which* the two variables move in opposite directions, one increasing as the other decreases.

Concept Check 4

1. more; less (or less; more)
2. survey; sample; randomly
3. naturalistic observation
4. positive
5. case study
6. positive; negative

Graphic Organizer 3

1. positive; positive
2. negative; negative
3. high; high; low; low
4. high; low; low; high

Matching Exercise 4

1. survey
2. descriptive research methods
3. sample
4. representative sample
5. correlational study
6. random selection

True/False Test 4

1. T   4. T
2. F   5. F
3. T

The Experimental Method and Ethics in Psychological Research

1. *The experimental method of investigation is used to* demonstrate cause-and-effect relationships by purposely manipulating one variable and observing the effect on a second variable.

2. *The independent variable is the* purposely manipulated factor thought to produce change in an experiment (also referred to as the treatment variable). *The dependent variable is the* factor that is observed and measured for change as a result of the manipulation of the independent variable in an experiment.

   Extraneous variables are factors other than the ones being studied that, if not controlled, could affect the outcome of the experiment (also called confounding variables).

3. *The experimental group (or experimental condition) is* the group of participants who are exposed to all experimental conditions, including the independent (treatment) variable.

   The placebo control group is a control group in which participants are exposed to a fake independent variable, or placebo. The effects of the placebo are compared to the effects of the actual independent variable (treatment variable) on the experimental group. This group serves as a check for practice effects and placebo effects (expectancy effects).

4. *A placebo is* a fake substance, treatment, or procedure that has no known effects (commonly called a sugar pill). *The placebo effect is* any change attributed to a person's beliefs and expectations rather than the actual drug, treatment, or procedure (also called expectancy effect).

5. *Random assignment means that* all participants in the study have an equal chance of being assigned to any of the groups or conditions in an experiment. *It helps ensure that* potential differences among participants are spread out across all experimental conditions and that assignment is done in an unbiased manner.

6. *The double-blind technique is* an experimental control in which neither the participants nor the researchers interacting with the participants is aware of the group or condition to which the participants have been assigned. *It is used to* guard against the possibility that the researcher will become an extraneous or confounding variable and display demand characteristics (that is, display subtle cues or signals that communicates the kind of response or

behavior that is expected). *Demand characteristics are* subtle cues or signals expressed by the researcher that communicate the kind of response or behavior that is expected from the participant. *Practice effects are* any changes in performance that result from mere repetition of a task. *Main effects are* any changes that can be directly attributed to the independent variable after controlling for other possible influences.

7. *The control group (or control condition) is* the group of participants who are exposed to all experimental conditions, except the independent variable or treatment variable, and against which changes in the experimental group are compared.

8. *A natural experiment is a study* investigating the effects of a naturally occurring event on the research participants.

9. *(Focus on Neuroscience) The major imaging techniques used to study the brain are* positron emission tomography (PET scan), magnetic resonance imaging (MRI), and functional magnetic resonance imaging (fMRI).

10. *(Focus on Neuroscience) Limitations of this technology are as follows:* First, most brain-imaging studies involve small groups of subjects, making it difficult to generalize the findings to a wider population. Second, most brain-imaging studies involve simple aspects of behavior and do not capture the extraordinary complexity of human behavior. Third, knowing what brain area is involved may reveal little about the psychological process under investigation. Finally, brain imaging techniques are not necessarily more scientific than other techniques used by psychologists, and to be truly useful, brain images of a particular behavior must be accurately interpreted within the context of existing knowledge about behavior.

11. *Comparative psychology* is a branch of psychology that studies the behavior of different animal species, including the study of animal learning, memory, thinking and language (animal cognition).

12. *Five key provisions of the APA ethical guidelines regulating research with human participants are*
    (a) Informed consent and voluntary participation is required.
    (b) Students must be given the option of not participating in research involving credits without being penalized in any way.
    (c) Psychologists are restricted in their use of deception.

(d) All records must be kept confidential.
(e) Participants must be allowed the opportunity to obtain information about the study once it is completed and must be debriefed about the nature of their involvement in the study.

Concept Check 5

1. the actual drug; the placebo (more precisely, THC, the active ingredient in marijuana, is the independent variable and the harmless, inert substance is the fake independent variable or placebo)

2. participants' scores on the memory tests

3. experimental; placebo control

4. double-blind; placebo (expectancy) effects; demand characteristics

5. random assignment

6. (a) *The hypothesis in this study was* that changing a person's belief about the exercise benefits of a particular activity would result in health benefits.
   (b) *The independent variable in this study was* being informed, or not being informed, that housekeeping work was good exercise. *The dependent variables were* participants' responses to the questionnaire and the measure of physical health (weight, percentage of body fat, body mass index, and blood pressure).

Matching Exercise 5

1. single-blind study
2. experimental method
3. dependent variable
4. comparative psychology
5. placebo effect (expectancy effect)
6. control group or control condition
7. demand characteristics
8. MRI
9. experimental controls
10. PET scan
11. natural experiment

True/False Test 5

1. T	5. T	9. T
2. T	6. T	10. T
3. T	7. T	
4. T	8. T	

Something to Think About

1. (a) Psychology tackles questions that people have grappled with for thousands of years. Instead of using anecdotal evidence, intuition, philosophical discussion, and speculation, psychology uses the scientific method to answer questions that are amenable to empirical testing. It uses four steps in generating empirical evidence. First, questions are formulated into testable hypotheses; next, the study is designed and the data are collected; then statistical analyses are prepared and conclusions are drawn; and finally, the results are reported. Psychologists operationally define all variables and precisely specify the method of measurement or manipulation. Following this process, they can have more confidence in the accuracy of their results.

(b) The difference between clinical psychologists and psychiatrists is training. Clinical psychologists have a doctorate in psychology and extensive training in the assessment, diagnosis, and treatment of people with psychological disorders. Psychiatrists, on the other hand, have an M.D. plus years of training in dealing with people with psychological disorders; because of their medical qualifications, they can prescribe drugs and order medical procedures such as electroshock therapy.

2. Many of the questions students have coming into psychology can be tested empirically, and quite a few have, in fact, been answered. For example, how would you test the claim that subliminal messages can influence our behavior? It turns out that psychologists have done just that.

The essence of their experimental design was the use of two subliminal tapes, one claiming to improve self-esteem and the other claiming to improve memory. They randomly assigned subjects to one of four groups and gave them all pretests on measures of self-esteem and memory. Members of group 1 were given the memory tape to listen to for a set period of time and told it would help improve their memory; those in group 2 were given the same memory tape but were told it would improve their self-esteem. (Remember, on subliminal tapes you can't, by definition, hear the messages, only the surface music.) Group 3 was given the self-esteem tape and told it would improve self-esteem, and group 4 was given the same self-esteem tape but were told that it would improve memory. All subjects listened to their respective tapes for exactly the same length of time, at the same times of the day, etc. Later they were given another test of self-esteem and memory. The pretest and posttest scores for all conditions were compared.

What do you think the results showed? If you believe the claims of those who promote the power of subliminal tapes, then groups 1 and 3 should have shown significant improvement in memory and self-esteem scores, respectively. And, one would assume, if the results were not due to some placebo effect, then groups 2 and 4 should have shown some change—memory improvement for group 2 and self-esteem improvement for group 4—because that is what they were actually exposed to.

The results were clear and unequivocal: there was no improvement in any of the groups between their pretest and posttest scores. In contrast to the claims of their promoters, subliminal tapes were shown to be of no value in improving memory or self-esteem.

This is a good example of how useful the scientific method is in answering questions of a psychological nature. Can you apply what you know about scientific psychology to answer other questions you may have?

Progress Test 1

1. d	6. d	11. a
2. d	7. b	12. d
3. b	8. d	13. a
4. c	9. a	14. a
5. d	10. c	15. b

Progress Test 2

1. a	6. a	11. c
2. c	7. b	12. b
3. c	8. d	13. b
4. a	9. c	14. a
5. b	10. a	15. a

Progress Test 3

1. c	6. c	11. a
2. d	7. a	12. a
3. c	8. d	13. b
4. c	9. a	14. e
5. b	10. c	15. d

CHAPTER 2

Neuroscience and Behavior

<table>
<tr>
<td>PREVIEW</td>
<td>Reading the section below first will give you a general sense of the chapter's contents and an initial introduction to some of the major concepts and terms. This will prime you for what you are about to read and help you to develop a "cognitive map" that will guide your study of the material in this chapter. Likewise, reading the preview questions at the beginning of each major section will improve your ability to understand, learn, and retain the information.</td>
</tr>
</table>

CHAPTER 2 . . . AT A GLANCE

Chapter 2 first outlines the scope and diversity of biological psychology and notes that it is one of the scientific disciplines that makes important contributions to neuroscience. Biological psychologists (biopsychologists or psychobiologists) investigate the physical processes underlying psychological experiences, mental processes, and behavior. The chapter begins with a description of the structure and functions of the neuron. Next, neural activation, synaptic transmission, and the role of neurotransmitters are outlined. The functions and effects of several neurotransmitters are discussed, as are the effects of certain drugs on neurotransmission.

The next section discusses the structures and functions of the divisions of the nervous system: the central nervous system, which consists of the brain and spinal cord; and the peripheral nervous system, which includes the somatic and autonomic nervous systems. The sympathetic and parasympathetic systems, which make up the autonomic nervous system, are described. This section ends by focusing on the endocrine system, its glands, and its chemical messengers, called hormones.

The section on the brain first discusses the neural pathways, functional and structural plasticity as well as neurogenesis. The tour of the brain then takes you through the regions of the hindbrain, midbrain, and forebrain, including their structures and functions. The different roles of the four lobes of the brain's cerebral hemispheres (temporal, occipital, parietal, and frontal) are explained, and the functions of forebrain structures in the limbic system—the hippocampus, thalamus, hypothalamus, and amygdala—are described.

The chapter ends with a discussion of hemispheric specialization and the part played by split-brain patients in discovering the specialized functions of the brain's hemispheres. The Application suggests ways of maximizing your brain's potential.

Introduction: Neuroscience and Behavior

Preview Questions

Consider the following questions as you study this section of the chapter.

- What is biological psychology?
- What is neuroscience?
- What systems and structures are of interest to biopsychologists?

*Read the section "Introduction: Neuroscience and Behavior" and **write** your answers to the following:*

1. Biological psychology is _____

   _____

2. Neuroscience is _____

   _____

   _____

3. The systems and structures that lay an important foundation for psychological principles discussed in later chapters are _____

   _____

   _____

The Neuron: The Basic Unit of Communication

Preview Questions

Consider the following questions as you study this section of the chapter.

- How is information in the nervous system transmitted?
- What are glial cells, and what are the three main types of neurons?
- What are the basic components of the neuron, and what are their functions?
- How is information communicated within and between neurons, and what are excitatory and inhibitory neurotransmitter messages?
- What are some common neurotransmitters, and what are their primary roles?
- How can drugs affect synaptic transmission?

*Read the section "The Neuron: The Basic Unit of Communication" and **write** your answers to the following:*

1. Glial cells (glia) are _____

   _____

2. Information is transmitted in the nervous system by the three basic types of neurons:

   _____

   _____

   Their functions are_____

   _____

   _____

3. The basic components of the neuron and their functions are _____

   _____

   _____

   _____

   _____

4. Within the neuron, information is communicated (describe the complete process) _____

   _____

   _____

   _____

   _____

   _____

5. Communication between neurons may be electrical or chemical. When communication is electrical (in less than 1 percent of synapses)

   _____

   _____

   Chemically, communication involves _____

   _____

   _____

   Reuptake is the process by which _____

   _____

   _____

6. An excitatory neurotransmitter message _____

   _____

   An inhibitory neurotransmitter message _____

   _____

7. Some important neurotransmitters (and their primary roles) are _____

   _____

   _____

   _____

8. Drugs can affect synaptic transmission by _____

_____

_____

_____

After you have carefully studied the preceding sections, complete the following exercises.

Concept Check 1

Read the following and decide which neurotransmitter is most likely involved:

1. Mrs. Cartwright's memory functions have deteriorated, and she has been diagnosed as suffering from Alzheimer's disease.

_____

2. The painkilling effect of morphine no longer worked after Hiu took the drug naloxone, which eliminated the effects of both _____ and _____ by blocking opiate receptors in his brain.

3. When Gerald was bitten by a black widow spider, he suffered severe, uncontrollable muscle spasms and had great difficulty breathing.

_____

4. When Melanie was suffering from severe depression, her doctor prescribed Prozac, which he said would help alleviate the symptoms of her mood disorder by increasing the availability of a particular neurotransmitter.

_____

5. Patients afflicted with Parkinson's disease suffer from rigidity, muscle tremors, and poor balance and have trouble initiating movements. These symptoms are believed to result from diminished production of the neurotransmitter

_____ .

6. George suffers from chronic anxiety. His doctor has prescribed the antianxiety drug Valium because it works by increasing

_____ , which inhibits action potentials and reduces brain activity.

7. Mr. Lee had his back pain treated by an ancient Chinese medical technique called acupuncture. Inserting needles in various parts of his body may have reduced his perception of pain because of the involvement of

_____ .

8. After being hit with an arrow coated with the drug curare, a person becomes paralyzed. This occurs because curare mimics a neurotransmitter called _____ and blocks its receptor sites.

Graphic Organizer 1

Identify the parts of the neuron in the figure below:

a. _____   f. _____

b. _____   g. _____

c. _____   h. _____

d. _____   i. _____

e. _____

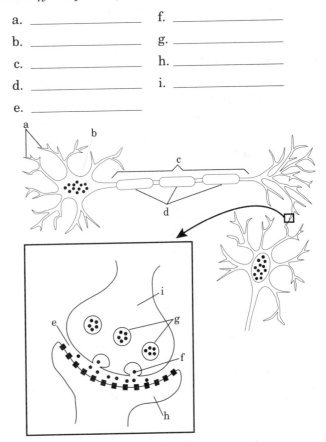

Review of Terms and Concepts 1

Use the terms in this list to complete the Matching Test, then to help you answer the True/False items correctly.

biological psychology (biopsychology or psychobiology)
neuroscience
neuron
glial cells (glia)
sensory neuron
motor neuron
interneuron
cell body (soma)
nucleus
chromosomes
dendrites
axon

myelin sheath
nodes of Ranvier (nodes)
multiple sclerosis
action potential
ions and ion channels
stimulus threshold
polarization
depolarization
resting potential
all-or-none law
refractory period
synapse
presynaptic neuron/
   postsynaptic neuron

synaptic gap
axon terminals
synaptic vesicles
neurotransmitter
synaptic transmission
reuptake
excitatory and
 inhibitory messages
acetylcholine
Alzheimer's disease
dopamine

Parkinson's disease
serotonin
norepinephrine
GABA (gamma-
 amniobutyric acid)
opiates
endorphins
acupuncture
curare
naloxone

Matching Exercise

Match the appropriate term from the list with its definition or description.

1. _____ Highly specialized cell that communicates information in electrical and chemical form.

2. _____ Neurotransmitter that usually communicates an inhibitory message.

3. _____ Neurotransmitters that regulate pain perception.

4. _____ Small gaps that separate segments of the myelin sheath that surrounds the axons of many neurons.

5. _____ Neurotransmitter that is involved in sleep, moods, and emotional states, including depression.

6. _____ The part of a neuron that contains the nucleus.

7. _____ Disease that involves the degeneration of patches of the myelin sheath that surrounds many neurons and causes such symptoms as muscular weakness, loss of coordination, and disturbances in speech and vision.

8. _____ Chemical messenger manufactured in the synaptic vesicles of a neuron.

9. _____ Neural condition in which the axon's interior is more negatively charged than the exterior fluid surrounding it, which occurs while the neuron is waiting for sufficient stimulation to activate it.

10. _____ The point of communication between two neurons.

11. _____ Tiny pouches, or sacs, in the axon terminals that contain chemicals called neurotransmitters.

12. _____ Neurotransmitter involved in the regulation of bodily movements and pleasurable or rewarding sensations.

13. _____ Minimum level of stimulation required to activate a particular neuron.

14. _____ The scientific study of the nervous system.

15. _____ Time period, lasting a thousandth of a second or less, that follows the action potential and during which the neuron is unable to fire.

16. _____ Disease characterized by progressive loss of memory and deterioration of intellectual functioning, caused by severe depletion of several neurotransmitters, most notably, acetylcholine.

17. _____ Specific group of painkilling drugs derived from the opium poppy that includes morphine, heroin, and codeine.

18. _____ Ancient Chinese medical technique that involves inserting needles at various locations in the body.

19. _____ Drug that eliminates the effects of both endorphins and opiates by blocking opiate receptor sites.

20. _____ Disease characterized by rigidity, muscle tremors, poor balance, and difficulty in initiating movements, caused by the degeneration of neurons in one brain area that produces dopamine.

21. _____ Twisted strands of DNA in the nucleus of the cell body.

22. _____ Structure in the cell body that contains the cell's genetic material.

True/False Test

Indicate whether each statement is true or false by placing T or F in the blank space next to each item.

1. ____ Norepinephrine is involved in activation of neurons throughout the brain, is critical in the body's response to danger, and is implicated in learning and memory retrieval.

2. ____ Biological psychology (biopsychology or psychobiology) is the specialized branch of psychology that studies the relationship between behavior and bodily processes and systems.

3. ____ Reuptake is the process in which neurotransmitters are released by one neuron, cross the synaptic gap, and affect adjoining neurons.

4. ____ Glial cells (glia) assist neurons by providing structural support, nutrition, and removal of cell wastes; they also enhance the speed of communication between neurons by manufacturing myelin.

5. ___ Interneurons communicate information from one neuron to the next.

6. ___ Synaptic transmission is the process by which neurotransmitter molecules detach from a postsynaptic neuron and are reabsorbed by a presynaptic neuron so that they can be recycled and used again.

7. ___ Axon terminals are branches at the end of the axon that contain tiny pouches, or sacs, called synaptic vesicles.

8. ___ Neurons that communicate information to the brain from specialized receptor cells in sense organs and internal organs are called motor neurons.

9. ___ Dendrites are multiple short fibers that extend from the neuron's cell body and receive information from other neurons or from sensory receptor cells.

10. ___ The myelin sheath is a white, fatty covering wrapped around the axons of some neurons that increases their speed of communication.

11. ___ The resting potential is a brief electrical impulse by which information is transmitted along the axon of a neuron.

12. ___ Acetylcholine is a neurotransmitter that produces muscle contractions and is involved in memory functions.

13. ___ The synaptic gap is a tiny space between the axon terminal of one neuron and the dendrite of an adjoining neuron.

14. ___ The all-or-none law states that either a neuron is sufficiently stimulated and an action potential occurs or a neuron is not sufficiently stimulated and an action potential does not occur.

15. ___ Sensory neurons are a type of neuron that signal muscles to contract or relax.

16. ___ The action potential is a state in which a neuron is prepared to activate and communicate its message if it receives sufficient stimulation.

17. ___ The long, fluid-filled tube that carries a neuron's messages to other body areas is called the axon.

18. ___ The message-sending neuron is called the presynaptic neuron, and the message-receiving neuron is called the postsynaptic neuron.

19. ___ The drug curare mimics acetylcholine and blocks acetylcholine receptor sites, causing almost instantaneous paralysis.

20. ___ An excitatory message increases the likelihood that the postsynaptic neuron will activate, and an inhibitory message decreases the likelihood that the postsynaptic neuron will activate.

21. ___ The axon membrane opens and closes ion channels that allow electrically charged particles (ions) to flow into and out of the axon.

22. ___ When the neuron is sufficiently stimulated by other neurons or sensory receptors, the action potential begins, a process called *depolarization*.

Check your answers and review any areas of weakness before going on to the next section.

The Nervous System and the Endocrine System: Communication Throughout the Body

Preview Questions

Consider the following questions as you study this section of the chapter.

- What are the two main divisions of the nervous system, and what does each include?
- What are spinal reflexes?
- What are the key components of the peripheral nervous system, and what are their functions?
- What is the endocrine system, and how does it transmit information?
- How does the endocrine system interact with the nervous system?
- What are the specific functions of the pituitary gland, the adrenal glands, and the gonads?

*Read the section "The Nervous System and the Endocrine System: Communication Throughout the Body" and **write** your answers to the following:*

1. The two main divisions of the nervous system and their components are _____

_____

_____

2. Spinal reflexes are _____

_____

3. The key components of the peripheral nervous system and their functions are_____

_____

_____

_____

_____

4. The two branches of the autonomic nervous system and their functions are _____

_____

_____

_____

5. The endocrine system is made up of_____

_____

_____

6. The endocrine system interacts with the nervous system in a number of ways: _____

_____

_____

_____

_____

_____

_____

7. The hypothalamus serves as _____

_____

_____

8. The pituitary gland's hormones affect _____

_____

_____

The adrenal glands (adrenal cortex and adrenal medulla) are involved in _____

_____

_____

The gonads are _____

_____

_____

_____

After you have carefully studied the preceding section, complete the following exercises.

Concept Check 2

Read the following and complete the sentence with the correct term:

1. Allison accidentally touched a hot stove top and immediately withdrew her hand before becoming consciously aware of the sensation or movement. She was able to do this because of her _____ .

2. Always a daredevil, Miguel dove off the cliff into the river below. Unfortunately, he landed on his head and is now paralyzed from the shoulders down. Fortunately, though, all his mental functions are intact, and he is attempting to complete his college degree. His present inability to move the lower part of his body is a result of permanent damage to his

_____ .

3. At home alone late one night, Jason had just finished watching the most frightening video he had ever seen when there was a knock on the door. His heart rate suddenly increased, his breathing accelerated, and he began to sweat. These physiological changes were most likely triggered by his

_____ .

4. When Jason answered the door, he discovered it was the pizza delivery; before long he calmed down and his blood pressure, heart rate, and breathing returned to their normal state. These physical reactions were most likely regulated by his _____ .

5. Jason's initial reaction to the knock on the door (his fight-or-flight response) resulted in his adrenal glands (in particular, the adrenal medulla) releasing the two hormones _____ and _____ .

6. When Munro tripped and fell headlong down the flight of stairs, he suffered only minor scrapes and bruises. His brain and spinal cord were protected from serious damage because they are suspended in _____ .

7. When Jannelle breast-feeds her baby, there is a complex interaction among the nervous system, the endocrine system, and behavior. The production of prolactin, which stimulates milk production, and oxytocin, which produces the

let-down reflex, is a function of the _____ gland, which is under the direction of a brain structure called the _____ .

8. In a discussion about the brain and nervous system, Tom contends that there is no difference between nerves and neurons. His roommate Salvador, who is taking introductory psychology, explains the difference by pointing out that _____ are made up of large bundles of _____ axons.

9. Before entering ninth grade, Kristofer had to have most of his clothes replaced because he had grown almost five inches since the previous spring. This relatively sudden increase in height was probably the result of his _____ gland producing _____ .

10. Young Minnie and Max are twins. Minnie's sexual development will be regulated by the hormones _____ and

_____ , which are produced by her ovaries, whereas Max's sexual development will be regulated by an androgen called _____ , which is produced by his testes.

11. As Estelle was searching for some change in her purse she accidentally dropped her keys on the floor. She quickly reached down, retrieved her keys, and put them back in her purse. This voluntary reaction involved _____ (motor/sensory) signals that were communicated to her muscles via the _____ (somatic/autonomic) nervous system.

12. While Randolf is relaxing on the couch after lunch, his heart rate, blood pressure, breathing, and digestion all are functioning without any conscious effort on his part. This is because a subdivision of the _____ nervous system called the _____ regulates these involuntary functions.

Graphic Organizer 2

Mapping the Divisions and Functions of the Nervous System

In the following organizational chart of the nervous system, write the name of each division and choose the appropriate function of each from the list below *(e.g., A is the appropriate choice for the nervous system).*

The nervous system (A)

```
                    ( )                              ( )
        ( )          ( )          ( )                    ( )
                          ( )                  ( )
```

A. Complex, organized communication system of nerves and neurons.
B. Maintains normal bodily functions and conserves physical resources.
C. Produces rapid physical changes to perceived threats and emergencies.
D. Includes all nerves lying outside the central nervous system.
E. Communicates sensory and motor information.
F. Consists of the brain and the spinal cord.
G. Regulates involuntary functions such as heartbeat and respiration.
H. Main organ of the nervous system; made up of billions of neurons.
I. System that handles both incoming and outgoing messages to and from the brain.

endocrine system
hormones
hypothalamus
pituitary gland
growth hormone
prolactin
oxytocin
adrenal glands

adrenal cortex
adrenal medulla
immune system
gonads
estrogen, progesterone, and testosterone (an androgen)

Review of Terms and Concepts 2

Use the terms in this list to complete the Matching Test, then to help you answer the True/False items correctly.

nervous system
nerves
central nervous system (CNS)
meninges
cerebrospinal fluid
ventricles
neural stem cells
spinal reflexes
withdrawal reflex

peripheral nervous system
somatic nervous system
autonomic nervous system
sympathetic nervous system
fight-or-flight response
parasympathetic nervous system

Matching Exercise

Match the appropriate term with its definition or description.

1. _____ Bundles of neuron axons that carry information in the peripheral nervous system.

2. _____ System composed of glands located throughout the body that secrete hormones into the bloodstream.

3. _____ Simple, automatic behaviors that are processed in the spinal cord without any brain involvement.

4. _____ Pair of endocrine glands that are involved in the human stress response.

5. _____ The brain and spinal cord are suspended in this fluid, which protects them from being jarred.

6. _____ Brain structure that regulates the release of hormones by the pituitary gland.

7. _____ Hormone secreted by the pituitary gland that stimulates normal skeletal growth during childhood.

8. _____ Division of the nervous system that includes all the nerves lying outside the central nervous system.

9. _____ In nursing mothers, the hormone produced by the pituitary gland that stimulates milk production.

10. _____ Body's defense system against invading viruses and bacteria.

11. _____ Hormone secreted by the pituitary gland that produces the let-down reflex, in which stored milk is "let down" into the nipple.

12. _____ Endocrine glands (ovaries in females and testes in males) that secrete hormones that regulate sexual characteristics and reproductive processes.

13. _____ The three layers of membranous tissue surrounding and protecting the brain and spinal cord.

14. _____ Specialized cells that line the inner surface of the ventricles in the adult brain and which produce neurons in the developing brain.

True/False Test

Indicate whether each statement is true or false by placing T or F in the blank space next to each item.

1. ____ The nervous system is the primary internal communication network of the body; it is divided into the central nervous system and the peripheral nervous system.

2. ____ The central nervous system is a major division of the nervous system and consists of the brain and the spinal cord.

3. ____ The pituitary gland is an endocrine gland attached to the base of the brain which secretes hormones that affect the function of other glands as well as hormones that act directly on physical processes.

4. ____ The fight-or-flight response refers to physiological changes such as increased heart rate, accelerated breathing, dry mouth, and perspiration that occur in response to perceived threats or danger.

5. ____ The parasympathetic nervous system is a branch of the autonomic nervous system that produces rapid physical arousal in response to perceived emergencies or threats.

6. ____ Hormones are chemical messengers that are secreted into the bloodstream by endocrine glands.

7. ____ The somatic nervous system is a subdivision of the peripheral nervous system that regulates involuntary functions such as heartbeat, digestion, breathing, and blood pressure.

8. ____ The adrenal medulla is the inner portion of the adrenal glands that secretes epinephrine and norepinephrine.

9. ____ The branch of the autonomic nervous system that maintains normal bodily functions and conserves the body's physical resources is called the sympathetic nervous system.

10. ____ The adrenal cortex is the outer portion of the adrenal glands.

11. ____ The autonomic nervous system is a subdivision of the peripheral nervous system that communicates sensory information to the central nervous system and carries motor messages from the central nervous system to the muscles.

12. ____ Testosterone, estrogen, and progesterone are sex hormones that regulate sexual characteristics and reproductive processes.

13. ____ The withdrawal reflex occurs when a painful stimulus, such as something hot, electrified, or sharp, is touched.

14. ____ Ventricles are the four hollow cavities in the brain that are filled with cerebrospinal fluid and lined with neural stem cells.

Check your answers and review any areas of weakness before going on to the next section.

A Guided Tour of the Brain

Preview Questions

Consider the following questions as you study this section of the chapter.

- What are neural pathways, and why are they important?

- What are functional plasticity and structural plasticity?

- What is neurogenesis?
- What are the key structures of the hindbrain and midbrain, and what functions are associated with each structure?
- What are the two main structures of the forebrain, and what functions have been identified with each of the four lobes of the cerebral cortex?
- What are the key limbic system structures, and what role do they play in behavior?

Read the section "A Guided Tour of the Brain" and **write** your answers to the following:

1. Neural pathways are _____

They are important because _____

2. Neuroplasticity refers to _____

They are important because _____

Structural plasticity is _____

3. Neurogenesis refers to _____

4. The key structures of the hindbrain and their functions are _____

5. The midbrain is _____

6. The forebrain includes _____

7. The four lobes and their functions are ____

8. The main structures of the limbic system and their functions are _____

After you have carefully studied the preceding sections, complete the following exercises.

Concept Check 3

Read the following and write the name of the brain part or the correct term in the space provided.

1. Marcel had a stroke on the *right* side of his brain in an area that controls motor movement; as a result, he has trouble moving limbs on the *left* side of his body. This is because incoming sensory messages and outgoing motor messages cross over at the _____ level of the brain.

2. If this area of your brain was electrically stimulated while you were fast asleep, you would wake up instantly. _____

3. After Larry was hit in the head by a baseball, his movements became jerky and uncoordinated, and he could no longer type or play his guitar. _____

4. In the third round of a boxing match, Bruno caught a right hook that snapped his head back; when he hit the canvas, his breathing stopped. _____

5. Ever since his automobile accident six months ago, Sam watches the same video day after day and each time responds to it as though he has never seen it before. All his other sensory functions appear to be intact, but it is clear that one brain area was damaged in the accident that prevents him from forming new memories.

_____

6. Because of a tumor growing in her brain, Janna has lost her senses of taste, sight, hearing, and touch, but not her sense of smell. The area of the brain involved in regulating these behaviors is the _____ .

7. Following an industrial accident, Harinder has lost his ability to plan, initiate, and execute voluntary movements, and he has problems with emotional control and in thinking clearly. It is most likely that the accident damaged his

_____ .

8. Mr. Endo has been diagnosed with Parkinson's disease. Many of his movement-related symptoms are associated with the degeneration of dopamine-producing neurons in a midbrain structure called the _____ .

9. When researchers electrically stimulated a forebrain structure in a cat, its back arched, its fur bristled, and it showed all the characteristic feline signs of rage and anger. The part of the cat's limbic system that was stimulated was the

_____ .

10. Morgana believes that you can tell a lot about a man's personality, character, and mental ability simply by examining the size and shape of his skull. Morgana's views are most like those of the popular nineteenth-century pseudoscience _____ , which, strangely enough, triggered scientific interest in the notion that specific psychological and mental functions are located or localized in specific brain areas, an idea called _____ .

11. Following a stroke, Bruce was unable to talk coherently and was partially paralyzed on his right side. However, through rehabilitation therapy he "relearned" to talk and walk. It appears that undamaged areas in his brain have gradually assumed the ability to process and execute these once routine tasks, a process called _____ .

12. Dr. Lassiter and her colleagues conduct research on brain areas such as the hippocampus, the thalamus, the hypothalamus, and the amygdala. These are all components of the area of the forebrain called

_____ .

13. During her ballet class, Emmalee executed a number of difficult moves, including a series of pirouettes on point. She is able to accomplish this difficult dance routine because somatosen-

sory information about her muscles and joints, and the position of her arms and legs, are relayed to the _____ lobe in her brain.

Graphic Organizer 3

Chart Diagram Exercise: The Key Structures of the Limbic System

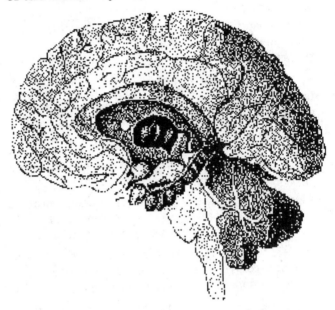

To help you develop the technique of creating your own graphic organizers, we encourage you to try to locate the structures listed below in the following outline of a brain. Then, on a separate piece of paper, write a description of each structure.
Locate and describe the following:
(a) Hippocampus
(b) Hypothalamus
(c) Thalamus
(d) Amygdala

Review of Terms and Concepts 3

Use the terms in this list to complete the Matching Test, then to help you answer the True/False items correctly.

neural pathways
neuroplasticity (or plasticity)
functional plasticity
structural plasticity
phrenology
cortical localization (localization of function)
neurogenesis
brainstem

hindbrain
contralateral organization
medulla
pons
cerebellum
reticular formation (reticular activating system)
midbrain
substantia nigra

forebrain
cerebral cortex
cerebral hemispheres
corpus callosum
temporal lobe
primary auditory cortex
occipital lobe
primary visual cortex
parietal lobe
somatosensory cortex
frontal lobe
primary motor cortex

association areas
prefrontal association
  cortex
limbic system
hippocampus
thalamus
hypothalamus
suprachiasmatic nucleus
  (SCN)
amygdala

Matching Exercise

Match the appropriate term with its definition or description.

1. _____ The nearly symmetrical left and right halves of the cerebral cortex.

2. _____ The area on each cerebral hemisphere located above the temporal lobe that processes somatosensory information.

3. _____ Midbrain area involved in motor control and containing a large concentration of dopamine-producing neurons.

4. _____ The part of the temporal lobe that enables hearing.

5. _____ Hindbrain structure that connects the medulla to the two sides of the cerebellum; helps coordinate and integrate movement on each side of the body.

6. _____ Forebrain structure that processes motor information and sensory information from all the senses, except smell, and relays it to higher brain centers.

7. _____ The part of the occipital lobe that receives information from the eyes.

8. _____ The curved forebrain structure that is part of the limbic system and is involved in learning and forming new memories.

9. _____ Region of the brain made up of the hindbrain and the midbrain.

10. _____ Band of tissue in the frontal lobe on which the movements of different parts of the body are represented.

11. _____ Large association area of the brain, situated in front of the primary motor cortex, that is involved in the planning of voluntary movements.

12. _____ Hindbrain structure that controls vital life functions such as breathing, circulation, heart rate, and digestion.

13. _____ Network of nerve fibers located at the center of the medulla and pons that helps regulate attention, arousal, and sleep.

14. _____ Area of the hypothalamus that plays a key role in regulating daily sleep–wake cycles and other body rhythms.

15. _____ The development of new neurons.

16. _____ The brain's ability to shift functions from damaged to undamaged brain areas.

17. _____ Pseudoscience based on the assumption that bumps on the skull reveal personality characteristics and abilities.

18. _____ Networks formed by groups of neuron cell bodies in one area of the brain projecting their axons to other brain areas, forming communication circuits and links between them.

True/False Test

Indicate whether each statement is true or false by placing T or F in the blank space next to each item.

1. ____ The frontal lobe is the largest lobe of the cerebral cortex; processes voluntary muscle movement and is involved in thinking, planning, and emotional expression and control.

2. ____ The somatosensory cortex is a band of tissue on the parietal lobe that receives information from touch receptors in different parts of the body.

3. ____ The midbrain is a region at the base of the brain that contains several structures that regulate basic life functions.

4. ____ The cerebellum is an almond-shaped forebrain structure that is part of the limbic system and involved in emotion and memory.

5. ____ The forebrain, the largest and most complex brain region, contains centers for complex behaviors and mental processes.

6. ____ The cerebral cortex is the wrinkled outer portion of the forebrain that contains the most sophisticated brain centers.

7. ____ The amygdala is the large, two-sided hindbrain structure at the back of the brain that is responsible for muscle coordination and maintaining posture and equilibrium.

8. ____ The occipital lobe is a region at the back of each cerebral cortex hemisphere that is the primary receiving area for visual information.

9. ____ The association areas, which make up the bulk of the cerebral cortex and are the regions in which sensory and motor information is combined, produce complex, sophisticated human behaviors.

10. ____ The temporal lobe is an area on each hemisphere that is the primary receiving area for auditory information.

11. ____ The hindbrain is the middle and smallest brain region that is involved in processing auditory and visual sensory information.

12. ____ Neuroplasticity (or plasticity) refers to the brain's ability to change structure and function.

13. ____ The limbic system is a group of forebrain structures that form a border around the brainstem and are involved in emotions, motivation, learning, and memory.

14. ____ The hypothalamus is a peanut-sized forebrain structure that is part of the limbic system and is involved in diverse functions such as eating, drinking, sexual activity, and fear and aggression; it exerts control over the secretion of endocrine hormones by directly influencing the pituitary gland.

15. ____ The thick band of nerve fibers that connects the two cerebral hemispheres and acts as a communication link between them, is called the corpus callosum.

16. ____ Cortical localization (also known as localization of function) refers to the notion that different functions are located or localized in different areas of the brain.

17. ____ Contralateral organization refers to the crossing over of the right and left sensory and motor pathways in the hindbrain.

18. ____ Structural plasticity refers to the brain's ability to change its structure in response to learning, active practice, or environmental stimulation.

Check your answers and review any areas of weakness before going on to the next section.

Specialization in the Cerebral Hemispheres

Preview Questions

Consider the following questions as you study this section of the chapter.

- What did Broca and Wernicke contribute to our knowledge of the brain?
- What is lateralization of function?
- What is aphasia, Broca's aphasia, and Wernicke's aphasia?
- What is the split-brain operation, and what did tests on split-brain patients reveal about differences in the abilities of the two hemispheres?
- What are the most important functions of each cerebral hemisphere?

*Read the section "Specialization in the Cerebral Hemispheres" and **write** your answers to the following:*

1. Broca and Wernicke provided the first evidence that _____

   _____

2. Lateralization of function (or lateralization) is

   _____

   _____

   _____

3. Aphasia refers to _____

   _____

   Broca's aphasia results in _____

   _____

   Wernicke's aphasia results in _____

   _____

4. The split-brain operation involves _____

   _____

5. In a specialized procedure, split-brain patients are directed to focus on a point in the middle of a screen and then _____

   _____

   Split-brain patients can _____

   _____

   _____

6. Tests on split-brain patients revealed that the left hemisphere is specialized for _____

_____

_____

and the right hemisphere is specialized for

_____

_____

_____

After you have carefully studied the preceding section, complete the following exercises.

Concept Check 4

Complete the following examples by placing the term right *or* left *in each blank:*

1. A blindfolded split-brain patient would be able to verbally identify an object placed in her _____ hand but not in her _____ hand.

2. When the picture of an apple was flashed to the _____ of the midpoint on the screen during an experiment with a split-brain patient, the patient was not able to say what he saw. However, he could draw a picture of the object with his _____ hand.

3. When a swear word was flashed to her _____ hemisphere, a split-brain patient could not say what she saw but showed some nonverbal signs of embarrassment.

4. The fact that a split-brain patient had trouble assembling colored blocks to match a design with his left hand but not his right hand suggests that the _____ hemisphere is superior to the _____ hemisphere at perceptual tasks that involve deciphering visual cues, reading maps, copying designs, and so on.

Review of Terms, Concepts, and Names 4

Use the terms in this list to complete the Matching Test, then to help you answer the True/False items correctly.

cortical localization
   (localization of
   function)
Pierre Paul Broca
Broca's area
Karl Wernicke
Wernicke's area
lateralization of function

aphasia
Broca's aphasia
   (expressive aphasia)
Wernicke's aphasia
   (receptive aphasia)
split-brain operation
Roger Sperry

Matching Exercise

Match the appropriate term/name with its definition or description.

1. _____ American psychologist who received the Nobel Prize in 1981 for his pioneering research on brain specialization in split-brain patients.

2. _____ The partial or complete inability to articulate ideas or understand spoken or written language due to brain damage or injury.

3. _____ The language area on the left temporal lobe concerned with speech comprehension.

4. _____ The notion that different functions are located, or localized, in different areas of the brain.

5. _____ Language area on the lower left frontal lobe of the cerebral cortex.

6. _____ The notion that specific psychological or cognitive functions are processed primarily on one side of the brain.

True/False Test

Indicate whether each statement is true or false by placing T or F in the blank space next to each item.

1. ____ Karl Wernicke was a German neurologist who discovered an area on the left temporal lobe that, when damaged, produces meaningless or nonsensical speech and difficulties in verbal or written comprehension.

2. ____ The split-brain operation is a surgical procedure that involves cutting the corpus callosum.

3. ___ People with Wernicke's aphasia find it difficult or impossible to produce speech, but their comprehension of verbal or written words is relatively unaffected.

4. ___ Pierre Paul Broca was a French surgeon and neuroanatomist who discovered an area on the lower left frontal lobe that, when damaged, produces speech disturbances but no loss of comprehension.

5. ___ Patients with Broca's aphasia can speak but may have problems finding the right words and typically have great difficulty understanding written or spoken communication.

Check your answers and review any areas of weakness before going on to the next section.

Something to Think About

1. A biological psychologist who specializes in the assessment and diagnosis of people with brain-related problems is faced with the following cases. On the basis of what you now know about biological psychology, the brain, and the functions of the nervous system, give some thought to what the specialist's assessment might be.
   (a) Fraser slipped on ice and hit the back of his head on the sidewalk, and now his vision is seriously affected. Which brain area is most likely affected?
   (b) Following an operation to remove a brain tumor, Yoko is able to read and understand written and spoken language but has difficulty speaking and expressing herself clearly. It is likely that she has damage in which part of the brain?
   (c) Ever since a part of her limbic system was destroyed, Vanessa has had trouble controlling her appetite and has had a constant urge to eat and drink. Which structure was most likely damaged?
   (d) Mr. Ashley has a disorder that is characterized by rigidity, muscle tremors, poor balance, and difficulty in initiating movements.

2. Family members and friends who know you are taking a psychology course may ask you some interesting and curious questions. One often-asked question is, "I know that regular exercise helps keep me in shape physically, but is there anything I can do to prevent mental

deterioration?" What advice would you give in response to that question?

Check your answers and review any areas of weakness before doing the following progress tests.

Progress Test 1

Review the complete chapter (including all boxed inserts), review all your study notes, and then test yourself on the following progress test. Check your answers. If you make a mistake, review your notes, check the appropriate section in the study guide, and, if necessary, go back and read the relevant part of the chapter in your textbook.

1. A hunter in a South American jungle uses the poisonous drug curare on the tip of his arrow. When the arrow strikes an animal, the animal becomes almost instantly limp and quickly suffocates because its respiratory system has become paralyzed. The curare has _____ the neurotransmitter acetylcholine.
   (a) blocked the release of
   (b) blocked the receptors for
   (c) increased the release of
   (d) increased the reuptake of

2. Miguel has been diagnosed with schizophrenia. His psychologist believes that Miguel's hallucinations and perceptual distortions may be caused, in part, by _____ amounts of the neurotransmitter _____ .
   (a) diminished; dopamine
   (b) excessive; dopamine
   (c) diminished; serotonin
   (d) excessive; serotonin

3. Jenny has just finished running a very tough marathon (26.22 miles) but seems to be very happy and elated. According to Focus on Neuroscience, one cause of her "runner's high" may be abnormally high levels of chemical substances in her brain called
   (a) acetylcholines.   (c) endorphins.
   (b) serotonins.   (d) dopamines.

4. Mrs. Danvers has multiple sclerosis. She experiences muscle weakness, loss of coordination and speech, and visual disturbances that result from the slowdown or interruption of neural transmission. The cause of these symptoms probably involves the degeneration of the
   (a) dendrites.   (c) myelin sheath.
   (b) corpus callosum.   (d) synaptic vesicles.

5. When Dr. Maxwell electrically stimulated a specific area of a patient's right cerebral hemisphere, the patient's left hand twitched. The part of the cortex that was stimulated was
   (a) Broca's area.
   (b) the primary motor cortex.
   (c) Wernicke's area.
   (d) the somatosensory cortex.

6. Neurotransmitters are to hormones as _____ is (are) to _____ .
   (a) nervous system; endocrine system
   (b) nerves; neurons
   (c) hypothalamus; pituitary gland
   (d) brain; spinal cord

7. When Mike was faced with a final exam worth 80 percent of his grade in his graduate statistics class, he was totally stressed out. The particular gland(s) in his endocrine system that is (are) likely to be stimulated is (are) the
   (a) thyroid.   (c) adrenal glands.
   (b) pituitary gland.   (d) nervous glands.

8. If researchers electrically stimulate the reticular formation in a sleeping cat, it is most likely that the cat will
   (a) aggressively attack the researchers.
   (b) stop breathing.
   (c) become paralyzed on both sides of the body.
   (d) instantly wake up, fully alert.

9. If researchers destroy the amygdala of a timid cat, it is likely that the cat will
   (a) become even more fearful.
   (b) lose its timidity and fearfulness.
   (c) become a vicious predator and start attacking large dogs.
   (d) stop breathing and die.

10. If a normal right-handed individual sustained severe damage to the right cerebral hemisphere, this would most likely reduce a number of abilities. Damage to the right hemisphere is NOT likely to affect his ability to
    (a) manipulate blocks to match a particular design.

    (b) recognize people's faces.
    (c) appreciate art and music.
    (d) decipher visual cues related to emotional expression.
    (e) produce and understand written and spoken language.

11. The occipital lobe is to _____ as the temporal lobe is to _____ .
    (a) planning; seeing
    (b) seeing; planning
    (c) seeing; hearing
    (d) hearing; seeing

12. If someone taps you on the back, you sense the touch because the _____ cortex in the _____ lobe receives this tactile information.
    (a) primary motor; frontal
    (b) primary visual; occipital
    (c) primary somatosensory; parietal
    (d) primary auditory; temporal

13. Gye-Min was so engrossed in studying for his upcoming midterm exam that he did not notice how hungry and thirsty he was until his stomach started growling. The brain structure responsible for regulating behavior related to survival, such as hunger and thirst, is called the _____ and is part of the _____ system.
    (a) hypothalamus; limbic
    (b) thalamus; endocrine
    (c) hippocampus; limbic
    (d) suprachiasmatic nucleus; endocrine
    (e) amygdala; limbic

14. According to the Application, rats were exposed to either an enriched environment or an impoverished environment. Researchers found that enrichment
    (a) increases the number and length of dendrites, enlarges the size of neurons, and produces more synaptic connections.
    (b) results in a dramatic increase in the number of neurons in the brain.
    (c) has profound effects on the brains of young rats but no effect on those of mature rats.
    (d) dramatically affects the limbic system but has little or no effect on the cerebral cortex.

15. After a tamping iron accidentally pierced his skull, Phineas Gage recovered physically but his personality was profoundly changed. He could no longer make rational decisions, he became emotionally unstable, and he could no longer work at his job. According to In Focus, his _____ were damaged.

    (a) frontal lobes
    (b) occipital lobes
    (c) parietal lobes
    (d) temporal lobes

Progress Test 2

After you have checked your understanding of the material in Progress Test 1 and have done a complete chapter review with special focus on any areas of weakness, you are ready to further assess your knowledge on Progress Test 2. Check your answers. If you make a mistake, review your notes, the appropriate parts of the study guide, and, if necessary, the relevant sections of your textbook.

1. Renata is suffering from a number of symptoms, including depression, sleep disturbances, and mood fluctuations; she also has problems in learning and memory retrieval. Her doctor prescribes Prozac and some other drugs because her problems are probably due to abnormal levels of the neurotransmitters

   (a) dopamine and acetylcholine.
   (b) serotonin and endorphins.
   (c) acetylcholine and norepinephrine.
   (d) serotonin and norepinephrine.

2. Signal reception is to _____ as signal transmission is to _____ .

   (a) myelin sheath; cell body
   (b) dendrite; axon
   (c) action potential; resting potential
   (d) axon; dendrite

3. As a result of a stroke, 75-year-old Mrs. Yee suffered brain damage. While she is no longer able to speak, she can understand what is being said to her. Mrs. Yee suffers from

   (a) damage to her occipital lobe.
   (b) Wernicke's aphasia.
   (c) damage to her left temporal lobe.
   (d) Broca's aphasia.

4. Your brain is involved in every perception, thought, and emotion, as are its neurons and their neurotransmitters. Neurotransmitters are chemical messengers that

   (a) carry information primarily in the endocrine system.
   (b) travel from the cell body along the axon and create an action potential.
   (c) assist neurons by providing physical support, nutrition, and waste removal.
   (d) travel across the synaptic gap and affect adjoining neurons.

5. If a patient suffers damage to the hippocampus, she is likely to have problems

   (a) learning and forming new memories.
   (b) remembering events and things that happened before her brain injury.
   (c) comprehending spoken and written language.
   (d) controlling emotions such as aggression, fear, anger, and disgust.

6. After Eduardo's serious skiing accident, doctors detected damage to his cerebellum. Eduardo is most likely to have trouble

   (a) swallowing, coughing, and breathing.
   (b) sleeping.
   (c) staying awake.
   (d) playing tennis, typing, and walking with a smooth gait.

7. In a typical test situation with a split-brain patient, a picture of an apple is briefly presented to the right of the center point. If the patient is asked to name what she sees, she will

   (a) be unable to say what she saw.
   (b) be able to draw a picture of the apple with her left hand.
   (c) report that she saw nothing.
   (d) say she saw an apple.

8. If a researcher anesthetizes the entire right hemisphere of a right-handed patient who is asked to recite the alphabet aloud while reclining on the operating table with both arms extended upward, it is most probable that the patient's

   (a) left arm will fall limp but she will continue saying the alphabet.
   (b) right arm will fall limp but she will continue saying the alphabet.
   (c) left arm will fall limp and she will become speechless.
   (d) right arm will fall limp and she will become speechless.

9. A champion athlete loses his medal after officials discover that he has taken anabolic steroids, a synthetic version of the male sex hormone testosterone. Anabolic steroids, like other hormones, circulate through the _____ and act as chemical messengers in the _____ .
   (a) cerebrospinal fluid; central nervous system
   (b) bloodstream; endocrine system
   (c) cerebrospinal fluid; peripheral nervous system
   (d) bloodstream; limbic system

10. In response to an exam question, Leilani carefully draws a picture of a neuron and indicates the sequence of events that are typically involved when a neuron communicates. She is likely to note that information is carried from
    (a) the axon terminals to the cell body and then down the dendrites to the synapse.
    (b) from the cell body to the dendrites and then down the axon to the axon terminals and the synapse.
    (c) from the dendrites to the axon and then down the axon to the cell body and the synapse.
    (d) the dendrites to the cell body and then along the axon to the axon terminals and the synapse.

11. The parietal lobe is to _____ as the frontal lobe is to _____ .
    (a) anticipatory thinking; hearing
    (b) sensing touch; planning
    (c) seeing; hearing
    (d) tasting; smelling

12. The chapter Prologue tells the story of Asha, who suffered a stroke. This story illustrates that the brain has a remarkable ability to gradually shift functions from damaged to undamaged areas, a phenomenon called
    (a) lateralization of function.
    (b) structural plasticity.
    (c) synaptic transmission.
    (d) functional plasticity.

13. According to Critical Thinking (His and Her Brains), which of the following is (are) false ?
    (a) Differences between male and female brains are innate and hardwired and are therefore fixed, permanent, and inevitable.
    (b) Men's brains tend to be much smaller than female brains.

    (c) In general, female brains are more asymmetrical and functions are more lateralized than in the male brain.
    (d) All of these statements are false.

14. According to Science Versus Pseudoscience (Brain Myths), which of the following is (are) a brain myth(s)?
    (a) Skilled teachers can educate the right hemisphere of the brain (in isolation from the left) to become more creative and intuitive.
    (b) The right hemisphere of the brain is solely responsible for creativity and intuition.
    (c) We use only 10 percent of our brain.
    (d) All of these are brain myths.

15. Despite the fact that phrenology was eventually dismissed as a pseudoscience, Science Versus Pseudoscience (Phrenology: The Bumpy Road to Scientific Progress) points out that phrenology played a significant role in advancing the scientific study of the brain by triggering interest in
    (a) split-brain operations for epilepsy.
    (b) the role neurotransmitters play in regulating behavior.
    (c) cortical localization, or localization of function.
    (d) how drugs affect synaptic transmission.

Progress Test 3

After you have checked your understanding of the material in Progress Tests 1 and 2 and have done a complete chapter review with special focus on any areas of weakness, you are ready to further assess your knowledge with Progress Test 3. Check your answers. If you make a mistake, review your notes, the appropriate parts of the study guide, and, if necessary, the relevant sections of your textbook.

1. When doctors removed a tumor from Andrew's occipital lobe, they also had to remove healthy brain tissue from the same area. When he recovers, Andrew is most likely to suffer some loss of
   (a) language comprehension.
   (b) muscular coordination.
   (c) visual perception.
   (d) taste perception.

2. Nancy suffers from severe epilepsy that so far has not responded to any treatment. As a final resort, her doctor operates on her brain and surgically cuts the
   - (a) amygdala.
   - (b) hippocampus.
   - (c) corpus callosum.
   - (d) adrenal cortex.

3. After a police car with flashing lights and blaring siren passes him and pulls over another driver for speeding, Jerry's heartbeat soon slows down, his blood pressure decreases, and he stops sweating so much. These calming physical reactions are most directly regulated by his
   - (a) sympathetic nervous system.
   - (b) parasympathetic nervous system.
   - (c) somatic nervous system.
   - (d) central nervous system.

4. While cooking dinner for a large family gathering, Mindy was so distracted by the conversations around her that she forgot to use an oven mitt when she grabbed a very hot roaster pan. She instantly withdrew her hand before becoming consciously aware of the sensation or her own hand movement. Mindy was able to do this because of her
   - (a) spinal reflexes.
   - (b) parasympathetic nervous system.
   - (c) high levels of endorphins.
   - (d) limbic system.

5. As a result of a stroke, Mr. Nelson can no longer understand what he reads or what is being said to him, and he often has trouble finding the right words when he tries to speak. Mr. Nelson suffers from
   - (a) Wernicke's aphasia.
   - (b) Broca's aphasia.
   - (c) Parkinson's disease.
   - (d) Alzheimer's disease.

6. If a picture of a hammer is flashed to the left of the midpoint during an experiment with a split-brain patient and she is asked to indicate what she saw, the patient will
   - (a) verbally report what she saw.
   - (b) be able to draw a picture of the hammer with her right hand.
   - (c) be unable to verbally report what she saw.
   - (d) most likely draw a picture of a nail with her right hand.

7. When reading about the brain in his psychology textbook, Damon was surprised to learn that the brain is made up of specialized cells that outnumber neurons by about 10 to 1. These cells assist neurons by providing structural support, nutrition, and removal of cell wastes. Damon was reading about
   - (a) glial cells.
   - (b) sensory cells.
   - (c) motor cells.
   - (d) interneuron cells.

8. Sonny suffered brain damage when he was knocked down in a boxing match; he can no longer hear in one ear. It is most probable that one of his _____ lobes was injured.
   - (a) ear
   - (b) occipital
   - (c) temporal
   - (d) frontal
   - (e) parietal

9. In an effort to relax after a stress-filled week, Joanne had a couple of glasses of wine, and her coworker Jim took a Valium. Both alcohol and Valium work by increasing the activity of the neurotransmitter _____ , which inhibits action potentials and slows brain activity.
   - (a) GABA
   - (b) dopamine
   - (c) norepinephrine
   - (d) serotonin

10. If Dr. Doonan's research showed that the left hemisphere is dominant for speech and language in virtually all right-handed people and the majority of left-handers, this would argue strongly for the notion of
    - (a) lateralization of function.
    - (b) the all-or-none law.
    - (c) structural plasticity.
    - (d) functional plasticity.

11. In his medical practice, Dr. Setiadi uses an ancient Chinese procedure, called _____ ,which involves inserting needles at various points in the body.
    - (a) acupuncture
    - (b) the split-brain procedure
    - (c) neurogenesis
    - (d) phrenology

12. During a lecture on the brain, Professor Chiga notes that an action potential will not occur unless a neuron is sufficiently stimulated. The principle that she is referring to is the
    (a) all-or-none law.
    (b) law of phrenology.
    (c) principle of lateralization.
    (d) principle of fight or flight.

13. Sangeeta wakes up at 7:00 A.M. every morning and is usually asleep by 11:00 P.M. at night. Her daily sleep–wake cycle is regulated by the area of her _____ called the _____ .
    (a) medulla; adrenal cortex
    (b) brainstem; pons
    (c) hypothalamus; suprachiasmatic nucleus (SCN)
    (d) hindbrain; corpus callosum

14. Researchers discovered that neural stem cells in the hippocampus developed into mature functioning neurons that appeared to become incorporated into the existing neural networks in the adult human brain. This development of new cells after birth is called
    (a) neurogenesis.
    (b) neurotransmission.
    (c) functional plasticity.
    (d) polarization.

15. For most right-handed people, the left hemisphere is dominant for language. According to Science Versus Pseudoscience (Brain Myths), for the majority of left-handed people (about 70 percent)
    (a) the right hemisphere is dominant for language.
    (b) language is processed equally in both hemispheres.
    (c) the left hemisphere is dominant for language.
    (d) language does not appear to be processed in either the left or the right hemisphere.

Answers

Introduction: Neuroscience and Behavior

1. *Biological psychology is* the specialized branch of psychology that studies the relationship between behavior and bodily processes and systems (also called biopsychology or psychobiology).

2. *Neuroscience is* the scientific study of the nervous system, especially the brain.

3. *The systems and structures that lay an important foundation for psychological principles discussed in later chapters are* the nervous system (the body's primary communication network), which is made up of neurons (the basic cells of the nervous system) and the endocrine system (a communication network closely linked to the nervous system). Also important are the major regions of the brain (hindbrain, midbrain, and forebrain) and how certain brain areas are specialized to handle different functions such as language, vision, and touch.

The Neuron: The Basic Unit of Communication

1. *Glial cells (glia) are* cells that assist neurons by providing structural support, nutrition, and removal of cell wastes; they also enhance the speed of communication between neurons by manufacturing myelin.

2. *Information is transmitted in the nervous system by the three basic types of neurons:* sensory neurons, motor neurons, and interneurons. *Their functions are* to convey information from sense organs to the brain (sensory), communicate information between neurons (interneuron), and communicate information to the body's muscles and glands (motor).

3. *The basic components of the neuron and their functions are* the cell body, which contains the nucleus and provides energy for the neuron to carry out its functions; the dendrites, which are short, branching fibers that extend out from the cell body and receive messages from other neurons or specialized cells; and the axon (often surrounded by a myelin sheath), which is a long, fluid-filled tube that carries information from the neuron to other cells in the body, including other neurons, glands, and muscles.

4. *Within the neuron, information is communicated* in the form of brief electrical impulses, called action potentials, which are produced by the movement of electrically charged particles, called ions, across the membrane of the axon. The resting potential is the state in which a neuron is prepared to activate and communicate its message if it receives sufficient stimulation. For an action potential to occur and a neuron to be activated (depolarized), stimulation must be above the stimulus threshold. In addition, neurons either respond or they don't, the all-or-none law.

5. *Communication between neurons may be electrical or chemical. When communication is electrical (in less than 1 percent of synapses),*

the synaptic gap is extremely narrow and special ion channels serve as a bridge between neurons, resulting in almost instantaneous communication. *Chemically, communication involves* neurotransmitters from the synaptic vesicles of one neuron diffusing across the synaptic gap, the space between two neurons, and affecting adjoining neurons. *Reuptake is the process by which* neurotransmitter molecules detach from a postsynaptic neuron and are reabsorbed by a presynaptic neuron so they can be recycled and used again.

6. *An excitatory neurotransmitter message* increases the likelihood that the postsynaptic neuron will activate and generate an action potential; *an inhibitory neurotransmitter message* decreases the likelihood that the postsynaptic neuron will activate.

7. *Some important neurotransmitters (and their primary roles) are* acetylcholine, which is involved in memory, learning, general intellectual functioning, and muscle contraction; dopamine, which is involved in movement, attention, learning, and pleasurable or rewarding sensations; serotonin, which is involved in sleep, moods, and emotional states; norepinephrine, which is involved in the activation of neurons, memory retrieval, learning, and physical arousal; GABA, which inhibits brain activity; and endorphins, which affect pain perceptions and positive emotions.

8. *Drugs can affect synaptic transmission by* increasing or decreasing the amount of neurotransmitter released by the neuron, by blocking the reuptake of the neurotransmitter by the sending neuron, by mimicking specific neurotransmitters and producing the same effects, or by mimicking a neurotransmitter and blocking its effect by occupying its receptor sites and preventing it from acting.

Concept Check 1

1. acetylcholine
2. endorphins; opiates
3. acetylcholine
4. serotonin
5. dopamine
6. GABA
7. endorphins
8. acetylcholine

Graphic Organizer 1

a. dendrites
b. cell body
c. axon
d. myelin sheath
e. synaptic gap
f. neurotransmitter
g. synaptic vesicles
h. postsynaptic neuron
i. presynaptic neuron

Matching Exercise 1

1. neuron
2. GABA (gamma-amniobutyric acid)
3. endorphins
4. nodes of Ranvier
5. serotonin
6. cell body
7. multiple sclerosis
8. neurotransmitter
9. polarization
10. synapse
11. synaptic vesicles
12. dopamine
13. stimulus threshold
14. neuroscience
15. refractory period
16. Alzheimer's disease
17. opiates
18. acupuncture
19. naloxone
20. Parkinson's disease
21. chromosomes
22. nucleus

True/False Test 1

1. T	7. T	13. T	18. T
2. T	8. F	14. T	19. T
3. F	9. T	15. F	20. T
4. T	10. T	16. F	21. T
5. T	11. F	17. T	22. T
6. F	12. T		

The Nervous System and the Endocrine System: Communication Throughout the Body

1. *The two main divisions of the nervous system and their components are* the central nervous system, which includes the brain and spinal cord, and the peripheral nervous system, which includes all the nerves lying outside the central nervous system.

2. *Spinal reflexes are* simple, automatic behaviors that are processed in the spinal cord.

3. *The key components of the peripheral nervous system and their functions are* the somatic nervous system, which communicates sensory information to the central nervous system and carries motor messages from the central nervous system to the muscles, and the autonomic nervous system, which regulates involuntary functions, such as heartbeat, blood pressure, breathing, and digestion.

4. *The two branches of the autonomic nervous system and their functions are* the sympathetic nervous system, which produces rapid physical arousal in response to perceived threats or emergencies, and the parasympathetic nervous system, which maintains normal bodily functions and conserves the body's physical resources.

5. *The endocrine system is made up of* glands that transmit information via chemical messengers called hormones. Hormones regulate such things as metabolism, growth rate, digestion, blood pressure, and sexual development and reproduction. Hormones are also involved in emotional responses and your response to stress.

6. *The endocrine system interacts with the nervous system in a number of ways:* Endocrine hormones can promote or inhibit the generation of nerve impulses; the release of hormones, in turn, can be stimulated or inhibited by certain parts of the nervous system; and finally, because some hormones and neurotransmitters are chemically identical, the same molecules can act as either a hormone or a neurotransmitter.

7. *The hypothalamus serves as* the main link between the endocrine system and the nervous system and directly regulates the release of hormones by the pituitary gland.

8. *The pituitary gland's hormones affect* the function of other glands as well as regulate the production of other hormones. *The adrenal glands (adrenal cortex and adrenal medulla) are involved in* the human stress response. *The gonads are* the sex organs: the ovaries in females, which secrete estrogen and progesterone, and the testes in males, which secrete androgens, the most important of which is testosterone (testosterone is also secreted by the adrenal glands in both males and females).

Concept Check 2

1. spinal reflex
2. spinal cord
3. sympathetic nervous system
4. parasympathetic nervous system
5. norepinephrine; epinephrine
6. cerebrospinal fluid
7. pituitary; hypothalamus
8. nerves; neuron
9. pituitary; growth hormone
10. estrogen; progesterone; testosterone
11. motor; somatic
12. peripheral; autonomic nervous system

Graphic Organizer 2

Mapping the Divisions and Functions of the Nervous System

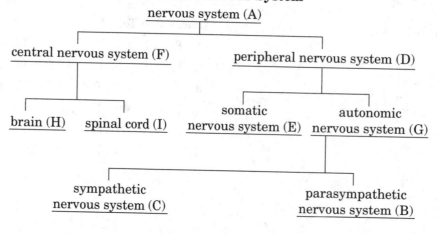

Matching Exercise 2

1. nerves
2. endocrine system
3. spinal reflexes
4. adrenal glands
5. cerebrospinal fluid
6. hypothalamus
7. growth hormone
8. peripheral nervous system
9. prolactin
10. immune system
11. oxytocin
12. gonads
13. meninges
14. neural stem cells

True/False Test 2

1. T	5. F	9. F	13. T
2. T	6. T	10. T	14. T
3. T	7. F	11. F	
4. T	8. T	12. T	

A Guided Tour of the Brain

1. *Neural pathways are* networks formed by groups of neuron cell bodies in one area of the brain that project their axons to other brain areas. *They are important because* they form communication networks and circuits that link different brain areas and are involved in many brain functions.

2. *Neuroplasticity refers to* the brain's ability to change structure and function. *Functional plasticity is* the brain's ability to shift functions from damaged to undamaged brain areas. *Structural plasticity is* the brain's ability to change its structure in response to learning, active practice, or environmental stimulation.

3. *Neurogenesis refers to* the development of new neurons in the brain.

4. *The key structures of the hindbrain and their functions are* the medulla, which controls breathing, heart rate, digestion, and other vital life functions; the pons, which connects the medulla to the two sides of the cerebellum and helps coordinate and integrate movements on each side of the body; and the cerebellum, which is responsible for muscle coordination and maintaining posture and equilibrium. The reticular formation, which is a network of nerve fibers at the center of the medulla, plays a role in regulating attention, arousal, and sleep.

5. *The midbrain is* an important relay station that contains centers important to the processing of auditory and visual sensory information and an area called the substantia nigra that is involved in motor control and contains a large concentration of dopamine-producing neurons.

6. *The forebrain includes* the cerebral cortex (the wrinkled outer portion of the forebrain) and the limbic system structures, which are involved in emotion, motivation, learning, and memory.

7. *The four lobes and their functions are* the temporal lobe, the primary receiving area for auditory information; the occipital lobe, the primary receiving area for visual information; the parietal lobe, which processes somatosensory information; and the frontal lobe, which processes voluntary muscle movements and is involved in thinking, planning, and emotional control.

8. *The main structures of the limbic system and their functions are* the hippocampus, which is involved in learning and forming new memories; the thalamus, which processes sensory information for all senses, except smell, and relays it to the cerebral cortex; the hypothalamus, which regulates behaviors related to survival, such as eating, drinking, and sexual behavior; and the amygdala, which is involved in emotions such as fear, anger, and disgust, and in learning and memory.

Concept Check 3

1. hindbrain (more specifically, the pons is the point at which neural messages cross over)
2. reticular formation
3. cerebellum
4. medulla
5. hippocampus
6. thalamus
7. frontal lobes
8. substantia nigra
9. amygdala
10. phrenology; cortical localization (or localization of function)

11. functional plasticity

12. the limbic system

13. parietal

Graphic Organizer 3
Chart Diagram Exercise: The Key Structures of the Limbic System

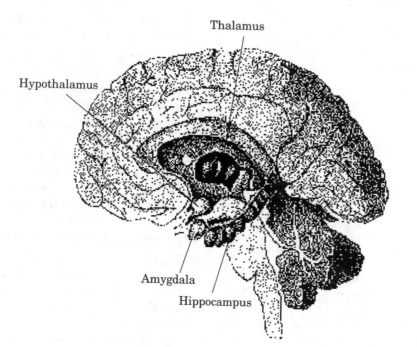

(a) Hippocampus: a curved forebrain structure that is involved in learning and forming new memories

(b) Hypothalamus: a peanut-sized forebrain structure that regulates both divisions of the autonomic nervous system as well as behaviors related to survival, such as eating, drinking, and sexual activity

(c) Thalamus: a forebrain structure that processes motor information and sensory information for all the senses except smell and relays it to the cerebral cortex

(d) Amygdala: an almond-shaped forebrain structure that is involved in emotion and in learning and forming memories

7. primary visual cortex

8. hippocampus

9. brainstem

10. primary motor cortex

11. prefrontal association cortex

12. medulla

13. reticular formation (reticular activating system)

14. suprachiasmatic nucleus (SCN)

15. neurogenesis

16. functional plasticity

17. phrenology

18. neural pathways

Matching Exercise 3

1. cerebral hemispheres

2. parietal lobe

3. substantia nigra

4. primary auditory cortex

5. pons

6. thalamus

True/False Test 3

1. T	7. F	13. T
2. T	8. T	14. T
3. F	9. T	15. T
4. F	10. T	16. T
5. T	11. F	17. T
6. T	12. T	18. T

Specialization in the Cerebral Hemispheres

1. *Broca and Wernicke provided the first evidence that* the left and right hemispheres were specialized for different functions (cortical localization or localization of function), and in particular that language and speech functions are processed primarily in the left hemisphere.

2. *Lateralization of function (or lateralization) is* the notion that specific psychological or cognitive functions are processed primarily on one side of the brain.

3. *Aphasia refers to* the partial or complete inability to articulate ideas or understand spoken or written language because of brain injury or damage. *Broca's aphasia results in* the inability to produce speech, but comprehension is relatively unaffected. *Wernicke's aphasia results in* problems in finding the correct word and difficulty in comprehension of written or spoken communication, but speech is relatively unaffected unless the damage is severe.

4. *The split-brain operation involves* surgically cutting the corpus callosum, the thick band of axons that connects the two hemispheres.

5. *In a specialized procedure, split-brain patients are directed to focus on a point in the middle of a screen and then* visual information is differentially projected either to the left or right hemisphere. *Split-brain patients can* verbally identify the object when it is projected to the left hemisphere but not the right; however, the left hand (which is controlled by the right hemisphere) can correctly pick out the object projected to the right hemisphere.

6. *Tests on split-brain patients revealed that the left hemisphere is specialized for* language abilities, speech, reading, and writing, and *the right hemisphere is specialized for* nonverbal emotional expression, visual-spatial tasks, deciphering complex visual cues, facial and emotional facial cue recognition, reading maps, copying designs, drawing, and musical appreciation or responsiveness (but not necessarily for musical ability, which involves the left hemisphere as well).

Concept Check 4

1. right; left
2. left; left
3. right
4. right; left

Matching Exercise 4

1. Roger Sperry
2. aphasia
3. Wernicke's area
4. cortical localization
5. Broca's area
6. lateralization of function

True/False Test 4

1. T   3. F   5. F
2. T   4. T

Something to Think About

1. (a) The occipital lobe is most likely affected because it includes the primary visual cortex where visual information is received, so damage to this area could affect vision.
   (b) Yoko probably has damage in the left frontal lobe, Broca's area. Damage here would not affect comprehension but would influence speech production.
   (c) Vanessa's hypothalamus was most likely damaged. The hypothalamus is part of the limbic system and regulates appetite, among its many functions.
   (d) Mr. Ashley suffers from Parkinson's disease, which is caused by the degeneration of neurons that produce dopamine in one brain area. Symptoms can be alleviated by the drug L-dopa, which converts to dopamine in the brain.

2. In answer to this question, the news is good. Because of the brain's structural plasticity, some brain structures can change in response to environmental stimulation. Research with rats has demonstrated that in addition to other changes, an enriched environment increases the number and length of dendrites, enlarges the size of neurons, and increases the number of neural connections. More important, there is an impressive amount of correlational research showing that the human brain also seems to benefit from enriched environments. Getting a good education, as long as the process is challenging, is one way to "exercise" the brain. Another piece of advice is to remain mentally active throughout the lifespan and to involve yourself in complex and stimulating activities rather than passively watching TV.

It is important to point out that intellectual decline is not the inevitable result of aging. To increase the number of synaptic connections and dendritic growth, the best advice is to get involved in novel, challenging, and unfamiliar pursuits. Keep pumping those neurons and remember, "If you don't use it, you lose it!"

Progress Test 1

1. b	6. a	11. c
2. b	7. c	12. c
3. c	8. d	13. a
4. c	9. b	14. a
5. b	10. e	15. a

Progress Test 2

1. d	6. d	11. b
2. b	7. d	12. d
3. d	8. a	13. d
4. d	9. b	14. d
5. a	10. d	15. c

Progress Test 3

1. c	6. c	11. a
2. c	7. a	12. a
3. b	8. c	13. c
4. a	9. a	14. a
5. a	10. a	15. c

CHAPTER 3

Sensation and Perception

PREVIEW	Reading the section below first will give you a general sense of the chapter's contents and an initial introduction to some of the major concepts and terms. This will prime you for what you are about to read and help you to develop a "cognitive map" that will guide your study of the material in this chapter. Likewise, reading the **preview questions** at the beginning of each major section will improve your ability to understand, learn, and retain the information.

CHAPTER 3 . . . AT A GLANCE

Chapter 3 describes both sensation and perception. Sensation refers to the response of sensory receptors in the sense organs to stimulation and the transmission of that information to the brain. Perception is the process through which the brain integrates, organizes, and interprets sensory information.

The chapter begins with the basic principles of sensation—transduction and absolute and difference thresholds, Weber's law, and sensory adaptation. It then explains the senses of vision and hearing and the chemical and body senses, including smell (olfaction), taste (gustation), touch, and position (the kinesthetic and vestibular senses). In addition, pain sensation, the role of nociceptors and Substance P, phantom limb pain, and the gate-control theory of pain are explored. Pain perception is the result of both physiological and psychological factors.

The discussion of perception first distinguishes between bottom-up (data-driven) processing and top-down (conceptually driven) processing. The Gestalt psychologists emphasized the perception of whole forms (gestalts). Figure–ground relationships and shape perception are then explained, followed by several principles of perceptual organization (laws of proximity, similarity, closure, good continuation, and Prägnanz). Depth perception, including monocular and binocular cues, is discussed next. The perception of motion is described; then perceptual constancies are explained. How we misperceive objects and events in our world is illustrated through various illusions. That perception is a psychological process is made clear through a discussion of how perceptual sets—expectations, learning experiences, and cultural factors—influence our interpretations.

The Application is devoted to how we can use various perceptual strategies and techniques in the control of pain.

Introduction: What Are Sensation and Perception?

Preview Questions

Consider the following questions as you study this section of the chapter.

- What are the definitions of *sensation* and *perception*?
- How do sensation and perception differ?

*Read the section "Introduction: What Are Sensation and Perception?" and **write** your answers to the following:*

1. The primary function of the nervous system is _____

2. Sensation refers to _____ and perception occurs when _____ _____

3. The difference between sensation and perception is _____ _____

Basic Principles of Sensation

Preview Questions

Consider the following questions as you study this section of the chapter.

- What are sensory receptors; how do they help us hear, taste, smell, feel, and see. What is transduction?
- What are the two types of sensory thresholds?
- How does Weber's law relate to the just noticeable difference (jnd)?
- Why does sensory adaptation occur, and why is it important?

*Read the section "Basic Principles of Sensation" and **write** the answers to the following:*

1. We are able to hear, taste, smell, feel, and see by _____ _____

2. Transduction is _____ _____

3. The two types of sensory threshold are (and what they refer to) _____ _____ _____ _____

4. Another name for the difference threshold is _____

5. Weber's law states _____ _____

6. Sensory adaptation occurs because _____ _____ _____

After you have carefully studied the preceding sections, complete the following exercises.

Concept Check 1

Read the following and write the correct term in the space provided.

1. When Anton went to have his hearing tested, different tones were transmitted through the earphones he was wearing. Some tones were at such a low level of intensity he could not detect them. These sounds were below Anton's _____ threshold.

2. When Jennifer was first presented with an auditory stimulus, she detected the sequence of sounds as only a series of different tones. After hearing the sequence of sounds a second time, she recognized them as a melody. This example illustrates the overlapping processes of _____ and _____ .

3. Jan was exposed to a 100-watt light. When its brightness was increased by 5 watts, she was not aware of the increase. However, when a 20-watt light was increased by 5 watts, she detected the increase immediately. Jan's ability to detect this difference is called the _____ , or _____ , and this may vary as a function of the size of the initial stimulus, a principle of sensation called _____ .

4. The school bell rings at lunchtime. The process by which our ears convert the sound waves from the bell into a coded neural signal that can be processed by the nervous system is called _____ .

5. Not realizing how cold it is after you have been on the ski slope for a while is an example of

_____ .

6. Dr. Jasenka's research demonstrated that simple information presented outside of conscious awareness influenced emotions, thoughts, and attitudes. These effects, however, were weak and short-lived. More complex messages had no effect. Dr. Jasenka's research is concerned with

_____ .

Review of Terms and Concepts 1

Use the terms in this list to complete the Matching Test, then to help you answer the True/False items correctly.

sensation
perception
sensory receptors
transduction
threshold
absolute threshold
difference threshold

(just noticeable difference or jnd)
Weber's law
subliminal perception
mere exposure effect
sensory adaptation

Matching Exercise

Match the appropriate term with its definition or description.

1. _____ The point at which a stimulus is strong enough to be detected because it activates sensory receptors.

2. _____ The process by which a form of physical energy is converted into a coded neural signal that can be processed by the nervous system.

3. _____ The smallest possible strength of a stimulus that can be detected half the time.

4. _____ Specialized cells unique to each sense organ that respond to a particular form of sensory stimulation.

5. _____ The smallest possible difference between two stimuli that can be detected half the time.

6. _____ The finding that repeated exposure to a stimulus increases a person's preference for that stimulus.

True/False Test

Indicate whether each statement is true or false by placing T or F in the blank space next to each item.

1. ____ Perception refers to the process of detecting a physical stimulus, such as sound, light, heat, or pressure.

2. ____ Sensory adaptation refers to the decline in sensitivity to a constant stimulus.

3. ____ Weber's law is a principle of sensation that holds that the size of the just noticeable difference will vary depending on its relation to the strength of the original stimulus.

4. ____ The process of integrating, organizing, and interpreting sensations is called sensation.

5. ____ The perception of stimuli that are below the threshold of conscious awareness is called subliminal perception.

Check your answers and review any areas of weakness before going on to the next section.

Vision: From Light to Sight
Preview Questions

Consider the following questions as you study this section of the chapter.

- How do we see, and what is the electromagnetic spectrum?
- What are the key structures of the eye, and what are their functions?
- What are the functions of the rods and cones, and how do the bipolar and ganglion cells process visual information for transmission to the brain?
- What properties of light determine our experience of color, and how do the two theories of color vision explain the process?

Read the section "Vision: From Light to Sight" and ***write*** *your answers to the following.*

1. The process of seeing begins with _____
_____
_____

2. The electromagnetic spectrum is _____
   _____
   _____

3. The key structures of the eye (and their functions) are _____
   _____
   _____
   _____
   _____
   _____

4. The function of rods is to _____
   _____
   The function of cones is to _____
   _____

5. The optic disk is _____
   _____

6. Bipolar cells process visual information by
   _____
   _____

7. Our experience of color involves _____
   _____
   _____
   _____

8. According to the trichromatic theory, _____
   _____
   _____
   _____
   This theory explains_____
   _____

9. According to the opponent-process theory,
   _____
   _____
   _____
   This theory explains_____
   _____

After you have carefully studied the preceding section, complete the following exercises.

Concept Check 2

Read the following and write the correct term in the space provided.

1. According to the trichromatic theory, if Mr. Colorado's red- and blue-sensitive cones are stimulated simultaneously, he should see
   _____ .

2. Constantino, who has normal vision, stares at a red circle for a couple of minutes, then shifts his eyes to a white surface. The afterimage of the circle will be _____ .

3. The fact that Constantino experiences an afterimage cannot be explained by the _____ theory of color vision, but it can be explained by the _____ theory.

4. Following an accident, the fovea in Harbinder's right eye was destroyed. Although he can still see with this eye, it is likely that he will have trouble seeing _____ and _____ when his left eye is closed.

5. Arica noted that her new T-shirt absorbed all the wavelengths of visible light and reflected none. The color of her T-shirt is
   _____ .

Graphic Organizer 1

Identify each part of the eye by writing the name on the appropriate line in the drawing below; then match its function by placing the corresponding number next to the name. (For example, "1. retina" is the first answer.)

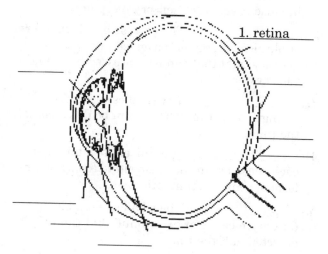

1. retina

1. A light-sensitive membrane located at the back of the eye that contains sensory receptors for vision.

2. The black opening in the middle of the eye that changes size to let in different amounts of light.

3. A clear membrane covering the visible part of the eye that helps gather and direct incoming light.

4. The colored part of the eye that is the muscle that controls the size of the pupil.

5. A transparent structure located behind the pupil that actively focuses, or bends, light as it enters the eye.

6. A small area in the center of the retina that contains cones but not rods.

7. The area of the retina without rods or cones, where the optic nerve leaves the eye.

Review of Terms and Concepts 2

Use the terms in this list to complete the Matching Test, then to help you answer the True / False items correctly.

wavelength	optic disk
cornea	blind spot
sclera	ganglion cells
pupil	bipolar cells
iris	visual acuity
lens	optic nerve
accommodation	optic chiasm
nearsightedness	feature detectors
(myopia)	color
farsightedness	hue
(hyperopia)	saturation
presbyopia	brightness
astigmatism	trichromatic theory of
retina	color vision
rods	color blindness
cones	afterimage
photoreceptors	opponent-process theory
fovea	of color vision

Matching Exercise

Match the appropriate term with its definition or description:

1. _____ The visual ability to see fine details.

2. _____ Visual experience that occurs after the original source of stimulation is no longer present.

3. _____ Distance from one wave peak to another.

4. _____ Process by which the lens changes shape to focus incoming light so that it falls on the retina.

5. _____ Perceived intensity of color that corresponds to the amplitude of the light wave.

6. _____ Thick nerve that exits from the back of the eye and carries visual information to the visual cortex in the brain.

7. _____ Theory that the sensation of color is due to cones in the retina that are especially sensitive to light that is red (long wavelengths), green (medium wavelengths), or blue (short wavelengths).

8. _____ Short, thick, pointed sensory receptors of the eye that detect color and are responsible for color vision and visual acuity.

9. _____ Property of wavelengths of light, what we know as color, in which different wavelengths correspond to our subjective experience of different colors.

10. _____ Long, thin, blunt sensory receptors that are highly sensitive to light but not to color and are primarily responsible for peripheral vision and night vision.

11. _____ Specialized neurons in the retina that collect sensory information from the rods and cones and then funnel it to other specialized neurons before it is transmitted to the brain.

12. _____ Perceptual experience of different wavelengths of light, involving hue, saturation (purity), and brightness (intensity).

13. _____ Area of the retina without rods or cones, where the optic nerve exits the back of the eye.

14. _____ A form of farsightedness caused when the lens becomes brittle and inflexible during middle age.

15. _____ A visual disorder in which an abnormally curved eyeball results in blurry vision for lines in a particular direction.

16. _____ Specialized neurons in the visual cortex that detect, or respond to, particular aspects of more complex visual stimuli.

True/False Test

Indicate whether each statement is true or false by placing T or F in the blank space next to each item.

1. ____ The cornea is the transparent structure located behind the pupil that actively focuses, or bends, light as it enters the eye.

2. ____ The opponent-process theory states that color vision is the product of opposing pairs of color receptors, red–green, black–white, and blue–yellow; when one member of a color pair is stimulated, the other is inhibited.

3. ____ The lens is the clear membrane covering the visible part of the eye that helps gather and direct incoming light.

4. ____ Ganglion cells are the specialized neurons in the retina that connect to the bipolar cells and whose bundled axons form the optic nerve.

5. ____ The retina is a small area in the center of the back of the eye that is composed entirely of cones, where visual information is most sharply focused.

6. ____ The colored part of the eye, which is actually a ring of muscles that controls the size of the pupil, is called the iris.

7. ____ The pupil is the opening in the middle of the iris that changes size to let in different amounts of light.

8. ____ The fovea is a thin, light-sensitive membrane located at the back of the eye that contains two kinds of sensory receptors for light and vision.

9. ____ The optic chiasm is the point in the brain where the optic fibers from each eye meet and partly cross over to the opposite side of the brain.

10. ____ Saturation is the property of color that corresponds to the purity of the light wave.

11. ____ Color blindness is one of several forms of color deficiency or weakness in which an individual cannot distinguish between certain colors.

12. ____ The blind spot is the point where the optic nerve leaves the eye, producing a small gap in the field of vision.

13. ____ Nearsightedness occurs when close objects are seen clearly but distant objects appear blurry because the light from distant objects is focused behind the retina.

14. ____ The sclera, or white portion of the eye, is a tough, fibrous tissue that covers the eyeball, except for the cornea.

15. ____ Farsightedness occurs when distant objects are seen clearly but close objects appear blurry because the light from close objects is focused in front of the retina.

16. ____ Photoreceptors are sensory receptors that respond to light and undergo a chemical reaction that results in a neural signal.

Check your answers and review any areas of weakness before going on to the next section.

Hearing: From Vibration to Sound

Preview Questions

Consider the following questions as you study this section of the chapter.

- What is audition, and how do we hear?
- What properties of a sound wave correspond to our perception of sound?
- What are the key structures of the ear, and what are their functions?
- How do place theory and frequency theory explain pitch perception?

*Read the section "Hearing: From Vibration to Sound" and **write** your answers to the following:*

1. Audition is _____

_____

2. Our perception of sound is directly related to the physical properties of _____

_____

_____

3. The key structures of the ear are _____

_____

_____

4. The process of hearing begins when _____

_____

It then involves _____

_____

_____

_____

5. According to frequency theory _____

_____

This theory explains _____

_____

_____

6. According to place theory _____

_____

_____

This theory explains _____

_____

_____

After you have carefully studied the preceding section, complete the following exercises.

Concept Check 3

Read the following and write the correct term in the space provided.

1. When Hamish whispered in Morag's ear, she could barely hear what he said. The loudness of his whisper was determined by the _____ of the sound waves, which are measured in units called

_____ .

2. Rita, who has suffered damage to the bones in her middle ear, has been told by the experts that a hearing aid that artificially amplifies sounds will help restore her hearing. Rita probably has _____ deafness.

3. The three tiny bones in Rita's middle ear are called the _____ , the _____ , and the _____ .

4 Within seconds of answering the phone, Lacey recognized her old friend's voice even though they had not spoken for years. Her ability to do this is due, in part at least, to the fact that every human voice has its own distinctive _____ , a quality produced by the complexity of several sound wave frequencies.

5. Dixon has attended so many rock concerts with extremely high decibel levels that he is now experiencing ringing in his ears. It is probable that this exposure to loud sounds has damaged the hair cells in his _____ ; he may eventually develop a form of deafness called _____ deafness.

6. During the first take in a recording session, Jelena adjusted the equipment in order to achieve a nice balance between the relative highness and lowness of the sounds produced by the musicians. Jelena is concerned with _____ , which is determined by the frequency of sound waves, measured in units called _____ .

7. Dr. Botchev's research is concerned with how sound waves produced by the rhythmic vibrations of air molecules are converted into neural messages in the inner ear, a process called _____ . He is most likely to be interested in the functions of two inner ear structures called the _____ and the _____ .

8. A researcher discovered that a sound wave of 100 hertz caused each hair along the basilar membrane to vibrate at 100 times per second and that neural impulses were sent to the brain at the same rate. This finding supports the _____ theory of pitch.

9. One question on the final exam required Seth to label three parts of the outer ear on a diagram. If he knows his material, he is likely to label these parts as the _____ , the _____ , and the _____ .

Graphic Organizer 2

Identify each part of the ear by writing the name on the appropriate line and then match its function by *placing the corresponding number next to the name. (For example, "1. pinna" is the first answer.)*

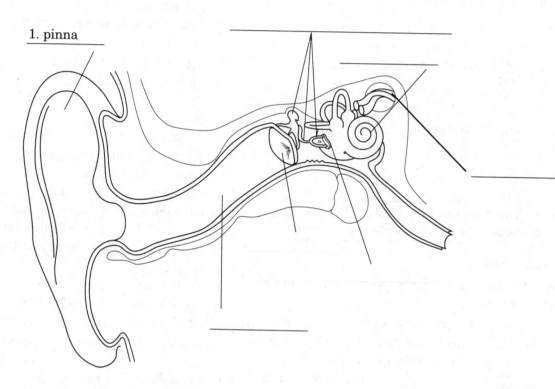

1. pinna

1. The oddly shaped flap of skin and cartilage that is attached to each side of the head.
2. A tightly stretched membrane at the end of the ear canal that vibrates when hit by sound waves.
3. A fluid-filled coiled structure that contains the sensory receptors for sound.
4. The tunnel through which sound waves travel to reach the eardrum.
5. The tightly stretched membrane that separates the middle ear from the inner ear.
6. The small structures of the middle ear whose joint action almost doubles the amplification of the sound.
7. The nerve that carries the neural information to the thalamus and the auditory cortex in the brain.

Review of Terms and Concepts 3

Use the terms in this list to complete the Matching Test, then to help you answer the True/False items correctly.

audition   decibel
sound waves   pitch
loudness   frequency
amplitude   hertz

timbre   conduction deafness
outer ear   inner ear
pinna   cochlea
ear canal   basilar membrane
eardrum   hair cells
middle ear   nerve deafness
hammer, anvil,   frequency theory
  and stirrup   place theory
oval window

Matching Exercise

Match the appropriate term with its definition or description.

1. _____ The intensity (or amplitude) of a sound wave measured in decibels.

2. _____ Technical term for the sense of hearing.

3. _____ Rate of vibration, or number of waves per second.

4. _____ Hairlike sensory receptors for sound embedded in the basilar membrane.

5. _____ Physical stimuli that produce our sensory experience of sound.

6. _____ The distinctive quality of a sound, determined by the complexity of the sound waves.

7. _____ Part of the ear that collects sound waves and consists of the pinna, the ear canal, and the eardrum.

8. _____ Relative highness or lowness of a sound, determined by the frequency of the sound wave.

9. _____ Unit of measurement for loudness.

10. _____ Intensity or amount of energy of a wave, reflected in the height of the wave; determines a sound's loudness.

11. _____ The part of the ear that amplifies sound waves; consists of three small bones—the hammer, the anvil, and the stirrup.

12. _____ The view that the basilar membrane vibrates at the same frequency as sound waves.

True/False Test

Indicate whether each statement is true or false by placing T or F in the blank space next to each item.

1. ____ Damage to the hair cells or auditory nerve can result in *conduction deafness.*

2. ____ The eardrum is a tightly stretched membrane that separates the middle ear from the inner ear.

3. ____ *Nerve deafness* results when the tiny bones of the middle ear are damaged or become brittle.

4. ____ The hammer, anvil, and stirrup are important structures in the middle ear that amplify sound.

5. ____ The cochlea is a coiled, fluid-filled structure that contains the sensory receptors for sound.

6. ____ Hertz refers to the number of wave peaks per second.

7. ____ The part of the outer ear that sound waves travel through to reach the eardrum is called the ear canal.

8. ____ The structure within the cochlea that contains the hair cells is called the basilar membrane.

9. ____ The oval window is a tightly stretched membrane at the end of the ear canal that vibrates when sound waves hit it.

10. ____ The pinna is the oddly shaped flap of skin and cartilage that is attached to each side of your head.

11. ____ The inner ear is the part of the ear where sound is transduced into neural impulses; it consists of the cochlea and semicircular canals.

12. ____ The view that different frequencies cause larger vibrations at different locations along the basilar membrane is called place theory.

Check your answers and review any areas of weakness before going on to the next section.

The Chemical and Body Senses: Smell, Taste, Touch, and Position

Preview Questions

Consider the following questions as you study this section of the chapter.

- How are olfaction and gustation defined, and what is meant by the chemical senses?

- How do airborne molecules result in the sensation of odor?

- What are the primary tastes, and how do we perceive different tastes?

- What are the skin and body senses, and what sensory receptors are involved in touch and temperature?

- How is the sensation of pain produced, and what causes pain?

- What nociceptors are involved in the fast and slow pain systems, and what is the gate-control theory of pain?

- What is phantom limb pain, and how can it be explained?

- What are the kinesthetic and vestibular senses, and where are their receptors located?

Read the section "The Chemical and Body Senses: Smell, Taste, Touch, and Position" and **write** *your answers to the following:*

1. Olfaction is the technical term for

_____

and gustation is the technical term for

_____

2. They are called chemical senses because _____

_____

3. Our sense of smell begins when _____

_____

It then involves _____

_____

4. Our sense of taste begins when _____

_____

It then involves _____

_____

_____

5. The five primary taste qualities are _____

_____

6. The skin and body senses include _____

_____

7. The skin responds to _____

_____

8. One receptor for touch is _____
and it works by _____

_____

_____

9. Pain is the unpleasant sensation of _____

_____

10. There are two types of nociceptors involved in
pain.
(a) _____ , which represent
the fast pain system, and transmit

_____

_____

(b) _____ , which represent
the slow pain system, and transmit

_____

_____

11. According to the gate-control theory, _____

_____

_____

_____

12. The experience of pain is also influenced by ___

_____

_____

13. Phantom limb pain refers to _____

_____

It is explained by _____

_____

_____

14. Our kinesthetic sense involves _____

_____

_____

15. Our vestibular sense provides us with _____

_____

16. The two sources of vestibular sensory information are _____

_____

_____

---

*After you have carefully studied the preceding
sections, complete the following exercises.*

Concept Check 4

*Read the following and write the correct term in the
space provided.*

1. After eating his salad with vinegar dressing,
Mario thinks that his very expensive vintage
wine tastes strange. This change in perceived
taste probably occurs because some vinegar
remains on his _____ .

2. Ever since he lost a finger in an industrial accident, Oswald experiences intense physical sensations in his nonexistent finger. Oswald is
experiencing _____ ,
which occurs because the neurons in the transmission pathways from the site of the amputation to the brain become _____ .

3. As the result of an accident, Chih Fan experienced damage to his thalamus. The one sense
that will be least affected by this brain damage
is his sense of _____ .

4. For dinner, Klara had a salad with lemon
dressing, a teriyaki steak with mushrooms, a
potato with sour cream, and ice cream for
dessert. It is very likely that she has experienced the five basic taste sensations of

_____ , _____ ,

_____ , _____ , and

_____ .

5. On the day of her final statistics exam, Nadia has a sore ankle. According to the gate-control theory, it is likely that Nadia's anxiety about the exam will _____ her perception of the pain in her ankle.

6. While fishing in a small boat, Mortimer becomes nauseated from the motion of the waves. Mortimer's _____ and _____ are most likely responsible for making him feel ill.

7. Dr. Farnaz conducts research on pain pathways. He is likely to be interested in small sensory fibers called_____ or _____ . In particular, he is interested in _____ fibers (fast pain system) and _____ fibers (slow pain system), which are triggered by bodily damage or injury.

8. If you are blindfolded and asked to touch your chin, nose, and forehead with your index finger, you probably will have no trouble doing so. This ability is due to your _____ sense.

9. Arleigh accidentally scrapes some skin off his knuckles while working on his car. The pain he feels following the injury is caused in part by the release of the neurotransmitter

_____ .

Review of Terms and Concepts 4

Use the terms in this list to complete the Matching Test, then to help you answer the True / False items correctly.

olfaction
gustation
anosmia
airborne chemical
  molecules
olfactory receptor cells
olfactory nerves
pheromones
olfactory bulb
olfactory cortex
olfactory tract

taste buds
umami
flavor
skin senses
body senses
Pacinian corpuscle
pain
nociceptors (free nerve
  endings)
A-delta fibers
C fibers

substance P
gate-control theory of
  pain
endorphins and
  enkephalins
phantom limb pain
sensitization

chronic pain
kinesthetic sense
proprioceptors
vestibular sense
semicircular canals
  and vestibular sacs

Matching Exercise

Match the appropriate term with its definition or description.

1. _____ Technical term for our sense of taste.

2. _____ Fluid-filled structures that are lined with hairlike receptor cells that shift in response to motion, changes in body position, or changes in gravity.

3. _____ Touch receptor located beneath the skin; when stimulated by pressure, it converts the stimulation into neural messages that are relayed to the brain.

4. _____ A condition characterized by a partial or complete loss of the sense of smell.

5. _____ Specialized sensory receptors for pain that are found in the skin, muscles, and internal organs.

6. _____ Cells located high in the nasal cavity that are stimulated by inhaled molecules in the air.

7. _____ Enlarged ending of the olfactory cortex at the front of the brain, where the sensation of smell is registered.

8. _____ Specialized sensory receptors for taste that are located on the tongue and inside the mouth and throat.

9. _____ Tract formed by bundles of axons from the olfactory bulb that projects to different brain areas, including the temporal lobe and structures in the limbic system.

10. _____ The sense of balance or equilibrium.

11. _____ The body's natural painkillers that are produced in many parts of the brain and the body.

12. _____ The sense of location and position of body parts in relation to one another.

13. _____ A taste category that involves the distinctive taste of monosodium glutamate, aged cheeses, mushrooms, seaweed, and protein-rich foods such as meat.

14. _____ A phenomenon in which a person continues to experience intense painful sensations in a limb that has been amputated.

15. _____ Myelinated nociceptors involved in the fast pain system that transmit sharp, intense, but short-lived pain signals, immediately following injury.

True/False Test

Indicate whether each statement is true or false by placing T or F in the space next to each item.

1. ____ Pain is the unpleasant sensation of physical discomfort or suffering that can occur in varying degrees of intensity.

2. ____ Gate-control theory suggests that pain is the product of both physiological and psychological factors that cause spinal "gates" to open and relay patterns of intense stimulation to the brain, which perceives them as pain.

3. ____ Airborne chemical molecules are emitted by the substances we smell and are inhaled through the nose and through the opening in the palate at the back of the throat.

4. ____ The olfactory nerves connect directly to the olfactory bulbs, where smells are perceived by the brain.

5. ____ Proprioceptors are neurotransmitters that are involved in the transmission of pain messages to the brain.

6. ____ Olfaction is the technical term for our sense of smell.

7. ____ Flavor involves several sensations, including the taste, aroma, temperature, texture, and appearance of food.

8. ____ The olfactory cortex is at the front of the brain and is directly linked to the outside world via neural pathways.

9. ____ The body senses provide essential information about our physical status and our physical interaction with objects in our environment.

10. ____ Substance P is found in the muscles and joints and provides information about body position and movement.

11. ____ The skin senses keep us informed as to our position and orientation in space.

12. ____ Pheromones are chemical signals released by animals that communicate information about social and sexual status and affect the behavior of other animals of the same species.

13. ____ C fibers are unmyelinated nociceptors that make up the slow pain system and create the longer-lasting, throbbing, burning kind of pain following injury.

14. ____ Sensitization is the opposite of sensory adaptation in that pain pathways in the brain become increasingly more responsive over time following severe injury or damage.

15. ____ Chronic pain involves the continuation of pain perception after the injury has healed; it may be caused by neurons in the pain pathways undergoing sensitization.

Check your answers and review any areas of weakness before going on to the next section.

Perception (Part 1)

Preview Questions

Consider the following questions as you study this section of the chapter.

- What is perception?
- How does bottom-up processing differ from top-down processing?
- What three questions does perception answer about the stimuli we sense?
- Who founded Gestalt psychology, and what is the main focus of this perspective?

*Read the section "Perception" (the introduction only) and **write** your answers to the following:*

1. Perception is the process of _____

_____

_____

2. Bottom-up processing refers to _____

_____

_____

3. Top-down processing refers to _____

_____

4. The three basic questions of perception are

_____

_____

_____

5. Gestalt psychology was founded by _____

_____

and is concerned with _____

_____

_____

Perception: The Perception of Shape (Part 2)

Preview Questions

Consider the following questions as you study this section of the chapter.

- What is the figure–ground relationship, and how significant is it to perception?
- What perceptual principles do we follow when we group visual elements?
- What is the law of Prägnanz, and what does it explain?

*Read the section "Perception: The Perception of Shape" (up to Depth Perception) and **write** your answers to the following:*

1. The figure–ground relationship describes

_____

_____

It is important because it demonstrates that

_____

_____

2. The perceptual principles involved in grouping visual elements include _____

_____

_____

_____

3. The law of Prägnanz states _____

_____

_____

It is important because it encompasses _____

_____

and suggests that_____

_____

_____

Perception: Depth Perception (Part 3)

Preview Questions

Consider the following questions as you study this section of the chapter.

- How is depth perception defined, and why is it important?
- What are monocular cues, and how do they contribute to depth perception?
- What are binocular cues, and how do they differ from monocular cues?
- How is binocular disparity involved in our ability to see three-dimensional images in, for example, stereograms?

*Read the section "Perception: Depth Perception" (up to Motion Perception) and **write** your answers to the following:*

1. Depth perception refers to _____

_____

It is important because _____

_____

2. Monocular cues are defined as _____

_____

_____

and include _____

_____

3. Binocular cues are defined as _____

_____

_____

and include _____

_____

_____

4. A stereogram is _____

_____

_____

After you have carefully studied the preceding sections, complete the following exercises.

Concept Check 5

Read the following and write the correct term in the space provided.

1. When Tsung looked at the 16 numbers on his credit card—2314 5634 8679 1357—he perceived them as four groups of four numbers each. The tendency to perceive things that are close together as a single unit is called the

   _____ .

2. At a noisy party, Ben focuses on his girlfriend's conversation, while tuning out the other conversations. Using a Gestalt perceptual principle to analyze this example, the noisy environment is the _____ and his girlfriend's voice is the _____ .

3. While viewing a stereogram, Nina experiences the perceptual illusion of three-dimensional depth from the two-dimensional scene. The binocular cue responsible for this phenomenon is _____ .

4. Chan knows that the red bicycle in the parking lot is closer to him than the green bicycle because the red one casts a larger retinal image. This illustrates the distance cue known as _____ .

5. Emily paints a long garden pathway bordered with flowers. She shows the flowers as decreasing in size as they approach the horizon, where they seem to meet; Emily is using

   _____ to convey depth on the canvas.

6. Although a number of individual lights had burned out on the flashing sign, Lizabet perceived the sign as complete and had no trouble reading the whole message. The tendency to fill in gaps in an incomplete image is called the

   _____ .

7. To make the task of completing the jigsaw puzzle more challenging, Zahra attempted to assemble it without the finished picture in front of her. Zahra is most likely to use

   _____ , or data-driven processing, to accomplish the task.

Review of Terms, Concepts, and Names 5

Use the terms in this list to complete the Matching Test, then to help you answer the True/False items correctly.

perception
bottom-up processing
  (data-driven
  processing)
top-down processing
  (conceptually driven
  processing)
Gestalt psychology
Max Wertheimer
figure–ground
  relationship
ESP (extrasensory
  perception)
parapsychology
figure–ground reversal
law of similarity
law of closure
law of good continuation

law of proximity
law of Prägnanz
  (law of simplicity)
depth perception
monocular cues
relative size
overlap (interposition)
aerial perspective
texture gradient
linear perspective
motion parallax
accommodation
binocular cues
convergence
binocular disparity
stereogram

Matching Exercise

Match the appropriate term with its definition or description.

1. _____ School of psychology founded in Germany in the early 1900s that maintained that our sensations are actively processed according to consistent perceptual rules that result in meaningful whole perceptions.

2. _____ Law that states that when several perceptual organizations are possible, the perceptual interpretation that will occur will be the one that produces the "best, simplest, and most stable shape."

3. _____ Monocular cue that suggests that faraway objects often appear hazy or slightly blurred by the atmosphere.

4. _____ Binocular cue that relies on the fact that our eyes are set a couple of inches apart and thus cast slightly different images on the retina of each eye.

5. _____ Gestalt principle of perceptual organization that states that we automatically separate the elements of a perception into the feature that clearly stands out from its less distinct background.

6. _____ Monocular cue in which an object partially blocked or obscured by another object is perceived as being farther away.

7. _____ Distance or depth cues that require the use of both eyes.

8. _____ Monocular cue that utilizes information about changes in the shape of the lens of the eye to help us gauge depth and distance.

9. _____ Gestalt principle of organization that refers to the tendency to perceive objects that are close to one another as a unit or figure.

10. _____ The use of monocular or binocular visual cues to perceive the distance or three-dimensional characteristics of objects.

11. _____ The perception of an image in which the ground can be perceived as the figure and the figure as the ground; underscores that our perception of figure and ground is a psychological phenomenon.

12. _____ German psychologist who founded Gestalt psychology in the early 1900s, studied the optical illusion of apparent movement, and described principles of perception.

13. _____ The scientific investigation of claims of various paranormal phenomena.

14. _____ Gestalt principle of organization that refers to the tendency to perceive objects of similar size, shape, or color as a unit or figure.

True/False Test

Indicate whether each statement is true or false by placing T or F in the space next to each item.

1. ____ Perception is defined as the process of integrating, organizing, and interpreting sensory information in a meaningful way.

2. ____ The law of good continuation, a Gestalt principle of organization, is the tendency to group elements that appear to follow in the same direction as a single unit or figure.

3. ____ The monocular cue of linear perspective refers to the fact that if two or more objects are assumed to be similar in size, the object that appears larger is perceived as being closer.

4. ____ Monocular cues are distance or depth cues that can be processed with either eye alone.

5. ____ The depth cue that occurs when parallel lines seem to meet in the distance (and the closer together the lines appear to be, the greater the perception of depth) is called relative size.

6. ____ Convergence is a binocular cue that relies on the degree to which muscles rotate the eyes to focus on an object; the less convergence, the farther away the object appears to be.

7. ____ When we are in motion, we can use the speed of passing objects to estimate their distance; nearby objects will appear to move much faster relative to distant objects. This monocular cue is called motion parallax.

8. ____ Texture gradient is a monocular cue in which the details of a surface with distinct texture become gradually less clearly defined as the surface extends into the distance; it appears crisp and distinct when close, and fuzzy and indistinct when farther away.

9. ____ Top-down processing is information processing that emphasizes the importance of sensory receptors in detecting the basic features of a stimulus in the process of recognizing a whole pattern; it involves analysis from the parts to the whole.

10. ____ A stereogram is a picture that uses the principle of binocular disparity to create the perception of a three-dimensional image.

11. ____ Bottom-up processing is information processing that emphasizes the importance of the observer's knowledge, expectations, and other cognitive processes in arriving at meaningful perceptions and involves analysis from the whole to the parts.

12. ____ ESP (extrasensory perception) is based on the idea that sensory information can be detected by some means other than through the normal processes of sensation.

13. ____ The law of closure, a Gestalt principle of organization, is the tendency to fill in gaps or contours in an incomplete image.

Check your answers and review any areas of weakness before going on to the next section.

Perception: The Perception of Motion (Part 4)

Preview Questions

Consider the following questions as you study this section of the chapter.

- Which sources of information contribute to our perception of motion?
- Who first studied induced motion, and how did he go about demonstrating this phenomenon?
- How does stroboscopic motion work, and how does it relate to the perception of motion?

*Read the section "Perception: The Perception of Motion" (up to perceptual constancies) and **write** your answers to the following:*

1. The perception of motion involves _____

   _____

   _____

2. Induced motion refers to _____

   _____

   It was first studied by   _____

3. Stroboscopic motion creates _____

   It is caused by   _____

   _____

   _____

   _____

Perception: Perceptual Constancies (Part 5)

Preview Questions

Consider the following questions as you study this section of the chapter.

- What is perceptual constancy?
- What principles guide our perception of size constancy?
- What is shape constancy?

*Read the section "Perception: Perceptual Constancies" and **write** your answers to the following:*

1. Perceptual constancy refers to _____

   _____

   _____

2. Size constancy is _____

   _____

   _____

   An important aspect of size constancy is _____

   _____

   _____

3. Shape constancy is _____

   _____

   _____

   _____

Perceptual Illusions and The Effects of Experience on Perceptual Interpretations

Preview Questions

Consider the following questions as you study this section of the chapter.

- What are perceptual illusions, and why are psychologists interested in them?
- How are the Müller-Lyer and moon illusions explained?
- What do illusions reveal about normal perceptual processes?
- How do perceptual sets influence the perceptual conclusions we reach?

*Read the sections "Perceptual Illusions" and "The Effects of Experience on Perceptual Interpretations" and **write** your answers to the following:*

1. A perceptual illusion involves _____

   _____

   _____

2. The Müller-Lyer illusion is _____

   _____

   _____

3. The moon illusion involves _____

   _____

   _____

   _____

   _____

and may be the result of _____
_____
_____

4. Perceptual illusions reveal that _____
_____
_____
_____

5. Perceptions can be influenced by _____
_____
_____

6. A perceptual set is _____
_____
_____
_____

After you have carefully studied the preceding sections, complete the following exercises.

Concept Check 6

Read the following and write the correct term in the space provided.

1. Stereotypes are mental conceptions that we have about individuals belonging to specific racial or ethnic groups and can influence how we interpret their behaviors. Stereotypes are most similar to the perceptual phenomenon of _____ , which is the tendency to perceive objects or situations from a particular frame of reference.

2. William noticed that the full moon seemed to be much larger on the horizon than when it was overhead. His friend Jane, a psychology major, explained that the illusion results from distance cues that make the horizon moon seem _____ (farther away/closer) than an overhead moon.

3. Your unopened introductory psychology textbook produces a trapezoidal retinal image, but you typically perceive the book as a rectangular object. This is due to _____ constancy.

4. When asked to judge the length of two equal lines, Desiree judged the one with outward-pointing arrows as being longer than the one

with inward-pointing arrows. Desiree has experienced the _____ illusion.

5. When Dave's dog runs down the lane to greet him after work, the image of the dog on his retinas gets bigger and bigger, yet Dave does not perceive Rex as the incredible growing dog. The general term for this tendency to perceive objects, particularly familiar objects, as constant and unchanging despite changes in sensory input is called _____ .

6. Ricardo uses sequentially flashing Christmas lights in front of his house to make it look as though Santa and his sleigh are moving from the garden to the roof. Ricardo is using the perceptual illusion of _____ .

Review of Terms, Concepts, and Names 6

Use the terms in this list to complete the Matching Test, then to help you answer the True/False items correctly.

induced motion
Karl Duncker
stroboscopic motion
perceptual constancy
size constancy
shape constancy
perceptual illusion

Müller-Lyer illusion
moon illusion
Shepard Tables
perceptual set
biofeedback
acupuncture

Matching Exercise

Match the appropriate term with its definition or description.

1. _____ The tendency to perceive objects or situations from a particular frame of reference.

2. _____ The tendency to perceive objects, especially familiar objects, as constant and unchanging despite changes in sensory input.

3. _____ Famous visual illusion involving the misperception of the identical length of two lines, one with arrows pointed inward and one with arrows pointed outward.

4. _____ The perception of an object as maintaining the same size despite changing images on the retina.

5. _____ German Gestalt psychologist who is best known for his studies on the perception of motion.

6. _____ Ancient Chinese medical procedure involving the insertion and manipulation of fine needles into specific locations on the body to alleviate pain and treat illness (may also involve stimulation of the needles with mild electrical current).

7. _____ Illusion in which one tabletop appears to be longer than another even though they are both identical in length.

True/False Test

Indicate whether each statement is true or false by placing T or F in the space next to each item.

1. ___ When we misperceive the true characteristics of an object or image, we experience a perceptual illusion.

2. ___ The moon illusion involves the misperception that the moon is larger when it is on the horizon than when it is directly overhead.

3. ___ The perception of a familiar object as maintaining the same shape regardless of the image produced on the retina is called shape constancy.

4. ___ Stroboscopic motion refers to an illusion of movement that results when two separate, carefully timed flashing lights are perceived as one light moving back and forth.

5. ___ Induced motion occurs because we have a strong tendency to assume that the background is stationary while the object or figure moves.

6. ___ Biofeedback is a technique that involves using auditory or visual feedback to learn to exert voluntary control over involuntary body functions, such as heart rate, blood pressure, blood flow, and muscle tension.

Check your answers and review any areas of weakness before going on to the next section.

Something to Think About

1. Many people have reported strange experiences that they interpret as extrasensory perception, or ESP. Suppose that a friend or family member told you about such an experience. This person might be convinced that something extraordinary has occurred. Based on what you have learned in this chapter, how would you go about explaining to your friend what has most likely taken place?

2. Imagine that you have decided to become an artist. You want to paint a picture that includes a variety of elements such as buildings, fields, a river, a mountain, and some people and animals. Using what you know about sensation and perception, think of all the monocular cues that you could use to give your masterpiece a sense of depth. In addition, can you think of any perceptual components that might add interest to your canvas?

Check your answers and review any areas of weakness before doing the progress tests.

Progress Test 1

Review the complete chapter (including all boxed inserts), review all your study notes, and then test yourself on the following progress test. Check your answers. If you make a mistake, review your notes, check the appropriate section in the study guide, and if necessary, go back and read the relevant part of the chapter in your textbook.

1. Dr. Kandola believes that we perceive whole objects as figures (gestalts) rather than isolated bits and pieces of sensory information. Dr. Kandola's research most likely focuses on
   (a) gate-control theory and the role of Substance P in the perception of pain.
   (b) top-down processing and basic perceptual principles such as the laws of similarity, closure, good continuation, proximity, and simplicity.
   (c) theories of color vision and phenomena such as afterimages, color blindness, and the experience of hue, brightness, and saturation.
   (d) bottom-up processing and basic sensory phenomena such as transduction, difference threshold, sensory adaptation, and accommodation.

2. Dr. Frankenstein's younger brother built a monster but omitted a very important part of his anatomy. As a result, the monster cannot transform sounds into neural messages. The missing part is the
   (a) eardrum.
   (b) middle ear with its tiny bones.
   (c) vestibular sacs.
   (d) basilar membrane.

3. A red pen is displayed in Roger's peripheral vision while he stares straight ahead. He correctly identifies the object but is unable to name the color. The reason for this is that
   (a) there are many rods but very few cones in the periphery of the retina.
   (b) there are many cones but very few rods in the periphery of the retina.
   (c) there are no receptor cells for vision in the periphery of the retina.
   (d) the stimulus was below Roger's difference threshold.

4. After staring at a blue light for a few minutes, Yoko shifts her gaze to a white wall and experiences an afterimage in the color _____ . Yoko's experience provides support for the _____ theory of color vision.
   (a) red; opponent-process
   (b) yellow; opponent-process
   (c) red; trichromatic
   (d) yellow; trichromatic

5. Neville is color-blind and cannot see red or green, yet he can see blue with no problem. Which theory of color vision can most easily explain this?
   (a) trichromatic theory
   (b) gate-control theory
   (c) opponent-process theory
   (d) gestalt theory

6. Ever since her operation, Madame Castellucci can no longer experience the flavors of the gourmet foods and wines she serves in her restaurant. It is most likely that she has suffered damage to her
   (a) kinesthetic sense.   (c) sense of humor.
   (b) sense of smell.   (d) vestibular sense.

7. The dizziness and disorientation Shelly felt after she rolled down the hill are a function of her
   (a) basilar membrane.
   (b) Pacinian corpuscles.

   (c) semicircular canals and vestibular sacs.
   (d) proprioceptors.

8. As Pancho gazed down the railway tracks it seemed to him that the two parallel rails actually met in the distance. Pancho is experiencing the monocular depth cue
   (a) linear perspective.   (c) motion parallax.
   (b) aerial perspective.   (d) texture gradient.

9. Many people have mistaken a floating log for Ogopogo, the alleged Okanagan Lake monster. The most likely reason for this misperception is
   (a) a perceptual set.
   (b) monocular vision.
   (c) rye whisky.
   (d) extrasensory perception.

10. If Fred holds a letter he is reading very close to his nose and Charlie holds it at arm's length when he reads it, Fred will experience _____ Charlie.
    (a) more convergence than
    (b) the identical level of convergence as
    (c) less convergence than
    (d) more motion parallax than

11. In an experiment, you are seated in a darkened room and shown a large lighted frame with a single dot of light inside it. The frame slowly moves to the left, and the dot remains stationary. It is very probable that you will perceive
    (a) induced motion.
    (b) the dot moving to the right.
    (c) the frame as remaining stationary.
    (d) all of these conditions.

12. As Demi moves away from the camera, her image in the viewfinder grows smaller and smaller, yet viewers do not perceive Demi as the incredible shrinking woman. This illustrates
    (a) convergence.   (c) size constancy.
    (b) binocular disparity. (d) motion parallax.

13. Researchers at State University study nociceptors (free nerve endings) and, in particular, the role played by A-delta fibers and C fibers. They are most likely to be interested in
    (a) olfaction and gustation.
    (b) the sensation and perception of pain.
    (c) proprioception and kinesthesis.
    (d) extrasensory perception.

14. People in industrialized societies are more susceptible to the Müller-Lyer illusion than those in nonindustrialized societies. According to Culture and Human Behavior (The Carpentered-World Hypothesis), these differences in susceptibility to the Müller-Lyer illusion are
    (a) the result of biological factors rather than cultural influences.
    (b) due to the mere exposure effect.
    (c) the result of cultural factors rather than biological influences.
    (d) due to innate or inborn perceptual sets.

15. According to Science Versus Pseudoscience (Subliminal Perception), if advertisers were to expose moviegoers to the subliminally flashed words EAT POPCORN and DRINK COKE during a movie
    (a) sales of popcorn and Coke would increase dramatically.
    (b) the moviegoers would feel hungry and thirsty for days after seeing the movie.
    (c) the subliminal messages are not likely to have any discernible effect on the sale of popcorn and Coke.
    (d) the moviegoers will have recurring nightmares involving popcorn and Coke.

Progress Test 2

After you have checked your understanding of the material in Progress Test 1 and have done a complete chapter review with special focus on any areas of weakness, you are ready to further assess your knowledge on Progress Test 2. Check your answers. If you make a mistake, review your notes, the relevant sections of the study guide, and if necessary, the appropriate parts of your textbook.

1. Detection of stimulus energy is to the interpretation of the information as _____ is to _____ .
    (a) transduction; accommodation
    (b) hue; saturation
    (c) hearing; vision
    (d) sensation; perception

2. When Julius returns from getting a drink of water, he resumes weightlifting a 150-pound free weight and doesn't notice that someone has added a 5-pound ring to each end. For Julius the additional 10 pounds
    (a) is not a just noticeable difference (jnd).
    (b) is below his absolute threshold.

    (c) is not sensed because of sensory adaptation.
    (d) is easy to lift because water releases endorphins.

3. When Vincent arrived home, the first thing he noticed was the smell of freshly baked bread. The process by which the odor of baking bread was converted into neural signals that Vincent's brain could interpret is called
    (a) sensory adaptation.
    (b) transduction.
    (c) accommodation.
    (d) conduction.

4. Malgorzata is wearing headphones and is asked to indicate when she is first aware of hearing a sound. It is very likely that the researchers are investigating
    (a) the difference threshold.
    (b) sensory adaptation.
    (c) the absolute threshold.
    (d) subliminal perception.

5. When Tony was painting a landscape, he used many different colors. The technical term for each of the different wavelengths of light that produce the subjective sensation of different colors in Tony's painting is
    (a) saturation.   (c) brightness.
    (b) hue.   (d) timbre.

6. As Rodney was setting up the equipment for the concert, he adjusted the amplitude of the speaker system. This is most likely to affect the _____ of the music.
    (a) pitch   (c) timbre
    (b) frequency   (d) loudness

7. Jasvir suffers from myopia; Carmen suffers from hyperopia. Both disorders involve abnormally shaped eyeballs that do not focus incoming light on the retina. In Jasvir's case, the light from a distant object is focused _____ ; for Carmen, the light is focused _____ .
    (a) on the cornea; on the optic disk
    (b) behind her retina; in front of her retina
    (c) on the optic disk; on the cornea
    (d) in front of her retina; behind her retina

8. When Derrick looked up from the newspaper he was reading to see if the bus was coming, the lenses in his eyes changed shape in order to focus on his retina the distant image of the street. This process is called
   (a) accommodation.
   (b) transduction.
   (c) sensory adaptation.
   (d) saturation.

9. In terms of the transduction of physical energy into coded neural messages, the _____ is to the eye as the _____ is to the ear.
   (a) lens; oval window
   (b) fovea; auditory nerve
   (c) retina; cochlea
   (d) iris; eardrum

10. On the day of an important job interview, Madeline wakes up with a slight toothache. As the time for the stressful interview approaches, her anxiety increases and so does her perception of the pain from her tooth. When the interview is over, Madeline is elated because she feels it has gone well and, to her surprise, she feels hardly any pain from her tooth. Madeline's experience is best explained by the _____ and the contribution of her psychological and emotional state.
    (a) opponent-process theory
    (b) gate-control theory
    (c) law of simplicity
    (d) law of good continuation

11. Astrid holds a pencil quite close to her nose and opens and closes her left and right eyes a couple of times in succession. She notices that the images are quite different. When she views the same pencil in a similar manner from across the room, she sees almost identical images. Astrid has demonstrated the _____ cue of _____ .
    (a) binocular; binocular disparity
    (b) monocular; motion parallax
    (c) binocular; overlap
    (d) monocular; convergence

12. With his eyes closed, Shahin can accurately touch his nose, lips, and ears with his right index finger. Shahin's ability to do this is due to specialized sensory neurons called _____ that are involved in his _____ sense.
    (a) Pacinian corpuscles; vestibular
    (b) ganglion cells; visual
    (c) proprioceptors; kinesthetic
    (d) pheromones; olfactory

13. At a police roadblock, drivers are randomly checked for seatbelt violations and other driving offenses. The police officer sometimes shines a light into the driver's eye. This typically results in the contraction of the _____ , which controls the size of the _____ and thus the amount of light entering the eye.
    (a) pupil; lens
    (b) iris; pupil
    (c) cornea; fovea
    (d) sclera; pupil
    (e) iris; optic disk

14. Culture and Human Behavior (Culture and the Müller-Lyer Illusion) discusses research on differences in perception between collectivistic cultures and individualistic cultures and concludes that
    (a) people from collectivistic cultures perceive the world in completely different ways from those in individualistic cultures,
    (b) people from different cultures do not differ significantly in the way they perceive things, in what they pay attention to, or in how they think about things.
    (c) people from individualistic cultures have a more holistic perceptual style than those from collectivistic cultures.
    (d) all people use the same neural processes to make perceptual judgments, but there are cultural differences in what people pay attention to and in how they think about what they see.

15. Willard believes he can influence the mechanical systems within slot machines with the power of his mind alone. According to Critical Thinking (ESP), Willard is claiming to possess the power of
    (a) telepathy.
    (b) clairvoyance.
    (c) psychokinesis.
    (d) precognition.

Progress Test 3

After you have checked your understanding of the material in Progress Tests 1 and 2 and have done a complete chapter review with special focus on any areas of weakness, you are ready to further assess your knowledge with Progress Test 3. Check your answers. If you make a mistake, review your notes, the appropriate parts of the study guide, and if necessary, the relevant sections of your textbook.

1. During a psychology lab demonstration, the instructor set up two flashing lights about three feet apart in a darkened room. About one-tenth of a second after the first light flashed, the second light flashed, and then the first light flashed again, and so on. Most of the students experienced the illusion of apparent motion, perceiving just one light traveling back and forth. The instructor is most likely to explain this phenomenon in terms of

   (a) the principles of stroboscopic motion.
   (b) the kinesthetic sense.
   (c) motion parallax.
   (d) binocular disparity.

2. You have just arrived at the beach and the texture of the sand toward the water appears smooth, even, and perfectly flat, yet the sand beneath your feet is rough and uneven, and you can see individual small stones, seashells, and other debris. You are experiencing the monocular distance cue of

   (a) motion parallax.
   (b) aerial perspective.
   (c) linear perspective.
   (d) texture gradient.

3. José notices that near the horizon the moon appears larger than when it is overhead in the sky. The effect is mainly the result of

   (a) distance cues that make the horizon moon seem farther away.
   (b) the retinal image of the horizon moon being larger than the retinal image of the overhead moon.
   (c) distance cues that make the horizon moon seem nearer.
   (d) having to tilt your head upward when looking at the overhead moon.

4. While carrying out a sensory demonstration in which a small object is positioned so that its retinal image would be cast on the exact spot where her optic nerve exits the eye, Deidre should expect the image of the object to

   (a) change to its opposite color.
   (b) look twice as large as it had before.
   (c) produce an afterimage if she shifts her gaze to a white surface.
   (d) disappear from sight.

5. Analysis that moves from the parts to the whole is to _____ as analysis that moves from the whole to the parts is to

   _____ .

   (a) figure–ground relationship; figure–ground reversal
   (b) bottom-up processing; top-down processing
   (c) size constancy; shape constancy
   (d) the moon illusion; the Müller-Lyer illusion

6. While strolling through the garden, Jamal suddenly noticed the wonderful odor of roses. Jamal is using her _____ sense, and the process by which the odor is converted into neural signals that her brain can understand is called _____ .

   (a) gustatory; saturation
   (b) olfactory: transduction
   (c) gustatory; adaptation
   (d) olfactory; accommodation

7. Whenever Robyn looks at her boyfriend, her pupils dilate. The eye structure responsible for this response is called the

   (a) retina.   (c) iris.
   (b) fovea.   (d) optic disk.

8. When looking carefully at a picture of a country scene, we are able to detect fine visual details, especially those that are focused on the fovea. One reason for this visual acuity is that

   (a) the fovea contains rods, which have many individual neural connections to the cortex.
   (b) the fovea contains cones, which have many individual neural connections to the cortex.
   (c) the fovea is the spot where the optic nerve leaves the eye.
   (d) there are only bipolar cells in the fovea, and these are specialized for feature detection.

9. After Jackson has been in the hot tub for a few minutes, he no longer notices how hot the water is. This is because of
   (a) sensory adaptation.
   (b) the just noticeable difference.
   (c) Jackson's thick skin.
   (d) sensory saturation.

10. After playing in a heavy metal rock band for most of his young adult life, Edwin has suffered a significant hearing loss. Unfortunately for Edwin, his hearing problem cannot be helped by a hearing aid. It is most likely that he is suffering from
    (a) damage to the auditory cortex in his left temporal lobe.
    (b) nerve deafness.
    (c) damage to his proprioceptors.
    (d) conduction deafness.

11. Graham is nearsighted and Grace is farsighted. Corrective lenses work for both of them because their respective visual disorders are caused by
    (a) the lack of rods and cones in the visual disk.
    (b) clouding or occlusion of the cornea.
    (c) smaller than normal ganglion and bipolar cells in the retina.
    (d) a failure of the lens to properly focus incoming light on the retina.

12. Mehnroosh believes that the size of the just noticeable difference varies depending on its relation to the strength of the original stimulus. Her views are most consistent with
    (a) Weber's law.
    (b) the law of Prägnanz.
    (c) the opponent-process theory.
    (d) gate-control theory.

13. After a small area near the stirrup end of her basilar membrane was damaged, Harriet could no longer hear high-frequency sounds. This particular loss of hearing can best be explained by
    (a) trichromatic theory.
    (b) place theory.
    (c) gate-control theory.
    (d) frequency theory.

14. To control the arthritic pain in his knees, Frederick now wears magnetic insoles in his shoes and magnetic bracelets on his wrists. Frederick is convinced that his pain has been somewhat reduced since he started wearing these magnets. According to the Application,

Frederick's self-administered strategy of pain control is an example of
   (a) mainstream medical health therapy (MMHT).
   (b) biofeedback therapy (BFT).
   (c) complementary and alternative medicines (CAM).
   (d) distraction and counterirritation pain control strategy (DCPCS).

15. Maxwell is a male pig and, like most male pigs, he releases a chemical substance in the sweat glands to communicate territorial boundaries and sexual receptiveness. According to In Focus, these chemical signals, common in the animal kingdom, are called
    (a) chemosignals.   (c) substance P.
    (b) pheromones.   (d) umami.

Answers

Introduction: What Are Sensation and Perception?

1. *The primary function of the nervous system is* communication—the transmission of information from one part of the body to another.

2. *Sensation refers to* the detection and basic sensory experience of environmental stimuli, *and perception occurs when* we integrate, organize, and interpret sensory information in a way that is meaningful.

3. *The difference between sensation and perception is* that sensation involves responding to stimulation and transmitting it in usable form to the brain, whereas perception involves the organization and interpretation of sensation. However, there is no clear definitive boundary between the two.

Basic Principles of Sensation

1. *We are able to hear, taste, smell, feel, and see by* using specialized cells called sensory receptors that respond to stimulation by some form of energy (e.g., sound waves, chemicals, pressure, and light waves).

2. *Transduction is* the process by which a form of physical energy is converted into a coded neural signal that can be processed by the nervous system.

3. *The two types of sensory threshold are (and what they refer to)* the absolute threshold, which is the smallest possible strength of a stimulus that can be detected half the time, and the difference threshold, which is the

smallest possible difference between two stimuli that can be detected half the time.

4. *Another name for the difference threshold is* the just noticeable difference (jnd).

5. *Weber's law states that* the size of the just noticeable difference (jnd) will vary depending on its relation to the strength of the original stimulus.

6. *Sensory adaptation occurs because* sensory receptor cells become less responsive to a constant stimulus; it is relative to the duration of exposure.

Concept Check 1

1. absolute

2. sensation; perception

3. difference threshold; just noticeable difference (jnd); Weber's law

4. transduction

5. sensory adaptation

6. subliminal perception

Matching Exercise 1

1. threshold

2. transduction

3. absolute threshold

4. sensory receptors

5. difference threshold

6. the mere exposure effect

True/False Test 1

1. F   3. T   5. T
2. T   4. F

Vision: From Light to Sight

1. *The process of seeing begins with* stimulation of visual receptor cells in the eye, which are sensitive to the physical energy of light.

2. *The electromagnetic spectrum is* made up of many different forms of electromagnetic energy, which vary in wavelength; humans are capable of visually detecting only a tiny portion of the spectrum (visible light).

3. *The key structures of the eye (and their functions) are* the cornea (helps gather and direct incoming light), the pupil (changes size to let in different amounts of light), the iris (the muscle that controls the size of the pupil), the lens (focuses or bends light as it enters the eye),

and the retina (contains the rods and cones, the photoreceptors that respond to light).

4. *The function of rods is to* detect light (but not color). They are especially sensitive in dim light and at night. *The function of cones is to* detect color and fine details (most cones are concentrated in the fovea, the point of central focus in the retina).

5. *The optic disk is* the point at which the fibers that make up the optic nerve exit the back of the eye and create a blind spot in our field of vision.

6. *Bipolar cells process visual information by* collecting information from the rods and cones and funneling it to the ganglion cells, whose bundled axons form the optic nerve; from the optic chiasm (the point of partial crossover of the optic nerves from each eye) information is sent to the thalamus and then on to the visual cortex.

7. *Our experience of color involves* three properties of light waves: hue (color), saturation (purity), and brightness (perceived intensity). Different wavelengths correspond to our subjective experience of different colors.

8. *According to the trichromatic theory,* there are three types of cones, each of which is especially sensitive to certain wavelengths: red light (long wavelengths), green light (medium wavelengths), or blue light (short wavelengths); other colors are a result of stimulation of a combination of cones. *This theory explains* the most common form of color blindness, red–green color blindness.

9. *According to the opponent-process theory,* there are four basic colors, which are divided into two pairs of color-sensitive neurons, red–green and blue–yellow (black and white also act as an opposing pair); when one member of a pair is stimulated, the other member is inhibited. *This theory explains* afterimages.

Concept Check 2

1. purple

2. green

3. trichromatic; opponent-process

4. color; fine detail

5. black

Graphic Organizer 1

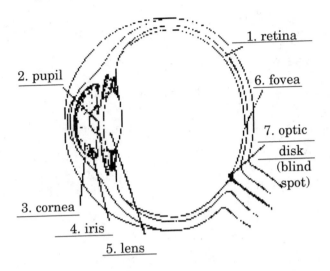

1. retina
2. pupil
3. cornea
4. iris
5. lens
6. fovea
7. optic disk (blind spot)

Matching Exercise 2

1. visual acuity
2. afterimage
3. wavelength
4. accommodation
5. brightness
6. optic nerve
7. trichromatic theory of color vision
8. cones
9. hue
10. rods
11. bipolar cells
12. color
13. optic disk
14. presbyopia
15. astigmatism
16. feature detectors

True/False Test 2

1. F	5. F	9. T	13. F
2. T	6. T	10. T	14. T
3. F	7. T	11. T	15. F
4. T	8. F	12. T	16. T

Hearing: From Vibration to Sound

1. *Audition is* the technical term for the sense of hearing.

2. *Our perception of sound is directly related to the physical properties of* sound waves and involves loudness as determined by intensity (amplitude, measured in decibels), pitch (the relative highness or lowness of a sound, determined by frequency), and timbre (the distinctive quality of a sound).

3. *The key structures of the ear are* the outer ear (pinna, ear canal, and eardrum), the middle ear (the hammer, anvil, and stirrup), and the inner ear (cochlea, basilar membrane, and semicircular canals).

4. *The process of hearing begins when* sound waves are caught by the pinna and funneled down the ear canal to the eardrum. *It then involves* the sound waves being amplified in the middle ear. Vibrations from the hammer, anvil, and stirrup vibrate the oval window, which relays the vibrations to the cochlea where the sound waves are transduced (transformed into neural messages) by hair cells in the basilar membrane, which runs the length of the cochlea in the inner ear.

5. *According to frequency theory,* the basilar membrane vibrates at the same frequency as sound waves. *This theory explains* how low-frequency sound waves (up to about 1,000 hertz) are transmitted to the brain but cannot explain transmission of higher-frequency sound waves.

6. *According to place theory,* different frequencies cause larger vibrations at different locations along the basilar membrane. *This theory explains* our discrimination of higher-pitched sounds, with the higher-pitched sounds being interpreted according to the place where the hair cells are most active; for intermediate frequencies or mid-range pitches, both place and frequency are involved.

Concept Check 3

1. amplitude; decibels
2. conduction
3. hammer; anvil; stirrup
4. timbre
5. basilar membrane; nerve
6. pitch; hertz
7. transduction; cochlea; basilar membrane
8. frequency
9. pinna; ear canal; eardrum

Graphic Organizer 2

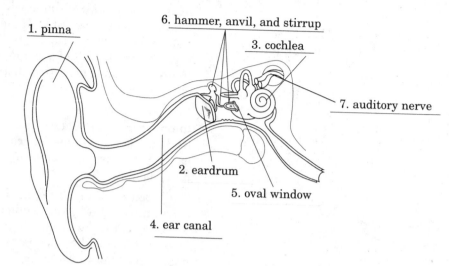

1. pinna
6. hammer, anvil, and stirrup
3. cochlea
7. auditory nerve
2. eardrum
5. oval window
4. ear canal

Matching Exercise 3

1. loudness
2. audition
3. frequency
4. hair cells
5. sound waves
6. timbre
7. outer ear
8. pitch
9. decibel
10. amplitude
11. middle ear
12. frequency theory

True/False Test 3

1. F	5. T	9. F
2. F	6. T	10. T
3. F	7. T	11. T
4. T	8. T	12. T

The Chemical and Body Senses: Smell, Taste, Touch, and Position

1. *Olfaction is the technical term for* the sense of smell, *and gustation is the technical term for* the sense of taste.

2. *They are called chemical senses because* the sensory receptors for taste and smell are specialized to respond to different types of chemical substances.

3. *Our sense of smell begins when* airborne molecules emitted by substances we inhale stimulate olfactory receptor cells high in the nasal cavity. *It then involves* the resulting neural messages being passed along the olfactory nerves, which are directly connected to the olfactory bulb (the enlarged ending of the olfactory cortex). Axons from the olfactory bulb form the olfactory tract, along which messages pass to various brain areas, including the temporal lobe and structures in the limbic system.

4. *Our sense of taste begins when* specialized receptors in the taste buds located on the tongue and inside the mouth and throat are stimulated. *It then involves* neural messages being sent along neural pathways to the thalamus, which, in turn, directs the information to several regions in the cortex.

5. *The five primary taste qualities are* sweet, sour, salty, bitter, and umami.

6. *The skin and body senses include* touch and temperature, pain, movement, position, and balance.

7. *The skin responds to* stimulation such as pressure, warmth, and cold.

8. *One receptor for touch is* the Pacinian corpuscle, *and it works by* converting pressure stimulation into a neural message that is relayed to the brain. If a pressure is constant, sensory adaptation takes place.

9. *Pain is the unpleasant sensation of* physical discomfort or suffering that can occur in varying degrees of intensity.

10. *There are two types of nociceptors involved in pain: (a)* myelinated A-delta fibers, *which represent the* fast pain system *and transmit* the sharp, intense, but short-lived pain of immediate injury (morphine and other opiates have virtually no effect on the system), and *(b)* unmyelinated C fibers, *which represent* the slow pain system *and transmit* the longer-lasting, throbbing, burning pain of injury (morphine and other opiates are effective with this system).

11. *According to the gate-control theory,* the sensation of pain is controlled by a series of gates in the spinal cord that open (pain is experienced or intensified) and close (pain is reduced). Pain results from both physiological and psychological factors and can be intensified by anxiety, fear, and a sense of helplessness.

12. *The experience of pain is also influenced by* positive emotions, laughter, distraction, and a sense of control, and by genetic factors, social and situational factors, and cultural learning experiences about the meaning of pain and how people should react to pain.

13. *Phantom limb pain refers to* the phenomenon in which a person continues to experience intense painful sensations in a limb that has been amputated. *It is explained by* sensitization, which is the opposite of sensory adaptation in that pain pathways from the site of the amputation to the brain become increasingly more responsive over time and produce the mental feeling of pain coming from the nonexistent limb.

14. *Our kinesthetic sense involves* stimulation of proprioceptors, which constantly communicate information to the brain about changes in body position and muscle tension and provide information about the location and position of body parts in relation to one another.

15. *Our vestibular sense provides us with* a sense of balance, or equilibrium, by responding to changes in gravity, motion, and body position.

16. *The two sources of vestibular sensory information are* the semicircular canals and the vestibular sacs, both of which are located in the ear.

Concept Check 4

1. taste buds
2. phantom limb pain; sensitized
3. smell (olfaction)
4. sweet; salty; sour; bitter; umami

5. intensify
6. semicircular canals; vestibular sacs
7. nociceptors; free nerve endings; A-delta; C
8. kinesthetic
9. substance P

Matching Exercise 4

1. gustation
2. semicircular canals and vestibular sacs
3. Pacinian corpuscle
4. anosmia
5. nociceptors (free nerve endings)
6. olfactory receptor cells
7. olfactory bulb
8. taste buds
9. olfactory tract
10. vestibular sense
11. endorphins and enkephalins
12. kinesthetic sense
13. umami
14. phantom limb pain
15. A-delta fibers

True/False Test 4

1. T	5. F	9. F	13. T
2. T	6. T	10. F	14. T
3. T	7. T	11. F	15. T
4. T	8. T	12. T	

Perception (Part 1)

1. *Perception is the process of* integrating, organizing, and interpreting sensory information in a meaningful way.

2. *Bottom-up processing refers to* the flow of information from the sensory receptors to the brain; this type of analysis moves from the parts to the whole (data-driven processing).

3. *Top-down processing refers to* analysis that moves from the whole to the parts; it occurs when we use our knowledge, experience, expectations, and other cognitive processes to arrive at meaningful perceptions (conceptually driven processing).

4. *The three basic questions of perception are* What is it?, How far away is it?, and Where is it going? (Bottom-up and top-down processing are both necessary for arriving at perceptual conclusions.)

5. *Gestalt psychology was founded by* Max Wertheimer *and is concerned with* the fact that we tend to perceive whole objects or figures (gestalts) rather than isolated bits and pieces of sensory information.

Perception: The Perception of Shape (Part 2)

1. *The figure–ground relationship describes* how we automatically separate the elements of perception into the feature that clearly stands out (the figure) and its less distinct background (the ground). *It is important because it demonstrates that* the separation of a scene into figure and ground is not a property of the actual elements in the scene but instead is a psychological accomplishment.

2. *The perceptual principles involved in grouping visual elements include* similarity, closure, good continuation, and proximity.

3. *The law of Prägnanz states* that when several perceptual organizations of an assortment of visual elements are possible, the perceptual interpretation that occurs will be one that produces the "best, simplest, and most stable shape" (also called the law of simplicity). *It is important because it encompasses* all other Gestalt principles, including the figure–ground relationship *and suggests that* we actively and automatically construct a perception that reveals the "essence of something."

Perception: Depth Perception (Part 3)

1. *Depth perception refers to* the ability to perceive the distance of an object as well as its three-dimensional characteristics. *It is important because* being able to perceive the distance of an object has obvious survival value, especially regarding potential threats or danger.

2. *Monocular cues are defined as* distance or depth cues that can be processed by either eye alone *and include* relative size, overlap, aerial perspective, texture gradient, linear perspective, motion parallax, and accommodation.

3. *Binocular cues are defined as* distance or depth cues that require the use of both eyes *and include* convergence and binocular disparity.

4. *A stereogram is* a picture that uses the principles of binocular disparity to create the perception of a three-dimensional image.

Concept Check 5

1. law of proximity
2. ground; figure

3. binocular disparity
4. relative size
5. linear perspective
6. law of closure
7. bottom-up processing

Matching Exercise 5

1. Gestalt psychology
2. law of Prägnanz
3. aerial perspective
4. binocular disparity
5. figure–ground relationship
6. overlap (interposition)
7. binocular cues
8. accommodation
9. law of proximity
10. depth perception
11. figure–ground reversal
12. Max Wertheimer
13. parapsychology
14. law of similarity

True/False Test 5

1. T	6. T	11. F
2. T	7. T	12. T
3. F	8. T	13. T
4. T	9. F	
5. F	10. T	

Perception: The Perception of Motion (Part 4)

1. *The perception of motion involves* the integration of information from several sources, including microfine eye-muscle movements, the changing retinal image, and the contrast of the moving object with its stationary background.

2. *Induced motion refers to* our strong tendency to assume that the background is stationary and that it is the object or figure that moves. *It was first studied by* Karl Duncker.

3. *Stroboscopic motion creates* an illusion of movement with two carefully timed flashing lights going on and off in succession. *It is caused by* the brain's visual system combining the rapid sequence of visual information (the two lights going on and off and being detected at two different points on the surface of the retina) and arriving at the conclusion of movement, even though no movement has occurred (the

perception of smooth motion in movies is due to the same phenomenon).

Perception: Perceptual Constancies (Part 5)

1. *Perceptual constancy refers to* the tendency to perceive objects as unchanging despite changes in sensory input.

2. *Size constancy is* the perception that an object remains the same size despite its changing image on the retina. *An important aspect of size constancy is* that if the retinal image of an object does not change, but the perception of its distance increases, the object is perceived as larger.

3. *Shape constancy is* the tendency to perceive familiar objects as having a fixed shape regardless of the image they cast on the retinas.

Perceptual Illusions and the Effects of Experience on Perceptual Interpretations

1. *A perceptual illusion involves* the misperception of the true characteristics of an object or image. Illusions are used to study perceptual principles.

2. *The Müller-Lyer illusion is* the misperception of the length of two identical lines, one with arrows pointing outward and one with arrows pointed inward.

3. *The moon illusion involves* the misperception that the moon is larger when it is on the horizon than when it is overhead *and may be the result of* the misapplication of the principles of overlap and size constancy—distance cues make the horizon moon seem farther away, and thus we perceive the moon as being larger, even though the retinal image of the moon remains constant.

4. *Perceptual illusions reveal that* what we see is not merely a reflection of the real world, but instead, it is our subjective interpretation of it; we actively construct perceptual conclusions about the information detected through our senses (in a way, believing is seeing).

5. *Perceptions can be influenced by* a variety of learning experiences, including educational, cultural, and life experiences.

6. *A perceptual set is* the tendency to perceive objects or situations from a particular frame of reference.

Concept Check 6

1. perceptual set
2. farther away
3. shape
4. Müller-Lyer
5. perceptual constancy
6. stroboscopic motion

Matching Exercise 6

1. perceptual set
2. perceptual constancy
3. Müller-Lyer illusion
4. size constancy
5. Karl Duncker
6. acupuncture
7. Shepard Tables

True/False Test 6

1. T	3. T	5. T
2. T	4. T	6. T

Something to Think About

1. First, you would note that these strange experiences happen to many people, that there is nothing particularly unique about them. The problem arises in the way people interpret these experiences. These experiences, of course, do not constitute proof of ESP, no matter how strongly someone believes they do. Two less extraordinary concepts can explain these occurrences: coincidence and the fallacy of positive instances. Coincidence, which refers to an event occurring simply by chance, can account for many of the experiences reported by people. Combine coincidence with our tendency to remember coincidental events that seem to confirm our belief about unusual phenomena—the fallacy of positive instances—and the feeling that something unusual has happened can be very strong, even though there are no rational grounds for that belief. Finally, there is no strong scientific evidence for the existence of ESP, despite years of intensive study by psychologists interested in this topic. To date, no parapsychology experiment, including those using the ganzfeld procedure, that has claimed to show evidence of ESP has been successfully replicated. This, of course, does not prove conclusively that ESP does not exist; however, although one should keep an open mind, there is no evidence or any rational reason to believe in its existence.

2. Some of the most common monocular cues that are useful in conveying a sense of depth on the canvas are overlap, in which "nearer" objects are depicted as blocking or obscuring more "distant" objects; linear perspective, in which parallel lines are depicted as converging toward the top of the painting, for instance; and texture gradient, in which surfaces that are supposed to be close to the observer have distinct, clearly defined textures and those that are gradually less and less clearly defined depict distance. Relative size and aerial perspective are also useful devices to convey depth.

   To make your picture more interesting you might want to attempt to incorporate some misleading depth cues (such as in Escher drawings) or perceptual illusions.

Progress Test 1

1. b	6. b	11. d
2. d	7. c	12. c
3. a	8. a	13. b
4. b	9. a	14. c
5. a	10. a	15. c

Progress Test 2

1. d	6. d	11. a
2. a	7. d	12. c
3. b	8. a	13. b
4. c	9. c	14. d
5. b	10. b	15. c

Progress Test 3

1. a	6. b	11. d
2. d	7. c	12. a
3. a	8. b	13. b
4. d	9. a	14. c
5. b	10. b	15. b

CHAPTER 4

Consciousness and Its Variations

PREVIEW	Reading the section below first will give you a general sense of the chapter's contents and an initial introduction to some of the major concepts and terms. This will prime you for what you are about to read and help you to develop a "cognitive map" that will guide your study of the material in this chapter. Likewise, reading the **preview questions** at the beginning of each major section will improve your ability to understand, learn, and retain the information.

CHAPTER 4 . . . AT A GLANCE

Chapter 4 examines the different forms of human consciousness, beginning with how biological and environmental "clocks" regulate our circadian rhythms and sleep–wake cycles. The discovery of REM sleep and how the EEG is used to measure brain-wave activity are discussed. This is followed by an examination of the different stages of sleep and their associated brain-wave activity and behavioral patterns. The next section is an exploration of dreams and mental activity during sleep. Two major theories of the meaning of dreams and their relevance to psychological and physiological functioning are presented. This section ends with a discussion of the various sleep disorders (dyssomnias, such as insomnia, obstructive sleep apnea, and narcolepsy, and parsomnias, such as sleepwalking, sleep terrors, sleep-related eating disorder, sleep-sex, and REM sleep behavior disorder).

Altered states of consciousness are introduced next, and both hypnosis and meditation are discussed in this context. Under hypnosis, profound sensory and perceptual changes may be experienced. This section focuses on phenomena such as posthypnotic suggestion, posthypnotic amnesia, and hypermnesia. Hilgard's notions of dissociation and the hidden observer are examined, and the controversy surrounding how to explain hypnosis is discussed. Finally, meditation is defined, and techniques for inducing a meditative state are presented along with research findings on transcendental meditation, or TM.

The final section is concerned with using drugs to alter consciousness. The psychoactive drugs are classified and listed along with their various effects on brain activity and physiological and psychological functioning. Drug dependence, drug tolerance, withdrawal symptoms, and drug abuse are discussed.

The Application offers some practical suggestions for improving sleep and mental alertness.

Introduction: Consciousness: Experiencing the "Private I"

Preview Questions

Consider the following questions as you study this section of the chapter.

- How is *consciousness* defined, and what did William James mean by *stream of consciousness*?
- Why was research on consciousness abandoned for a time, and why did it regain legitimacy?

*Read the section "Introduction: Consciousness: Experiencing the 'Private I'" and **write** your answers to the following:*

1. *Consciousness* is defined as the _____
   _____

2. William James's idea of "stream of consciousness" refers to the fact that _____
   _____
   _____

3. Research on consciousness was abandoned because _____
   _____

   Psychologists turned instead to _____
   _____

4. Psychologists returned to studying consciousness in the late 1950s for two reasons: _____
   _____
   _____

Biological and Environmental "Clocks" That Regulate Consciousness

Preview Questions

Consider the following questions as you study this section of the chapter.

- What are circadian rhythms?
- What roles do the suprachiasmatic nucleus (SCN), sunlight, and melatonin play in regulating circadian rhythms?
- How do "free-running" conditions affect circadian rhythms?
- Why do people suffer jet lag symptoms, and what role does melatonin play in producing these symptoms?

*Read the section "Biological and Environmental 'Clocks' Regulating Consciousness" and **write** the answers to the following:*

1. Circadian rhythms are _____
   _____

2. The suprachiasmatic nucleus (SCN) is _____
   _____
   _____

   Its role in sleep–wake cycles and other circadian rhythms is to _____
   _____
   _____

3. Melatonin is a _____
   _____

4. Free-running conditions are created by _____
   _____

   They have two distinct effects: First, _____
   _____

   Second, _____
   _____

5. People suffer from jet lag symptoms because
   _____
   _____

6. Melatonin plays a key role in jet lag symptoms by _____
   _____

After you have carefully studied the preceding sections, complete the following exercises.

Concept Check 1

Read the following and write the correct term in the space provided.

1. Sheena works the night shift and has had trouble sleeping during the day. But now that she has hung heavy curtains in her bedroom that effectively block out any daylight, she is able to get restful sleep in the daytime. This is because her _____ are staying in sync with her night work schedule, and she has prevented sunlight from resetting her

   _____ .

2. Although Marvin was very tired after pulling an "all-nighter" to finish a paper, he began to feel much less drowsy as the morning proceeded. His reaction is probably due to decreased levels of the hormone _____ .

3. David typically experiences a slump in mental alertness around midafternoon but feels very energetic in the early evening. These daily highs and lows are examples of

_____ .

4. During a history lecture, Alfie is listening and taking notes but at times he is also thinking about his girlfriend and the argument they had last night. He wonders what he will say to her when he phones her that afternoon, which gets him thinking about how often his parents fight and whether arguing is genetic, which reminds him about his biology exam next week. This description reflects Alfie's _____ .

5. Dr. Parizeau arranges for volunteers to spend several weeks in special isolation units without exposure to sunlight, clocks, or other environmental time cues; during this time he monitors their sleep–wake cycles and other biological events. Dr. Parizeau is attempting to create _____ in his research on circadian rhythms.

Review of Terms, Concepts, and Names 1

Use the terms in this list to complete the Matching Test, then to help you answer the True/False items correctly.

consciousness
William James
introspection
overt behavior
circadian rhythm
suprachiasmatic nucleus
  (SCN)

melatonin
pineal gland
free-running condition
jet lag

Matching Exercise

Match the appropriate term/name with its definition or description:

1. _____ Personal awareness of mental activities, internal sensations, and the external environment.

2. _____ Verbal self-reports that try to capture the "structure" of conscious experiences.

3. _____ Cluster of neurons in the brain's hypothalamus that governs the timing of circadian rhythms.

4. _____ Symptoms such as physical and mental fatigue, depression or irritability, disrupted sleep, and fuzziness in concentration, thinking, and memory that result from circadian rhythms being out of sync with daylight and darkness cues.

5. _____ Hormone manufactured by the pineal gland that produces sleepiness.

True/False Test

Indicate whether each statement is true or false by placing T or F in the blank space next to each item.

1. ___ Overt behavior refers to any response that can be directly observed, measured, and verified.

2. ___ William James was the American psychologist and philosopher who proposed that the subjective experience of consciousness is an ongoing stream of mental activity.

3. ___ The pineal gland is an endocrine gland located in the brain that regulates the production of the hormone melatonin.

4. ___ A free-running condition exists when the body's internal clock runs freely and independently of external time cues, such as daylight, darkness, clocks, or schedules.

5. ___ Circadian rhythm refers to a cycle or rhythm that is roughly 24 hours long and involves cyclical daily fluctuations in biological and psychological processes.

Check your answers and review any areas of weakness before going on to the next section.

Sleep

Preview Questions

Consider the following questions as you study this section of the chapter.

- How did the invention of the electroencephalograph and the discovery of REM sleep contribute to modern sleep research?
- What are the characteristics of the NREM sleep stages and REM sleep?
- How do sleep patterns change over the lifespan?

Read the section "Sleep" (up to "Do We Need to Sleep?") and **write** *your answers to the following:*

1. An electroencephalograph is _____
_____
_____

2. By studying EEGs, sleep researchers established that _____
_____

3. Use of the EEG led to the discovery of _____
_____

4. Beta brain waves are associated with _____
_____
_____

   Alpha brain waves are associated with _____
_____
_____

5. Hypnagogic hallucinations are _____
_____

6. The four NREM sleep stages are characterized by different brain and body activity:

   Stage 1 NREM: _____
_____

   Stage 2 NREM: _____
_____

   Stage 3 and 4 NREM:_____
_____

7. REM sleep is characterized by _____
_____
_____

8. Over the course of the lifespan, the quantity and quality of our sleep _____
_____
_____

Do We Need to Sleep?

Preview Questions

Consider the following questions as you study this section of the chapter.

- Why do we need sleep, and what is the evidence that we have a biological need for sleep?
- What do the phenomena of REM and NREM rebound indicate?
- How do the restorative and adaptive theories of sleep explain the function of sleep?

Read the section "Do We Need Sleep?" and **write** *your answers to the following:*

1. Sleep deprivation and sleep restriction studies demonstrate that _____
_____
_____
_____

2. The phenomena of REM and NREM rebound seem to indicate that _____
_____

3. The restorative theory of sleep suggests that
_____
_____

4. The adaptive theory of sleep suggests that
_____
_____
_____

Concept Check 2

Read the following and write the correct term in the space provided.

1. James went to bed a short while ago; although his eyes are closed and he is very relaxed, he has not yet fallen asleep. If James's brain is relatively normal, it is probably generating _____ brain waves.

2. Shortly after falling asleep, James experiences a muscle spasm that jolts him awake. James

has most likely experienced the most common hypnagogic hallucination of _____ accompanied by a _____ .

3. Every day during the past week, Richie got only about half his usual night's sleep. As a result, he is likely to be not only _____ deprived but also _____ deprived. When he is finally able to get a full night's sleep, he will probably experience _____ .

4. Mrs. Eastman has just turned 65 and is worried because she is waking up more easily nowadays, sleeps less than 7 hours most nights, and feels less rested and less satisfied after sleeping. A sleep specialist is most likely to say that she _____ .

5. Azra has been asleep for about 10 minutes and is now in stage 2 sleep. Her brain-wave activity

is likely to be predominantly _____ waves and is defined by the appearance of _____ and _____ .

6. Dr. Ayle believes that the different sleep patterns exhibited by different species of animals evolved as a way of preventing certain species from interacting with the environment when doing so is most hazardous. Dr. Ayle's view is most consistent with the _____ theory of sleep.

7. Vladimir was having a very frightening dream that heavily armed, masked burglars were breaking into his house and trying to kill him. He woke up suddenly and was even more alarmed because he was unable to move, a phenomenon called _____ .

Graphic Organizer 1

The diagram below shows the brain waves typical of each stage in a 90-minute (approximately) sleep cycle. Match the term or description with the correct brain-wave pattern.

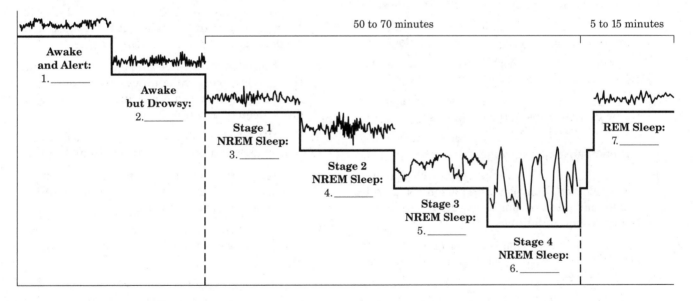

A. Brain waves associated with dreaming

B. Sleep spindles and K complexes

C. Beta brain waves

D. Mixture of theta and delta brain waves

E. Alpha brain waves

F. Delta brain waves

G. Mixture of alpha and theta brain waves

Review of Terms and Concepts 2

Use the terms in this list to complete the Matching Test, then to help you answer the True/False items correctly.

electroencephalograph
brain waves
EEG (electroencephalo-
    gram)
REM sleep (active sleep
    or paradoxical sleep)
NREM sleep (quiet
    sleep)
beta brain waves
alpha brain waves
hypnagogic
    hallucinations
myoclonic jerk
    (sleep start)
theta brain waves

sleep spindles
K complexes
delta brain waves
slow-wave sleep
sleep paralysis
sleep deprivation studies
microsleeps
sleep restriction studies
REM rebound
NREM rebound
restorative theory of
    sleep
adaptive (evolutionary)
    theory of sleep

Matching Exercise

Match the appropriate term with its definition or description.

1. _____ Brain-wave pattern associated with relaxed wakefulness and drowsiness.

2. _____ Graphic record of brain activity produced by an electroencephalograph.

3. _____ Short bursts of brain activity that characterize stage 2 NREM sleep.

4. _____ Vivid sensory phenomena that can occur during the onset of sleep.

5. _____ Term applied to the combination of stage 3 and stage 4 sleep.

6. _____ Involuntary muscle spasm of the whole body that jolts the person completely awake and often accompanies the hypnagogic hallucination of falling.

7. _____ Single but large high-voltage spikes of brain activity that characterize stage 2 NREM sleep.

8. _____ Phenomenon in which a person who is deprived of REM sleep greatly increases the amount of time spent in REM sleep at the first opportunity for uninterrupted sleep.

9. _____ Instrument that uses electrodes placed on the scalp to measure and record the brain's electrical activity.

10. _____ The rhythmical patterns of electrical brain activity.

11. _____ Studies that reduce the amount of time people are allowed to sleep to as little as four hours per night, and which continue for a few nights or for more than six months.

True/False Test

Indicate whether each statement is true or false by placing T or F in the blank space next to each item.

1. ___ NREM rebound is a phenomenon in which a person who is deprived of stage 3 and 4 NREM sleep spends more time in these stages when permitted to sleep undisturbed.

2. ___ The restorative theory of sleep suggests that the unique sleep patterns of different animals evolved over time to help promote survival and environmental adaptation.

3. ___ During REM sleep, rapid eye movements and dreaming occur, and voluntary muscle activity is suppressed; also called *active sleep* or *paradoxical sleep*.

4. ___ The view that sleep and dreaming are essential to normal physical and mental functioning is called the adaptive (evolutionary) theory of sleep.

5. ___ Beta brain waves are patterns of electrical activity that begin in stage 1 NREM sleep and predominate in stage 2 NREM sleep.

6. ___ Episodes of sleep lasting only a few seconds that occur during wakefulness are called microsleeps; they can occur after as little as one day's sleep deprivation.

7. ___ NREM sleep, or quiet sleep, is divided into four stages and does not involve dreaming.

8. ___ Theta brain waves are small, fast brain waves that reflect an awake and reasonably alert state of consciousness.

9. ___ Delta brain waves are the long, slow waves associated with stage 3 and stage 4 NREM sleep.

10. ___ Sleep paralysis is a temporary condition in which a person is unable to move upon awakening in the morning or during the night.

11. ___ Sleep deprivation studies, in which people are not allowed to sleep, demonstrate a biological need for sleep.

Check your answers and review any areas of weakness before going on to the next section.

Dreams and Mental Activity During Sleep

Preview Questions

Consider the following questions as you study this section of the chapter.

- What is the difference between sleep thinking and dreaming?
- How many dream episodes do people typically have each night, and how long do they last?
- What patterns of brain activity are associated with dreaming sleep?
- What is memory consolidation, and how do the different stages of sleep aid memory consolidation?
- What do people dream about, and what are nightmares?
- What is Freud's theory of the meaning of dreams and how does it differ from the activation–synthesis model?
- What conclusions can we draw about the meaning of dreams?

*Read the section "Dreams and Mental Activity During Sleep" and **write** your answers to the following:*

1. Sleep thinking (sleep mentation) refers to

   _____

   whereas a dream is _____

   _____

2. People usually have _____

   _____

   _____

   _____

3. Brain activity during REM sleep is _____

   _____

   _____

4. Memory consolidation refers to _____

   _____

   _____

5. NREM slow-wave sleep contributes to _____

   _____

   whereas REM sleep and NREM stage 2 sleep seem to help _____

   _____

Research has also shown that sleep (before and after learning) plays a role in _____

_____

_____

_____

6. Sleep strengthens memories by _____

   _____

   _____

   _____

   Sleep before learning is _____

7. Most dreams are _____

   _____

   _____

8. The most common patterns and themes of dreams are as follows: _____

   _____

9. Nightmares are _____

   _____

   _____

   _____

   The frequency of nightmares is closely related to _____

   _____

   _____

10. Freud's explanation for dreams suggests that

    _____

    _____

11. The manifest content refers to _____

    _____

    The latent content is the _____

    _____

    Freud believed that _____

    _____

    were phallic symbols, and that _____

    _____

    symbolized the vagina.

12. The activation–synthesis model of dreaming maintains that _____

    _____

13. Current research concludes that dreams reflect

_____

_____

_____

_____
*After you have carefully studied the preceding
section, complete the following exercises.*

Concept Check 3

*Read the following and write the correct term in the
space provided.*

1. Meredith recalls having a dream about dancing
   in a ballet with a very big, strong, muscular
   male dancer when suddenly the music switches
   to loud rock music and the man disappears.
   According to Freud, Meredith's account represents the _____ of the
   dream.

2. Dr. Dormo believes that Meredith's dream could
   be the result of a burst of neural activity that
   spread upward from the brainstem and activated more sophisticated brain areas. This interpretation is most consistent with the
   _____ model of dreaming.

3. While Ricardo is asleep, his mind keeps returning to the material he has been studying all day
   in preparation for an exam the next morning.
   Ricardo is experiencing the most common form
   of mental activity during sleep, called

   _____ .

4. Sometimes when she is asleep, Madeline is
   aware that she is dreaming and can often deliberately guide the course of the dream, including
   backing it up and making it go in a different
   direction. These dreams are called

   _____ .

5. Maxwell claims that he has no recollection of
   any dream when he wakes up in the morning,
   and he is convinced that he never dreams. One
   way to demonstrate to Maxwell that he does
   dream is to wake him up after he has been
   asleep for about _____ minutes,
   when he is clearly in _____ sleep.

6. After a visit to the natural history museum,
   young Jamila had a scary dream about
   dinosaurs, which caused her to wake up in a
   very frightened state. Jamila has experienced
   an unpleasant anxiety dream called a(n)

   _____ .

7. A PET scan of Danya's brain while she is in
   REM sleep is likely to reveal _____
   (increased/decreased) activity in the frontal
   lobes and primary visual cortex and

   _____(increased/decreased) activi-

   ty in areas of the limbic system and in associa-

   tion areas involved with generating visual

   images.

Review of Terms, Concepts, and Names 3

*Use the terms in this list to complete the Matching
Test, then to help you answer the True/False items
correctly.*

sleep thinking (sleep mentation)	manifest content
dream	latent content
memory consolidation	phallic symbols
episodic memories	J. Allan Hobson
procedural memories	and Robert W.
spatial memories	McCarley
nightmare	activation–synthesis
Sigmund Freud	model of dreaming

Matching Exercise

*Match the appropriate term/name with its definition
or description:*

1. _____ American psychiatrists and
   neuroscientists who have extensively
   researched the brain controls and neuropsycho-
   logical events involved in sleep and dreaming;
   proposed the activation–synthesis model of
   dreaming.

2. _____ Austrian physician and
   founder of psychoanalysis, who proposed that
   dream images are disguised and symbolic
   expressions of unconscious wishes and urges.

3. _____ Vague, bland, thought-like
   ruminations about real-life events that usually
   occur during NREM slow-wave sleep.

4. _____ The gradual process of converting new memories, through the simple passage of time, into long-term, relatively permanent form.

5. _____ A vivid and disturbing dream that typically involves fear, anxiety, or terror, and that often awakens the sleeper.

6. _____ Dream images of sticks, swords, brooms, and other elongated objects that Freud believed represented the penis.

7. _____ Memories of personally experienced events that tend to be consolidated during NREM slow-wave sleep.

True/False Test

Indicate whether each statement is true or false by placing T or F in the space next to each item

1. ___ REM sleep and NREM stage 2 sleep contribute to the consolidation of procedural memories, which are memories involved in learning a new skill or task until it can be preformed automatically.

2. ___ In Freud's psychoanalytic theory, the latent content of a dream refers to the elements that are consciously experienced and remembered by the dreamer.

3. ___ A dream is an unfolding sequence of perceptions, thoughts, and emotions during sleep that is experienced as a series of real-life events.

4. ___ The activation–synthesis model of dreaming states that dreaming is our subjective awareness of the brain's internally generated signals during sleep, which the activated brain synthesizes and imposes meaning on.

5. ___ In Freud's psychoanalytic theory, the manifest content of a dream refers to the unconscious wishes, thoughts, and urges that are concealed in the latent content of a dream.

6. ___ *Spatial memories* are memories that involve the location of places or objects, including the directions to them and the distance between them.

Check your answers and review any areas of weakness before going on to the next section.

Sleep Disorders: Troubled Sleep

Preview Questions

Consider the following questions as you study this section of the chapter.

- What are sleep disorders and what is the difference between dyssomnias and parasomnias?

- How is insomnia defined, and what are transient insomnia and chronic insomnia?

- What are the characteristics of obstructive sleep apnea (OSA), narcolepsy, and cataplexy?

- What are sleep terrors, and how do they differ from nightmares?

- How are some of the other important parasomnias (sleepsex, sleepwalking, sleep-related eating disorder, and REM sleep behavior disorder) defined?

*Read the section "Sleep Disorders: Troubled Sleep" and **write** your answers to the following:*

1. Sleep disorders involve _____
_____

2. Dyssomnias are _____
_____
_____

They include _____
_____
_____

Parasomnias are _____
_____
_____

They include _____
_____
_____
_____

3. Insomnia is characterized by _____
_____
_____

Transient insomnia lasts _____
_____

Symptoms of chronic insomnia occur _____
_____
_____

4. In obstructive sleep apnea (OSA) _____
_____
_____
_____

5. Narcolepsy is characterized by _____
_____
_____
_____

Cataplexy is the _____

_____

_____

6. A parasomnia called sleep terrors typically

occurs _____

_____

_____

They involve _____

_____

They differ from nightmares _____

_____

7. Sleepsex is a parasomnia that involves _____

_____

_____

_____

8. Sleepwalking or somnambulism is character-

ized by _____

_____

_____

9. Sleep-related eating disorder (SRED) involves

_____

_____

10. REM sleep behavior disorder involves _____

_____

_____

_____

**After you have carefully studied the preceding
section, complete the following exercises.**

Concept Check 4

*Read the following and write the correct term in the
space provided.*

1. Bjorn, who has been under a lot of stress ever
   since he started college, is having trouble sleeping. He repeatedly complains about the quality
   and duration of his sleep, and worrying about
   not sleeping well often keeps him awake at
   night. Bjorn is most likely to be diagnosed as
   suffering from _____ .

2. Researchers who study insomnia, obstructive
   sleep apnea, and narcolepsy are interested in
   disorders involving disruptions in the amount,

quality, or timing of sleep, a broad category of
sleep disorders called _____ .

3. Salim is enjoying a night out with several university friends at Yuk Yuks Comedy Club.
   While laughing heartily at a very funny act, he
   suddenly goes limp and falls asleep for a few
   minutes. It is likely that Salim is suffering from
   _____ and is experiencing

   _____ .

4. Ivana sometimes sleepwalks to the kitchen and
   compulsively eats mainly cake and cookies; typically, she has no memory of the nocturnal
   events when she awakens in the morning.
   Ivana is suffering from a parasomnia called

   _____ .

5. After being asleep for about 2 hours, 8-year-old
   Soo Mee suddenly sits up in bed screaming
   incoherently. Her mother has trouble waking
   her and calming her down. Soo Mee is experiencing a _____ and is probably in
   stage _____ or _____
   of NREM sleep.

6. When Mr. Granger was diagnosed with severe
   obstructive sleep apnea (OSA), he was treated
   with the aid of a machine and a special mask
   that gently blows air into his throat, stopping
   the airway from becoming too narrow or
   blocked, while he sleeps. Mr. Granger's treatment is called _____ .

7. Young Dominic suffers from sleep terrors, and
   sometimes has episodes of, sleepwalking. He is
   likely to be diagnosed with a general category
   of sleep disorders called _____ .

8. Both Percy and Patty have narcolepsy and both
   experience sleep paralysis accompanied by vivid
   and frightening hallucinations. Percy's hallucinations occur during sleep onset, and so they
   are called _____ hallucinations.
   Patty's hallucinations occur as she is waking
   up, and so they are called _____
   hallucinations.

Review of Terms and Concepts 4

Use the terms in this list to complete the Matching Test, then to help you answer the True/False items correctly.

sleep disorders
dyssomnias
parasomnias
insomnia
transient insomnia
chronic insomnia
obstructive sleep apnea
(OSA)
continuous positive air-
way pressure (CPAP)
narcolepsy
sleep attacks
(microsleeps)
cataplexy
hypnagogic
hallucina-tions
(related to narcolepsy)

hypnopompic
hallucinations (related
to narcolepsy)
hypocretins (orexins)
modafinil (Provigil) and
sodium oxybate
(Xyrem)
sleep terrors (night
terrors)
sleepsex (sexsomnia)
sleepwalking
(somnambulism)
sleep-related eating
disorder (SRED)
REM sleep behavior
disorder (RBD)

Matching Exercise

Match the appropriate term/name with its definition or description:

1. _____ Condition in which people repeatedly complain about the quality or duration of their sleep, have difficulty going to sleep or staying asleep, or wake up before it is time to get up.

2. _____ Sleep disorder in which the sleeper's airway becomes narrowed or blocked, causing shallow breathing or repeated pauses in breathing.

3. _____ Sleep disorder caused by a failure of the brain mechanisms that normally suppress voluntary actions during sleep, in which the sleeper verbally and physically responds to the dream story.

4. _____ A parasomnia that involves abnormal sexual behaviors and experiences during sleep.

5. _____ A therapy used to treat obstructive sleep apnea (OSA) that involves a special mask and a machine that gently blows air into the sleeper's throat, stopping the airway from becoming too narrow or blocked.

6. _____ A sudden loss of voluntary muscle strength and control that is usually triggered by an intense emotion and often occurs during episodes of narcolepsy.

7. _____ A sleep disorder characterized by excessive daytime sleepiness and brief, uncontrollable episodes of sleep.

8. _____ Consistent abnormal sleep patterns that cause subjective distress and interfere with a person's daytime functioning.

9. _____ Broad category of sleep disorders involving disruptions in the amount, quality, or timing of sleep that includes insomnia, obstructive sleep apnea, and narcolepsy.

10. _____ Parasomnia in which the sleeper will sleepwalk and eat compulsively.

True/False Test

Indicate whether each statement is true or false by placing T or F in the space next to each item

1. ___ Hypocretins (orexins) are a special class of neurotransmitter produced during daytime to maintain a steady state of wakefulness.

2. ___ People who suffer from narcolepsy experience overwhelming bouts of excessive sleepiness and brief, uncontrollable episodes of sleep called *microsleeps* or *sleep attacks*.

3. ___ Sleepwalking (somnambulism) is a sleep disturbance characterized by an episode of walking or performing other actions during stage 3 or stage 4 NREM sleep.

4. ___ Approximately 1 out of 10 adults experience *transient insomnia* with symptoms that occur at least three nights each week and persist for a month or longer.

5. ___ Sleep terrors (night terrors) typically occur during stage 3 or 4 NREM sleep and are characterized by increased physiological arousal, intense fear and panic, frightening hallucinations, and no recall of the episode the next morning.

6. ___ Modafinil (Provigil) and sodium oxybate (Xyrem) are drugs used in the treatment of narcolepsy that reduce daytime sleepiness.

7. ___ About 1 out of 3 people occasionally experience *chronic insomnia*, which can last from one or two nights to a couple of weeks.

8. ___ People with narcolepsy can experience nighttime sleep disruptions, such as sleep paralysis and hallucinations, when these hallucinations occur as a person is waking up, they are called *hypnopompic hallucinations*.

9. ___ Parasomnias are sleep disorders involving undesirable physical arousal, behaviors, or events during sleep or sleep transitions, and include sleep terrors, sleepsex, sleepwalking, sleep-related eating disorder, and REM sleep behavior disorder.

10. ___ People with narcolepsy can experience nighttime sleep disruptions, such as sleep paralysis and hallucinations; when these hallucinations occur during sleep onset, they are called *hypnagogic hallucinations*.

Check your answers and review any areas of weakness before going on to the next section.

Hypnosis

Preview Questions

Consider the following questions as you study this section of the chapter.

- What is hypnosis, and what are the characteristics of the hypnotic state?
- What are the main characteristics of people who are susceptible to hypnosis?
- What are some effects of hypnosis?
- How has hypnosis been explained?
- What are the limits of hypnosis?

Read the section "Hypnosis" and **write** *your answers to the following:*

1. Hypnosis is a _____
   _____
   _____

2. Hypnosis is characterized by _____
   _____

   During hypnosis, the person _____
   _____

3. The best candidates for hypnosis are _____
   _____
   _____
   _____

4. The effects of hypnosis include _____
   _____
   _____
   _____
   _____

5. Hilgard's neodissociation theory of hypnosis suggests that _____
   _____
   _____
   _____
   _____

6. The limits of hypnosis are that _____
   _____
   _____
   _____

Meditation

Preview Questions

Consider the following questions as you study this section of the chapter.

- What is meditation, and what is it intended to accomplish?
- What are the two general categories of meditation?
- What are the effects of meditation?

Read the section "Meditation" and **write** *your answers to the following:*

1. Meditation refers to _____
   _____
   _____

2. The two general types of meditation differ in that _____
   _____
   _____
   _____
   _____

3. The effects of meditation include _____
   _____
   _____
   _____

Concept Check 5

Read the following and write the correct term in the space provided.

1. Janna quickly becomes deeply absorbed while reading novels or watching movies. It is very likely that Janna is among the 15 percent of adults who are _____ to hypnosis.

2. While under hypnosis, Karl describes a frightening experience of being lost at the fairgrounds when he was 6 years old. When his therapist makes the suggestion that Karl will soon forget this traumatic event, he is attempting to induce _____ .

3. During every final exam period, Declan gets uptight and anxious. At the suggestion of a friend, he has tried using a meditation technique in which he focuses his awareness and attention by repeating a simple phrase over and over to himself. Declan is using a _____ technique of meditation.

4. A researcher suggests to a hypnotized subject that the letter D does not exist. Afterward, the subject is asked to recite the alphabet; when she does, she skips the letter D. This example illustrates the use of

   _____ .

5. An eyewitness to a robbery (who couldn't remember much of the incident) was hypnotized. When the hypnotherapist suggested that there had been three white men and one black woman involved in the robbery, the subject agreed and described them in some detail. All the other five witnesses reported that only one white male robber was involved. The hypnotherapist has created a

   _____ .

6. Lynda has an irrational fear and dislike of cats but has no conscious memory of when or how her phobia developed. In an attempt to enhance her memory, Lynda's therapist hypnotizes her.

If the therapist's hypnotic suggestions actually work, this would demonstrate _____ .

7. Neuroscientists used PET scanners to investigate brain activity while hypnotized subjects performed three cognitive tasks as they viewed rectangular images: They were asked to see the images as they were, to mentally "drain" color from the images, and to mentally "add" color to the gray images. If the researchers' results are consistent with previous research, they are likely to conclude that hypnosis involves a distinct _____ and is not simply _____ , as the social-cognitive view of hypnosis proposes.

Review of Terms, Concepts, and Names 5

Use the terms in this list to complete the Matching Test, then to help you answer the True/False items correctly.

hypnosis
posthypnotic suggestion
posthypnotic amnesia
hypermnesia
pseudomemories
Ernest R. Hilgard
dissociation
neodissociation theory of hypnosis

hidden observer
meditation
concentration techniques
opening-up techniques
transcendental meditation (TM)

Matching Exercise

Match the appropriate term/name with its definition or description.

1. _____ Theory proposed by Ernest Hilgard that explains hypnotic effects as being due to the splitting of consciousness into two simultaneous streams of mental activity, only one of which is available to the consciousness of the hypnotized subject.

2. _____ Meditative technique that has been widely used in research in which practitioners sit quietly with eyes closed, mentally repeat the mantra they have been given, and practice a strategy for getting rid of distracting thoughts.

3. _____ A cooperative social interaction in which the hypnotized person responds to the hypnotist's suggestions with changes in perception, memory, thoughts, and behavior.

4. _____ The splitting of consciousness into two or more simultaneous streams of mental activity.

5. _____ Suggestion made during hypnosis that the person carry out a specific instruction following the hypnotic session.

6. _____ Hypnotic suggestion that supposedly enhances the person's memory for past events.

7. _____ Hilgard's term for the dissociated stream of mental activity that continues during hypnosis.

True/False Test

Indicate whether each statement is true or false by placing T or F in the space next to each item.

1. ___ Ernest Hilgard is the American psychologist who studied hypnosis extensively and advanced the neodissociation theory of hypnosis.

2. ___ The opening-up meditative technique involves a present-centered awareness of the passing moment without mental judgment, it does not involve concentrating on a mantra, visual image, or activity.

3. ___ The inability to recall specific information because of a posthypnotic suggestion is called posthypnotic amnesia.

4. ___ Pseudomemories are false memories (even though the person may be very confident that the memories are real) that result when suggestions are made during hypnosis that create distortions and inaccuracies in recall.

5. ___ Concentration meditative techniques involve focusing awareness on a visual image or your breathing, or mentally repeating a sound called a mantra.

6. ___ Meditation is any of a number of sustained concentration techniques that focus attention and heighten awareness.

Check your answers and review any areas of weakness before going on to the next section.

Psychoactive Drugs

Preview Questions

Consider the following questions as you study this section of the chapter.

- What are psychoactive drugs, and what properties do they have in common?

- What factors influence the effects of a drug, and what factors influence drug-taking behavior?

- How do depressants work, and what effects do alcohol, barbiturates, inhalants, and tranquilizers have?

- What are opiates, and what effects do they have?

- How do stimulants affect the brain and psychological functioning?

- How do the most common psychedelic drugs influence perception, mood, and thinking?

- What are designer "club" drugs, and what effects do they have?

*Read the section "Psychoactive Drugs" and **write** your answers to the following:*

1. Psychoactive drugs are _____

_____

They include _____

_____

2. Addiction is a broad term that refers to

_____

_____

More specific terms for addiction-related conditions are _____

_____

3. The effects of a drug may be influenced

_____

_____

_____

4. Drug abuse refers to _____

_____

_____

Drug-taking behavior is influenced by _____

_____

5. Depressants have several effects: _____

_____

_____

Examples of depressants include _____
_____

6. Alcohol depresses _____
_____

and impairs _____
_____
_____
_____

7. Inhalants are _____
_____
_____

They include _____
_____

8. Barbiturates are depressant drugs that _____
_____

9. Tranquilizers are depressants that _____
_____
_____

10. The opiates are a group of addictive drugs that
_____
_____

Examples of opiates include _____
_____

11. Stimulant drugs _____
_____

Examples include _____
_____

12. The psychedelic drugs create _____
_____
_____

Examples of psychedelic drugs include _____
_____

LSD and psilocybin mimic _____
_____
_____

13. Marijuana and its active ingredient, THC,

produce _____
_____
_____

THC has been shown to be useful in _____
_____
_____

14. Designer "club" drugs are _____
_____

Examples (and their effects) include _____
_____
_____
_____
_____
_____

After you have carefully studied the preceding section, complete the following exercises.

Concept Check 6

Read the following and write the correct term in the space provided.

1. Sian regularly drinks five or six cups of strong coffee a day. If she is like most people, she would probably be surprised to find out that caffeine is a _____ drug and is _____ addictive.

2. Zachary has been using a mood-altering, euphoria-enhancing psychoactive drug; with continued use, he needs to take larger and larger doses in order to experience its original effects. Zachary is developing

   _____ .

3. At a party where he has had too much to drink, the normally shy Darryl keeps people entertained with his silly antics. Darryl probably behaves in this unusual way because alcohol lessens inhibitions by depressing the brain centers responsible for _____ and

   _____ .

4. If he continues drinking at the party, Darryl will probably lose his coordination and balance; the next day, he might _____ (remember/not remember) very clearly the events of the evening before.

5. While undergoing chemotherapy for cancer, Brendan is given marijuana to help prevent nausea and vomiting. Most likely, Brendan _____ (will/will not) develop drug tolerance and physical dependence.

6. Dora has been suffering from severe anxiety, so her doctor prescribes a depressant drug called Valium, which is a commonly prescribed

   _____ .

7. Shortly after "snorting" an illegal psychoactive drug, Samuel experiences intense euphoria, mental alertness, and self-confidence that lasts for several minutes. It is most likely that Samuel has inhaled the stimulant drug

   _____ .

8. After taking a designer drug at a party, Nadine experienced a combination of stimulant and mild psychedelic effects. It is most likely that Nadine has taken a club drug called

   _____ , or _____ .

9. After an accident, Trent was given medication to reduce his perception of pain. It is probable that he has been prescribed Oxycontin, Percodan, or Demerol, drugs that belong to the category of psychoactive drugs called

   _____ , or _____ .

Graphic Organizer 2

Read the following examples, identify the drug involved, and indicate the type of drug it is.

Example	Drug Name	Drug Class
1. During a party Jordy becomes less and less inhibited as the night wears on, and by the time the party is nearly over, he is very uncoordinated and unbalanced and has trouble walking.		
2. After taking her prescription drug for a number of weeks, Janet no longer feels the intense anxiety she used to suffer.		
3. Mrs. Smothers, who suffers from glaucoma, and Mr. Hartley, who has asthma, have both been given an ordinarily illegal drug at the university hospital.		
4. Harold has used a powerful synthetic drug for a number of years to create sensory and perceptual distortions and to alter his mood, but now he is experiencing flashbacks, depression, and occasional psychotic reactions.		
5. Henrietta was a very heavy coffee drinker until she quit cold turkey. She is now experiencing headaches, irritability, drowsiness, and fatigue.		
6. Following surgery, Gregory was given a common prescription drug under medical supervision in order to alleviate his pain.		
7. Just before his exam, Juan smokes a couple of cigarettes and finds he is less tired, more mentally alert, and yet fairly relaxed.		

Review of Terms and Concepts 6

Use the terms in this list to complete the Matching Test, then to help you answer the True/False items correctly.

psychoactive drug
addiction
physical dependence
drug tolerance
withdrawal symptoms
drug rebound effect
drug abuse
depressants
additive
binge drinking
delirium tremens (DTs)
inhalants
barbiturates
tranquilizers
opiates (narcotics)
opium
morphine
codeine

stimulants
caffeine
nicotine
amphetamines
methamphetamine
 (meth)
cocaine
stimulant-induced
 psychosis (amphetamine psychosis or
 cocaine psychosis)
psychedelic drugs
mescaline
psilocybin
LSD (lysergic acid
 diethylamide)
marijuana

THC
 (tetrahydrocannabinol)
hashish
anandamide
designer "club" drugs
MDMA (ecstasy)

dissociative anesthetics
 (PCP and ketamine)
stimulus control therapy
relaxation training
progressive relaxation
autogenic training

Matching Exercise

Match the appropriate term with its definition or description.

1. _____ The active ingredient of marijuana and other preparations derived from the hemp plant.

2. _____ Category of psychoactive drugs that inhibit brain activity.

3. _____ Stimulant drug found in tobacco products.

4. _____ Recurrent drug use that results in disruptions in academic, social, or occupational functioning or in legal or psychological problems.

5. _____ Drug that alters normal consciousness, perception, mood, and behavior.

6. _____ Schizophrenia-like symptoms that can occur as the result of prolonged amphetamine or cocaine use.

7. _____ Psychedelic drug derived from the peyote cactus.

8. _____ Condition in which increasing amounts of a physically addictive drug are needed to produce the original, desired effect.

9. _____ Potent form of marijuana made from the resin of the hemp plant.

10. _____ Unpleasant physical reactions, combined with intense drug cravings, that occur when a person abstains from a drug on which he or she is physically dependent.

11. _____ Stimulant drug derived from the coca tree.

12. _____ Class of stimulant drugs that arouse the central nervous system and suppress appetite.

13. _____ The collective term for withdrawal symptoms associated with high levels of alcohol dependence; may involve confusion, hallucinations, severe tremors, or seizures.

14. _____ A relaxation technique that involves systematically tensing, then relaxing, a progressive sequence of muscle groups.

15. _____ A natural opiate that can be derived from either opium or morphine.

16. _____ Synthetic "club" drug that combines stimulant and mild psychedelic effects.

17. _____ Naturally occurring brain chemical, structurally similar to THC, involved in pain sensations, mood, and memory.

18. _____ Chemical substances that produce an alteration in consciousness and include paint solvents, model airplane glue, spray paint and paint thinner, gasoline, nitrous oxide, and aerosol sprays.

19. _____ Treatment for insomnia involving specific guidelines to create a strict association between the bedroom and rapid sleep onset.

20. _____ A relaxation technique that involves breathing control, focused attention on physical sensations, and mental imagery.

True/False Test

Indicate whether each statement is true or false by placing T or F in the space next to each item.

1. ___ Marijuana is a psychoactive drug derived from the hemp plant.

2. ___ Opiates are a category of depressant drugs that reduce anxiety and produce sleepiness.

3. ___ The occurrence of withdrawal symptoms that are the opposite of a physically addictive drug's action is referred to as the drug rebound effect.

4. ___ Caffeine is the stimulant drug found in coffee, tea, cola drinks, chocolate, and many over-the-counter medications.

5. ___ Opium is a natural opiate derived from the opium poppy.

6. ___ Binge drinking is defined as five or more drinks in a row for men, or four or more drinks in a row for women.

7. ___ Psilocybin is a psychedelic drug derived from the psilocybe mushroom, which is sometimes called "magic mushroom."

8. ___ LSD is a synthetic psychedelic drug.

9. ___ Morphine is the active ingredient of the natural opiate called opium.

10. ___ Tranquilizers such as Valium and Librium are depressants that are prescribed to relieve anxiety.

11. ___ Psychedelic drugs are a category of psychoactive drugs that increase brain activity, as reflected in aroused behavior and increased mental alertness.

12. ___ Physical dependence is a condition in which a person who has physically adapted to a drug must take the drug regularly in order to avoid withdrawal symptoms.

13. ___ Barbiturates are a category of psychoactive drugs that have strong pain-relieving properties and are chemically similar to morphine.

14. ___ Stimulants are a category of psychoactive drugs that create profound perceptual distortions, alter mood, and affect thinking.

15. ___ Designer "club" drugs are drugs that are synthesized in a laboratory rather than being derived from naturally occurring compounds.

16. ___ Dissociative anesthetics are a class of drugs that reduce sensitivity to pain and produce feelings of detachment and dissociation.

17. ___ Methamphetamine is an illegal, highly addictive drug that provides an intense high that is longer-lasting than one from cocaine; it also causes brain damage and tissue loss.

18. ___ Addiction is a condition in which a person feels psychologically and physically compelled to take a specific drug.

19. ___ Relaxation training refers to any number of techniques designed to diminish muscle tension, reduce physical arousal, and decrease intrusive thoughts.

20. ___ When depressants are combined, their sedative effects are *additive,* meaning that they are increased.

Check your answers and review any areas of weakness before going on to the next section.

Something to Think About

1. We've all heard the complaint, "There's so much to do, and so little time!" When people are busy and feel pressured, they are often also sleep-deprived, making them less efficient or productive than well-rested people. More important, they are more likely to make potentially dangerous mistakes. Those most at risk are shift workers or people who suffer jet lag symptoms for other reasons.

   Imagine you are a consultant and have been asked to prepare a report for an organization concerned with these problems among its employees. Based on what you have learned about the sleep–wake cycle, circadian rhythms, biological and environmental clocks, and so on, what would you recommend in your report?

2. Almost everybody is fascinated by dreams and what they mean. Some people believe that dreams can foretell the future or are important in other mysterious ways. Suppose a friend tells you that she has dreamed that she could not understand a single question on a very important math exam. She just stared at the exam until the professor announced the exam was over and removed the paper from in front of her. At this point, she awoke in a very anxious state. Now she is worried that when she takes the real exam next week, her dream will come true. What would you say to her about dreams and their meaning, theories of dreams, and such?

Check your answers and review any areas of weakness before doing the progress tests.

Progress Test 1

Review the complete chapter (including all boxed inserts), review all your study notes, and then test yourself on the following progress test. Check your answers. If you make a mistake, review your notes, check the appropriate section in the study guide, and if necessary, go back and read the relevant part of the chapter in your textbook.

1. Nightmares are to _____ as sleep terrors are to _____ .
   (a) sleep spindles; beta waves
   (b) alpha waves; beta waves
   (c) REM sleep; slow-wave NREM sleep
   (d) slow-wave NREM sleep; REM sleep

2. Bernita witnessed a robbery, but her recall of the event was vague. Police investigators used hypnosis in an attempt to enhance her memory. The hypnotic effect that the investigators hope for is called _____ , which research shows is _____ to be successful.
   (a) hypermnesia; very likely
   (b) posthypnotic suggestion; not very likely
   (c) hypermnesia; not very likely
   (d) posthypnotic suggestion; very likely

3. After ingesting a small dose of a psychoactive drug, Graham experiences vivid visual hallucinations and other perceptual distortions; he feels as though he is floating above his body. Graham is most likely experiencing the effects of
   (a) cocaine.   (d) LSD.
   (b) barbiturates.   (e) cappuccino.
   (c) tranquilizers.

4. Curtis has been diagnosed with a sleep disorder after his wife complained about his sporadic abnormal sexual behaviors during the night. These episodes included behaviors such as masturbation, sleepsex-talking, groping or fondling his wife's genitals, and sometimes very rough sexual intercourse. Curtis has no memory of these incidents. He has a parasomnia called
   (a) cataplexy.
   (b) sexsomnia (sleepsex).
   (c) transient insomnia.
   (d) somnambulism.

5. After flying from San Diego to New York, Jasmine experiences a restless, sleepless night; the next day, she is irritable and cannot concentrate on her work. Jasmine's problems are likely due to

    (a) disruption in her circadian rhythms.
    (b) high blood levels of melatonin.
    (c) jet lag.
    (d) all of these factors.

6. Justine believes that dreaming is simply our subjective awareness of the brain's internally generated signals during sleep, which start with automatic activation of brainstem circuits that then arouse more sophisticated brain areas. Justine's views are most consistent with which theory of dreams?

    (a) adaptive theory
    (b) restorative theory
    (c) activation–synthesis theory
    (d) wish-fulfillment theory

7. To find out what goes on in people's brains during a typical night's sleep, researchers are most likely to

    (a) ask people to try to remember as much as possible when they awake in the morning.
    (b) closely watch the actions of subjects sleeping in the sleep research lab.
    (c) wake people up every 15 minutes and ask them what is going on in their minds.
    (d) use an electroencephalograph to measure their brain-wave activity throughout the night.

8. Just as you are about to fall asleep, you have the sudden feeling of falling and your body gives an involuntary spasm. You have experienced

    (a) a sleep spindle.
    (b) a myoclonic jerk.
    (c) sexsomnia.
    (d) cataplexy.

9. Harry has been asleep for about an hour or so, and his heart begins to beat faster, his breathing becomes irregular, his voluntary muscle activity is suppressed, and his closed eyes move rapidly back and forth. It is most probable that Harry is in _____ and is therefore experiencing _____ .

    (a) REM sleep; a myoclonic jerk
    (b) NREM; sleep spindles
    (c) REM; paradoxical sleep
    (d) NREM; quiet sleep

10. Eight-year-old Billy gets out of bed at 1 A.M. and starts to sleepwalk. He is most likely

    (a) in slow-wave stage 3 or 4 NREM sleep.
    (b) suffering from narcolepsy.
    (c) in REM sleep.
    (d) experiencing elevated brain levels of hypocretins.

11. After Zufina has been asleep for a period of time in the sleep lab, the EEG monitor indicates the presence of theta waves, sleep spindles, and K complexes. Zufina is in _____ sleep.

    (a) stage 3 NREM   (c) stage 2 NREM
    (b) REM   (d) stage 4 NREM

12. Mr. Jensen repeatedly complains about the quality and duration of his sleep; he claims that he can't fall asleep and stay asleep and usually wakes up before it is time to get up. Mr. Jensen apparently suffers from

    (a) obstructive sleep apnea (OSA).
    (b) narcolepsy.
    (c) cataplexy.
    (d) insomnia.

13. While participating in a research project to create free-running conditions, Teddy was confined to an isolation unit for a number of weeks. During this experiment, it is very probable that

    (a) Teddy's internal body clock will drift to its natural or intrinsic rhythm, which is about 24.2 hours long.
    (b) Teddy's SCN will keep his circadian cycles synchronized on a 24-hour schedule.
    (c) Teddy's internal body clock will drift to its natural or intrinsic rhythm, which is about 25.2 hours long.
    (d) Teddy will suffer major depression, irritability, memory loss, and both mental and physical fatigue because his SCN is no longer being entrained by sunlight.

14. According to the Application (Can't Sleep? Read This!), which of the following is NOT one of the recommendations for improving the quality of sleep and minimizing sleep problems?

    (a) continuous positive airway pressure (CPAP)
    (b) stimulus control therapy
    (c) progressive relaxation training
    (d) autogenic training

15. According to Critical Thinking (Is Hypnosis a Special State of Consciousness?), _____ theory suggests that hypnotic subjects are responding to social demands by acting the way they think good hypnotic subjects should act and by conforming to expectations and situational cues.

    (a) neodissociation
    (b) social-cognitive
    (c) imaginative suggestibility
    (d) adaptive

Progress Test 2

After you have checked your understanding of the material in Progress Test 1 and have done a complete chapter review with special focus on any areas of weakness, you are now ready to assess your knowledge on Progress Test 2. Check your answers. If you make a mistake, review your notes, the relevant section of the study guide, and, if necessary, the appropriate part of your textbook.

1. Dr. Benjamin hypnotizes a client and suggests that she will no longer feel a craving for chocolates. Dr. Benjamin is making use of

    (a) posthypnotic suggestion.
    (b) hypermnesia.
    (c) posthypnotic amnesia.
    (d) meditation.

2. Amber sits in a relaxed position, closes her eyes, and begins to recite her mantra. Amber is practicing

    (a) hypnosis.   (d) dissociation.
    (b) meditation.   (e) laziness.
    (c) stimulus control therapy.

3. Researchers who have found evidence that subjects appear to have a "hidden observer" are likely to suggest that hypnosis involves

    (a) dissociation.
    (b) social factors.
    (c) stages 3 and 4 NREM sleep.
    (d) experimenter bias.

4. John drinks five or six cups of coffee every day; if he doesn't, he feels irritable, drowsy, and fatigued. John is _____ a(n) _____ drug.

    (a) addicted to; psychedelic
    (b) physically dependent on; opiate
    (c) addicted to; depressant
    (d) physically dependent on; stimulant

5. Richard has just finished his fourth night shift and is driving home from work in the bright morning light. The most likely effect of this exposure is that

    (a) the bright light will reset his body clock to a day schedule.
    (b) he will become very drowsy and sleepy.
    (c) he will experience an increase in the production of melatonin.
    (d) all of these events will occur.

6. Nancy's husband took her to the doctor because she frequently sleepwalks to the kitchen and compulsively eats food from the cupboard and fridge but has no memory of doing so in the morning. The doctor is likely to diagnose her with a _____ called _____ .

    (a) parasomnia; sexsomnia
    (b) dyssomnia; somnambulism
    (c) parasomnia; sleep-related eating disorder (SRED)
    (d) dyssomnia; cataplexy

7. Phelan has just had a very painful operation. His doctors are most likely to prescribe _____ for pain relief.

    (a) a tranquilizer   (c) morphine
    (b) marijuana   (d) alcohol

8. Mr. Godfrey has cancer and was given marijuana to counter the nausea and vomiting following chemotherapy. The active ingredient that makes this a useful drug in such cases is

    (a) psilocybin.   (c) LSD.
    (b) cannabis.   (d) THC.

9. Sleep researchers deprive subjects of REM sleep for a number of nights but allow them an otherwise normal sleep; the subjects are likely to experience _____ when next allowed to sleep uninterrupted.

    (a) narcolepsy   (c) sleep terrors
    (b) REM rebound   (d) NREM rebound

10. Harold dreams that he is on a train traveling through mountains in what he thinks is Switzerland. He can see the train very clearly going in and out of tunnels over and over again. Harold's therapist suggests that the dream is not about travel in a foreign country but about Harold's concern with his sexual performance. The therapist adheres to _____ theory of dreams and is attempting to reveal the _____ of Harold's dream.
    (a) the evolutionary; adaptive aspects
    (b) Freud's wish-fulfillment; manifest content
    (c) Freud's wish-fulfillment; latent content
    (d) the activation–synthesis; restorative aspects

11. During a very intense game of pool, Gary is attempting a difficult shot that will win him the game. However, he suddenly loses complete muscle control and falls fast asleep on the pool table. Gary probably suffers from _____ and is experiencing _____ .
    (a) obstructive sleep apnea (OSA); a sleep attack
    (b) narcolepsy; cataplexy
    (c) insomnia; somnambulism
    (d) REM sleep behavior disorder; sleep paralysis

12. Nicotine is to alcohol as a _____ drug is to a _____ .
    (a) stimulant; depressant
    (b) psychedelic; stimulant
    (c) depressant; stimulant
    (d) depressant; psychedelic

13. Dr. Tirian's research is concerned with the effects of psychedelic drugs on brain functioning. Which of the following is she most likely to test in her experiments?
    (a) LSD, psilocybin, and mescaline
    (b) amphetamines and cocaine
    (c) alcohol, nicotine, and caffeine
    (d) barbiturates and tranquilizers

14. According to In Focus (What You Really Wanted to Know About Sleep), which of the following is true?
    (a) Research suggests that high levels of a naturally occurring compound in the body called adenosine cause sleepiness.
    (b) It is not dangerous to wake a sleepwalker.

(c) In a relatively common phenomenon called sleep paralysis, the paralysis of REM sleep carries over to the waking state for up to 10 minutes.
(d) All of these statements are true.

15. According to In Focus (What You Really Want to Know About Dreams), which of the following is true?
    (a) People who have been blind all their lives don't dream.
    (b) Up until the widespread use of color TV, most people dreamed in black and white.
    (c) Virtually all mammals experience sleep cycles in which REM sleep alternates with slow-wave NREM sleep, and it is reasonable to conclude that they all dream.
    (d) Dreams can often be used to accurately predict the future.

Progress Test 3

After you have checked your understanding of the material in Progress Tests 1 and 2, and have done a complete chapter review with special focus on any areas of weakness, you are ready to further assess your knowledge with Progress Test 3. Check your answers. If you make a mistake, review your notes, the appropriate parts of the study guide, and if necessary, the relevant sections of your textbook.

1. Mrs. Cadogan complains that her overweight 65-year-old husband snores and snorts throughout the night and appears to be gasping for breath. She notes that this happens most often when he is sleeping on his back. Mr. Cadogan suffers from
    (a) ovstructive sleep apnea.
    (b) sleep terrors.
    (c) sleep-related eating disorder.
    (d) somnambulism.

2. Dr. Gerhardt believes that sleep promotes physiological processes that repair and rejuvenate the body and mind. Dr. Gerhardt's view is consistent with the _____ theory of sleep.
    (a) evolutionary
    (b) activation–synthesis
    (c) wish-fulfillment
    (d) restorative

3. Brianna, who has a very warm, loving relationship with her husband, dreamed that she had an intense, emotional argument with him in which she shouted and screamed and called him horrible names. Her psychoanalyst suggested that Brianna must have some deeply repressed anger and frustration toward her father that is expressed symbolically in the dream about her husband. Brianna's account of the dream represents the _____ , and her therapist's account represents the _____ .
   (a) latent content; manifest content
   (b) activation phase; synthesis phase
   (c) manifest content; latent content
   (d) synthesis phase; activation phase

4. Stage 2 sleep is to _____ as stage 4 is to _____ .
   (a) beta waves; alpha waves
   (b) alpha waves; beta waves
   (c) sleep spindles and K complexes; delta waves
   (d) dreams; nightmares

5. Dr. Hayward uses hypnosis on a patient during a root canal procedure. When he asks her to raise her hand if some part of her can feel pain, she raises her hand. This illustrates
   (a) the hidden observer.
   (b) paradoxical sleep.
   (c) posthypnotic amnesia.
   (d) tolerance.

6. In a class discussion of sleep and dreams, Anouk suggests that different sleep patterns exhibited by various animals, including humans, evolved as a way of preventing a particular species from interacting with the environment when it is most dangerous to do so. Anouk is promoting the
   (a) restorative theory.
   (b) the activation–synthesis model.
   (c) the adaptive theory.
   (d) the neodissociation theory.

7. Due to prolonged and heavy use of cocaine, Andrew suffered schizophrenia-like symptoms, including auditory hallucinations of "voices" and bizarre paranoid ideas. Andrew's symptoms suggest that he has
   (a) stimulant-induced psychosis.
   (b) delirium tremens (DTs).
   (c) hypermnesia.
   (d) a parasomnia.

8. During a rave, Drake was given a substance that reduced his sensitivity to pain and produced feelings of detachment and dissociation. He is most likely to have used a class of club drug called _____ , and, in particular, either _____ or _____ .
   (a) psychedelics; LSD; mescaline
   (b) the dissociative anesthetics; PCP (angel dust); ketamine (Special K)
   (c) depressants; methaqualone; quaalude
   (d) tranquilizers; Valium; Librium

9. After he abruptly stops taking a depressant drug, Ernie suffers from sleep problems, excitability, and restlessness. Ernie is suffering from
   (a) drug rebound effect.
   (b) parasomnia.
   (c) dyssomnia.
   (d) stimulant-induced psychosis.

10. Maya uses the zazen, or the "just sitting" technique of Zen Buddhism, in which she engages in quiet awareness of the "here and now" without any distracting thoughts. Maya is using a type of _____ meditation.
    (a) opening-up
    (b) autogenic
    (c) concentration
    (d) stimulus control

11. According to his wife, 70-year-old Hugo sometimes jumps out of bed during the night and appears to be acting out his dreams. It is very likely that Hugo suffers from a sleep disorder called
    (a) narcolepsy.
    (b) REM sleep behavior disorder.
    (c) obstructive sleep apnea.
    (d) hypnopompic hallucinogenic disorder.

12. Gaetan is a subject in a sleep research lab experiment. A PET scan reveals that, compared to when he is awake or in slow-wave sleep, his brain activity while in REM is likely to show decreased activity in _____ , and increased activity in association areas of _____ .
    (a) the limbic system; the frontal lobes and primary visual cortex
    (b) the left parietal lobe; both frontal lobes
    (c) the frontal lobes and primary visual cortex; the limbic system
    (d) brain areas associated with visual imagery; the temporal lobes

\ 13. Farhana often becomes aware that she is dreaming while she is still asleep. Sometimes she can consciously guide the direction of the dream: even if she wakes up, she can go back to sleep and continue her interrupted dream. This example illustrates

(a) lucid dreaming.

(b) sleep mentation.

(c) cataplexy.

(d) parasomnia.

14. Sleep researchers have developed guidelines to assess the likelihood that violent actions were sleep related and happened while the offender was sleepwalking. Based on those guidelines, which of the following is not one of the key points presented in Scott Falater's murder trial as discussed in Critical Thinking (Sleep-Related Violence: Is Sleep Murder Possible?)?

(a) There is no apparent motivation for the behavior, which is usually abrupt, immediate, impulsive, and senseless.

(b) The sleep-related violence was brought on by one or more precipitating factors, such as situational stress, sleep deprivation, alcohol, medications, or fever.

(c) There is almost always total awareness of the event and immediately upon waking the person has a clear, vivid memory of what happened during the sleepwalking incident.

(d) The victim is usually someone who merely happened to be present and inadvertently provoked the behavior.

15. Jason suffers from a number of work- and school-related sleeping problems. According to the Application, Jason could improve the situation by

(a) monitoring his intake of stimulants, especially those containing caffeine.

(b) establishing a quite bedtime routine and avoiding stimulating mental or physical activity for at least an hour before his bedtime.

(c) creating the conditions for restful sleep; keeping the bedroom quiet, dark, and cool; and turning off his cell phone and computer so that they can't disrupt his sleep.

(d) doing all of these things.

Answers

Introduction: Consciousness: Experiencing the "Private I"

1. Consciousness *is defined as the* personal awareness of mental activities, internal sensations, and the external environment.

2. *William James's idea of "stream of consciousness" refers to the fact that* although consciousness is always changing, it is perceived as unified and unbroken, in much the same way that a stream or river is seen as one thing, yet is constantly changing.

3. *Research on consciousness was abandoned because* introspective self-reports were not objectively verifiable. *Psychologists turned instead to* overt behavior that could be directly observed, measured, and verified.

4. *Psychologists returned to studying consciousness in the late 1950s for two reasons:* first, because it became clear that a complete understanding of behavior would not be possible without considering the role of conscious mental processes in behavior, and second, because psychologists devised more objective ways to study the phenomenon (technological advances in studying brain activity and more objective means of inferring conscious experience from behavior).

Biological and Environmental "Clocks" That Regulate Consciousness

1. *Circadian rhythms are* biological and psychological processes that systematically vary over a roughly 24-hour period.

2. *The suprachiasmatic nucleus (SCN) is a* tiny cluster of neurons in the hypothalamus that governs the timing of circadian rhythms, including the sleep–wake; thus, it is considered the master biological clock. *Its role in sleep–wake cycles and other circadian rhythms is to* detect, through its connections with the visual system, decreases in sunlight and, in turn, to trigger an increase in the production of melatonin, which makes you sleep. Exposure to sunlight suppresses melatonin levels.

3. *Melatonin is a* hormone manufactured by the pineal gland (an endocrine gland in the brain), which produces sleepiness.

4. *Free-running conditions are created by* the absence of environmental time cues like sunlight and clocks. *They have two distinct effects: First,* in the absence of normal light, darkness,

and other time cues, people tend to drift to the natural, or intrinsic, rhythm of the SCN, which is approximately 24.2 hours long; consequently, people go to sleep a little later each night. *Second,* the sleep–wake, body temperature, and melatonin circadian rhythms become desynchronized so that they are no longer coordinated with one another.

5. *People suffer from jet lag symptoms because* time cues are out of sync with their internal biological clocks; these symptoms can be produced by travel across multiple time zones, working night shifts, or working rotating shifts.

6. *Melatonin plays a key role in jet lag symptoms by* causing sleepiness, grogginess, etc., at a time when the external environmental cues suggest that you should be alert and awake (your internal body clock says it is 3:00 A.M., so melatonin levels are high, but the external time is 10:00 A.M. and you need to be awake).

Concept Check 1

1. circadian rhythms; SCN (the body's clock)
2. melatonin
3. circadian rhythms
4. consciousness
5. free-running conditions

Matching Exercise 1

1. consciousness
2. introspection
3. suprachiasmatic nucleus (SCN)
4. jet lag
5. melatonin

True/False Test 1

1. T	3. T	5. T
2. T	4. T	

Sleep

1. *An electroencephalograph is* an instrument that uses electrodes placed on the scalp to measure and record the brain's electrical activity and produces an electroencephalogram (EEG).

2. *By studying EEGs, sleep researchers established that* brain-wave activity systematically changes throughout sleep.

3. *Use of the EEG led to the discovery of* rapid-eye-movement sleep, or REM sleep, and this

marked the beginning of modern sleep research.

4. *Beta brain waves are associated with* being alert and awake and are small, fast brain waves. *Alpha brain waves are associated with* drowsiness and relaxation and are slightly larger and slower than beta waves.

5. *Hypnagogic hallucinations are* vivid sensory phenomena that occur during the onset of sleep.

6. *The four NREM sleep stages are characterized by different brain and body activity:*

   Stage 1 NREM: a mixture of alpha and theta waves, lasts only a few minutes, and is a transitional stage from wakefulness to being asleep.

   Stage 2 NREM: the appearance of sleep spindles (bursts of brain activity that last a second or two), K complexes (single but large high-voltage spikes of brain activity), and mainly theta brain waves although the slower delta waves begin to emerge.

   Stages 3 and 4 NREM: delta brain-wave activity (20 percent in stage 3, and 50 percent in stage 4); in combination, these stages are referred to as slow-wave sleep.

7. *REM sleep is characterized by* increased brain activity (smaller, faster brain waves), activation of visual and motor neurons, dreaming, suppression of voluntary muscle activity, and considerable physiological arousal.

8. *Over the course of the lifespan, the quantity and quality of our sleep* changes considerably; from birth onward, the average amount of time spent sleeping gradually decreases, and the amount of time devoted to slow-wave NREM also gradually decreases.

Do We Need to Sleep?

1. *Sleep deprivation studies and sleep restriction studies demonstrate that* we have a biological need to sleep; after a day or more without sleep we will experience impairments in mood, mental abilities (such as concentration and vigilance), reaction time, the ability to gauge risks, perceptual skills, and complex motor skills. Metabolic and hormonal disruptions also occur, and the immune system's effectiveness is diminished. All these changes become more pronounced as sleep restriction continues night after night. When people are deprived of sleep (either REM or stage 3 and 4 NREM), they will experience rebound effects if allowed to sleep undisturbed.

2. *The phenomena of REM and NREM rebound seem to indicate that* the brain needs to make up for missing components of sleep.

3. *The restorative theory of sleep suggests that* sleep promotes physiological processes that restore and rejuvenate the body and the mind.

4. *The adaptive theory of sleep suggests that* the sleep patterns exhibited by different animals, including humans, are the result of evolutionary adaptation and that different sleep patterns evolved as a way of preventing a particular species from interacting with the environment when it may be dangerous to do so.

Concept Check 2

1. alpha

2. falling; myoclonic jerk

3. sleep; REM; REM rebound

4. is experiencing sleep disturbances that are normal for her age

5. theta; sleep spindles; K complexes

6. adaptive (evolutionary)

7. sleep paralysis

Graphic Organizer 1

1. C   4. B   6. F
2. E   5. D   7. A
3. G

Matching Exercise 2

1. alpha brain waves
2. electroencephalogram (EEG)
3. sleep spindles
4. hypnagogic hallucinations
5. slow-wave sleep
6. myoclonic jerk (sleep starts)
7. K complexes
8. REM rebound
9. electroencephalograph
10. brain waves
11. sleep restriction studies

True/False Test 2

1. T   5. F   9. T
2. F   6. T   10. T
3. T   7. T   11. T
4. F   8. F

Dreams and Mental Activity During Sleep

1. *Sleep thinking (sleep mentation) refers to* vague, bland, thoughtlike ruminations about real-life events that usually occur during NREM slow-wave sleep, *whereas a dream is* an unfolding sequence of perceptions, thoughts, and emotions during sleep (usually REM) that is experienced as a series of real-life events; even if bizarre and illogical, they are accepted because disbelief is suspended when we dream.

2. *People usually have* four or five dreaming episodes each night; the first REM period is the shortest (about 10 minutes) and subsequent REM episodes average about 30 minutes and tend to get longer as the night continues, with early morning dreams the longest (40 minutes or longer) and most likely to be recalled.

3. *Brain activity during REM sleep is* different from waking and NREM sleep. Activity in the primary visual cortex and the frontal lobes is diminished, while activity in association areas of the visual cortex and the limbic centers associated with emotion, motivation, and memory increase.

4. *Memory consolidation refers to* the gradual process of converting a new memory, through the simple passage of time, into a long-term, relatively permanent form.

5. *NREM slow-wave sleep contributes to* forming new episodic memories of personally experienced events, consolidate new procedural memories, which involve learning a new skill or task until it can be performed automatically. *Research has also shown that sleep (before and after learning) plays a role in* the consolidation and performance of new spatial memories (memories of the location of places and objects, directions to them, the distances between them, and so on).

6. *Sleep strengthens memories by* reactivating daytime memories during the 90-minute cycles of sleep that occur throughout the night, and this repeated reactivation of newly encoded memories during sleep helps strengthen neuronal connections that contribute to forming long-term memories; it also helps integrate them into existing networks of memories. *Sleep before learning is* also critical to the formation of new memories; the capacity to learn and form new memories is greatly reduced if you have had too little sleep or are completely sleep deprived.

7. *Most dreams are* fairly coherent, patterned, thoughtful, and by and large, a realistic

simulation of waking life; they are overwhelmingly about everyday settings, people, activities, and events. They involve some unusual and perhaps nonsensical aspects, but only a relatively small amount of bizarreness.

8. *The most common patterns and themes of dreams are as follows:* Women report males and females in equal proportion but men are more likely to report other males as the story characters; negative feelings and events are more common than positive ones; instances of aggression, with the dreamer being the victim, are more common than instances of friendliness; physical aggression in dreams is more common for males than females but females report more emotions; sex or sexual behaviors seldom occur as elements of the dream story; and apprehension or fear is the most frequently reported dream emotion for both sexes, followed by happiness and confusion.

9. *Nightmares are* vivid and disturbing dreams that often awaken the sleeper and typically involve feelings of helplessness or powerlessness in the face of being aggressively attacked or pursued. Some nightmares involve intense feelings of sadness, anger, disgust, or embarrassment. *The frequency of nightmares is closely related to* age: nightmares occurr most often during middle and late childhood (25 percent of 5- to 11-year-olds have at least one per week), then decrease in frequency during adolescence and adulthood (about 5 to 10 percent of adults experience nightmares on a weekly basis). Genetics and gender (females have more nightmares than men) are factors, but nightmares are not indicative of psychological or sleep disorders unless they occur frequently, cause difficulties returning to sleep, or cause daytime distress.

10. *Freud's explanation for dreams suggests that* because the sexual and aggressive instincts that motivate human behavior are so unacceptable to the conscious mind, they are pushed into the unconscious mind, or repressed. He believed that these repressed urges and wishes could surface in dream imagery.

11. *The manifest content refers to* the elements of a dream that are consciously experienced and remembered by the dreamer; *the latent content is the* disguised psychological meanings of the dream that are concealed in the manifest content. *Freud believed that* dream images of sticks, swords, and other elongated objects *were phallic symbols, and that* dream images of cupboards, boxes, and ovens *symbolized the vagina.*

12. *The activation–synthesis model of dreaming maintains that* dreaming is our subjective awareness of the brain's internally generated signals during sleep; brain activity produces dream images (activation); these are combined by the brain into a dream story (synthesis) and meaning is imposed on them.

13. *Current research concludes that dreams reflect* the waking concerns and preoccupations of the dreamer and the active process of trying to make sense of stimuli produced by the brain during sleep; dream interpretation occurs when we are awake, and it may reveal more about the psychological characteristics of the interpreter than about the dream itself.

Concept Check 3

1. manifest content
2. activation–synthesis
3. sleep thinking (sleep mentation)
4. lucid dreams
5. 75; REM
6. nightmare
7. decreased; increased

Matching Exercise 3

1. J. Allan Hobson and Robert W. McCarley
2. Sigmund Freud
3. sleep thinking
4. memory consolidation
5. nightmare
6. phallic symbols
7. episodic memories

True/False Test 3

1. T	4. T
2. F	5. F
3. T	6. T

Sleep Disorders: Troubled Sleep

1. *Sleep disorders involve* consistent abnormal sleep patterns that cause subjective distress and interfere with a person's daytime functioning.

2. *Dyssomnias are* sleep disorders involving disruptions in the amount, quality, or timing of

sleep. *They include* insomnia, obstructive sleep apnea, and narcolepsy. *Parasomnias are* sleep disorders involving undesirable physical arousal, behaviors, or events during sleep or sleep transitions. *They include* sleep terrors, sleepsex, sleepwalking, sleep-related eating disorder, and REM sleep behavior disorder.

3. *Insomnia is characterized by* complaints about the quality or duration of sleep, difficulty going to sleep or staying asleep, or waking before it is time to get up. *Transient insomnia lasts* from one or two nights to a couple of weeks. *Symptoms of chronic insomnia occur* three nights each week and persist for a month or longer.

4. *In obstructive sleep apnea (OSA),* the sleeper's airway becomes narrowed or blocked causing very shallow breathing or repeated pauses in breathing that can happen from 5 to 30 or more times per hour disrupting sleep.

5. *Narcolepsy is characterized by* overwhelming bouts of excessive daytime sleepiness and brief uncontrollable episodes of sleep, which are called microsleeps or sleep attacks. *Cataplexy is the* sudden loss of voluntary muscle strength and control, lasting from several seconds to several minutes; it is usually triggered by a sudden intense emotion, such as laughter, anger, fear, or surprise.

6. *A parasomnia called sleep terrors typically occurs* during stage 3 or 4 NREM sleep and lasts only a few seconds. *They involve* sharply increased physiological arousal, restlessness, sweating, a racing heart, and intense fear accompanied by a panic-stricken scream or cry for help with no recollection of the episode in the morning. *They differ from nightmares* in that nightmares are anxiety dreams that typically occur during REM sleep.

7. *Sleepsex is a parasomnia that involves* abnormal sexual behaviors and experiences during NREM stage 3 and 4 slow-wave sleep, such as masturbation, sleepsex-talking, groping or fondling their bed partner's genitals, or sexual intercourse.

8. *Sleepwalking or somnambulism is characterized by* an episode of walking or performing other actions, which may include elaborate and complicated behavior, and can range from calm or benign to agitated or aggressive behavior; episodes typically occur during NREM stage 3 or 4 slow-wave sleep.

9. *Sleep-related eating disorder (SRED) involves*

episodes of frequent sleepwalking to the kitchen and compulsive eating during stage 3 and 4 NREM slow-wave sleep, with no memory of the episodes upon awakening in the morning.

10. *REM sleep behavior disorder involves* a failure of the brain mechanisms that normally suppress voluntary actions during REM sleep; thus the person verbally and physically responds to the unfolding dream story, which they remember in vivid detail upon awakening.

Concept Check 4

1. insomnia (or chronic insomnia)
2. dyssomnias
3. narcolepsy; cataplexy
4. sleep-related eating disorder (SRED)
5. sleep (night) terrors; 3; 4
6. continuous positive airway pressure (CPAP)
7. parasomnias
8. hypnagogic; hynopompic

Matching Exercise 4

1. insomnia
2. obstructive sleep apnea (OSA)
3. REM sleep behavior disorder (RBD)
4. sleepsex (sexsomnia)
5. continuous positive airway pressure (CPAP)
6. cataplexy
7. narcolepsy
8. sleep disorders
9. dyssomnias
10. sleep-related eating disorder (SRED)

True/False Test 4

1. T	5. T	9. T
2. T	6. T	10. T
3. T	7. F	
4. F	8. T	

Hypnosis

1. *Hypnosis is a* cooperative social interaction in which the hypnotized person responds to the hypnotist's suggestions with changes in perception, memory, thoughts, and behavior.

2. *Hypnosis is characterized by* highly focused attention, increased responsiveness to suggestions, vivid images and fantasies, and a willing-

ness to accept distortions of logic or reality. *During hypnosis, the person* temporarily suspends a sense of initiative and voluntarily accepts and follows the hypnotist's instructions.

3. *The best candidates for hypnosis are* individuals who approach the experience with positive, receptive attitudes and expect it to work and people who easily become absorbed in fantasy and imaginary experience—for example, they become absorbed in reading fiction, watching movies, or listening to music.

4. *The effects of hypnosis include* sensory and perceptual changes (temporary blindness, deafness, or loss of sensation in some body part), hallucinations, and such outside behaviors as carrying out posthypnotic suggestions, posthypnotic amnesia, hypermnesia, and possibly creating false memories or pseudomemories.

5. *Hilgard's neodissociation theory of hypnosis suggests that* hypnotic effects are due to the splitting of consciousness into two simultaneous streams of memory activity, only one of which the hypnotic participant is consciously aware of during hypnosis (the dissociated stream is called the hidden observer).

6. *The limits of hypnosis are that* you cannot be hypnotized against your will, you cannot become physically stronger than you are, you cannot exhibit talents that you don't already possess, and you cannot be made to perform behaviors that are contrary to your morals and values.

Meditation

1. *Meditation refers to* a group of sustained concentration techniques that induce an altered state of focused attention and heightened awareness.

2. *The two general types of meditation differ in that* concentration techniques involve focusing awareness on a visual image, your breathing, a word, or a phrase, and opening-up techniques involve a present-centered awareness of the passing moment, without mental judgment.

3. *The effects of meditation include* a state of lowered physiological arousal, including a decrease in heart rate, lowered blood pressure, and changes in brain waves, as well as enhanced physical and psychological functioning beyond that provided by relaxation alone.

Concept Check 5

1. highly susceptible
2. posthypnotic amnesia
3. concentration
4. posthypnotic suggestion
5. pseudomemory
6. hypermnesia
7. brain state; role-playing

Matching Exercise 5

1. neodissociation theory of hypnosis
2. transcendental meditation (TM)
3. hypnosis
4. dissociation
5. posthypnotic suggestion
6. hypermnesia
7. hidden observer

True/False Test 5

1. T
2. T
3. T
4. T
5. T
6. T

Psychoactive Drugs

1. *Psychoactive drugs are* chemical substances that alter consciousness, perception, mood, and behavior. *They include* depressants, opiates, stimulants, and psychedelic drugs.

2. *Addiction is a broad term that refers to* a condition in which a person feels psychologically and physically compelled to take a specific drug. *More specific terms for addiction-related conditions are* physical dependence, drug tolerance, withdrawal symptoms, and the drug rebound effect.

3. *The effects of a drug may be influenced* not only by biological factors but also by psychological and environmental factors, including personality characteristics, mood, expectations, experience with the drug, and the setting in which the drug is taken.

4. *Drug abuse refers to* recurrent drug use that leads to disruptions in academic, social, or occupational functioning or in legal or psychological problems. *Drug-taking behavior is influenced by* cultural norms.

5. *Depressants have several effects:* they inhibit central nervous system activity; produce drowsiness, sedation, or sleep; relieve anxiety; and lower inhibitions. *Examples of depressants include* alcohol, barbiturates, inhalants, and tranquilizers.

6. *Alcohol depresses* the activity of neurons throughout the brain *and impairs* cognitive abilities, such as concentration, memory, and speech, and physical abilities, such as muscle coordination and balance.

7. *Inhalants are* chemical substances that are inhaled to produce an alteration in consciousness. *They include* paint solvents, model airplane glue, spray paint and paint thinner, gasoline, nitrous oxide, and aerosol sprays.

8. *Barbiturates are depressant drugs that* reduce anxiety and promote sleep by depressing activity in the brain centers that control arousal, wakefulness, and alertness. They also depress the brain's respiratory centers.

9. *Tranquilizers are depressants that* relieve anxiety; while chemically different from barbiturates, they produce similar, although less powerful, effects.

10. *The opiates are a group of addictive drugs that* relieve pain and produce euphoria by mimicking the brain's own natural painkillers called endorphins. *Examples of opiates include* opium, morphine, codeine, heroin, methadone, oxycodone, and the prescription painkillers OxyContin, Vicodin, Percodan, Tylox, Demerol, and Fentanyl.

11. *Stimulant drugs* increase brain activity, arouse behavior, and increase mental alertness. *Examples include* caffeine, nicotine, amphetamines, and cocaine.

12. *The psychedelic drugs create* profound perceptual distortions, alter mood, and affect thinking. *Examples of psychedelic drugs include* mescaline, psilocybin, LSD, and marijuana. LSD and psilocybin mimic the neurotransmitter serotonin (which is involved in regulating moods and sensations) and stimulate serotonin receptor sites in the somatosensory cortex.

13. *Marijuana and its active ingredient, THC, produce* a sense of well-being, mild euphoria, and a dreamy state of relaxation. *THC has been shown to be useful in* the treatment of pain, epilepsy, hypertension, nausea, glaucoma, and asthma.

14. *Designer "club" drugs are* synthetic drugs used at dance clubs, parties, and "raves." *Examples*

(and their effects) include MDMA (ecstasy), which acts as a stimulant and produces mild psychedelic effects, and the dissociative anesthetics PCP (angel dust) and ketamine (Special K), which reduce sensitivity to pain and produce feelings of detachment and dissociation.

Concept Check 6

1. psychoactive; physically
2. drug tolerance
3. judgment; self-control
4. not remember
5. will not
6. tranquilizer
7. cocaine
8. MDMA; ecstasy
9. opiates; narcotics

Graphic Organizer 2

1. alcohol; depressant
2. tranquilizer; depressant
3. marijuana; psychedelic
4. LSD; psychedelic
5. caffeine; stimulant
6. morphine; opiate
7. nicotine; stimulant

Matching Exercise 6

1. THC
2. depressants
3. nicotine
4. drug abuse
5. psychoactive drug
6. stimulant-induced psychosis
7. mescaline
8. drug tolerance
9. hashish
10. withdrawal symptoms
11. cocaine
12. amphetamines
13. delirium tremens (DTs)
14. progressive relaxation
15. codeine
16. MDMA (ecstasy)

17. anandamide

18. inhalants

19. stimulus control therapy

20. autogenic training

True/False Test 6

1. T	6. T	11. F	16. T
2. F	7. T	12. T	17. T
3. T	8. T	13. F	18. T
4. T	9. T	14. F	19. T
5. T	10. T	15. T	20. T

Something to Think About

1. Generally speaking, humans are very adaptable; in fact, most people can easily adapt to shift work. If shifts are scheduled to take into account our natural tendencies and use knowledge about sleep–wake cycles, circadian rhythms, and the role of the SCN, they need not produce the usual jet lag symptoms.

   Begin your report with a discussion of how to rotate a person's shifts. Because we tend to drift to longer days (the 24.2-hour day rather than the 24-hour day), as we often do on weekends, it would seem best to rotate shifts forward: first shift, 8 A.M. to 4 P.M., second shift 4 P.M. to 12 midnight, and then midnight to 8 A.M. for the third shift.

   The length of the shift rotation is the next issue to address. Every shift change is going to take some time to get used to and will be accompanied by some jet-lag symptoms, so the less someone has to change the better. It would probably be best to have people do the same shift for at least a month before changing to the next shift.

   Shift workers should be given as much information as possible about circadian rhythms, sleep–wake cycles, and the role of the SCN in the production of melatonin. People finishing a night shift, for example, could be told the value of blackout curtains to avoid having their biological clock reset by bright light. Or, having bright lights, especially in the early part of the shift, can help people adjust to the night shift. For more specific suggestions, see the Application (Can't Sleep? Read This!).

2. This dream sounds like a real nightmare. The first thing to tell your friend is that dreams cannot predict the future. She is not likely to fail the exam because of her dream. Her dream reflects the fact that she is concerned and worried about the course. The best way to do well on the exam, and to deal with exam anxiety, is to study the material completely. The text presents two theories of dreams. Freud's view is that the manifest content is relatively unimportant; he would suggest looking for disguised symbolic meaning that reflects the latent content. The activation–synthesis theory suggests that if someone is worried and anxious, these concerns are likely to show up in a dream if these well-worn neural pathways are activated. In other words, the brain produces dream images that are synthesized into a meaningful story, using memories about daily events, past experiences, concerns, and worries.

   The person's interpretation of the dream may tell us more about the dreamer than anything else. If that is the case, it would be fairly safe to assume that this dreamer is experiencing some perceived difficulty with the course (or some aspect of it) and/or the course material itself.

Progress Test 1

1. c	6. c	11. c
2. c	7. d	12. d
3. d	8. b	13. a
4. b	9. c	14. a
5. d	10. a	15. b

Progress Test 2

1. a	6. c	11. b
2. b	7. c	12. a
3. a	8. d	13. a
4. d	9. b	14. d
5. a	10. c	15. c

Progress Test 3

1. a	6. c	11. b
2. d	7. a	12. c
3. c	8. b	13. a
4. c	9. a	14. c
5. a	10. a	15. d

CHAPTER 5

Learning

PREVIEW

Reading the section below first will give you a general sense of the chapter's contents and an initial introduction to some of the major concepts and terms. This will prime you for what you are about to read and help you to develop a "cognitive map" that will guide your study of the material in this chapter. Likewise, reading the **preview questions** at the beginning of each major section will improve your ability to understand, learn, and retain the information.

CHAPTER 5 . . . AT A GLANCE

Chapter 5 answers the question "What is learning?" Conditioning focuses on how we form associations between environmental events and behavioral responses. Classical conditioning (discovered by Ivan Pavlov) involves repeatedly pairing a neutral stimulus with a stimulus that naturally elicits a response until the neutral stimulus elicits the same response. Behaviorism (founded by John B. Watson) is concerned with the scientific study of observable behaviors, especially as they pertain to learning. Classical conditioning is used to explain conditioned emotional reactions, conditioned drug effects, and placebo responses. Contemporary psychology has modified the basics of classical conditioning to account for cognitive functioning and biological predispositions.

Operant conditioning (developed by B. F. Skinner) demonstrates how voluntary, active behaviors are acquired through reinforcement, punishment, and shaping. Once acquired, behaviors are maintained through different schedules of reinforcement. Behaviors that are partially reinforced are more resistant to extinction than are behaviors that are continuously reinforced. Behavior modification is the application of principles of operant conditioning to help people develop more adaptive behaviors. Operant conditioning principles have also been modified by contemporary cognitive and biological views.

Observational learning (studied by Albert Bandura) shows how new behaviors can be acquired through watching the actions of others. It involves the processes of attention, memory, motor skills, and motivation and has been applied in education, vocational and job training, psychotherapy, counseling, and entertainment–education programs to promote healthy behaviors and social change.

The Application suggests ways that learning principles can be used to improve self-control.

Introduction: What Is Learning?

Preview Questions

Consider the following questions as you study this section of the chapter.

- How is learning defined?
- What is conditioning?
- What are three basic types of learning?

*Read the section "Introduction: What Is Learning?" and **write** your answers to the following:*

1. Learning refers to _____
_____

2. Conditioning is the _____
_____

3. Three basic types of learning are
_____
_____

Classical Conditioning: Associating Stimuli

Preview Questions

Consider the following questions as you study this section of the chapter.

- Who discovered classical conditioning, and how did he investigate it?
- What is the basic process of classical conditioning?
- What factors can affect the strength of a classically conditioned response?
- What phenomena did Pavlov discover when he varied the stimuli during conditioning?

*Read the section "Classical Conditioning: Associating Stimuli" and **write** your answers to the following:*

1. The person who discovered classical conditioning was _____
He investigated the phenomenon by _____
_____
_____
_____

2. Classical conditioning is the process of (describe the elements involved in the process)
_____
_____
_____

3. The two factors that can affect the strength of a classically conditioned response are _____
_____
_____

4. The five other conditioning phenomena that Pavlov discovered were
_____
_____
_____
_____
_____

From Pavlov to Watson: The Founding of Behaviorism

Preview Questions

Consider the following questions as you study this section of the chapter.

- Who founded behaviorism, and what were its basic assumptions?
- How can classical conditioning be used to create and explain conditioned emotional responses?
- How is classical conditioning involved in responses to drugs, and how are these effects involved in placebo responses?

*Read the section "From Pavlov to Watson: The Founding of Behaviorism" and **write** your answers to the following:*

1. Behaviorism was founded by _____
and was defined as _____
_____
_____

2. The fundamental assumptions of behaviorism as formulated by Watson are _____
_____
_____

3. Watson identified three innate emotions, which are _____ , each of which could be _____

_____

With regard to these emotions, Watson showed that classical conditioning could be used to

_____

_____

4. Classical conditioning can be used to create a conditioned emotional response (CR) to a previously neutral stimulus by_____

_____

_____

5. The classical conditioning components in the Little Albert study were as follows:

CS: _____

UCS: _____

UCR: _____

CR: _____

6. Some people acquire classically conditioned responses to drugs such as caffeine, an active ingredient in coffee. In this example, the CS is _____ ; the UCS is _____ ; the UCR is _____ ; and the CR is

_____ .

7. A placebo response is _____

_____ .

Contemporary Views of Classical Conditioning
Preview Questions

Consider the following questions as you study this section of the chapter.

- How does the cognitive explanation of learning differ from the behavioral explanation?
- What kinds of cognitive processes are involved in classical conditioning, and how have they been demonstrated experimentally?
- How does the evolutionary perspective account for the conditioning process?
- How do taste aversions challenge the principles of classical conditioning, and how can they be explained?
- What is biological preparedness?

*Read the section "Contemporary Views of Classical Conditioning" and **write** your answers to the following:*

1. According to the cognitive perspective, learning

_____

_____

On the other hand, the traditional behavioral perspective holds that _____

_____

_____

2. In his research with rats, Robert Rescorla demonstrated that _____

_____

_____

3. According to the evolutionary perspective,

_____

This is because_____

_____

_____

4. Taste aversion is a _____

_____

Taste aversions violate two basic principles of classical conditioning: _____

_____

_____

_____

5. John Garcia demonstrated that taste aversions could be produced under controlled laboratory conditions by _____

_____

He found that _____

_____

_____

6. Biological preparedness refers to _____

_____

_____

After you have carefully studied the preceding sections, complete the following exercises.

Concept Check 1

Read the following and write the correct term in the space provided.

1. Dr. Munchausen believes that the general principles of learning apply to virtually all species and all learning situations, whereas his colleague Dr. Milstein believes that an animal's natural behavioral patterns and unique characteristics can influence what it is capable of learning. Dr. Munchausen supports the traditional _____ perspective, and Dr. Milstein's views are consistent with a(n) _____ perspective.

2. Dr. Wells decided to classically condition some rats. He used a tone (CS) followed by a shock (UCS) for group 1; for group 2, he used a taste (CS) followed by a shock. It is very _____ (likely/unlikely) that the rats in group 1 will be classically conditioned; it is very _____ (likely/unlikely) that the rats in group 2 will be classically conditioned.

3. It appears that Dr. Wells in the above example is investigating how _____ affects learning through classical conditioning.

4. Dr. Manly believes that classical conditioning depends on the information the CS provides about the UCS and that for learning to occur, the CS must be a reliable signal that predicts the presentation of the UCS. Dr. Manly's views are most consistent with the _____ perspective.

5. About five hours after extinguishing the classically conditioned response (CR) in an experimental animal, Dr. Taylor presented the conditioned stimulus (CS) and obtained a CR. Dr. Taylor has demonstrated _____ .

6. Fido drools whenever he hears the sound of the electric can opener but does not drool when he hears the sound of the blender, which makes a similar noise. It appears that Fido has learned to _____ between the two sounds.

7. Ahmood, who has recently started drinking a lot of hot chocolate, notices that he now feels a positive emotional reaction at just the sight and smell of hot chocolate. In classical conditioning terms, Ahmood's response to these cues is called a _____ .

8. Ahmood also observes that he has a similar emotional response to the smell of other beverages such as herbal tea and coffee. In this situation, he is experiencing a phenomenon called _____ .

9. During basic training, Tremaine felt that the drill sergeant was very unfair in the way he demeaned and threatened him and some of the other new recruits. Tremaine was constantly angry and fearful during this period; today, although it's years later, just the mention of the sergeant's name is enough to elicit a strong negative emotional reaction. In this example of classical conditioning, the demeaning and threatening behavior was the _____ , Tremaine's response of fear and anger was the _____ , and the present negative emotional reaction to the sergeant's name is the _____ .

10. In a research study, patients with high blood pressure regularly received a drug that reduced their hypertension. The drug was always given in the same location. When a similar-looking fake pill was given in the same place, the patients' blood pressure was reduced, much as it had been with the real drug. This example illustrates a _____ .

Graphic Organizer 1

*In his classic experiment, Pavlov repeatedly present-
ed a neutral stimulus, such as a tone, just before
putting food in the dog's mouth, which automatically*
*elicited salivation. After several repetitions the tone
alone triggered the salivation. Label the following
graph using the correct terms (UCS, UCR, CS, CR):*

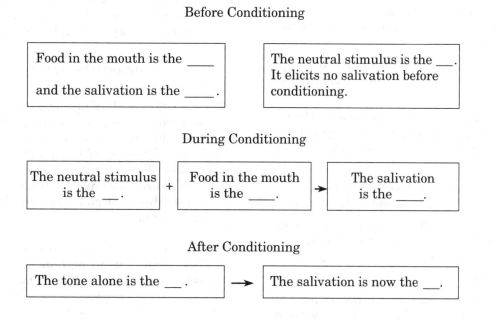

Before Conditioning

Food in the mouth is the ____

and the salivation is the ____ .

The neutral stimulus is the __.
It elicits no salivation before
conditioning.

During Conditioning

The neutral stimulus
is the __ . + Food in the mouth
is the ____ . → The salivation
is the ____ .

After Conditioning

The tone alone is the __ . → The salivation is now the __.

Review of Terms, Concepts, and Names 1

*Use the terms in this list to complete the Matching
Test, then to help you answer the True/False items
correctly.*

learning
conditioning
Ivan Pavlov
reflex
stimulus
classical conditioning
    (respondent or
    Pavlovian
    conditioning)
elicit
unconditioned stimulus
    (UCS)
unconditioned response
    (UCR)
conditioned stimulus
    (CS)
conditioned response
    (CR)

stimulus generalization
stimulus discrimination
higher order
    conditioning (second-
    order conditioning)
extinction
spontaneous recovery
John B. Watson
behaviorism
placebo response
    (placebo effect)
cognitive perspective
Robert A. Rescorla
taste aversion
John Garcia
biological preparedness

Matching Exercise

*Match the appropriate term/name with its definition
or description.*

1. _____ The gradual weakening and
apparent disappearance of conditioned behavior; in classical conditioning, it occurs when the
conditioned stimulus is repeatedly presented
without the unconditioned stimulus.

2. _____ The process of learning associations between environmental events and
behavioral responses.

3. _____ A process that produces a
relatively enduring change in behavior or
knowledge as a result of experience.

4. _____ Classically conditioned dislike for and avoidance of a particular food that
develops when an organism becomes ill after
eating the food.

5. _____ School of psychology and
theoretical viewpoint that emphasizes the scientific study of observable behaviors, especially
as they pertain to the process of learning.

6. _____ American psychologist who founded behaviorism in the early 1900s.

7. _____ Natural stimulus that reflexively elicits a response without the need for prior learning.

8. _____ Russian physiologist who first described the basic learning process of associating stimuli that is now called classical conditioning.

9. _____ Unlearned, reflexive response that is elicited by an unconditioned stimulus.

10. _____ In learning theory, the idea that an organism is innately predisposed to form associations between certain stimuli and responses.

11. _____ A largely involuntary, automatic response to an external stimulus.

12. _____ An individual's psychological and physiological response to what is actually a fake treatment or drug.

True/False Test

Indicate whether each statement is true or false by placing T or F in the blank space next to each item.

1. ____ Classical conditioning is the basic learning process that involves repeatedly pairing a neutral stimulus with a response-producing stimulus until the neutral stimulus elicits the same response.

2. ____ Elicit means to draw out or bring forth; a stimulus causes an existing behavior to occur.

3. ____ The American psychologist who experimentally demonstrated the involvement of cognitive processes in classical conditioning is John Garcia.

4. ____ The occurrence of a learned response not only to the original stimulus but also to other, similar stimuli as well is called stimulus discrimination.

5. ____ The conditioned stimulus is a formerly neutral stimulus that acquires the capacity to elicit a reflexive response.

6. ____ The reappearance of a previously extinguished conditioned response after a period of time without exposure to the conditioned stimulus is called spontaneous recovery.

7. ____ Stimulus generalization occurs when a learned response is made to a specific stimulus but not to other, similar stimuli.

8. ____ Robert A. Rescorla is the American psychologist who experimentally demonstrated the learning of taste aversions in animals.

9. ____ The conditioned response is the learned, reflexive response to a conditioned stimulus.

10. ____ The cognitive perspective holds that mental processes as well as external events are an important component in the learning of new behaviors.

11. ____ Anything perceptible to the senses is a stimulus.

12. ____ The procedure in which a conditioned stimulus from one learning trial functions as the unconditioned stimulus in a new conditioning trial and the second conditioned stimulus comes to elicit the conditioned response, even though it has never been directly paired with the unconditioned stimulus is called higher-order conditioning.

Check your answers and review any areas of weakness before going on to the next section.

Operant Conditioning: Associating Behaviors and Consequences (Part 1)

Preview Questions

Consider the following questions as you study the first three parts of this section of the chapter (through Discriminative Stimuli).

- What was Thorndike's contribution to learning theory?

- What were B. F. Skinner's key assumptions, and what is the fundamental premise of operant conditioning?

- How are positive and negative reinforcement similar, and how are they different?

- What are primary and conditioned (secondary) reinforcers?

- What is punishment, and what factors influence its effectiveness?

- What negative effects are associated with the use of punishment?

- What are discriminative stimuli, and what important role do they play in operant conditioning?

*Read the section "Operant Conditioning: Associating Behaviors and Consequences" (through Discriminative Stimuli) and **write** your answers to the following:*

1. Edward L. Thorndike was the first person to _____

   _____

   He concluded that _____

   _____

   _____

   _____

2. B. F. Skinner believed that _____

   _____

   _____

   _____

3. Operant conditioning is _____

   _____

   It explains _____

   _____

4. The basic premise of operant conditioning is

   _____

5. Reinforcement refers to _____

   _____

   _____

6. Positive reinforcement involves _____

   _____

   _____

   Negative reinforcement involves _____

   _____

   Negative and positive reinforcement are similar in that _____

   _____

   They differ in that _____

   _____

7. A primary reinforcer is _____

   _____

   and a conditioned reinforcer (secondary reinforcer) is _____

   _____

8. Punishment is a _____

   _____

   _____

9. The factors that influence the effectiveness of punishment are _____

   _____

   _____

   _____

   The drawbacks of punishment are that

   _____

   _____

   _____

   _____

10. Discriminative stimuli are _____

    _____

    _____

    _____

    According to Skinner, they are important because _____

    _____

    _____

___

After you have carefully studied the preceding section, complete the following exercises.

Concept Check 2

Read the following and write the correct term in the space provided.

1. Ashley holds the view that responses followed by a satisfying state of affairs are strengthened and are more likely to occur again in the same situation and that responses followed by an unpleasant or annoying state of affairs are less likely to recur. This view is most consistent with a fundamental principle of learning called the _____ .

2. April burned her fingers when she picked up a hot saucepan with her bare hands. She now always dons her oven mitts before touching any hot pan or pot. The aversive stimulus of getting burned reduced her tendency to pick up pots with her bare hands and is therefore an example of _____ ; her increased tendency to use oven mitts because doing so reduces the possibility of getting burned is an example of _____ .

3. Whenever young Simon wants something, such as a new toy or candy, he cries and screams until his parents give him what he wants. Simon's whining behavior is _____ reinforced by his parents' giving him what he wants, and the parents' behavior is _____ reinforced because it stops Simon's annoying crying and screaming.

4. While researching a term paper for his history of psychology class, Rupert discovered the name of the first psychologist to investigate how voluntary behaviors are influenced by their consequences. That psychologist was _____ .

5. The following are examples of negative reinforcement. Decide which illustrate *escape* and which illustrate *avoidance*.

(a) You go to the dentist on a regular basis; as a result, you don't experience problems such as toothaches. This an example of

_____ .

(b) Your partner is complaining about your messy habits, so you put on your running gear and go for a five-mile jog. This is an example of _____ .

(c) You study hard all semester because you don't want to end up with a low grade-point average. This is an example of

_____ .

(d) You turn the air conditioner on when the temperature in your room gets too hot and uncomfortable. This is an example of

_____ .

6. For each of the following, decide whether the example illustrates negative reinforcement (NR), punishment by application (P/A), or punishment by removal (P/R).

(a) _____ Marco always wears his seatbelt when he drives his car because he doesn't want to be thrown against the windshield if his car is hit from behind.

(b) _____ Darryl has tried some new aftershave lotion. "It smells like diesel oil!" complains his girlfriend. Darryl never uses that aftershave lotion again.

(c) _____ Maria does not misbehave at the dinner table because she knows that misbehavior will result in her forfeiting dessert.

(d) _____ Greta's cigarette lighter ignites the hair spray she has just put on her hair and burns her bangs and eyebrows. Greta no longer smokes when she is doing her hair.

(e) _____ Jim no longer picks up hitchhikers after the last one robbed him at gun point.

(f) _____ Before pouring milk on her cereal, Carmelita smells the carton to make sure the milk has not gone sour.

(g) _____ Astrid brushes her teeth after every meal because she wants to cut down on the number of visits she needs to make to the dentist.

7. A ringing telephone is a

_____ for picking up the receiver.

Graphic Organizer 2

The following is a very useful way to organize the procedures used in operant conditioning. The arrow

(↑ or ↓) indicates whether the behavior increases or decreases. Fill in the blanks in cells 1, 2, 3, and 4.

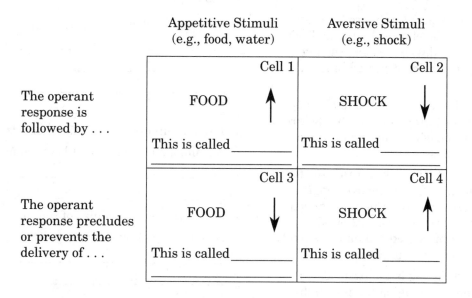

Review of Terms, Concepts, and Names 2

Use the terms in this list to complete the Matching Test, then to help you answer the True/False items correctly.

Edward L. Thorndike
law of effect
B. F. Skinner
operant
operant conditioning
reinforcement
positive reinforcement
negative reinforcement
aversive stimuli
escape behavior
avoidance behavior

primary reinforcer
conditioned reinforcer
(secondary reinforcer)
punishment
punishment by
application (positive
punishment)
punishment by removal
(negative punishment)
discriminative stimulus

Matching Exercise

Match the appropriate term/name with its definition or description.

1. _____ American psychologist who developed the operant conditioning model of learning.

2. _____ Situation in which a response results in the removal of, avoidance of, or escape from a punishing stimulus, increasing the likelihood of the response being repeated in similar situations.

3. _____ American psychologist who was the first to study animal behavior

systematically and document how active behaviors are influenced by their consequences.

4. _____ Presentation of a stimulus or event following a behavior that acts to decrease the likelihood of the behavior being repeated.

5. _____ Stimulus or event that has acquired reinforcing value by being associated with a primary reinforcer.

6. _____ Occurrence of a stimulus or event following a response that increases the likelihood of the response being repeated.

7. _____ Skinner's term for an actively emitted behavior that operates on the environment to produce consequences.

8. _____ A specific stimulus in the presence of which a particular response is more likely to be reinforced and in the absence of which a particular response is not reinforced.

9. _____ In negative reinforcement, behavior that removes an aversive stimulus that is already present.

True/False Test

Indicate whether each statement is true or false by placing T or F in the blank space next to each item.

1. ____ A primary reinforcer is a stimulus or event that is naturally or inherently reinforcing for a given species such as food, water, and other biological necessities.

2. ___ Punishment by application refers to a situation in which an operant is followed by the removal or subtraction of a reinforcing stimulus.

3. ___ Positive reinforcement refers to a situation in which a response is followed by the addition of a reinforcing stimulus, increasing the likelihood of the response being repeated in similar situations.

4. ___ Punishment by removal refers to a situation in which an operant is followed by the presentation or addition of an unpleasant or aversive event or stimulus.

5. ___ The law of effect states that responses followed by a satisfying effect become strengthened and are more likely to recur in a particular situation, whereas responses followed by a dissatisfying effect are weakened and less likely to recur in a particular situation.

6. ___ Operant conditioning is the basic learning process that involves changing the probability that a response will be repeated by manipulating the consequences of that response.

7. ___ Aversive stimuli involve physical or psychological discomfort that an organism seeks to escape or avoid.

8. ___ In negative reinforcement, behavior that precludes the delivery of an aversive stimulus is called avoidance behavior.

Check your answers and review any areas of weakness before going on to the next section.

Operant Conditioning: Associating Behaviors and Consequences (Part 2)

Preview Questions

Consider the following questions as you study the last parts of this section of the chapter (through Applications of Operant Conditioning).

- What is shaping, and how does it work?
- How does partial reinforcement affect behavior?
- What are the four basic schedules of reinforcement?
- How has behavior modification been used to change human behavior?

*Read the section "Operant Conditioning: Associating Behaviors and Consequences" (through Applications of Operant Conditioning) and **write** your answers to the following:*

1. Shaping involves _____

_____

_____

_____

2. Partial reinforcement is more effective than continuous reinforcement because it _____

_____

3. The four basic schedules of reinforcement are (and their patterns of responding) _____

_____

_____

_____

4. Behavior modification is _____

_____

_____

_____

_____

After you have carefully studied the preceding section, complete the following exercises.

Concept Check 3

Read the following and write the correct term in the space provided.

1. Your instructor, Dr. Jones, gives surprise quizzes throughout the semester. Your studying will be reinforced on a _____ schedule.

2. Your instructor, Dr. Wong, schedules a quiz every two weeks throughout the semester. Your studying will be reinforced on a _____ schedule.

3. A rat gets a food pellet for every 20 responses. It is reinforced on a _____ schedule.

4. If parents use praise and encouragement to gradually teach a child how to dress herself, they are using a _____ procedure.

5. Maria sells magazine subscriptions over the phone. She makes many calls but only gets paid for making a sale. She is reinforced on a _____ schedule.

6. Juanita and her colleagues assemble TV sets in a factory. They get paid a bonus for every ten TVs they produce. They are being rewarded on a _____ schedule.

Graphic Organizer 3

Fill in each cell with the name of the appropriate partial reinforcement schedule.

	Based on the number of responses made	Based on the elapsed time
Fixed	Cell 1 _____	Cell 2 _____
Variable	Cell 3 _____	Cell 4 _____

Review of Terms, Concepts, and Names 3

Use the terms in this list to complete the Matching Test, then to help you answer the True/False items correctly.

operant chamber (Skinner box)
shaping
continuous reinforcement
partial reinforcement
extinction
partial reinforcement effect
schedule of reinforcement
fixed-ratio schedule
variable-ratio schedule
fixed-interval schedule
variable-interval schedule
behavior modification

Matching Exercise

Match the appropriate term/name with its definition or description:

1. _____ The application of learning principles to help people develop more effective or adaptive behaviors.

2. _____ Schedule of reinforcement in which every occurrence of a particular response is reinforced.

3. _____ The name of the experimental apparatus invented by B. F. Skinner to study the relationship between environmental events and active behaviors.

4. _____ Reinforcement schedule in which a reinforcer is delivered after a fixed number of responses has occurred.

5. _____ Operant conditioning procedure in which successively closer approximations of a goal behavior are selectively reinforced until the goal behavior is displayed.

6. _____ Reinforcement schedule in which a reinforcer is delivered for the first response that occurs after a preset time interval has elapsed.

True/False Test

Indicate whether each statement is true or false by placing T or F in the blank space next to each item.

1. ____ Partial reinforcement refers to a situation in which the occurrence of a particular response is only sometimes followed by a reinforcer.

2. ____ A variable-ratio schedule is one in which a reinforcer is delivered for the first response that occurs after an average time interval has elapsed, but the time varies unpredictably from trial to trial.

3. ____ A variable-interval schedule is one in which a reinforcer is delivered after an average number of responses, but the number varies unpredictably from trial to trial.

4. ____ The partial reinforcement effect refers to the fact that continuously reinforced behaviors are more resistant to extinction than behaviors that are only sometimes reinforced.

5. ____ The gradual weakening and disappearance of conditioned behavior in operant conditioning is called extinction; it occurs when an emitted behavior is no longer followed by a reinforcer.

6. ____ Schedule of reinforcement refers to the delivery of a reinforcer according to a preset pattern based on the number of responses or the time interval between responses.

Check your answers and review any areas of weakness before going on to the next section.

Contemporary Views of Operant Conditioning

Preview Questions

Consider the following questions as you study this section of the chapter.

- What factors do contemporary learning researchers suggest are involved in operant conditioning?
- How did Tolman's research demonstrate the involvement of cognitive processes in learning?
- What are cognitive maps, latent learning, and learned helplessness?
- How is operant conditioning influenced by an animal's natural behavior patterns?
- How does the phenomenon of instinctive drift challenge the traditional behavioral view of operant conditioning?

*Read the section "Contemporary Views of Operant Conditioning" and **write** your answers to the following:*

1. Contemporary learning researchers confirm the basic principles of operant conditioning but also acknowledge _____

_____

2. Unlike Skinner and Thorndike, Tolman believed that _____

_____

3. A cognitive map is _____

_____

Latent learning is _____

_____

_____

4. Learned helplessness demonstrates the role of cognitive factors in learning in that _____

_____

_____

_____

5. Operant conditioning may also be influenced by

_____

_____

_____

6. The phenomenon of instinctive drift challenged the traditional behavioral view by _____

_____

_____

_____

Observational Learning: Imitating the Actions of Others

Preview Questions

Consider the following questions as you study this section of the chapter.

- What type of learning is indirect?
- What four mental processes are involved in observational learning?
- How has observational learning been applied?

*Read the section "Observational Learning: Imitating the Actions of Others" and **write** your answers to the following:*

1. Observational learning is _____

_____

The person most strongly identified with work in this area is _____

2. The four cognitive processes that interact to determine if imitation will occur are _____

_____

_____

_____

_____

3. Observational learning has been applied in a variety of settings, including _____

_____

_____

_____

_____

After you have carefully studied the preceding sections, complete the following exercises.

Concept Check 4

Read the following and write the correct term in the space provided.

1. Maria watches a popular cooking show on public TV on Saturday afternoons and often cooks one of the dishes she sees the chef prepare. Maria's culinary ability is the result of _____ learning.

2. Dr. Bristow believes that reinforcement is not necessary for learning to occur but that the *expectation* of reinforcement can affect the performance of what has been learned. Dr. Bristow is emphasizing the importance of _____ factors in learning.

3. If a rat has been allowed to explore a maze for a number of trials without ever getting a reinforcer, when food is made available in the goal box, it is very _____ (likely/unlikely) that the rat will find the food very quickly with few errors.

4. An animal trainer has a hard time operantly conditioning a pig to pick up a large wooden penny and put it in a big "piggy bank" because the pig seems to prefer to push the coin with its snout even though it is not reinforced for this behavior. The Brelands called this phenomenon _____ .

5. Mr. and Mrs. Delbrook both stopped smoking when they started a family because they wanted to model healthy behavior patterns for their children. They are apparently aware of the importance of _____ learning in children's development.

Review of Terms, Concepts, and Names 4

Use the terms in this list to complete the Matching Test, then to help you answer the True/False items correctly.

Edward C. Tolman	instinctive drift
cognitive map	observational learning
latent learning	Albert Bandura
learned helplessness	mirror neurons

Matching Exercise

Match the appropriate term/name with its definition or description:

1. _____ Learning that occurs through observing the actions of others.

2. _____ Tolman's term for learning that occurs in the absence of reinforcement but is not behaviorally demonstrated until a reinforcer becomes available.

3. _____ American psychologist whose experimental findings strongly suggested that cognitive factors play a role in animal learning.

4. _____ Tolman's term for the mental representation of the layout of a familiar environment.

5. _____ American psychologist who experimentally investigated observational learning, emphasizing the role of cognitive factors.

6. _____ The tendency of an animal to revert to instinctive behaviors, which can interfere with the performance of an operantly conditioned response.

7. _____ A phenomenon in which exposure to inescapable and uncontrollable aversive events produces passive behavior.

8. _____ Neurons that fire both when an action is performed and when the action is simply perceived.

Check your answers and review any areas of weakness before going on to the next section.

Something to Think About

1. Imagine that you are a behavioral therapist whose client has a real fear of going to the dentist. Despite the need for some important dental work, he can't bring himself to make an appointment. Using what you know about classical conditioning, explain how his phobia might have come about, and describe how to extinguish the fear.

2. Mrs. Denton can't understand why scolding her ten-year-old son for misbehaving only seems to make the problem worse. Using what you know about operant conditioning techniques, what advice would you give Mrs. Denton about how she might (a) reduce the disruptive behavior and (b) encourage more appropriate behavior?

3. Imagine that your family has decided to adopt a puppy. Using what you know about operant conditioning techniques, what advice would you give them about how they should train the dog to be obedient and do some neat pet tricks?

Check your answers and review any areas of weakness before doing the progress tests.

Progress Test 1

Review the complete chapter (including all boxed inserts), review all your study notes, and then test yourself on the following progress test. Check your answers. If you make a mistake, review your notes, check the appropriate section in the study guide, and if necessary, go back and read the relevant part of the chapter in your textbook.

1. Dr. Ramos is a behavioral psychologist who conducts basic research using animals in carefully controlled laboratory studies. The goal of his research is most probably to
   (a) train animals to do tricks.
   (b) collect and sell saliva from dogs and other animals.
   (c) identify the general principles of learning that apply across a wide range of species, including humans.
   (d) observe changes in animal behavior that result from biological maturation.

2. Dr. Frolov classically conditioned a dog to flex his hind leg at the sound of a bell by pairing the ringing of a bell with a mild electric shock to the leg. In this example, the ringing bell is the
   (a) unconditioned stimulus (UCS).
   (b) conditioned response (CR).
   (c) unconditioned response (UCR).
   (d) conditioned stimulus (CS).

3. Some forms of chemotherapy make patients sick. A patient who has eaten a pizza just before the therapy (and is then sick) later feels ill when she sees or smells pizza. In this example of taste aversion learning, the conditioned response is the
   (a) pizza.
   (b) chemotherapy.
   (c) illness induced by the therapy.
   (d) nausea felt at the sight or smell of pizza.

4. After establishing a classically conditioned response (CR) to a tone, the experimenter presents a new conditioned stimulus, a red light, followed repeatedly by the original conditioned stimulus, the tone. As a result the conditioned response (CR) is elicited by the red light alone, even though it had never been paired with the original UCS. The experimenter has demonstrated
   (a) spontaneous recovery.
   (b) higher order conditioning (second-order conditioning).
   (c) a placebo response (placebo effect).
   (d) punishment by application.

5. Dr. Redner believes that classical conditioning depends on the information the conditioned stimulus provides about the unconditioned stimulus. Also, for learning to occur, the conditioned stimulus must be a reliable signal that predicts the presentation of the unconditioned stimulus. Dr. Redner's views are most consistent with those of the learning theorist
   (a) Robert A. Rescorla.
   (b) Edward L. Thorndike.
   (c) Ivan Pavlov.
   (d) B. F. Skinner.

6. Ricardo always gets nervous and apprehensive when his professor uses the word *exam,* but he seldom feels the same anxiety when the word *quiz* is mentioned. Assuming that classical conditioning is involved in these two different reactions at the mention of tests, it appears that Ricardo is exhibiting
   (a) stimulus discrimination.
   (b) spontaneous recovery.
   (c) latent learning.
   (d) stimulus generalization.

7. About five hours after she had successfully extinguished a dog's classically conditioned response of salivating to the sound of a bell, Dr. Sheckenov discovered that the dog once again salivated in the presence of the bell. This example illustrates the phenomenon of
   (a) stimulus generalization.
   (b) spontaneous recovery.
   (c) latent learning.
   (d) instinctive drift.

8. Dr. Radersched conducts research on the phenomenon of biological preparedness. She is most likely to discover that

    (a) organisms are innately predisposed to form associations between some stimuli and responses and not to others.

    (b) the general principles of learning apply to virtually all animal species and all learning situations.

    (c) classical conditioning occurs because two stimuli are associated closely in time and that frequency and contiguity are the only variables that affect learning.

    (d) mental processes, but not innate predispositions, are the crucial variables involved in classical conditioning.

9. Sasha studied very hard last semester and earned good grades in all her courses. This semester, Sasha is once again studying hard. It appears that good grades are _____ for Sasha's studying behavior.

    (a) conditioned stimuli

    (b) discriminative stimuli

    (c) positively reinforcing

    (d) negatively reinforcing

10. Rachel studies a lot to avoid getting bad grades because for her a bad grade is devastating. Rachel's studying behavior is maintained by

    (a) negative reinforcement.

    (b) primary reinforcement.

    (c) positive reinforcement.

    (d) punishment by removal.

11. Helmut is employed by his university as a telephone solicitor for a fund-raising drive. He is paid a set amount of money for every 10 calls he makes whether or not he gets any donations. Helmut's telephoning is reinforced on a _____ schedule of reinforcement.

    (a) fixed-interval (FI)

    (b) variable-interval (VI)

    (c) fixed-ratio (FR)

    (d) variable-ratio (VR)

12. Ever since Thelma used her phone line to hook up her computer to the Internet, her phone line is often busy. Her parents don't know the best time to call her, so they try at random times. It appears that phoning Thelma is reinforced on a _____ schedule.

    (a) fixed-interval (FI)

    (b) variable-interval (VI)

    (c) fixed-ratio (FR)

    (d) variable-ratio (VR)

13. After they had been watching Superman cartoons all morning, 5-year-old Jim and 6-year-old John, each using a beach towel as a cape, climbed on top of the garage roof and got ready to fly. Their startled mother stopped them in time and realized the powerful influence of _____ on behavior.

    (a) observational learning

    (b) classical conditioning

    (c) operant conditioning

    (d) stimulus generalization

14. Researchers, interested in training rats using operant conditioning principles, implanted electrodes in the rats' medial forebrain bundle (MFB), and in brain areas processing signals from the rats' whiskers. If the outcome of their research is similar to results presented in the Focus on Neuroscience (Virtual Operant Conditioning), it is very likely that

    (a) the rats will go into convulsions once the electrodes are stimulated.

    (b) once the electrodes are stimulated, the rats will eat and drink excessively and become very obese.

    (c) by using radio signals from a laptop computer, the researchers can command the rats to run, turn, jump, and climb through pipes and concrete rubble.

    (d) the rats will lose their appetites and stop eating and drinking whenever the electrodes are activated.

15. According to Critical Thinking (Is Human Freedom Just an Illusion?), B. F. Skinner maintained that

    (a) human freedom is an illusion.

    (b) all behavior arises from causes that are within the individual, and environmental factors have little or no influence.

    (c) cognitive factors are the crucial elements in all learning and that how we think about things determines our actions.

    (d) people should be held responsible for their actions because they have individual freedom (free will) and are self-determined.

Progress Test 2

After you have checked your understanding of the material in Progress Test 1 and have done a complete chapter review with special focus on any areas of weakness, you are now ready to assess your knowledge on Progress Test 2. Check your answers. If you make a mistake, review your notes, the relevant section of the study guide, and, if necessary, the appropriate part of your textbook.

1. Which of the following best illustrates classical conditioning?
   (a) Henry feels ill when he smells peanut butter because it once made him sick.
   (b) Annalee studies hard because she wants to get good grades.
   (c) Virginia goes shopping for new clothes fairly frequently because it makes her feel good.
   (d) Lyndle drives at the posted speed limit after getting a number of speeding tickets.

2. Erv developed a fear of attics after he was accidentally locked in his own attic by his wife. Erv's present fear of the attic is a(n)
   (a) example of instinctive drift.
   (b) conditioned emotional response.
   (c) form of observational learning.
   (d) operantly conditioned response.

3. Little Richard receives attention from his teacher in the form of a scolding every time he misbehaves. As a result, Richard misbehaves quite frequently. In this instance, it would appear that the teacher's scolding is a
   (a) form of punishment by application.
   (b) positively reinforcing stimulus.
   (c) form of punishment by removal.
   (d) negatively reinforcing stimulus.

4. A group of 4-year-old children watch a video showing an adult hitting, kicking, and punching a large Bobo doll. These children are later asked to imitate the model and are promised a reward for every behavior they can imitate. It is very probable that the children will
   (a) not imitate the adult model.
   (b) verbally describe what they saw but will refuse to imitate the adult model.
   (c) quite readily imitate the adult's aggressive behavior.
   (d) become very upset as a result of watching the aggressive behavior.

5. Lauren spent the first week of the semester exploring the campus. Later, she had no trouble locating the library, although she had never been there before. According to Tolman, Lauren
   (a) has developed biological preparedness.
   (b) has formed a cognitive map.
   (c) is suffering from instinctive drift.
   (d) has developed a sense of direction.

6. Gerry puts up her umbrella soon after it starts to rain in order to prevent her clothes from getting any wetter. This example illustrates _____ behavior and _____ reinforcement.
   (a) avoidance; positive
   (b) escape; negative
   (c) avoidance; negative
   (d) escape; positive

7. When Juanita gets paid, she uses her money to buy food to feed her family. For Juanita, money is a _____ reinforcer and food is a _____ reinforcer.
   (a) conditioned; primary
   (b) primary; negative
   (c) conditioned; secondary
   (d) primary; positive

8. At dinner one night, Amanda started using her spoon as a drumstick. Her mother told her that she would get no dessert if she persisted with her bad behavior. Amanda soon stopped the banging. This example most clearly illustrates
   (a) negative reinforcement.
   (b) punishment by removal.
   (c) positive reinforcement.
   (d) punishment by application.

9. When Cal first attended college, he either barely passed or failed almost all his courses despite his efforts to do well. After working at a low-paying job for a couple of years, Cal has returned to school. Overwhelmed with the demands of exams, term papers, library assignments, and the need to concentrate on his studies, Cal finds himself procrastinating and engaging in other self-defeating passive behaviors. This example illustrates the phenomenon of
   (a) observational learning.
   (b) spontaneous recovery.
   (c) learned helplessness.
   (d) biological preparedness.

10. Zeno uses operant conditioning principles to train animals to perform a variety of behaviors. However, he discovered that some behaviors were difficult, if not impossible, to condition because an animal's natural behavior patterns, even though never reinforced, tended to interfere with the response he was trying to condition. This phenomenon is called

    (a) instinctive drift.
    (b) stimulus discrimination.
    (c) spontaneous recovery.
    (d) extinction.

11. Ashlynn loves playing the slot machines even though she wins money only once in a while. Ashlynn's gambling behavior is likely to be very resistant to extinction because of

    (a) the partial reinforcement effect.
    (b) spontaneous recovery.
    (c) the law of effect.
    (d) instinctive drift.

12. Dalbir believes that although reinforcement is not necessary for learning to occur, it does affect the performance of what has been learned. Dalbir's view is most consistent with the phenomenon of

    (a) instinctive drift.
    (b) biological preparedness.
    (c) shaping.
    (d) latent learning.

13. According to Critical Thinking (Does "Reel" Violence Cause Real Aggressive Behavior?), which of the following is (are) true?

    (a) There is a great deal of violence depicted on American TV.
    (b) In general, the more a person is exposed to media violence, the greater the likelihood that the person will behave aggressively.
    (c) TV depictions of violence fulfill the criteria that are most likely to lead to imitation, especially by children.
    (d) Research using children has shown that reduced exposure to TV depictions of violence can reduce aggressive behavior in the real world.
    (e) All of these statements are true.

14. According to the Application, we often choose a short-term reinforcer over a more valuable long-term goal. Your text suggests that we do this because

    (a) the relative value of a reinforcer can shift over time.
    (b) as a reinforcer becomes more available, the subjective value of the reinforcer increases.
    (c) when we make our decision, we'll choose whichever reinforcer has the greatest subjective value.
    (d) of all of these reasons.

15. According to Martin Seligman (In Focus: Evolution, Biological Preparedness, and Conditioned Fears), people are more likely to develop phobias of spiders, snakes, or heights—as compared to doorknobs, knives, washing machines, and ladders—because

    (a) of instinctive drift.
    (b) we are biologically prepared to do so.
    (c) doorknobs, knives, and ladders are inherently safer than spiders, snakes, and heights.
    (d) of latent learning.

Progress Test 3

After you have checked your understanding of the material in Progress Tests 1 and 2, and have done a complete chapter review with special focus on any areas of weakness, you are ready to further assess your knowledge with Progress Test 3. Check your answers. If you make a mistake, review your notes, the appropriate parts of the study guide, and, if necessary, the relevant sections of your textbook.

1. Arturo, a psychology major, was asked by his roommate to explain conditioning. He is most likely to point out that

    (a) conditioning is the process of learning associations between environmental events and behavioral responses.
    (b) there are two basic types of conditioning, operant conditioning and classical conditioning.
    (c) contemporary learning theorists also consider the process of observational learning.
    (d) all of these statements are true.

2. A monkey watches another monkey pick up and eat a peanut. Researchers discovered that the neuronal activity in this monkey's brain was the same as that of the monkey actually performing these actions. These researchers are investigating
    (a) cognitive maps and latent learning.
    (b) biological preparedness.
    (c) mirror neurons and the mirror neuron system.
    (d) higher order conditioning.

3. Justine got sick after eating a chicken burger. Now she not only has an intense dislike of chicken burgers but also feels nauseated at the sight of beef burgers, fish burgers, soybean burgers, or anything that even resembles a burger. It would appear that Justine has experienced the phenomenon Pavlov called
    (a) stimulus discrimination.
    (b) spontaneous recovery.
    (c) extinction.
    (d) stimulus generalization.

4. By presenting the CS over and over again without the UCS, Dr. Laslove discovered that the research participant's conditioned response (CR) gradually weakened and seemed to disappear. This decrease in responding is called
    (a) latent learning.
    (b) spontaneous recovery.
    (c) extinction.
    (d) stimulus discrimination.

5. Rolando got very sick after eating a big plate of oysters. Ever since that experience, Rolando feels ill whenever he sees or smells oysters. It appears that Rolando
    (a) has developed a taste aversion.
    (b) has experienced latent learning.
    (c) is suffering from instinctive drift.
    (d) is experiencing spontaneous recovery.

6. Dr. Alonzo takes a cognitive perspective in his research on learning. He is most likely to suggest that classical conditioning
    (a) involves learning the relations between events and that the CS must be a reliable predictor of the UCS.
    (b) results from simply pairing the CS with the UCS for a number of trials.
    (c) is constrained by biological predispositions.
    (d) follows general principles of learning that apply to virtually all animal species and all learning situations.

7. Positive reinforcement is to _____ as negative reinforcement is to _____ .
    (a) increased responding; decreased responding
    (b) decreased responding; decreased responding
    (c) increased responding; decreased responding
    (d) increased responding; increased responding

8. When Billy used his knife to release a piece of toast that was jammed in the toaster he got a severe electric shock. Billy has never used his knife to get toast out of the toaster again. It appears that Billy's behavior has been changed by
    (a) punishment by application.
    (b) negative reinforcement.
    (c) punishment by removal.
    (d) extinction.

9. Whenever the doorbell rings, Rex runs to the door and barks and growls. For Rex the ringing doorbell is a(n) _____ for his growling and barking behavior.
    (a) discriminative stimulus
    (b) unconditioned stimulus
    (c) reinforcing stimulus
    (d) primary reinforcer

10. Tammy wants to train her dog to "shake hands" with people, so she reinforces closer and closer approximations to the desired behavior. First she rewards him for sitting on command, then for slightly raising his front paw, then for fully raising his paw, then for moving his paw up and down until it is grasped, and so on. Tammy has used a process called
    (a) latent learning.
    (b) extinction.
    (c) partial reinforcement.
    (d) shaping.

11. Arnie always drives at the posted speed limit and obeys all the rules of the road because he can't afford to pay fines for driving offenses. Arnie's good driving habits are maintained by
    (a) positive reinforcement.
    (b) partial reinforcement.
    (c) secondary reinforcement.
    (d) negative reinforcement.

12. Harry works on an assembly line as part of a team of eight workers. They get paid a bonus for every one hundred products they assemble. Harry and his coworkers are being rewarded on a _____ schedule of reinforcement.
    (a) fixed-interval (FI)
    (b) variable-interval (VI)
    (c) fixed-ratio (FR)
    (d) variable-ratio (VR)

13. Wilma's psychology instructor schedules tests every two weeks throughout the semester, but her sociology instructor has surprise quizzes throughout the semester. The psychology instructor is using a _____ schedule, and the sociology instructor is using a _____ schedule.
    (a) fixed-interval (FI); variable-interval (VI)
    (b) variable-interval (VI); variable-ratio (VR)
    (c) fixed-ratio (FR); variable-ratio (VR)
    (d) variable-ratio (VR); fixed-interval (FI)

14. According to In Focus (Watson, Classical Conditioning, and Advertising), John B. Watson
    (a) believed that punishment was the best and most desirable way to change behavior.
    (b) vehemently opposed Skinner's idea that freedom is just an illusion.
    (c) was a pioneer in the application of classical conditioning principles to advertising.
    (d) discovered the phenomenon of latent learning.

15. According to In Focus (Changing the Behavior of Others), which of the following is true?
    (a) Punishment by removal is the most effective way to change undesirable behavior.
    (b) Punishment by application works better than any other behavioral strategy in changing undesirable behavior.
    (c) There are no effective strategies for reducing undesirable behaviors.
    (d) Several strategies other than punishment can be used to change undesirable behavior.

Answers

Introduction: What Is Learning?

1. *Learning refers to* a process that produces a relatively enduring change in behavior or knowledge as a result of past experience.

2. *Conditioning is the* process of learning associations between environmental events and behavioral responses.

3. *Three basic types of learning are* classical conditioning, operant conditioning, and observational learning.

Classical Conditioning: Associating Stimuli

1. *The person who discovered classical conditioning was* Ivan Pavlov. *He investigated the phenomenon by* studying how dogs learned to salivate to the presence of a stimulus (that would not normally elicit saliva) after it had been associated with food in the mouth, which reflexively elicits saliva.

2. *Classical conditioning is the process of (describe the elements involved in the process)* learning an association between two stimuli: the neutral stimulus (later to be the conditioned stimulus, or CS) that does not normally produce the response of interest and the unlearned natural stimulus (the unconditioned stimulus, or UCS), which automatically elicits the response (the unconditioned response, or UCR). Following this association, the CS will elicit a new learned response (the conditioned response, or CR).

3. *The two factors that can affect the strength of a classically conditioned response are* the frequency of the presentations of the two stimuli (the more frequently the CS and UCS are paired, the stronger the conditioning) and the timing of the stimulus presentations (the CS needs to be presented about a half-second before the UCS).

4. *The five other conditioning phenomena that Pavlov discovered were* stimulus generalization, the ability to respond to new stimuli that were similar to the CS; stimulus discrimination, the ability to distinguish between two stimuli, responding only to one stimulus but not to other, similar stimuli; higher order conditioning, in which a conditioned stimulus from one learning trial functions as the unconditioned stimulus in a new conditioning trial; extinction, the gradual weakening and apparent disappearance of the CR after repeated exposure to the CS alone (without the UCS); and spontaneous recovery, the reappearance of a previously extinguished conditioned response following a rest period when the CS is again presented.

From Pavlov to Watson: The Founding of Behaviorism

1. *Behaviorism was founded by* John B. Watson *and was defined as* the scientific study of observable behaviors, especially as they pertain to the process of learning.

2. *The fundamental assumptions of behaviorism as formulated by Watson are that* psychology is an objective experimental branch of natural science, the goals of which are the prediction and control of behavior; introspection and the study of consciousness are not part of scientific psychology; overt, observable, measurable behavior is the subject matter; and virtually all human behavior is a result of conditioning and learning.

3. *Watson identified three innate emotions, which are* fear, rage, and love, *each of which could be* reflexively triggered by a small number of specific stimuli. *With regard to these emotions, Watson showed that classical conditioning could be used to* deliberately establish a conditioned emotional response (i.e., a new learned response).

4. *Classical conditioning can be used to create a conditioned emotional response (CR) to a previously neutral stimulus by* pairing the neutral stimulus (now called the CS) with a stimulus (the UCS) that naturally and reflexively elicits the emotion in question (the UCR).

5. *The classical conditioning components in the Little Albert study were as follows: CS:* the sight of the white rat (initially neutral); *UCS:* the loud noise caused by clanging a steel bar; *UCR:* the fear experienced to the loud noise; *CR:* the fear experienced to the white rat after conditioning had taken place.

6. *Some people acquire classically conditioned responses to drugs such as caffeine, an active ingredient in coffee. In this example, the CS is* the sight, smell,, and/or taste of coffee; *the UCS is* the caffeine; *the UCR is* increased arousal and alertness elicited by the caffeine; *and the CR is* the increased arousal and alertness in response to the CS (sight, smell, and/or taste of coffee) following a number of pairings of the CS and UCS.

7. *A placebo response is* an individual's psychological and physiological response to what is actually a fake treatment or drug; it is also called the placebo effect.

Contemporary Views of Classical Conditioning

1. *According to the cognitive perspective, learning* involves mental processes as well as external events. *On the other hand, the traditional behavioral perspective holds that* conditioning results from a simple association of the CS and the UCS.

2. *In his research with rats, Robert Rescorla demonstrated that* classical conditioning involves cognitive processes such as learning the relationship between events, assessing the reliability of signals, and actively processing information about the predictive value of stimuli in the environment.

3. *According to the evolutionary perspective, bio*logical predispositions, shaped by evolution, affect the conditioning process. *This is because* animals have developed unique forms of behavior to adapt to their natural environment, and so some responses and behavioral patterns are more readily conditioned than others.

4. *Taste aversion is a* classically conditioned dislike for and avoidance of a particular food that develops when an organism becomes ill after eating the food. *Taste aversions violate two basic principles of classical conditioning:* first, conditioning requires only a single pairing of the CS and UCS, not multiple pairings; second, the time span between the CS and UCS can be several hours, not necessarily a matter of seconds, as Pavlov claimed.

5. *John Garcia demonstrated that taste aversions could be produced under controlled laboratory conditions by* pairing saccharin-flavored water (the CS) with a drug (the UCS), which produced illness (the UCR). *He found that* even though the interval between the presentation of the two stimuli was several hours, the rats developed a taste aversion (CR) to the CS and refused to drink the saccharin-flavored water.

6. *Biological preparedness refers to* the idea that organisms are innately predisposed to form associations between certain stimuli and responses.

Concept Check 1

1. behavioral; evolutionary
2. likely; unlikely
3. biological preparedness
4. cognitive
5. spontaneous recovery
6. discriminate
7. conditioned response (CR)
8. stimulus generalization
9. UCS; UCR; CR
10. placebo response (placebo effect)

Graphic Organizer 1

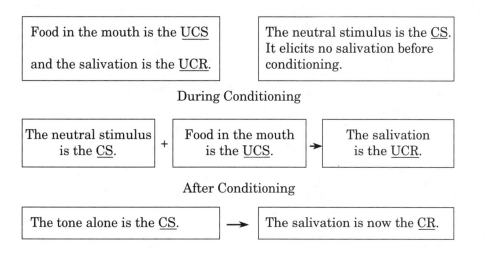

Before Conditioning

| Food in the mouth is the <u>UCS</u> and the salivation is the <u>UCR</u>. | The neutral stimulus is the <u>CS</u>. It elicits no salivation before conditioning. |

During Conditioning

| The neutral stimulus is the <u>CS</u>. | + | Food in the mouth is the <u>UCS</u>. | → | The salivation is the <u>UCR</u>. |

After Conditioning

| The tone alone is the <u>CS</u>. | → | The salivation is now the <u>CR</u>. |

Matching Exercise 1

1. extinction
2. conditioning
3. learning
4. taste aversion
5. behaviorism
6. John B. Watson
7. unconditioned stimulus (UCS)
8. Ivan Pavlov
9. unconditioned response (UCR)
10. biological preparedness
11. reflex
12. placebo response (placebo effect)

True/False Test 1

1. T	5. T	9. T
2. T	6. T	10. T
3. F	7. F	11. T
4. F	8. F	12. T

Operant Conditioning: Associating Behaviors and Consequences (Part 1)

1. *Edward L. Thorndike was the first person to* systematically study how voluntary behaviors are influenced by their consequences. *He concluded that* (according to his law of effect) animals use the process of trial and error, rather than reasoning, to acquire new behaviors and that behaviors followed by satisfying outcomes were "strengthened" (more likely to occur again), and behaviors followed by unpleasant consequences were "weakened" (less likely to occur).

2. *B. F. Skinner believed that* psychology should restrict itself to studying only outwardly observable behavior and environmental events that could be objectively measured and verified; that internal factors such as thoughts, expectations, and perceptions should not be included in psychology; and that the most important form of learning was demonstrated by new behaviors that were actively emitted by the organism (operants).

3. *Operant conditioning is* the basic learning process that involves changing the probability that a response will be repeated by manipulating the consequences of that response. *It explains* how we acquire everyday voluntary behaviors.

4. *The basic premise of operant conditioning is* that behavior is shaped and maintained by its consequences.

5. *Reinforcement refers to* the occurrence of a stimulus or event following a response that increases the likelihood of that response being repeated.

6. *Positive reinforcement involves* following an operant with a reinforcing stimulus, thus increasing the likelihood that the response will be repeated in similar situations. *Negative reinforcement involves* the removal of an aversive, punishing, or unpleasant stimulus from a situation, thereby increasing the likelihood that the behavior that brought about the removal of the stimulus will be repeated in similar situations

(can involve escape from, or avoidance of, the stimulus). *Negative and positive reinforcement are similar in that* they both increase the probability of the behavior occurring again. *They differ in that* positive reinforcement involves the addition of a reinforcing stimulus, and negative reinforcement involves the removal of, avoidance of, or escape from an aversive or punishing stimulus.

7. *A primary reinforcer is* one that is naturally reinforcing for a given species, *and a conditioned reinforcer (secondary reinforcer) is* one that has acquired reinforcing value by being associated with a primary reinforcer.

8. *Punishment is a* process in which a behavior is followed by an aversive consequence that decreases the occurrence of that behavior; it may involve punishment by application (of an aversive stimulus) or punishment by removal (of a reinforcing stimulus).

9. *The factors that influence the effectiveness of punishment are* the consistency and immediacy of the delivery of the punishment following the response. *The drawbacks of punishment are that* it doesn't teach the correct response, it may produce undesirable results, and its effects are likely to be temporary.

10. *Discriminative stimuli are* specific stimuli in the presence of which a particular response is more likely to be reinforced, and in the absence of which a particular response is not reinforced. *According to Skinner, they are important because* behavior is determined and controlled by the stimuli that are present in a given situation (discriminative stimuli) and not by personal choice or conscious decisions.

Concept Check 2

1. law of effect
2. punishment by application; negative reinforcement
3. positively; negatively
4. Edward L. Thorndike
5. (a) avoidance
   (b) escape
   (c) avoidance
   (d) escape
6. (a) NR   (e) P/A
   (b) P/A   (f) NR
   (c) P/R   (g) NR
   (d) P/A
7. discriminative stimulus

Graphic Organizer 2

	Appetitive Stimuli (e.g., food, water)	Aversive Stimuli (e.g., shock)
The operant response is followed by . . .	**Cell 1** FOOD ↑ This is called <u>positive reinforcement</u>	**Cell 2** SHOCK ↓ This is called <u>punishment by application</u>
The operant response precludes or prevents the delivery of . . .	**Cell 3** FOOD ↓ This is called <u>punishment by removal</u>	**Cell 4** SHOCK ↑ This is called <u>negative reinforcement</u>

Matching Exercise 2

1. B. F. Skinner
2. negative reinforcement
3. Edward L. Thorndike
4. punishment
5. conditioned reinforcer
6. reinforcement
7. operant
8. discriminative stimulus
9. escape behavior

True/False Test 2

1. T	3. T	5. T	7. T
2. F	4. F	6. T	8. T

Operant Conditioning: Associating Behaviors and Consequences (Part 2)

1. *Shaping involves* reinforcing successively closer approximations of a behavior until the correct behavior is displayed; it works by allowing the animal to gradually learn the correct response by making reinforcement dependent on getting closer and closer to the target behavior with each attempt.

2. *Partial reinforcement is more effective than continuous reinforcement because it* makes the target behavior more resistant to extinction than behavior that has been continuously reinforced (called the partial reinforcement effect).

3. *The four basic schedules of reinforcement are* fixed-ratio (FR), in which a fixed number of responses are required for reinforcement; variable-ratio (VR), in which an average number of responses, which varies from trial to trial, are needed for reinforcement; fixed-interval (FI), in which a reinforcer is delivered for the first response after a preset amount of time; and variable-interval (VI), in which a reinforcer is delivered for the first response after an average, and unpredictable, amount of time.

4. *Behavior modification is* the application of learning principles to help people develop more effective or adaptive behaviors; it has been used in such diverse situations as reducing public smoking by teenagers, improving student behavior in school cafeterias, reducing tantrums in preschool children, improving social skills and reducing self-destructive behaviors in people with autism and related disorders, increasing productivity in employees, and training animals to help the physically challenged.

Concept Check 3

1. variable-interval (VI)
2. fixed-interval (FI)
3. fixed-ratio (FR)
4. shaping
5. variable-ratio (VR)
6. fixed-ratio (FR)

Graphic Organizer 3

	Based on the number of responses made	Based on the elapsed time
Fixed	Cell 1 Fixed ratio	Cell 2 Fixed interval
Variable	Cell 3 Variable ratio	Cell 4 Variable interval

Matching Exercise 3

1. behavior modification
2. continuous reinforcement
3. operant chamber (Skinner box)
4. fixed-ratio (FR) schedule
5. shaping
6. fixed-interval (FI) schedule

True/False Test 3

1. T	3. F	5. T
2. F	4. F	6. T

Contemporary Views of Operant Conditioning

1. *Contemporary learning researchers confirm the basic principles of operant conditioning but also acknowledge* the importance of both cognitive factors and natural behavior patterns in operant conditioning.

2. *Unlike Skinner and Thorndike, Tolman believed that* cognitive processes played an important role in the learning of complex behavior, and he demonstrated their importance with his research on cognitive maps and latent learning.

3. *A cognitive map is* Tolman's term for the mental representation of the layout of a familiar environment. *Latent learning is* Tolman's term for learning that occurs in the absence of reinforcement but is not demonstrated in overt behavior until a reinforcer becomes available.

4. *Learned helplessness demonstrates the role of cognitive factors in learning in that* this behavior reflects a cognitive expectation that the organism cannot avoid the painful stimulus, no matter what it does to avoid or escape it. Exposure to inescapable and uncontrollable aversive events produces passive behavior.

5. *Operant conditioning may also be influenced by* biological predispositions to perform natural, or instinctive, behaviors that can interfere with the performance of an operantly conditioned response, a tendency called instinctive drift.

6. *The phenomenon of instinctive drift challenged the traditional behavioral view by* demonstrating that reinforcement is not the sole determinant of behavior and that instinctive behavior patterns can interfere with the operant conditioning of arbitrary responses.

Observational Learning: Imitating the Actions of Others

1. *Observational learning is* learning that occurs through observing the action of others. *The person most strongly identified with work in this area is* Albert Bandura.

2. *The four cognitive processes that interact to determine if imitation will occur are* attention (you must pay attention to the model), memory (you must remember the model's behavior), motor skills (you must be able to transform the mental representation into actions that you are capable of reproducing), and motivation (you must have some expectation of the outcome of your imitation of the behavior).

3. *Observational learning has been applied in a variety of settings, including* education, vocational and job training, psychotherapy, and counseling. It has also been used effectively in entertainment–education programs to promote healthy behaviors and social change.

Concept Check 4

1. observational
2. cognitive
3. likely
4. instinctive drift
5. observational

Matching Exercise 4

1. observational learning
2. latent learning
3. Edward C. Tolman
4. cognitive map
5. Albert Bandura
6. instinctive drift
7. learned helplessness
8. mirror neurons

Something to Think About

1. The first assumption that someone who adheres to the behavioral perspective would make is that the irrational fear, or phobia, was the result of a classical conditioning process. In the past, the client had had a very unpleasant experience at a dentist's office. One could speculate that as a child he was taken to the dentist and experienced pain and fear when a hypodermic needle was inserted into his gum or a drill struck a nerve. If this were the case, the dentist (CS) has become associated with the needle or drill (UCS), which elicited pain and fear (UCR). The dentist (CS) now evokes a fear response (CR), which may have generalized to all dentists.

   One way to get rid of the irrational fear would be to use an extinction procedure in which the CS (the dentist) is presented over and over without the UCS until the fear subsides. This might mean that the client will have to find a very understanding dentist who will allow him to make many visits to the office without having any work done. The behavioral perspective predicts that this would eventually result in a reduction of the irrational fear and therefore allow the client to get some much-needed dental work done. It would also be important to point out that following a prolonged absence from the dentist, spontaneous recovery may occur.

2. It is possible that Mrs. Denton's "scolding" may in fact be reinforcing the undesirable behavior. Attention, in almost any form, from an adult can be a powerful positive reinforcer for a child. If this is the case, then withholding reinforcement (scolding) will tend to extinguish the target behavior, but only if it is consistent. Inconsistent or intermittent reinforcement will make the behavior very resistant to extinction.

   In addition, she should encourage desirable behavior. She should pay attention to any instance of good behavior, or any close approximation of the goal behavior, by praising her son or providing some other positive reinforcer. In other words, she should use a shaping procedure initially, then use partial reinforcement to ensure that the desirable behavior becomes resistant to extinction. It is also important that she model the appropriate behavior and avoid punishing the child, especially using punishment by application.

3. Operant conditioning techniques can be used to train animals. Decide on the target behavior(s) and start by using a shaping procedure and continuous positive reinforcement. Pick one of the behaviors you want to train—for example, having the dog sit at the command "sit"—and use a reinforcer such as "good dog!" while patting the dog on the head or rubbing his chest. The command "sit" should be followed with gentle pressure on the dog's rear end to make him sit; he should be reinforced immediately. After just a few trials, the dog will sit on command without the application of pressure to his back; he should always be immediately reinforced. It is important to let the dog know who is in command at all times without using punishment. After the dog is obeying the commands regularly, then switch to a partial reinforcement schedule, only occasionally reinforcing the dog for obeying. This will ensure greater resistance to extinction. Dogs can be trained to do many tricks in this manner, but remember to work with the animal's natural repertoire of behaviors (biological predispositions). Dogs can learn some behaviors more easily than others.

Progress Test 1

1. c	6. a	11. c
2. d	7. b	12. b
3. d	8. a	13. a
4. b	9. c	14. c
5. a	10. a	15. a

Progress Test 2

1. a	6. b	11. a
2. b	7. a	12. d
3. b	8. b	13. e
4. c	9. c	14. d
5. b	10. a	15. b

Progress Test 3

1. d	6. a	11. d
2. c	7. d	12. c
3. d	8. a	13. a
4. c	9. a	14. c
5. a	10. d	15. d

CHAPTER 6

Memory

PREVIEW   Reading the section below first will give you a general sense of the chapter's contents and an initial introduction to some of the major concepts and terms. This will prime you for what you are about to read and help you to develop a "cognitive map" that will guide your study of the material in this chapter. Likewise, reading the **preview questions** at the beginning of each major section will improve your ability to understand, learn, and retain the information.

CHAPTER 6 . . . AT A GLANCE   Chapter 6 examines memory and the mechanisms involved in remembering and forgetting. The first section begins with the fundamental processes of encoding, storage, and retrieval, followed by a discussion of sensory memory, short-term memory, and long-term memory.

Short-term memory provides temporary storage for information transferred from sensory memory and from long-term memory; its effectiveness can be improved by maintenance rehearsal and chunking. The three components of Baddeley's model of working memory (the part of short-term memory involving active manipulation of information) are explained.

Elaborative rehearsal and the three categories of information stored in long-term memory are explained. Explicit and implicit memory are then explored, and the ways in which information is organized in long-term memory are discussed.

How retrieval works and the problems associated with retrieval failure are examined. The serial position effect, the encoding specificity principle, and flashbulb memories all contribute to our ability to remember, or not remember, and these topics are explored next.

Retrieval failure (forgetting) and theories of forgetting (encoding failure, divided attention, decay of memory traces, retroactive and proactive interference, suppression and repression) are covered in this section. Following this is a discussion of the constructive nature of memory and how the misinformation effect, source confusion, schemas, scripts, and imagination inflation all contribute to errors, distortions, and false memories.

Finally, the biological basis of memory is explained and the contributions of empirical research and case studies of people with amnesia are presented. The chapter ends with an examination of the role in memory played by several brain structures. The Application presents several effective strategies for improving memory.

What Is Memory?

Preview Questions

Consider the following questions as you study this section of the chapter.

- How is memory defined?
- What are encoding, storage, and retrieval?
- What is the stage model of memory, and what are the characteristics of the three stages?
- How do the stages interact?

Read the section "What Is Memory?" and **write** *your answers to the following:*

1. Memory refers to _____

   _____

   _____

2. Encoding is the process of _____

   _____

   Storage is the process of _____

   _____

   Retrieval is the process of _____

   _____

3. The stage model of memory describes memory

   as _____

   _____

   _____

   _____

4. The three stages interact by _____

   _____

   _____

   _____

Sensory Memory: Fleeting Impressions of the World

Preview Questions

Consider the following questions as you study this section of the chapter.

- How long is information from the environment held in sensory memory?
- How did Sperling's experiment establish the duration of visual sensory memory?
- What are the functions of sensory memory?

Read the section "Sensory Memory: Fleeting Impressions of the World" and **write** *your answers to the following:*

1. Information is held in sensory memory for

   _____

2. Sperling's classic experiment demonstrated

   _____

   _____

   _____

3. An important function of sensory memory (iconic and echoic) is _____

   _____

   _____

Short-Term, Working Memory: The Workshop of Consciousness

Preview Questions

Consider the following questions as you study this section of the chapter.

- What is the main function of short-term memory?
- What are the duration and capacity of short-term memory?
- How do we overcome the limitations of short-term memory?
- What is working memory, and what are the three components of Baddeley's model?

Read the section "Short-Term, Working Memory: The Workshop of Consciousness" and **write** *your answers to the following:*

1. Short-term memory is the stage of memory in

   which _____

   _____

2. The duration of short-term memory is _____

   _____

3. The capacity of short-term memory is _____

   _____

   It can be increased by _____

   _____

   _____

4. Working memory is _____

_____

5. The three components of Baddeley's model of working memory are _____

_____

_____

_____

_____

Long-Term Memory

Preview Questions

Consider the following questions as you study this section of the chapter.

- How much information can be stored in long-term memory?
- What factors increase the efficiency of encoding?
- What are the characteristics of procedural, episodic, and semantic memory?
- What is the difference between explicit memory and implicit memory?
- How is information organized in long-term memory, and what is one of the best-known models of organization?

Read the section "Long-Term Memory" and **write** *your answers to the following:*

1. The amount of information that can be held in long-term memory is _____

2. Three ways to increase the efficiency of encoding are _____

_____

_____

3. Procedural memory refers to _____

_____

Episodic memory refers to _____

_____

Semantic memory refers to _____

_____

4. Explicit memory is _____

_____

Implicit memory is _____

_____

5. Information is organized in long-term memory by _____

_____

6. The best-known model of how information is organized in memory is _____

_____

which describes long-term memory as _____

_____

_____

After you have carefully studied the preceding sections, complete the following exercises.

Concept Check 1

Read the following and write the correct term in the space provided.

1. During a math exam, Trevor is desperately trying to think of the correct formula for the area of a triangle. Although he knew the formula when he was studying last week, it just won't come to mind, despite all his efforts. Trevor is experiencing trouble with one of the three fundamental processes of memory, called

_____ .

2. To help learn the number of days in each month, 8-year-old Gloria has been reciting a short rhyme over and over: "Thirty days hath September, April, June, and November; all the rest have thirty-one excepting February alone; and that has twenty-eight days clear; and twenty-nine in each leap year." She is using the fundamental process of _____ to transform the information into a form that can be entered and retained by the memory system.

3. In the above example, Gloria is using a type of rehearsal that is giving some meaning to an otherwise hard-to-remember string of numbers; this is called _____ rehearsal.

4. After looking up a phone number, Alysha is able to remember it only long enough to press all the correct numbers on the keypad. The phone number is in her _____ memory and is briefly stored there by the use of _____ rehearsal.

5. Vito is an excellent chess player and can easily recall the exact positions of most of the chess pieces after a brief glance at the board. He explains his ability by pointing out that he does not try to memorize the locations of all the individual pieces but instead focuses on their relatively few attack patterns. Vito is using _____ to improve the capacity of his short-term memory.

6. Fifty-five-year-old Mr. Adams puts on roller skates for the first time in over 40 years; much to his surprise, he has no trouble remembering how to skate. In this instance, Mr. Adams is using one of the three categories of long-term memory, called _____ memory.

7. When Stephan was consciously reviewing the information he had researched for a term paper, he was using a dimension of long-term memory called _____ (or declarative memory); later, when he was typing his paper without conscious awareness of the exact layout of the letters on the keyboard, he was using _____ (or nondeclarative memory).

8. During an interview about his military accomplishments, General Rooyakkers described specific wartime episodes in which he was directly involved. He went on to reminisce about events in his early life that eventually led him to a career in the army. In the first instance, he was using _____ memory to recall the time and place of wartime events; in the second case, he was using _____ memory to recall his personal life history.

Review of Terms, Concepts, and Names 1

Use the terms in this list to complete the Matching Test, then to help you answer the True/False items correctly.

memory	visuospatial sketchpad
encoding	central executive
storage	elaborative rehearsal
retrieval	self-reference effect
stage model of memory	visual imagery
sensory memory	procedural memory
short-term memory	episodic memory
long-term memory	autobiographical
George Sperling	memory
visual sensory memory	semantic memory
(iconic memory)	explicit memory
auditory sensory	(declarative memory)
memory	implicit memory
(echoic memory)	(nondeclarative
maintenance rehearsal	memory)
chunking	clustering
working memory	association
phonological loop	semantic network model

Matching Exercise

Match the appropriate term/name with its definition or description.

1. _____ Rehearsal that involves focusing on the meaning of information to help encode and transfer it to long-term memory.

2. _____ Model that describes units of information in long-term memory as being organized in a complex network of associations.

3. _____ The process of recovering information stored in memory so that we are consciously aware of it.

4. _____ Organizing items into related groups during recall from long-term memory.

5. _____ The use of mental representations, or pictures, especially vivid ones, to enhance encoding.

6. _____ Active stage of memory in which information is stored for about 20 seconds.

7. _____ Category of long-term memory that includes memories of particular events.

8. _____ The process of transforming information into a form that can be entered into and retained by the memory system.

9. _____ Model that describes memory as consisting of three distinct stages: sensory

memory, short-term memory, and long-term memory.

10. _____ The mental processes that enable us to acquire, retain, and use information over time.

11. _____ Category of long-term memory that includes memories of different skills, operations, and actions.

12. _____ American psychologist who identified the duration of visual sensory memory in a series of classic experiments in 1960.

13. _____ Memory that is closely related to episodic memory and involves memories of events in our lives and our personal life history.

14. _____ Short-term memory system involved in the temporary storage and active manipulation of information that has three main components capable of operating independently of each other.

15. _____ Component of Baddeley's working memory that initiates retrieval and decision processes, integrates information, controls attention, and manages the activities of the other two components.

True/False Test

Indicate whether each statement is true or false by placing T or F in the blank space next to each item.

1. ____ Information or knowledge that can be consciously recollected is called implicit, or nondeclarative, memory.

2. ____ Auditory sensory memory is sometimes referred to as iconic memory because it is a brief memory of an image, or icon.

3. ____ Applying information to yourself to help you remember that information is called the self-reference effect.

4. ____ Semantic memory is the category of long-term memory that includes memories of general knowledge of facts, names, and concepts.

5. ____ When people are presented with the stimulus word *salt*, they frequently respond with the word *pepper,* this suggests that there is some logical association between bits of information in long-term memory.

6. ____ Storage is the process of retaining information in memory so that it can be used at a later time.

7. ____ Sensory memory is the stage of memory that registers information from the environment and holds it for a very brief period of time.

8. ____ Maintenance rehearsal involves the mental or verbal repetition of information in order to maintain it beyond the usual 20-second duration of short-term memory.

9. ____ Increasing the amount of information that can be held in short-term memory by grouping related items together as a single unit is called chunking.

10. ____ Visual sensory memory is sometimes referred to as echoic memory, because it is a brief memory that is like an echo.

11. ____ Information or knowledge that affects behavior or task performance but cannot be consciously recollected is called explicit, or declarative, memory.

12. ____ Long-term memory is the stage of memory that represents the storage of information over extended periods of time.

13. ____ The phonological loop is the component of Baddeley's working memory that is specialized for spatial or visual material.

14. ____ The visuospatial sketchpad is the component of Baddeley's working memory that is specialized for verbal material.

Check your answers and review any areas of weakness before going on to the next section.

Retrieval: Getting Information from Long-Term Memory

Preview Questions

Consider the following questions as you study this section of the chapter.

- How is retrieval defined, and what is a retrieval cue?

- What does the TOT experience tell us about the nature of memory?

- How is retrieval tested, and what is the serial position effect?

- What is the encoding specificity principle, and how is it reflected in context effects and mood congruence?

- What role does distinctiveness play in retrieval, and how accurate are flashbulb memories?

Read the section "Retrieval: Getting Information from Long-Term Memory" and **write** *your answers to the following:*

1. Retrieval refers to _____

   _____

   A retrieval cue is _____

   _____

   Retrieval cue failure refers to _____

   _____

2. The tip-of-the-tongue (TOT) experience is

   _____

   _____

   It illustrates the fact that _____

   _____

   _____

   _____

3. Retrieval is tested by _____

   _____

   _____

   _____

4. The serial position effect is _____

   _____

   _____

5. The encoding specificity principle states that

   _____

   _____

6. The context effect, an encoding specificity phenomenon, refers to _____

   _____

   _____

   Mood congruence, another example of encoding specificity, refers to _____

   _____

7. Distinctiveness plays a role in retrieval because

   _____

   _____

8. A flashbulb memory is _____

   _____

After you have carefully studied the preceding sections, complete the following exercises.

Concept Check 2

Read the following and write the correct term in the space provided.

1. When Cathy feels depressed, she remembers certain sad childhood events that she otherwise never thinks about. Cathy is experiencing the effects of _____ .

2. Hendrik vividly remembers exactly what he was doing when he felt the vibrations of the earthquake shake his house. This example illustrates a _____ memory.

3. Although Jessie cannot remember the newer name of the small Central American country that was formerly called British Honduras, she has the distinct feeling that she knows the name. Jessie is experiencing a memory phenomenon called the _____ .

4. When Jessie is told that the name of the country starts with the letter B she quickly remembers the name. The letter B acts as a _____ for the name *Belize*.

5. Professor Patheiger's exams consist of both multiple-choice questions and short essay questions. The multiple-choice questions involve retrieval that requires _____ , whereas the short essay questions measure the ability to _____ information from long-term memory.

6. Research subjects memorized long lists of words while in a room full of fresh flowers. Later, half the subjects were tested in the same room, and half were tested in a room with no flowers. Those tested in the same room recalled significantly more words than those in the different room. This is one form of the _____ principle, called the _____ .

7. When Beata was given a free recall test of a list of 20 words, she recalled words from the beginning and end of the list more easily than those in the middle of the list. The tendency to remember the first items is called the _____ , and the tendency to remember the final items is called the _____ .

8. The pattern of responses in the above example is called the _____ .

Graphic Organizer 1

Read the definitions and fill in the correct term next to the appropriate number in the puzzle below (items 1–6). When you have finished, the letters in the boxes will spell a significant memory term. Write out the definition of this term (item 7).

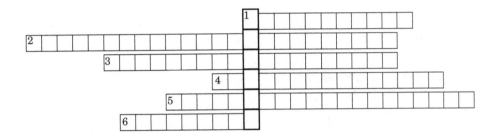

1. A test of long-term memory that involves identifying correct information out of several possible choices.

2. A memory phenomenon that involves the sensation of knowing that specific information is stored in long-term memory but being temporarily unable to retrieve it.

3. The inability to recall long-term memories because of inadequate or missing retrieval cues.

4. The recall of very specific images or details surrounding a vivid, rare, or significant personal event.

5. The tendency to remember items at the beginning and end of a list better than the items in the middle.

6. The process of accessing stored information.

7. Write the definition of the memory term:

_____

_____

Review of Terms, Concepts, and Names 2

Use the terms in this list to complete the Matching Test, then to help you answer the True/False items correctly.

retrieval
retrieval cue
retrieval cue failure
tip-of-the-tongue (TOT) experience
recall (free recall)
cued recall
recognition
serial position effect

primacy effect
recency effect
serial recall
encoding specificity principle
context effect
mood congruence
distinctiveness
flashbulb memory

Matching Exercise

Match the appropriate term with its definition or description.

1. _____ Tendency to recover information more easily when the retrieval occurs in the same setting as the original learning of the information.

2. _____ The process of accessing stored information.

3. _____ Recall of very specific images or details surrounding a vivid, rare, or significant personal event.

4. _____ The tendency to remember items at the beginning and end of a list better than items in the middle.

5. _____ Test of long-term memory that involves remembering an item of information in response to a retrieval cue.

6. _____ Clue, prompt, or hint that helps trigger recall of a given piece of information stored in long-term memory.

7. _____ Encoding specificity phenomenon in which a given mood tends to evoke memories that are consistent with that mood.

8. _____ Principle that when the conditions of information retrieval are similar to the conditions of information encoding, retrieval is more likely to be successful.

True/False Test

Indicate whether each statement is true or false by placing T or F in the blank space next to each item.

1. ____ The primacy effect refers to the tendency to recall the final items in a list during serial recall.

2. ___ A test of long-term memory that involves retrieving information without the aid of retrieval cues is called recall, or free recall.

3. ___ The tip-of-the-tongue (TOT) experience involves the sensation of knowing that specific information is stored in long-term memory but being temporarily unable to retrieve it.

4. ___ Serial recall refers to remembering a list of items in their original order.

5. ___ When the encoded information represents a unique, different, or unusual memory, it is said to be characterized by a high degree of distinctiveness.

6. ___ The inability to recall long-term memories because of inadequate or missing retrieval cues is called retrieval cue failure.

7. ___ The recency effect refers to the tendency to recall the first items in a list during serial recall.

8. ___ Recognition refers to a test of long-term memory that involves identifying correct information from several possible choices.

Check your answers and review any areas of weakness before going on to the next section.

Forgetting: When Retrieval Fails

Preview Questions

Consider the following questions as you study this section of the chapter.

- How is forgetting defined?
- What did Ebbinghaus contribute to the study of forgetting?
- What are encoding failure, prospective memory, decay theory, and interference theory, and how do they contribute to forgetting?
- What is motivated forgetting (suppression and repression), and why is this topic controversial?

Read the section "Forgetting: When Retrieval Fails" and **write** *your answers to the following:*

1. Forgetting is the _____

   _____

2. The Ebbinghaus forgetting curve reveals two distinctive patterns about forgetting:

   (a) _____

   _____

   (b) _____

   _____

3. Encoding failure refers to _____

   _____

   It may contribute to _____

4. Prospective memory is _____

   _____

   Prospective memory failure may be due to ____

   _____

   _____

5. According to decay theory _____

   _____

   _____

6. Interference theory is the theory that _____

   _____

   The two basic types of interference affect memory in the following ways: _____

   _____

   _____

7. Motivated forgetting refers to the idea that __

   _____

   _____

   There are two forms of motivated forgetting:

   _____

   _____

8. Motivated forgetting is a controversial topic

   because _____

   _____

   _____

Imperfect Memories: Errors, Distortions, and False Memories

Preview Questions

Consider the following questions as you study this section of the chapter.

- Why do errors and distortions in memory occur during the process of retrieval?

- What are the misinformation effect and source confusion, and how can they distort memories?
- What are schemas and scripts, and how can they contribute to memory distortions?
- What techniques can create false memories for events that never happened?
- How does imagination inflation contribute to the formation of false memories?

Read the section "Reconstructing Memories: Sources of Potential Errors" and **write** *your answers to the following:*

1. Errors and distortions occur during the process of retrieval because _____

   _____

   _____

   _____

2. The misinformation effect (one phenomenon that can reduce the accuracy of eyewitness testimony) refers to _____

   _____

   _____

3. Source confusion is _____

   _____

   _____

4. A false memory is _____

   _____

5. A schema is _____

   _____

   Research has demonstrated that _____

   _____

   _____

   _____

6. A script is _____

   _____

   _____

7. The lost-in-the-mall technique is _____

   _____

   _____

   _____

   It demonstrates that _____

   _____

   _____

   _____

8. Imagination inflation is _____

   _____

   _____

   _____

   _____

After you have carefully studied the preceding sections, complete the following exercises.

Concept Check 3

Read the following and write the correct term in the space provided.

1. When he first moved to his new apartment, Adam could not remember his new phone number; instead, he would give people his old phone number. Adam's inability to remember his new number is due to _____ interference.

2. At a recent orientation meeting, Juan was introduced to five of the company's directors; much to his embarrassment, after a short while he could not remember their names. Juan's memory lapse is probably due to

   _____ .

3. Later that night, while thinking about his embarrassment at the meeting, Juan decided that because it was normal to forget names under such circumstances, he was just not going to think about it any more. Juan is using a form of motivated forgetting called

   _____ .

4. When Mr. Melvin questioned a witness, he deliberately kept referring to the murder weapon as a large pair of scissors instead of garden shears. When the witness was later asked to identify the garden shears as the murder weapon, he appeared slightly confused and said that he believed the weapon was a large pair of scissors. Mr. Melvin had successfully used the _____ .

5. Giselle planned to return the library book before the due date but forgot to do so. Her inability to remember to do what she had planned is an example of prospective memory failure and was probably caused by

_____ .

6. Jackson has just finished a course in Spanish and is having problems remembering the Italian he learned last semester. Jackson's memory problem is a result of _____ interference.

7. Cecil parked his car on the fifth floor of the parking garage; with flowers, chocolates, and magazines in hand he made his way to the hospital ward to visit his wife. When he was ready to go home, he could not remember where he had parked his car. This type of forgetting (resulting from divided attention) is called _____ and is probably due to _____ failure.

8. Mrs. Gerber's first phone was a rotary dial telephone. Now she uses a state-of-the-art cell phone with all the latest features. Most likely, Mrs. Gerber's _____ for "telephone" has been changed to integrate all these recent technological innovations.

9. During one phase of an experiment a participant is encouraged to actively envision shaking hands with Bugs Bunny during a childhood visit to Disneyland. When asked about her visit to Disneyland later in the experiment she was quite confident that she had met Bugs Bunny and shaken his hand (an event that never actually happened). This example illustrates an effect called _____ .

10. Ferdie promised to phone his girlfriend during the class break. Because he was distracted, he did not remember to call her. This example most clearly illustrates a failure in _____ memory.

Graphic Organizer 2

Use the following to review forgetting due to interference in the test phase. Write in the type of interference that is responsible for forgetting in the test phase.

Memorizing Phase	Test Phase	Type of Interference
1. Learn A first; later learn B	Test A	
2. Learn A first; later learn B	Test B	

Review of Terms, Concepts, and Names 3

Use the terms in this list to complete the Matching Test, then to help you answer the True/False items correctly.

forgetting
Hermann Ebbinghaus
nonsense syllable
forgetting curve
encoding failure
absent-mindedness
prospective memory
déjà vu
source memory (source
   monitoring)
decay theory
interference theory
retroactive interference
proactive interference

motivated forgetting
suppression
repression
psychoanalysis
Elizabeth Loftus
misinformation effect
source confusion
false memory
schema
script
pseudoevent
lost-in-the-mall
   technique
imagination inflation

Matching Exercise

Match the appropriate term/name with its definition or description.

1. _____ Motivated forgetting that occurs consciously.

2. _____ The inability to recall information previously available.

3. _____ Theory that forgetting is due to normal metabolic processes that occur in the brain over time.

4. _____ Motivated forgetting that occurs unconsciously.

5. _____ The theory that forgetting is caused by one memory competing with or replacing another.

6. _____ German psychologist who originated the scientific study of forgetting and plotted the first forgetting curve, which describes the basic pattern of forgetting learned information over time.

7. _____ Inability to recall specific information because of insufficient encoding of the information for storage in long-term memory.

8. _____ Organized cluster of information about a particular topic.

9. _____ Research strategy of using information from family members to help create or induce false memories of childhood experiences.

10. _____ American psychologist who has conducted extensive research on the memory distortions that can occur in eyewitness testimony.

11. _____ Memory distortion phenomenon in which a person's existing memories can be altered if the person is exposed to misleading information.

12. _____ Memory failure that occurs when attention is divided and the relevant information is not encoded.

13. _____ Remembering to do something in the future.

True/False Test

Indicate whether each statement is true or false by placing T or F in the space next to each item.

1. ____ Déjà vu is a brief but intense feeling of remembering a scene or an event that is actually being experienced for the first time.

2. ____ With retroactive interference, an old memory interferes with remembering a new memory; forward-acting memory interference.

3. ____ Motivated forgetting refers to the idea that we forget because a memory is unpleasant or disturbing.

4. ____ A distorted or inaccurate memory that feels completely real and is often accompanied by all the emotional impact of a real memory is called a false memory.

5. ____ Imagination inflation refers to a memory phenomenon in which vividly imagining an event markedly increases confidence that the event actually occurred.

6. ____ Hermann Ebbinghaus used nonsense syllables to study memory and forgetting of completely new material, and to avoid the potential bias of using words that had preexisting associations in memory.

7. ____ Proactive interference is forgetting in which a new memory interferes with remembering an old memory; backward-acting memory interference.

8. ____ Source memory (source monitoring) refers to a memory distortion that occurs when the true source of the memory is forgotten.

9. ____ The forgetting curve reveals two distinct patterns in the relationship between forgetting and the passage of time; much of what is learned is forgotten relatively quickly, and the amount of forgetting eventually levels off.

10. ___ A pseudoevent is an event that never really happened and is used in memory research to induce inaccurate or false childhood memories.

11. ___ A script is a schema for the typical sequence of actions and behaviors involved in an everyday event.

12. ___ Sigmund Freud's famous theory of personality and psychotherapy is called psychoanalysis.

13. ___ Source confusion refers to our ability to remember the original details or features of a memory, including when, where, and how a particular piece of information was acquired.

Check your answers and review any areas of weakness before going on to the next section.

The Search for the Biological Basis of Memory

Preview Questions

Consider the following questions as you study this section of the chapter.

- How did research by Karl Lashley and Richard Thompson contribute to our understanding of the physical basis of memory?

- How do neurons change when a memory is formed?

- What did Eric Kandel's research demonstrate, and what is long-term potentiation?

- What is amnesia, and how have case studies of people with retrograde and anterograde amnesia provided important insights into the brain structures involved in memory?

- What brain structures are involved in normal memory, and what roles do they play?

- What are dementia and Alzheimer's disease (AD)?

*Read the section "The Search for the Biological Basis of Memory" and **write** your answers to the following:*

1. Lashley and Thompson contributed to our understanding of the physical basis of memory by _____

_____

_____

2. When a new memory is formed, neurons change in two ways: _____

_____

3. Eric Kandel showed that _____

_____

_____

_____

Long-term potentiation refers to _____

_____

_____

4. Amnesia refers to _____

_____

Retrograde amnesia is _____

_____

_____

Anterograde amnesia is _____

_____

_____

5. Research with patients such as H.M. has enabled investigators to _____

_____

_____

_____

6. The brain structures (and their functions) involved in normal memory are _____

_____

_____

_____

_____

_____

_____

7. Dementia is the _____

_____

_____

Alzheimer's disease (AD) is a _____

_____

_____

After you have carefully studied the preceding sections, complete the following exercises.

Concept Check 4

Read the following and write the correct term in the space provided.

1. Bruno, who was knocked out in his last boxing match, cannot remember anything about the fight or events that happened before the bout. Bruno is most likely suffering from a form of amnesia called _____ amnesia.

2. Bruno's inability to remember details of events that happened before the knockout blow was most likely caused by the disruption of the process of _____ .

3. Mrs. O'Meara, whose hippocampus was removed during a recent brain operation, is most likely to have trouble forming _____ (short-term/long-term) memories.

4. After many training trials, Pookie the dog will now sit on her hind legs and "beg" for food. Learning this new behavior has probably involved functional and structural neuronal changes in her brain that are collectively called _____ .

5. Mr. Usselman has been diagnosed with a condition characterized by impairment of memory and intellectual functions. He is likely suffering from _____ , a condition most often caused by _____ .

6. MRI images of Mr. Usselman's brain are likely to show an abundance of _____ , which are dense deposits of proteins and other cell materials outside and around the neurons, and _____ , which are twisted fibers that build up inside the neuron.

7. Reiner suffers from anterograde amnesia and has virtually no new memories (episodic or semantic) since a tumor destroyed his hippocampus. However, just like H.M., he is able to learn the procedures involved in solving certain puzzles, which suggests that he can form new _____ memories. His lack of conscious awareness of his new ability indicates that these memories are _____ memories.

Review of Terms, Concepts, and Names 4

Use the terms in this list to complete the Matching Test, then to help you answer the True/False items correctly.

Karl Lashley
memory trace (engram)
cerebral cortex
Richard F. Thompson
cerebellum
Eric Kandel
long-term potentiation
amnesia
retrograde amnesia
memory consolidation
anterograde amnesia
hippocampus

Brenda Milner
Suzanne Corkin
amygdala
frontal lobes
prefrontal cortex
medial temporal lobes
dementia
Alzheimer's disease (AD)
beta-amyloid plaques
  and neurofibrillary
  tangles

Matching Exercise

Match the appropriate term/name with its definition or description.

1. _____ Outermost covering of the brain that contains the most sophisticated brain areas.

2. _____ American physiological psychologist who attempted to find the specific brain location of particular memories.

3. _____ The brain changes associated with a particular stored memory.

4. _____ Severe memory loss.

5. _____ American psychologist and neuroscientist who conducted extensive research on the neurobiological foundations of learning and memory.

6. _____ The gradual, physical process of converting new long-term memories to stable, enduring long-term memory codes.

7. _____ Long-lasting increase in synaptic strength between two neurons.

8. _____ A lower-brain structure involved in classically conditioned simple reflexes, procedural memories, and motor skill memories.

9. _____ A brain structure that plays an important role in working memory.

10. _____ American neurobiologist, born in Austria, who won the Nobel Prize in 2000 for his work on the neural basis of learning and memory in the sea snail *Aplysia*.

11. _____ Canadian neuropsychologist whose groundbreaking research on the role of brain structures and functions in cognitive processes helped establish neuropsychology as a field; extensively studied the famous amnesia patient, H.M.

True/False Test

Indicate whether each statement is true or false by placing T or F in the space next to each item.

1. ____ Anterograde amnesia is the loss of memory, especially for episodic information; backward-acting amnesia.

2. ____ Suzanne Corkin is an American neuropsychologist who has extensively investigated the neural basis of memory, including studying the famous amnesia patient H.M.

3. ____ Beta-amyloid plaques are dense deposits of protein and other cell materials outside and around neurons, and neurofibrillary tangles are twisted fibers that build up inside the neuron.

4. ____ The frontal lobes are involved in retrieving and organizing information that is associated with autobiographical and episodic memories.

5. ____ Retrograde amnesia is the loss of memory caused by the inability to store new memories; forward-acting amnesia.

6. ____ Damage or destruction of the hippocampus can affect the ability to transfer short-term memories into long-term memories.

7. ____ The amygdala is involved in encoding and storing the emotional qualities associated with particular memories.

8. ____ Dementia is a condition characterized by impairment of memory and intellectual functions.

9. ____ The medial temporal lobes are involved in encoding complex memories by forming links among pieces of information stored in multiple brain regions.

10. ____ The symptoms of Alzheimer's disease are caused by the progressive degeneration of neurons in the brain; this disease is the most common cause of dementia.

Check your answers and review any areas of weakness before going on to the next section.

Something to Think About

1. You may have met that rare person who seems to have a perfect memory—seldom forgetting anything. Most of us, however, have to struggle to learn and retain at least some of the vast amount of material we are constantly exposed to in the "information age." If someone were to ask you what you have learned about memory and forgetting that could be of help, what would you say?

2. Suppose a friend of yours is falsely identified as being the culprit in a grocery store hold-up and comes to you for help. Based on what you know about eyewitness testimony and related phenomena, what advice would you give him?

Check your answers and review any areas of weakness before doing the progress tests.

Progress Test 1

Review the complete chapter (including all boxed inserts), review all your study notes, and then test yourself on the following progress test. Check your answers. If you make a mistake, review your notes, check the appropriate section in the study guide, and if necessary, go back and read the relevant part of the chapter in your textbook.

1. In preparation for his biology exam, Lionel repeats the list of terms and their definitions over and over. Lionel's rehearsal strategy involves the fundamental memory process of
   (a) encoding.   (c) retrieval.
   (b) storage.   (d) wasting his time.

2. Michael, whose aggressive, arrogant behavior and indifferent attitude have resulted in the break-up of many relationships, is contemplating getting married for the third time. Michael is confident that this time it will work and that his previous relationship problems were never his fault. Michael is either actively _____ or unconsciously _____ memory of his own behavior.

    (a) consolidating; schematizing
    (b) schematizing; consolidating
    (c) suppressing; repressing
    (d) repressing; suppressing

3. Five-year-old Betty can recite the alphabet perfectly every time she is asked to do so. Betty's ability to do this involves the fundamental memory process of

    (a) repression.   (c) retrograde amnesia.
    (b) retrieval.   (d) encoding.

4. Sarina repeated the 10-digit telephone number over and over in her mind as she walked from the living room to the kitchen to make her call. Paige created an acronym for the names of the different brain waves associated with various states of wakefulness and sleep, BATD—Beta, Alpha, Theta, Delta. Sarina is using _____ rehearsal, and Paige is using _____ rehearsal.

    (a) distributed; massed
    (b) maintenance; elaborative
    (c) massed; distributed
    (d) elaborative; maintenance

5. Dirk can remember in vivid detail where he was and what he was doing when he heard about the terrorist attacks in New York City and Washington, D.C. Dirk's flashbulb memory is stored in his

    (a) iconic memory.   (c) long-term memory.
    (b) short-term memory. (d) echoic memory.

6. Whenever Killian is introduced to someone, he usually remembers the name by repeating it over and over to himself. Killian is using a memory strategy called

    (a) rehearsal.
    (b) retroactive interference.
    (c) clustering.
    (d) chunking.

7. One conclusion that can be drawn from Ebbinghaus's work on forgetting is that

    (a) we can remember only about seven nonsense syllables at one time.
    (b) when we memorize new information, most forgetting occurs relatively soon after we learn it.
    (c) the duration of visual sensory memory is less than half a second.
    (d) the capacity of long-term memory is large but temporary.

8. Mrs. Carson phoned her husband and quickly listed the 12 items she wanted him to pick up at the store. After she hung up, Mr. Carson attempted to write down the items. It is likely that he will

    (a) forget the items in the middle.
    (b) remember only the middle and the last items.
    (c) remember only the first and middle items.
    (d) forget the first and last items and remember the items in the middle.

9. At her high school reunion, Chychi met a girl who used to sit next to her in tenth grade, but she could not recall the girl's name. In an attempt to jog her memory, Chychi began reciting the alphabet. When she came to the letter M, she immediately remembered that her schoolfriend's name was Maureen. In this example, the letter of the alphabet

    (a) eliminated source confusion.
    (b) served as a retrieval cue.
    (c) provoked a flashbulb memory.
    (d) reversed encoding failure.

10. Charlie finds it easier to remember a list of words that includes *automobile, cigarettes, encyclopedia, lampshade, geranium,* and *seashell,* compared to a list of the same length that includes *philosophy, processes, justice, abstraction, fundamental,* and *inherent.* This is because with the first list it is easier to use

    (a) echoic processing.
    (b) maintenance rehearsal.
    (c) procedural memory.
    (d) visual imagery.

11. Karen can remember very clearly when and where she met Jim and how she felt when he first spoke to her. This information, which is stored in Karen's long-term memory, is called
    (a) procedural memory.
    (b) episodic memory.
    (c) semantic memory.
    (d) retroactive memory.

12. After his hippocampus was destroyed by a tumor, Mr. Locke is likely to experience problems _____ and is likely to be classified as suffering from _____ .
    (a) forming procedural memories; retrograde amnesia
    (b) recognizing common objects; Alzheimer's disease
    (c) correctly repeating items over and over; Alzheimer's disease
    (d) transferring short-term memories into long-term memory; anterograde amnesia

13. When Mitra entered the famous cathedral for the first time she had a brief but intense feeling that she had walked through the doorway before but could not recall when or where. According to In Focus (Déjà Vu), which of the following is true?
    (a) Déjà vu is the result of precognition, clairvoyance, telepathy, or a past-life experience.
    (b) Déjà vu can be explained by basic memory concepts such as disruptions in source memory, encoding failure, or inattentional blindness.
    (c) The remembered feeling of familiarity is caused by an overabundance of beta-amyloid plaques and neurofibrillary tangles in the brain.
    (d) Frequent episodes of déjà vu are associated with early-onset dementia and, in particular, Alzheimer's disease (AD).

14. According to the Application, one way to make memories last is to learn material over several sessions rather than cramming learning into one long session. This method of study is called
    (a) distributed practice.
    (b) massed practice.
    (c) maintenance rehearsal.
    (d) serial position learning.

15. According to Critical Thinking (The Memory Wars), which of the following regarding childhood sexual abuse is true?
    (a) Physical and sexual abuse in childhood is a serious social problem and can contribute to psychological problems in adulthood.
    (b) It is possible that memories of abuse can become repressed in childhood and surface later in life.
    (c) Repressed memories recovered in therapy need to be regarded with caution.
    (d) A person's confidence in a memory is no guarantee that the memory is accurate.
    (e) All of these statements are true.

Progress Test 2

After you have checked your understanding of the material in Progress Test 1 and have done a complete chapter review with special focus on any areas of weakness, you are ready to assess your knowledge on Progress Test 2. Check your answers. If you make a mistake, review your notes, the relevant section of the study guide, and, if necessary, the appropriate part of your textbook.

1. When Gary was preparing for an exam, he tried to make the material more meaningful by using strategies such as visual imagery, creating short stories involving the terms, self-referencing, and so on. Gary is using _____ to help him remember the information.
   (a) elaborative rehearsal
   (b) maintenance rehearsal
   (c) clustering
   (d) the encoding specificity principle

2. Shortly after he finished reading an exciting novel, Sean fell down the stairs and suffered a concussion; now, he has no recall of ever having read the novel. Sean's memory problem is probably the result of _____ , and he is most likely to be classified as suffering from _____ .
   (a) retrieval cue failure; anterograde amnesia
   (b) source confusion; dementia
   (c) disruption of memory consolidation; retrograde amnesia
   (d) mood incongruence; Alzheimer's disease

3. Dr. Chung's research is concerned with three components of memory: the phonological loop, the visuospatial sketchpad, and the central executive. He is most likely investigating aspects of

   (a) memory consolidation and long-term potentiation.
   (b) the encoding specificity principle.
   (c) Baddeley's model of working memory.
   (d) motivated forgetting such as suppression and repression.

4. Richard F. Thompson classically conditioned rabbits to eye-blink to a tone. He found that after learning the brain activity in the rabbit's cerebellum changed. This result suggests that some long-term memories

   (a) are stored in a localized region of the brain.
   (b) are distributed and stored across multiple brain locations.
   (c) have no biological or physical basis in the brain.
   (d) are very vulnerable if they are not given enough time to consolidate.

5. Dr. Dement believes that forgetting is due to memory traces being eroded by normal metabolic processes in the brain. Dr. Dement supports the

   (a) interference theory.
   (b) motivated forgetting theory.
   (c) semantic network theory.
   (d) decay theory.

6. When Manfred, who used to be a compulsive gambler, is asked how much money he won or lost, he recalls losing much less money than was actually the case. Manfred's memory failure best illustrates

   (a) motivated forgetting.
   (b) retrieval cue failure.
   (c) retroactive interference.
   (d) proactive interference.

7. Natasha has memorized the new personal identity code she was given by security; now, she can't remember her old personal identity code. Natasha is experiencing the effects of

   (a) mood congruence.
   (b) source confusion.
   (c) proactive interference.
   (d) retroactive interference.

8. Jeffery, who was an eyewitness to a robbery, initially thought the robber looked like a female. During questioning, a police detective suggested to him many times that the robber was probably a man with long hair. Later, when he was giving testimony on the witness stand, Jeffery was quite sure that it was a man who robbed the store. This example illustrates

   (a) the serial position effect.
   (b) mood congruence.
   (c) a flashbulb memory.
   (d) the misinformation effect.

9. Faizal was given a list of words to remember; on a later test of his long-term memory, he recalled the words according to how he had grouped them into categories, such as vegetables, furniture, and colors. When Korina is given a list of letters to study and recall—CPADNIDCTMVDASABM—she groups them into familiar units—CD PC ATM DVD NASA and IBM. Faizal is using a strategy for improving long-term memory called _____ , and Korina is using _____ to increase the amount of information she can hold in short-term memory.

   (a) clustering; chunking
   (b) echoic memory; iconic memory
   (c) chunking; clustering
   (d) long-term potentiation; memory consolidation

10. The smell of cherry blossoms awakened in Mrs. Yamomoto vivid memories of her childhood in Osaka. The aroma of the blossoms apparently acted as an effective

   (a) schema.   (c) flashbulb cue.
   (b) echoic cue.   (d) retrieval cue.

11. During a discussion about old movies, Grace could not bring to mind the name of the actor who played Sidney Greenstreet's sidekick in *The Maltese Falcon*, despite the fact that she felt she knew the name and had, in fact, talked about his role in the movie on other occasions. Grace is experiencing

   (a) the serial position effect.
   (b) encoding failure.
   (c) the tip-of-the-tongue (TOT) phenomenon.
   (d) anterograde amnesia.

12. Harold, who was in the kitchen, asked Jane, who was reading a book in the living room, whether she wanted a diet or a regular soft drink. Jane replied, "What did you say?" Before Harold could respond, Jane said, "Make it a regular Coke, please." This example illustrates
    (a) iconic memory.
    (c) echoic memory.
    (b) repression.
    (d) a flashbulb memory.

13. According to Culture and Human Behavior (Cultural Differences in Early Memories), which of the following is true?
    (a) Autobiographical memories may be shaped by cultural and social contexts.
    (b) European American and Taiwanese and Chinese college students' earliest memories were very similar in content, and both groups had their earliest memories at the same average age.
    (c) Autobiographical memories are relatively independent of culture and context and reflect universal and innate biological developments in the brain.
    (d) The memories of Asian students tended to be longer, more elaborate, and more self-focused than those of the American students.

14. When his hippocampus was removed, H.M. lost the ability to quickly encode new semantic and episodic memories. According to In Focus (H.M. and Famous People), recent research with H.M. (and the famous people test) demonstrated that
    (a) most of H.M.'s memory problems were related to retrograde amnesia.
    (b) most of H.M.'s new memories were the result of source confusion and imagination inflation.
    (c) his brain had an abundance of two abnormal structures, beta-amyloid plaques and neurofibrillary tangles.
    (d) some limited declarative semantic learning can occur without the hippocampus.

15. Regarding the critical issue of recovered memories versus false memories, Critical Thinking (The Memory Wars) notes that
    (a) every act of remembering involves reconstructing a memory.
    (b) the details of memory can be distorted with disturbing ease.
    (c) a person's confidence in a memory is no guarantee that the memory is accurate.
    (d) false or fabricated memories can seem just as detailed, vivid, and real as accurate ones.
    (e) all of these statements are true.

Progress Test 3

After you have checked your understanding of the material in Progress Tests 1 and 2 and have done a complete chapter review with special focus on any areas of weakness, you are ready to further assess your knowledge with Progress Test 3. Check your answers. If you make a mistake, review your notes, the appropriate parts of the study guide, and, if necessary, the relevant sections of your textbook.

1. Memory with awareness is to _____ as memory without awareness is to
   _____ .
   (a) explicit memory; implicit memory
   (b) retroactive interference; proactive interference
   (c) implicit memory; explicit memory
   (d) proactive interference; retroactive interference

2. Dr. Rhodes believes that when the conditions of information retrieval are similar to the conditions of information encoding, retrieval is more likely to be successful. This view is most consistent with
   (a) the stage model of memory.
   (b) the semantic network model.
   (c) the encoding specificity principle.
   (d) interference theory.

3. Elizabeth Loftus's story, presented in the Prologue, demonstrates how it is possible to form an extremely vivid, but inaccurate, memory. A common cause of such false memories is
   (a) retrograde amnesia.
   (b) source confusion.
   (c) anterograde amnesia.
   (d) retrieval cue failure.

4. The _____ is to encoding emotional aspects of memory as the _____ is to the encoding and transfer of new information from short-term to long-term memory.
   (a) amygdala; hippocampus
   (b) prefrontal cortex; amygdala
   (c) hippocampus; amygdala
   (d) cerebellum; hippocampus

5. Research participants were first presented with a visual stimulus (a picture of a cat and the word *cat*). Another group heard an auditory stimulus (the sound of a dog barking and the word *dog*). Next, they were given a retrieval cue (cat or dog) and asked to recall the original stimulus (visual or auditory). If the results of this experiment are similar to those in the Focus on Neuroscience, fMRI scans during the recall phase are likely to show that remembering the sound activates the _____ and remembering the picture activates the

   _____ .

   (a) visual cortex; auditory cortex
   (b) prefrontal cortex; cerebellum
   (c) auditory cortex; visual cortex
   (d) hippocampus; amygdala

6. Neddy cannot accurately remember the order of the numbers on the small calculator he has owned for 10 years and uses quite frequently. Neddy's problem in recall is most likely a function of

   (a) retrieval cue failure.
   (b) proactive interference.
   (c) encoding failure.
   (d) retroactive interference.

7. Most subjects in an experiment responded with *sky* and *grass* to the stimulus words *blue* and *green*. Results such as these support

   (a) the semantic network model.
   (b) decay theory.
   (c) the tip-of-the-tongue (TOT) experience.
   (d) interference theory.

8. Emelia can quite easily list all 50 U.S. states and Canada's 10 provinces and 2 territories. This type of information in long-term memory is called _____ information.

   (a) procedural   (c) semantic
   (b) episodic   (d) implicit

9. During a memory experiment, Amy was given lists of words to remember. Which component of her working memory is most likely to be used for this verbal task?

   (a) the phonological loop
   (b) visual sensory memory
   (c) the visiospatial sketchpad
   (d) auditory sensory memory

10. Lisa took a strong mood-altering prescription drug while studying for her exam; the following week, she took the same pills before the exam because she wanted to be in the same positive emotional state on both occasions. Lisa appears to believe in the effects of

    (a) maintenance rehearsal.
    (b) elaborative rehearsal.
    (c) mood congruence.
    (d) source confusion.

11. When Kirk was given a long list of items to memorize, he found it easier to remember them when he regrouped all the items according to whether they were plants, animals, minerals, and so on. Kirk is using a memory aid called

    (a) the serial position effect.
    (b) the self-referencing technique.
    (c) the context effect.
    (d) chunking.

12. When she first transferred from a college to a university, Kelly had trouble remembering her new student number; she would always recall her old college student number instead. Kelly's memory problem is an example of

    (a) retrograde amnesia.
    (b) proactive interference.
    (c) anterograde amnesia.
    (d) retroactive interference.

13. Mrs. Kahn experienced no trouble skiing despite the fact that she had not been on the slopes for almost 15 years. Mrs. Kahn's current skiing ability is probably due to a category of long-term memory called _____ memory.

    (a) procedural
    (b) episodic
    (c) semantic
    (d) repressed

14. Professor Isernia uses short essay questions on all her exams. In contrast, Professor Stregger relies on multiple-choice questions to test his students. Professor Isernia's exams involve a test of long-term memory called _____ , whereas Professor Stregger's exam questions involve _____ .

    (a) cued recall; chunking
    (b) recall (free recall); recognition
    (c) cued recall; clustering
    (d) recognition; recall (free recall)

15. According to the Application, which of the following strategies is NOT good for boosting memory?
    (a) Focus your attention and avoid distractions.
    (b) Use massed practice and take ginkgo biloba.
    (c) Organize the information and elaborate on it.
    (d) Use visual imagery and mnemonic devices.
    (e) Use contextual cues to jog your memory, and sleep after studying.

Answers

What Is Memory?

1. *Memory refers to* a group of related mental processes that enable us to acquire, retain, and use information over time.

2. *Encoding is the process of* transforming information into a form that can be entered into and retained by the memory system. *Storage is the process of* retaining information in memory so that it can be used at a later time. *Retrieval is the process of* recovering information stored in memory so that we are consciously aware of it.

3. *The stage model of memory describes memory as* consisting of three distinct stages: sensory memory (the stage that registers information from the environment for a brief period of time), short-term memory (the active, working stage in which information is stored for up to about 20 seconds), and long-term memory (the stage that represents the long-term storage of information).

4. *The three stages interact by* transferring information from one stage to another, with transfer between short-term and long-term memory going two ways.

Sensory Memory: Fleeting Impressions of the World

1. *Information is held in sensory memory for* a few seconds.

2. *Sperling's classic experiment demonstrated that* our visual sensory memory holds a great deal of information very briefly (for about half a second); this information is available just long enough for us to pay attention to specific elements that are significant to us at that moment.

3. *An important function of sensory memory (iconic and echoic) is* to store sensory impressions very briefly so that they overlap slightly with

one another. Consequently, we perceive the world around us as continuous, rather than as a series of disconnected images or disjointed sounds.

Short-Term, Working Memory: The Workshop of Consciousness

1. *Short-term memory is the stage of memory in which* information transferred from sensory memory and retrieved from long-term memory is temporarily stored and enters conscious awareness.

2. *The duration of short-term memory is* approximately 20 seconds, unless the information is rehearsed (maintenance rehearsal).

3. *The capacity of short-term memory is* limited to about seven items, or bits of information (plus or minus two), although some psychologists have found that four plus or minus one is more likely. *It can be increased by* maintenance rehearsal and by chunking (grouping related items together into a single unit or chunk).

4. *Working memory is* the short-term memory system involved in the temporary storage and active manipulation of information.

5. *The three components of Baddeley's model of working memory are* the phonological loop (specialized for verbal material), the visuospatial sketchpad (specialized for spatial or visual material), and the central executive (controls attention, integrates information, initiates retrieval and decision processes, and manages the activities of the other two components).

Long-Term Memory

1. *The amount of information that can be held in long-term memory is* essentially unlimited.

2. *Three ways to increase the efficiency of encoding are* to engage in elaborative rehearsal (focus on the meaning of information), use self-referencing (apply information to yourself), and use visual imagery.

3. *Procedural memory refers to* the long-term memory of how to perform different skills, operations, and actions. *Episodic memory refers to* the long-term memory of specific events or episodes, including the time and place that they occurred (autobiographical memory is closely related and refers to memory of events in your life). *Semantic memory refers to* memory of general knowledge that includes facts, names, definitions, concepts, and ideas.

4. *Explicit memory is* information or knowledge that can be consciously recollected (also called declarative memory). *Implicit memory is* information or knowledge that affects behavior or task performance but cannot be consciously recollected (also called nondeclarative memory).

5. *Information is organized in long-term memory by* clustering and by association.

6. *The best-known model of how information is organized in memory is* the semantic network model, *which describes long-term memory as* units of information organized in a complex network of associations.

Concept Check 1

1. retrieval
2. encoding
3. elaborative
4. short-term; maintenance
5. chunking
6. procedural
7. explicit memory; implicit memory
8. episodic; autobiographical

Matching Exercise 1

1. elaborative rehearsal
2. semantic network model
3. retrieval
4. clustering
5. visual imagery
6. short-term memory
7. episodic memory
8. encoding
9. stage model of memory
10. memory
11. procedural memory
12. George Sperling
13. autobiographical memory
14. working memory
15. central executive

True/False Test 1

1. F	6. T	11. F
2. F	7. T	12. T
3. T	8. T	13. F
4. T	9. T	14. F
5. T	10. F	

Retrieval: Getting Information from Long-Term Memory

1. *Retrieval refers to* the process of accessing stored information. *A retrieval cue is* a clue, prompt, or hint that helps trigger recall of a given piece of information stored in long-term memory. *Retrieval cue failure refers to* the inability to recall long-term memories because of inadequate or missing retrieval cues.

2. *The tip-of-the-tongue (TOT) experience is* a memory phenomenon that involves the sensation of knowing that specific information is stored in long-term memory but being temporarily unable to retrieve it. *It illustrates the fact that* retrieving information is not an all-or-nothing process; in many instances, information is stored in memory but is not accessible without the right retrieval cues. It also shows that information stored in memory is organized and connected in relatively logical ways.

3. *Retrieval is tested by* recall (retrieving information without the aid of retrieval cues), cued recall (remembering an item of information in response to a retrieval cue), and recognition (identifying correct information out of several possible choices).

4. *The serial position effect is* the tendency to remember items at the beginning of a list (primacy effect) and at the end of a list (recency effect) better than items in the middle of the list.

5. *The encoding specificity principle states that* when the conditions of information retrieval are similar to the conditions of information encoding, retrieval is more likely to be successful.

6. *The context effect, an encoding specificity phenomenon, refers to* the tendency to recover information more easily when retrieval occurs in the same setting as the original learning of the information. *Mood congruence, another example of encoding specificity, refers to* the idea that a given mood tends to evoke memories that are consistent with that mood.

7. *Distinctiveness plays a role in retrieval because* highly unusual, surprising, or even bizarre experiences are easier to retrieve from memory than are routine events.

8. *A flashbulb memory is* the recall of very specific images or details surrounding a vivid, rare, or significant event; although confidence about the recollection is usually high, accuracy is not (confidence in a memory is no guarantee of accuracy).

Concept Check 2

1. mood congruence
2. flashbulb
3. tip-of-the-tongue phenomenon
4. retrieval cue
5. recognition; recall
6. encoding specificity; context effect
7. primacy effect; recency effect
8. serial position effect

Graphic Organizer 1

1. RECOGNITION
2. TIPOFTHETONGUEEXPERIENCE
3. RETRIEVALCUEFAILURE
4. FLASHBULBMEMORY
5. SERIALPOSITIONEFFECT
6. RETRIEVAL

7. Recall is a test of long-term memory that involves retrieving information without the aid of retrieval cues (also called free recall).

Matching Exercise 2

1. context effect
2. retrieval
3. flashbulb memory
4. serial position effect
5. cued recall
6. retrieval cue
7. mood congruence
8. encoding specificity principle

True/False Test 2

1. F   5. T
2. T   6. T
3. T   7. F
4. T   8. T

Forgetting: When Retrieval Fails

1. *Forgetting is the* inability to recall information that was previously available.

2. *The Ebbinghaus forgetting curve reveals two distinct patterns about forgetting: (a)* much of what we forget is lost relatively soon after we originally learned it; *(b)* the amount of forgetting eventually levels off, with information that is not quickly forgotten remaining quite stable in memory over long periods of time.

3. *Encoding failure refers to* the inability to recall specific information because of insufficient encoding of the information for storage in long-term memory. *It may contribute to* absent-mindedness, which occurs when attention is divided at the time of encoding and the relevant information is therefore not transferred into long-term memory.

4. *Prospective memory is* remembering to do something in the future. *Prospective memory failure may be due to* retrieval cue failure rather than encoding failure.

5. *According to decay theory,* forgetting is due to normal metabolic processes that occur in the brain over time.

6. *Interference theory is the theory that* forgetting is caused by one memory competing with or replacing another memory. *The two basic types of interference affect memory in the following ways:* in retroactive interference, a new memory interferes with remembering an old memory (backward-acting memory interference); in proactive interference, an old memory interferes with remembering a new memory (forward-acting memory interference).

7. *Motivated forgetting refers to the idea that* we forget because we are motivated to forget, usually because a memory is unpleasant or disturbing. *There are two forms of motivated forgetting:* suppression (a deliberate, conscious effort to forget) and repression (unconscious motivation to forget).

8. *Motivated forgetting is a controversial topic because* (a) it is based on the Freudian (psychoanalytic) belief that psychologically threatening emotions, conflicts, and urges (especially those

from childhood) can become repressed, yet can still unconsciously influence a person's thoughts, behavior, and personality, often in maladaptive or unhealthy ways; and (b) The construct of repression has not been scientifically validated and, while many clinical psychologists and others believe in the notion, the evidence from research on false and distorted memories suggests that claims of recovered repressed memories in psychotherapy should be regarded with caution.

Imperfect Memories: Errors, Distortions, and False Memories

1. *Errors and distortions occur during the process of retrieval because* retrieval involves the active construction and reconstruction of memories and may be affected by the information stored before and after the memory occurred.

2. *The misinformation effect (one phenomenon that can reduce the accuracy of eyewitness testimony) refers to* a memory-distortion phenomenon in which a person's existing memories can be altered if the person is exposed to misleading information. *It is a problem because* postevent exposure to misinformation can distort the recollection of the original event.

3. *Source confusion is* a memory distortion that occurs when the true source of the memory is forgotten.

4. *A false memory is* a distorted or fabricated recollection of something that did not actually occur.

5. *A schema is* an organized cluster of information about a particular topic. *Research has demonstrated that* our schemas can influence what we remember; that once a memory is formed, it has the potential to be changed by new information; and that memories can easily become distorted.

6. *A script is* one kind of schema that involves the typical sequence of actions and behaviors at a common event.

7. *The lost-in-the-mall technique is* a research strategy using information from family members to help create or induce false memories of childhood experiences (pseudoevents). *It demonstrates that* people are capable of developing beliefs and memories for events that definitely did not happen to them.

8. *Imagination inflation is* a memory phenomenon in which vividly imagining an event markedly increases confidence that the event (pseudoevent) actually happened.

Concept Check 3

1. proactive
2. encoding failure
3. suppression
4. misinformation effect
5. retrieval cue failure
6. retroactive
7. absent-mindedness; encoding
8. schema
9. imagination inflation
10. prospective

Graphic Organizer 2

1. retroactive interference
2. proactive interference

Matching Exercise 3

1. suppression
2. forgetting
3. decay theory
4. repression
5. interference theory
6. Hermann Ebbinghaus
7. encoding failure
8. schema
9. lost-in-the-mall technique
10. Elizabeth Loftus
11. misinformation effect
12. absent-mindedness
13. prospective memory

True/False Test 3

1. T	5. T	9. T	13. F
2. F	6. T	10. T	
3. T	7. F	11. T	
4. T	8. F	12. T	

The Search for the Biological Basis of Memory

1. *Lashley and Thompson contributed to our understanding of the physical basis of memory by* demonstrating that memories have the potential to be both localized and distributed: Very simple memories are localized in a specific area, and more complex memories appear to be distributed throughout the brain.

2. *When a new memory is formed, neurons change in two ways:* functionally, they increase the amount of neurotransmitters they produce, and structurally, they show an increase in the number of interconnecting branches between neurons as well as in the number of synapses on each branch.

3. *Eric Kandel showed that* functional and structural changes in neurons are associated with acquiring a classically conditioned response (in the sea snail *Aplysia). Long-term potentiation refers to* a long-lasting increase in synaptic strength between two neurons.

4. *Amnesia refers to* severe memory loss. *Retrograde amnesia is* loss of memory, especially for episodic information (backward-acting amnesia). *Anterograde amnesia is* loss of memory caused by the inability to store new memories (forward-acting amnesia).

5. *Research with patients such as H.M. has enabled investigators to* relate the type and extent of amnesia to the specific brain areas that have been damaged and has also contributed to our understanding of the distinction between implicit and explicit memory.

6. *The brain structures (and their functions) involved in normal memory are* the cerebellum (motor skill memories, classically conditioned simple reflexes, and procedural memories), amygdala (associates memories involving different senses with rewards and punishments and encodes the emotional aspects of memories), prefrontal cortex (plays an important role in working memory), the frontal lobes (retrieve and organize information associated with autobiographical and episodic memories), the medial temporal lobes (encode complex memories by forming links among multiple brain regions), and the hippocampus (encodes and transfers new explicit memories to long-term memory).

7. *Dementia is the* progressive deterioration and impairment of memory, reasoning, and other cognitive functions occurring as the result of a disease or a condition. *Alzheimer's disease (AD) is a* progressive disease that destroys the brain's neurons, gradually impairing memory, thinking, language, and other cognitive functions, resulting in the complete inability to care for oneself. It is the most common cause of dementia.

Concept Check 4

1. retrograde

2. memory consolidation

3. long-term

4. long-term potentiation

5. dementia; Alzheimer's disease (AD)

6. beta-amyloid plaques; neurofibrillary tangles

7. procedural; implicit

Matching Exercise 4

1. cerebral cortex

2. Karl Lashley

3. memory trace (engram)

4. amnesia

5. Richard F. Thompson

6. memory consolidation

7. long-term potentiation

8. cerebellum

9. prefrontal cortex

10. Eric Kandel

11. Brenda Milner

True/False Test 4

1. F	5. F	9. T
2. T	6. T	10. T
3. T	7. T	
4. T	8. T	

Something to Think About

1. We are all vulnerable to forgetting, and sometimes the consequences can be serious. What can we do to improve memory? Fortunately, a number of strategies can help us to remember important information. You might begin your answer with a discussion of the fundamental processes of encoding, storage, and retrieval, then explain the function, capacity, and duration of each of the three stages of memory. Of course, no discussion of the topic of memory would be complete without mentioning Ebbinghaus's work on forgetting as well as the contributions of the various theories of forgetting to our understanding of memory. Finally, mention the important strategies that could help improve memory, as described in the Application.

2. It is a real nightmare to contemplate the prospect of being falsely accused of a crime and having an eyewitness point at you and say very confidently, "Yes, that is the person. There's no doubt about it, he (or she) did it!" What can be done in such a situation? If you don't have an

alibi, the jury is very likely to believe a confident eyewitness who, under oath, points a finger at the accused. First, you might consider hiring an expert witness, such as Elizabeth Loftus, to testify to the problems inherent in eyewitness testimony. Such testimony, based on scientific evidence, is difficult to refute.

If your friend cannot afford the testimony of an expert witness, then we suggest he or she try to educate his defense lawyer about the relevant research findings in this important area of psychology. These include source confusion, the personal schema of the eyewitness, the power of the misinformation effect, suggestion, and imagination inflation, evidence related to false memories, and relevant aspects of the encoding specificity principle.

Progress Test 1

1. a	6. a	11. b
2. c	7. b	12. d
3. b	8. a	13. b
4. b	9. b	14. a
5. c	10. d	15. e

Progress Test 2

1. a	6. a	11. c
2. c	7. d	12. c
3. c	8. d	13. a
4. a	9. a	14. d
5. d	10. d	15. e

Progress Test 3

1. a	6. c	11. d
2. c	7. a	12. b
3. b	8. c	13. a
4. a	9. a	14. b
5. c	10. c	15. b

Thinking, Language, and Intelligence

CHAPTER 7. . . AT A GLANCE

Chapter 7 combines thinking, language, and intelligence, three closely related cognitive functions. The section on thinking begins with discussions of the use of mental imagery and concept formation. This leads to a description of problem-solving strategies, followed by an explanation of two common obstacles to effective problem solving: functional fixedness and mental sets. The section concludes with a discussion of different decision-making models.

The next section, on our remarkable cognitive capacity for language, first explains the characteristics of language, then explores ways in which language influences thought. Animal communication and the controversial debate over whether animals are capable of language finishes up this section.

Our ability to think and use language are aspects of what we call intelligence. Because the measurement of intelligence has been a controversial issue, this section provides some background into the development of intelligence testing and the contributions of various psychologists. The difference between aptitude tests and achievement tests is explained, and the requirements of standardization, reliability, and validity are described as a way of understanding the problems of testing.

The debate over the nature of intelligence centers on whether intelligence is a single, general ability or a cluster of different abilities, and on whether intelligence should be narrowly or broadly defined. Four theories regarding this issue are presented. The heredity–environment debate regarding the origins of intelligence is examined in detail. The Application presents a number of suggestions for enhancing our ability to think creatively.

Introduction: Thinking, Language, and Intelligence

Preview Questions

Consider the following questions as you study this section of the chapter.

- What is cognition?
- How is *thinking* defined, and what does it typically involve?
- What are mental images, and how do we manipulate them?
- What are concepts, and how are they formed?
- What are prototypes and exemplars, and what role do they play in concept formation?

Read the section "Introduction: Thinking, Language, and Intelligence" and **write** *your answers to the following:*

1. Cognition is _____

   _____

2. Thinking is defined as _____

   _____

   It typically involves _____

   _____

3. A mental image is _____

   _____

4. We manipulate mental images

   _____

   Mental images are potentially subject to error and distortion because _____

   _____

   _____

5. Concepts are _____

   _____

   The two ways of forming concepts are _____

   _____

   _____

6. A prototype is _____

   _____

   The more closely an item matches a prototype,

   _____

7. Exemplars are _____

   _____

When we encounter a new object, _____

_____

_____

Solving Problems and Making Decisions

Preview Questions

Consider the following questions as you study this section of the chapter.

- How is problem solving defined?
- What are four problem-solving strategies, and what are the advantages and/or disadvantages of each?
- What are functional fixedness and mental sets, and how do they interfere with problem solving?

Read the section "Solving Problems and Making Decisions" and **write** *your answers to the following:*

1. Problem solving is defined as _____

   _____

2. The trial-and-error strategy involves _____

   _____

3. An algorithm involves _____

   _____

4. A heuristic is a _____

   _____

   _____

5. Insight is the _____

   _____

   Intuition means _____

   _____

6. Functional fixedness is _____

   _____

7. A mental set is _____

   _____

Decision-Making Strategies

Preview Questions

Consider the following questions as you study this section of the chapter.

- What are the single-feature, additive, and elimination by aspects models of decision making?
- Under what conditions is each strategy appropriate?
- When are the availability and representativeness heuristics used, and what potential problems are associated with each?

*Read the section "Decision-Making Strategies" and **write** your answers to the following:*

1. The single-feature model involves _____

   _____

   It is appropriate when _____

   _____

2. Using the additive model, you first _____

   _____

   It is appropriate for _____

   _____

3. Using the elimination by aspects model, you

   _____

   _____

   _____

   It is appropriate when _____

   _____

4. The availability heuristic is a strategy _____

   _____

   _____

5. The representativeness heuristic is a strategy

   _____

   _____

After you have carefully studied the preceding sections, complete the following exercises.

Concept Check 1

Read the following and write the correct term in the space provided.

1. After a chimpanzee tries unsuccessfully to get bananas that are out of reach, she sits for a long time staring at them. Suddenly, she looks around the cage, picks up a stick, and uses it to pull the bananas within her reach, something she has never done before. Her solution to the banana problem is probably the result of

   _____ .

2. You learn that one of the Russell children is taking ballet classes; you immediately conclude that it is their one daughter rather than any of their three sons. You reached a possibly erroneous conclusion by using the

   _____ .

3. Dr. Mendleson studies how people manipulate mental representations to draw inferences and conclusions. Dr. Mendleson is most likely a _____ psychologist interested in people's _____ ability.

4. You are asked to decide which city is farther north, Edinburgh, Scotland, or Stockholm, Sweden, so you try to picture a map of Europe in your mind. You are using a

   _____ .

5. Marisa has learned the rules and features that define a square, a rectangle, and a right-angle triangle. Marisa has learned a _____ concept.

6. Henry, an avid fisherman, had trouble recognizing that a seahorse is a fish because it does not closely resemble his _____ concept of fish.

7. To convert liters into U.S. gallons, Natalie multiplies the number of liters by 0.264178. She is using a(n) _____ to arrive at the correct answer.

8. Hilda is asked to complete the sequence "J, F, M, A, _, _, _, _, _, _, _, _." After trying a few different possibilities, she comes up with the correct answer—M, J, J, A, S, O, N, D (the first letter of the months of the year). It appears that Hilda is using a(n)

_____ strategy to solve the problem.

9. Anatole is trying to decide which of two equally affordable and attractive cars to purchase, so he makes a list of the advantages and disadvantages of each using an arbitrary rating scale. Anatole is using the _____ model to help him make a decision.

10. When he first tried an avocado, Keeton compared his memory of other individual types of fruits in order to decide whether an avocado is a fruit. In this case, Keeton is using an

_____ to help him categorize the food item.

Review of Terms and Concepts 1

Use the terms in this list to complete the Matching Test, then to help you answer the True/False items correctly.

cognition
thinking
mental image
concept
formal concept
natural concept
prototype
exemplars
problem solving
trial and error
algorithm
heuristic
analysis of subgoals
working backward

insight
intuition
guiding stage and
    integrative stage
functional fixedness
mental set
single-feature model
additive model
elimination by aspects
    model
availability heuristic
representativeness
    heuristic

Matching Exercise

Match the appropriate term with its definition or description.

1. _____ Decision-making model in which all the alternatives are evaluated one characteristic at a time, starting with the most important feature and scratching each alternative off the list of possible choices if it fails to meet the criterion.

2. _____ The manipulation of mental representations of information in order to draw inferences or conclusions.

3. _____ Most typical instance of a particular concept.

4. _____ Sudden realization of how a problem can be solved.

5. _____ Decision-making strategy in which the choice among many alternatives is simplified by basing the decision on a single feature.

6. _____ Strategy in which the likelihood of an event is estimated by comparing how similar it is to the typical prototype of the event.

7. _____ A problem-solving strategy that involves following a specific rule, procedure, or method that inevitably produces the correct solution.

8. _____ Problem-solving strategy that involves attempting different solutions and eliminating those that do not work.

9. _____ Mental category that is formed by learning the rules or features that define it.

10. _____ The mental activities involved in acquiring, retaining, and using knowledge.

11. _____ Mental category of objects or ideas based on properties that they share.

12. _____ Problem-solving strategy that involves following a general rule of thumb to reduce the number of possible solutions.

True/False Test

Indicate whether each statement is true or false by placing T or F in the blank space next to each item.

1. ___ Working backward is a common heuristic used to break a problem down into a series of smaller problems; as each subproblem is solved, you get closer to solving the larger problem.

2. ___ A mental representation of objects or events that are not physically present is called a mental image.

3. ___ Problem solving is thinking and behavior directed toward attaining a goal that is not readily available.

4. ___ The tendency to persist in solving problems with solutions that have worked in the past is called functional fixedness.

5. ___ The additive model of decision making involves generating a list of the most important factors, then using an arbitrary rating scale to rate each alternative on each factor, and finally adding the ratings together for comparison purposes.

6. ___ The availability heuristic is a strategy in which the likelihood of an event is estimated on the basis of how easily other instances of the event are available in memory.

7. ___ A natural concept is a mental category that is formed as a result of everyday experience.

8. ___ A useful heuristic in which you start at the end point and determine the steps necessary to reach your goal uses the analysis of subgoals.

9. ___ A mental set is the tendency to view objects as functioning only in their usual or customary manner.

10. ___ Intuition refers to the process of coming to a conclusion or making a judgment without conscious awareness.

11. ___ The two-stage model of intuition involves a guiding stage (a pattern in the information is perceived unconsciously) and an integrative stage (a representation of the pattern becomes conscious).

12. ___ Exemplars are individual instances of a concept or category, held in memory.

Check your answers and review any areas of weakness before going on to the next section.

Language and Thought

Preview Questions

Consider the following questions as you study this section of the chapter.

- How is *language* defined?
- What are the five most important characteristics of language?
- In what ways does language influence thinking?
- Can nonhuman animals use language?

Read the section "Language and Thought" and **write** *your answers to the following:*

1. Language is defined as _____
   _____

2. The five most important characteristics of language are as follows:
   (a) _____
   _____
   (b) _____
   _____
   (c) _____
   _____
   (d) _____
   _____
   (e) _____
   _____

3. Language influences thinking by _____
   _____
   _____
   _____

4. Animals communicate with each other and with other species, but _____
   _____
   _____
   _____

Measuring Intelligence

Preview Questions

Consider the following questions as you study this section of the chapter.

- How is *intelligence* defined?
- What roles did Binet, Terman, and Wechsler play in the development of intelligence tests?

Read the section "Measuring Intelligence" and **write** *your answers to the following:*

1. Intelligence is defined as _____

   _____

   _____

2. Alfred Binet, along with psychiatrist Théodore Simon, devised _____

   _____

   _____

   _____

3. Lewis Terman translated and adapted _____

   _____

   _____

   _____

   _____

4. David Wechsler developed a new intelligence test, _____

   _____

   _____

   _____

Principles of Test Construction: What Makes a Good Test?

Preview Questions

Consider the following questions as you study this section of the chapter.

- How do achievement tests differ from aptitude tests?
- What does it mean to standardize a test?
- What is the role of norms in standardization, and what is the normal curve?
- How are *reliability* and *validity* defined, and how are they determined?

Read the section "Principles of Test Construction: What Makes a Good Test?" and **write** *your answers to the following:*

1. Achievement tests are designed to _____

   _____

   Aptitude tests are designed to _____

   _____

2. Standardization refers to _____

   _____

   _____

3. The normal curve, or normal distribution, is

   _____

   _____

4. Reliability is defined as _____

   _____

   It is determined by _____

   _____

5. Validity is defined as _____

   _____

   One way to determine validity is by _____

   _____

After you have carefully studied the preceding sections, complete the following exercises.

Concept Check 2

Read the following and write the correct term in the space provided.

1. A Norwegian visitor to England asks the hotel clerk, "Can you please my key to my room give me?" This visitor has apparently not yet mastered the _____ of the English language.

2. In order to fulfill one of the three requirements of good test design, Dr. Houseman administered his new test, under uniform conditions, to a large number of people who were representative of the population of interest. Dr. Houseman has gone through a procedure called

   _____ , and the scores of this representative group will be used to establish the

   _____ against which an individual score will be compared and interpreted.

3. Ten-year-old Jean performed at the same level as most 12-year-olds on Binet's test. Her _____ age is different from her _____ age.

4. According to his score on the Stanford-Binet test, Marcel's mental age is identical to his chronological age. Marcel's IQ score is likely to be _____ .

5. When 25-year-old Dagmar applied for a position with the Department of Defense, she was given a test; she scored slightly above the norm on overall verbal ability but well above the norm in overall performance for her age group. The test Dagmar was given was a(n) _____ called the _____ .

6. The test and retest scores on the new Zander jealousy scale were highly similar but lacked predictive value; furthermore, it was not clear exactly what human attribute it was measuring. The Zander test was high in _____ but low in _____ .

7. Marta is thoroughly enjoying reading the latest book in a series that recounts the adventures of children who attend a special school for wizards and witches. The author of these books has an extraordinary talent for telling interesting and exciting tales about nonexistent places and people. This ability to communicate meaningfully about imaginary events and characters demonstrates two important characteristics of language; one is called _____ , and the second is that language is _____ or _____ .

8. Twelve-year-old Golnaz was given a standardized intelligence test, specially designed for children. She is most likely to have taken the _____ .

Review of Terms, Concepts, and Names 2

Use the terms in this list to complete the Matching Test, then to help you answer the True/False items correctly.

language
syntax
generative
displacement
linguistic relativity
  hypothesis (Whorfian
  hypothesis)
animal cognition
  (comparative cognition)
intelligence
Alfred Binet
mental age
Lewis Terman
Stanford-Binet
  Intelligence Scale
intelligence quotient
  (IQ)
David Wechsler

Wechsler Adult
  Intelligence Scale
  (WAIS)
verbal score
performance score
Wechsler Intelligence
  Scale for Children
  (WISC),
  Wechsler Preschool
  and Primary Scale of
  Intelligence (WPPSI)
achievement test
aptitude test
standardization
norms
normal curve (normal
  distribution)
reliability
validity

Matching Exercise

Match the appropriate term/name with its definition or description.

1. _____ Every language's unique rules for combining words.

2. _____ The French psychologist who, along with French psychiatrist Théodore Simon, developed the first widely used intelligence test.

3. _____ The ability to communicate meaningfully about ideas, objects, and activities that are not physically present.

4. _____ Measure of intelligence in which an individual's mental level is expressed in terms of the average abilities of a given age group.

5. _____ Name of Lewis Terman's translation and revision of the Binet-Simon intelligence test.

6. _____ The ability of a test to measure what it is intended to measure.

7. _____ Characteristic of language that allows one to create an infinite number of new and different phrases and sentences.

8. _____ The study of animal learning, memory, thinking, and language.

9. _____ Bell-shaped distribution of individual differences in a normal population in which most scores cluster around the average score.

10. _____ The global capacity to think rationally, act purposefully, and deal effectively with the environment.

11. _____ System for combining arbitrary symbols to produce an infinite number of meaningful statements.

12. _____ Two tests developed by David Wechsler for testing children's intelligence.

True/False Test

Indicate whether each item is true or false by placing T or F in the space next to each item.

1. ____ Lewis Terman was the American psychologist who translated and adapted the Binet-Simon intelligence test for use in the United States.

2. ____ David Wechsler was the American psychologist who developed the Wechsler Adult Intelligence Scale (WAIS), the most widely used intelligence scale.

3. ____ An aptitude test is designed to measure a person's level of knowledge, skill, or accomplishments in a particular area, such as mathematics or a foreign language.

4. ____ The intelligence quotient (IQ) is a measure of general intelligence derived by comparing an individual's score with that of others in the same age group.

5. ____ The *verbal score* on the WAIS reflects scores on subtests such as identifying missing parts in incomplete pictures, arranging pictures to tell a story, or arranging blocks to match a given pattern.

6. ____ Reliability refers to the ability of a test to produce consistent results when administered on repeated occasions under similar conditions.

7. ____ Standardization is the process of administering a test to a large, representative sample of people under uniform conditions for the purpose of establishing norms.

8. ____ An achievement test is designed to measure a person's capacity to benefit from education or training.

9. ____ The *performance score* on the WAIS represents scores on subtests of vocabulary, comprehension, knowledge of general information, and other similar tasks.

10. ____ The Wechsler Adult Intelligence Scale (WAIS) is an adult intelligence test with scores on 11 subtests that are grouped to provide an overall verbal score and a performance score.

11. ____ The scores of the large number of representative subjects for whom the test is designed establish the norms or the standards against which an individual score is compared and interpreted.

12. ____ The notion that differences among languages causes differences in the thoughts of their speakers is called the linguistic relativity hypothesis.

Check your answers and review any areas of weakness before going on to the next section.

The Nature of Intelligence

Preview Questions

Consider the following questions as you study this section of the chapter.

- What are the two key issues involved in the debate over the nature of intelligence?

- What is the *g* factor (general intelligence), and who first proposed a theory regarding its existence?

- What was Louis L. Thurstone's contribution to the debate about the nature of intelligence?

- Who proposed the idea of "multiple intelligences," and what are the eight distinct intelligences?

- What is the triarchic theory of intelligence, and who proposed it?

*Read the section "The Nature of Intelligence" and **write** your answers to the following:*

1. The two key issues involved in the debate over the nature of intelligence are as follows:

   (a) _____

   _____

   (b) _____

   _____

2. The *g* factor (or general intelligence) is the notion _____

_____

It was proposed by _____

3. Louis L. Thurstone proposed the notion that

_____

_____

4. The idea of multiple intelligences was proposed by_____

The eight intelligences are _____

_____

5. The triarchic theory of intelligence proposes that_____

_____

_____

It was developed by _____

The Roles of Genetics and Environment in Determining Intelligence

Preview Questions

Consider the following questions as you study this section of the chapter.

- What is the heredity–environment issue?
- How are twin studies used to measure genetic and environmental influences?
- What is heritability, and why can't heritability estimates be used to explain differences between groups?
- Are IQ tests culturally biased?

*Read the section "The Roles of Genetics and Environment in Determining Intelligence" and **write** your answers to the following:*

1. The basic heredity–environment issue is concerned with_____

_____

_____

_____

2. Twin studies have been used because _____

_____

_____

_____

3. Heritability is defined as _____

_____

_____

_____

Heritability estimates cannot be used to explain differences between groups because _____

_____

_____

_____

4. It is virtually impossible to create a culture-free IQ test because _____

_____

_____

_____

After you have carefully studied the preceding sections, complete the following exercises.

Concept Check 3

Read the following and write the correct term in the space provided.

1. Although Dr. Bowman recognizes that particular individuals might excel in specific areas, she believes that a factor, called general intelligence, or the *g* factor, is responsible for overall performance on mental ability tests. Her belief about the nature of intelligence is most consistent with the approach taken by psychologist

_____ .

2. Jamal is a highly valued maintenance worker because of his almost uncanny ability to fix nearly any piece of equipment that breaks down. Jamal is demonstrating what Robert Sternberg would call _____ intelligence.

3. Selma is a very successful, highly motivated, goal-directed, and creative graphic designer. These aspects of her intelligence are _____ (not likely/very likely) to be assessed and measured on a conventional intelligence test.

4. Dicky and Ricky are identical twins and have almost identical IQ scores despite the fact that they were separated at birth and raised in different environments. Fraternal twins Joel and Joanna were raised together but their IQ scores are much less similar than Dicky and Ricky's scores. This example provides the most support for the _____ side in the heredity–environment debate.

5. Compared with the scores of two randomly selected unrelated people of the same age, the IQ scores of fraternal twins Joel and Joanna are much more similar. This finding provides the most support for the _____ side in the heredity–environment debate.

6. Dr. Yokomoto, like the majority of experts on intelligence testing, is most likely to attribute the finding that Japanese and Chinese children outperform American children on mathematics achievement tests to _____ factors.

7. When Dr. Parsei, an expert on intelligence testing, was asked if a completely culture-free intelligence test could be designed, he replied that it _____ (was possible/was not possible) because group ability tests reflect the values, knowledge, and communication strategies of their culture of origin.

8. Professor Kensington suggests that there are seven "primary mental abilities," which are relatively independent elements of intelligence. These abilities include verbal comprehension, numerical ability, reasoning, and perceptual speed. Dr. Kensington's views of intelligence are most consistent with those of
_____ .

9. Yan is an expert chess player with an exceptional ability to mentally visualize the relationship of the various chess pieces following different moves. Howard Gardner labeled this type of intelligence _____ .

10. Constantino is a very successful salesperson. His success is due, in part at least, to his ability to understand and respond appropriately to other people's emotions, motives, and intentions. Constantino demonstrates _____ intelligence, one of the eight intelligences proposed by _____ .

11. Before taking a challenging math test Chung Yee was reminded of the cultural stereotype that Asian Americans have superior math skills. She scored significantly higher than her equally gifted friend Jee Young, who was reminded before the same test of the stereotype that females are poor at math. The unexpected difference in their performance on the same test may be the result of what psychologist Claude Steele called the
_____ .

12. Researchers calculated that approximately 50 percent of the differences in IQ scores within a given population was due to genetic factors. They have calculated the _____ of the variation within that group that is due to heredity.

13. According to the Prologue, Tom is intellectually gifted but has a number of problems, including cognitive rigidity, inflexible thinking, a tendency toward functional fixedness, and some impairments in social aspects of his life. Tom has been diagnosed with a condition called
_____ .

Graphic Organizer 1

Read the following statements and decide which psychologist is most associated with each.

Statement	Psychologist
1. I define intelligence as the global capacity to think rationally, act purposefully, and deal effectively with the environment; a good IQ test should have both verbal and performance scores representing subtests that measure a variety of abilities.	
2. My theory of intelligence emphasizes both universal aspects of intelligent behavior and the importance of adapting to the individual's particular social and cultural environment; there are essentially three forms of intelligence: analytical, creative, and practical intelligence.	
3. I'm not sure I have a fully developed theory of intelligence, but I do believe that we can help children do better in school if we devise tests that can identify those who need help and then provide that help. There is a great deal of variation in intelligence in any age group of children.	
4. I am convinced that a factor called general intelligence, or the g factor, is responsible for overall performance on mental ability tests. Furthermore, I would go so far as to say that intelligence can be accurately expressed as a single number that reflects an individual's intellectual abilities.	
5. I disagree with those who say that intelligence is a single, general mental capacity. On the basis of my observations of what is valued in different cultures, I've concluded that there are eight intelligences, each independent of the other, and these must be viewed in the context of a particular culture.	
6. I tend to agree with statement 4 above. In addition, I believe that intelligence can best be expressed by a number I call the intelligence quotient, or IQ, which is derived by dividing the mental age by the chronological age and multiplying the result by 100.	
7. I do not agree with the notion that intelligence is a single general mental capacity. Instead, I believe that there are a number of different "primary mental abilities" such as verbal comprehension, numerical ability, reasoning, and perceptual speed, and that each one is a relatively independent element of intelligence. In my view, the so-called g factor is simply an overall average score of these independent abilities and is therefore less important than an individual's specific pattern of mental abilities.	

Review of Terms, Concepts, and Names 3

Use the terms in this list to complete the Matching Test, then to help you answer the True/False items correctly.

Charles Spearman
general intelligence,
   or the *g* factor
Louis L. Thurstone
Howard Gardner
Robert Sternberg
triarchic theory of
   intelligence
successful intelligence
analytic intelligence
creative intelligence
practical intelligence

heredity
environment
identical twins
fraternal twins
heritability
autism
Asperger's syndrome
mental retardation
Claude Steele
stereotype threat
creativity

Matching Exercise

Match the appropriate term/name with its definition or description.

1. _____ Contemporary American psychologist whose triarchic theory of intelligence identifies three forms of intelligence (analytical, creative, and practical).

2. _____ The percentage of variation within a given population that is due to heredity.

3. _____ Factor of intelligence that is responsible for a person's overall performance on tests of mental ability.

4. _____ Group of cognitive processes used to generate useful, original, and novel ideas or solutions.

5. _____ American psychologist who advanced the theory that intelligence is composed of several primary mental abilities and cannot be accurately described by a general intelligence, or *g*, factor.

6. _____ Sternberg's type of intelligence that involves the ability to adapt to the environment and often reflects what is commonly described as street smarts.

7. _____ British psychologist who advanced the theory that a general intelligence factor, called the *g* factor, is responsible for overall intellectual functioning.

8. _____ Form of intelligence that involves the ability to deal with novel situations by drawing on existing skills and knowledge.

9. _____ Psychological predicament in which fear that you will be evaluated in terms of a negative stereotype about a group to which you belong creates anxiety and self-doubt, lowering performance in a particular domain that is important to you.

10. _____ Psychological disorder characterized by communication problems, lack of social responsiveness, tendency to engage in repetitive or odd motor behaviors, and highly restricted routines and interests.

11. _____ Psychological disorder characterized by normal, even advanced language development, narrow interests, and inflexible behavior.

True/False Test

Indicate whether each item is true or false by placing T or F in the space next to each item.

1. ____ Howard Gardner is a contemporary American psychologist whose theory of intelligence states that there is not one intelligence but multiple independent intelligences.

2. ____ Identical twins develop from two different fertilized eggs and are 50 percent genetically similar to each other.

3. ____ Heredity refers to the traits, capacities, and intellectual potential that we inherit from our parents, grandparents, and great-grandparents.

4. ____ Analytic intelligence refers to the mental processes used in learning how to solve problems, that is, in picking a problem-solving strategy and applying it to solve problems.

5. ____ In the debate over what determines intelligence, environment refers to factors such as type of upbringing, nutritional and health standards, social and cultural factors, and other influences that may have an effect on intellectual development.

6. ____ Fraternal twins share exactly the same genes because they developed from a single fertilized egg that split into two.

7. ____ Sternberg's theory that there are three forms of intelligence—analytic, creative, and practical—is called the triarchic theory of intelligence.

8. ____ Successful intelligence involves three distinct types of mental ability—analytic, creative, and practical.

9. ___ Claude Steele is a contemporary American psychologist whose research has focused on the effects of stereotypes and is credited with coining the term *stereotype threat.*

10. ___ An IQ is 70 or below is characteristic of mental retardation.

Check your answers and review any areas of weakness before going on to the next section.

Something to Think About

1. Many people mistakenly believe that creativity is restricted to a few gifted, genius-level, artistic people. What would you tell someone who wants to be creative but does not believe he or she possesses an artistic temperament?

2. People vary in their IQ test scores, but about 68 percent of scores on tests such as the WAIS-III are between 85 and 115, the range for normal intelligence. A friend comes up to you and says, "Wouldn't it be great if we all had above-average IQ scores? Just think how wonderful life would be and how happy and successful we'd be!" How might you enlighten your friend about IQ tests and IQ scores?

Check your answers and review any areas of weakness before doing the progress tests.

Progress Test 1

Review the complete chapter (including all boxed inserts), review all your study notes, and then test yourself on the following progress test. Check your answers. If you make a mistake, review your notes, check the appropriate section in the study guide, and if necessary, go back and read the relevant part of the chapter in your textbook.

1. In applying for a job at O'Hare Airport, Lynda is given a test to see if she is suited to be an air traffic controller. This is an example of _____ testing.
   - (a) intelligence
   - (b) achievement
   - (c) aptitude
   - (d) motivational

2. When Aaron is asked to define *weapon,* he responds that it is anything you could use to beat someone with. Aaron is using the word *weapon* as a
   - (a) natural concept.
   - (b) algorithm.
   - (c) formal concept.
   - (d) heuristic.

3. When Michelle is asked the same question as Aaron, she replies that a weapon is one of a variety of instruments, or objects, that can be used to defend, attack, hurt, maim, or kill. Furthermore, the term *weapon* can even refer to words in a phrase, as in "the pen is mightier than the sword." Michelle is using the word *weapon* as a
   - (a) natural concept.
   - (b) prototype.
   - (c) formal concept.
   - (d) heuristic.

4. When 3-year-old Claudia is asked which letter of the alphabet comes before *g*, she recites the alphabet from the beginning until she arrives at the solution. Claudia is using _____ to solve the problem.
   - (a) trial and error
   - (b) insight
   - (c) an algorithm
   - (d) a heuristic

5. Louis forgot to bring his pillow when he went camping for the weekend, so he spent a very uncomfortable night. It didn't occur to Louis that he could use his down-filled jacket as a pillow. This example best illustrates
   - (a) functional fixedness.
   - (b) mental set.
   - (c) the availability heuristic.
   - (d) use of an algorithm.

6. When Vasilis is faced with the decision of which of two equally attractive apartments to rent, he makes a list of what is most important and gives each factor a numerical rating. It appears that Vasilis is using the _____ model of decision making.
   - (a) elimination by aspects
   - (b) additive
   - (c) single-feature
   - (d) heuristic

7. Jerome recently saw a TV special in which most of the psychologists interviewed were middle-aged, bearded males. When he took his first psychology class, he was surprised to find that his professor was a young female rather than an older, bearded male. Jerome's surprise is probably due to his use of the

   (a) availability heuristic.
   (b) representativeness heuristic.
   (c) single-feature model.
   (d) additive model.

8. When Heidi tells Hans that she is going to enter a foot race to raise funds to end the arms race, he has no trouble understanding that she is going to run in a race to generate support for an anti-weapons cause. Hans's correct interpretation best illustrates the importance of

   (a) syntax.   (c) generativity.
   (b) displacement.   (d) prototypes.

9. In the course of doing some research for a term paper, Anet read about the psychologist who is best known for developing the first intelligence test. She also discovered that this psychologist believed his test could help identify children who needed special help. Anet was reading about

   (a) Charles Spearman. (c) Alfred Binet.
   (b) Lewis Terman.   (d) Louis L. Thurstone.

10. Six-year-old Bruce's performance on an intelligence test is at a level characteristic of an average 4-year-old. Bruce's mental age is

    (a) 8.   (c) 6.
    (b) 4.   (d) 5.

11. Scott is a very bright 10-year-old with a mental age of 13. If tested on the Stanford-Binet Intelligence Scale, his IQ score would most likely be

    (a) 100.   (c) 150.
    (b) 77.   (d) 130.

12. Twenty-year-old Val has just taken a test that includes vocabulary, comprehension, general knowledge, object assembly, and other subtests. Val has completed the

    (a) WAIS.   (c) WISC.
    (b) WPPSI.   (d) Stanford-Binet.

13. In his research on very young black children adopted into white middle-class families, Dr. Wilson found that their IQ scores were several points above the average of both blacks and whites. Dr. Wilson, like most experts in this area, is most likely to conclude that

    (a) intelligence is determined primarily by heredity.
    (b) IQ scores cannot be improved by environmental factors.
    (c) improved diet and health standards are the crucial factor in improving IQ scores.
    (d) socioeconomic conditions, cultural values, and other such environmental factors can affect IQ scores.

14. As discussed in the Prologue, Tom has been diagnosed with Asperger's Syndrome. According to Critical Thinking (Neurodiversity), Tom is likely to

    (a) have a low score on the Raven's Progressive Matrices test (50 or below) and a high score on the WAIS (100 or above).
    (b) have an IQ score of 70 or below accompanied by a high level of social competence.
    (c) show abnormal and retarded language development, to have narrow interests and inflexible behavior, and by definition, have an IQ of 70 or below
    (d) show normal, even advanced language development, to have narrow interests and inflexible behavior, and by definition, have an IQ in the normal to genius level.

15. Critical Thinking (The Persistence of Unwarranted Beliefs) discusses how unwarranted beliefs in pseudosciences or other areas can persist, and how contradictory evidence can actually strengthen a person's established beliefs. A number of obstacles to logical thinking about unwarranted beliefs are discussed. Which of the following is NOT one of those obstacles?

    (a) the belief bias effect
    (b) the confirmation bias
    (c) the underestimation effect
    (d) the fallacy of positive instances
    (e) the overestimation effect

Progress Test 2

After you have checked your understanding of the material in Progress Test 1 and have done a complete chapter review with special focus on any areas of weakness, you are now ready to assess your knowledge on Progress Test 2. Check your answers. If you make a mistake, review your notes, the relevant section of the study guide, and, if necessary, the appropriate part of your textbook.

1. As part of his overall vocational assessment, Steven took a test that measured his level of knowledge, skills, and accomplishments in particular areas such as mathematics and writing ability. Steven took a(n) _____ test.
   - (a) aptitude
   - (b) achievement
   - (c) intelligence
   - (d) motivational

2. When Katrina is asked to identify the letters of the alphabet that do not have curved lines, she tries to mentally picture each letter as she completes the task. Katrina is using
   - (a) mental imagery.
   - (b) a natural concept.
   - (c) a formal concept.
   - (d) a prototype.

3. Shawn is asked to memorize a map of an island that has a hut, a lake, a tree, a beach, and a grassy area, all clearly marked at distinct locations. Later, he is asked to imagine a specific location, such as the hut; when a second location, the tree, is named, he has to press a button when he reaches the tree on the visual image in his mind. What are the results of this experiment most likely to reveal about the relationship between the distance between the two points and the time it will take Shawn to scan the mental image of the map?
   - (a) The greater the distance, the more time it will take Shawn to scan the mental image.
   - (b) The greater the distance, the less time it will take Shawn to scan the mental image.
   - (c) The shorter the distance, the more time it will take Shawn to scan the mental image.
   - (d) All of these statements are false; there is no relationship between distance and time taken to mentally scan points on a map.

4. When Earl is asked what object or objects come to mind in response to the word *vegetable,* he answers "potatoes and carrots." For Earl, potatoes and carrots are
   - (a) formal concepts.
   - (b) prototypes.
   - (c) algorithms.
   - (d) heuristics.

5. Dr. Naidu's research is concerned with the study of animal learning, memory, thinking, and language. Dr. Naidu is most likely interested in
   - (a) understanding the stereotype threat.
   - (b) investigating the triarchic theory of intelligence.
   - (c) heritability and heritability estimates.
   - (d) comparative cognition.

6. When Elana got her new DVD recorder, she spent a lot of time trying different approaches to programming the machine rather than consulting the manual. Elana is using the _____ approach to problem solving.
   - (a) algorithm
   - (b) trial-and-error
   - (c) heuristic
   - (d) insight

7. After spending weeks studying a variety of sources and materials, Terry still couldn't decide on a topic for her seminar presentation. However, when she was out for her daily jog, she suddenly had a flash of inspiration about her topic. Terry solved her problem
   - (a) through insight.
   - (b) by using an algorithm.
   - (c) through functional fixedness.
   - (d) by using the representativeness heuristic.

8. Whenever his TV picture became fuzzy, Lloyd would bang the top of the TV set, which usually cleared the picture. Recently, when he was viewing a film on his new DVD player, tracking problems created a fuzzy picture; Lloyd banged the top of the TV over and over but to no avail. Lloyd appears to be experiencing a problem-solving obstacle called
   - (a) functional fixedness.
   - (b) subgoal analysis.
   - (c) a mental set.
   - (d) confirmation bias.
   - (e) prototypical male stupidity.

9. When writing term papers, assignments, and exams, Gary is very careful to use "he or she" in place of the masculine pronoun and "people" instead of "man." Gary is apparently aware of the relationship between language and
   - (a) prototypes.
   - (b) gender bias.
   - (c) mental sets.
   - (d) functional fixedness.

10. Dr. Peerless has designed a test to measure the level of scientific knowledge in high school graduates. To establish a norm against which individual scores may be interpreted and compared, she is presently administering the test to a large representative sample of high school graduates. Dr. Peerless is in the process of
    (a) establishing the test's reliability.
    (b) establishing the test's validity.
    (c) standardizing the test.
    (d) determining the test's aptitude.

11. Dr. Peerless needs to check whether her test on the level of scientific knowledge measures what it was designed to measure. She does this by comparing scores on her test with the scores and grades obtained by students in high school science courses. In this instance, Dr. Peerless is in the process of
    (a) establishing the test's reliability.
    (b) establishing the test's validity.
    (c) standardizing the test.
    (d) determining the test's aptitude.

12. Arnie is very adept at dealing with novel situations by drawing on previous experience and can often find unusual ways to relate old information to solve new problems. Robert Sternberg would call this _____ intelligence.
    (a) analytic   (c) creative
    (b) practical   (d) motivational

13. As part of a bizarre experiment in a science fiction story, Dr. Igor places 100 genetically identical individual infants in different homes. Because the infants are all identical, the heritability of intelligence (that is, the percentage of variation within the group that is due to genetic factors) should be _____ percent.
    (a) 0   (c) 65
    (b) 50   (d) 100

14. According to In Focus (Does a High IQ Score Predict Success in Life?), which of the following is true?
    (a) IQ scores reliably predict academic success.
    (b) Academic success is no guarantee of success beyond school.
    (c) Many different personality factors are involved in achieving success, such as motivation, emotional maturity, commitment to goals, creativity, and a willingness to work hard.
    (d) All of these statements are true.

15. According to the Application, which of the following is NOT a way to increase your creative potential?
    (a) Focus almost exclusively on extrinsic motivation.
    (b) Choose the goal of creativity.
    (c) Try different approaches.
    (d) Acquire relevant knowledge.
    (e) Engage in problem finding.

Progress Test 3

After you have checked your understanding of the material in Progress Tests 1 and 2, and have done a complete chapter review with special focus on any areas of weakness, you are ready to further assess your knowledge with Progress Test 3. Check your answers. If you make a mistake, review your notes, the appropriate parts of the study guide, and, if necessary, the relevant sections of your textbook.

1. Adrian took the WAIS test. One aspect of his general cognitive ability that is NOT likely to have been measured is his
   (a) linguistic ability.
   (b) problem-solving ability.
   (c) general knowledge.
   (d) creativity.

2. Dr. Larch is a renowned researcher and theorist in the area of intelligence testing. Like most experts in his field, Dr. Larch is most likely to agree that
   (a) genetic factors, rather than environmental influences, are the primary cause of any IQ differences found between racial groups.
   (b) within a given racial group, the differences among people are due at least as much to environmental influences as they are to genetic influences.
   (c) the IQ of any individual, regardless of his or her race, is determined almost exclusively by genetic factors and is relatively uninfluenced by environmental influences.
   (d) the IQ of any given individual, regardless of his or her race, is determined almost exclusively by environmental factors and is relatively uninfluenced by genetics.

3. With little or no hesitation, Matthew was able to state that cats and dogs are both examples of the concept of mammal; he was slower to respond when asked whether dolphins and whales were also examples of mammals. This example suggests that
   (a) formal concepts have fuzzy boundaries and that cats and dogs are prototypes of the category.
   (b) natural concepts have fuzzy boundaries and that cats and dogs are prototypes of the category.
   (c) formal concepts have fuzzy boundaries and that dolphins and whales are prototypes of the category.
   (d) natural concepts have fuzzy boundaries and that dolphins and whales are prototypes of the category.

4. Tom created the novel sentence, "The faceless bureaucrat was finally faced with making a face-saving decision but could not face up to the fact that he was in a fatal face-off with his favorite facetious faculty." Tom's ability to do this illustrates the _____ nature of language.
   (a) syntactic
   (b) inflexible
   (c) generative
   (d) practical

5. Dr. Adatia, a cross-cultural psychologist, discovered that children of immigrant Buraku families living in the United States had IQ scores no different from other Japanese Americans, but that the Burakumin in Japan had IQ scores 10 to 15 points lower than those of other Japanese. Dr. Adatia is most likely to conclude that
   (a) IQ scores are genetically determined.
   (b) social discrimination can affect IQ scores.
   (c) better nutrition is the main factor that influences IQ scores.
   (d) the U.S. educational system is better than that of Japan.

6. Dr. Bishop assesses the correlation between scores obtained on two halves of her new abstract reasoning test in order to measure the _____ of her test.
   (a) reliability   (c) norms
   (b) validity   (d) aptitude

7. Miguel is extremely adept at learning how to solve problems; that is, he is very good at picking problem-solving strategies and applying them to problems. Robert Sternberg would call this ability a form of
   (a) analytic intelligence.
   (b) creative intelligence.
   (c) practical intelligence.
   (d) general intelligence, or the g factor.

8. Dr. Welch believes that there are multiple independent intelligences that cannot be reflected in a single measure of mental ability and that each intelligence must be viewed within a cultural context. Dr. Welch's position is most consistent with the views of
   (a) Charles Spearman.
   (b) L. L. Thurstone.
   (c) Howard Gardner.
   (d) Robert Sternberg.

9. When Allison goes to graduate school, she plans to investigate aspects of the heredity–environment debate as it relates to intelligence. She is most likely to
   (a) use animals, such as rats and pigeons, in her research.
   (b) get involved in twin studies.
   (c) study the language abilities of primates.
   (d) explore creativity and intuition.

10. Maja is writing a paper for her course in comparative cognition. After reviewing all the relevant research on animal language, Maja is likely to conclude that
    (a) only humans possess language capabilities.
    (b) animals can communicate with each other but are not capable of mastering any aspect of language.
    (c) some species have demonstrated an elementary understanding of syntax and certain other aspects of language.
    (d) many animal species can "think," use language, and possess self-awareness.

11. Martin has had some difficulties in school and has fallen behind in academic achievement. His chronological age is 10 and his IQ score on the Stanford-Binet is 70. Martin's mental age is therefore
    (a) 7.   (c) 13.
    (b) 10.   (d) 5.

12. Cynthia always buys the brand of paper towels that is on sale, even if it is not the highest quality towel. Cynthia makes her decision about which paper towel to purchase based on the _____ model of decision making.
    (a) single-feature
    (b) additive
    (c) elimination by aspects
    (d) heuristic

13. Jan is orderly, neat, quiet, and shy. She enjoys reading in her spare time and is an avid chess player. Given this description, most people would guess that she is a librarian rather than a real estate agent. This tendency to classify Jan as a librarian illustrates the influence of
    (a) the availability heuristic.
    (b) belief bias.
    (c) the representativeness heuristic.
    (d) the elimination by aspects strategy.

14. According to Culture and Human Behavior (The Effect of Language on Perception), the linguistic relativity hypothesis (Whorfian hypothesis)
    (a) proposes that the differences among languages cause differences in the thoughts of their speakers.
    (b) has been supported by the results of dozens of cross-cultural studies.
    (c) suggests that the ability to count and use numerical concepts is an innate capacity of all human beings.
    (d) proposes that color perception does not depend on the language used and that people from cultures that vary in the number of color words used will perceive differences between colors in much the same manner.

15. According to Culture and Human Behavior (How Stereotypes Undermine Performance), which of the following is (are) true?
    (a) Older people always score lower on memory tests than younger people because forgetfulness and an inability to remember new material is the inevitable consequence of growing old.
    (b) Performance on relatively fair and objective tests may be susceptible to social and cultural influences such as the stereotype threat.
    (c) What other people expect and believe about a person's performance on a test will have no influence on his or her score as long as the test has been standardized.

    (d) Females always score lower than males on advanced math tests because they do not possess the same level of logical-mathematical intelligence as males.
    (e) All of these statements are true.

Answers

Introduction: Thinking, Language, and Intelligence

1. *Cognition is* a general term that refers to the mental activities involved in acquiring, retaining, and using knowledge.

2. *Thinking is defined as* the manipulation of mental representations of information in order to draw inferences and conclusions. *It typically involves* active mental processes and is often directed toward some goal, purpose, or conclusion.

3. *A mental image is* a mental representation of objects or events that are not physically present.

4. *We manipulate mental images* in much the same way as we manipulate the actual objects they represent. *Mental images are potentially subject to error and distortion because* they are not perfect duplicates of our actual sensory experience; instead, they are memories of visual images and are actively constructed.

5. *Concepts are* mental categories of objects, events, or situations based on properties they share. *The two ways of forming concepts are* learning the rules or features that define the particular concept (formal concept) and as a result of everyday experiences (natural concept).

6. *A prototype is* the most typical instance of a particular concept. *The more closely an item matches a prototype,* the more quickly we can identify it as being an example of the concept.

7. *Exemplars are* individual instances of a concept or category, held in memory. *When we encounter a new object,* we compare it to the exemplars that we have stored in memory to determine whether it belongs to that category.

Solving Problems and Making Decisions

1. *Problem solving is defined as* thinking and behavior directed toward attaining a goal that is not readily available.

2. *The trial-and-error strategy involves* attempting different solutions and eliminating those that do not work; it is useful when there is a limited range of possible solutions.

3. *An algorithm involves* following a specific rule, procedure, or method that inevitably produces the correct solution (such as a mathematical formula). Using an algorithm may not always be practical because of the amount of time it can take to solve some problems.

4. *A heuristic is a* general rule-of-thumb strategy that reduces the number of possible solutions. While it tends to simplify problem solving, it is not guaranteed to solve a given problem.

5. *Insight is the* sudden realization of how a problem can be solved. *Intuition means* coming to a conclusion without conscious awareness of the thought processes involved. Insights, intuitions, or hunches are likely to be accurate only in contexts in which you already have a broad base of knowledge and experience.

6. *Functional fixedness is* the tendency to view objects as functioning only in their usual or customary way; it may prevent us from seeing the full range of ways in which an object can be used.

7. *A mental set is* the tendency to persist in solving problems with solutions that have worked in the past; it may prevent us from coming up with new and possibly more effective solutions.

Decision-Making Strategies

1. *The single-feature model involves* making a decision based on a single feature. *It is appropriate when* the decision is a minor one.

2. *Using the additive model, you first* generate a list of factors that are most important to you, next you rate each alternative using an arbitrary rating scale, and finally, you add up the ratings for each alternative. *It is appropriate for* complex decisions and useful in identifying the most acceptable choice from a range of possible decisions.

3. *Using the elimination by aspects model, you* evaluate all the alternatives one characteristic at a time (starting with what you consider to be the most important feature) and systematically eliminate all alternatives that don't meet that criterion until only the one choice that satisfies your criteria remains. *It is appropriate when* the decision is complex and there is a need to narrow down a range of choices with multiple features.

4. *The availability heuristic is a strategy* in which the likelihood of an event is estimated on the basis of how readily available other instances of the event are in memory.

5. *The representative heuristic is a strategy* in which the likelihood of an event is estimated by comparing how similar it is to the typical prototype of the event.

Concept Check 1

1. insight
2. representativeness heuristic
3. cognitive; thinking
4. mental image
5. formal
6. natural
7. algorithm
8. trial-and-error
9. additive
10. exemplar

Matching Exercise 1

1. elimination by aspects model
2. thinking
3. prototype
4. insight
5. single-feature model
6. representativeness heuristic
7. algorithm
8. trial and error
9. formal concept
10. cognition
11. concept
12. heuristic

True/False Test 1

1. F	5. T	9. F
2. T	6. T	10. T
3. T	7. T	11. T
4. F	8. F	12. T

Language and Thought

1. *Language is defined as* a system for combining arbitrary symbols to produce an infinite number of meaningful statements.

2. *The five most important characteristics of language are as follows:* (a) The purpose of language is to communicate; to do so, language requires the use of symbols; their connection to meaning is arbitrary. (b) The meaning of these

arbitrary symbols is shared by others.
(c) Language is a highly structured system that follows rules for combining words (syntax).
(d) Language is creative, allowing for the generation of an infinite number of new and different phrases and sentences (generative). *(e)* Language involves displacement, the ability to communicate meaningfully about ideas, objects, and activities that are not physically present.

3. *Language influences thinking by* affecting our perceptions of others. For example, when the masculine pronoun is used, it tends to produce images of males and excludes females (it is not really a gender-neutral pronoun).

4. *Animals communicate with each other and with other species, but* some critics contended that they were simply responding to their trainers' nonverbal cues. However, recent studies have produced compelling demonstrations of animal language learning.

Measuring Intelligence

1. *Intelligence is defined as* the global capacity to think rationally, act purposefully, and deal effectively with the environment.

2. *Alfred Binet, along with psychiatrist Théodore Simon, devised* a series of tests to measure different elementary mental abilities, such as memory, attention, and the ability to understand similarities and differences; his research led Binet to the idea of a mental age.

3. *Lewis Terman translated and adapted* Binet's intelligence test (the Stanford-Binet Intelligence Scale) and developed the concept of the intelligence quotient, or IQ.

4. *David Wechsler developed a new intelligence test,* the Wechsler Adult Intelligence Scale (WAIS), which was designed specifically for adults, and its 11 subtest scores (measuring a variety of abilities) can be grouped to provide an overall verbal score and performance score. He also devised the WISC and WPPSI.

Principles of Test Construction: What Makes a Good Test?

1. *Achievement tests are designed to* measure a person's level of knowledge, skill, or accomplishment in a particular area. *Aptitude tests are designed to* assess a person's capacity to benefit from education or training.

2. *Standardization refers to* the administration of a test to a large, representative sample of

people under uniform conditions for the purpose of establishing norms.

3. *The normal curve, or normal distribution, is* a bell-shaped distribution of individual differences in a normal population in which most scores cluster around the average score.

4. *Reliability is defined as* the ability of a test to produce consistent results when administered on repeated occasions under similar conditions. *It is determined by* administering two similar, but not identical, versions of the test at different times, or by comparing the scores on one half of the test to the scores on the other half of the test.

5. *Validity is defined as* the ability of a test to measure what it is intended to measure. *One way to determine validity is by* demonstrating the predictive value of a test.

Concept Check 2

1. syntax
2. standardization; norms
3. mental; chronological
4. 100
5. IQ test; WAIS
6. reliability; validity
7. displacement; creative; generative
8. Wechsler Intelligence Scale for Children (WISC)

Matching Exercise 2

1. syntax
2. Alfred Binet
3. displacement
4. mental age
5. Stanford-Binet Intelligence Scale
6. validity
7. generative
8. animal cognition (comparative cognition)
9. normal curve (normal distribution)
10. intelligence
11. language
12. Wechsler Intelligence Scale for Children (WISC) and Wechsler Preschool and Primary Scale of Intelligence (WPPSI)

True/False Test 2

1. T	5. F	9. F
2. T	6. T	10. T
3. F	7. T	11. T
4. T	8. F	12. T

The Nature of Intelligence

1. *The two key issues involved in the debate over the nature of intelligence are as follows: (a)* Is intelligence a single, general ability or is it better described as a cluster of different mental abilities? *(b)* Should the definition of intelligence be restricted to the mental abilities measured by IQ and other intelligence tests, or should it be defined more broadly?

2. *The g factor (or general intelligence) is the notion* of a general intelligence factor that is responsible for a person's overall performance on tests of mental ability. *It was proposed by* Charles Spearman.

3. *Louis L. Thurstone proposed the notion that* intelligence is a cluster of seven different primary mental abilities, each a relatively independent element of intelligence.

4. *The idea of multiple intelligences was proposed by* Howard Gardner. *The eight intelligences are* linguistic, logical-mathematical, musical, spatial, bodily-kinesthetic, interpersonal, intrapersonal, and naturalist intelligence.

5. *The triarchic theory of intelligence proposes that* there are three distinct forms of intelligence: analytic, creative, and practical. *It was developed by* Robert Sternberg.

The Roles of Genetics and Environment in Determining Intelligence

1. *The basic heredity–environment issue is concerned with* whether we inherit our intelligence from our parents (genes, or nature) or whether our intellectual potential is primarily determined by our environment and upbringing (nurture). (Because of research by molecular biologists, the issue has become one of how environment influences gene expression.)

2. *Twin studies have been used because* identical twins share exactly the same genes, and any differences between them must be due to environmental factors rather than to hereditary differences.

3. *Heritability is defined as* the percentage of variation within a given population that is due to heredity. *Heritability estimates cannot be used to explain differences between groups because* unless the environmental conditions of the two groups are identical, it is impossible to estimate the overall genetic differences between the groups; even if intelligence were primarily determined by heredity, which is not the case, IQ differences between groups could still be due entirely to the environment (socioeconomic conditions, cultural values, and so on).

4. *It is virtually impossible to create a culture-free IQ test because* ability tests reflect the values, knowledge, and communication strategies of their culture of origin. Cultural differences in test-taking behavior may also affect results. Finally, the stereotype threat can cause students to perform as they think they are expected to perform.

Concept Check 3

1. Charles Spearman
2. practical
3. not likely
4. heredity
5. environment
6. environmental
7. was not possible
8. Louis L. Thurstone
9. spatial intelligence
10. interpersonal intelligence; Howard Gardner
11. stereotype threat
12. heritability (or heritability estimate)
13. Asperger's Syndrome

Graphic Organizer 1

1. David Wechsler
2. Robert Sternberg
3. Alfred Binet
4. Charles Spearman
5. Howard Gardner
6. Lewis Terman
7. Louis L. Thurstone

Matching Exercise 3

1. Robert Sternberg
2. heritability
3. *g* factor (general intelligence)

4. creativity

5. Louis L. Thurstone

6. practical intelligence

7. Charles Spearman

8. creative intelligence

9. stereotype threat

10. autism

11. Asperger's syndrome

True/False Test 3

1. T	4. T	7. T	10. T
2. F	5. T	8. T	
3. T	6. F	9. T	

Something to Think About

1. Many people would like to be more creative. Fortunately, much can be done to increase our creative potential. The first thing to tell someone is that creativity is hard to define precisely but that most cognitive psychologists agree that creativity is a group of cognitive processes used to generate useful, original, novel ideas and solutions. Creativity is not confined to artistic expression; as indicated in the definition, creativity involves usefulness as well as originality. Based on information in the Application, you could then conduct your own mini-workshop on creativity. You can summarize the workshop by using the letters of the word **CREATE** as an acronym: **C**hoose the goal of creativity; **R**einforce creative behavior; **E**ngage in problem finding; **A**cquire relevant knowledge; **T**ry different approaches; **E**xert effort and expect setbacks.

2. First, you could tell your friend that we can't all be above average. The distribution of intelligence scores tends to follow a normal, or bell-shaped, curve, with about 50 percent above average and 50 percent below average. Next, you could talk a little about the problems involved in defining intelligence. Not even the experts agree. Some think that performance on mental ability tests reflects a general intelligence, or g factor; others think there are three forms of intelligence; and some postulate multiple intelligences. Despite these disagreements, psychologists do agree that intelligence involves such elements as abstract thinking, problem solving, and the capacity to acquire knowledge. They also tend to agree that aspects of intelligent behavior such as creativity, motivation, goal-directed behavior, and adaptation to one's environment are not measured by conventional intelligence tests. Thus, IQ scores reflect the limitations of existing intelligence tests. Finally, although IQ scores may predict academic success, doing well in school is no guarantee of success and happiness in life in general. Many different personality factors are involved in achieving success, such as motivation, emotional maturity, commitment to goals, creativity, and, perhaps most important of all, a willingness to work hard. None of these attributes are measured by traditional IQ tests.

Progress Test 1

1. c	6. b	11. d
2. a	7. a	12. a
3. c	8. a	13. d
4. c	9. c	14. d
5. a	10. b	15. c

Progress Test 2

1. b	6. b	11. b
2. a	7. a	12. c
3. a	8. c	13. a
4. b	9. b	14. d
5. d	10. c	15. a

Progress Test 3

1. d	6. a	11. a
2. b	7. a	12. a
3. b	8. c	13. c
4. c	9. b	14. a
5. b	10. c	15. b

CHAPTER 8

Motivation and Emotion

PREVIEW	Reading the section below first will give you a general sense of the chapter's contents and an initial introduction to some of the major concepts and terms. This will prime you for what you are about to read and help you to develop a "cognitive map" that will guide your study of the material in this chapter. Likewise, reading the **preview questions** at the beginning of each major section will improve your ability to understand, learn, and retain the information.

CHAPTER 8 . . . AT A GLANCE	Chapter 8 is concerned with motivation and emotion. Motivation refers to the forces that act on or within an organism to initiate and direct behavior. Instinct theories, drive theories, incentive theories, arousal theory, and humanistic theories are introduced.

The motivation to eat is influenced by psychological, biological, social, and cultural factors. Set-point theory and the rate at which the body uses energy (basal metabolic rate, or BMR) are discussed in relation to the regulation of body weight. Settling-point models of weight regulation help explain why baseline body weight can change over time. Factors involved in becoming overweight or obese are presented.

The section on psychological needs as motivators covers Maslow's hierarchy of needs and Deci and Ryan's self-determination theory (SDT). Competence motivation and achievement motivation are compared, and the Thematic Apperception Test (TAT) is introduced.

Emotions have three basic components: subjective experience, a physiological response, and a behavioral or expressive response. They are associated with distinct patterns of responses by the sympathetic nervous system and in the brain. Emotional intelligence is discussed along with an evolutionary account of the value and function of emotions. Facial expressions for some basic emotions seem to be universal and innate, but expression is also influenced by cultural display rules. The major theories of emotion—the James–Lange theory, the two-factor theory of emotion, and cognitive appraisal theory—are examined. Emotion researchers tend to agree that emotions can be triggered in multiple ways and that instinctive emotional responses may not require a conscious cognitive appraisal.

The Application discusses Albert Bandura's concept of self-efficacy and describes methods for turning our goals into reality.

Introduction: Motivation and Emotion

Preview Questions

Consider the following questions as you study this section of the chapter.

- How is *motivation* defined?
- What three characteristics are associated with motivation?
- How is emotion related to motivation?

*Read the section "Introduction: Motivation and Emotion" and **write** your answers to the following:*

1. Motivation refers to _____
   _____

2. The three characteristics associated with motivation are _____
   _____
   _____

3. Emotions are closely tied to motivational processes (and vice versa) because both involve
   _____
   _____
   _____

Motivational Concepts and Theories

Preview Questions

- What five categories of theories have historically been included in the study of motivation?
- How does each theory explain motivation, and what are some of the limitations of these theories?
- What lasting ideas did each theory contribute to the study of motivation?

*Read the section "Motivational Concepts and Theories" and **write** your answers to the following:*

1. According to the earliest theories of motivation, instinct theories, people are motivated to
   _____
   _____

   The limitation of these theories is _____
   _____
   _____
   _____

2. According to drive theories, behavior is motivated by _____
   _____
   _____

   Their limitations are _____
   _____
   _____

3. Incentive theories proposed that behavior is motivated by _____
   _____

   Their limitation is _____
   _____

4. Arousal theory is based on the notion that people are motivated _____
   _____

   The limitation of this theory is that _____
   _____
   _____
   _____

5. Humanistic theories emphasize the importance of _____
   _____
   _____

   (Limitations of this model are covered later in the chapter.)

6. The key ideas and concepts from each theory that were incorporated into newer models include _____
   _____
   _____

After you have carefully studied the preceding section, complete the following exercises.

Concept Check 1

Read the following and write the correct term in the space provided.

1. Amber is a graduate student studying the biological, emotional, cognitive, and social forces that activate and direct behavior. Her area of research is _____ .

2. When Trevor is hungry, he eats. The consumption of food serves to maintain

   _____ .

3. Gurjinder loves bungee jumping, skydiving, and hang-gliding. Because of her need for novel and exciting sensory stimulation, she is likely to be dubbed a _____ .

4. Mrs. Lewis gives a gold star to any child in her class who gets 100 percent on the weekly spelling test. This example illustrates _____ theory.

5. Bruno the bear hibernates every winter. This behavior is an example of a(n)

   _____ .

6. When Bernice finished her first 10-mile race in less than 100 minutes, she felt totally exhilarated and overjoyed by having achieved her goal. Her intense feelings suggest that _____ are closely tied to motivation.

Review of Terms and Concepts 1

Use the terms in this list to complete the Matching Test, then to help you answer the True/False items correctly.

motivation	drive theories
activation	homeostasis
persistence	drive
intensity	incentive theories
emotion	arousal theory
instinct theories	sensation seeking
fixed action patterns	humanistic theories of
evolutionary perspective	motivation

Matching Exercise

Match the appropriate term/name with its definition or description.

1. _____ Theories that emphasize the importance of psychological and cognitive components in human motivation, especially the notion that people are motivated to realize their personal potential.

2. _____ The biological, emotional, cognitive, or social forces that activate and direct behavior.

3. _____ Basic characteristic commonly associated with motivation that is seen in a person's continued efforts or determination to achieve a particular goal, often in the face of obstacles.

4. _____ Automatic and innate instinctual behavior patterns, such as migration or mating rituals, displayed by animals.

5. _____ Need or internal motivational state that activates behavior to reduce the need and restore homeostasis.

6. _____ Theories that view certain human behaviors as innate and due to evolutionary programming.

7. _____ Degree to which an individual is motivated to experience high levels of sensory and physical arousal associated with varied and novel activities.

8. _____ Point of view that considers how our heritage influences human behaviors such as eating habits or the expression of emotions.

True/False Test

Indicate whether each statement is true or false by placing T or F in the blank space next to each item.

1. ____ Incentive theories propose that behavior is motivated by the pull of external goals, such as rewards.

2. ____ Arousal theory is the view that people are motivated to maintain a level of arousal that is optimal—neither too high nor too low.

3. ____ Activation, one of the basic characteristics commonly associated with motivation, is seen in the greater vigor of responding that usually accompanies motivated behavior.

4. ____ Drive theories propose that behavior is motivated by the desire to reduce internal tension caused by unmet biological needs.

5. ____ Homeostasis refers to the notion that the body monitors and maintains internal states, such as body temperature and energy supplies, at relatively constant levels; in general, the tendency to reach or maintain equilibrium.

6. ___ Intensity, one of the basic characteristics commonly associated with motivation, is seen in the initiation or production of behavior.

7. ___ Emotion is a complex psychological state that involves subjective experience, a physiological response, and a behavioral or expressive response.

Check your answers and review any areas of weakness before going on to the next section.

Biological Motivation: Hunger and Eating

Preview Questions

Consider the following questions as you study this section of the chapter.

- What factors interact and influence the motivation to eat?
- What is energy homeostasis, and how does it relate to energy balance?
- What are glucose, insulin, the basal metabolic rate, and adipose tissue, and what role do they play in energy homeostasis?
- What are the short-term signals that regulate eating, and what roles do ghrelin, satiation, cholecystokinin (CCK), and sensory-specific satiety play?
- What are the long-term chemical signals that regulate body weight, and what influences do leptin, insulin, and neuropeptide Y (NPY) have in the long-term regulation of stable body weight?
- What are set-point and settling-point theories, and how do they differ?

*Read the section "Biological Motivation: Hunger and Eating" and **write** your answers to the following:*

1. Eating behavior reflects the complex interaction of _____

2. Energy homeostasis refers to _____

3. Energy homeostasis (energy balance) involves
   (a) glucose (blood sugar), which is a _____

   (b) insulin, which is a _____

   (c) basal metabolic rate (BMR), which is

   (d) adipose tissue, which is _____

4. A positive energy balance occurs when

   A negative energy balance occurs when

5. In terms of physiological changes, about 30 minutes before eating there is _____

   Once a meal has begun _____

6. An important internal signal involved in eating is provided by the hormone ghrelin, which is

   Blood levels of ghrelin _____

7. Psychological factors that trigger eating behavior involve
   (a) classical conditioning, in which _____

   (b) operant conditioning, in which _____

8. Satiation refers to _____

   Satiation involves signals from _____

   and _____

9. Sensory-specific satiety refers to _____
_____
_____

10. Long-term chemical signals that regulate body weight are

(a) leptin, a hormone secreted by the _____
_____
_____

(b) insulin, a hormone secreted by the _____
_____
_____

(c) neuropeptide Y (NPY), a neurotransmitter manufactured _____
_____
_____

The two factors correlated with how much of each hormone is secreted are _____
_____

and _____
_____

11. According to set-point theory _____
_____
_____
_____

According to settling-point models of weight regulation _____
_____
_____
_____

After you have carefully studied the preceding section, complete the following exercises.

Excess Weight and Obesity

Preview Questions

Consider the following questions as you study this section of the chapter.

- What is the body mass index (BMI), and what is the difference between being obese and being overweight?
- What factors contribute to people becoming overweight?
- What factors contribute to people becoming obese?

- How do genetics and environment interact in people susceptible to becoming obese, and what factors are involved in obesity?

Read the section "Excess Weight and Obesity" and **write** *your answers to the following:*

1. The body mass index (BMI) is a _____
_____

2. People are considered overweight if _____
_____

Obesity is a condition characterized by _____
_____
_____

3. A number of factors are involved in creating a positive energy balance (when caloric intake consistently exceeds energy expenditure) and in becoming overweight:

(a) Going without sleep disrupts _____
_____
_____

(b) the positive incentive value of certain foods, defined as _____
_____

(c) the "SuperSize It" syndrome, a relatively recent phenomenon in which _____
_____

(d) the cafeteria diet effect, which is_____
_____

(e) the sedentary lifestyle of many people (40 percent of Americans) who never
_____
_____

(f) individual differences and lifespan changes are involved because _____
_____
_____

4. Several factors contribute to obesity:

   (a) The interaction of genetics and environment, because _____

   _____

   _____

   (b) leptin resistance, which refers to

   _____

   _____

   (c) weight cycling (yo-yo dieting), which is

   _____

   _____

   (d) and finally, as noted in Focus on Neuroscience, obese people's brains tend to have fewer _____

   _____

   which may lead to _____

   _____

After you have carefully studied the preceding section, complete the following exercises.

Concept Check 2

Read the following and write the correct term in the space provided.

1. Shortly before lunch Farah begins to feel hungry. It is likely that blood levels of the hormone _____ , which is primarily manufactured by cells lining the stomach, have _____ (increased/decreased).

2. By the end of her family's holiday dinner Federicca declared that she was so full she couldn't eat another bite. Federicca is experiencing _____ , a feeling that is promoted, in part at least, by the chemical _____ .

3. Although she was feeling full after her turkey dinner, Federicca was still able to eat a plate of her favorite dessert. It appears that her feeling of being full after eating the main course was a _____ satiety.

4. Although he leads a somewhat sedentary lifestyle, 35-year-old Joshua has been about the same weight, give or take a pound or two, since his late teens. Joshua's relatively consistent weight is called his _____ ; instances of stable weight over time, such as Joshua's, provide support for _____ theory.

5. The regulatory process of matching food intake with energy expenditure that allows Joshua to maintain his typical body weight over time is called _____ .

6. If Dr. Hamagoochi studies the long-term signals that regulate body weight, he is most likely to investigate the effects of three chemical messengers: _____

   _____ .

7. Bruno the bear eats large quantities of food during the summer months in order to help him survive hibernation in the winter. His reserve of stored energy or calories is called _____ or _____ .

8. Benjamin, a lively 60-year-old, noted that as he aged his weight tended to increase somewhat, then stabilize, increase again, and stabilize once again, and so on. Now he is 30 pounds heavier than when he was a young adult. This phenomenon can best be accounted for by _____ theory.

9. Mikka multiplied her weight in pounds by 703 and divided the product by her height in inches squared. She has just calculated her _____ . If the resulting number is 30.0 or greater, she is considered _____ .

10. During his afternoon statistics lecture, Dimitri's mind wandered as he contemplated the pleasure of having souvlaki, salad, olives, feta cheese, and pita bread for dinner. These foods obviously have a high _____ for Dimitri.

11. Alice has experienced weight cycling (yo-yo dieting) throughout most of the time she has been attempting to lose weight. Her inability to

maintain weight loss may be due in part to

_____ .

12. Whenever Saul and his friends eat at the International Self-Serve Smorgasbord Deli, which has a wide variety of wonderful foods, they tend to consume substantially more food than they would at the school cafeteria. This phenomenon is called the

_____ .

13. Charles' calculated BMI is 27.7. Assuming that his BMI is due to fat rather than muscle or bone, he would be considered _____ (normal/overweight/obese).

Review of Terms and Concepts 2

Use the terms in this list to complete the Matching Test, then to help you answer the True/False items correctly.

glucose (blood sugar)
glycogen
insulin
basal metabolic rate
  (BMR)
adipose tissue
baseline body weight
energy homeostasis
  (energy balance)
positive energy balance
negative energy balance
ghrelin
positive incentive value
satiation
stretch receptors
cholecystokinin (CCK)

sensory-specific satiety
leptin
neuropeptide Y (NPY)
set-point theory and
  set-point weight
settling-point models of
  weight regulation and
  settling-point weight
body mass index (BMI)
overweight
obese (or obesity)
cafeteria diet effect
leptin resistance
weight cycling
  (yo-yo dieting)

Matching Exercise

Match the appropriate term with its definition or description.

1. _____ An organism's typical body weight.

2. _____ When the body is at rest, the rate at which it uses energy for vital functions, such as heartbeat and respiration.

3. _____ Compound formed and stored in the liver and the muscles that can easily be reconverted into glucose for energy.

4. _____ A numerical scale indicating adult height in relation to weight that is calculated by multiplying weight in pounds by 703 and dividing the product by height in inches squared.

5. _____ Body fat that is the main source of stored or reserve energy.

6. _____ Hormone produced by the pancreas that regulates blood levels of glucose and signals the hypothalamus, regulating hunger and eating behavior.

7. _____ In the stomach, specialized sensory receptors that communicate sensory information to the brainstem.

8. _____ In eating behavior, the long-term matching of caloric intake and caloric energy expenditure.

9. _____ Reduced desire to continue consuming a particular food.

10. _____ A condition in which higher-than-normal blood levels of the hormone leptin does not produce the expected physiological response.

11. _____ Repeated cycles of dieting, weight loss, and weight regain.

12. _____ Hormone manufactured primarily by the stomach that stimulates appetite and the secretion of growth hormone by the pituitary gland.

13. _____ Neurotransmitter found in several brain areas, most notably the hypothalamus, that stimulates eating behavior and reduces metabolism, promoting positive energy balance and weight gain.

True/False Test

Indicate whether each statement is true or false by placing T or F in the blank space next to each item.

1. ____ Set-point theory suggests that body weight (the set-point weight) settles, or stabilizes, around the point at which there is a balance between the factors influencing energy intake and energy expenditure.

2. ____ Glucose is the simple sugar that provides energy and is primarily produced by conversion of carbohydrates and fats.

3. ____ In eating behavior, a negative energy balance occurs when caloric intake exceeds calories expended for energy; produced by overeating or overconsumption.

4. ____ In eating behavior, satiation is the feeling of fullness and diminished desire to eat that accompanies eating a meal, and in general, refers to fully or excessively satisfying an appetite or desire.

5. ____ Leptin is a hormone produced by fat cells that signals the hypothalamus, regulating hunger and eating behavior.

6. ____ Cholecystokinin (CCK) is a chemical that is secreted primarily by the small intestines that promotes satiation; also found in the brain.

7. ____ Settling-point models of weight regulation propose that humans and other animals have a natural or optimal body weight (the settling-point weight) that the body defends from becoming higher or lower by regulating feelings of hunger and metabolism.

8. ____ In eating behavior, positive incentive value is the anticipated pleasure of consuming a particular food and, in general, the expectation of pleasure or satisfaction in performing a particular task.

9. ____ In eating behavior, a positive energy balance occurs when calories expended for energy exceed caloric intake; produced by fasting, dieting, or starvation.

10. ____ Obesity is a condition characterized by excessive body fat and a body mass index (BMI) equal to or greater than 30.0.

11. ____ People are considered overweight if their BMI is between 25 and 29.9, and is due to fat and not muscle or bone.

12. ____ The tendency to eat more when a wide variety of palatable foods is available is called the cafeteria diet effect.

Check your answers and review any areas of weakness before going on to the next section.

Psychological Needs as Motivators

Preview Questions

Consider the following questions as you study this section of the chapter.

- What are the key questions associated with theories that emphasize the motivation to satisfy fundamental psychological needs?
- How does Maslow's hierarchy of needs explain human motivation?
- What are some important criticisms of Maslow's theory?
- Which psychologists are associated with self-determination theory, and what are its basic premises?
- What roles do intrinsic and extrinsic motivation play in human behavior?

*Read the section "Psychological Needs as Motivators" and **write** your answers to the following:*

1. Some of the key questions associated with motivational theories that emphasize fundamental psychological needs are

   (a) _____

   (b) _____

   _____

   (c) _____

   _____

2. Maslow's hierarchy of needs divides motivation

   into _____

   _____

   _____

   Maslow believed that people _____

   _____

   _____

   _____

3. Criticisms of Maslow's model of motivation are

   (a) The concept of self-actualization is _____

   _____

   _____

   (b) Maslow's initial studies on self-actualization

   _____

   _____

(c) Despite the claim that self-actualization is an innate motivational goal of all people,

_____

_____

(d) Maslow's notion that we must satisfy needs at one level before moving to the next level

_____

_____

4. Self-determination theory is associated with psychologists _____ _____, who contend that in order to realize optimal psychological functioning we must meet three innate and universal psychological needs:

   (a) autonomy, which is _____

   _____

   _____

   (b) competence, which is _____

   _____

   _____

   (c) relatedness, which is _____

   _____

   _____

5. Intrinsic motivation refers to _____

   _____

   Extrinsic motivation refers to _____

   _____

Competence and Achievement Motivation

Preview Questions

Consider the following questions as you study this section of the chapter.

- How does competence motivation differ from achievement motivation, and how is achievement motivation measured?
- What characteristics are associated with a high level of achievement motivation, and how does culture affect achievement motivation?

*Read the section "Competence and Achievement Motivation" and **write** your answers to the following:*

1. Competence motivation is displayed when

   _____

   _____

2. Achievement motivation refers to _____

   It is measured by the _____

   _____

3. People who score high in achievement motivation tend to _____

   _____

   _____

   _____

4. In individualistic cultures, the need to achieve emphasizes _____

   _____

   _____

   whereas in collectivistic cultures _____

   _____

   _____

After you have carefully studied the preceding sections, complete the following exercises.

Concept Check 3

Read the following and write the correct term in the space provided.

1. Young Alec practices at the golf range for at least two or three hours most days because he plans to become a professional golfer. His goal and behavior suggest that Alec has a high level of _____ motivation.

2. Yen Shih and her fellow students believe that it is unacceptable to express pride for personal achievements, but it is acceptable to feel pride in achievements that benefit others. Yen Shih most likely lives in a _____ culture.

3. Young Mindy loves painting and spends many enjoyable hours carefully drawing and coloring flowers, butterflies, and birds. Her focused behavior is most likely a result of _____ motivation.

4. Allison wants to prove to herself that she is capable of mastering basic mathematical concepts, so she enrolls in an algebra course and an introductory statistics course. Allison is demonstrating _____ motivation.

5. Dr. Rosenbaum believes that people are actively growth-oriented and that to realize optimal psychological functioning and growth, three innate and universal psychological needs must be satisfied. Dr. Rosenbaum's views are most consistent with _____ theory.

6. Sarah studies and rehearses her spelling list because those children who get 100 percent on the weekly test receive a gold star and have their name and prize posted on the bulletin board. Sarah's studying behavior appears to be a function of _____ motivation.

7. In her counseling practice, Dr. Harrar is often interested in her clients' achievement motivation; to measure their need for achievement (nAch) she is likely to use the

    _____ .

Graphic Organizer 1

Identify the theory associated with each of the following statements:

Statement	Theory
1. I support the view that behavior is motivated by the desire to reduce internal tension caused by unmet biological needs that push us to behave in certain ways.	
2. I believe in the importance of psychological and cognitive factors in motivation, and especially the notion that people are motivated to realize their personal potential.	
3. I take my lead from Charles Darwin and support the perspective that we are motivated to engage in certain behaviors because of evolutionary programming.	
4. We are of the opinion that people are actively growth-oriented and that optimal human functioning can occur only if the psychological needs of autonomy, competence, and relatedness are satisfied.	
5. We do what we do because of the pull of external goals, such as obtaining rewards, money, or recognition. I believe that learning and cognitive theorists have it right when they say reinforcement, and the expectation of reinforcement, are key factors in motivation.	
6. In my view, people are motivated to maintain an optimal level of arousal that is neither too high nor too low. When arousal is too low, we experience boredom and try to increase arousal by seeking out stimulating experiences; when it is too high, we seek to reduce arousal in less stimulating environments.	

Review of Terms, Concepts, and Names 3

Use the terms in this list to complete the Matching Test, then to help you answer the True/False items correctly.

Abraham Maslow
hierarchy of needs
self-actualization
Edward L. Deci and
 Richard M. Ryan
self-determination
 theory (SDT)
autonomy
competence
relatedness

intrinsic motivation
extrinsic motivation
internalize and
 integrate
competence motivation
achievement motivation
Thematic Apperception
 Test (TAT)
power motivation

Matching Exercise

Match the appropriate term with its definition or description:

1. _____ The theory that optimal functioning can occur only if the psychological needs for autonomy, competence, and relatedness are satisfied.

2. _____ Maslow's division of motivation into levels that progress from basic physical needs to psychological needs to self-fulfillment needs.

3. _____ To incorporate societal expectations, rules, and regulations as values or rules that one personally endorses.

4. _____ A projective test developed by Henry Murray and his colleagues that involves creating stories about vague scenes that can be interpreted in a variety of ways.

5. _____ Behavior motivated by the desire to attain power or control or influence the behavior of other people or groups.

6. _____ American humanistic psychologist who developed a hierarchical model of human motivation in which basic needs must first be satisfied before people can strive for self-actualization.

7. _____ In self-determination theory (SDT), the need to effectively learn and master appropriately challenging tasks.

8. _____ In self-determination theory (SDT), the need to determine, control, and organize one's own behavior and goals so that they are in harmony with one's own interests and values.

True/False Test

Indicate whether each statement is true or false by placing T or F in the blank space next to each item.

1. ____ Edward L. Deci and Richard M. Ryan developed self-determination theory, which contends that optimal psychological functioning and growth can occur only if the psychological needs of autonomy, competence, and relatedness are satisfied.

2. ____ Extrinsic motivation refers to the desire to engage in tasks that the person finds inherently satisfying and enjoyable, novel, or optimally challenging.

3. ____ Self-actualization was defined by Maslow as "a person's full use and exploitation of talents, capacities, and potentialities."

4. ____ In self-determination theory (SDT), the need to feel attached to others and experience a sense of belongingness, security, and intimacy is called relatedness.

5. ____ The desire to direct one's behavior toward demonstrating competence and exercising control in a situation is called achievement motivation.

6. ____ Intrinsic motivation refers to external factors or influences on behavior, such as rewards, consequences, or social expectations.

7. ____ The desire to direct one's behavior toward excelling, succeeding, or outperforming others at some task is called competence motivation.

Check your answers and review any areas of weakness before going on to the next section.

Emotion

Preview Questions

Consider the following questions as you study this section of the chapter.

- How is *emotion* defined, and what are the three components of emotion?

- How do emotions and moods differ, what functions do emotions serve, and what is emotional intelligence?

- How do evolutionary psychologists view emotions?

- What are the basic emotions, and how are they classified?

- How do culture and individual differences influence emotional experience?

*Read the section "Emotion" and **write** your answers to the following:*

1. Emotion is defined as _____
   _____
   _____

2. Emotions tend to be _____
   _____
   _____

   Moods involve _____
   _____

3. Emotions have many functions, including triggering_____
   _____
   _____
   _____

4. Emotional intelligence is the capacity to
   _____
   _____
   _____

5. According to evolutionary psychologists, emotions are the _____
   _____
   _____
   _____

6. The most common basic emotions that all humans, in every culture, experience are
   _____
   _____

7. Cross-cultural research has shown _____
   _____
   _____

8. Cross-cultural researchers have noted that Japanese subjects also categorized emotions along a dimension of _____
   _____
   which reflects _____
   _____
   _____

The Neuroscience of Emotion

Preview Questions

Consider the following questions as you study this section of the chapter.

- How is the sympathetic nervous system involved in intense emotional responses?
- What brain structures are involved in emotional experience, and what neural pathways make up the brain's fear circuit?
- How does the evolutionary perspective explain the dual brain pathways for transmitting fear-related information?

*Read the section "The Neuroscience of Emotion" and **write** your answers to the following:*

1. The physiological component of emotions such as fear and anger involves the _____
   _____
   _____
   _____

2. The amygdala, which is part of the limbic system, is an _____
   _____
   _____

3. From an evolutionary perspective, evidence of a direct thalamus→amygdala pathway makes adaptive sense because the amygdala can be activated by _____
   _____
   _____

   When the amygdala is activated, it sends information to _____
   _____

   The second (indirect) pathway, thalamus→cortex→amygdala, allows more complex stimuli to be_____
   _____
   _____
   _____

The Expression of Emotions: Making Faces

Preview Questions

Consider the following questions as you study this section of the chapter.

- What evidence supports the notion that facial expressions for basic emotions are universal?
- How does culture affect the behavioral expression of emotion?
- How can emotional expression be explained in terms of evolutionary theory?

*Read the section "The Expression of Emotions: Making Faces" and **write** your answers to the following:*

1. Research on facial expressions (and emotions expressed vocally) suggests that _____ _____ _____

2. Display rules are social and cultural rules that _____ _____

3. Display rules can vary greatly from culture to culture (and even for different groups within a given culture, such as males and females); consequently, _____ _____ _____

4. The overall conclusion is that the expression of emotions serves the _____ _____ _____ _____

Theories of Emotion: Explaining Emotion

Preview Questions

Consider the following questions as you study this section of the chapter.

- What are the basic principles and key criticisms of the James–Lange theory of emotion?
- What challenges did Cannon present to the James–Lange theory?

- What is the facial feedback hypothesis, and how does this hypothesis and other contemporary research support aspects of the James–Lange theory?
- What are the two-factor theory and the cognitive appraisal theory of emotion, and how do the two theories differ?

Read the section "Theories of Emotion: Explaining Emotion" and write your answers to the following:

1. The James–Lange theory of emotions states that _____ _____

2. Walter Cannon criticized the James–Lange theory on a number of grounds:
   (a) Bodily reactions are _____ _____
   (b) Our emotional reaction to a stimulus is _____
   (c) When physiological changes are artificially induced, _____ _____
   (d) People cut off from feeling bodily changes _____

3. Support for some aspects of the James–Lange theory comes from
   (a) Damasio's work, which demonstrated that _____ _____
   (b) the facial feedback hypothesis, which states that _____ _____ _____

4. Schachter and Singer's two-factor theory of emotion suggests that _____ _____ _____

5. The cognitive appraisal theory proposes that _____ _____ _____

6. Although both two-factor theory and the cognitive appraisal theory emphasize the importance of cognitive appraisal, two-factor theory states _____

_____

_____

while the cognitive appraisal model stresses that _____

_____

_____

_____

After you have carefully studied the preceding sections, complete the following exercises.

Concept Check 4

Read the following and write the correct term in the space provided.

1. Since the end of the semester, Ellen had been feeling very content and relaxed. When she received her transcript in the mail and discovered that she had received an A+ in statistics, she was overwhelmed with excitement and relief. Ellen's two different states (contentment and excitement) illustrate the difference between a(n) _____ and a(n) _____ .

2. Walking to the parking lot late at night, Camellia suddenly hears footsteps behind her. Her heartbeat and blood pressure increase, her muscles tense, her mouth goes dry, and she begins to perspire. These physiological reactions were activated by her _____ nervous system and are called the _____ response.

3. Mr. Kobayashi is very careful to hide his true feelings and control his facial expressions when in the presence of his company's chief executive officers. This example illustrates the _____ of his culture.

4. Although Kasper is known for his superior reasoning skills, he appears to lack the ability to manage his own emotions and does not seem to

understand or respond appropriately to the emotions of others. It is probable that Kasper is low in _____ .

5. When Pavel got his layoff notice after five years with the company, he simultaneously experienced a number of emotions—anger, sadness, anxiety, and even relief and a degree of excitement about what the future would hold for him. Pavel has experienced _____ emotions.

6. Opening what he thought was simply a can of peanuts, generously given to him by his older sister, young Kyle was totally startled and alarmed by the "jack-in-the-box" snake that flew out of the can. His instantaneous startle response was most likely the result of stimulation of the _____ neural pathway in his brain.

7. In an experiment testing the two-factor theory of emotion, Milbourne was injected with a hormone called _____ that activated his sympathetic nervous system, causing accelerated heartbeat, rapid breathing, trembling, and so on.

8. Dr. Rhienhard believes that the cognitive interpretation of an event or situation and the personal meaning of that appraisal for the individual determine the emotion experienced. Dr. Rhienhard's view is most consistent with the _____ theory of emotion.

9. As the result of an accident that damaged her spinal cord, Gerri is paralyzed from the waist down. The fact that her experience of fear, anger, grief, sentimentality, and joyfulness has not been affected by her injury is _____ (consistent/not consistent) with the proposal made by William James.

10. Whenever she feels a bit gloomy, Danica sings the song "Pretend You're Happy When You're Blue." If she follows the advice of the song, she actually experiences an elevation in her mood. This example is consistent with the

    _____ .

11. When Harbinder first rode on the High Peak ski lift, he looked down at the steep slopes beneath him and became aware of his high level of physiological arousal. Suddenly, he felt fearful. Harbinder's experience is best explained by the

    _____ theory of emotion.

12. Cecelia decided to tackle the challenging task of becoming a proficient piano player. Although she knew that progress would likely be gradual and that there would be some setbacks along the way, she nevertheless felt that engaging in what Bandura called a _____ would help strengthen her sense of self-efficacy.

Graphic Organizer 2

Identify the emotion (relaxation, alarm, annoyance, boredom, astonishment) associated with each of the following descriptions and indicate where it should go on the matrix below.

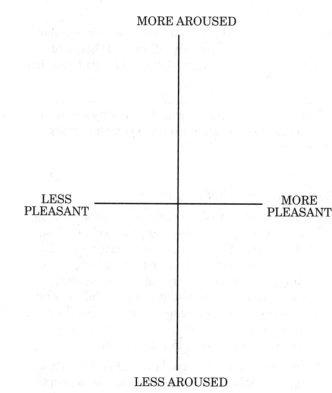

MORE AROUSED

LESS PLEASANT ————————————— MORE PLEASANT

LESS AROUSED

1. Natasha receives an A+ in her third-year history course and can hardly believe it.

   _____

2. In the middle of the night, Harry, who lives alone, is startled out of a deep sleep by strange noises coming from the basement.

   _____

3. During his three o'clock calculus class, Nathan finds the topic totally uninteresting and starts losing his concentration. _____

4. On Saturday, Dawn sleeps in and spends most of the morning propped up on comfortable pillows reading a romantic novel.

   _____

5. Five minutes after the meter has expired Dhillon arrives at his car only to find he has been given a $20 ticket. _____

Review of Terms, Concepts, and Names 4

Use the terms in this list to complete the Matching Test, then to help you answer the True/False items correctly.

emotion	anthropomorphism
mood	William James
emotional intelligence	James–Lange theory of
Charles Darwin	emotion
basic emotions	Walter Cannon
mixed emotions	epinephrine (adrenaline)
interpersonal	facial feedback
engagement	hypothesis
fight-or-flight response	two-factor theory of
amygdala	emotion
Paul Ekman	cognitive appraisal
emblems	theory of emotion
display rules	self-efficacy

Matching Exercise

Match the appropriate term/name with its definition or description:

1. _____ English naturalist and scientist whose theory of evolution through natural selection was first published in *On the Origin of the Species by Natural Selection* in 1859.

2. _____ The most fundamental set of emotion categories, which are biologically innate, evolutionarily determined, and culturally universal.

3. _____ The capacity to understand and manage your own emotional experiences and to perceive, comprehend, and respond appropriately to the emotional responses of others.

4. _____ The almond-shaped cluster of neurons in the brain's temporal lobe, involved in memory and emotional responses, especially fear.

5. _____ American psychologist and emotion researcher who is best known for his work in classifying basic emotions, analyzing facial expressions, and demonstrating that basic emotions and facial expressions are culturally universal.

6. _____ View that expressing a specific emotion, especially facially, causes the subjective experience of that emotion.

7. _____ Specific gestures or other nonverbal behaviors that have a particular meaning in a given culture but may vary across cultures.

8. _____ Schachter and Singer's theory that emotion is the interaction of physiological arousal and the cognitive label that we apply to explain the arousal.

9. _____ The attribution of human traits, motives, emotions, or behaviors to non-human animals or inanimate objects.

10. _____ Hormone secreted by the adrenal glands that is released into the bloodstream in response to physical or emotional stress or excitement.

11. _____ A complex psychological state that involves subjective experience, a physiological response, and a behavioral or expressive response.

True/False Test

Indicate whether each item is true or false by placing T or F in the space next to each item.

1. ____ The fight-or-flight response is a rapidly occurring series of automatic physical reactions, including accelerated breathing and heart rate, a surge in blood pressure, increased perspiration, dilation of the pupils, and dryness of the mouth.

2. ____ Display rules are social and cultural regulations governing the expression of emotions, especially facial expressions.

3. ____ In more complex situations we may experience mixed emotions, in which very different emotions are experienced simultaneously or in rapid succession.

4. ____ In comparison to an emotion, a mood involves a milder emotional state that is more general and pervasive and may last for a few hours or even days.

5. ____ Interpersonal engagement is a dimension of emotion reflecting the degree to which emotions involve a relationship with another person or people.

6. ____ Walter Cannon was an American psychologist who developed an influential theory of emotion called the Cannon–Bard theory of emotion.

7. ____ The James–Lange theory suggests that emotions arise from the perception of bodily changes.

8. ____ The cognitive appraisal theory of emotion proposes that emotions result from the cognitive appraisal of a situation's effect on personal well-being.

9. ____ Self-efficacy refers to the degree to which a person is convinced of his or her ability to effectively meet the demands of a particular situation.

10. ____ William James was an American psychologist who developed an influential theory of emotion called the James–Lange theory of emotion.

Check your answers and review any areas of weakness before doing the progress tests.

Something to Think About

1. Many Americans are obsessed with achieving, or at least getting closer to, the socially desirable goal of thinness. Approximately one-third of all American women and one-quarter of all American males are trying to lose weight, and the weight-loss industry is a multibillion-dollar-a-year enterprise. Based on what you have read in the text, what advice would you give to a friend who is trying to lose weight?

2. Imagine that you have been asked to write a report outlining ways that would help people

actually accomplish their goals. Using psychological research presented in the text, consider the various strategies that you might include in your paper on motivation and behavior.

Check your answers and review any areas of weakness before doing the progress tests.

Progress Test 1

Review the complete chapter (including Concept Reviews and the boxed inserts), review all your study notes, and then test yourself on the following progress test. Check your answers. If you make a mistake, review your notes, review the relevant section of the study guide, and, if necessary, go back and read the appropriate part of your textbook.

1. It is an innate characteristic of the European cuckoo to lay her eggs in other birds' nests. This behavior is called _____ and is an example of _____ .
   (a) a fixed action pattern; an instinct
   (b) energy homeostasis; a drive
   (c) a drive; incentive motivation
   (d) anthropomorphism; competence motivation

2. Harland got up in the middle of the night to go to the bathroom; in the dark, he accidentally tripped over his sleeping dog. Both the dog and Harland were instantaneously startled and frightened; the dog barked and Harland screamed. In this instance, it is very probable that the neural pathway involved in their immediate emotional reactions was the
   (a) thalamus→cortex→amygdala pathway.
   (b) hypothalamus→pituitary→cortex pathway.
   (c) thalamus→amygdala pathway.
   (d) amygdala→cortex→thalamus pathway.

3. About 10 or 15 minutes into his weightlifting routine Scott usually begins to perspire heavily. His body's tendency to maintain a steady temperature through the cooling action of sweating is a function of
   (a) instinct.
   (b) incentive motivation.
   (c) energy homeostasis.
   (d) self-actualization.

4. Dr. Range's views are consistent with self-determination theory (SDT). He believes that for people to realize optimal psychological functioning and growth throughout the lifespan, a number of innate and universal needs must be met, namely,
   (a) autonomy, competence, and relatedness.
   (b) competence, interpersonal engagement, and self-efficacy.
   (c) self-actualization, mastery, and self-efficacy.
   (d) relatedness, satiation, and homeostasis.

5. Morrie is a very successful business consultant. His success, in part at least, is due to his capacity to manage and understand his own emotional experiences, and his ability to correctly perceive, comprehend, and respond appropriately to the emotional reactions of his clients. Morrie has a high level of
   (a) emotional intelligence.
   (b) self-determination.
   (c) interpersonal engagement.
   (d) power motivation.

6. Tim buys a lottery ticket every Friday with the expectation that he is going to win some money. His behavior illustrates
   (a) competence motivation.
   (b) incentive motivation.
   (c) drive theory.
   (d) self-actualization.

7. Nicole feels that she has all the material possessions she needs in life and is now determined to devote all her energy to her art. According to Maslow's hierarchy of needs, Nicole is probably striving
   (a) to fulfill her fundamental biological need to paint.
   (b) to fulfill her basic safety needs.
   (c) toward the realization of her personal potential.
   (d) toward the realization of her social needs.

8. Fast-Fat-Fuds offers a double helping of fries with its Sooper Dooper Whooper Burger for only an extra 15 cents; not surprisingly, many people buy the larger meal. This phenomenon is referred to as
   (a) the "SuperSize It" syndrome.
   (b) the cafeteria diet effect.
   (c) positive incentive value.
   (d) the energy homeostasis effect.

9. Whenever he sees Amanda, Richard's heart beats faster and he gets a trembling feeling inside. Richard's personal interpretation of his physiological reaction to the sight of Amanda led him to experience the emotion of romantic love. Which theory of emotion is represented in this example?

    (a) self-determination theory (SDT)
    (b) drive theory
    (c) facial feedback theory
    (d) cognitive appraisal theory

10. Michael's achievement motivation reflects his North American individualistic culture. Compared to people in collectivistic cultures, Michael is more likely to

    (a) express pride for personal achievements that benefit others.
    (b) persevere and aspire to do well in order to fulfill the expectations of family members and to fit into the larger group.
    (c) emphasize personal success rather than the success of the group.
    (d) display a very low level of competence motivation.

11. Zomobia is easily bored and constantly seeks new and stimulating situations; she loves the outdoors and includes among her many interests skydiving, downhill skiing, white water kayaking, and hang-gliding. Based on this information about her, it is most probable that Zomobia would be classified as

    (a) a sensation seeker.
    (b) fully self-actualized.
    (c) emotionally intelligent.
    (d) having high extrinsic motivation.

12. As part of his overall vocational assessment, Bertram took the Thematic Apperception Test (TAT). His score on this test is most likely to reveal his level of

    (a) competence motivation.
    (b) need for achievement (nAch).
    (c) self-actualization.
    (d) emotional intelligence.

13. When Willard's relationship with Rebecca ended, he felt pretty confused and experienced a combination of relief, sadness, nostalgia, anger, and jealousy. Willard's experience illustrates

    (a) basic emotions.
    (b) mixed emotions.
    (c) mood fluctuations.
    (d) interpersonal engagement.

14. According to In Focus (Detecting Lies), the polygraph is a machine that

    (a) measures deception by tracking radioactive chemical "tags" that bind to dopamine receptors in the brain.
    (b) detects lies or deception with high reliability and few errors.
    (c) measures nonverbal cues such as microexpressions, nervous body movements, and fleeting facial changes.
    (d) measures physiological changes associated with emotions such as fear, tension, and anxiety.

15. Tracylynne usually starts the semester with the intention of studying hard, achieving high grades, eating a properly balanced diet, and getting lots of exercise. Unfortunately, these good intentions are rarely translated into actual behavior. According to the Application, which of the following strategies might help Tracylynne?

    (a) Transform general intentions into specific, concrete, measurable goals.
    (b) Create implementation intentions, such as specifying exactly where, when, and how the behaviors will be carried out.
    (c) Use mental rehearsal by visualizing successful outcomes.
    (d) Strengthen self-efficacy through mastery experiences and by observing and imitating the behavior of those already competent at these tasks.
    (e) All of these strategies would be useful.

Progress Test 2

After you have checked your understanding of the material in Progress Test 1 and reviewed the chapter with special focus on any areas of weakness, you are ready to assess your knowledge on Progress Test 2. Check your answers. If you make a mistake, review your notes, the relevant section of the study guide, and, if necessary, the appropriate part of your textbook.

1. Sachiyo had lunch more than an hour later than usual. Before lunch, she probably had high blood levels of the "hunger hormone"

    (a) ghrelin.
    (b) cholecystokinin (CCK).
    (c) neuropeptide Y (NPY).
    (d) leptin.

2. Farina was curious about the physiological changes that correlate with eating behavior. A review of the relevant literature would likely reveal that
   (a) eating is triggered by a drastic drop in blood glucose levels and a drastic increase in blood levels of insulin.
   (b) about 30 minutes before eating there is a *slight* decrease in blood glucose levels and a *slight* increase in blood levels of insulin.
   (c) eating is triggered by a drastic increase in blood glucose levels and a drastic decrease in blood levels of insulin.
   (d) about 30 minutes before eating there is a *slight* increase in blood glucose levels and a *slight* decrease in blood levels of insulin.

3. If he's feeling sad or unhappy, Milton "puts on a happy face." When he does this, his mood often improves. This result is best predicted by the
   (a) cognitive appraisal theory.
   (b) two-factor theory.
   (c) self-determination theory.
   (d) facial feedback hypothesis.

4. After his fifth slice of pizza, Massimo felt quite full. His feeling of satiation was most likely triggered by
   (a) stretch receptors in his stomach and cholecystokinin (CCK).
   (b) leptin, ghrelin, and insulin.
   (c) homeostasis, adipose, and insulin.
   (d) glycogen, leptin, ghrelin, and insulin.

5. Professor DeVoir's area of research is concerned with the long-term signals that regulate body weight. The chemical messengers of most interest to the professor are likely to be
   (a) leptin, insulin, and neuropeptide Y (NPY).
   (b) glucose, insulin, glycogen, and adipose.
   (c) CCK, BMR, and BMI.
   (d) BMR, NPY, and CCK.

6. Dr. Ushiro scanned the brains of his subjects using positron emission tomography (PET) while they recalled emotionally charged memories that made them feel sad, happy, angry, disgusted, and so on. If his research is consistent with neuroscience data reported in the text, he is likely to find that
   (a) there is a single "emotional center" in the brain that controls all emotions.
   (b) negative emotions such as fear and anger have distinct circuits in the brain, but positive emotions such as happiness and joy are governed by a single emotion center.
   (c) each emotion involves distinct neural circuits in the brain.
   (d) negative emotions such as fear and anger are governed by a single emotion center, but positive emotions such as happiness and joy have distinct circuits in the brain.

7. Dr. Zascow conducts research on the facial feedback hypothesis. Her results are consistent with previous research showing that expressing a specific emotion, especially facially, causes people to subjectively experience that emotion. Collectively, this evidence provides support for the _____ theory of emotion.
   (a) arousal
   (b) cognitive appraisal
   (c) two-factor
   (d) James–Lange

8. While writing a term paper for her motivation course, Cara notes that the majority of people do not experience or achieve self-actualization, despite the claim that it is a goal common to all people. She decides that this is an important limitation of
   (a) instinct theories.
   (b) drive theories.
   (c) incentive theories.
   (d) Maslow's hierarchy of needs.

9. Set-point theory provides the best explanation for which of the following?
   (a) Gladys finds that when she is alone and feeling bored her arousal level is uncomfortably low; in order to regain her normal or optimal level of arousal she seeks a more stimulating environment.
   (b) At age 60, Edwina noted that her weight had fluctuated over the years and had progressively increased to the point where she is now about 25 pounds heavier than she was 35 years ago.
   (c) After eating a very filling and satisfying main meal, Ken manages to eat and enjoy a delicious slice of banana cream pie.
   (d) Although she leads a somewhat sedentary lifestyle, 40-year-old Andrea has been about the same weight, give or take a pound or two, since her late teens.

10. In an investigation of culture and emotional experience, researchers discovered that Japanese people categorize emotions not only along pleasantness and activation dimensions but also along a third dimension. This dimension, called _____ , reflects the idea that some emotions result from relationships and interactions with other people.
    (a) interpersonal engagement
    (b) the self-efficacy dimension
    (c) anthropomorphism
    (d) emotional intelligence

11. Nithya has been carrying extra pounds for many years. If she is like most of the obese experimental subjects examined by neuroscientists who were studying obesity and the brain (Focus on Neuroscience), a PET scan is likely to reveal _____ in her brain, compared to normal-weight control subjects.
    (a) higher levels of cholecystokinin (CCK)
    (b) more dopamine receptors
    (c) lower levels of neuropeptide Y (NPY)
    (d) fewer dopamine receptors

12. Sidney believes that women are "naturally" more emotional than men. Which of the following is (are) true regarding gender and emotions?
    (a) males and females do not differ significantly in their experience of emotion.
    (b) women are more emotionally expressive compared to men.
    (c) men are more likely than women to mask their emotions.
    (d) all of these statements are true.

13. Dr. Heilbron studies a neurotransmitter, manufactured throughout the brain, that increases during periods of negative energy balance and triggers eating behavior, reduces body metabolism, and promotes fat storage. If there is a positive energy balance, the activity of this neurotransmitter decreases. Dr. Heilbron's research is concerned with
    (a) ghrelin.
    (b) leptin.
    (c) cholecystokinin (CCK).
    (d) neuropeptide Y (NPY).

14. According to Critical Thinking (Has Evolution Programmed Us to Overeat?), the tendency for people in industrialized countries to overeat and become overweight or obese is the result of
    (a) the high positive incentive value of many of our foods.
    (b) an evolutionary propensity to eat a wide variety of foods, which promoted survival by ensuring that essential nutrients, vitamins, and minerals were obtained.
    (c) a tendency to overeat when food is available, which was adaptive in our ancestral past.
    (d) all of these things.

15. Doyne typically approaches any difficult task as a challenge to be mastered; he exerts a strong motivational effort, persists in the face of obstacles, and looks for creative ways to solve the problem. According to the Application, Doyne has a high level of
    (a) self-efficacy.
    (b) self-actualization.
    (c) power motivation.
    (d) interpersonal engagement.

Progress Test 3

After you have checked your understanding of the material in Progress Tests 1 and 2, and have done a complete chapter review with special focus on any areas of weakness, you are ready to further assess your knowledge with Progress Test 3. Check your answers. If you make a mistake, review your notes, the appropriate parts of the study guide, and, if necessary, the relevant sections of your textbook.

1. When Sean went for his annual medical checkup, his doctor calculated his body mass index (BMI) and told him that he was overweight but not obese. Sean's BMI is most likely
   (a) between 25 and 29.9.
   (b) less than 20.
   (c) between 30 and 39.9.
   (d) less than 15.

2. Five-year-old Nemanja was excited and very curious about the various animals he saw when he was taken to the zoo for the first time. His exploratory behavior and curiosity were quickly inhibited, however, when he was suddenly startled and frightened by a loud roar from the lion's enclosure. According to the _____ theory of emotion, Nemanja's negative emotions were the result of cognitive appraisal of the meaning of the event or stimulus, whereas the _____ theory would say that they were the result of the perception of the physiological response to the event or stimulus.

   (a) arousal; two-factor
   (b) James–Lange; arousal
   (c) cognitive appraisal; James–Lange
   (d) two-factor; cognitive appraisal

3. The desire to drink when thirsty is to _____ as the desire to avoid boredom is to _____ .

   (a) sensory-specific satiety; sensation seeking
   (b) set-point theory; settling-point theory
   (c) drive theory; arousal theory
   (d) two-factor theory; cognitive appraisal theory

4. As Leopold aged he had to pay more attention to how much he ate in order to maintain his typical weight. One factor that may be involved in this tendency to gain weight as we age is that

   (a) the positive incentive value of food increases substantially over time.
   (b) leptin resistance increases with age.
   (c) as age increases the basal metabolic rate (BMR) decreases.
   (d) as age increases the basal metabolic rate (BMR) increases.

5. Dr. Fleming studies how food is converted into energy in the body. She is very likely to be interested in

   (a) glucose.
   (b) insulin.
   (c) basal metabolic rate (BMR).
   (d) all of these factors.

6. Lazy Lou's food intake tends to exceed the amount of calories he expends on energy. On the other hand, Frenetic Frank's caloric intake is often less than the calories he expends on energy. It is likely that Lou has _____ and Frank has _____ .

   (a) a low set-point weight; a high set-point weight
   (b) a positive energy balance; a negative energy balance
   (c) a low settling-point weight; a high settling-point weight
   (d) a negative energy balance; a positive energy balance

7. Despite minor seasonal fluctuations, Phil's weight has been fairly consistent all his adult life. One reason for this stability over time is that the number of calories he consumes tends to match the number of calories he expends, a process called

   (a) positive incentive value.
   (b) satiation.
   (c) fixed action pattern.
   (d) energy homeostasis.

8. Kramer argues that from an evolutionary perspective, our need for autonomy, competence, and relatedness had an adaptive advantage. The need for relatedness, for example, promoted resource sharing, mutual protection, and the division of labor; it thus increased the likelihood that both the individual and the group would survive. Kramer's views of motivation are most like those of

   (a) Maslow's self-actualization theory.
   (b) Ryan and Deci's self-determination theory.
   (c) Bandura's self-efficacy theory.
   (d) Schachter's two-factor theory.

9. Graham, an assistant manager, has a strong need to attain more power and status so that he can control and influence the behavior of other employees; he has his heart set on becoming general manager. It is probable that Graham has a high level of

   (a) self-actualization.
   (b) emotional intelligence.
   (c) anthropomorphism.
   (d) power motivation.

10. When Keiho first arrived in North America from Japan, she was surprised to find that people vigorously nodded their heads in answer to a question to indicate the affirmative "Yes" instead of "Maybe" or "No way." Nodding the head is a specific gesture called _____ that can have a different meaning in different cultures.

    (a) an emblem
    (b) anthropomorphism
    (c) a fixed action pattern
    (d) self-efficacy

11. Ulricke lost 20 pounds on her latest diet, and her weight fell below her set-point weight. She is likely to experience a(n) _____ in her basal metabolic rate and energy level; when she goes off the diet she is likely to _____ .

    (a) increase; maintain her weight loss
    (b) decrease; regain the lost pounds
    (c) increase; regain the lost pounds
    (d) decrease; maintain her weight loss

12. When Bryce was too afraid to jump off the top diving board at the pool, his friends accused him of having "cold feet." Later, when he was telling his Dad about the episode, he became angry and "hot under the collar." The two different descriptions of these basic emotions could have arisen because

    (a) anger produces an increase in skin temperature, and fear produces a decrease in skin temperature.
    (b) anger is associated with a decrease in heart rate and blood pressure, and fear is associated with an increase in heart rate and blood pressure.
    (c) anger produces a decrease in skin temperature and blood pressure, and fear produces an increase in skin temperature.
    (d) anger is associated with a decrease in heart rate and blood pressure, and fear is associated with an increase in heart rate and blood pressure.

13. Miguella was born blind and deaf. Despite her inability to observe or hear others, she still expresses joy, anger, and pleasure using the same expressions as sighted children. This example provides support for

    (a) the idea that basic emotions are innate.
    (b) the notion that emotional expressions are culturally determined.

    (c) the idea that both genetics and the environment are involved in the expression of basic emotions.
    (d) all of these ideas.

14. April is convinced that her cats experience the same emotions as humans. She argues that they can be happy or sad, anxious or content, frightened or fearless, and they can feel embarrassment, grief, love, and shame. According to Critical Thinking (Emotion in Nonhuman Animals), April is engaging in

    (a) interpersonal engagement.
    (b) anthropomorphism.
    (c) sensation-seeking behavior.
    (d) homeostasis.

15. When Alfie applied for a job with a government agency, he was told that he would have to take a polygraph test to evaluate his honesty. According to In Focus (Detecting Lies), Alfie should be concerned about taking the test because

    (a) the polygraph does not detect lies, only physiological changes associated with emotions like fear, tension, and anxiety.
    (b) there is no unique pattern of physiological arousal associated with lying.
    (c) the test itself can lead to increased physiological arousal and produce false positive results (an innocent person can be judged guilty).
    (d) interpreting polygraph results can be highly subjective.
    (e) of all of these reasons.

Answers

Introduction: Motivation and Emotion

1. *Motivation refers to* the biological, emotional, cognitive, or social forces that activate and direct behavior.

2. *The three characteristics associated with motivation are* activation (the initiation of behavior), persistence (continued efforts to achieve a goal), and intensity (the vigor of responding).

3. *Emotions are closely tied to motivational processes (and vice versa) because both involve* the complex interaction of physical, behavioral, cognitive, and social factors. We may be motivated to achieve certain emotions, and emotions may motivate us to take action.

Motivational Concepts and Theories

1. *According to the earliest theories of motivation, instinct theories, people are motivated to* engage in certain behaviors because of evolutionary programming. *The limitation of these theories is* that they merely describe and label behaviors rather than actually explain them.

2. *According to drive theories, behavior is motivated by* the desire to reduce internal tension caused by unmet biological needs, such as hunger or thirst. *Their limitations are that* people engage in behaviors that are not a reflection of internal drives (we sometimes eat when we are not hungry or don't eat when we are hungry) and that many behaviors involve psychological influences, such as buying a lottery ticket, that are not related to filling unmet biological needs.

3. *Incentive theories proposed that behavior is motivated by* the pull of external goals, such as rewards. In addition, cognitive factors, such as the expectation that a behavior will lead to a particular reward, may be involved. *Their limitation is* that many behaviors are not primarily motivated by any kind of external incentive (we sometimes engage in behaviors for their own sake without any obvious reinforcement).

4. *Arousal theory is based on the notion that people are motivated* to maintain an optimal level of arousal. When arousal is too low, we are motivated to seek stimulation; when it is too high, we seek to reduce arousal in a less stimulating environment. *The limitation of this theory is that* what constitutes an optimal level of arousal varies from person to person, time to time, and from one situation to another. For example, some people (called sensation seekers) seek out varied, novel, and unique sensory experiences because they find high levels of arousal pleasurable.

5. *Humanistic theories emphasize the importance of* psychological and cognitive components in human motivation, especially the notion that people are motivated to realize their personal potential.

6. *The key ideas and concepts from these theories that were incorporated into newer models include* drive, homeostasis, incentive, and arousal.

Concept Check 1

1. motivation

2. homeostasis

3. sensation seeker

4. incentive

5. instinct

6. emotions

Matching Exercise 1

1. humanistic theories of motivation

2. motivation

3. persistence

4. fixed action patterns

5. drive

6. instinct theories

7. sensation seeking

8. evolutionary perspective

True/False Test 1

1. T	3. F	5. T	7. T
2. T	4. T	6. F	

Biological Motivation: Hunger and Eating

1. *Eating behavior reflects the complex interaction of* psychological, biological, and social factors.

2. *Energy homeostasis refers to* the long-term matching of food intake to energy expenditure.

3. *Energy homeostasis (energy balance) involves (a) glucose (blood sugar), which is a* simple sugar that provides energy and is primarily produced by the conversion of carbohydrates and fats;
(b) insulin, which is a hormone produced by the pancreas that regulates blood levels of glucose and signals the hypothalamus, regulating hunger and eating behavior;
(c) basal metabolic rate (BMR), which is the rate at which your body at rest uses energy for vital body functions such as generating body heat, heartbeat, respiration, and brain activity;
(d) adipose tissue, which is body fat that is the main source of stored, or reserve, calories (energy).

4. *A positive energy balance occurs when* caloric intake exceeds the amount of calories expended for energy and the excess glucose is stored as fat (reserve energy). *A negative energy balance occurs when* caloric intake falls short of the calories expended as energy; if continued, body fat stores will shrink.

5. *In terms of physiological changes, about 30 minutes before eating there is* a slight increase in blood levels of insulin, a slight decrease in blood levels of glucose, body temperature

increases, and metabolism decreases. *Once a meal has begun,* blood glucose levels return to baseline, body temperature decreases, and metabolism increases.

6. *An important internal signal involved in eating is the hormone ghrelin, which is* manufactured primarily by the stomach and stimulates appetite and the secretion of growth hormone by the pituitary gland. *Blood levels of ghrelin* rise sharply before meals and fall abruptly after meals.

7. *Psychological factors that trigger eating behavior involve*
(a) *classical conditioning, in which* the conditioned stimulus or CS (the time you normally eat, the setting, the sight of food cues, etc.) elicits the conditioned response or CR (internal physiological changes, such as changes in blood levels of insulin, glucose, and ghrelin, increased body temperature, and decreased metabolism).
(b) *operant conditioning, in which* voluntary eating behaviors are followed by a reinforcing stimulus (food) and are thus positively reinforced (preferred foods acquire positive incentive value).

8. *Satiation refers to* the feeling of fullness and diminished desire to eat that accompanies eating a meal. *Satiation involves signals from* stretch receptors in the stomach that communicate sensory information to the brainstem *and* cholecystokinin (CCK), a hormone/neurotransmitter that promotes satiety effects.

9. *Sensory-specific satiety refers to* the reduced desire to continue consuming a particular food, especially the food that is being eaten; this may be due to a decline in the food's positive incentive value.

10. *Long-term chemical signals that regulate body weight are*
(a) *leptin, a hormone secreted by the* body's adipose tissue (fat) into the bloodstream and detected by receptors in various locations in the hypothalamus and also by neurons in the stomach and gut that have leptin receptors.
(b) *insulin, a hormone secreted by the* pancreas; high brain levels of insulin are associated with reduced food intake and body weight.
(c) *neuropeptide Y (NPY), a neurotransmitter manufactured* throughout the brain, including the hypothalamus; increased levels trigger eating behavior, reduce body metabolism, and promote fat storage. *The two factors correlated with how much of each hormone is secreted are*

the amount of body fat and the degree of negative or positive energy balance.

11. *According to set-point theory,* the body has a natural or optimal body weight, called the set-point weight, that the body defends from becoming higher or lower by regulating feelings of hunger and body metabolism. *According to settling-point models of weight regulation,* the body weight tends to settle, or stabilize, around the point at which an equilibrium, or balance, is achieved between energy expenditure and calorie consumption; settling-point weight may go up or down depending on whether the factors affecting food consumption and energy expenditure change.

Excess Weight and Obesity

1. *The body mass index (BMI) is a* numerical scale indicating adult height in relation to weight; it is calculated as $703 \times$ weight (in pounds) divided by height in inches squared.

2. *People are considered overweight if* they have a BMI between 25 and 29.9 that is due to fat and not to muscle or bone. *Obesity is a condition characterized by* an abnormally high proportion of body fat and a body mass index equal to or greater than 30.0.

3. *A number of factors are involved in creating a positive energy balance (when caloric intake consistently exceeds energy expenditure) and in becoming overweight:*
(a) *Going without adequate sleep disrupts* the hunger-related hormones leptin (appetite-suppressing) and ghrelin (appetite-increasing), resulting in increased feelings of hunger, especially for foods with high carbohydrate content.
(b) *the positive incentive value of certain foods, defined as* the anticipated pleasure of consuming particular highly palatable foods.
(c) *the "SuperSize It" syndrome, a relatively recent phenomenon in which* restaurants, fast-food outlets, etc., offer substantially increased portions of food for very little extra money, an offer many find hard to resist.
(d) *the cafeteria diet effect, which is* the tendency to eat more when a wide variety of palatable foods is available.
(e) *the sedentary lifestyle of many people (40 percent of Americans) who never* exercise, play sports, or engage in physically active hobbies.
(f) *individual differences and lifespan changes are involved because* people vary greatly in their basal metabolic rate (which accounts for about two-thirds of energy expenditure),

females have a slightly lower BMR than males, metabolism decreases slightly over the lifespan (2 to 3 percent per decade), and weight gain will occur over time if food intake is not reduced.

4. *Several factors contribute to obesity:*
(a) *the interaction of genetics and environment, because* when a genetic predisposition to become obese is combined with a high-risk environment characterized by ample easily obtainable high-fat, high-calorie, palatable food, obesity is more likely to occur.
(b) *leptin resistance, which refers to* a condition in which higher than normal blood levels of the hormone leptin do not produce the expected physiological response of reduced eating behavior and weight loss.
(c) *weight cycling (yo-yo dieting), which is* the repeated cycles of dieting, weight loss, and weight regain experienced by many overweight and obese dieters.
(d) *and finally, as noted in Focus on Neuroscience, obese people's brains tend to have fewer* dopamine receptors than normal-weight individuals, *which may lead to* compulsive eating to stimulate brain reward centers.

Concept Check 2

1. ghrelin; increased
2. satiation; cholecystokinin (CCK)
3. sensory-specific
4. baseline body weight; set-point
5. energy homeostasis or energy balance
6. leptin, insulin, and neuropeptide Y (NPY)
7. adipose tissue; body fat
8. settling-point
9. body mass index (BMI); obese
10. positive incentive value
11. her body defending against weight loss by decreasing her basal metabolic rate and energy level
12. cafeteria diet effect
13. overweight

Matching Exercise 2

1. baseline body weight
2. basal metabolic rate (BMR)
3. glycogen
4. body mass index (BMI)
5. adipose tissue

6. insulin
7. stretch receptors
8. energy homeostasis (energy balance)
9. sensory-specific satiety
10. leptin resistance
11. weight cycling
12. ghrelin
13. NPY (neuropeptide Y)

True/False Test 2

1. F	5. T	9. F	13. T
2. T	6. T	10. T	
3. F	7. F	11. T	
4. T	8. T	12. T	

Psychological Needs as Motivators

1. *Some of the key questions associated with motivational theories that emphasize fundamental psychological needs are*
(a) Are there universal psychological needs?
(b) Are we internally or externally motivated to satisfy psychological needs?
(c) What psychological needs must be satisfied for optimal human functioning?

2. *Maslow's hierarchy of needs divides motivation into* levels that progress from basic physiological needs to psychological needs to self-fulfillment needs. *Maslow believed that people* are motivated to satisfy the needs at each level of the hierarchy before moving up to the next level and that they are ultimately motivated by the desire to achieve self-actualization (the full use and exploitation of talents, capacities, and potentialities).

3. *Criticisms of Maslow's model of motivation are*
(a) *The concept of self-actualization is* very vague and difficult to define in a way that would allow it to be tested scientifically.
(b) *Maslow's initial studies on self-actualization* had limited samples and many were based on biographical and autobiographical accounts of famous historical figures that Maslow selected.
(c) *Despite the claim that self-actualization is an innate motivational goal of all people,* most people do not experience or achieve self-actualization.

(d) Maslow's notion that we must satisfy needs at one level before moving to the next level has not been supported (has not stood the test of time).

4. *Self-determination theory is associated with psychologists* Edward L. Deci and Richard M. Ryan, *who contend that in order to realize optimal psychological functioning we must meet three innate and universal psychological needs: (a) autonomy, which is* the need to determine, control, and organize one's own behavior and goals so that they are in harmony with one's own interests and values.
(b) competence, which is the need to effectively learn and master appropriately challenging tasks.
(c) relatedness, which is the need to feel attached to others and experience a sense of belongingness, security, and intimacy.

5. *Intrinsic motivation refers to* the desire to engage in tasks that the person finds inherently satisfying and enjoyable, novel, or optimally challenging (the desire to do something for its own sake). *Extrinsic motivation refers to* external factors or influences on behavior, such as rewards, consequences, or social expectations.

Competence and Achievement Motivation

1. *Competence motivation is displayed when* a person strives to use his or her cognitive, social, and behavioral skills to be capable and exercise control in a situation (provides much of the "push" for tackling new challenges).

2. *Achievement motivation refers to* the desire to direct one's behavior toward excelling, succeeding, or outperforming others at some task. *It is measured by* the Thematic Apperception Test (TAT).

3. *People who score high in achievement motivation tend to* expend their greatest efforts when faced with moderately challenging tasks, work long hours, display original thinking, seek expert advice, value feedback about their performance, and have the capacity to delay gratification. They also tend to be independent and to attribute their successes to their own abilities and efforts and explain their failures as being due to external factors or bad luck.

4. *In individualistic cultures, the need to achieve emphasizes* personal, individual success rather than the success of the group, *whereas in collectivistic cultures* there is a social orientation

with a focus on the well-being of others and a desire to fulfill the expectations of family members and to fit into the larger group.

Concept Check 3

1. achievement
2. collectivistic
3. intrinsic
4. competence
5. self-determination
6. extrinsic
7. Thematic Apperception Test (TAT)

Graphic Organizer 1

1. drive theory
2. humanistic theory
3. instinct theory
4. self-determination theory (SDT)
5. incentive theory
6. arousal theory

Matching Exercise 3

1. self-determination theory (SDT)
2. hierarchy of needs
3. internalize and integrate
4. Thematic Apperception Test (TAT)
5. power motivation
6. Abraham Maslow
7. competence
8. autonomy

True/False Test 3

1. T	4. T	7. F
2. F	5. F	
3. T	6. F	

Emotion

1. *Emotion is defined as* a complex psychological state involving three distinct components: subjective experience, a physiological response, and a behavioral or expressive response.

2. *Emotions tend to be* intense and rather short-lived, and they have a specific cause, are directed toward a particular object, and motivate a person to take some form of action. *Moods*

involve a milder emotional state that is more general and pervasive, such as gloominess or contentment, and they may last for a few hours or days.

3. *Emotions have many functions, including triggering* motivated behavior, and they contribute to rational decision making, purposeful behavior, and setting appropriate goals. People who have lost the capacity to feel emotion tend to make disastrous decisions.

4. *Emotional intelligence is the capacity to* understand and manage your own emotional experiences, and to perceive, comprehend, and respond appropriately to the emotional responses of others.

5. *According to evolutionary psychologists, emotions are the* product of evolution, they help us solve important adaptive problems posed by the environment, they move us toward potential resources and away from potential dangers, ultimately they help survival and reproductive success, and their expression informs other organisms about our internal state.

6. *The most common basic emotions that all humans, in every culture, experience are* happiness, sadness, anger, fear, surprise, and disgust.

7. *Cross-cultural research has shown* general agreement among cultures regarding the "pleasant/unpleasant" and "activated/not activated" emotional dimensions.

8. *Cross-cultural researchers have noted that Japanese subjects also categorized emotions along a dimension of* interpersonal engagement, *which reflects* the degree to which emotions involve a relationship with another person or other people.

The Neuroscience of Emotion

1. *The physiological component of emotions such as fear and anger involves the* activation of the sympathetic branch of the autonomic nervous system, which gears people for action, affecting heart rate, blood pressure, respiration, perspiration, and other bodily activities (the fight-or-flight response).

2. *The amygdala, which is part of the limbic system, is an* almond-shaped cluster of neurons in the brain's temporal lobe, is involved in memory and emotional responses, especially fear, and has connections with other brain structures, including the cortex, the thalamus, and the hypothalamus.

3. *From an evolutionary perspective, evidence of a direct thalamus→amygdala pathway makes adaptive sense because the amygdala can be activated by* a threatening stimulus, even before we become consciously aware of the stimulus, an adaptive response. *When the amygdala is activated, it sends information to* the hypothalamus, then to the medulla, which, in combination, trigger arousal of the sympathetic nervous system and the release of stress hormones. *The second (indirect) pathway, thalamus→cortex→amygdala, allows more complex stimuli to be* evaluated in the cortex before triggering the amygdala's alarm system.

The Expression of Emotions: Making Faces

1. *Research on facial expressions (and emotions expressed vocally) suggests that* expressions of the basic emotions are innate and probably hard-wired in the brain, and appear to be universal across different cultures.

2. *Display rules are social and cultural rules that* regulate the expression of emotions, particularly facial expressions.

3. *Display rules can vary greatly from culture to culture (and even for different groups within a given culture, such as males and females); consequently,* the expression of different emotions may vary depending on the culture and its display rules.

4. *The overall conclusion is that the expression of emotions serves the* adaptive function of communicating internal states to friends and enemies, helps us recognize and respond quickly to the emotional state of others, and ultimately helps in survival.

Theories of Emotion: Explaining Emotion

1. *The James–Lange theory of emotions states that* emotions arise from the perception and interpretation of body changes; in other words, the experience of emotion results from the perception of the internal physical responses to a stimulus—you feel afraid because your heart pounded.

2. *Walter Cannon criticized the James–Lange theory on a number of grounds:*

   (a) *Body reactions are* similar for many emotions, yet our subjective experience of various emotions is very different.

   (b) *Our emotional reaction to a stimulus is* often faster than our physiological reaction; the subjective experience of emotion is often virtually instantaneous.

(c) *When physiological changes are artificially induced,* people do not necessarily report feeling a related emotion.

(d) *People cut off from feeling bodily changes* do experience true emotions (the perception of physical arousal does not seem to be essential to the experience of emotion).

3. *Support for some aspects of the James–Lange theory comes from (a) Damasio's work, which demonstrated that* each of the basic emotions produced a distinct pattern of brain activity and that the subjective sense of feeling an emotion follows from physiological feedback from the skin, muscles, internal organs, and the sympathetic nervous system, and *(b) the facial feedback hypothesis, which states that* expressing a specific emotion, especially facially, causes the subjective experience of that emotion.

4. *Schachter and Singer's two-factor theory of emotion suggests that* emotion is a result of the interaction of physiological arousal and the cognitive label that we apply to explain the arousal.

5. *Cognitive appraisal theory proposes that* the most important aspect of an emotional experience is our cognitive interpretation, or appraisal, of the personal meaning of events and experiences.

6. *Although both two-factor theory and the cognitive appraisal model emphasize the importance of cognitive appraisal, two-factor theory states that* emotion results from physiological arousal plus a cognitive label, *while the cognitive appraisal model stresses that* appraisal is the essential trigger for an emotional response, and all other components of emotion, including physiological arousal, follow from the initial cognitive appraisal.

Concept Check 4

1. mood; emotion
2. sympathetic; fight-or-flight
3. display rules
4. emotional intelligence
5. mixed
6. thalamus→amygdala
7. epinephrine
8. cognitive appraisal
9. not consistent

10. facial feedback hypothesis
11. James–Lange
12. mastery experience

Graphic Organizer 2

1. astonishment
2. alarm
3. boredom
4. relaxation
5. annoyance

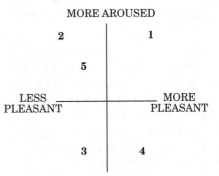

Matching Exercise 4

1. Charles Darwin
2. basic emotions
3. emotional intelligence
4. amygdala
5. Paul Ekman
6. facial feedback hypothesis
7. emblems
8. two-factor theory of emotion
9. anthropomorphism
10. epinephrine (adrenaline)
11. emotion

True/False Test 4

1. T	5. T	9. T
2. T	6. T	10. T
3. T	7. T	
4. T	8. T	

Something to Think About

1. Losing weight and keeping it off is a big problem for many people. You might begin your discussion by noting that our motivation to eat is influenced by psychological, biological, and

social factors. For example, biologically, hunger and satiation are regulated by oral signals from taste buds, stretch receptors in the stomach, and chemicals such as CCK, insulin, ghrelin, and leptin. Of course, genetic factors also play a role, but there is usually an interaction between genetic susceptibility and environmental factors. Psychological factors include classically conditioned stimuli, the positive incentive value of certain foods acquired through operant conditioning and reinforcement, and memory of previous meals eaten. Socially, people are affected by the cultural norms and attitudes about what constitutes the ideal weight.

First, knowing a little about how food is converted to energy in the body is useful in understanding the regulation of hunger and eating behavior. Food provides glucose, the main source of the body's energy, which is regulated by insulin. Excess glucose is stored in adipose tissue (fat) and the basal metabolic rate reflects the rate at which your body at rest uses energy for vital body functions. Energy homeostasis and chemicals such as leptin, insulin, and neuropeptide Y (NPY) help people maintain their baseline body weight, which tends to remain stable over time unless conditions of positive or negative energy balance occur. When the former happens, we gain weight. Body mass index (BMI) is one way to calculate weight status, and someone with a BMI of 30.0 or more is classified as obese.

So what are the major factors involved in becoming overweight and what might we do to minimize or prevent weight gain?

First is the positive incentive value of many easily available and very palatable foods, which can easily lead to overeating. You have to become aware of this factor and try to avoid these foods.

Second, when faced with the opportunity of a double portion of a tasty food for only a few cents more (the "SuperSize It" syndrome) most people can't resist. These situations are optimized to pack on those extra calories, so do your best to stay away from them.

Third is the cafeteria diet effect. This happens when a wide variety of highly palatable foods are offered, such as at a cafeteria or an all-you-can-eat buffet. Your "eyes are bigger than your stomach," as the expression goes, and sure enough people tend to pile up their plates with food, a sure-fire formula for packing on the pounds.

Fourth are individual differences in BMR. Two people, matched on all the essential variables, can maintain the same approximate weight even though one of the pair consumes twice as much as the other. Yes, it's true, and no, life is not fair. In addition, your BMR decreases with age, so as you get older you have to watch carefully what you eat or you'll gain weight (the old "middle-age spread" idea). People also differ in the amount of energy they use for normal daily activities.

Finally, weight gain for many people is a result of a sedentary lifestyle. Forty percent of Americans report that they never exercise, play sports, or engage in physical activities such as walking the dog or gardening. Make exercise a regular part of your routine and give the time spent doing some physical activity the highest priority. When you get busy and anxiety levels are high, the very last thing you should give up is your regular exercise program.

Having said all that, it is important to note that this is a complex problem with no magic bullet or easy solution. For example, obesity certainly involves genetic susceptibility, but environmental factors also play a role. Obese people also develop leptin resistance, a condition in which higher-than-normal blood levels of the hormone leptin do not produce the expected physiological response of reduced hunger and eating. Frequent dieting may lead to weight cycling, a phenomenon in which the weight lost during dieting is regained in a matter of weeks or months and is then maintained until the next attempt at dieting begins. Research has also shown that obese people tend to have fewer dopamine receptors in their brains than normal weight people, which may lead some individuals to engage in compulsive eating to stimulate brain reward centers. And, as Critical Thinking: Has Evolution Programmed Us to Overeat points out, we may be programmed by evolution for the propensity to overeat and store energy as fat. Obviously, obesity is not a simple problem with a simple solution.

So, the best advice for losing weight is to become aware of all the factors (especially those just mentioned) that can contribute to weight gain, modify your eating patterns accordingly, and follow a regular exercise program. It's an uphill battle, and despite the gloomy statistics, many people have successfully kept weight off by following this advice.

2. You might first want to define the two important and related topics of motivation and emotion. Motivation refers to the forces that act on or within an organism to initiate and direct

behavior and involves three characteristics: activation, persistence and intensity. It is closely related to emotion because we are often motivated to achieve certain emotional states, and emotions, in turn, may motivate us to achieve certain goals.

As the text makes clear, these are complicated topics involving a variety of theories and a large volume of research findings. Fortunately, there is some relevant psychological research that directly addresses the issue of how to change our goals (usually easy to formulate) into actual accomplishments (much harder to achieve).

Psychologist Albert Bandura has investigated this topic and proposed the notion of self-efficacy—the degree to which a person believes his or her ability can meet the demands of a specific situation and produce the desired results. Those who have an optimistic sense of self-efficacy tend to approach a tough task as a challenge to be overcome rather than an aversive event that needs to be avoided. Those who view themselves as capable, competent, and effective in dealing with obstacles and challenges are more likely to pursue higher personal goals than those who have self-doubts about their abilities. The big question for most of us, then, is how do we build our sense of self-efficacy, especially when confronted with tough challenges and when our confidence level is not as high as it might be. The Application provides a number of strategies and suggestions that can help motivate people to pursue and achieve their goals, and these should be a central part of your report.

Bandura noted that one of the most effective ways to build self-efficacy is through mastery experiences. Experiencing success at moderately challenging tasks can lead to the desire to tackle somewhat harder goals. In addition, realizing that setbacks can and do occur can teach us that success usually requires persistent effort. Social modeling (observational learning)

is a useful strategy because it allows us to observe and imitate the behavior of those who are already competent at the task of interest. Gaining knowledge about what works and what doesn't work is a very important part of building a sense of self-efficacy. The two steps for turning goals into actions, forming a goal intention, and creating implementations, should be discussed next in your report. Finally you should provide information about the power of mental rehearsal in improving performance. Mentally rehearsing the process (the skills that will be effectively used and the steps that will be taken in achieving the desired outcome) is better than simply imagining a positive outcome.

Progress Test 1

1. a		6. b		11. a	
2. c		7. c		12. b	
3. c		8. a		13. b	
4. a		9. d		14. d	
5. a		10. c		15. e	

Progress Test 2

1. a		6. c		11. d	
2. b		7. d		12. d	
3. d		8. d		13. d	
4. a		9. d		14. d	
5. a		10. a		15. a	

Progress Test 3

1. a		6. b		11. b	
2. c		7. d		12. a	
3. c		8. b		13. a	
4. c		9. d		14. b	
5. d		10. a		15. e	

CHAPTER 9

Lifespan Development

PREVIEW

Reading the section below first will give you a general sense of the chapter's contents and an initial introduction to some of the major concepts and terms. This will prime you for what you are about to read and help you to develop a "cognitive map" that will guide your study of the material in this chapter. Likewise, reading the **preview questions** at the beginning of each major section will improve your ability to understand, learn, and retain the information.

CHAPTER 9 . . . AT A GLANCE

Chapter 9 examines the scope of developmental psychology and major themes such as the stages of lifespan development, the nature of change, and the interaction between heredity and environment. The first two sections describe genetic contributions to development and the stages of prenatal development.

Development during infancy and childhood and the capacities and capabilities of the newborn are explored, including social and personality development. Special attention is paid to the nature of temperament, the concept of attachment, and the stages of language development. The section concludes with a detailed analysis of Piaget's theory of cognitive development and an examination of Vygotsky's sociocultural theory and the information-processing model.

Adolescence, the transition from childhood to adulthood, involves important changes in physical, sexual, and social development. Adolescent–parent relationships undergo some changes during this period, and peer relationships and influence become increasingly relevant. Erikson's theory of psychosocial development is examined.

The final sections describe early, middle, and late adult development, including physical, social, and cognitive changes typical of each stage. Love and work are the key themes that dominate adult development. Late adulthood does not necessarily involve a steep decline in physical and cognitive functioning. In discussing dying and death, the text outlines Kübler-Ross's five-stage model of dying, noting that dying is an individual process, like any other during the lifespan.

The Application presents some basic principles of parenting that have been shown to foster the development of psychologically well-adjusted and competent children who are in control of their own behavior.

Introduction: Your Life Story

Preview Questions

Consider the following questions as you study this section of the chapter.

- What do developmental psychologists study?
- What are the major themes in developmental psychology?

*Read the section "Introduction: Your Life Story" and **write** your answers to the following:*

1. Developmental psychology is the _____
   _____
   _____

2. The major themes in developmental psychology
   are _____
   _____
   _____
   _____
   _____

Genetic Contributions to Your Life Story

Preview Questions

Consider the following questions as you study this section of the chapter.

- What is a zygote?
- What are chromosomes, DNA, and genes?
- How do genes guide the development of living organisms?
- What are genotypes, alleles, and phenotypes?
- What role does the environment play in the relationship between genotype and phenotype, and what are genetic predispositions?

*Read the section "Genetic Contributions to Your Life Story" and **write** your answers to the following:*

1. A zyogte is _____
   _____

2. Chromosomes are_____
   _____

3. DNA (deoxyribonucleic acid) is _____
   _____
   _____

4. Genes are _____
   _____

   Genes direct the manufacture of _____
   _____

5. Genotype refers to the _____
   _____

   The human genome is _____
   _____
   _____

6. Alleles are _____
   _____

   The best-known pattern of allele variation is
   _____

7. Phenotype refers to the _____

   Rather than being fixed or inevitable, gene
   expression is _____
   _____
   _____
   _____

8. The environment plays a role in the relationship between genotype and phenotype as
   follows: _____
   _____
   _____
   _____

9. Genetic predispositions are _____
   _____
   _____

Prenatal Development

Preview Questions

Consider the following questions as you study this section of the chapter.

- What happens to the single-cell zygote during prenatal development?
- What are the three phases of prenatal development?
- What are teratogens?

*Read the section "Prenatal Development" and **write** your answers to the following:*

1. During prenatal development, the single-cell zygote _____
   _____
   _____

2. The three phases of the prenatal stage are_____
   _____
   _____
   _____
   _____

3. Teratogens are _____
   _____

After you have carefully studied the preceding sections, complete the following exercises.

Concept Check 1

Read the following and write the correct term in the space provided.

1. Dr. Dalliwhal's research focuses on the relationship between various teratogens and birth defects. Dr. Dalliwhal is most likely a _____ psychologist.

2. From the day Franco was born, people have always responded very positively to his good looks. Now that he is growing older, it is clear that he is developing a socially confident and outgoing personality. This best illustrates the interaction of _____ and _____ .

3. Dr. Markowitz, who is a behavioral geneticist, believes that rather than a simple "genetic blueprint" for fixed, inevitable development, genotypes react differently to different environmental factors. He is most likely to suggest that we have _____ for developing in particular ways.

4. It is now six weeks since Jennifer conceived. The human organism she is carrying is called a(n) _____ ; at the third month, it will be called a(n) _____ .

5. When Myra became pregnant, she decided that she would not drink any alcohol because she did not want to risk causing abnormal development or birth defects in her unborn child. Myra is aware that alcohol is a _____ .

6. Dr. Zhang conceptualizes the lifespan in terms of eight basic stages of development. She is most likely to label the stage from birth to 2 years of age as _____ , the stage from 2 to 6 years as _____ , and the stage from 6 to 12 years as
   _____ .

7. When answering an exam question about what makes each individual unique, Philipa is most likely to note that every cell in the body has 23 pairs of _____ , each of which is a long, threadlike structure composed of twisted strands of _____ , which are arranged in thousands of segments called
   _____ .

8. Sapna read that the development of freckles appears to be controlled by a single gene, which can be dominant or recessive. In order to have the potential for freckles you need to inherit a dominant version of the freckles gene from either or both your parents. Sapna is reading about one of the best-known patterns of variation in a gene called an _____ .

Graphic Organizer 1

Identify the parts of the cell in the diagram below.

1. cell nucleus
2. chromosome
3. gene
4. DNA

Then match each numbered part with one of the following descriptions.

A. ____ Unit of DNA on a chromosome that encodes instructions for making a particular molecule.

B. ____ Double-stranded molecule that encodes genetic instructions.

C. ____ Long, threadlike structure composed of twisted parallel strands of DNA.

D. ____ Part of the cell that contains the 23 pairs of chromosomes.

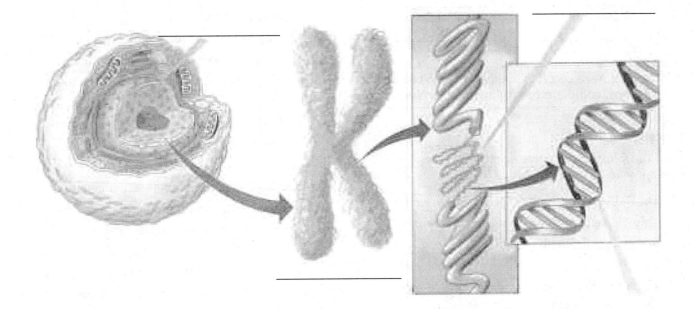

Review of Terms and Concepts 1

Use the terms in this list to complete the Matching Test, then to help you answer the True/False items correctly.

developmental psychology
critical period
nature–nurture issue
zygote
chromosome
deoxyribonucleic acid (DNA)
gene
genotype
human genome
sex chromosomes
allele
phenotype

genetic predispositions
mutation
prenatal stage
germinal period (zygotic period)
embryo
embryonic period
amniotic sac
umbilical cord
placenta
teratogens
fetal period
fetus
quickening

Matching Exercise

Match the appropriate term with its definition or description.

1. _____ The stage of development before birth; divided into the germinal, embryonic, and fetal periods.

2. _____ The basic unit of heredity that directs the development of a particular characteristic; the individual unit of DNA instructions on a chromosome.

3. _____ The branch of psychology that studies how people change over the lifespan.

4. _____ Particular genetic configurations that are more or less sensitive to specific environmental factors and influence how development unfolds.

5. _____ Harmful agents or substances that can cause malformations or defects in an embryo or a fetus.

6. _____ Long, threadlike structure composed of twisted parallel strands of DNA; found in the cell nucleus.

7. _____ Spontaneous change in genes from one generation to another.

8. _____ The first two weeks of prenatal development.

9. _____ Cluster of cells that develops from the single-cell zygote by the end of the two-week germinal period.

10. _____ The scientific description of the complete set of DNA in the human organism, including gene locations.

11. _____ One of the different forms of a particular gene.

12. _____ Disk-shaped vascular organ that acts as a filter to prevent the mother's blood from directly mingling with that of the developing embryo.

13. _____ Chromosomes, designated as X or Y, that determine biological sex and are the 23rd pair of chromosomes in humans.

True/False Test

Indicate whether each statement is true or false by placing T or F in the blank space next to each item.

1. ___ The fetus is the name given to the growing organism at the beginning of the third month.

2. ___ A critical period during development is a time during which the child is maximally sensitive to environmental influences.

3. ___ Deoxyribonucleic acid (DNA) is the double-stranded molecule that encodes genetic instructions and is the chemical basis of heredity.

4. ___ The fetal period is the second period of prenatal development, extending from the third week through the eighth week.

5. ___ The single cell formed at conception from the union of the egg cell and sperm cell is called a zygote.

6. ___ The umbilical cord delivers nourishment, oxygen, and water to the embryo and carries away carbon dioxide and other wastes.

7. ___ The embryonic period is the third and longest period of prenatal development, extending from the ninth week until birth.

8. ___ An important theme in developmental psychology is the interaction between heredity and environment; traditionally called the nature–nurture issue.

9. ___ Genotype refers to observable traits or characteristics of an organism as determined by the interaction of genetic and environmental factors.

10. ___ Phenotype refers to the genetic makeup of an individual organism.

11. ___ The embryo is protectively housed in the fluid-filled amniotic sac.

12. ___ During the fourth month of pregnancy, the mother can feel the fetus moving, an experience called quickening.

Check your answers and review any areas of weakness before going on to the next section.

Development During Infancy and Childhood: Physical Development

Preview Questions

Consider the following questions as you study this section of the chapter.

- What reflexes and sensory capabilities are physically helpless infants equipped with that enhance their chances for survival?

- How do the sensory capabilities of the newborn promote the development of relationships with caregivers?

- How does the brain develop after birth?

*Read the section "Development During Infancy and Childhood" and **write** your answers to the following:*

1. Newborn infants enter the world equipped with

_____

_____

Their senses of vision, hearing, smell, and

touch are _____

_____

_____

2. The infant's sensory capabilities promote the development of relationships with caregivers, as evidenced by the fact that they _____

_____

_____

_____

3. After birth, a number of physical changes in he brain and body take place: _____

_____

_____

Development During Infancy and Childhood: Social and Personality Development

Preview Questions

Consider the following questions as you study this section of the chapter.

- What is temperament, and what temperamental patterns have been identified?
- What is attachment, and what is the basic premise of attachment theory?
- How is attachment measured?

*Read the section "Social and Personality Development" and **write** your answers to the following:*

1. Temperament refers to _____

_____

The three broad temperamental patterns are

_____

Two other temperamental patterns that have been identified are _____

_____

2. Attachment is the _____

_____

The basic premise of attachment theory is

_____

_____

_____

_____

3. Attachment is measured using a procedure called the _____
In this technique, _____

_____

_____

_____

_____

Development During Infancy and Childhood: Language Development

Preview Questions

Consider the following questions as you study this section of the chapter.

- How does a biological predisposition to learn language function in language development?
- How is language development encouraged by caregivers?
- What are the stages of language development?

*Read the section "Language Development" and **write** your answers to the following:*

1. According to Noam Chomsky _____

_____

_____

_____

2. Language development is encouraged by _____

_____

3. The stages of language development are _____

_____

_____

_____

After you have carefully studied the preceding sections, complete the following exercises.

Concept Check 2

Read the following and write the correct term in the space provided.

1. Dr. Snow is interested in the abilities of newborn children. While testing visual perception, she is likely to find that newborns will look longer at the image of a(n) _____ compared to other visual patterns.

2. To determine whether a child is securely or insecurely attached, researchers are likely to use _____ .

3. Kathy just gave birth to a normal, healthy, eight-and-a-half-pound baby. In terms of brain development, the baby's brain weighs _____ (25 percent/50 percent/ 75 percent/100 percent) of its adult weight.

4. When Kathy touched her newborn's right cheek, the baby turned to the right and opened her mouth, a response called the _____ ; touching her lips elicited the _____ ; and when Kathy put a finger on each of the baby's palms, she grasped them tightly, a response called the _____ .

5. As Kathy's baby develops, she readily adapts to new experiences, displays positive moods and emotions, and has regular sleeping and eating patterns. She is likely to be classified as a temperamentally _____ baby.

6. In contrast, Kathy's first child Kamron tended to be tense, frightened, and somewhat shy when exposed to new experiences, strangers, and novel objects. According to Jerome Kagan, who classified temperament in terms of reactivity, Kamron is likely to be categorized as a(n) _____ infant.

7. Kathy and her husband are consistently warm, responsive, and sensitive to their infant's needs, and the baby has developed the expectation that her needs will be met. It is very probable that the baby will form a(n) _____ attachment to her parents.

8. When Kathy tells 12-month-old Kaila to "Bring Mommy the dolly," Kaila immediately does so, even though she cannot say the words *bring, Mommy,* or *dolly.* This suggests that Kaila's _____ vocabulary is larger than her _____ vocabulary.

Review of Terms, Concepts, and Names 2

Use the terms in this list to complete the Matching Test, then to help you answer the True/False items correctly.

rooting reflex	multiple attachments
sucking reflex	secure attachment
grasping reflex	insecure attachment
temperament	Strange Situation
easy temperament	motherese (infant-directed speech)
difficult temperament	
slow-to-warm-up temperament	cooing and babbling stage
high-reactive infant	comprehension vocabulary
low-reactive infant	
attachment	production vocabulary
Mary D. Salter Ainsworth	one-word stage
	two-word stage
secure base	

Matching Exercise

Match the appropriate term/name with its definition or description.

1. _____ Kagan's term for infants who react to new experiences, strangers, and novel objects by being fearful, tense, shy, and inhibited.

2. _____ Measure of attachment devised by Mary D. Salter Ainsworth, typically used with infants who are between 1 and 2 years old.

3. _____ Automatic response elicited by touching a newborn's lips.

4. _____ Temperamental category for babies who have a low activity level, who withdraw from new situations and people, and who adapt to new experiences very gradually.

5. _____ Universal style of speech used with babies and characterized by very distinct pronunciation, a simplified vocabulary, short sentences, a high pitch, and exaggerated intonation and expression.

6. _____ Biologically programmed stage in language development that occurs between about 3 and 9 months of age.

7. _____ Emotional bond that forms between infants and their caregiver(s), especially parents.

8. _____ Words that are understood by an infant or child.

9. _____ Form of attachment that may develop when parents are neglectful, inconsistent, or insensitive to their infant's moods or behaviors and reflects an ambivalent or detached emotional relationship between the infant and his or her parents.

10. _____ Universal stage in language development, starting around 2 years of age, in which infants combine two words to construct simple "sentences" that reflect the first understanding of grammar.

11. _____ Bonds that are formed between the infant and other consistent caregivers in his or her life, such as relatives or workers at day-care centers.

True/False Test

Indicate whether each statement is true or false by placing T or F in the blank space next to each item.

1. ___ Mary D. Salter Ainsworth is the psychologist who devised the Strange Situation procedure to measure attachment; contributed to attachment theory.

2. ___ Production vocabulary refers to the words that an infant or child can speak.

3. ___ An infant's response to having his or her palms touched is called the rooting reflex.

4. ___ Babies with a difficult temperament tend to be intensely emotional, are irritable and fussy, cry a lot, and have irregular sleeping and eating patterns.

5. ___ During the one-word stage, babies use a single word and vocal intonation to stand for an entire sentence.

6. ___ Secure attachment is likely to develop when parents are consistently warm, responsive, and sensitive to their infant's needs.

7. ___ According to attachment theory, parents or caregivers function as a secure base for the infant, providing a sense of comfort, security, and a safe haven from which the infant can explore and learn about the environment.

8. ___ Babies with an easy temperament readily adapt to new experiences, generally display positive moods and emotions, and have regular sleeping and eating patterns.

9. ___ Touching the newborn's cheek elicits the grasping reflex; the infant turns toward the source of the touch and opens the mouth.

10. ___ Temperament is the inborn predisposition to consistently behave and react in a certain way.

11. ___ A low-reactive infant tends to be calm, uninhibited, sociable, not shy, and shows interest rather than fear when exposed to new people, experiences, and objects.

Check your answers and review any areas of weakness before going on to the next section.

Development During Infancy and Childhood: Cognitive Development

Preview Questions

Consider the following questions as you study this section of the chapter.

- What are Piaget's four stages of cognitive development, and what are the characteristics of each stage?
- What are three criticisms of Piaget's theory?
- What factors did Vygotsky emphasize in his theory of cognitive development?
- What is the zone of proximal development?
- What is the information-processing model of cognitive development?

*Read the section "Cognitive Development" and **write** your answers to the following:*

1. The four stages (and their characteristics) in Piaget's theory are

   (a) _____

   _____

   (b) _____

   _____

   (c) _____

   _____

   (d) _____

   _____

2. Piaget's theory has been criticized because ____

_____

_____

_____

_____

3. Vygotsky believed that _____

_____

_____

The zone of proximal development refers to

_____

_____

4. The information-processing model of cognitive development views cognitive development as

_____

_____

_____

After you have carefully studied the preceding sections, complete the following exercises.

Concept Check 3

Read the following and write the correct term in the space provided.

1. Four-year-old Tiborg is not completely egocentric, and 5-year-old Natasha exhibits some understanding of conservation. Observations such as these suggest that Piaget may have _____ (overestimated/underestimated) the cognitive abilities of infants and children.

2. Eight-year-old Nadia has the ability to think logically about visible and tangible objects and situations. She is in the _____ stage of cognitive development.

3. Young Adrienne attempts to retrieve her toy bear after her father hides it under a blanket. This suggests that Adrienne has developed a sense of _____ .

4. When Mrs. Goodley cut Janet's hot dog into eight pieces and Simon's into six pieces, Simon started to cry and complained that he wasn't getting as much hot dog as Janet. Piaget would say that Simon doesn't understand the principle of _____ .

5. Three-year-old Rita calls all unfamiliar four-legged animals "doggies." She appears to be _____ these new experiences into her existing concept of a dog.

6. Piaget would call Rita's mental representation or concept of dog a _____ .

7. During a tutorial devoted to the pros and cons of genetic engineering, Vasilis raised some important issues about the ownership of fertilized eggs and whether destroying them constitutes taking a life. Piaget would say that Vasilis is in the _____ operational stage of cognitive development.

8. While Coral was still in high school, she imagined that most of her college professors would be older bearded males. During her first year, she was surprised to find that many were relatively young females. Because of these new experiences, she has changed her way of thinking about college professors, a process Piaget called _____ .

9. Dr. Ramenian believes that infants have limited physical coordination and are therefore incapable of clearly demonstrating their mental abilities in tasks involving manual responses. The results of Dr. Ramenian's research using visual tasks suggest that Piaget confused _____ limitations with _____ limitations.

10. Dr. Ramenian also believes that cognitive development is a process of continuous change over the lifespan, not a series of distinct stages, as Piaget proposed. His views are consistent with the _____ model of cognitive development.

Review of Terms, Concepts, and Names 3

Use the terms in this list to complete the Matching Test, then to help you answer the True/False items correctly.

Jean Piaget
qualitatively different
    thinking
assimilation
accommodation
sensorimotor stage
object permanence
schemas
preoperational stage
operations
symbolic thought
egocentrism
irreversibility

centration
conservation
concrete operational
    stage
formal operational stage
Renée Baillargeon
Lev Vygotsky
zone of proximal
    development
information-processing
    model of cognitive
    development

Matching Exercise

Match the appropriate term/name with its definition or description.

1. _____ The ability to use words, images, and symbols to represent the world.

2. _____ Canadian-born psychologist whose studies of cognitive development during infancy using visual rather than manual tasks challenged beliefs about the age at which object permanence first appears.

3. _____ The understanding that an object continues to exist even when it can no longer be seen.

4. _____ Piaget's fourth stage of cognitive development, which lasts from adolescence through adulthood and is characterized by the ability to think logically about abstract principles and hypothetical situations.

5. _____ Swiss child psychologist whose influential theory proposed that children progress through distinct stages of cognitive development.

6. _____ The model that views cognitive development as a process of continuous change over the lifespan and that studies the development of basic mental processes such as attention, memory, and problem solving.

7. _____ Piaget's term for the mental representations of the world that children acquire as their memories improve and as they gain an understanding of object permanence.

8. _____ Piaget's first stage of cognitive development, from birth to about age 2; the period during which the infant explores the environment and acquires knowledge through sensing and manipulating objects.

9. _____ In Piaget's theory, the inability to take another person's perspective or point of view.

10. _____ Russian psychologist who stressed the importance of social and cultural influences on cognitive development.

True/False Test

Indicate whether each statement is true or false by placing T or F in the blank space next to each item.

1. ____ In Piaget's theory, the word *operations* refers to logical, mental activities.

2. ____ Changing one's mental representation of the world, and the way one thinks about things on the basis of new information and experiences, is a process Piaget called accommodation.

3. ____ In Piaget's theory, the concrete operational stage is the second stage of cognitive development, which lasts from about age 2 to age 7 and is characterized by increasing use of symbols and prelogical thought processes.

4. ____ In Piaget's theory, irreversibility is the inability to reverse a sequence of events or logical operations mentally.

5. ____ In Piaget's theory, centration refers to the understanding that two equal quantities remain equal even though the form or appearance is rearranged, as long as nothing is added or subtracted.

6. ____ According to Piaget, as children advance to a new stage, their thinking is *qualitatively different* from that used in the previous stage; each new stage represents a fundamental shift in *how* children think and understand the world.

7. ____ In Piaget's theory, the tendency to focus on only one aspect of a situation and ignore other important aspects of the situation is called conservation.

8. ____ Assimilation is the process of incorporating and interpreting new information in terms of existing mental representations of the world.

9. ___ In Piaget's theory, the preoperational stage is the third stage of cognitive development, which lasts from about age 7 to adolescence and is characterized by the ability to think logically about concrete objects and situations.

10. ___ Zone of proximal development refers to the gap between what children can accomplish on their own and what they can accomplish with the help of others who are more competent.

Check your answers and review any areas of weakness before going on to the next section.

Adolescence

Preview Questions

Consider the following questions as you study this section of the chapter:

- How is adolescence defined?
- What is puberty, and what are primary and secondary sex characteristics?
- What is the adolescent growth spurt, and, in females, what is menarche?
- What factors affect the timing of puberty?
- What characterizes adolescent relationships with parents and peers?
- What factors are involved in romantic and sexual relationships during adolescence?
- How do adolescents begin the process of identity formation?
- What is Erikson's psychosocial theory of life-span development?

*Read the section "Adolescence" and **write** your answers to the following:*

1. Adolescence is _____

2. Puberty is the _____

3. Puberty involves the development of primary sex characteristics, which are _____

and secondary sex characteristics, which are

_____

4. The adolescent growth spurt is _____

5. Menarche refers to _____

6. Factors that affect the timing of puberty include _____

When adolescents are "off time" in maturation, they _____

7. The relationship between parents and their adolescent children is _____

8. Factors involved in romantic and sexual relationships during adolescence include

_____

9. Identity refers to _____

10. Adolescents begin the process of identity formation by _____

11. According to Erikson's psychosocial theory of lifespan development _____

The key psychosocial conflict facing adolescents is _____

After you have carefully studied the preceding section, complete the following exercises.

Concept Check 4

Read the following and write the correct term in the space provided.

1. Thomas, who is now a young adult, had a typical adolescent period of conflict over identity issues but now feels comfortable with the choices and commitments he has made. According to Erikson, Thomas has achieved an _____ , and the next psychosocial task he is facing is likely to be _____ .

2. Seventeen-year-old Brendan questions his parents' values but is not sure that his peer group's standards are totally correct either. His confusion about what is really important in life suggests that Brendan is struggling with the problem of _____ .

3. Prior to adolescence, Brendan very likely struggled with other conflicts. According to Erikson, his first psychosocial conflict during infancy was about _____ ; his second, during toddlerhood (18 months to 3 years), involved _____ ; his third, which is likely to have happened during early childhood (3 to 6 years), was concerned with _____ ; and his fourth psychosocial conflict in middle to late childhood (6 to 12 years) dealt with _____ .

4. Mr. and Mrs. Atkins have three adolescent children. If they are like most American parents, their relationships with their children are likely to be generally _____ (negative/ positive).

5. When she was almost 13, Manjit experienced her first menstrual period. She has reached _____ .

6. Adam is 15 and has gained both height and weight, some body hair, and a deeper voice during the past year. These changes are referred to as _____ sex characteristics.

7. During the final months of Darrel's prenatal development, there was fierce competition among the neurons in his brain to make connections, and those that did not make connections were eliminated. According to Focus on Neuroscience (The Adolescent Brain), this process is called _____ .

8. Mr. and Mrs. Kartwright both have jobs they enjoy, are involved in community activities, and have two young children. Erikson would say that they have successfully dealt with the psychosocial conflict called _____ , which is typical of the _____ stage of life.

Review of Terms, Concepts, and Names 4

Use the terms in this list to complete the Matching Test, then to help you answer the True/False items correctly.

adolescence	menarche
puberty	identity
primary sex characteristics	Erik Erikson role confusion
secondary sex characteristics	moratorium period integrated identity
adolescent growth spurt	

Matching Exercise

Match the appropriate term/name with its definition or description.

1. _____ A person's self-definition or description, including the values, beliefs, and ideals that guide the individual's behavior.

2. _____ In Erikson's theory, the period following role confusion, during which the adolescent experiments with different roles, values, and beliefs.

3. _____ Transitional stage between late childhood and the beginning of adulthood, during which sexual maturity is reached.

4. _____ The stage of adolescence in which an individual reaches sexual maturity and becomes physiologically capable of sexual reproduction.

5. _____ A female's first menstrual period, which occurs during puberty.

6. _____ Period of accelerated growth during puberty, involving rapid increases in height and weight.

True/False Test

Indicate whether each item is true or false by placing T or F in the space next to each item.

1. ___ Secondary sex characteristics are the sexual organs that are directly involved in reproduction, such as the uterus, ovaries, penis, and testicles.

2. ___ In Erikson's theory, the adolescent's path to successfully achieving an identity begins with role confusion, which is characterized by little sense of commitment to the various issues he or she has to grapple with and the social demands made on him or her.

3. ___ Following the moratorium period, during which the adolescent experiments with different roles, values, and beliefs, he or she may then choose among alternatives and make commitments, gradually arriving at an *integrated identity*.

4. ___ Erik Erikson was the German-born American psychoanalyst who proposed an influential theory of psychosocial development throughout the lifespan.

5. ___ Primary sex characteristics are sexual characteristics that develop during puberty and are not directly involved in reproduction but differentiate between the sexes, such as male facial hair and female breasts.

Check your answers and review any areas of weakness before going on to the next section.

Adult Development

Preview Questions

Consider the following questions as you study this section of the chapter.

- What physical changes take place in adulthood?
- What are some general patterns of adult social development?
- How does the transition to parenthood affect adults?
- What are some of the variations in the paths of adult social development?
- What characterizes career paths in adulthood?

*Read the section "Adult Development" and **write** your answers to the following:*

1. The physical changes that take place during adulthood include _____

2. According to Erikson, the primary psychosocial task of middle adulthood is _____

3. The most general pattern of social development includes _____

4. In relation to having children, marital satisfaction _____

5. The nature of intimate relationships and family structures varies widely in the United States. For example, _____

6. In terms of careers in adulthood, _____

Late Adulthood and Aging

Preview Questions

- What cognitive and physical changes take place in late adulthood?
- What factors can influence social development during this period?

Read the section "Late Adulthood and Aging" and **write** *your answers to the following:*

1. Regarding mental and physical abilities in late adulthood _____

   _____

   _____

   _____

2. According to the activity theory of aging _____

   _____

   _____

   _____

3. According to Erikson, the psychosocial conflict of late adulthood is_____

   _____

The Final Chapter: Dying and Death

Preview Question

- How did Kübler-Ross describe the stages of dying, and how valid is her theory?

Read the section "The Final Chapter: Dying and Death" and **write** *your answers to the following:*

1. According to Kübler-Ross's theory of dying and death, the five stages are _____

   _____

   _____

   _____

   _____

   _____

2. Problems with Kübler-Ross's theory are that _____

   _____

   _____

   _____

After you have carefully studied the preceding sections, complete the following exercises.

Concept Check 5

Read the following and write the correct term in the space provided.

1. Forty-eight-year-old Dr. Gretinger has three grown children, a thriving dental practice, and is very involved in local community activities. Dr. Gretinger is in the _____ stage of life and, according to Erikson, has achieved the psychosocial task of

   _____ .

2. Compared with their grandparents, Mr. and Mrs. Belmont's children are likely to marry for the first time at _____ (an earlier/a later) age.

3. David, a 65-year-old retired civil servant, feels that his life has been unproductive and ultimately meaningless. David is in the

   _____ stage of life and, according to Erikson, is experiencing

   _____ .

4. Andrew, a 45-year-old accountant, has just learned he has a terminal illness. According to Kübler-Ross, as soon as Andrew gets over his initial denial, he will experience

   _____ .

5. Sarah is a 25-year-old, white, middle-class, well-educated, moderately religious person. If she is typical, she will marry someone very _____ (different from/similar to) herself.

6. The last of the Sandwells' four children has just left home to pursue a career with NASA. If the Sandwells are like most parents whose children have left home, they are likely to experience a steady _____ (decline/increase) in marital satisfaction.

7. Mort and Harry, who are in their seventies, belong to a club called the "Active Ancients Association." Both men feel that their lives have been meaningful and satisfying and feel no disappointment about their accomplishments. Erikson would say that Mort and Harry have achieved _____ .

8. Harry and Mort pursue hobbies, such as fishing, golf, and chess, travel occasionally, take an interest in their grandchildren and great-grandchildren, and do occasional volunteer work. Mort and Harry appear to epitomize the _____ theory of aging.

Graphic Organizer 2

Identify the theorist related to each of the following statements. (Note: This covers theorists discussed throughout the chapter.)

Statement	Theorist
1. I believe that social and cultural influences are the most important factors in cognitive development.	
2. I study attachment, and I have devised a measure of attachment called the Strange Situation.	
3. In my view people have an innate understanding of the basic principles of language, which I call a "universal grammar."	
4. I believe that development continues throughout the lifespan and that individuals pass through eight distinct stages during which they are faced with resolving important psychosocial conflicts.	
5. My primary interest is in how children develop intellectually and cognitively, and my theory proposes that children progress through four distinct stages in succession, each stage characterized by a qualitatively different way of thinking from the previous stage.	

Review of Terms and Concepts 5

Use the terms in this list to complete the Matching Test, then to help you answer the True/False items correctly.

early adulthood
middle adulthood
late adulthood
menopause
generativity
activity theory of aging
ego integrity
despair
life review

Kübler-Ross's stages of dying (denial, anger, bargaining, depression, acceptance)
authoritarian parenting style
permissive parenting style
authoritative parenting style
induction

Matching Exercise

Match the appropriate term/name with its definition or description.

1. _____ Discipline technique that combines parental control with explaining why a behavior is prohibited.

2. _____ The natural cessation of menstruation and the end of reproductive capacity in women.

3. _____ Baumrind's term for a parenting style in which parents are extremely tolerant and not demanding.

4. _____ Stage of adulthood, roughly from the forties to the mid-sixties, when physical strength and endurance gradually decline.

5. _____ Psychosocial theory that life satisfaction in late adulthood is highest when people maintain the level of activity they displayed earlier in life.

6. _____ Erikson's eighth psychosocial task that involves the feeling that one's life has been meaningful.

7. _____ Process through which the themes of ego integrity or despair emerge as older adults think about or retell their life story to others.

True/False Test

Indicate whether each item is true or false by placing T or F in the space next to each item.

1. ____ In Erikson's theory, the primary psychosocial task of middle adulthood in which the person contributes to future generations through children, career, and other meaningful activity is called generativity.

2. ____ Early adulthood refers to the stage of development during the twenties and thirties when physical strength typically peaks.

3. ____ Authoritarian parenting style is Diana Baumrind's term for describing parents who set clear standards for their children's behavior but are also responsive to the children's needs and wishes.

4. ____ Late adulthood refers to the stage of development beginning in the mid-sixties, when physical stamina and reaction time tend to decline further and faster.

5. ____ According to Baumrind, authoritative parents are demanding of and unresponsive toward their children's needs or wishes.

6. ____ According to Kübler-Ross, people who are facing death go through five stages—denial, anger, bargaining, depression, and acceptance.

7. ____ During Erikson's eighth stage of psychosocial development, older adults who are filled with regrets or bitterness about past mistakes, missed opportunities, or bad decisions experience despair.

Check your answers and review any areas of weakness before going on to the next section.

Something to Think About

1. A popular and controversial topic in any discussion of raising children is the effect of day care on a child's development. Such discussions can become quite heated, with people holding strong views on both sides of the debate. On the basis of what you have read in this chapter, what light could you shed on this controversial topic?

2. You may be planning to have a family one day, if you haven't already started one. For most people this is quite a responsibility and a lot of work. Unlike many other areas in life, no formal training is available or required for the job of parent. You, however, are fortunate because you are taking an introductory psychology course and have learned a few things about child development. What advice would you give to people who are planning to have a family?

Check your answers and review any areas of weakness before doing the progress tests.

Progress Test 1

Review the complete chapter (including all boxed inserts), review all your study notes, and then test yourself on the following progress test. Check your answers. If you make a mistake, review your notes, check the appropriate section in the study guide, and if necessary, go back and read the relevant part of the chapter in your textbook.

1. When Thomas was conceived, he was a single fertilized egg called a(n)
   (a) zygote.   (c) fetus.
   (b) embryo.   (d) infant.

2. Young Misty has dark curly hair and freckles; her friend Paige has straight blonde hair and no freckles. In both children, the underlying genetic makeup and genetic instructions for these traits are their _____ , and the observable traits that they actually display are their _____ .
   (a) dominant characteristics; recessive characteristics
   (b) phenotypes; genotypes
   (c) recessive characteristics; dominant characteristics
   (d) genotypes; phenotypes

3. In her research, Dr. Joacim found that a pregnant mother's use of a certain chemical substance caused harm to the fetus. The chemical substance could be classified as
   (a) deoxyribonucleic acid.
   (b) a chromosome.
   (c) a phenotype.
   (d) a teratogen.

4. When Samira was an infant, she was usually calm, uninhibited, sociable, and typically showed interest rather than fear when exposed to new people, novel experiences, and unfamiliar objects. In terms of Kagan's classification of temperamental patterns, Samira is likely to be categorized as

(a) a low-reactive infant.

(b) a slow-to-warm-up infant.

(c) a high-reactive infant.

(d) an insecurely attached infant.

5. When Mrs. Euland touched her newborn's lips, he produced an automatic response called the _____ reflex.

(a) rooting   (c) grasping

(b) sucking   (d) greedy

6. It has become apparent to Mr. and Mrs. Euland that their baby has a low activity level, tends to withdraw from new situations and people, and adapts to new experiences very gradually. The baby would be classified as a(n) _____ baby.

(a) easy   (c) slow-to-warm-up

(b) difficult   (d) securely attached

7. When 2-year-old Kerry was tested in the Strange Situation, she did not explore the environment even when her mother was present. She appeared very anxious, and she became extremely distressed when her mother left the room. Kerry is a(n)

(a) insecurely attached infant.

(b) securely attached infant.

(c) conventional infant.

(d) concrete operational infant.

8. Between the ages of 15 and 16, Sean grew almost five inches. Sean experienced _____ during this year.

(a) irreversibility

(b) conservation

(c) the adolescent growth spurt

(d) centration

9. When Neil's mother hides his favorite toy under a blanket, Neil acts as though it no longer exists and makes no attempt to retrieve it. Neil is in Piaget's _____ stage, and his behavior suggests that he _____ .

(a) sensorimotor; has developed object permanence

(b) preoperational; has not developed object permanence

(c) concrete operational; is capable of reversible thinking

(d) formal operational; understands the principle of conservation

10. Lincoln is a normal 8-month-old infant. According to Chomsky's theory of language development, Lincoln

(a) has a biological predisposition to learn any language and can distinguish among speech sounds of all the world's languages.

(b) has a much larger production vocabulary than comprehension vocabulary.

(c) can only distinguish among the speech sounds of the language spoken by his parents.

(d) is capable of speaking quite clearly but only in motherese (infant-directed speech).

11. Danielle has switched college majors four times and does not know what she wants to do after she gets her degree. Erikson would suggest that Danielle has not achieved

(a) an integrated identity.

(b) a sense of generativity.

(c) the zone of proximal development.

(d) the concrete operational stage of development.

12. Like most developmental psychologists, Dr. Ladner is likely to divide the lifespan into

(a) continuous and abrupt aspects of development.

(b) genetic and environmental phases of development.

(c) eight age-related stages of development.

(d) four distinct psychosocial stages of development and six physical stages of development.

13. Gordon, a 50-year-old lawyer, has just learned from his physician that he has only one year to live. According to Kübler-Ross, his first reaction to hearing the news is likely to be

(a) "No, it's not possible, there's obviously been some mix-up, some terrible mistake."

(b) "Life is not worth living any more."

(c) "Why me? This is very unfair and makes me mad."

(d) "Well, that's the way it goes, I guess."

14. According to the Application, a parenting style in which parents set clear standards for their children's behavior but are also responsive to the children's needs and wishes is called
    (a) authoritarian.
    (b) permissive-indulgent.
    (c) permissive-indifferent.
    (d) authoritative.

15. According to Culture and Human Behavior (Where Does the Baby Sleep?), infants typically sleep in their own bed and in a separate room from their parents in
    (a) all cultures.
    (b) all Western cultures.
    (c) the United States.
    (d) all Latin cultures.

Progress Test 2

After you have checked your understanding of the material in Progress Test 1 and have done a complete chapter review with special focus on any areas of weakness, you are ready to assess your knowledge on Progress Test 2. Check your answers. If you make a mistake, review your notes, the relevant section of the study guide, and, if necessary, the appropriate part of your textbook.

1. Dr. Strayer is conducting longitudinal research on factors that correlate with getting older. She is likely to find that
    (a) intelligence declines sharply with age.
    (b) there is severe memory impairment as people reach late adulthood.
    (c) most people maintain their intellectual abilities as they age.
    (d) no matter how much older people practice their mental skills, they still do very poorly on intellectual tasks.

2. Mr. Danzig is a 68-year-old retired accountant. If he is typical of people his age, he is probably living
    (a) in his own home.
    (b) in a nursing home.
    (c) with his grown-up children.
    (d) in a mental health facility.

3. When he was 13, Kyle experienced several physical changes: his testicles started to enlarge, his height and weight increased, and his voice deepened. Kyle experienced
    (a) menarche.
    (b) a germinal period.
    (c) puberty.
    (d) irreversibility.

4. Miguel is a 25-year-old, college-educated middle-class engineer. Like his Mexican parents, he is a devout Catholic. If Miguel is like most people, he will probably marry someone who is
    (a) completely different from him in every way as long as she is Catholic.
    (b) very much like he is.
    (c) much older than he is.
    (d) much richer than he is.

5. Mrs. Grant is 49 years old and has recently ceased to menstruate. Mrs. Grant has experienced
    (a) moratorium.   (c) induction.
    (b) menopause.   (d) centration.

6. According to Erikson's psychosocial theory of development, late adulthood is to _____ as adolescence is to _____ .
    (a) ego integrity; generativity
    (b) generativity; intimacy
    (c) intimacy; ego integrity
    (d) ego integrity; integrated identity

7. Mary and Martin are fraternal twins who will be celebrating their sixth birthday very soon. If they are typical of children at this age, Mary will ask for _____ and Martin will ask for _____ as birthday presents.
    (a) dolls and a dollhouse; toy cars and trucks
    (b) sports equipment; dolls and a dollhouse
    (c) toy cars and trucks; sports equipment
    (d) toy guns and toy soldiers; dolls and a dollhouse

8. Sixteen-year-old Jade is reading books about different religions and philosophies and is trying out different approaches to how one should live one's life. Jade is in Erikson's
    (a) moratorium period.
    (b) generativity stage.
    (c) ego integrity period.
    (d) formal operational stage.

9. According to Focus on Neuroscience (The Adolescent Brain), MRI studies of normal children and adolescents
    (a) demonstrated clearly that there was a causal connection between high levels of sex hormones and emotional problems in adolescents.
    (b) indicated that only about 10 percent of the neurons in adolescent brains were ever active or were ever used.

(c) showed overproduction of a second wave of gray matter just prior to puberty, followed by a second round of neuronal pruning during the teenage years.

(d) showed that all of these statements are true.

10. Marcel is researching a paper for his child development course and discovers the work of Lev Vygotsky. In summarizing Vygotsky's contribution to developmental psychology, Marcel is likely to note that the theorist emphasized

(a) genetic factors.

(b) clearly defined biological stages of cognitive development.

(c) clearly defined biological stages of physical development.

(d) social and cultural factors in cognitive development.

11. Kelly is 5 years old and has a good imagination. Recently, for example, she used a discarded box as a make-believe castle and made up a very interesting dialogue between the "king" and "queen" of her castle. This illustrates

(a) centration.   (c) symbolic thought.

(b) conservation.   (d) object permanence.

12. In the Strange Situation procedure, little Anthony used his mother as a safe base from which to explore the environment, showed distress when she left the room, and greeted her warmly when she returned. Anthony would be classified as a(n)

(a) difficult baby.

(b) securely attached baby.

(c) insecurely attached baby.

(d) slow-to-warm-up baby.

13. The development of freckles appears to be controlled by a single gene, which can be either dominant or recessive. Colleen has freckles, just like her mother, so it is likely that she inherited a dominant version of the freckle gene from her mother. The simple dominant–recessive pattern is a fairly common example of gene variation. The different versions of genes are called

(a) alleles.   (c) sex chromosomes.

(b) phenotypes.   (d) karyotypes .

14. According to Critical Thinking (The Effects of Child Care on Attachment and Development), putting young children in a high-quality daycare facility

(a) is detrimental to their physical health.

(b) severely disrupts the attachment process.

(c) has no detrimental effect on the children.

(d) is detrimental to their psychological health.

15. According to the Application, psychologist Diana Baumrind has described a number of basic parenting styles. In her research, she found that children of _____ parents were likely to be moody, unhappy, fearful, withdrawn, unspontaneous, and irritable.

(a) permissive-indulgent

(b) permissive-indifferent

(c) authoritative

(d) authoritarian

Progress Test 3

After you have checked your understanding of the material in Progress Tests 1 and 2, and have done a complete chapter review with special focus on any areas of weakness, you are ready to further assess your knowledge with Progress Test 3. Check your answers. If you make a mistake, review your notes, the appropriate parts of the study guide, and, if necessary, the relevant sections of your textbook.

1. In looking back at his life, 70-year-old Redner experiences regret, dissatisfaction, and disappointment about his accomplishments. According to Erikson, Redner, who is in late adulthood, is experiencing _____ and has failed to achieve a sense of

_____ .

(a) inferiority; generativity

(b) despair; ego integrity

(c) stagnation; ego identity

(d) isolation; intimacy

2. Nine-year-old Adam has acquired the mental operations to comprehend such things as conservation and reversibility and can solve tangible problems in a logical manner. Adam is in Piaget's _____ stage of development.

(a) sensorimotor   (c) concrete operational

(b) preoperational   (d) formal operational

3. Piaget is to _____ development as Erikson is to _____ development.

   (a) cognitive; language
   (b) psychosocial; cognitive
   (c) language; cognitive
   (d) cognitive; psychosocial

4. Despite the fact that he uses only one-word utterances when he attempts to talk, 1-year-old Vincent immediately does what he is told when his mother says, "Bring Mommy the teddy bear, Vincent." This suggests that

   (a) Vincent's comprehension vocabulary is much larger than his production vocabulary.
   (b) Vincent is in the embryonic stage of language development.
   (c) Vincent has reached the concrete opertional stage of development.
   (d) Vincent's production vocabulary is much larger than his comprehension vocabulary.

5. When asked if he had a brother, 3-year-old Kiran said, "Yes, and his name is Mike." When Kiran was asked if Mike had a brother, he replied, "No." This example illustrates Kiran's preoperational way of thinking and demonstrates

   (a) conservation.
   (b) egocentrism.
   (c) a problem in production vocabulary.
   (d) that he has not yet entered the zone of proximal development.

6. Nine months after conception, baby Tracy is born. The stages of her prenatal development, from first to last, were

   (a) embryonic, fetal, germinal.
   (b) fetal, embryonic, germinal.
   (c) germinal, embryonic, fetal.
   (d) germinal, fetal, embryonic.

7. Mrs. Hoff uses very distinct pronunciation, a simplified vocabulary, short sentences, a high pitch, and exaggerated intonation and expression whenever she interacts with her baby. This is an example of

   (a) motherese, or infant-directed speech.
   (b) comprehension vocabulary.
   (c) an insecurely attached mother.
   (d) cooing and babbling.

8. Dr. Kalbiar believes that there is a gap between what children can accomplish on their own and what they can accomplish with the help of others who are more competent. Vygotsky's theory suggested that such guidance can help "stretch" the child's cognitive abilities to new levels, an idea he called

   (a) induction.
   (b) event-specific expectations.
   (c) centration.
   (d) the zone of proximal development.

9. During Mr. Guerno's seventieth birthday party his grandchildren had a chance to ask him about some of his many adventures and travels. While listening to his colorful stories, they realized that their grandfather had lived a very meaningful life and was very satisfied with his many accomplishments. Mr. Guerno is in the _____ stage of life and has achieved what Erikson called _____.

   (a) middle adulthood; generativity
   (b) late adulthood; ego integrity
   (c) middle adulthood; initiative
   (d) late adulthood; ego identity

10. According to Focus on Neuroscience, neuroscientists studying brain changes during childhood are likely to find that between age 6 and early adolescence

   (a) there is a steady increase in the actual number of neurons in the brain.
   (b) unused dendrites, synaptic connections, and neurons are selectively pruned and discarded, and those neurons that are most used strengthen their interconnections with other neurons.
   (c) the neurons that are least used tend to proliferate and those that are most used tend to wear out and decrease in number.
   (d) there is an explosive proliferation of synaptic connections in all neurons regardless of whether they are used or not.

11. Young Allison doesn't understand that adding together one and three is the same as adding together three and one. Allison is demonstrating _____ and is in Piaget's _____ stage of development.

   (a) conservation; concrete operational
   (b) egocentrism; preoperational
   (c) centration; sensorimotor
   (d) irreversibility; preoperational

12. Fourteen-year-old Jason has the ability to reason abstractly and think logically even about hypothetical situations. Jason is in Piaget's _____ stage of cognitive development.
    (a) sensorimotor
    (b) preoperational
    (c) concrete operational
    (d) formal operational

13. Noreen is almost 13 and has just had her first menstrual period. Noreen has experienced
    (a) menopause.   (c) menarche.
    (b) conservation.   (d) centration.

14. According to Culture and Human Behavior (Conflict Between Adolescents and Their Parents)
    (a) the level of conflict between parents and adolescents tends to be higher in Chinese families, compared with European-American families.
    (b) although the level of conflict may vary, parent–adolescent conflict is a common dimension of family life in all cultures.
    (c) regardless of which culture they belonged to, adolescents showed a high level of respect for parental authority, a strong sense of family obligation, and a keen desire for harmony within the family.
    (d) there is significantly less parent–adolescent conflict in individualistic cultures, compared with collectivistic cultures.

15. According to the Application, which of the following is *not* recommended for raising psychologically healthy children?
    (a) Work with your children's temperamental qualities.
    (b) Use induction to teach as you discipline.
    (c) Let your children know that you love them.
    (d) Strive to be an authoritarian parent.

Answers

Introduction: Your Life Story

1. *Developmental psychology is the* study of how people change physically, mentally, and socially over the lifespan.

2. *The major themes in developmental psychology are* the common patterns of growth and development people share and how they differ in terms of social, occupational, and interpersonal accomplishment; the abrupt age-related stages people go through over the lifespan and those aspects of development that reflect gradually unfolding changes; and the nature of the interaction between heredity (nature) and environment (nurture) throughout development.

Genetic Contributions to Your Life Story

1. *A zygote is* a single cell formed at conception from the union of the egg cell and the sperm cell that contains the unique set of genetic instructions inherited from our biological parents.

2. *Chromosomes are* long, threadlike structures composed of twisted parallel strands of DNA; they are found in the cell nucleus.

3. *DNA (deoxyribonucleic acid) is* the double-stranded molecule that is the chemical basis of heredity and carries genetic instructions in the cell.

4. *Genes are* the basic units of heredity and consist of segments of DNA strung like beads along the chromosomes; each gene is a unit of DNA code for making a particular protein molecule. *Genes direct the manufacture of* proteins, which are used in virtually all body functions, such as building cells, producing hormones, and regulating brain activity.

5. *Genotype refers to the* underlying genetic make-up of a particular organism, including the genetic instructions for traits that are not actually displayed. *The human genome is* the scientific description of the complete set of DNA in the human organism, including the location of the genes.

6. *Alleles are* different versions of a particular gene; the combination of these makes our unique genotype (some genes have only a few different versions, others have 50 or more). *The best-known pattern of allele variation is* the dominant–recessive gene pair; the dominant gene contains genetic instructions that may be expressed when paired with another dominant gene or with a recessive gene, and the recessive gene contains genetic instructions that will not be expressed unless paired with another recessive gene.

7. *Phenotype refers to the* observable traits or characteristics of an organism as determined by the interaction of genetics and environmental factors. *Rather than being fixed or inevitable, gene expression is* flexible, responding to fluctuations in the organism's internal state or the external environment (genetic activity can be triggered by the activity of other genes as well as by environmental factors).

8. *The environment plays a role in the relationship between genotype and phenotype as follows:* Different genotypes may react differently to the same environmental factors (the phenotypic expressions are not the same even though the environmental influences are very similar), and similar genotypes may react differently to very different environmental factors (the phenotypic expressions are different even when the underlying genotypes are much the same).

9. *Genetic predispositions are* particular genetic configurations that are more or less sensitive to specific environmental factors and so influence development in certain ways.

Prenatal Development

1. *During prenatal development, the single-cell zygote* undergoes rapid cell division before it is implanted on the wall of the mother's uterus. Eventually, it develops into a full-term fetus.

2. *The three phases of the prenatal stage are* the germinal period, which is also called the zygotic period (the first two weeks), the embryonic period (from the third through the eighth week), and the fetal period (from the ninth week until birth).

3. *Teratogens are* harmful agents or substances that can cross the placenta and cause malformations or defects in an embryo or fetus. The greatest vulnerability to teratogens is during the embryonic stage.

Concept Check 1

1. developmental
2. nature (heredity); nurture (environment)
3. genetic predispositions
4. embryo; fetus
5. teratogen
6. infancy; early childhood; middle childhood
7. chromosomes; deoxyribonucleic acid (DNA); genes
8. allele

Graphic Organizer 1

1. cell nucleus: D
2. chromosome: C
3. gene: A
4. DNA: B

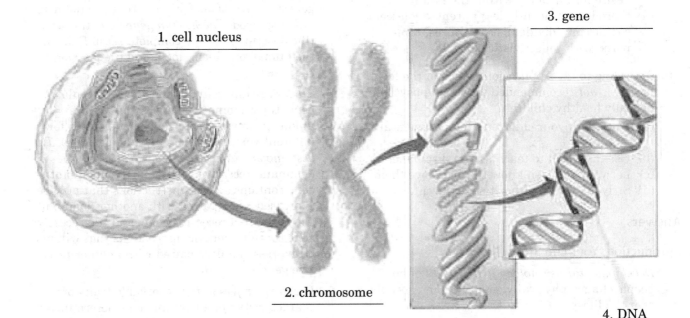

1. cell nucleus

2. chromosome

3. gene

4. DNA

Matching Exercise 1

1. prenatal stage
2. gene
3. developmental psychology
4. genetic predisposition
5. teratogens
6. chromosome
7. mutation

8. germinal period (zygotic period)

9. embryo

10. human genome

11. allele

12. placenta

13. sex chromosomes

True/False Test 1

1. T	5. T	9. F
2. T	6. T	10. F
3. T	7. F	11. T
4. F	8. T	12. T

Development During Infancy and Childhood: Physical Development

1. *Newborn infants enter the world equipped with* the rooting reflex, the sucking reflex, and the grasping reflex. *Their senses of vision, hearing, smell, and touch are* keenly attuned to people, and this ability helps them differentiate between their mothers and other people.

2. *The infant's sensory capabilities promote the development of relationships with caregivers, as evidenced by the fact that they* stare at human faces longer than other images, make eye contact with adults who position themselves close to the newborn (about 6 to 12 inches), and display a preference for their mother's voice and face.

3. *After birth, a number of physical changes in the brain and body take place:* At birth, the brain is about 25 percent of its adult weight, whereas birth weight is only about 5 percent of its eventual adult weight. During infancy, the brain will grow to about 75 percent of its adult weight, whereas body weight will reach approximately 20 percent of adult weight.

Development During Infancy and Childhood: Social and Personality Development

1. *Temperament refers to* the inborn predispositions to consistently behave and react in a certain way. *The three broad temperamental patterns are* easy, difficult, and slow-to-warm-up. *Two other temperamental patterns that have been identified are* high and low reactivity. High-reactive infants react intensely to new experiences, strangers, and novel objects and tend to be tense, fearful, and inhibited (shy); low-reactive infants tend to be calmer, uninhibited, bolder, and more sociable and show

interest rather than fear when exposed to new people, experiences, and objects.

2. *Attachment is the* emotional bond that forms between the infant and his or her caregivers, especially the parents. *The basic premise of attachment theory is* that an infant's ability to thrive physically and psychologically depends in part on the quality of attachment. When parents are consistently warm, responsive, and sensitive to their infant's needs, the infant develops a secure attachment; if parents are neglectful, inconsistent, or insensitive, an infant may suffer insecure attachment.

3. *Attachment is measured using a procedure called the* Strange Situation. *In this technique,* the baby and mother are brought into an unfamiliar room with a variety of toys, and a few minutes later a stranger enters. The mother stays with the child for a few moments, then departs and returns a short time later, she spends a little time with the child, and then departs and returns again. Observers record the infant's behavior through a one-way window.

Development During Infancy and Childhood: Language Development

1. *According to Noam Chomsky,* all children are born with a biological predisposition to learn language; in effect, they possess a "universal grammar," which allows them to easily extract grammatical rules from what they hear.

2. *Language development is encouraged by* the use of infant-directed speech (motherese) that adults instinctively use with babies.

3. *The stages of language development are* the cooing and babbling stage, the one-word stage (in which comprehension vocabulary is usually much larger than production vocabulary), the two-word stage, and finally, fully developed language comprehension and production.

Concept Check 2

1. human face

2. the Strange Situation

3. 25 percent

4. rooting reflex; sucking reflex; grasping reflex

5. easy

6. high-reactive infant

7. secure

8. comprehension; production

Matching Exercise 2

1. high-reactive infant
2. Strange Situation
3. sucking reflex
4. slow-to-warm-up temperament
5. motherese (infant-directed speech)
6. cooing and babbling stage
7. attachment
8. comprehension vocabulary
9. insecure attachment
10. two-word stage
11. multiple attachments

True/False Test 2

1. T	5. T	9. F
2. T	6. T	10. T
3. F	7. T	11. T
4. T	8. T	

Development During Infancy and Childhood: Cognitive Development

1. *The four stages (and their characteristics) in Piaget's theory are*

   (a) the sensorimotor stage, from birth to about age 2, during which the infant explores the environment and acquires knowledge through experiencing and manipulating objects. The development of object permanence is characteristic of this stage.

   (b) the preoperational stage, from about age 2 to age 7, during which the use of symbols and prelogical thought processes increase. Characteristics of this stage include the increasing use of symbolic thought; the tendency for egocentrism, irreversibility, and centration; and the inability to understand conservation.

   (c) the concrete operational stage, from about age 7 to adolescence, during which the child develops the ability to think logically about concrete objects and situations. Characteristics of this stage are the tendency to be less egocentric in their thinking, the ability to reverse mental problems, and the ability to understand the principle of conservation.

   (d) the formal operational stage, from adolescence through adulthood, during which the person acquires the ability to think logically about abstract principles and hypothetical situations.

This stage is characterized by more systematic and logical problem-solving abilities.

2. *Piaget's theory has been criticized because* he underestimated the cognitive abilities of infants and young children, confusing motor skill limitations with cognitive limitations; he underestimated the impact of social and cultural factors on cognitive development; and he overestimated the degree to which people achieve formal operational thought processes.

3. *Vygotsky believed that* cognitive development is strongly influenced by social and cultural factors, such as the support and guidance that children receive from parents, other adults, and older children. *The zone of proximal development refers to* the gap between what children can accomplish on their own and what they can accomplish with the help of others who are more competent.

4. *The information-processing model of cognitive development views cognitive development as* a process of continuous change over the lifespan. Researchers in this area focus on the development of basic mental processes, such as attention, memory, and problem solving.

Concept Check 3

1. underestimated
2. concrete operational
3. object permanence
4. conservation
5. assimilating
6. schema
7. formal
8. accommodation
9. motor skill; cognitive
10. information-processing

Matching Exercise 3

1. symbolic thought
2. Renée Baillargeon
3. object permanence
4. formal operational stage
5. Jean Piaget
6. information-processing model of cognitive development
7. schemas
8. sensorimotor stage
9. egocentrism
10. Lev Vygotsky

True/False Test 3

1. T   6. T
2. T   7. F
3. F   8. T
4. T   9. F
5. F   10. T

Adolescence

1. *Adolescence is* the transitional stage between late childhood and the beginning of adulthood, during which sexual maturity is reached.

2. *Puberty is the* physical process of attaining sexual maturation and reproductive capacity that begins during the early adolescent years.

3. *Puberty involves the development of primary sex characteristics, which are* the sexual organs that are directly involved in reproduction, such as the uterus, ovaries, penis, and testicles, *and secondary sex characteristics, which are* not directly involved in reproduction but differentiate between the sexes, such as male facial hair and female breasts.

4. *The adolescent growth spurt is* the period of accelerated growth during puberty, involving rapid increases in height and weight (occurs about two years earlier in females than in males).

5. *Menarche refers to* a female's first menstrual period (typically occurs around 12 or 13, but can be as early as 9 or 10 or as late as 16 or 17).

6. *Factors that affect the timing of puberty include* gender, nutrition, health, body size, degree of physical activity, family stress, and absence of the biological father. *When adolescents are "off time" in maturation, they* experience maturation noticeably earlier or later than the majority of their peers.

7. *The relationship between parents and their adolescent children is* generally positive, and parents remain influential, but relationships with friends and peers become increasingly important.

8. *Factors involved in romantic and sexual relationships during adolescence include* the physical changes of puberty, which prime the adolescent's interest in sexuality; social and cultural factors also have an influence on when, why, and how adolescents initiate sexual behavior. By the late teens, romantic relationships can lead to overall feelings of enhanced self-worth, feelings of competence, and enhanced relationships with friends and peers.

9. *Identity refers to* a person's definition or description of himself or herself, including the values, beliefs, and ideals that guide the individual's behavior.

10. *Adolescents begin the process of identity formation by* evaluating themselves on several different dimensions, such as social acceptance by peers, academic and athletic abilities, work abilities, personal appearance, and romantic appeal.

11. *According to Erikson's psychosocial theory of lifespan development,* each of the eight stages of life is associated with a particular psychosocial conflict that can be resolved in either a positive or negative direction. *The key psychosocial conflict facing adolescents is* identity versus role confusion.

Concept Check 4

1. integrated identity; intimacy versus isolation
2. identity
3. trust versus mistrust; autonomy versus doubt; initiative versus guilt; industry versus inferiority
4. positive
5. puberty
6. secondary
7. pruning
8. generativity versus stagnation; middle adulthood

Matching Exercise 4

1. identity
2. moratorium period
3. adolescence
4. puberty
5. menarche
6. adolescent growth spurt

True/False Test 4

1. F   4. T
2. T   5. F
3. T

Adult Development

1. *The physical changes that take place during adulthood include* genetically influenced changes such as menopause (the cessation of

menstruation) and thinning, graying hair; and environmentally influenced changes such as the formation of wrinkles, a decrease in the efficiency of various body organs, and a decline in physical strength and endurance.

2. *According to Erikson, the primary psychosocial task of middle adulthood is* generativity.

3. *The most general pattern of social development includes* love and work, which means forming a long-term committed relationship, becoming parents, and pursuing a career or careers. However, there is great variability in the path to intimacy.

4. *In relation to having children, marital satisfaction* tends to decline after the first child is born and to increase after children leave home.

5. *The nature of intimate relationships and family structures varies widely in the United States. For example,* the number of unmarried couples living together increased dramatically at the end of the twentieth century; more than 30 percent of children are being raised by a single parent; more than half of all first marriages end in divorce, and remarrying and starting a second family later in life is not uncommon; among married couples some are opting for a child-free life together; and there are many gay and lesbian couples committed to a long-term monogamous relationship.

6. *In terms of careers in adulthood,* about one-third of people in their late twenties and early thirties not only change jobs within a particular field, but completely switch occupational fields; dual-career families have become more common; and although the combination of work and family roles can be demanding, especially for women, multiple roles can lead to increased feelings of self-esteem, happiness, and competence. The career tracks of men and women often differ, especially if they have children.

Late Adulthood and Aging

1. *Regarding mental and physical abilities in late adulthood,* they do not necessarily show a steep decline. A small but steadily increasing percentage of older adults show a slight decline beginning around age 60, and these declines can be minimized or eliminated with an active and mentally stimulating lifestyle.

2. *According to the activity theory of aging,* life satisfaction in late adulthood is highest when you maintain your previous level of activity, either by continuing old activities or by finding new ones.

3. *According to Erikson, the psychosocial conflict of late adulthood is* ego integrity versus despair.

The Final Chapter: Dying and Death

1. *According to Kübler-Ross's theory of death and dying, the five stages are* denial (people deny that death is imminent); anger (people feel and express indignation and rage); bargaining (people try to work out a deal with doctors, relatives, or God); depression (people become despondent about their fate); and acceptance (people realize what lies ahead and resign themselves to their fate).

2. *Problems with Kübler-Ross's theory are that* dying individuals do not necessarily progress through the predictable sequence of stages that she described. Dying is as individual a process as living; people cope with the prospect of dying much as they have coped with other stresses in their lives.

Concept Check 5

1. middle adulthood; generativity
2. a later
3. late adulthood; despair
4. anger
5. similar to
6. increase
7. ego integrity
8. activity

Graphic Organizer 2

1. Lev Vygotsky
2. Mary D. Salter Ainsworth
3. Noam Chomsky
4. Erik Erikson
5. Jean Piaget

Matching Exercise 5

1. induction
2. menopause
3. permissive parenting style
4. middle adulthood
5. activity theory of aging
6. ego integrity
7. life review

True/False Test 5

1. T	4. T	7. T
2. T	5. F	
3. F	6. T	

Something to Think About

1. Most psychologists today agree that the *quality* of the child-care arrangements is the key factor in promoting secure attachment in early childhood and preventing problems in later childhood. In fact, many studies have found that children who experience high-quality day care tend to be more sociable, better adjusted, and more academically competent than children who experience poor-quality day care. In addition, some researchers have found that grade school children enrolled in high-quality day care from infancy experience no negative effects of their day-care experience. Research in Sweden has supported these findings.

   High-quality day care is characterized by a number of key factors: caregivers should be warm and responsive, developmentally appropriate activities and a variety of play materials should be available, caregivers should have some training and education in child development, low staff turnover is important, and the ratio of caregivers to children should be low.

2. A short discussion of the various stages of cognitive and psychosocial development would be appropriate. Raising psychologically healthy children is possible if parents adopt some of the strategies suggested by the experts. Psychologist Diana Baumrind has described three basic parenting styles: authoritarian, permissive, and authoritative. Research has shown that the authoritative style produces the best results. Can parents learn to be authoritative in their parenting style? The Application has a number of practical suggestions: let your children know that you love them, listen to your children, use induction to teach as you discipline, work with your children's temperamental qualities, understand your children's age-related cognitive abilities and limitations, and don't expect perfection and learn to go with the flow.

   Although all children inherit genetic predispositions from both parents, research has shown that environmental factors, such as the social and cultural influences, educational experiences, and parenting style have very powerful effects on a child's development.

Progress Test 1

1. a	6. c	11. a
2. d	7. a	12. c
3. d	8. c	13. a
4. a	9. b	14. d
5. b	10. a	15. c

Progress Test 2

1. c	6. d	11. c
2. a	7. a	12. b
3. c	8. a	13. a
4. b	9. c	14. c
5. b	10. d	15. d

Progress Test 3

1. b	6. c	11. d
2. c	7. a	12. d
3. d	8. d	13. c
4. a	9. b	14. b
5. b	10. b	15. d

CHAPTER 10

Gender and Sexuality

<table>
<tr>
<td>PREVIEW</td>
<td>Reading the section below first will give you a general sense of the chapter's contents and an initial introduction to some of the major concepts and terms. This will prime you for what you are about to read and help you to develop a "cognitive map" that will guide your study of the material in this chapter. Likewise, reading the preview questions at the beginning of each major section will improve your ability to understand, learn, and retain the information.</td>
</tr>
</table>

CHAPTER 10 . . . AT A GLANCE

To help you distinguish between sex and gender, the text first defines all the relevant terms *sex, gender, gender roles, gender identity, sexual orientation,* and *gender-role stereotype*. Similarities and differences in the personalities, cognitive abilities, and sexual attitudes and behaviors of men and women are discussed. Gender-role development and the influence of social and cultural factors are examined. Two theories of gender-role development—social learning theory and gender schema theory—explain current thinking about how gender roles develop.

Human sexuality is discussed next. The four stages of the human sexual response cycle are presented, and sexual motivation in both humans and other animals is explored. Sexual orientation appears to develop at an early age, and genetics and brain structure may be involved.

Details of human sexual behavior are presented, including the frequency and type of sexual behavior people engage in, and people's fantasies about sexual activity.

The chapter ends with a discussion of various sexual disorders and problems, including the paraphilias. The most common types of sexual dysfunctions in men and women are described. Sexually transmitted diseases (STDs), including genital herpes and AIDS, are discussed. The Application looks at the communication differences and conflicts of people in intimate relationships and offers some important practical tips for dealing with them.

Introduction: Gender and Sexuality

Preview Questions

Consider the following questions as you study this section of the chapter.

- How is sex defined, and how does it differ from gender?
- How do the terms *gender role, gender identity,* and *sexual orientation* differ in meaning?

Read the section "Introduction: Gender and Sexuality" and **write** *your answers to the following:*

1. Sex refers to _____

   _____

   Gender refers to _____

   _____

2. Gender roles consist of _____

   _____

   Gender identity refers to _____

   _____

   Sexual orientation refers to _____

   _____

   _____

Gender Stereotypes and Gender Roles

Preview Questions

Consider the following questions as you study this section of the chapter.

- What are gender-role stereotypes?
- How do men and women compare in terms of personality characteristics, cognitive abilities, and sexual attitudes and behaviors?
- What important qualifications about gender differences need to be made?

Read the section "Gender Stereotypes and Gender Roles" and **write** *your answers to the following:*

1. Gender-role stereotypes are _____

   _____

   _____

   _____

2. Important qualifications about gender differences are as follows: _____

   _____

   _____

   _____

   _____

   _____

   _____

3. Research on gender differences has shown that

   (a) _____

   _____

   (b) _____

   _____

   _____

   _____

   (c) _____

   _____

Gender-Role Development: Blue Bears and Pink Bunnies

Preview Questions

Consider the following questions as you study this section of the chapter.

- What role does gender play in our culture?
- How are boys and girls treated differently, and what gender differences develop during childhood?
- How do social learning theory and gender schema theory explain the development of gender roles?

*Read the section "Gender-Role Development: Blue Bears and Pink Bunnies" and **write** your answers to the following:*

1. Some gender differences that develop during childhood in our culture are as follows:

   (a) _____

   _____

   (b) _____

   _____

   (c) _____

   _____

   (d) _____

   _____

2. According to social learning theory _____

   _____

   _____

3. Gender schema theory contends that _____

   _____

   _____

After you have carefully studied the preceding section, complete the following exercises.

Concept Check 1

Read the following and write the correct term in the space provided.

1. During a sex-education talk, the teacher describes the differences in genetic composition and reproductive anatomy that define a person as biologically male or female. The teacher is describing _____ .

2. Sheila contends that children actively develop cognitive categories for masculinity and femininity, and that these mental representations influence how children perceive, interpret, and remember relevant aspects of what is appropriate for boys and girls. Sheila's views are most consistent with _____ theory.

3. Liam describes his girlfriend's behavior as gentle, caring, empathic, and very feminine. Liam is referring to his girlfriend's _____ .

4. Pat and Les are fraternal twins. Pat consistently scores higher than Les on tests of verbal fluency, reading comprehension, and basic writing skills; Les outscores Pat on spatial skills and tests of advanced mathematical ability. It is very probable that Pat is _____ (male/female) and Les is _____ (male/female).

5. As part of an experiment investigating gender-role development, Dr. Beach decides to dress a number of male and female one-year-olds in identical clothes. It is very likely that adults _____ (will/will not) be able to tell male and female infants apart but that other one-year-olds _____ (will/will not) be able to do so.

6. Frank is very fit and works out in the gym almost every day. He is considered by many to be very masculine, especially by his boyfriend. Frank's sense of maleness is his _____ , and his attraction to members of the same sex is his _____ .

7. Mr. and Mrs. Morganthaler were window shopping in the mall when they saw the devastating aftermath of a terrorist attack on TV. Both were overcome with emotion. Mrs. Morganthaler started to cry but Mr. Morganthaler masked his feelings. This gender difference in the *expression* of emotion is probably a result of _____ .

8. After watching an action-packed movie on TV, young Ho Wai started practicing kung fu kicks and karate chops. According to _____ theory, Ho Wai's present behavior is the result of observing and imitating the movie characters, a process called _____ .

9. When Julian was a child, he loved playing with dolls and joining in girls' games; as a teenager, he shaved his legs and under his arms. Now, he frequently dresses in women's clothes and

hopes one day to undergo sex-reassignment surgery. Julian is a _____ individual, who might also be classified as a _____ .

Review of Terms, Concepts, and Names 1

Use the terms in this list to complete the Matching Test, then to help you answer the True/False items correctly.

sex
gender
gender roles
gender identity
sexual orientation
gender-role stereotypes
benevolent sexism

social learning theory
Sandra Bem
gender schema theory
schemas
intersex
transgendered
transsexual

Matching Exercise

Match the appropriate term/name with its definition or description.

1. _____ American psychologist who has conducted extensive research on sex roles and gender identity; proposed gender schema theory to explain gender-role development.

2. _____ The cultural, social, and psychological meanings that are associated with masculinity and femininity.

3. _____ The direction of a person's emotional and erotic attraction toward members of the opposite sex, the same sex, or both sexes.

4. _____ The beliefs and expectations that people hold about the typical characteristics, preferences, and behaviors of men and women.

5. _____ In gender schema theory, the mental categories or representations of masculinity and femininity.

6. _____ Form of prejudice that results from accepting positive stereotypes of women.

7. _____ Condition in which a person's biological sex is ambiguous, often combining aspects of both male and female anatomy and/or physiology.

True/False Test

Indicate whether each statement is true or false by placing T or F in the blank space next to each item.

1. ____ Social learning theory contends that gender roles are acquired through the basic processes of learning, including reinforcement, punishment, and modeling.

2. ____ Sex refers to (1) the biological category of male or female as defined by physical differences in genetic composition and in reproductive anatomy and function and (2) the behavioral manifestations of the sexual urge; sexual intercourse.

3. ____ Gender identity refers to the behaviors, attitudes, and personality traits that are designated as either masculine or feminine in a given culture.

4. ____ Gender schema theory states that gender-role development is influenced by the formation of schemas, or mental representations, of masculinity and femininity.

5. ____ Gender roles refer to people's psychological sense of being male or female.

6. ____ A transgendered individual is a person whose psychological gender identity conflicts with his or her biological sex.

7. ____ A transsexual is a transgendered person who undergoes surgery and hormone treatment to physically transform his or her body into the opposite sex.

Check your answers and review any areas of weakness before going on to the next section.

Human Sexuality

Preview Questions

Consider the following questions as you study this section of the chapter.

- What factors are involved in human sexuality?
- What are the four stages of the human sexual response?
- How does sexual motivation differ for lower and higher animals?
- What biological factors are involved in sexual motivation?

*Read the section "Human Sexuality" and **write** your answers to the following:*

1. The scientific study of sexuality is _____

_____

_____

2. The four stages of the human sexual response (and the characteristics of each) are _____

_____

_____

_____

_____

_____

3. In nonhuman animals, sexual behavior is _____

_____

_____

In higher animals, sexual behavior is _____

_____

_____

Sexual Orientation

Preview Questions

Consider the following questions as you study this section of the chapter.

- What does sexual orientation refer to?
- Why is sexual orientation sometimes difficult to identify?
- What factors have been associated with sexual orientation?

*Read the section "Sexual Orientation" and **write** your answers to the following:*

1. Sexual orientation refers to _____

_____

_____

2. Sexual orientation is difficult to identify because _____

_____

_____

_____

_____

_____

_____

3. Factors associated with sexual orientation are as follows: _____

_____

_____

_____

_____

Sexual Behavior

Preview Questions

Consider the following questions as you study this section of the chapter.

- What characterizes the sexual behavior patterns of adults?
- What have neuroscientists shown about activity in the brains of people in love?
- What are some important aspects of sexual relationships in late adulthood?

*Read the section "Sexual Behavior over the Lifespan" and **write** your answers to the following:*

1. The most general conclusions about sexuality in early and middle adulthood are

   (a) _____

   _____

   (b) _____

   _____

   (c) _____

   _____

   (d) _____

   _____

2. Neuroscientists have shown that romantic love activates _____

_____

_____

_____

3. In late adulthood, people experience _____

_____

_____

_____

After you have carefully studied the preceding section, complete the following exercises.

Concept Check 2

Read the following and write the correct term in the space provided.

1. Mary and her husband James have just shared a fulfilling sexual experience. Unlike Mary, James is not likely to be able to experience another orgasm for a period of time; this is called the _____ period.

2. Mrs. Jacobson had her ovaries removed because of cancer and is now in perfect health. As a result of the operation, the level of the female sex hormone estrogen will _____ ; the level of her interest in sexual activity will _____ (increase/decrease/stay the same).

3. Dr. Jamison surgically removed the testes of an experimental laboratory rat. It is very probable that the rat will experience a(n) _____ in sexual activity and interest.

4. Hamish, a 25-year-old medical student, is heterosexual; his brother Stuart, a 21-year-old philosophy major, is homosexual. The two brothers differ in their _____ .

5. Mr. and Mrs. Dempster are in their seventies and enjoy good health and an active lifestyle. If they are like many adults in their age range, they are very _____ (unlikely/likely) to have an interest in sex.

6. Young Simon has a rather passive, weak-willed father and a strong-willed, assertive mother. Research on early life experiences and sexual orientation indicates that such atypical family relationships _____ (are/are not) one of the main causes of homosexuality.

Review of Terms, Concepts, and Names 2

Use the terms in this list to complete the Matching Test, then to help you answer the True/False items correctly.

William H. Masters and
  Virginia E. Johnson
excitement phase
plateau phase
orgasm
resolution phase
refractory period
estrus
estrogen
testosterone
sexual orientation
heterosexual
homosexual
bisexual
lesbian
gay
retrospective study
prospective study

Matching Exercise

Match the appropriate term/name with its definition or description.

1. _____ American behavioral scientists who conducted pioneering research in the field of human sexuality and sex therapy.

2. _____ The second stage in the human sexual response cycle in which physical arousal builds as pulse and breathing rates continue to rise; the penis becomes fully erect, the testes enlarge, the clitoris withdraws but remains sensitive, the vaginal entrance tightens, and vaginal lubrication continues.

3. _____ A person who is sexually attracted to individuals of the other sex.

4. _____ For a male, a period of time following orgasm during which he is incapable of having another erection or orgasm.

5. _____ A person who is attracted to individuals of the same sex.

6. _____ The first stage in the human sexual response cycle that marks the beginning of sexual arousal and can occur in response to sexual fantasies or other sexually arousing stimuli, physical contact with another person, or masturbation.

7. _____ Term typically used by male homosexuals to describe their sexual orientation.

8. _____ Type of study in which a group of people are systematically observed over time in order to discover what factors are associated with a particular trait, characteristic, or behavior.

9. _____ The direction of a person's emotional and erotic attraction toward members of the opposite sex, the same sex, or both sexes.

True/False Test

Indicate whether each statement is true or false by placing T or F in the blank space next to each item.

1. ____ Estrus refers to the cyclical period during which a nonhuman female animal is fertile and receptive to male sexual advances.

2. ___ The fourth stage of the sexual response cycle, during which both sexes tend to experience a warm physical glow and sense of well-being and arousal returns to normal, is called the resolution phase.

3. ___ A bisexual is sexually attracted to individuals of both sexes.

4. ___ Testosterone, the female sex hormone produced by the ovaries, influences a woman's monthly reproductive cycle.

5. ___ Orgasm is the third and shortest phase of the sexual response cycle, during which blood pressure and heart rate reach their peak and muscles in the vaginal walls and uterus contract rhythmically, as do the muscles in and around the penis as the male ejaculates.

6. ___ Estrogen, the male sex hormone produced by the testes, is responsible for male sexual development.

7. ___ Female homosexuals are usually called lesbians.

8. ___ A retrospective study involves asking people to recall or remember childhood events and behaviors.

Check your answers and review any areas of weakness before going on to the next section.

Sexual Disorders and Problems

Preview Questions

Consider the following questions as you study this section of the chapter.

- How common are sexual problems?
- What are sexual dysfunctions, and what characterizes these disorders?
- What are the paraphilias, and how do they differ from dysfunctions?
- What are sexually transmitted diseases (STDs), and what causes genital herpes and AIDS?
- Who is at greatest risk of contracting AIDS, and how common is AIDS worldwide?

Read the section "Sexual Disorders and Problems" and **write** *your answers to the following:*

1. .The incidence of sexual dysfunction among

   women is _____ ; among men, it is

   _____ . For women the most common

sexual problems are _____

_____

for men the most common sexual problems are

_____

Overall, married and college-educated men and

women have _____

_____

2. A sexual dysfunction is _____

_____

_____

3. The eight categories of sexual dysfunctions and their characteristics are

   (a) _____

   _____

   (b) _____

   _____

   (c) _____

   _____

   (d) _____

   _____

   (e) _____

   _____

   (f) _____

   _____

   (g) _____

   _____

   (h) _____

   _____

4. A paraphilia is _____

_____

_____

5. The eight most common paraphilias and their characteristics are

   (a) _____

   _____

   (b) _____

   _____

   _____

   (c) _____

   _____

   _____

(d) _____

_____

(e) _____

_____

(f) _____

_____

(g) _____

_____

(h) _____

_____

6. Unlike a person with a sexual dysfunction, a person who has a paraphilia is _____

_____

_____

_____

7. Sexually transmitted diseases (STDs) are

_____

_____

They include _____

_____

_____

_____

_____

8. Genital herpes is a disease mostly caused by

_____

_____

9. AIDS (acquired immune deficiency syndrome) is a disease caused by _____

_____

_____

_____

10. In the United States, the three groups at greatest risk of becoming infected by HIV are

_____

_____

Most infections occur among _____

_____

Blacks account for approximately _____ percent of new infections each year, whites for _____ percent, and Hispanics _____ percent. Worldwide more than _____ are cur-

rently living with HIV and AIDS, and _____ have died because of AIDS.

After you have carefully studied the preceding section, complete the following exercises.

Concept Check 3

Read the following and write the correct term in the space provided.

1. Marshall went to his doctor because his complete lack of sexual desire was causing interpersonal problems with his wife. He is most likely to be diagnosed as having a condition called _____ disorder.

2. Recently, Herbert was arrested when he was caught peering through the window of a woman who was getting undressed. It turned out that Herbert had a long history of similar behavior. Herbert suffers from _____ .

3. Axel uses public transport during rush hour because he gets sexually aroused from touching and rubbing against strangers. Axel has a paraphilia called _____ .

4. Marjorie went to her doctor when she experienced symptoms that included vaginal discharge and painful urination. If she is diagnosed with a bacterial sexually transmitted disease (STD), it is likely to be _____ or

_____ .

5. Jennifer sought medical help for a problem she noticed after she started living with her boyfriend. After she described her symptoms of chronic genital pain during intercourse, her doctor diagnosed her condition as

_____ .

6. Marek has been diagnosed with AIDS. When the HIV virus became active, it selectively attacked a key component of his immune system called _____ , which mobilize other immune system cells to fight off diseases and infections. He is most likely to be prescribed _____ , which work by slowing down HIV's reproductive cycle.

Graphic Organizer 1

Identify the following paraphilias.

1. Sexual arousal achieved by exposing one's genitals to shocked strangers:

   _____

2. Sexual arousal from touching and rubbing against a nonconsenting person, usually in a crowded public situation, such as a crowded bus or subway car:

   _____

3. Sexual arousal in response to inanimate objects or body parts that are not primarily associated with sexual arousal:

   _____

4. For a heterosexual male, sexual arousal from cross-dressing in women's clothes:

   _____

5. Sexual fantasies, urges, or behavior involving sexual activity with a prepubescent child (generally age 13 or younger):

   _____

6. Sexual arousal from observing an unsuspecting person who is disrobing, naked, or engaged in sexual activity:

   _____

7. Sexual arousal achieved through intentionally inflicting psychological or physical suffering on another person:

   _____

8. Sexual arousal in response to actually being humiliated, beaten, bound, or otherwise made to suffer:

   _____

Graphic Organizer 2

Read the following and decide whether the statement is more characteristic of a paraphilia (P) or a sexual dysfunction (SD):

Statement	P	SD
1. Consistent disturbances in sexual desire, arousal, or orgasm.		
2. Much more prevalent among men than women.		
3. Is not usually accompanied by psychological distress.		
4. Sexual gratification is almost always dependent on fantasies, urges, or behaviors that fall outside the socially accepted range of sexual behavior.		
5. Is usually accompanied by psychological distress and interpersonal difficulties.		
6. Typically come to the attention of mental health professionals when a person's behavior causes problems for his or her partner, family member, or coworker or has resulted in the person's arrest.		
7. Can be successfully treated by psychologists and physicians who have received specialized training in sex therapy.		
8. Some forms of the disturbance are illegal.		
9. Although biological and psychological theories have been proposed, the cause or causes remain obscure.		
10. While there are no reliable data on the prevalence of these problems, it is known that they affect both men and women about equally.		

Review of Terms and Concepts 3

Use the terms in this list to complete the Matching Test, then to help you answer the True/False items correctly.

sexual dysfunction
hypoactive sexual desire
  disorder
sexual aversion disorder
dyspareunia
erectile dysfunction
male orgasmic disorder
premature ejaculation
female orgasmic
  disorder
vaginismus
paraphilia
exhibitionism
frotteurism
fetishism
transvestic fetishism
pedophilia
voyeurism
sexual sadism

sexual masochism
sexually transmitted
  diseases (STDs)
gonorrhea, syphilis, and
  chlamydia
pubic lice
genital herpes
herpes simplex virus
  type 1 and 2 (HSV-1
  and HSV-2)
AIDS (acquired immune
  deficiency syndrome)
(HIV) human
  immunodeficiency
  virus
CD4 positive helper
  T cells
antiretroviral drugs

Matching Exercise

Match the appropriate term with its definition or description.

1. _____ Paraphilia characterized by sexual arousal in response to inanimate objects (for example, female undergarments, shoes, leather) or body parts that are not typically associated with sexual arousal (for example, feet, hair, legs).

2. _____ Infectious diseases that are transmitted primarily through sexual intercourse or other intimate sexual contact.

3. _____ In males, sexual dysfunction characterized by a recurring inability to achieve or maintain an erect penis.

4. _____ In females, sexual dysfunction characterized by consistent delays in achieving orgasm or the inability to achieve orgasm.

5. _____ Paraphilia in which a heterosexual male achieves sexual arousal from cross-dressing in women's clothes.

6. _____ Sexual dysfunction characterized by persistent, involuntary contractions or spasms of the vaginal muscles, which result in uncomfortable or painful intercourse.

7. _____ Nontraditional sexual behavior in which a person's sexual gratification depends on an unusual sexual experience, object, or fantasy.

8. _____ Retrovirus that infects, destroys, and reduces the number of helper T cells in the immune system, producing AIDS.

9. _____ Consistent disturbance in sexual desire, arousal, or orgasm that causes psychological distress and interpersonal difficulties.

10. _____ In males, sexual dysfunction characterized by delayed orgasm during intercourse or the inability to achieve orgasm during intercourse.

11. _____ In males, sexual dysfunction characterized by orgasm occurring before it is desired, often immediately or shortly after penetration.

12. _____ Disease caused by the human immunodeficiency virus (HIV), which selectively attacks CD4 positive helper T cells in the immune system, progressively weakening the body's ability to fight infections and diseases.

13. _____ Parasitic sexually transmitted disease (STD).

14. _____ Cells that mobilize other immune system cells to fight off diseases or infections and are selectively attacked by the HIV virus, weakening the immune system.

True/False Test

Indicate whether each item is true or false by placing T or F in the space next to each item.

1. ____ A paraphilia in which sexual arousal is achieved through intentionally inflicting psychological or physical suffering on another person is called sexual masochism.

2. ____ A paraphilia in which sexual fantasies, urges, or behavior involve sexual activity with a prepubescent child is called pedophilia.

3. ____ Dyspareunia is a sexual dysfunction characterized by active avoidance of genital sexual contact because of extreme anxiety, fear, or disgust.

4. ____ Most cases of genital herpes are caused by herpes simplex virus type 2 (HSV-2), but the disease may also be caused by HSV-1.

5. ___ Voyeurism is a paraphilia in which sexual arousal is obtained from observing an unsuspecting person disrobing, naked, or engaging in sexual activity.

6. ___ Hypoactive sexual desire disorder is a sexual dysfunction characterized by abnormally high and persistent levels of sexual desire.

7. ___ A paraphilia in which sexual arousal is achieved by exposing one's genitals to shocked strangers is called exhibitionism.

8. ___ Sexual sadism is a form of paraphilia in which sexual arousal is achieved in response to actually being humiliated, beaten, bound, or otherwise made to suffer.

9. ___ Frotteurism is a paraphilia in which the person achieves sexual arousal from touching and rubbing against a nonconsenting person, usually in a crowded public situation, such as a crowded bus or subway car.

10. ___ A sexual dysfunction characterized by genital pain before, during, or after sexual intercourse is called sexual aversion disorder.

11. ___ Gonorrhea, syphilis, and chlamydia are bacterial sexually transmitted diseases (STDs).

12. ___ Genital herpes is a sexually transmitted disease (STD) caused by the herpes simplex virus that can produce outbreaks of painful blisters in the genital and anal regions.

13. ___ Antiretroviral drugs work together by slowing down HIV's reproductive cycle.

Check your answers and review any areas of weakness before going on to the next section.

Something to Think About

1. Just about everyone experiences some kind of relationship problem at one time or another. Most frequently, problems tend to arise in intimate relationships between men and women. Imagine you are a therapist and a couple comes to you for help in resolving their ongoing interpersonal conflicts. Based on what you have discovered in this chapter, what advice would you give them?

2. The French saying "Vive la différence!" refers to the differences between men and women. When

people use it, they may simply be celebrating the most obvious anatomical features and behaviors associated with masculinity and femininity. Male–female differences, however, continue to be a topic of debate. For instance, some popular books and the media have suggested that male and female brains are fundamentally different and that men and women are like creatures from two different planets (Mars and Venus, respectively). Now that you know quite a bit about gender and sexuality, what would you add to a discussion of the issue?

Check your answers and review any areas of weakness before doing the progress tests.

Progress Test 1

Review the complete chapter (including Concept Reviews and the boxed inserts), review all your study notes, and then test yourself on the following progress test. Check your answers. If you make a mistake, review your notes, review the relevant section of the study guide, and, if necessary, go back and read the appropriate part of your textbook.

1. In a recent tutorial discussion, Michael stated that women are more nurturing, patient, and emotional than men, and that men are more logical, rational, and aggressive than women. Michael's beliefs about male and female differences best illustrates
   (a) sexual orientation.
   (b) gender identity.
   (c) sex.
   (d) gender-role stereotypes.

2. Aldred believes that gender roles develop as young children observe others modeling particular gender-appropriate behaviors and that children are rewarded when they behave accordingly and are punished when they don't. Aldred's view is most consistent with the _____ theory of gender-role development.
   (a) gender schema
   (b) Masters and Johnson
   (c) social learning
   (d) evolutionary

3. When Kathy's baby was born, the doctor took one look at its genitals and said "It's a girl!" By definition, the doctor was referring to the newborn's
   (a) gender.
   (b) sex.
   (c) sexual orientation.
   (d) gender role.

4. In order to avoid the potential problems of memory bias in the recall of childhood events, researchers followed the development of two groups of boys for approximately 15 years, then compared them on a number of different traits and characteristics. These researchers are trying to avoid the problems associated with _____ by conducting a(n) _____ .
   (a) prospective studies; retrospective study
   (b) correlational research; experimental study
   (c) retrospective studies; prospective study
   (d) experimental research; correlational study

5. Because of an illness, 30-year-old Mandy had her ovaries surgically removed. As a result of this operation, Mandy is likely to experience
   (a) homosexual feelings and urges.
   (b) an increase in estrogen production.
   (c) a steep drop in sexual activity and interest.
   (d) a decrease in estrogen production.

6. Laureen is a lesbian. It is very probable that
   (a) her sexual orientation was determined before adolescence and before any sexual activity occurred.
   (b) she experienced some early childhood sexual abuse by a member of the opposite sex.
   (c) her father was overly domineering and her mother was ineffectual and provided her with a poor feminine role model.
   (d) her first sexual experience occurred in childhood with a member of the same sex.

7. Thomas and Shauna have just completed a number of tests of cognitive abilities. If they are typical, Thomas is likely to score _____ than Shauna on spatial skills, and Shauna is likely to score _____ than Thomas on verbal, reading, and writing skills.
   (a) lower; higher
   (b) lower; lower
   (c) higher; lower
   (d) higher; higher

8. When he was 18 months old, Garreth had sex-reassignment surgery after his penis was accidentally severed during a routine medical procedure. Although he was given hormone treatments and brought up as a girl, he has never been comfortable with the role; he was dressed and treated in every way like a female but he always felt like a male. Garreth's psychological sense of being a male is his _____ , and the way he was dressed and treated represents his _____ .
   (a) gender identity; gender role
   (b) sex; sexual orientation
   (c) gender role; gender identity
   (d) gender-role stereotype; sex

9. After her husband died, 68-year-old Mrs. Jaspers started dating 70-year-old Sidney. At their age
   (a) it is very unlikely that they will engage in sexual activity.
   (b) they will want to get married almost immediately.
   (c) dating fills their needs for companionship and sexual intimacy.
   (d) all of these statements are true.

10. Frank and his wife Joanne have not managed to start a family yet. This is because Frank is unable to achieve orgasm during intercourse; he is only able to do so through other means. Frank has a problem called
    (a) premature ejaculation.
    (b) erectile dysfunction.
    (c) dyspareunia.
    (d) male orgasmic disorder.

11. Nancy and Bruce are newlyweds. They are going to a sex therapist because Nancy experiences persistent, involuntary contraction of the vaginal muscles, resulting in painful intercourse. Nancy suffers from
    (a) female orgasmic disorder.
    (b) vaginismus.
    (c) hypoactive sexual desire disorder.
    (d) frotteurism.

12. When Desmond and Mona met, they found that they shared certain sexual interests. Desmond achieves sexual arousal through intentionally inflicting psychological or physical suffering on another person, and Mona is sexually aroused by being humiliated, beaten, bound, or otherwise made to suffer. Desmond is a(n) _____ and Mona is a _____ .

    (a) exhibitionist; voyeur
    (b) sexual sadist; sexual masochist
    (c) pedophile; frotteurist
    (d) sexual masochist; sexual sadist

13. Although Steve is anatomically normal (he is biologically a male), he is uncomfortable with his own assigned gender, fantasizes about being a woman, frequently dresses in female clothes, and displays the mannerisms typical of an "extremely feminine" female. According to In Focus (Beyond Male and Female), Steve would be considered a(n)

    (a) exhibitionist.
    (b) person with a fetish.
    (c) person with hypoactive sexual desire disorder.
    (d) transgendered individual.

14. According to the Application, a key ingredient in successful intimate relationships is

    (a) suppressing one's true emotions.
    (b) resolving conflict.
    (c) stonewalling.
    (d) flooding.

15. According to Culture and Human Behavior (Evolution and Mate Preferences), the evolutionary explanation of sex differences

    (a) has been criticized on the grounds that it is overly deterministic and does not sufficiently acknowledge the role of culture, gender-role socialization, and other social factors.
    (b) provides clear evidence that sexual inequality is natural, correct, and justified.
    (c) proposes that kindness, intelligence, emotional stability, health, and a pleasing personality are much less important than a prospective mate's financial resources or good looks.
    (d) theorizes that men are more likely to look for a mate who has high status and wealth and will be a "good provider," and women are more attracted to males who are young and fertile and would make good "trophy husbands."

Progress Test 2

After you have checked your understanding of the material in Progress Test 1 and have done a complete chapter review with special focus on any areas of weakness, you are ready to assess your knowledge on Progress Test 2. Check your answers. If you make a mistake, review your notes, the relevant section of the study guide, and, if necessary, the appropriate part of your textbook.

1. Julian is a heterosexual male who has a transvestic fetishism. Cross-dressing in women's clothes and wearing women's cosmetics sexually arouses him. Because his behavior falls outside the socially accepted range of sexual behaviors, he is likely to be classified as having

    (a) dyspareunia.
    (b) male orgasmic disorder.
    (c) hypoactive sexual desire disorder.
    (d) a paraphilia.

2. Elsie is thinking of going to a sex therapist. She is worried because she has never experienced an orgasm during sexual intercourse with her husband, despite having an otherwise very warm and loving relationship. Elsie probably has a sexual dysfunction called

    (a) dyspareunia.
    (b) sexual aversion disorder.
    (c) female orgasmic disorder.
    (d) vaginismus.

3. Mary and Martin are fraternal twins who will be celebrating their sixth birthday very soon. If they are typical of children at this age, Mary will ask for _____ and Martin will ask for _____ as birthday presents.

    (a) dolls and a dollhouse; toy cars and trucks
    (b) sports equipment; dolls and a dollhouse
    (c) toy cars and trucks; sports equipment
    (d) toy guns and soldiers; sports equipment

4. Dr. Poon's research indicates that the annual rate of new HIV infections has been stable in the United States for over a decade. In addition, she has found that approximately _____ Americans are newly infected with HIV each year, and approximately _____ of these newly infected people are unaware of their HIV infection.

    a. 1.2 million; one-half
    b. 55,000; one-quarter
    c. 15,000; three-quarters
    d. 25 million; one-quarter

5. Kaleigh and Graeme are madly and passionately in love. A brain scan of their brains using functional magnetic resonance imaging (fMRI) is likely to show activation in four brain areas associated with the emotion of happiness. According to Focus on Neuroscience (Romantic Love and the Brain), these four brain areas are also activated in response to
   (a) antidepressant drugs such as Prozac, Paxil, and Zoloft.
   (b) lithium, a commonly used medication for treating bipolar disorder.
   (c) antipsychotic drugs such as Thorazine.
   (d) euphoria-producing drugs such as opiates and cocaine.

6. Blair has a sexually transmitted disease whose signs include flu-like symptoms, swollen glands, and outbreaks of painful blisters in the genital area. Blair has a disease called _____, which is usually caused by _____ .
   (a) AIDS (acquired immune deficiency syndrome); the human immunodeficiency virus (HIV)
   (b) chlamydia; a bacterium
   (c) genital herpes; the herpes simplex virus 2 (HSV-2)
   (d) pubic lice; a parasite

7. Brandilyn and Travis both took standardized math tests. If they are like most females and males in studies investigating gender differences in math ability, their overall scores
   (a) will be drastically different; Travis's score will be about 25 percent higher than Brandilyn's.
   (b) are likely to be very similar.
   (c) will be drastically different; Brandilyn's score will be about 25 percent higher than Travis's.
   (d) will differ only if they are in the very lowest range (bottom 3 percent) of math achievement test results; then, Travis's score will be twice as high as Brandilyn's.

8. In summarizing research on certain gender differences, Dr. Tigglewerth noted that, in general, women tend to be socially sensitive, friendly, and concerned with others' welfare, whereas men tend to be dominant, controlling, and independent. Dr. Tigglewerth is describing
   (a) gender-role stereotypes found only in North American culture.

   (b) gender differences on two cognitive abilities.
   (c) gender differences in sexual behavior and attitudes.
   (d) gender differences on two personality dimensions.

9. Corey has AIDS and is taking a combination of antiretroviral drugs. These drugs
   (a) actively seek out and selectively kill CD4 positive helper T cells.
   (b) work by slowing down HIV's reproductive cycle.
   (c) increase the probability of Corey's contracting an opportunistic infection.
   (d) actively seek out and selectively kill the human immunodeficiency virus (HIV).

10. In a term paper on child development, Sima made the case that children actively develop categories for masculinity and femininity and suggested that these mental representations influence how children perceive, interpret, and remember relevant aspects of what is appropriate for girls and boys. Sima's position is most consistent with the _____ theory of gender-role development.
    (a) gender schema   (c) Masters and Johnson
    (b) evolutionary   (d) social learning

11. Barney and Bailey are identical twins. Barney is gay. Therefore, there is
    (a) about a 50 percent chance that Bailey will also be homosexual.
    (b) almost 100 percent chance that Bailey will also be homosexual.
    (c) about a 20 percent chance that Bailey will also be homosexual.
    (d) no way to predict Bailey's sexual orientation because there is no correlation between genetic factors and sexual behavior.

12. In the human sexual response cycle, the first phase is _____ and the last phase is _____ .
    (a) plateau; resolution
    (b) excitement; orgasm
    (c) orgasm; plateau
    (d) excitement; resolution

13. Dr. MacKinnon is doing cross-cultural research on gender-role stereotypes. She is likely to discover that
    (a) across cultures, there is a high degree of agreement on the characteristics associated with each sex.
    (b) in every culture, the characteristics associated with the male stereotype are identical.
    (c) across cultures, there is a high degree of disagreement on the characteristics associated with each sex.
    (d) in every culture, the female stereotype is more widely believed than is the male stereotype.

14. According to In Focus (Everything You Wanted to Know About Sexual Fantasies), which of the following is true?
    (a) Sexual fantasies are psychologically unhealthy.
    (b) Male and female sexual fantasies are almost identical in content and frequency.
    (c) Sexual fantasies are a sign of sexual frustration and dissatisfaction with a relationship.
    (d) None of these statements are true.

15. One of the most persistent and pervasive gender stereotypes is that women are more emotional than men. Critical Thinking (Are Women Really More Emotional Than Men?) concludes that
    (a) women are more emotionally *expressive* than men, and men tend to mask their emotions more than women do.
    (b) males and females differ significantly in their *experience* of emotion.
    (c) the expression of emotions is strongly influenced by genes and inherited tendencies and relatively unaffected by culturally determined display rules.
    (d) all of these statements are true.

Progress Test 3

After you have checked your understanding of the material in Progress Tests 1 and 2, and have done a complete chapter review with special focus on any areas of weakness, you are ready to further assess your knowledge with Progress Test 3. Check your answers. If you make a mistake, review your notes, the appropriate parts of the study guide, and if necessary, the relevant sections of your textbook.

1. When Oliver played with dolls and domestic toys, his mother would show her disapproval; when he played with toy vehicles and building blocks, his mother would respond in a positive manner. As Oliver grew older, he played less and less with dolls, dollhouses, and domestic toys and more and more with stereotypical "boys" toys. This description of gender-role development illustrates
    (a) gender identity theory.
    (b) gender schema theory.
    (c) social learning theory.
    (d) evolutionary theory.

2. When Rex was a young pup, his owners took him to the vet to have him neutered. If Rex is like most animals, the removal of his testes will very likely result in a(n) _____ in the levels of the hormone testosterone, and a(n) _____ in sexual interest and sexual activity.
    (a) increase; decrease
    (b) decrease; decrease
    (c) decrease; increase
    (d) increase; increase

3. Dr. LaSage conducted twin studies on sexual orientation. If his findings are consistent with previous research on this topic, he is likely to conclude that
    (a) sexual orientation is at least partly influenced by genetics.
    (b) having an inadequate male role model or having an overly dominant mother is the primary cause of homosexuality.
    (c) sexual orientation is almost completely influenced by environmental factors.
    (d) homosexuality is the result of unpleasant early heterosexual experiences.

4. Barbara and Bob have decided to live together. She discovers that he can achieve sexual arousal only from contact with her stockings, shoes, or underwear. It appears that Bob has a disorder called
    (a) voyeurism.   (c) exhibitionism.
    (b) pedophilia.   (d) fetishism.

5. Heinz has a passive, weak father who provides a poor masculine role model. His mother, on the other hand, is a very strong, assertive, domineering woman. On the basis of research on early life experiences and sexual orientation, you would be justified in concluding that
   (a) Heinz's experiences with his parents are not likely to cause him to become homosexual.
   (b) by the time he is a young adult Heinz is almost certain to be a homosexual.
   (c) Heinz will be a heterosexual during his teens, a bisexual in his early adult years, and eventually a homosexual in middle to late adulthood.
   (d) by the time he reaches puberty, Heinz will suffer from gender identity disorder and one or more of the paraphilias.

6. Robert is very distressed and embarrassed because he frequently reaches sexual climax within minutes of becoming sexually aroused and before he has intercourse with his partner. Robert's problem is called
   (a) hypoactive sexual desire disorder.
   (b) premature ejaculation.
   (c) male orgasmic disorder.
   (d) erectile dysfunction.

7. Doug was infected with HIV from contaminated blood during a blood transfusion many years ago. It is very likely that he will develop
   (a) chlamydia.
   (b) herpes.
   (c) syphilis.
   (d) acquired immune deficiency syndrome (AIDS).

8. If research investigating sexual problems in the adult population is consistent with data reported in the text, it is likely to show that for women the most common sexual problems are _____ and for men the most common sexual problems are _____ .
   (a) low sexual desire and arousal problems, including the inability to achieve orgasm; premature ejaculation and problems achieving and maintaining an erection
   (b) sexual aversion disorder and vaginismus; male orgasmic disorder and dyspareunia
   (c) dyspareunia and hyperactive sexual desire disorder; hypoactive sexual desire disorder and sexual aversion disorder
   (d) female orgasmic disorder and vaginismus; erectile dysfunction and hyperactive sexual desire disorder

9. Larry is married, but he and his wife rarely have intercourse because the thought of any genital contact with his wife fills him with fear, anxiety, and disgust. Larry suffers from
   (a) hypoactive sexual desire disorder.
   (b) dyspareunia.
   (c) sexual aversion disorder.
   (d) male orgasmic disorder.

10. John is now serving a long jail sentence after his third conviction for engaging in sexual activities with prepubescent girls. John suffers from a paraphilia called
    (a) frotteurism.   (c) voyeurism.
    (b) pedophilia.   (d) fetishism.

11. Sharina is writing a term paper on human sexuality. Her library research is likely to indicate that the normal order of the four stages in the human sexual response cycle is
    (a) excitement, resolution, plateau, and orgasm.
    (b) excitement, orgasm, plateau, and resolution.
    (c) plateau, excitement, resolution, and orgasm.
    (d) excitement, plateau, orgasm, and resolution.

12. Elizabeth has had to seek treatment because of persistent itching due to pubic lice. Elizabeth has contracted
    (a) a parasitic STD.
    (b) AIDS (acquired immune deficiency syndrome).
    (c) a bacterial STD.
    (d) chlamydia.

13. Mary has a syndrome called congenital adrenal hyperplasia, and Marty was diagnosed with androgen insensitivity syndrome. According to In Focus (Beyond Male and Female), both Mary and Marty would be classified as
    (a) exhibitionists.
    (b) transgendered individuals.
    (c) pedophiles.
    (d) intersex individuals.

14. The Application suggests that couples who want to to break the vicious circle of flooding-stonewalling-flooding should
    (a) call a time-out whenever either one begins to feel overwhelmed or in danger of flooding.

(b) spend the time-out period thinking about ways to resolve the conflict, not about ways to mount a more effective counterattack.

(c) recognize that males need to try to stop avoiding conflict and females should try to raise issues in need of resolution in a calm manner and without personal attack.

(d) do all of these things.

15. According to research by David Buss (Culture and Human Behavior: Evolution and Mating Preferences)

(a) mutual attraction and love are the most important factors in selecting a mate in all cultures studied.

(b) men are more likely than women to value youth and physical attractiveness in a potential mate.

(c) women value financial security, access to material resources, and high status and education in a potential mate.

(d) all of these conditions are true.

Answers

Introduction: Gender and Sexuality

1. *Sex refers to* biologically determined physical characteristics, such as differences in genetic composition and reproductive anatomy and function. It also refers to the behavioral manifestation of the sexual urge. *Gender refers to* the cultural, social, and psychological meanings that are associated with masculinity or femininity.

2. *Gender roles consist of* the behaviors, attitudes, and personality traits that a given culture designates as either masculine or feminine. *Gender identity refers to* a person's psychological sense of being either male or female. *Sexual orientation refers to* whether a person's emotional and erotic attraction is directed toward members of the opposite sex, the same sex, or both sexes.

Gender Stereotypes and Gender Roles

1. *Gender-role stereotypes are* the beliefs and expectations that people hold about the typical characteristics, preferences, and behaviors of men and women.

2. *Important qualifications about gender differences are as follows:* First, gender differences are not gender deficiencies. Second, differences between men and women are average differences, not absolute differences (no single

finding applies to all men and women, there is a wide range of individual variation within each group, and there is a great deal of overlap between the two groups). Third, finding that a gender difference exists does not explain what caused the difference (differences are not necessarily natural, inevitable, or unchangeable).

3. *Research on gender differences has shown that* (a) Men are more assertive than women and women are more nurturant than men, but men and women are otherwise similar in their personality characteristics. (b) On average, women outscore men on tests of verbal fluency, spelling, reading comprehension, and basic writing skills; men outscore women on mental rotation tasks, but women are better at remembering the location of objects. The average scores of males and females on national tests of math ability are similar, but twice as many males as females score in the very highest range on math achievement tests. (c) Men and women are largely similar in their sexual attitudes and behaviors, except that men masturbate more often, are more accepting of casual sex than are women, and have more sexual partners.

Gender-Role Development: Blue Bears and Pink Bunnies

1. *Some gender differences that develop during childhood in our culture are as follows:* (a) Girls and boys are treated differently from birth (pink for girls and blue for boys.) (b) Toddler girls play more with soft toys and dolls and ask for adult help, whereas toddler boys play more with blocks and trucks or wagons, and play more actively than do girls. (c) Between the ages of 2 and 3, preschoolers start acquiring gender-role stereotypes for toys, clothes, household objects, games, and work; they also develop a strong preference for playing with members of their own sex, tendencies that continue throughout childhood. (d) Girls tend to be less rigid than boys in adhering to gender stereotypes.

2. *According to social learning theory,* gender roles are developed through the basic processes of learning, including reinforcement, punishment, and modeling.

3. *Gender schema theory contends that* children actively develop mental categories, or schemas, for masculinity and femininity, and these mental representations influence gender-role development.

Concept Check 1

1. sex
2. gender schema
3. gender role
4. female; male
5. will not; will
6. gender identity; sexual orientation
7. culturally determined display rules
8. social learning; modeling
9. transgender; transsexual

Matching Exercise 1

1. Sandra Bem
2. gender
3. sexual orientation
4. gender-role stereotypes
5. schemas
6. benevolent sexism
7. intersex

True/False Test 1

1. T	4. T	7. T
2. T	5. F	
3. F	6. T	

Human Sexuality

1. *The scientific study of sexuality is* multidimensional and involves biological, psychological, social, and cultural factors.

2. *The four stages of the human sexual response (and the characteristics of each) are* excitement (which can occur in response to sexual fantasies or other sexually arousing stimuli, physical contact with another person, or masturbation), plateau (physical arousal builds as pulse and breathing rates continue to increase), orgasm (blood pressure and heart rate reach their peak), and resolution (arousal slowly subsides and returns to normal; at this point, males experience a refractory period during which they are incapable of having another erection or orgasm).

3. *In nonhuman animals, sexual behavior is* biologically determined and triggered by hormonal changes in the female (during estrus, females are fertile and receptive to male sexual advances). *In higher animals, sexual behavior is* more strongly influenced by learning and environmental factors and is less limited to the goal of reproduction; in some species, sexual interactions serve important social functions.

Sexual Orientation

1. *Sexual orientation refers to* whether a person is sexually aroused by members of the same sex, the opposite sex, or both sexes; a heterosexual is sexually attracted to individuals of the other sex, a homosexual is attracted to individuals of the same sex, and a bisexual is attracted to individuals of both sexes.

2. *Sexual orientation is difficult to identify because* there is not always a perfect correspondence between a particular person's sexual identity, sexual desires, and sexual behaviors. In addition, determining accurate numbers depends on how researchers structure survey questions, how they define their criteria, where the survey is conducted, and how survey participants are selected.

3 *Factors associated with sexual orientation are as follows:* First, twin studies suggest that genetics may play a role in determining sexual orientation, but genetic predisposition alone is not a sufficient explanation. Second, genetic influences are complex and involve multiple genes (not a single "gay" gene). Beyond heredity, other biological influences, such as prenatal exposure to sex hormones or other aspects of the prenatal environment may play a role. Third, the more older biologically related brothers a man has the more likely he is to be homosexual. Research suggests that carrying successive male children might trigger an immune response in the mother, which, in turn, might influence brain development in the male fetus. Fourth, some small and inconclusive studies have found differences in brain function and structure among gay, lesbian, and heterosexual males and females, but it is not known if these differences are the cause or the effect of different patterns of sexual behavior. Fifth, homosexuality is not the result of disturbed or abnormal family relationships. Finally, research has shown that sexual orientation is determined before adolescence and long before the beginning of sexual activity.

Sexual Behavior

1. *The most general conclusions about sexuality in early and middle adulthood are (a)* Most adults are married or cohabiting with someone by the age of 30. *(b)* Young adults today tend to have

more sexual partners than previous generations, and they become sexually active at an earlier age but marry at a later average age. *(c)* Married and cohabiting people tend to have the most active sex lives, and married people are the most satisfied with their sex lives. *(d)* Vaginal intercourse is the most widely practiced sexual activity.

2. *Neuroscientists have shown that romantic love activates* brain areas (anterior cingulate cortex, caudate nucleus, putamen, and insula) that are involved in positive emotions, such as happiness, and that respond to euphoria-producing drugs, such as opiates and cocaine.

3. *In late adulthood, people experience* physical changes that affect the sexual response, but satisfying sexual relationships can continue throughout the lifespan.

Concept Check 2

1. refractory
2. decrease; stay the same
3. decrease
4. sexual orientation
5. likely
6. are not

Matching Exercise 2

1. William H. Masters and Virginia E. Johnson
2. plateau phase
3. heterosexual
4. refractory period
5. homosexual
6. excitement phase
7. gay
8. prospective study
9. sexual orientation

True/False Test 2

1. T	4. F	7. T
2. T	5. T	8. T
3. T	6. F	

Sexual Disorders and Problems

1. *The incidence of sexual dysfunction among women is* 43 percent, *and among men it is* 31 percent. *For women the most common sexual problems are* low sexual desire (hypoactive sexual desire disorder) and arousal problems, including the inability to achieve orgasm (female orgasmic disorder); *for men the most common sexual problems are* premature ejaculation and problems achieving and maintaining an erection (erectile dysfunction). *Overall, married and college educated men and women have* a much lower incidence of sexual problems than unmarried people or people with less education.

2. *A sexual dysfunction is* a consistent disturbance in sexual desire, arousal, or orgasm that causes psychological distress.

3. *The eight categories of sexual dysfunctions and their characteristics are (a)* hypoactive sexual desire disorder (characterized by little or no sexual desire); *(b)* sexual aversion disorder (characterized by active avoidance of genital sexual contact because of extreme anxiety, fear, or disgust); *(c)* dyspareunia (characterized by genital pain before, during, or after intercourse); *(d)* erectile dysfunction (characterized by a recurring inability to achieve or maintain an erect penis); *(e)* male orgasmic disorder (characterized by delayed orgasm during intercourse or the inability to achieve orgasm during intercourse); *(f)* premature ejaculation (characterized by orgasm occurring before it is desired, often immediately or shortly after sexual stimulation or penetration); *(g)* female orgasmic disorder (characterized by consistent delays in achieving orgasm or the inability to achieve orgasm); and *(h)* vaginismus (characterized by persistent, involuntary contractions or spasms of the vaginal muscles, which result in uncomfortable or painful intercourse).

4. *A paraphilia is* any of several forms of nontraditional sexual behavior in which a person's sexual gratification depends on an unusual sexual experience, object, or fantasy.

5. *The eight most common paraphilias and their characteristics are (a)* exhibitionism (sexual arousal achieved by exposing one's genitals to shocked strangers); *(b)* frotteurism (sexual arousal from touching or rubbing against a nonconsenting person, usually in a crowded public situation, such as a crowded bus or subway car); *(c)* fetishism (sexual arousal in response to inanimate objects, or body parts that are not typically associated with sexual arousal); *(d)* transvestic fetishism (in heterosexual males, sexual arousal from cross-dressing in women's clothes); *(e)* pedophilia (sexual fantasies, urges, or behavior involving sexual activity with a prepubescent child, generally age 13 or younger); *(f)* voyeurism (sexual arousal from observing an unsuspecting person who is disrobing, naked, or

engaged in sexual activity); *(g)* sexual sadism (sexual arousal achieved through intentionally inflicting psychological or physical suffering on another person); *(h)* sexual masochism (sexual arousal in response to actually being humiliated, beaten, bound, or otherwise made to suffer).

6. *Unlike a person with a sexual dysfunction, a person who has a paraphilia is* often not psychologically distressed by it. These individuals typically come to the attention of mental health professionals only when their behavior has created a conflict with their sexual partner, has been discovered by a family member or co-worker, or has resulted in arrest (some paraphilias, such as voyeurism and pedophilia, are illegal).

7. *Sexually transmitted diseases (STDs)* are any of several infectious diseases that are transmitted primarily through sexual intercourse or other intimate sexual contact. *They include* bacterial infections (gonorrhea, syphilis, and chlamydia), parasitic infections (pubic lice), and viral infections (genital herpes and AIDS).

8. *Genital herpes is a disease mostly caused by* a virus called genital herpes virus type 2 (HSV-2) and is one of the most common sexually transmitted diseases in the United States. It may also be caused by HSV-1.

9. *AIDS (acquired immune deficiency syndrome) is a disease caused by* the exchange of bodily fluids (semen, vaginal fluids, or blood) containing the human immunodeficiency virus (HIV), which selectively attacks CD4 positive helper T cells in the immune system, progressively weakening the body's ability to fight infections and diseases.

10. *In the United States, the three groups at greatest risk of becoming infected by HIV are* men who have sex with men, intravenous drug users, and heterosexuals who have sex with people who are already at high risk for HIV infection. *Most infections occur among* adolescents and young adults under the age of 30 (34%): *Blacks account for approximately* 45 percent *of new infections each year, whites for* 35 percent, *and Hispanics* 17 percent. *Worldwide more than* 33 million people *are currently living with HIV and AIDS, and* 25 million people *have died because of AIDS.*

Concept Check 3

1. hypoactive sexual desire
2. voyeurism

3. frotteurism
4. gonorrhea; chlamydia
5. dyspareunia
6. CD4 positive helper T cells; a combination of antiretroviral drugs

Graphic Organizer 1

1. exhibitionism
2. frotteurism
3. fetishism
4. transvestic fetishism
5. pedophilia
6. voyeurism
7. sexual sadism
8. sexual masochism

Graphic Organizer 2

1. SD	5. SD	9. P
2. P	6. P	10. SD
3. P	7. SD	
4. P	8. P	

Matching Exercise 3

1. fetishism
2. sexually transmitted diseases (STDs)
3. erectile dysfunction
4. female orgasmic disorder
5. transvestic fetishism
6. vaginismus
7. paraphilia
8. (HIV) human immunodeficiency virus
9. sexual dysfunction
10. male orgasmic disorder
11. premature ejaculation
12. AIDS (acquired immune deficiency syndrome)
13. pubic lice
14. CD4 positive helper T cells

True/False Test 3

1. F	5. T	9. T	13. T
2. T	6. F	10. F	
3. F	7. T	11. T	
4. T	8. F	12. T	

Something to Think About

1. Resolving conflicts is a key ingredient in successful intimate relationships. Men and women differ significantly in the way they communicate, especially when they are trying to deal with emotional issues and interpersonal conflicts; these fundamental differences can sabotage conflict resolution. There is hope, however. John Gottman's research provides evidence of a number of constructive ways for overcoming these communication differences.

   First, conflict can play a key role in a healthy, happy relationship; a couple's relationship will grow if the couple successfully reconciles the inevitable differences that occur. Men and women react differently to conflict, particularly if it involves strong emotions. Typically, men have learned to suppress and contain their emotions, whereas women tend to be more comfortable with emotional expression. During emotional conflicts, people may experience flooding (the feeling of being overwhelmed emotionally); in reaction to this intense physiological arousal, they may engage in stonewalling (withdrawing to contain their uncomfortable emotions). Men tend to get more physiologically aroused during relationship conflicts than do women and are therefore more likely to engage in stonewalling. Women tend to experience stonewalling as disapproval and rejection and typically react by flooding. And that's how the vicious circle of flooding-stonewalling-flooding begins.

   A number of things can be done to break this vicious circle. First, both parties need to become aware of the gender differences in handling emotion. Men need to remember that women experience stonewalling as rejection, disapproval, and abandonment, and women need to accept men's need to temporarily withdraw from the situation. Second, calling for a 20- to 30-minute time-out period during a conflict is a good idea so long as both parties use the time to think about ways to resolve the conflict, rather than rehearsing or preparing vengeful comments and counterattack strategies. Third, men need to make a conscious effort to embrace, rather than avoid, the problem; sidestepping the issue won't make it go away. If the woman didn't care about the relationship, she wouldn't keep confronting her partner; generally, she wants both people to resolve the issue together. Fourth, women should try raising the issue in a more calm and less emotionally confrontational manner. Frame the problem in the context of maintaining a loving relationship and avoid personal attacks. Finally, tell the couple to buy, read, and discuss John Gottman's book—together!

2. The first point to make in any discussion of differences between men and women is that the sexes are much more alike than they are different. The similarities extend across many different and important aspects of behavior and ability, including brain structure. We tend to overlook these similarities when we focus on the differences that have been found between men and women. In addition, if we examine the data on sex differences, we are very likely to find a great deal of overlap between men and women.

   Second, any sex differences in behavior and cognitive functioning are not necessarily because male and female brains are structurally different. There is considerable *individual* variation in brain structure and function; thus, the average range of differences *within* each sex is larger than the average differences between the sexes. Indeed, some individual females are found to be more similar to the average male pattern than average female pattern, and vice versa. There are more similarities than differences between male and female brains.

   Third, even if we assume, for the sake of argument, that there are reliable sex differences in brain structure, no one knows the functional significance of those differences. The human brain is incredibly complex, and researchers have not yet managed to unravel all the interrelated organizational and functional aspects of this complicated organ. Clearly, we know a lot more than we used to, but we are still a long way from being able to specify the precise significance of any subtle sex difference that has been found or may be found in the future. It certainly can't be concluded that males and females "think differently" because of structural differences in their brains, as some headlines have claimed.

   If we accept that there may be some small and inconsistent differences in the structure of male and female brains, it does not necessarily follow that we are born with these differences. The brain's structure changes in response to experience, so it is entirely possible that any sex differences in the brain could be due to men's and women's different environmental and learning experiences.

Finally—and this is worth repeating—male and female brains are much more alike than they are dissimilar.

Progress Test 1

1. d	6. a	11. b
2. c	7. d	12. b
3. b	8. a	13. d
4. c	9. c	14. b
5. d	10. d	15. a

Progress Test 2

1. d	6. c	11. a
2. c	7. b	12. d
3. a	8. d	13. a
4. b	9. b	14. d
5. d	10. a	15. a

Progress Test 3

1. c	6. b	11. d
2. b	7. d	12. a
3. a	8. a	13. d
4. d	9. c	14. d
5. a	10. b	15. d

CHAPTER 11

Personality

PREVIEW

Reading the section below first will give you a general sense of the chapter's contents and an initial introduction to some of the major concepts and terms. This will prime you for what you are about to read and help you to develop a "cognitive map" that will guide your study of the material in this chapter. Likewise, reading the **preview questions** at the beginning of each major section will improve your ability to understand, learn, and retain the information.

CHAPTER 11 . . . AT A GLANCE

Chapter 11 focuses on the four major perspectives on personality. Freud's psychoanalysis stresses the unconscious, the importance of sex and aggression, and the influences of early childhood experiences. The major defense mechanisms, as well as the psychosexual stages of development and the various conflicts associated with each, are examined. The contributions of Freud's early followers, the neo-Freudians, are explored, and criticisms of Freud's theory are discussed.

Humanistic theory and its optimistic view of human nature are examined, including Carl Rogers's ideas about the self-concept, unconditional positive regard, the actualizing tendency, and the fully functioning person.

The social cognitive perspective stresses the role of conscious thought processes, goals, self-regulation, and reciprocal determinism. The influence of self-efficacy on behavior, performance, motivation, and persistence is explored. The notion that the interaction of multiple factors determines personality and behavior is examined.

The trait perspective focuses on measuring and describing individual differences. Cattell initially suggested 16 basic personality factors, then Eysenck proposed three dimensions. The five-factor model is the current view of the number of source traits. The text concludes that traits are generally stable over time and across situations. Behavioral genetics research uses twin and adoption studies to measure the relative influences of genetics and environment. Personality factors that appear to have a genetic basis are identified.

The final section examines projective tests and self-report inventories, noting their strengths and weaknesses. The Application discusses the concept of "possible selves" and explains how we can apply research findings regarding this concept to our own lives.

Introduction: What Is Personality?

Preview Questions

Consider the following questions as you study this section of the chapter.

- How is personality defined, and what is a personality theory?
- What are the four major theoretical perspectives on personality?

*Read the section "Introduction: What Is Personality?" and **write** your answers to the following:*

1. Personality is defined as _____ _____

2. A personality theory is _____ _____ _____

3. The four basic perspectives on personality (and the main emphasis of each) are _____ _____ _____ _____ _____ _____ _____

The Psychoanalytic Perspective on Personality

Preview Questions

Consider the following questions as you study this section of the chapter.

- Who was the founder of psychoanalysis, and what did he consider to be the main factors that influenced personality development?
- What were some of the key influences on Freud's thinking?

*Read the section "The Psychoanalytic Perspective on Personality" and **write** your answers to the following:*

1. Psychoanalysis—Freud's theory of personality— stresses _____ _____ _____

2. Some of the key factors in the development of Freud's ideas were _____ _____ _____ _____ _____

The Psychoanalytic Perspective on Personality: Freud's Dynamic Theory of Personality

Preview Questions

Consider the following questions as you study this section of the chapter.

- How do we access unconscious mental processes?
- What are the three basic structures of personality, and what are their functions?
- What are the main defense mechanisms, and what role do they play?

*Read the section "The Psychoanalytic Perspective: Freud's Dynamic Theory of Personality" and **write** your answers to the following:*

1. The content of the unconscious can surface in disguised form in _____ _____

2. The three basic structures of personality (and their functions) are _____ _____ _____ _____ _____ _____ _____

3. The three main ego defense mechanisms (and the roles they play) are _____ _____ _____ _____

Other ego defense mechanisms include _____ _____ _____

The Psychoanalytic Perspective: Personality Development

Preview Questions

Consider the following questions as you study this section of the chapter.

- What are the five psychosexual stages of personality development, and what is the focus of each?
- What are the consequences of fixation?
- What role does the Oedipus complex play in personality development?

Read the section "The Psychoanalytic Perspective: Personality Development" and **write** *your answers to the following:*

1. The psychosexual stages are age-related developmental periods in which _____
   _____
   _____

2. The five psychosexual stages (and the focus of each) are _____
   _____
   _____
   _____
   _____

3. If the developmental conflict of a particular stage is not resolved _____
   _____
   _____

4. The Oedipus complex refers to _____
   _____
   _____

5. Identification (which is one way of resolving the Oedipus complex) is an ego defense mechanism that _____
   _____

After you have carefully studied the preceding sections, complete the following exercises.

Concept Check 1

Read the following and write the correct term in the space provided.

1. Birkley was feeling irritable and bad-tempered all day. When she arrived home from work, she accused her husband of being moody and grumpy. According to Freud, Birkley may be using an ego defense mechanism called

   _____ .

2. Colleen, who is suffering from some puzzling physical and psychological symptoms that don't appear to have any physiological cause, has decided to seek help from a Freudian psychoanalyst. The therapist is most likely to use

   _____ in an attempt to explore Colleen's unconscious.

3. During a heated argument, David inadvertently called his wife Joanne by his mother's name. From the psychoanalytic perspective, this "Freudian slip" reveals something about David's

   _____ (conscious/preconscious/unconscious) motivation.

4. Amelia had a very strange dream in which she was with a very handsome man on a train traveling through the Swiss Alps. The train kept going in and out of tunnels and going faster and faster as it made its way through the mountains. According to Freudian theory, the

   _____ (manifest/latent) content of the dream should give some clue to Amelia's unconscious conflicts.

5. When 2-year-old Tyler was told that he would get no dessert unless he finished eating all his vegetables, he turned the plate upside down and said he hated his Mom and Dad. Freud would have said that Tyler was responding to the demands of the _____ .

6. Kato found a wallet containing $200 in cash. For just a moment he was tempted to keep the money, but the thought of doing so made him feel guilty and anxious, and he immediately took the wallet to the lost-and-found office. According to Freud, Kato's good deed was motivated by his _____ .

7. Leslie sometimes thinks that the real reason her husband became a psychotherapist was to provide himself with a socially acceptable way to indulge his excessive curiosity about other people's private lives. Leslie is suggesting that her husband's unconscious sexual urges are being rechanneled into productive work, a special form of displacement called _____ .

8. Nine-year-old Danny looks up to his father and wants to be an engineer just like him. Freud would suggest that Danny is exhibiting signs of the process of _____ .

9. When Gregory did not get the promotion he applied for, he told his family and colleagues that, in retrospect, he was much happier staying in his present position and glad he didn't have to deal with all the hassles associated with the higher-paying position. It appears that Gregory is using an ego defense mechanism called _____ .

Graphic Organizer 1

Read the following and match each one with the appropriate stage of psychosexual development:

Description	Stage
1. Sixteen-year-old Graham has started going steady with Julie and is experiencing all the sensations of being in love.	
2. Five-year-old Annette has become very competitive with her mother for her father's affections and quite defiantly states that she is "Going to marry Daddy when I grow up!"	
3. Vivian is 8 years old and does not like boys very much. In fact, she plays with her girlfriends almost exclusively.	
4. No matter what Marie gives her baby to play with, the baby immediately puts it in her mouth.	
5. Darcy is not quite 2 but seems to take great pleasure in refusing to obey his parents and asserting his control and independence. His favorite word is "No!"	

Review of Terms, Concepts, and Names 1

Use the terms in this list to complete the Matching Test, then to help you answer the True / False items correctly.

personality
personality theory
Sigmund Freud
psychoanalysis
catharsis
free association
conscious
preconscious
unconscious
manifest content
latent content
id
Eros (life instinct)
libido
Thanatos (death instinct)
pleasure principle
ego
reality principle
superego
ego defense mechanisms
repression
displacement
sublimation
psychosexual stages
oral stage
anal stage
phallic stage
fixation
Oedipus complex
castration anxiety
identification
penis envy
latency stage
genital stage

Matching Exercise

Match the appropriate term / name with its definition or description.

1. _____ In Freud's theory, the psychological and emotional energy associated with expressions of sexuality; the sex drive.

2. _____ An individual's unique and relatively consistent patterns of thinking, feeling, and behaving.

3. _____ In Freud's theory, the partly conscious, self-evaluative, moralistic component of personality that is formed through the internalization of parental and societal rules.

4. _____ In Freud's theory, a child's unconscious sexual desire for the opposite-sex parent, usually accompanied by hostile feelings toward the same-sex parent.

5. _____ Latin for "I"; in Freud's theory, the partly conscious, rational component of personality that regulates thoughts and behavior and is most in touch with the demands of the external world.

6. _____ Level of awareness that contains information not currently in conscious awareness but easily accessible.

7. _____ Psychosexual stage of development during which the child derives pleasurable and gratifying sensations through feeding and exploring objects with his or her mouth.

8. _____ In psychoanalytic theory, the ego defense mechanism that involves unconsciously shifting the target of an emotional urge to a substitute target that is less threatening or dangerous.

9. _____ Austrian neurologist who founded psychoanalysis and emphasized the role of unconscious determinants of behavior and early childhood experiences in the development of personality and psychological problems.

10. _____ Psychosexual stage of development during which the infant derives pleasurable sensations through acquiring control over elimination via toilet training.

11. _____ Theory that attempts to describe and explain similarities and differences in people's patterns of thinking, feeling, and behaving.

12. _____ Latin for "the it"; in Freud's theory, the completely unconscious, irrational component of personality that seeks immediate satisfaction of instinctual urges and drives; ruled by the pleasure principle.

13. _____ Psychosexual stage of development during which sexual urges become repressed and dormant as the child develops same-sex friendships with peers and focuses on school, sports, and other activities.

14. _____ Sigmund Freud's theory of personality, which emphasizes unconscious determinants of behavior, sexual and aggressive instinctual drives, and the enduring effects of early childhood experiences on later personality development.

15. _____ In psychoanalytic theory, largely unconscious distortions of thought or perception that act to reduce anxiety.

16. _____ In Freud's theory, age-related developmental periods in which the child's sexual urges are focused on different areas of the body and are expressed through the activities associated with those areas.

17. _____ In Freud's psychoanalytic theory, the elements of a dream that are consciously experienced and remembered by the dreamer.

True/False Test

Indicate whether each statement is true or false by placing T or F in the blank space next to each item.

1. ____ During the phallic psychosexual stage of development, the adolescent reaches physical sexual maturity and the genitals become the primary focus of pleasurable sensations, which the person seeks to satisfy in heterosexual relationships.

2. ____ As the Oedipus complex unfolds, the little boy feels affection for his mother and hostility and jealousy toward his father but realizes that his father is more physically powerful than he is; the boy experiences *castration anxiety,* or the fear that his father will punish him by castrating him.

3. ____ Fixation occurs if the child is frustrated or overindulged in his or her attempts to resolve the conflict associated with a psychosexual stage; the individual will continue to seek pleasure through behaviors that are similar to those associated with that stage.

4. ____ In Freud's theory, the death instinct, reflected in aggressive, destructive, and self-destructive actions, is called Eros.

5. ____ In psychoanalytic theory, repression refers to the unconscious exclusion of anxiety-provoking thoughts, feelings, and memories from conscious awareness; the most fundamental ego defense mechanism.

6. ____ The term *unconscious* is used in Freud's theory to describe thoughts, feelings, wishes, and drives that are operating below the level of conscious awareness.

7. ____ Catharsis is a phenomenon that occurs when puzzling physical and psychological problems disappear after a person expresses pent-up emotions associated with traumatic events that may have been related to his or her problems.

8. ____ As part of the resolution of her Oedipus complex, the little girl discovers that little boys have a penis and that she does not; she experiences a sense of loss, or deprivation, that Freud referred to as *penis envy.*

9. ____ During the genital stage of psychosexual development, the genitals are the primary focus and the child derives pleasurable sensations through sexual curiosity, masturbation, and sexual attraction toward the opposite-sex parent.

10. ____ In psychoanalytic theory, sublimation is an ego defense mechanism that involves reducing anxiety by imitating the behavior and characteristics of another person.

11. ____ The reality principle refers to the awareness of environmental demands and the capacity to accommodate them by postponing gratification until the appropriate time or circumstances exist.

12. ____ In Freud's theory, Thanatos refers to the self-preservation, or life, instinct, reflected in the expression of basic psychological urges that perpetuate the existence of the individual as well as the species.

13. ____ Free association is a psychoanalytic technique in which the patient spontaneously reports all thoughts, feelings, and mental images as they come to mind.

14. ____ All thoughts, feelings, and sensations that a person is aware of at any given moment represent the conscious level of awareness.

15. ____ The pleasure principle refers to the motive to obtain pleasure and avoid tension or discomfort; the most fundamental human motive and the guiding principle of the id.

16. ____ In psychoanalytic theory, identification is the ego defense mechanism that involves redirecting sexual urges toward productive, socially acceptable, nonsexual activities.

17. ____ In Freud's psychoanalytic theory, the latent content of a dream refers to the unconscious wishes, thoughts, and urges that are concealed as symbols in a dream.

Check your answers and review any areas of weakness before going on to the next section.

The Psychoanalytic Perspective: The Neo-Freudians

Preview Questions

Consider the following questions as you study this section of the chapter.

- What are the similarities and differences in the approaches taken by Freud and the neo-Freudians?

- What are the key ideas of Jung, Horney, and Adler?

Read the section "The Psychoanalytic Perspective: The Neo-Freudians" and **write** *your answers to the following:*

1. The neo-Freudians followed Freud in stressing

   _____

   _____

   However, they developed independent personality theories, because they disagreed with Freud on three key points:

   (a) _____

   _____

   (b) _____

   _____

   (c) _____

   _____

2. Carl Jung emphasized _____

   _____

   _____

3. Karen Horney stressed _____

   _____

   _____

4. Alfred Adler believed _____

   _____

   _____

The Psychoanalytic Perspective: Evaluating Freud and the Psychoanalytic Perspective on Personality

Preview Questions

Consider the following questions as you study this section of the chapter.

- What are three criticisms of Freud's theory and, more generally, the psychoanalytic perspective?
- Which Freudian ideas have been substantiated by empirical research?

Read the section "Evaluating Freud and the Psychoanalytic Perspective on Personality" and **write** *your answers to the following:*

1. Although Sigmund Freud's ideas have had a profound and lasting effect on psychology and

on society, the main criticisms of Freud's theory and psychoanalysis are

   (a) _____

   _____

   (b) _____

   _____

   _____

   _____

   (c) _____

   _____

   _____

2. Several of Freud's ideas have been substantiated by empirical evidence, including

   _____

   _____

   _____

   _____

After you have carefully studied the preceding sections, complete the following exercises.

Concept Check 2

Read the following and write the correct term in the space provided.

1. Wilfred suffered physical hardship and abuse as a child; as an adult, he lacks confidence, can't hold a job for long, and feels that nothing is really worth striving for. Adler would have said that Wilfred suffers from feelings of

   _____ .

2. In a class discussion, Louanne disputed Freud's assumption that women are inferior to men and that they suffer from penis envy; instead, she suggested that men suffer from womb envy and feel inadequate because they are incapable of bearing children. Louanne's views are most consistent with those of personality theorist

   _____ .

3. During a lecture on personality, Dr. Shornagel suggested that the deepest aspect of the individual psyche is a part inherited from previous generations, which contains universally shared experiences and ideas called archetypes. Dr. Shornagel is describing the

   _____ , which is

   central to _____ theory of personality.

4. Terry has an excessive need to exert power over people; his competitiveness and need to feel superior to others stem from his childhood feelings of being isolated and helpless in a potentially hostile world. Horney would have suggested that Terry is attempting to deal with

   _____ by moving

   _____ (toward/against/away from) others.

5. Frank is very sociable and outgoing and has a keen interest in sports and outdoor activities. Jung would probably describe Frank as an

   _____ personality type.

6. When Merrilee recently watched the video *Star Wars,* she became aware of some of the universal themes and preoccupations depicted in the movie. In particular, she noted the hero's quest for psychological growth, self-knowledge, selfhood, and wisdom. According to Jung, these inherited images of human instincts, themes, and preoccupations are called

   _____ and are the main components of the _____.

7. According to his psychotherapist, Adrian can achieve psychological harmony only if he recognizes and accepts the feminine aspect of his personality. The therapist is referring to the

   _____ , an important archetype in

   _____ theory of personality.

8. Shelby is always trying to improve himself, to master challenges, to grow and develop intellectually and psychologically, and to move forward toward self-realization. Adler would say that

Shelby is exhibiting the most fundamental human motive of _____ .

Review of Terms, Concepts, and Names 2

Use the terms in this list to complete the Matching Test, then to help you answer the True/False items correctly.

neo-Freudians	Karen Horney
Carl Jung	basic anxiety
collective unconscious	womb envy
archetypes	Alfred Adler
anima	striving for superiority
animus	feelings of inferiority
introvert	inferiority complex
extravert	superiority complex

Matching Exercise

Match the appropriate term/name with its definition or description.

1. _____ German-born American psychoanalyst who emphasized the role of social relationships and culture in personality; sharply disagreed with Freud's characterization of female psychological development, especially his notion that women suffer from penis envy.

2. _____ In Jung's theory, the inherited mental images of universal human instincts, themes, and preoccupations that are the main components of the collective unconscious.

3. _____ In Adler's theory, the desire to improve oneself, master challenges, and move toward self-perfection and self-realization, considered to be the most fundamental human motive.

4. _____ Fundamental emotion that Horney described as a child's feeling of being isolated and helpless in a potentially hostile world.

5. _____ Adler's term for the personality characteristic developed by people who are unable to compensate for specific weaknesses; it includes a general sense of inadequacy, weakness, and helplessness.

6. _____ In Jung's theory, the basic personality type that focuses attention and energy toward the outside world.

7. _____ In Jung's theory, the hypothesized part of the unconscious mind that is inherited from previous generations and that

contains universally shared ancestral experiences and ideas.

8. _____ According to Jung, an important archetype that represents the feminine side of every person.

True/False Test

Indicate whether each statement is true or false by placing T or F in the blank space next to each item.

1. ___ The term *neo-Freudians* was given to the early followers of Freud who developed their own theories yet still recognized the importance of many of Freud's basic notions, such as the influence of unconscious processes and early childhood experiences.

2. ___ Alfred Adler was an Austrian physician who broke with Freud and developed his own psychoanalytic theory of personality, which emphasized social factors and motivation toward self-improvement and self-realization, and overcoming feelings of inferiority.

3. ___ According to Adler's theory, people can overcompensate for their feelings of inferiority and develop a *superiority complex,* which is characterized by exaggeration of one's accomplishments and importance in an effort to cover up weaknesses and limitations.

4. ___ Horney used the term *womb envy* to describe the envy that men feel about women's capacity to bear children.

5. ___ In Jung's theory, the introvert is a basic personality type that focuses attention inward.

6. ___ Carl Jung was the Swiss psychiatrist who broke with Freud to develop his own psychoanalytic theory of personality, which stressed striving toward psychological harmony and included the key ideas of the collective unconscious and archetypes.

7. ___ According to Adler's theory, striving for superiority arises from universal *feelings of inferiority* that are experienced during infancy and childhood, when the child is helpless and dependent on others.

8. ___ In Jung's theory of personality, the animus is the archetype that represents the masculine side of every person.

Check your answers and review any areas of weakness before going on to the next section.

The Humanistic Perspective on Personality

Preview Questions

Consider the following questions as you study this section of the chapter.

- Who were the major contributors to humanistic psychology?
- What is the focus of the humanistic perspective?
- What role do the self-concept, the actualizing tendency, and unconditional positive regard play in Rogers's personality theory?
- What are the key strengths and weaknesses of the humanistic perspective?

*Read the section "The Humanistic Perspective on Personality" and **write** your answers to the following:*

1. The major contributors to humanistic psychology were _____ and _____ .

2. The humanistic perspective emphasizes _____ _____

3. The actualizing tendency is _____ _____

4. The self-concept is _____ _____ _____

5. Conditional positive regard is _____ _____ _____

   Unconditional positive regard is _____ _____ _____

6. The fully functioning person experiences _____ _____

7. The humanistic perspective has been criticized on two particular points: _____ _____ _____ _____

The Social Cognitive Perspective on Personality

Preview Questions

Consider the following questions as you study this section of the chapter.

- What is the focus of the social cognitive perspective?
- What is the principle of reciprocal determinism, and what is the role of self-efficacy beliefs in personality, according to this perspective?
- What are the key strengths and weaknesses of the social cognitive perspective?

*Read the section "The Social Cognitive Perspective on Personality" and **write** your answers to the following:*

1. The social cognitive perspective stresses _____
   _____
   _____

2. Bandura's social cognitive theory emphasizes
   _____
   _____
   _____
   _____

3. Reciprocal determinism suggests that human
   functioning and personality _____
   _____
   _____

4. Self-efficacy is _____
   _____

5. Key strengths of the social cognitive perspective
   are _____
   _____
   _____
   _____
   _____

6. Some weaknesses of the social cognitive perspective are that _____
   _____
   _____
   _____

The Trait Perspective on Personality

Preview Questions

Consider the following questions as you study this section of the chapter.

- What is the focus of trait theories?
- How are traits defined, and what is the difference between surface traits and source traits?
- What models of personality did Cattell and Eysenck propose, and what is the five-factor model of personality?
- What is the focus of behavioral genetics?
- To what degree are personality traits inherited?
- What are the key strengths and weaknesses of the trait perspective?

*Read the section "The Trait Perspective on Personality" and **write** your answers to the following:*

1. Trait theories focus on _____
   _____

2. Traits are _____
   _____

   Surface traits are _____
   _____

   Source traits are _____
   _____

3. Cattell believed that _____
   _____

4. Hans Eysenck proposed that _____
   _____
   _____

5. According to the five-factor model _____
   _____
   _____

6. The field of behavioral genetics studies _____
   _____

7. Factors that seem to have a significant genetic
   component are _____
   _____
   _____
   _____

8. The trait perspective is useful in _____
   _____

9. Some criticisms of the trait theories are _____
   _____
   _____
   _____
   _____
   _____

_____

After you have carefully studied the preceding sections, complete the following exercises.

_____

Concept Check 3

Read the following and write the correct term in the space provided.

1. Dunja is confident in her ability to service her own car but is less sure of her ability to bake cakes and cookies. According to Bandura, Dunja's different beliefs about her own abilities are her _____ beliefs.

2. Eileen is consistently cheerful, optimistic, talkative, and impulsive. These traits, which are inferred from her observable behavior, are referred to as _____ traits.

3. Navi is viewed by her family and friends as a flexible, creative, spontaneous, open, caring person who likes and is liked by most people. Carl Rogers would probably describe her as a(n) _____ person.

4. Alfred believes that from an early age we develop a set of perceptions and beliefs about ourselves, our nature, and our personal qualities and are motivated to act in accordance with these perceptions. Alfred's belief about personality development is most consistent with _____ theory.

5. Dr. Bhatt is concerned with describing, classifying, and measuring the many ways in which individuals may differ from one another. Her approach is most characteristic of the _____ perspective on personality.

6. Whenever her son misbehaves, Rochelle makes sure he clearly understands that his behavior is not acceptable while taking care to reassure him that he is loved and valued. Rochelle is using Rogers's concept of

   _____ .

7. Dr. Lavalle studies the effects of heredity on behavior. In his research, he studies identical and fraternal twins who were separated at birth, identical and fraternal twins raised together, and the similarities and differences between adopted children and their adoptive and biological parents. Dr. Lavalle works in the field of _____ .

8. While Madeline and Charlene watched positive and negative images, fMRI scans of Madeline's brain showed greater reactivity to positive images, especially in areas that control emotion, whereas Charlene's fMRI scans showed more brain activation in response to negative images, but in fewer areas that control emotions. According to Focus on Neuroscience, on a personality test to determine their level of extraversion or neuroticism, Madeline is likely to score high on _____ ,
   while Charlene is likely to score high on

   _____ .

9. Dr. Porter collected data on a large sample of people who were rated on each of 150 personality characteristics. He then used a statistical technique called factor analysis to identify the traits that were most closely related to one another and eventually reduced his list to 12 key personality factors. Dr. Porter's approach is most similar to that of trait theorist

   _____ , who developed one of the most widely used personality tests called the _____ .

Graphic Organizer 2

Read the following statements and match the personality theorist and theory/perspective associated with each. This chart covers the entire chapter.

Statement	Theorist	Theory/ Perspective
1. I believe that people can be classified into four basic types: introverted–neurotic, introverted–stable, extraverted–neurotic, and extraverted–stable.		
2. It is my belief that people have an innate drive to maintain and enhance themselves. This actualizing tendency is the most basic human motive, and all other motives, whether biological or social, are secondary.		
3. I reduced Allport's 4,000 terms to 171, and then, by using factor analysis, I eventually came up with 16 personality factors that represent the essential source of human personality.		
4. My theory of personality stresses the influence of unconscious mental processes, the importance of sexual and aggressive instincts, and the enduring effects of early childhood experiences on personality.		
5. For me the most fundamental human motive is striving for superiority, which arises from universal feelings of inferiority. Depending on how people deal with these feelings, they may develop either an inferiority complex or a superiority complex.		
6. My research suggests that human functioning is caused by the interaction of behavioral, cognitive, and environmental factors, a process I call reciprocal determinism.		
7. For me the impact of social relationships and the nature of the parent–child interaction are the main determinants of personality. Different patterns of behavior develop as people try to deal with their basic anxiety. Males have an additional problem to deal with, womb envy.		
8. I am most well known for my theory of motivation and the notion of a hierarchy of needs. I also identified the qualities most associated with self-actualized people.		
9. It is apparent to me, from my observations of different cultures and my own patients, that the deepest part of the individual psyche is the collective unconscious, which contains universal archetypes. Personality can be described on two basic dimensions, introversion and extraversion.		

Review of Terms, Concepts, and Names 3

Use the terms in this list to complete the Matching Test, then to help you answer the True/False items correctly.

humanistic psychology	self-system
Abraham Maslow	self-efficacy
Carl Rogers	mastery experience
actualizing tendency	trait
self-concept	trait theory
positive regard	surface trait
conditional positive	source traits
regard	Raymond Cattell
incongruence	Hans Eysenck
unconditional positive	introversion
regard	extraversion
fully functioning person	neuroticism
congruence	stability
Albert Bandura	psychoticism
observational learning	five-factor model of
social cognitive theory	personality
reciprocal determinism	behavioral genetics

Matching Exercise

Match the appropriate term/name with its definition or description.

1. _____ A relatively stable, enduring predisposition to consistently behave in a certain way.

2. _____ People's beliefs about their ability to meet the demands of a specific situation; feelings of self-confidence or self-doubt.

3. _____ Contemporary American psychologist who is best known for his research on observational learning and his social cognitive theory of personality.

4. _____ In Rogers's theory, the innate drive to maintain and enhance the human organism.

5. _____ Trait theory of personality that identifies five basic source traits (extraversion, neuroticism, agreeableness, conscientiousness, and openness to experience) as the fundamental building blocks of personality.

6. _____ American psychologist who was one of the founders of humanistic psychology and emphasized the study of healthy personality development; developed a hierarchical theory of motivation based on the idea that people will strive for self-actualization, the highest motive, only after more basic needs have been met.

7. _____ In Eysenck's theory, a third dimension of personality; a person high on this trait is antisocial, cold, hostile, and unconcerned about others, whereas a person low on this trait is warm and caring toward others.

8. _____ In Rogers's theory, the term for the sense of being loved and valued by other people, especially one's parents.

9. _____ Bandura's theory of personality, which emphasizes the importance of observational learning, conscious cognitive processes, social experiences, self-efficacy beliefs, and reciprocal determinism.

10. _____ Theory of personality that focuses on identifying, describing, and measuring individual differences in behavioral predispositions.

11. _____ In Eysenck's theory, the dimension of personality that describes people who direct their energies outward toward the environment and other people; a person high on this dimension would be outgoing and sociable, enjoying new experiences and stimulating environments.

12. _____ American psychologist who was one of the founders of humanistic psychology; developed a theory of personality and form of psychotherapy that emphasized the inherent worth of people, the innate tendency to strive toward one's potential, and the importance of the self-concept in personality development.

13. _____ Theoretical viewpoint on personality that generally emphasizes the inherent goodness of people, human potential, self-actualization, the self-concept, and healthy personality development.

14. _____ Albert Bandura's model that explains human functioning and personality as caused by the interaction of behavioral, cognitive, and environmental factors.

15. _____ In Eysenck's theory, a personality dimension in which the person directs his or her energies inward, toward inner, self-focused experiences; a person high on this dimension might be quiet, solitary, and reserved, avoiding new experiences.

16. _____ In Bandura's theory, the term for the successful performance of a task that results in enhanced self-efficacy.

True/False Test

Indicate whether each statement is true or false by placing T or F in the blank space next to each item.

1. ___ Behavioral genetics is an interdisciplinary field that studies the effects of genes and heredity on behavior.

2. ___ In Rogers's theory, people are in a state of congruence when their feelings and experiences are denied and distorted because they contradict or conflict with their self-concept.

3. ___ Raymond Cattell was a British-born American psychologist who developed a trait theory that identifies 16 essential source traits or personality factors; also developed the widely used self-report personality test, the Sixteen Personality Factor Questionnaire (16PF).

4. ___ Personality characteristics or attributes that can easily be inferred from observable behavior are called source traits.

5. ___ In Rogers's theory, the sense that you will be valued and loved only if you behave in a way that is acceptable to others is called conditional positive regard.

6. ___ Self-concept is the set of perceptions and beliefs that you hold about yourself.

7. ___ In Eysenck's theory, neuroticism refers to a person's predisposition to become emotionally upset.

8. ___ In Rogers's theory, the fully functioning person has a flexible, constantly evolving self-concept and is realistic, open to new experiences, and capable of changing in response to new experiences.

9. ___ Unconditional positive regard, in Rogers's theory, is the sense that you will be valued and loved even if you don't conform to the standards and expectations of others.

10. ___ A surface trait is the most fundamental dimension of personality; these broad basic traits are hypothesized to be universal and relatively few in number.

11. ___ In Rogers's theory, people are in a state of incongruence when their sense of self (their self-concept) is consistent with their emotions and experiences.

12. ___ Hans Eysenck was a German-born British psychologist who developed a trait theory of personality that identifies the three basic dimensions of personality as neuroticism–emotional stability, introversion–extraversion, and psychoticism.

13. ___ In Eysenck's theory, stability reflects a person's predisposition to be emotionally even.

14. ___ Cognitive skills, abilities, and attitudes that emerge through developmental experiences involving the interaction of behavioral, cognitive, and environmental factors represent the person's self-system.

15. ___ In Bandura's theory, observational learning refers to learning that occurs through watching and then imitating the behavior of other people.

Check your answers and review any areas of weakness before going on to the next section.

Assessing Personality: Psychological Tests

Preview Questions

Consider the following questions as you study this section of the chapter.

- What are projective tests and self-report inventories, and how are they used to measure personality?

- What are the key strengths and limitations of projective tests and self-report inventories?

*Read the section "Assessing Personality: Psychological Tests" and **write** your answers to the following:*

1. A psychological test is _____

   _____

   _____

2. A projective test is _____

   _____

   _____

3. A self-report inventory is _____

   _____

   _____

4. Projective tests provide qualitative data but their limitations are that _____

   _____

   _____

5. The strengths of self-report inventories are that

   _____

   _____

   _____

6. Problems with self-report inventories are that

_____

_____

_____

After you have carefully studied the preceding section, complete the following exercises.

Concept Check 4

Read the following and write the correct term in the space provided.

1. Michelle was given a psychological test in which she was asked to look at a series of cards with ambiguous scenes and make up stories for each one. She was told to give as much detail as possible about what the characters are feeling and how the story ends. Michelle was given a(n) _____ test called the

_____ .

2. When Roger was assessed for his suitability to be a police officer, he was given a 500-item test that was used to evaluate his mental health. The test he was given was most likely the

_____ .

3. Mr. and Mrs. Sheldrake want to get some idea of how their son is going to do in high school. The test that is best at predicting their son's high school grades is the _____ .

4. In his psychoanalytic practice, Dr. Coles tries to understand his client's unconscious conflicts, motives, psychological defenses, and personality traits. It is very probable that Dr. Coles uses either the _____ or the

_____ , which are both

_____ tests.

5. Dr. Cera sees a lot of married couples in his counseling practice. In an effort to help them resolve their conflicts, he frequently administers a test to each partner, which generates a profile of their personality characteristics. Dr. Cera most likely uses the

_____ .

Review of Terms and Concepts 4

Use the terms in this list to complete the Matching Test, then to help you answer the True/False items correctly.

psychological test
projective test
projection
Rorschach Inkblot Test
Thematic Apperception
  Test (TAT)
graphology
validity
reliability
self-report inventory
  (objective personality
  test)

Minnesota Multiphasic
  Personality Inventory
  (MMPI)
California Personality
  Inventory (CPI)
Sixteen Personality
  Factor Questionnaire
  (16PF)
possible selves

Matching Exercise

Match the appropriate term with its definition or description.

1. _____ Type of psychological test in which a person's responses to standardized questions are compared with established norms.

2. _____ Projective test that uses inkblots, developed by Swiss psychiatrist Hermann Rorschach in 1921.

3. _____ Self-report inventory that assesses personality characteristics in normal populations.

4. _____ Test that assesses a person's abilities, aptitudes, interests, or personality on the basis of a systematically obtained sample of behavior.

5. _____ Self-report inventory developed by Raymond Cattell that generates a personality profile with ratings on 16 trait dimensions.

6. _____ The consistency of test results on repeated occasions under similar conditions.

7. _____ Pseudoscience that claims to assess personality, social, and occupational attributes based on a person's distinctive handwriting, doodles, and drawing styles.

True/False Test

Indicate whether each statement is true or false by placing T or F in the blank space next to each item.

1. ____ A projective test is a type of personality test that involves a person's interpreting an ambiguous image and is used to assess unconscious motives, conflicts, psychological defenses, and personality traits.

2. ____ Possible selves refers to an aspect of the self-concept that includes images of the selves that you hope, fear, or expect to become in the future.

3. ____ The Minnesota Multiphasic Personality Inventory (MMPI) is a projective personality test that involves creating stories about each of a series of ambiguous scenes.

4. ____ The Thematic Apperception Test (TAT) is a self-report inventory that assesses personality characteristics and psychological disorders; used to assess both normal and disturbed populations.

5. ____ Projection is a major ego defense mechanism that involves attributing one's own unacceptable urges or qualities to others.

6. ____ Validity is the ability of a test to measure what it is intended to measure.

Check your answers and review any areas of weakness before going on to the next section.

Something to Think About

1. The use of psychological tests has been and will continue to be an interesting topic of discussion for most people. Almost everyone has heard of the famous inkblot test, but not everyone knows its purpose or its limitations. Considering what you have learned about psychological tests in this chapter, what would you tell someone about the inkblot test and psychological tests in general?

2. The history of astrology can be traced back over 4,000 years. Astrology's basic premise is that the positions of the planets and stars at the time and place of your birth determine your personality and destiny. Today, belief in astrological predictions remains widespread. Indeed, you probably know a number of people who, even if they are not true believers, at least read their daily horoscope in the paper. How do you think scientific psychologists might go about testing the claims of astrologers, and how might you enlighten these people about scientific research on astrology?

Check your answers and review any areas of weakness before completing the progress tests.

Progress Test 1

Review the complete chapter (including all boxed inserts), review all your study notes, and then test yourself on the following progress test. Check your answers. If you make a mistake, review your notes, check the appropriate section in the study guide, and if necessary, go back and read the relevant part of the chapter in your textbook.

1. Marvin is angry and upset after an argument with his boss. At home that evening he is harshly and unreasonably critical of his son for not getting all his homework assignments completed. According to Freud, Marvin is using an ego defense mechanism called

   (a) identification.   (c) rationalization.
   (b) repression.   (d) displacement.

2. Seven-year old Salvatore prefers to play with his male friends and does not like playing with girls very much. Salvatore is probably in the _____ stage of psychosexual development.

   (a) anal   (c) latency
   (b) phallic   (d) genital

3. Although Tim has many fond memories of his college days, he only vaguely remembers the girl he was engaged to but who left him suddenly for another man. Tim's unconscious forgetting is an ego defense mechanism called

   (a) identification.   (c) displacement.
   (b) sublimation.   (d) repression.

4. Every time 2-year-old Kate is given a bath, she plays with her genital area. If her parents chastise or punish her, she is likely to experience frustration and so be unable to resolve the developmental conflict of that stage. The result is

(a) fixation.   (c) displacement.
(b) undoing.   (d) denial.

5. Zachary considers himself to be an outgoing, fun-loving type of person, and he goes to a lot of parties. Sondra, on the other hand, thinks of herself as fairly quiet and shy, and enjoys being by herself, reading a book and listening to classical music. In Jung's theory, Zachary's and Sondra's different behaviors reflect

(a) the two basic personality types, the extravert and the introvert.
(b) the two important archetypes, the hero and the nurturing mother.
(c) a superiority complex and an inferiority complex.
(d) penis envy and womb envy.

6. Mary is an outgoing, extraverted person, and John is introverted and shy. According to social cognitive theory, the different personalities of Mary and John reflect the interaction of behavioral, cognitive, and environmental factors, a process Bandura called

(a) identification.
(b) striving for superiority.
(c) the actualizing tendency.
(d) reciprocal determinism.

7. As part of a research project, Jasbinder was given the same psychological test three times at 2-month intervals by three different therapists. Her results on the tests were all very different. It is most probable that she was given the

(a) MMPI.   (c) CPI.
(b) 16PF.   (d) TAT.

8. The actualizing tendency and the self-concept are to _____ as reciprocal determinism and self-efficacy are to _____ .

(a) Abraham Maslow; Hans Eysenck
(b) Alfred Adler; Albert Bandura
(c) Raymond Cattell; Carl Jung
(d) Carl Rogers; Albert Bandura

9. When asked to describe her husband, Mrs. Roech said that he is prone to exaggerating his accomplishments and importance, seems unaware of the reality of his limitations, and tends to overcompensate for his feelings of inferiority and weakness. Adler would probably have said that Mr. Roech has

(a) an inferiority complex.
(b) an extraverted personality.
(c) a superiority complex.
(d) an anal fixation.

10. Katrina thinks of herself as fairly laid back, easygoing, and relatively calm. She believes that she is above average academically and intellectually and sees herself as very conscientious at work and caring and loving with her family. Carl Rogers's term for Katrina's perceptions and beliefs about herself would be

(a) self-efficacy.   (c) self-system.
(b) self-concept.   (d) possible selves.

11. Miguel is giving a lecture on the five-factor model of personality. Which of the following personality dimensions is NOT likely to be included in his talk?

(a) anal retentiveness
(b) extraversion
(c) neuroticism
(d) agreeableness
(e) openness to experience

12. Dr. Markowitz studies the effects of heredity on behavior. One of his areas of research focuses on similarities and differences in identical twins who were separated at birth or early infancy and raised by different families. Dr. Markowitz is most probably a

(a) psychoanalyst.
(b) humanistic psychologist.
(c) social cognitive psychologist.
(d) behavioral geneticist.

13. In Freudian theory, retreating to a behavior pattern characteristic of an earlier stage of development is to _____ as thinking or behaving in a way that is the extreme opposite of unacceptable urges or impulses is to

_____ .

(a) rationalization; projection
(b) regression; reaction formation
(c) sublimation; displacement
(d) repression; undoing

14. According to the Application, the term *possible selves* refers to
    (a) the unconscious part of the mind that motivates our behavior.
    (b) the major symptom of a fixated personality.
    (c) the aspect of the self-concept that includes images of the selves that you hope, fear, or expect to become in the future.
    (d) delusional thought processes.

15. According to Critical Thinking (Freud Versus Rogers on Human Nature), which of the following is true?
    (a) Freud's view of human nature was deeply pessimistic.
    (b) Rogers's view of human nature was deeply pessimistic.
    (c) Freud believed that humans are positive, forward-moving, constructive, realistic, and trustworthy.
    (d) Rogers believed that the essence of human nature is destructive but that societal, religious, and cultural restraints make people behave in good and moral ways.

Progress Test 2

After you have checked your understanding of the material in Progress Test 1 and have done a complete chapter review with special focus on any areas of weakness, you are ready to assess your knowledge on Progress Test 2. Check your answers. If you make a mistake, review your notes, the relevant section of the study guide, and, if necessary, the appropriate part of your textbook.

1. Nathan chews the end of his pen, bites his nails, overeats, smokes cigarettes, and talks incessantly. According to Freud, Nathan has probably fixated at the _____ stage of psychosexual development due to some unresolved conflict.
   (a) oral   (c) phallic
   (b) anal   (d) genital

2. Dr. Jivraj, like many contemporary trait theorists, believes that the 16 trait model is too complex, and that the three-dimensional trait theory is too limited. Instead, he favors a model in which five basic dimensions represent the structural organization of personality traits. These five factors are
    (a) extraversion, neuroticism, agreeableness, conscientiousness, and openness to experience.

    (b) submissiveness, apprehensiveness, dominance, sociability, and venturesomeness.
    (c) inferiority, superiority, introversion, extraversion, and actualizing tendencies.
    (d) self-efficacy, self-concept, reciprocal determining tendencies, defensiveness, and openness to experience.

3. Sheila was often rejected by her parents; as a result, she mistrusts other people and treats them with hostility, which leads to their rejection of her. This cycle of rejection, mistrust, hostility, and further rejection illustrates what Bandura called
    (a) self-efficacy.
    (b) identification.
    (c) displacement.
    (d) reciprocal determinism.

4. During a class discussion of various perspectives on personality, Sasha points to all the evidence that human beings are destructive and aggressive. He points to the millions who died in two world wars and the ongoing killings and massacres that continue in many parts of the world today. Sasha's observation about basic human nature supports the _____ perspective and is a criticism of the _____ perspective.
    (a) humanistic; psychoanalytic
    (b) trait; social cognitive
    (c) social cognitive; trait
    (d) psychoanalytic; humanistic

5. Dr. Sheenan is a clinical psychologist who wants to assess the extent to which a client is suffering from depression, delusions, and other mental health problems. Dr. Sheenan is most likely to use the
    (a) 16PF.   (c) MMPI.
    (b) CPI.   (d) TAT.

6. When Cindy was given the Rorschach Inkblot Test, she reported seeing a number of inanimate objects and some animal figures and tended to concentrate on very small details in each inkblot. Her therapist observed her behavior, gestures, and reactions as she responded to each card. It is most probable that her therapist is
    (a) interested in her unconscious conflicts, motives, and psychological defenses.
    (b) assessing her suitability for a particular occupation, such as police officer or pilot.

(c) trying to generate a personality profile based on a number of personality traits.

(d) trying to predict how she will perform academically when she goes to college.

7. Lukasz was given a forced-choice personality test in which he was required to respond to each item by choosing one of three alternatives. The results generated a personality profile with ratings on a number of trait dimensions that helped Lukasz decide which career path he should pursue. Lukasz was most likely given the

(a) Thematic Apperception Test (TAT).

(b) Minnesota Multiphasic Personality Inventory (MMPI).

(c) California Personality Inventory (CPI).

(d) Sixteen Personality Factor Questionnaire (16PF).

8. Five-year-old Dunstan has recently become very possessive of his mother and appears to be jealous of his father. He is sometimes openly hostile, telling his father, "Don't kiss my Mommy!" According to Freud, Dunstan is in the _____ stage of psychosexual development and showing manifestations of _____ .

(a) oral; fixation

(b) anal; fixation

(c) phallic; the Oedipus complex

(d) latency; the Oedipus complex

9. Wendy believes that the most fundamental human motive is striving for superiority. She thinks that this drive arises from global feelings of inferiority and that human personality and behavior reflect our attempts to compensate for or overcome our perceived weaknesses. Which personality theorist is most likely to agree with Wendy's views?

(a) Freud   (c) Horney

(b) Jung   (d) Adler

10. David is very quiet, pessimistic, anxious, and moody and becomes emotionally upset very easily. In terms of Eysenck's four basic personality types, he would be classified as

(a) introverted–neurotic.

(b) introverted–stable.

(c) extraverted–neurotic.

(d) extraverted–stable.

11. In a term paper on Carl Jung's theory of personality, Justin quoted Jung as saying that the _____ contains "the whole spiritual heritage of mankind's evolution, born anew in the brain structure of every individual."

(a) personal preconscious

(b) collective conscious

(c) personal unconscious

(d) collective unconscious

12. Ursula's therapist instructs her to relax, close her eyes, and state aloud whatever thoughts come to mind no matter how trivial, silly, or absurd they seem. The therapist is using a technique called

(a) free association.

(b) displacement.

(c) unconditional positive regard.

(d) repression.

13. Leanne studies very hard, but she always feels that she hasn't studied enough. If she takes a break to socialize with her friends, she starts feeling guilty and anxious. Freud would say that Leanne has a

(a) strong superego.   (c) weak superego.

(b) strong id.   (d) weak id.

14. According to Science Versus Pseudoscience (Graphology), graphologists' claims that handwriting reveals temperament, personality traits, intelligence, and reasoning ability

(a) have been tested and supported by numerous scientific studies.

(b) have not been supported by scientific research.

(c) should be believed because thousands of companies have used graphologists to assist in hiring new employees.

(d) have been compared to astrologers' claims, and graphology has been shown clearly to have greater validity and reliability.

15. According to In Focus (Explaining Those Amazing Identical-Twin Similarities), which of the following is true?

(a) Any two randomly chosen people of the same age, sex, and culture will likely have absolutely no similarities.

(b) Some similarities between separated identical twins may be genetically influenced.

(c) Personality is almost completely determined by genes.

(d) Personality is almost completely determined by environmental factors.

Progress Test 3

After you have checked your understanding of the material in Progress Tests 1 and 2, and have done a complete chapter review with special focus on any areas of weakness, you are ready to further assess your knowledge with Progress Test 3. Check your answers. If you make a mistake, review your notes, the appropriate parts of the study guide, and if necessary, the relevant sections of your textbook.

1. During a class reunion, Adeil reminisced with some of his high school friends about their last year at school. He had no problem recalling many of the fun times they had together. In terms of Freud's theory of personality, Adeil's ability to recall these events would suggest that they are stored at the _____ level of awareness.
   - (a) unconscious
   - (b) conscious
   - (c) latency
   - (d) preconscious

2. Researchers conducting twin and adoption studies are likely to conclude that
   - (a) in general, the influence of environmental factors on personality traits is at least equal to the influence of genetic factors.
   - (b) certain personality traits, such as extraversion and neuroticism, are significantly influenced by genetics.
   - (c) identical twins are more alike early in life, but as they grow up, leave home, and have different experiences in different environments, their personalities become more different.
   - (d) all of these statements are true.

3. Juan is an experienced car mechanic who believes he can fix just about any problem in any make of car or truck. According to Bandura, Juan's confidence in his ability to handle mechanical problems is his
   - (a) self-concept.
   - (b) superiority complex.
   - (c) self-efficacy.
   - (d) actualizing tendency.

4. When Romwaldo was given the results of his psychological test, he was told that he scored high on the extraverted–stable dimension and that he has a tendency to be sociable, outgoing, talkative, and responsive. This description of Romwaldo's source and surface traits is most consistent with
   - (a) Hans Eysenck's view of personality.
   - (b) Rorschach's theory of personality.
   - (c) Alfred Adler's model of personality.
   - (d) Carl Rogers's humanistic approach to personality.

5. The pleasure principle is to _____ as the reality principle is to _____ .
   - (a) the oral stage; the anal stage
   - (b) Thanatos; Eros
   - (c) the id; the ego
   - (d) the ego; the superego

6. When Kaysone was researching a term paper for her history of psychology course, she was intrigued by the ideas of neo-Freudian Alfred Adler. She noted that for Adler the most fundamental human motive was _____ , which arises from universal _____ .
   - (a) driven by basic anxiety; feelings of womb and penis envy
   - (b) the need to achieve psychological growth, self-realization, and psychic harmony; archetypes in the collective unconscious
   - (c) sexual and aggressive in nature; feelings of guilt and anxiety repressed in the unconscious
   - (d) striving for superiority; feelings of inferiority

7. Dr. Selnick believes in the importance of unconscious psychological conflicts, sexual and aggressive drives, and the formative influence of early childhood experiences. Dr. Selnick's views are most consistent with the _____ perspective.
   - (a) psychoanalytic
   - (b) humanistic
   - (c) social cognitive
   - (d) trait

8. Raffi is shown a series of cards with ambiguous scenes and is told to make up a story about each one, describing the characters' feelings and their motives. Raffi has been given the
   - (a) Thematic Apperception Test (TAT).
   - (b) Rorschach Inkblot Test.
   - (c) California Personality Inventory (CPI).
   - (d) Minnesota Multiphasic Personality Inventory (MMPI).

9. Sheldon has frequently been rebellious, inconsiderate, and self-centered. His parents are consistent in disciplining him for his inappropriate behaviors while communicating to him that they value and love him. The person most likely to agree with their parenting approach and use of unconditional positive regard is
   - (a) Sigmund Freud.
   - (b) Carl Rogers.
   - (c) Joseph Breuer.
   - (d) Carl Jung.

10. Dr. Welch is a clinical psychologist who uses the MMPI and the 16PF. If asked to identify the key strength of these tests, he is most likely to note that
    (a) they provide a wealth of qualitative information about the individual.
    (b) scoring relies on the examiner's subjective judgment and clinical experience and expertise.
    (c) they accurately measure the individual's unconscious motives and conflicts.
    (d) they are standardized and objectively scored.

11. Research participants were first given a personality test; then, as they viewed very positive or very negative images, they underwent fMRI brain scans. It is very probable that those who scored high on extraversion showed _____ and those who scored high on neuroticism showed _____ .
    (a) less activity in the brain areas that control emotion; more activity in the brain areas that control emotion
    (b) damage to the frontal and temporal cortical areas; damage to the temporal lobe and the amygdala
    (c) more activity in the brain areas that control emotion; less activity in the brain areas that control emotion
    (d) damage to the temporal lobe and the amygdala; damage to the frontal and temporal cortical areas

12. Dr. Sharma stresses the importance of identifying, measuring, and describing individual differences in terms of various personality characteristics. His views are most representative of the _____ perspective on personality.
    (a) psychoanalytic (c) social cognitive
    (b) humanistic   (d) trait

13. When Dr. Mainprize was going through a very painful divorce, he tended to mark students' papers more harshly than usual and he also constructed much tougher exams. A psychoanalyst would most likely view the professor's treatment of his students as an example of
    (a) reciprocal determinism.
    (b) repression.
    (c) Thanatos (death instinct).
    (d) displacement.

14. Dr. Abrahams believes that people experience psychological problems when their self-concept conflicts with their actual experience and they continually have to defend against genuine feelings and experiences. Consistent with humanistic theory, Dr. Abrahams is likely to say that such people are _____ , which is caused by _____ .
    (a) extraverted-neurotics; a lack of self-efficacy
    (b) in a state of congruence; unconditional positive regard
    (c) overcompensating; feelings of inferiority
    (d) in a state of incongruity; conditional positive regard

15. After reading Freud's theory, Edwin was convinced that there are two conflicting instinctual drives. One consists of biological urges that perpetuate the existence of the individual and the species, and the other is destructive energy reflected in aggressive, reckless, and life-threatening, self-destructive behavior. Freud called these two constructs _____ and _____ .
    (a) introversion; extraversion
    (b) neuroticism; psychoticism
    (c) the pleasure principle; the reality principle
    (d) Eros; Thanatos

Answers

Introduction: What Is Personality?

1. *Personality is defined as* an individual's unique and relatively consistent pattern of thinking, feeling, and behaving.

2. *A personality theory is* an attempt to describe and explain similarities and differences in people's patterns of thinking, feeling, and behavior—in other words, how people are similar, how they are different, and why every individual is unique.

3. *The four basic perspectives on personality (and the main emphasis of each) are* the psychoanalytic perspective, which emphasizes the importance of unconscious processes and the influence of early childhood experience; the humanistic perspective, which represents an optimistic look at human nature, emphasizing the self and the fulfillment of a person's unique potential; the social cognitive perspective, which emphasizes learning and conscious

cognitive processes, including the importance of beliefs about the self, goal setting, and self-regulation; and the trait perspective, which emphasizes the description and measurement of specific personality differences among individuals.

The Psychoanalytic Perspective on Personality

1. *Psychoanalysis—Freud's theory of personality—stresses* the influence of unconscious mental processes, the importance of sexual and aggressive instincts, and the enduring effects of early childhood experiences on later personality development.

2. *Some of the key factors in the development of Freud's ideas were* his collaboration with Joseph Breuer on the cause of hysteria and the concept of catharsis; the development of free association to study the unconscious; the importance of dreams and their interpretation; and the impact of war on culture and society.

The Psychoanalytic Perspective: Freud's Dynamic Theory of Personality

1. *The content of the unconscious can surface in disguised form in* free association, dreams, slips of the tongue, mistakes, instances of forgetting, and what, on the surface, appear to be accidental or unintentional actions.

2. *The three basic structures of personality (and their functions) are* the id (the completely unconscious, irrational component of personality that seeks immediate satisfaction of instinctual urges and is ruled by the pleasure principle); the ego (the partly conscious rational component of personality that regulates thoughts and behavior, that is most in touch with the real world, and that is governed by the reality principle); and the superego (the partly conscious, self-evaluative, moralistic component of personality that is formed through the internalization of parental and societal rules).

3. *The three main ego defense mechanisms (and the roles they play) are* repression (the unconscious exclusion of anxiety-provoking thoughts, feelings, and memories from conscious awareness, which is involved in all other ego defense mechanisms), displacement (unconscious shifting of the target of an emotional urge to a substitute target that is less threatening or dangerous), and sublimation (a form of displacement in which sexual urges are rechanneled into productive, sociably acceptable, nonsexual activities). *Other ego defense mechanisms include* rationalization, projection, reaction formation, denial, undoing, and regression.

The Psychoanalytic Perspective: Personality Development

1. *The psychosexual stages are age-related developmental periods in which* the child's sexual impulses are focused on different bodily zones and are expressed through the activities associated with these areas.

2. *The five psychosexual stages (and the focus of each) are* the oral stage (the mouth is the primary focus of pleasurable and gratifying sensations, which are achieved via feeding and exploring objects with the mouth); the anal stage (the anus is the primary focus of pleasurable sensations, which are derived from developing control over elimination via toilet training); the phallic stage (the genitals are the primary focus of pleasurable sensations derived through sexual curiosity, masturbation, and sexual attraction to the opposite-sex parent); the latency stage (sexual impulses become repressed and dormant as the child develops same-sex friendships with peers and focuses on school, sports, and other activities); and the genital stage (at physical sexual maturity, the genitals become the focus of pleasurable sensations, which are satisfied in heterosexual relationships).

3. *If the developmental conflict of a particular stage is not resolved,* the result may be fixation, and the person will continue to seek pleasure through behaviors that are similar to those associated with that psychosexual stage.

4. *The Oedipus complex refers to* a child's unconscious sexual desire for the opposite-sex parent, usually accompanied by hostile feelings toward the same-sex parent.

5. *Identification (which is one way of resolving the Oedipus complex) is an ego defense mechanism that* involves reducing anxiety by imitating the behavior and characteristics of another person.

Concept Check 1

1. projection
2. free association
3. unconscious
4. latent
5. id
6. superego

7. sublimation

8. identification

9. rationalization

Graphic Organizer 1

1. genital

2. phallic

3. latency

4. oral

5. anal

Matching Exercise 1

1. libido

2. personality

3. superego

4. Oedipus complex

5. ego

6. preconscious

7. oral stage

8. displacement

9. Sigmund Freud

10. anal stage

11. personality theory

12. id

13. latency stage

14. psychoanalysis

15. ego defense mechanisms

16. psychosexual stages

17. manifest content

True/False Test 1

1. F	6. T	11. T	16. F
2. T	7. T	12. F	17. T
3. T	8. T	13. T	
4. F	9. F	14. T	
5. T	10. F	15. T	

The Psychoanalytic Perspective: The Neo-Freudians

1. *The neo-Freudians followed Freud in stressing* the importance of the unconscious and early childhood experiences. *However, they developed independent personality theories, because they disagreed with Freud on three key points: (a)* They took issue with Freud's belief that behavior was primarily motivated by sexual desires. *(b)* They disagreed with Freud's contention that personality is fundamentally determined by early childhood experiences; instead, they believed that personality can also be influenced by experiences throughout the lifespan. *(c)* They departed from Freud's generally pessimistic view of human nature and society.

2. *Carl Jung emphasized* psychological growth, self-realization, and psychic wholeness and harmony. He proposed the existence of the collective unconscious, which contains archetypes of universal human instincts, themes, and preoccupations. He was the first to describe two basic personality types: introverts and extraverts.

3. *Karen Horney stressed* the role of social relationships in protecting against basic anxiety; she objected to Freud's views of female development, particularly his idea of penis envy (she proposed that males often have womb envy).

4. *Alfred Adler believed* that the most fundamental human motive was to strive for superiority, which arose from universal feelings of inferiority. He proposed the notions of the inferiority complex and the superiority complex.

The Psychoanalytic Perspective: Evaluating Freud and the Psychoanalytic Perspective on Personality

1. *Although Sigmund Freud's ideas have had a profound and lasting effect on psychology and on society, the main criticisms of Freud's theory and psychoanalysis are*

   (a) Freud's theory relies wholly on data derived from a relatively small sample of patients and from self-analysis. He did not take notes during his private therapy sessions, and so we have only Freud's interpretations of the cases; this problem has to do with the ability to objectively evaluate the evidence.

   (b) Many psychoanalytic concepts, because they are so vague and ambiguous, are very difficult to measure or confirm scientifically. In addition, because even seemingly contradictory information can be used to support Freud's theory, psychoanalytic concepts are often impossible to disprove. Psychoanalysis is also better at explaining past behavior than at predicting future behavior.

   (c) Many people feel that Freud's theories reflect a sexist view of women; Freud's theory uses male psychology as a prototype, and women are essentially viewed as a deviation from the norm of masculinity.

2. *Several of Freud's ideas have been substantiated by empirical evidence, including* the idea that much of mental life is unconscious; that early childhood experiences have a critical influence on interpersonal relationships and psychological adjustment; and that people differ significantly in the degree to which they are able to regulate their impulses, emotions, and thoughts toward adaptive and socially acceptable ends.

Concept Check 2

1. inferiority
2. Karen Horney
3. collective unconscious; Jung's
4. basic anxiety; against
5. extravert
6. archetypes; collective unconscious
7. anima; Jung's
8. striving for superiority

Matching Exercise 2

1. Karen Horney
2. archetypes
3. striving for superiority
4. basic anxiety
5. inferiority complex
6. extravert
7. collective unconscious
8. anima

True/False Test 2

1. T	4. T	7. T
2. T	5. T	8. T
3. T	6. T	

The Humanistic Perspective on Personality

1. *The major contributors to humanistic psychology were* Abraham Maslow *and* Carl Rogers.

2. *The humanistic perspective emphasizes* free will, self-awareness, and human potential.

3. *The actualizing tendency is* the innate drive to maintain and enhance the human organism.

4. *The self-concept is* the set of perceptions and beliefs that you have about yourself, including your nature, your personal qualities, and your typical behavior.

5. *Conditional positive regard is* the sense that you will be loved and valued only if you behave in a way that is acceptable to others; this can cause a person to deny or distort genuine feelings and experience, leading to a state of incongruence with regard to the self-concept. *Unconditional positive regard is* the sense that you will be valued and loved even if you don't conform to the standards and expectations of others; this leads to a state of congruence, where your sense of self is consistent with your emotions and experiences.

6. *The fully functioning person experiences* congruence, the actualizing tendency, and psychological growth.

7. *The humanistic perspective has been criticized on two particular points*: first, humanistic theories are hard to validate or test scientifically; second, according to many psychologists, the humanistic perspective's view of human nature is too optimistic.

The Social Cognitive Perspective on Personality

1. *The social cognitive perspective stresses* the role of conscious thought processes, self-regulation, and the importance of situational influences.

2. *Bandura's social cognitive theory emphasizes* the importance of observational learning, conscious cognitive processes, social experiences, self-efficacy beliefs, and reciprocal determinism.

3. *Reciprocal determinism suggests that human functioning and personality* are caused by the interaction of behavioral, cognitive, and environmental factors.

4. *Self-efficacy is* a person's belief about his or her ability to meet the demands of a specific situation (feelings of self-confidence or self-doubt); self-efficacy influences behavior, performance, motivation, and persistence.

5. *Key strengths of the social cognitive perspective are* that it is grounded in empirical, laboratory research; it is built on research in learning, cognitive psychology, and social psychology rather than on clinical impressions. Unlike the vague psychoanalytic and humanistic concepts, the concepts of social cognitive theory are scientifically testable; they can be operationally defined and measured.

6. *Some weaknesses of the social cognitive perspective are that* real-life, everyday situations are not adequately captured in the typical laboratory research situation because they are more

complex, with multiple factors converging to affect behavior and personality. Other psychologists argue that the social cognitive perspective ignores unconscious influences, conflicts, or emotions.

The Trait Perspective on Personality

1. *Trait theories focus on* identifying, measuring, and describing individual differences in behavioral predispositions.

2. *Traits are* relatively stable, enduring predispositions to consistently behave in certain ways. *Surface traits are* personality characteristics or attributes that can easily be inferred from observing behavior. *Source traits are* the most fundamental dimensions of personality and are thought to be universal and relatively few in number.

3. *Cattell believed that* there are 16 basic personality factors (he developed the 16PF personality test).

4. *Hans Eysenck proposed that* there are three personality dimensions, introversion–extraversion, neuroticism–emotional stability, and psychoticism.

5. *According to the five-factor model,* there are five basic personality dimensions: extraversion, neuroticism, agreeableness, conscientiousness, and openness to experience.

6. *The field of behavioral genetics studies* the effects of genes and heredity on behavior.

7. *Factors that seem to have a significant genetic component are* extraversion and neuroticism, but openness to experience, conscientiousness, and agreeableness are also influenced by genetics, although to a lesser extent. However, the influence of environmental factors on personality traits is at least equal to the influence of genetic factors.

8. *The trait perspective is useful in* describing and comparing people.

9. *Some criticisms of the trait theories are* that they don't really explain human personality or how or why individual differences develop, and they generally fail to address other important personality factors, such as the basic motives that drive human personality, the role of unconscious mental processes, how beliefs about the self influence personality, or how psychological change and growth occur.

Concept Check 3

1. self-efficacy
2. surface
3. fully functioning
4. social cognitive
5. trait
6. unconditional positive regard
7. behavioral genetics
8. extraversion; neuroticism
9. Raymond Cattell; Sixteen Personality Factor Questionnaire (16PF)

Graphic Organizer 2

1. Hans Eysenck; trait
2. Carl Rogers; humanistic
3. Raymond Cattell; trait
4. Sigmund Freud; psychoanalytic
5. Alfred Adler; psychoanalytic (neo-Freudian)
6. Albert Bandura; social cognitive
7. Karen Horney; psychoanalytic (neo-Freudian)
8. Abraham Maslow; humanistic
9. Carl Jung; psychoanalytic (neo-Freudian)

Matching Exercise 3

1. trait
2. self-efficacy
3. Albert Bandura
4. actualizing tendency
5. five-factor model of personality
6. Abraham Maslow
7. psychoticism
8. positive regard
9. social cognitive theory
10. trait theory
11. extraversion
12. Carl Rogers
13. humanistic psychology
14. reciprocal determinism
15. introversion
16. mastery experience

True/False Test 3

1. T	6. T	11. F
2. F	7. T	12. T
3. T	8. T	13. T
4. F	9. T	14. T
5. T	10. F	15. T

Assessing Personality: Psychological Tests

1. *A psychological test is* a test that assesses a person's abilities, aptitudes, interests, or personality on the basis of a systematically obtained sample of behavior.

2. *A projective test is* a type of personality test that involves the client's interpreting an ambiguous image; it is used to assess unconscious motives, conflicts, psychological defenses, and personality traits. The Rorschach Inkblot Test and the Thematic Apperception Test are examples.

3. *A self-report inventory is* a type of psychological test in which a person's responses to standardized questions are compared to established norms. The Minnesota Multiphasic Personality Inventory (MMPI), the California Personality Inventory (CPI), and the Sixteen Personality Factor Questionnaire (16PF) are examples.

4. *Projective tests provide qualitative data but their limitations are that* responses may be affected by the examiner or the situation, scoring is very subjective, results may be inconsistent, and they do not predict behavior well.

5. *The strengths of self-report inventories are that* they are objectively scored, they differentiate among people on particular personality characteristics, and they have high reliability, validity, and predictive value.

6. *Problems with self-report inventories are that* people do not always respond honestly or accurately, people can successfully fake responses and answer in socially desirable ways, and some people may respond in a set way to all questions.

Concept Check 4

1. projective; Thematic Apperception Test (TAT)
2. MMPI
3. CPI
4. Rorschach Inkblot Test; TAT; projective
5. 16PF

Matching Exercise 4

1. self-report inventory
2. Rorschach Inkblot Test
3. California Personality Inventory (CPI)
4. psychological test
5. Sixteen Personality Factor Questionnaire (16PF)
6. reliability
7. graphology

True/False Test 4

1. T	3. F	5. T
2. T	4. F	6. T

Something to Think About

1. In any discussion of psychological testing it is always a good idea to point out the important characteristics of a good test, namely, reliability and validity. In terms of personality testing, you should first describe the two categories of tests, projective tests and self-report inventories.

   The famous Rorschach Inkblot Test is, of course, a projective test. In other words, it is assumed that people will project their unconscious feelings, motives, drives, thoughts, and so on in their responses to the series of inkblots. Similarly, the Thematic Apperception Test (TAT) gives subjects an opportunity to project unconscious information into the stories they make up about ambiguous scenes. Both tests developed out of the psychoanalytic approaches to personality, and scoring involves the subjective interpretations of the examiner. A brief discussion of Freud's theory as it relates to personality would probably be in order. A review of the most damaging criticisms of psychoanalysis may shed light on the topic, and the issue of the validity and reliability of projective tests should not be overlooked. Despite the criticisms, projective tests are widely used and can provide a wealth of qualitative data about an individual.

   Self-report inventories are used by clinical psychologists to evaluate both normal and abnormal populations in a variety of settings and for a variety of purposes. The most common are the MMPI, the CPI, and the 16PF. These are often called objective personality tests because they are standardized and objectively scored and measured against established norms. Self-report inventories are far more reliable and valid than are projective tests. These tests do have some drawbacks, including a person's ability to fake responses and answer in a socially desirable manner, some people's tendency to answer in a set way to all questions, and the fact that people are not always the best judges of their own behavior.

Personality tests are generally useful strategies that can provide insights about the psychological makeup of a person. However, no personality test, by itself, is likely to provide a definitive description of a given individual. In addition, because people can and often do change over time, any personality test provides a profile of the person only at the time of the test.

2. One of the oldest personality theories is based on the premise that the position of the planets and stars at the time and place of your birth determine your personality and destiny. This explanation of personality is called *astrology*. However, just because its origins are ancient and belief in it has persisted over a long period of time does not mean that it is true or accurate. In fact, astrology is considered by most scientists to be a pseudoscience.

Nevertheless, many people believe in astrology, and a large number consult professional astrologers to find out what they should do and to predict the future. Belief in astrology is not restricted to any class or group of individuals. People from all walks of life, from senior managers to assembly line workers, from government leaders to junior clerks, consult their horoscopes on a regular basis. However, popularity does not always equal truth.

As is the case with many strongly held beliefs, it is often difficult to get true believers in astrology to listen to any information that might contradict what they feel is a valid point of view. It is always important to be aware of this and to respect their right to believe whatever they wish. However, if the opportunity does arise to have an open-minded discussion, presenting the results of Shawn Carlson's (1985) carefully designed study could be useful. In this study, a panel of astrological advisers were involved in helping Carlson design the study, and 30 of the top American and European astrologers who were considered by their peers to be among the best, were also consulted. All the participating astrologers agreed beforehand that Carlson's study was a fair test of astrological claims. In the study, the astrologers developed astrological profiles for all the participants based on each person's

time, date, and place of birth. Each person also completed the California Personality Inventory (CPI), a widely used and valid test of personality that all the astrologers were familiar with. The astrologers were then given an individual's astrological profile along with three CPI profiles, two were random and one was the correct CPI profile for the person. All the astrologer had to do was match the person's astrological profile with the correct CPI profile. Although the astrologers who approved the design predicted that 50 percent was the minimum effect they would expect to see, the results showed that astrologers performed at a chance level—they were correct only 34 percent of the time. In other words, anybody simply guessing would have done as well as the astrologers.

Carlson's results are consistent with those of many other researchers. A careful review of the scientific research on astrology came to the conclusion that astrology has absolutely no reliable basis in scientific fact and cannot stand up to any valid statistical test. Of course, if the astrologers had any real insight from their reading of the planets, they could easily have foreseen the outcome of Carlson's study!

Progress Test 1

1. d	6. d	11. a
2. c	7. d	12. d
3. d	8. d	13. b
4. a	9. c	14. c
5. a	10. b	15. a

Progress Test 2

1. a	6. a	11. d
2. a	7. d	12. a
3. d	8. c	13. a
4. d	9. d	14. b
5. c	10. a	15. b

Progress Test 3

1. d	6. d	11. c
2. d	7. a	12. d
3. c	8. a	13. d
4. a	9. b	14. d
5. c	10. d	15. d

CHAPTER 12

Social Psychology

PREVIEW	Reading the section below first will give you a general sense of the chapter's contents and an initial introduction to some of the major concepts and terms. This will prime you for what you are about to read and help you to develop a "cognitive map" that will guide your study of the material in this chapter. Likewise, reading the **preview questions** at the beginning of each major section will improve your ability to understand, learn, and retain the information.

CHAPTER 12 . . . AT A GLANCE

Chapter 12 discusses social psychology—the scientific study of the way individuals think, feel, and behave in social situations—as broadly divided into two major research areas: social cognition and social influence. The chapter first explores person perception, including the factors that influence our perceptions of others. This is followed by a discussion of the process of attribution, including three important attributional biases and the influence of culture on attributional processes.

Once we form impressions of people, we tend to interpret their behavior in terms of our attitudes about them. The conditions under which attitudes determine behavior are identified. The role of cognitive dissonance in behavior and cognition is explored. In discussing prejudice, the text describes such cognitive influences as stereotypes, in-groups, out-groups, the out-group homogeneity effect, in-group bias, and ethnocentrism. The emotional roots of prejudice and techniques for reducing prejudice are also considered.

Conformity occurs when people change their behavior, attitudes, or beliefs in response to real or imagined group pressure. The original experimental design and the results of Stanley Milgram's research on obedience are presented in detail. Conditions that influence people to obey and to resist obeying authority figures are identified.

Latané and Darley's research on helping behavior, bystander intervention, and diffusion of responsibility is discussed, and their model of bystander intervention is presented. In this context, individual behavior can be strongly influenced by the presence of others. The phenomena of social loafing, social striving, social facilitation, and deindividuation are examined.

The Application discusses various techniques used by professional persuaders and provides some practical suggestions that will help you to avoid being taken in by such techniques.

Introduction: What Is Social Psychology?

Preview Questions

Consider the following questions as you study this section of the chapter.

- What is social psychology?
- What is meant by social cognition and social influence?

*Read the section "Introduction: What Is Social Psychology?" and **write** your answers to the following:*

1. Social psychology is _____

   _____

2. Social cognition refers to _____

   _____

3. Social influence focuses on _____

   _____

Person Perception: Forming Impressions of Other People

Preview Questions

Consider the following questions as you study this section of the chapter.

- What is person perception?
- What four principles does the mental process of forming judgments of others follow?
- How do social categories, implicit personality theories, and physical attractiveness influence person perception?

*Read the section "Person Perception: Forming Impressions of Other People" and **write** your answers to the following:*

1. Person perception refers to _____

   _____

   _____

2. The four basic principles of person perception are

   (a) _____

   (b) _____

   (c) _____

   (d) _____

3. In combination, these four basic principles underscore that person perception is _____

   _____

   _____

4. Social categorization is _____

   _____

   _____

   Its advantages and disadvantages are _____

   _____

   _____

5. An implicit personality theory is _____

   _____

   _____

   Like social categories, implicit personality theories are useful _____

   _____

   _____

6. Physical attractiveness is correlated with ____

   _____

   _____

   It is not correlated with _____

   _____

   _____

   Neuroscientists have shown that when people make direct eye contact with a physically attractive person _____

   _____

   _____

   _____

Attribution: Explaining Behavior

Preview Questions

Consider the following questions as you study this section of the chapter.

- How is *attribution* defined?
- What are the fundamental attribution error, blaming the victim, the just-world hypothesis, the actor–observer discrepancy, and the self-serving bias?

Read the section "Attribution: Explaining Behavior" and **write** *your answers to the following:*

1. Attribution is _____
_____
_____

2. The fundamental attribution error is the tendency to _____
_____
_____

3. Blaming the victim is the tendency to _____
_____
_____

4. The just-world hypothesis is _____
_____
_____

5. The actor–observer discrepancy is the tendency to _____
_____

6. The self-serving bias is the tendency to _____
_____
_____

After you have carefully studied the preceding sections, complete the following exercises.

Concept Check 1

Read the following and write the correct term in the space provided.

1. Adam earned an A in his philosophy class and concluded that he had quite a talent for writing coherently and thinking logically. When he earned a C in his sociology class, he expressed dissatisfaction with the course content, the teaching ability of the professor, and the quality and clarity of the exams. This best illustrates the _____ .

2. Rachel has just learned that her neighbor's teenage son Brad was involved in an automobile accident at a nearby intersection. She said to her husband, "Well, Brad's recklessness has finally got him into trouble!" Rachel's comment suggests that she has made the

_____ .

3. When Allen observed Mark missing what looked to him like an easy point, Allen concluded that Mark was not a skilled basketball player. Later, in an identical position, Allen also failed to score. However, this time he concluded that it was the strong opposing team that prevented him from scoring. It would appear that Allen has succumbed to a common attributional bias called the _____ .

4. When Cheryl first met Charles, who is an archivist in the university library, she concluded that he was probably very quiet, introverted, and introspective. She was later surprised to learn that he was the lead singer in a heavy metal band. Cheryl's surprise is probably the result of using a(n)

_____

to judge people on the basis of certain traits and characteristics associated with certain types of people.

5. After learning about some interesting social psychology phenomena in his introductory class, Patrick decided he would like to test one of the concepts by facing the back instead of the front while riding the elevator. Much to his surprise, he found that he could not carry out his plan. After a second or two, he was overcome with embarrassment and ended up facing the front like everyone else. Patrick's behavior was governed by the _____ of the situation.

6. Grover does not support any charities because he believes that people who are poor, hungry, or homeless did something to deserve their situation. Grover's explanatory style is called

_____ ; it probably reflects his strong need to believe the world is fair, an assumption called the

_____ .

7. Byron is tall, dark, and handsome. Like most physically attractive people, he is likely to be *perceived* as being _____

_____ than less attractive people.

8. When people make direct eye contact with Byron, an area of their brain called the ventral striatum is likely to _____ ; if he disengages from eye contact and averts his gaze, it is likely _____ .

9. Gustini has a strong belief in a just world and finds it distressing to think that the bomb attack could just as easily have killed him as the innocent victims. He feels strongly that the perpetrators should be brought to justice and severely punished. In this case, it is _____ (very likely/not likely) that Gustini will blame the victim.

Graphic Organizer 1

The following statements represent attributional processes. Decide which is (A) the fundamental attribution error, (B) the actor–observer discrepancy, or (C) the self-serving bias, and decide whether the attribution is to the self or to others or to both and whether it is internal (INT) or external (EXT).

Statement	Process	Attribution
1. I solved the local newspaper puzzle because I'm smart; I couldn't solve the *Times* puzzle because it was tricky and unfair and asked questions about facts unknown to most people.		
2. My sister had a fender-bender because she is a typical female driver; when I had a fender-bender, it was because the other driver was an idiot.		
3. I don't care what he said about his car breaking down; he was 15 minutes late for the first class, so he must be one of those inconsiderate professors who is more concerned with his research than with his students.		

Review of Terms and Concepts 1

Use the terms in this list to complete the Matching Test, then to help you answer the True / False items correctly.

social psychology
social cognition
social influence
person perception
interpersonal context
social norms
social categorization
implicit personality
  theory
schemas

attribution
fundamental attribution
  error
blaming the victim
just-world hypothesis
actor–observer
  discrepancy
self-serving bias
self-effacing bias
  (modesty bias)

Matching Exercise

Match the appropriate term with its definition or description.

1. _____ The "rules," or expectations, for appropriate behavior in a particular social situation.

2. _____ Mental process of inferring the causes of people's behavior, including one's own. Also used to refer to the explanation made for a particular behavior.

3. _____ Tendency to attribute successful outcomes of one's own behavior to internal causes and unsuccessful outcomes to external, situational causes.

4. _____ Branch of psychology that studies how people think, feel, and behave in social situations.

5. _____ Network of assumptions or beliefs about the relationships among various types of people, traits, and behaviors.

6. _____ Tendency to attribute one's own behavior to external, situational causes while attributing the behavior of others to internal, personal causes; especially likely to occur with regard to behaviors that lead to negative outcomes.

7. _____ Tendency to blame an innocent victim of misfortune for having somehow caused the problem or for not having taken steps to avoid or prevent it.

8. _____ The assumption that the world is fair and that therefore people get what they deserve and deserve what they get.

True/False Test

Indicate whether each statement is true or false by placing T or F in the blank space next to each item.

1. ____ The effect that situational factors and other people have on an individual's behavior is called social cognition.

2. ____ The fundamental attribution error refers to the tendency to attribute the behavior of others to internal, personal characteristics while ignoring or underestimating the effects of external, situational factors; an attributional bias that is common in individualistic cultures.

3. ____ Person perception refers to the mental processes we use to form judgments and draw conclusions about the characteristics and motives of others.

4. ____ Social categorization refers to the mental process of classifying people into groups (or social categories) on the basis of their shared characteristics.

5. ____ Social influence refers to the mental processes people use to make sense of their social environment; it includes the study of person perception, attribution, attitudes, and prejudice.

6. ____ The self-effacing bias (modesty bias) involves blaming failure on internal, personal factors while attributing success to external, situational factors; more common in collectivistic cultures than in individualistic cultures.

7. ____ Interpersonal context has three components: the characteristics of the person being perceived, your own characteristics, and the specific situation in which the process occurs.

8. ____ Through previous social experiences, we form cognitive *schemas,* or mental frameworks, about the traits and behaviors associated with different types of people.

Check your answers and review any areas of weakness before going on to the next section.

The Social Psychology of Attitudes

Preview Questions

Consider the following questions as you study this section of the chapter.

- How is the term *attitude* defined, and what are its three components?

- Under what conditions are attitudes most likely to determine behavior?

- What is cognitive dissonance, and how does it affect behavior?

Read the section "The Social Psychology of Attitudes" and **write** *your answers to the following:*

1. An attitude is defined as _____
   _____

2. The three components of an attitude are
   (a) _____
   (b) _____
   (c) _____

3. You are most likely to behave in accordance with your attitudes in any of five conditions:
   (a) _____
   (b) _____
   (c) _____
   (d) _____
   (e) _____

4. Cognitive dissonance is _____
   _____
   _____

It commonly occurs in situations in which

_____

_____

_____

_____

5. Cognitive dissonance can also change _____

_____

6. Cognitive dissonance also operates when you
    have to choose _____

_____

_____

_____

_____

_____

Understanding Prejudice

Preview Questions

*Consider the following questions as you study this
section of the chapter.*

- How is *prejudice* defined?
- What are in-groups, out-groups, the out-group
  homogeneity effect, the in-group bias, discrimination, and ethnocentrism?
- What conditions are necessary for reducing
  tension between groups?
- How can prejudice be overcome?

*Read the section "Understanding Prejudice" and
write your answers to the following:*

1. Prejudice is defined as _____

_____

2. A stereotype is _____

_____

_____

3. An in-group is _____

_____

An out-group is _____

_____

4. The out-group homogeneity effect refers to ___

_____

_____

The in-group bias is _____

5. Ethnocentrism is the belief _____

_____

6. The emotional component of prejudice includes
    negative feelings such as _____

_____

Behaviorally, prejudice can result in _____

_____

7. In his classic study on overcoming prejudice,
    psychologist Muzafer Sherif demonstrated that

_____

_____

_____

In the educational system _____

_____

_____

_____

_____

*After you have carefully studied the preceding
sections, complete the following exercises.*

Concept Check 2

*Read the following and write the correct term in the
space provided.*

1. In Zeegland, where Majib grew up, women
    manage all the household finances, make all
    the major decisions regarding the family, and
    earn most of the family income. The men, on
    the other hand, tend to spend their time
    "hanging out" and trying to impress each other
    with the way they dress. Majib's belief that all
    women are naturally more assertive and domi-
    neering than men reflects her
    _____ about gender.

2. In a discussion about gun control laws,
    Jerrilee said, "In my opinion, easy access to
    guns is the major contributing factor to the
    high homicide rate in the United States." This
    statement reflects the _____ com-
    ponent of Jerrilee's attitude about gun control.

3. At lunch one day, a group of fine arts majors happened to sit next to a group of engineering students. During a discussion after lunch, one of the fine arts students remarked, "Boy, those engineering students are all alike. They are so loud, pushy, and aggressive, and, unlike us, they haven't got a scrap of creativity among them!" This statement reflects the

_____

effect.

4. During a sociology class, the instructor mentioned that the Heckawe tribe considers chopped-up earthworms, sheep's eyeballs, water buffalo testicles, and live caterpillars to be delicacies. Later, while having a hamburger and fries for lunch, a student remarked that the Heckawe diet was disgusting and repulsive. Another suggested that the tribe would someday become civilized and maybe even start eating good food "just like us." These remarks illustrate a form of in-group bias called

_____ .

5. When Sylvester decided to buy the very expensive Z5000 Spartan computer, he was happy with all the features of this model but was also very concerned about the cost. However, after talking with many enthusiastic Z5000 Spartan owners, he is now convinced that he made the right decision. It is very likely that Sylvester experienced _____ when he purchased his PC, and his subsequent behavior was an attempt to _____ this unpleasant state of psychological tension.

6. Miss Graham's elementary class is made up of students from a variety of backgrounds and cultures. In order to increase cooperation and decrease negative stereotypes and intergroup hostility, Miss Graham has students cooperate in small ethnically diverse groups in which each individual has responsibility for one aspect of the overall project. This is called the

_____ .

7. Dr. Gandham believes that stereotypes are closely related to the tendency, in person perception, to view others in terms of two very basic social categories, "us" and "them," referred to as the _____ and the _____ .

8. In a class discussion, Klarissa points out that negative attitudes toward people who belong to a specific group are ultimately based on the exaggerated notion that members of other social groups are very different from members of our own social group. Klarissa is discussing the topic of _____ .

9. In response to Klarissa's comment, Selena suggests that certain groups *are* different from others. She notes that Italians are emotional and passionate, the English are cold and aloof, the Japanese are inscrutable, and the Scots are hairy and argumentative. These comments indicate that Selena is engaging in the process of _____ these particular groups.

Graphic Organizer 2

The following statements reflect attitudes about certain topics. Decide which component—cognitive, affective, or behavioral— is represented by each statement.

Statement	Component
1. I believe that the automobile is the single most destructive element on this planet.	
2. I consistently recycle paper, plastic, soda cans, glass, and other waste.	
3. I vote for antigun control advocates and give them my full support.	
4. I get really angry when I see people carelessly throwing their litter on the ground.	
5. I don't want to contribute to the pollution of our city, so I ride my bicycle or take public transportation.	
6. I am very happy when I see women doing well in what used to be male-dominated occupations.	
7. In my opinion, a woman's place is in the home, raising the kids and doing housework.	
8. I get really upset when motorists are rude and inconsiderate.	
9. I believe that the automobile is the greatest invention ever and that we need to elect politicians who will promise to build more roads and freeways.	

Review of Terms, Concepts, and Names 2

Use the terms in this list to complete the Matching Test, then to help you answer the True/False items correctly.

attitude
cognitive component
affective component
behavioral component
Philip Zimbardo
cognitive dissonance
prejudice
stereotype
in-group
out-group

out-group homogeneity
    effect
heterogeneous
in-group bias
ethnocentrism
discrimination
Muzafer Sherif
jigsaw classroom
    technique

Matching Exercise

Match the appropriate term/name with its definition or description.

1. _____ American social psychologist who is best known for his "Robbers Cave" experiments to study prejudice, conflict resolution, and group processes.

2. _____ The belief that one's own culture or ethnic group is superior to all others and the related tendency to use one's own culture as a standard by which to judge other cultures.

3. _____ Learned tendency to evaluate some object, person, or issue in a particular way; such evaluations may be positive, negative, or ambivalent.

4. _____ A social group to which one belongs.

5. _____ Unpleasant state of psychological tension or arousal that occurs when two thoughts or perceptions are inconsistent; typically results from awareness that attitudes and behavior are in conflict.

6. _____ A social group to which one does not belong.

7. _____ Component of an attitude that involves thoughts, ideas, and conclusions about a given topic or object.

8. _____ Cluster of characteristics that are associated with all members of a specific social group, often including qualities that are unrelated to the objective criteria that define the group.

9. _____ American social psychologist who is known for his research on cognitive dissonance and social influence, and especially for the Stanford Prison Experiment, which demonstrated how situational factors can impact human behavior.

True/False Test

Indicate whether each statement is true or false by placing T or F in the blank space next to each item.

1. ____ Prejudice is a negative attitude toward people who belong to a specific social group.

2. ____ When prejudice is displayed behaviorally, it is called discrimination.

3. ____ The out-group homogeneity effect refers to the tendency to judge the behavior of in-group members favorably and out-group members unfavorably.

4. ____ The jigsaw classroom technique is a teaching technique that stresses cooperative, rather than competitive, learning situations.

5. ____ The in-group bias refers to the tendency to see members of out-groups as very similar to one another.

6. ____ The affective component of an attitude is reflected in the feelings that people have about a given event, object, or topic.

7. ____ Members of an in-group typically see themselves as being quite varied, or *heterogeneous*.

8. ____ The behavioral component of an attitude is reflected in people's actions.

Check your answers and review any areas of weakness before going on to the next section.

Conformity: Following the Crowd

Preview Questions

Consider the following questions as you study this section of the chapter.

- What is social influence, and how is *conformity* defined?

- Which psychologist first studied conformity, and what did he find?

- Why do people conform, and what factors influence the degree to which people conform?

- How does culture affect conformity?

Read the section "Conformity: Following the Crowd" and **write** *your answers to the following:*

1. Social influence is _____
   _____
   _____

2. Conformity is the tendency to _____
   _____
   _____

3. In studying the degree to which people would conform to the group even when the group opinion was clearly wrong, Asch found that _____
   _____
   _____

4. We conform to the larger group for two basic reasons:
   (a) _____
   _____
   (b) _____
   _____

5. In a cross-cultural meta-analysis, British psychologists found that _____
   _____
   _____

Obedience: Just Following Orders

Preview Questions

Consider the following questions as you study this section of the chapter.

- How is *obedience* defined?
- What was the basic procedure in Milgram's original obedience experiment, and what were the results?
- What aspects of the experimental situation increased the likelihood of obedience?
- What factors did Milgram later discover that decreased the level of obedience?

Read the section "Obedience: Just Following Orders" and **write** *your answers to the following:*

1. Obedience is defined as _____

_____

2. The basic design of Milgram's obedience experiment was as follows: _____

_____

_____

_____

3. In contrast to predictions, the results of Milgram's original experiment showed that

_____

_____

4. Aspects of the experimental situation that had a strong impact on the subjects' willingness to continue obeying the experimenter's orders were as follows: _____

_____

_____

_____

_____

_____

5. Some of the situational factors that made people less willing to obey were_____

_____

_____

_____

_____

Helping Behavior: Coming to the Aid of Strangers

Preview Questions

Consider the following questions as you study this section of the chapter.

- What is altruism, and how does it differ from prosocial behavior?
- What factors increase or decrease the likelihood that people will help a stranger?
- What is the bystander effect, and what causes it?
- What factors decrease the likelihood that people will help a stranger?

Read the section "Helping Behavior: Coming to the Aid of Strangers" and **write** *your answers to the following:*

1. Altruism is _____

_____

_____

whereas prosocial behavior is _____

_____

_____

2. According to Latané and Darley's general model, six factors increase the likelihood of bystander intervention:

(a) _____

_____

(b) _____

_____

(c) _____

_____

(d) _____

_____

(e) _____

_____

(f) _____

3. The bystander effect refers to _____

_____

_____

4. There are two reasons for the bystander effect:

(a) _____

_____

_____

(b) _____

_____

_____

5. Other factors that decrease the likelihood of helping behavior are

(a) _____

_____

(b) _____

_____

(c) _____

_____

The Influence of Groups on Individual Behavior

Preview Questions

Consider the following questions as you study this section of the chapter.

- What is social loafing, and what factors reduce or eliminate it?
- What is social striving, and how is it affected by cultural factors?
- What are social facilitation and deindividuation?

*Read the section "The Influence of Groups on Individual Behavior" and **write** your answers to the following:*

1. Social loafing is _____

_____

Social loafing is reduced or eliminated when

_____

_____

_____

2. Social striving is_____

_____

_____

Cross-cultural psychologists have found that social striving is very common

_____

_____

_____

3. Social facilitation is _____

_____

_____

4. Deindividuation refers to _____

_____

_____

_____

After you have carefully studied the preceding sections, complete the following exercises.

Concept Check 3

1. Trent hates to wear ties but wears one to his sister's wedding to avoid the disapproval of his family. Trent's behavior illustrates the importance of _____ social influence.

2. Harold is a subject in a replication of Milgram's obedience experiment. If he is like most of the subjects in the experiment, he _____ (will/will not) administer high levels of shock to the learner.

3. If Harold was allowed to act as his own authority and freely choose the shock level, it is very _____ (likely/unlikely) that he will use a shock over 150 volts, the first point at which the learner is likely to protest.

4. At the end of a music concert featuring his *favorite* group, Jason joined everyone else in giving the group a standing ovation. Jason's behavior _____ (is/is not) an example of conformity.

5. Carmichael was elated when he won $1,000 in the lottery. Later that day, he gladly volunteered to spend a few hours over the weekend to help collect food for the local food bank. This illustrates the "_____" effect.

6. While about 20 people were filling out a questionnaire in a classroom, an odorless vapor started seeping into the room from one of the heating vents. The room slowly began to fill with the vapor, yet none of them stopped what they were doing, and no one went to report the incident. This bystander effect occurred because the presence of other people creates a(n)

_____ .

7. Leonarda volunteers for the crisis line at her university because she believes that not only is the work experience valuable but it will also look good on her application to graduate school. Leonarda's volunteer work would be considered an example of _____ .

8. When Jaffar, the student representative, attended the first meeting of the College Education Committee, a vote was taken on an agenda item that he knew little about. Jaffar voted for the motion because he assumed that the rest of the committee members, who voted in favor of the motion, must have accurate information about the proposal. Jaffar's conformity in this case was the result of

_____ .

9. Bryan is short of cash and needs about another $20 for an evening out with his girlfriend. He asks his friend Jared if he can borrow $150; before Jared can say no, Bryan appears to back off and makes a much smaller request—to borrow $20. Jared says, "OK, I can't lend you $150, but I guess I can cough up $20." Bryan has cleverly utilized a strategy called the

_____

technique, which is based on the rule of

_____ .

10. Kaila read about Zimbardo's controversial Stanford Prison Experiment and was surprised at how quickly the participants adopted their randomly assigned roles as either guards or prisoners. She realized that when people are not certain about what to do, they tend to rely on cues provided by others and conform their behavior to those in their immediate social group, showing that implied _____ can be just as powerful as explicit orders.

11. When practicing for an upcoming bike race, Vernice's best time was 47 minutes and 12 seconds. In the actual race, her time improved by almost 3 minutes. Vernice's improvement in front of an audience may be the result of

_____ .

12. In a social psychology experiment, U.S. college students pulled less hard on a rope if they believed others were pulling on the same rope. They pulled harder if they thought they were pulling alone. This example illustrates the phenomenon of _____ .
In a replication of this experiment in a collectivistic culture, the reverse pattern, called

_____ , was observed.

13. Keith and his friends, who are normally law-abiding teenagers, put on masks and costumes on Halloween and smashed a number of pumpkins in the neighborhood. Social psychologists suggest that acts of vandalism such as this may be the result of _____ .

Graphic Organizer 3

Describe the main research findings of the following social psychologists. (For example, Zimbardo's grasshopper study showed how behavior can change attitude through the process of cognitive dissonance.)

Researcher	Main Research Findings
1. Asch	
2. Sherif	
3. Milgram	
4. Latané and Darley	

Review of Terms, Concepts, and Names 3

Use the terms in this list to complete the Matching Test, then to help you answer the True/False items correctly.

conformity
Solomon Asch
normative social
  influence
informational social
  influence
Stanley Milgram
obedience
Bibb Latané and
  John M. Darley
altruism

prosocial behavior
"feel good, do good"
  effect
bystander effect
diffusion of
  responsibility
social loafing
social striving
social facilitation
deindividuation
persuasion

Matching Exercise

Match the appropriate term/name with its definition or description.

1. _____ American social psychologist who is best known for his controversial investigation of destructive obedience to an authority figure.

2. _____ The tendency to adjust one's behavior, attitudes, or beliefs to group norms in response to real or imagined group pressure.

3. _____ Contemporary American social psychologists who are best known for their pioneering studies of bystander intervention in emergency situations.

4. _____ Performance of an action in response to the direct orders of an authority or person of higher status.

5. _____ American social psychologist who is best known for his pioneering studies of conformity.

6. _____ Helping another person with no expectation of personal reward or benefit.

7. _____ Any behavior that helps another, whether the underlying motive is self-serving or selfless.

8. _____ The reduction of self-awareness and inhibitions that can occur when a person is part of a group whose members feel anonymous.

9. _____ The tendency of the presence of other people to enhance individual performance.

True/False Test

Indicate whether each item is true or false by placing T or F in the space next to each item.

1. ____ Persuasion is the deliberate attempt to influence the attitudes or behavior of another person in a situation in which that person has some freedom of choice.

2. ____ The bystander effect refers to a phenomenon in which the greater the number of people present, the less likely each individual is to help someone in distress.

3. ____ A phenomenon in which the presence of other people makes it less likely that any individual will help someone in distress because the obligation to intervene is shared among all the onlookers is called diffusion of responsibility.

4. ____ Source of behavior that is motivated by the desire to gain social acceptance and approval is called informational social influence.

5. ____ The "feel good, do good" effect refers to the fact that when people feel good, successful, happy, or fortunate, they are more likely to help others.

6. ____ Source of behavior that is motivated by the desire to be correct is called normative social influence.

7. ____ Social striving refers to the tendency to expend less effort on a task when it is a group effort.

8. ____ The tendency, especially in collectivistic cultures, of individuals to work harder when they are in a group than when they are working alone is called social loafing.

Check your answers and review any areas of weakness before going on to the next section.

Something to Think About

1. People often ask, "Why are so many people reluctant to help others who are in distress and need help?" The most usual responses are that people suffer from apathy and that big cities alienate and depersonalize people. What would you say if someone asked you that question?

2. We are subjected to a wide variety of situations and stimuli that are designed to influence our attitudes or behavior. The most obvious of these are media advertisements, but we regularly encounter many other more subtle sources of attempted influence. These attempts to influence us all use techniques of persuasion. Imagine that you are hired by a company, and management wants you to write a brief summary of the factors that are most powerful in changing people's attitudes or behaviors. What would you put in your report?

Check your answers and review any areas of weakness before completing the progress tests.

Progress Test 1

Review the complete chapter (including all boxed inserts), review all your study notes, and then test yourself on the following progress test. Check your answers. If you make a mistake, review your notes, check the appropriate section in the study guide, and if necessary, go back and read the relevant part of the chapter in your textbook.

1. Dr. Lopez is a social psychologist who studies the mental processes people use to make sense of their social environment, including person perception, attribution, attitudes, and prejudice. His specific area of research is called

   (a) social cognition.
   (b) perception.
   (c) social influence.
   (d) personality.

2. About a dozen students were sitting in a small research laboratory room filling out a questionnaire when they heard a crash followed by groaning from the room next door. While many of them appeared to notice, nobody went to inform the researcher, who said he would be in his office just down the hall. This example illustrates

   (a) the actor–observer discrepancy.
   (b) diffusion of responsibility.
   (c) obedience.
   (d) informational social influence.

3. Michael, who is an accountant, often wonders why people are surprised when they find out that he is also a skydiving instructor on the weekends. The most obvious explanation is that people form cognitive schemas for different types of people and occupations. The use of these types of assumptions is called

   (a) the fundamental attribution error.
   (b) ethnocentrism.
   (c) implicit personality theory.
   (d) the self-serving bias.

4. In her field research, Dr. Safarian observes that people generally do not sit next to strangers on trains. She also notices a similar pattern in movie theaters, airport lounges, and cafeterias. Dr. Safarian is documenting the effects of _____ on behavior.

   (a) stereotypes
   (b) ethnocentrism
   (c) prejudice
   (d) social norms

5. Sally did very poorly on her last math test. If her fifth-grade teacher concludes that Sally did poorly because she is not motivated to do well in school, the teacher may be committing the

   (a) fundamental attribution error.
   (b) actor–observer discrepancy.
   (c) self-serving bias.
   (d) social categorization error.

6. When Allison landed a big contract for her firm, she accepted the credit for her hard work and smart "wheeling and dealing." When she failed to get the contract in another situation, she blamed the sneaky and dishonest tactics of the competition. This illustrates

   (a) informational social influence.
   (b) the self-serving bias.
   (c) the self-effacing bias.
   (d) the actor–observer discrepancy.

7. During a discussion on fast food and fast-food outlets, Reginald stated, "Fast food is great. I just love southern fried chicken, fries, coleslaw, and milkshakes." This statement represents the _____ component of Reginald's positive attitude toward fast-food restaurants.

   (a) cognitive   (c) behavioral
   (b) affective   (d) ambivalent

8. When Jill tried on the very fashionable but expensive coat, she thought it looked great on her. However, she initially felt guilty about buying the coat because she couldn't really afford it. Later that night she rationalized her decision by saying that the coat was one of a kind, and, considering how lovely it looked on her, it was surely quite a bargain. This example illustrates

   (a) diffusion of responsibility.
   (b) conformity.
   (c) prejudice.
   (d) cognitive dissonance.

9. One of Manfred's college classmates was from Turkey, and he loved turkey sandwiches, turkey pizza, turkey burgers, and turkey sausages. Manfred now believes that all people from Turkey eat mostly foods made from turkey meat, and so he has little doubt why the country is called Turkey. Manfred's beliefs about the culture of Turkey reflect

   (a) ethnic stereotyping.
   (b) ethnocentrism.
   (c) informational social influence.
   (d) in-group bias.

10. Jackson joined the Alpine cross-country ski club because he couldn't afford the cost of downhill skiing. Many members of his club think that downhill skiing is destroying the natural environment, and they often make derogatory remarks about downhillers. Since joining the club, Jackson has changed his attitude about downhill skiing; he now promotes the benefits of cross-country skiing and joins his new buddies in categorizing all downhill skiers as self-centered, uncaring destroyers of the environment. This example illustrates

    (a) the out-group homogeneity effect.
    (b) in-group bias.
    (c) stereotyping.
    (d) all of these effects.

11. Greg, who is a new faculty member, is on a college committee concerned with student evaluation. Greg disagrees with the proposal to institute a collegewide percentage system for grading. The other five members have already stated that they are in favor of the proposal. Greg decides that it would be in his best interests to go along with his colleagues and not risk antagonizing them, so he votes in favor of the proposed policy. This example best illustrates
    (a) obedience.
    (b) informational social influence.
    (c) in-group bias.
    (d) normative social influence.

12. All the members of the MacGregor household are enthusiastic supporters of the new community recycling program. They consistently sort their garbage by placing paper, plastic, glass, and aluminum in their respective bins. The actions of the MacGregors best illustrate the _____ component of attitudes.
    (a) emotional   (c) biological
    (b) behavioral   (d) cognitive

13. Just moments after dozens of people get off a crowded bus, a badly dressed man stumbles and falls on the sidewalk near the bus stop. Research on bystander intervention would suggest that
    (a) he will get immediate help from many people.
    (b) the presence of others will decrease the diffusion of responsibility.
    (c) if one person stops to help him, other people are likely to help as well.
    (d) no one in the crowd will perceive that he may need help.

14. According to Critical Thinking (Abuse at Abu Ghraib), which of the following factors contributed to the events that occurred at Abu Ghraib prison?
    (a) prejudice
    (b) negative stereotypes
    (c) dehumanization
    (d) in-group versus out-group thinking
    (e) all of these factors

15. According to the Application, which of the following is correct?
    (a) Persuasion refers to the deliberate attempt to influence the attitudes or behaviors of another person in a situation in which the person has some freedom of choice.

(b) Persuasion techniques are not effective in manipulating people in any way.
(c) Professional persuaders can easily manipulate and change the attitudes and behaviors of the vast majority of people.
(d) Because of the flexible nature of social norms, the vast majority of people can resist conforming to any societal standards.

Progress Test 2

After you have checked your understanding of the material in Progress Test 1 and have done a complete chapter review with special focus on any areas of weakness, you are ready to assess your knowledge on Progress Test 2. Check your answers. If you make a mistake, review your notes, the relevant section of the study guide, and, if necessary, the appropriate part of your textbook.

1. Jake lost his job two months ago when his company downsized its operations. Despite his efforts, he has not yet found another job. One of his neighbors stated that Jake is just like most unemployed people—irresponsible, unmotivated, and basically lazy. The neighbor has committed the
    (a) self-serving bias.
    (b) actor–observer discrepancy.
    (c) social categorization error.
    (d) fundamental attribution error.

2. When their town was threatened by a flood, two families who had been enemies for years ended up working together to try to save the town from the overflowing river. Generalizing from Sherif's findings, you might conclude that this act of cooperative behavior may lead to
    (a) increased antagonism once the danger has passed.
    (b) an increase in cognitive dissonance.
    (c) reduced conflict and increased harmony between the two families.
    (d) diffusion of responsibility.

3. Liliana thinks that people her parents' age are old-fashioned, critical, intolerant, and unconcerned about important social issues. Liliana is assuming that people in a particular age category have certain characteristics, even though these qualities may be unrelated to the objective criteria that define this particular age group. This example illustrates
   (a) the just-world hypothesis.
   (b) stereotyping.
   (c) ethnocentrism.
   (d) the self-effacing (modesty) bias.

4. When Rachel found out that she had straight As in all her courses, she was elated. Later that day, when she was asked if she could donate some money to the restore-the-church fund, she readily made a donation, even though she is not religious and does not go to church. This illustrates
   (a) cognitive dissonance.
   (b) the "feel good, do good" effect.
   (c) conformity.
   (d) informational social influence.

5. When young Tia saw the movie *Snow White,* she thought that Snow White was very pretty and sweet and that her evil stepmother was ugly and cruel. Tia's beliefs about the characters in the movie represent _____ called _____ .
   (a) a form of social categorization; the self-serving bias
   (b) a type of fundamental attribution error; blaming the victim
   (c) an implicit personality theory; the "what is beautiful is good" myth
   (d) a form of person perception; the actor–observer discrepancy

6. When Inge was first elected to the student finance committee, she was asked to make a decision on an important but unfamiliar financial matter. All the other members of the committee stated that they were going to vote against the proposal. Inge voted with the group because she assumed that they must have the correct information. This example illustrates
   (a) the bystander effect.
   (b) normative social influence.
   (c) informational social influence.
   (d) diffusion of responsibility.

7. Martha is participating in a replication of Milgram's original obedience experiment that involves female subjects only. Compared with a similar study involving only male subjects,
   (a) at least 60 percent of the females will refuse to continue with the experiment at the 300-volt level.
   (b) a much higher percentage of the females will obey the experimenter and progress to the 450-volt level.
   (c) only about 10 percent of the female subjects will obey the experimenter and progress to the 450-volt level.
   (d) the results of the all-female replication will be the same as the all-male condition.

8. Wolfgang's best typing speed was 80 words a minute while practicing alone. However, in a speed-typing competition with 10 other people he improved his speed to 90 words a minute. Wolfgang's improved performance in the presence of others reflects
   (a) social striving.
   (b) normative social influence.
   (c) social facilitation.
   (d) the bystander effect.

9. In preparing a term paper on conformity and obedience, Quincy has reviewed all the relevant literature. He is most likely to conclude that
   (a) virtually nobody is capable of resisting group or authority pressure.
   (b) all people are innately predisposed to be cruel and aggressive.
   (c) conformity and obedience are not necessarily bad in and of themselves and are important for an orderly society.
   (d) all of these statements are true.

10. Jorge thought that either horse, Con Brio or White Lightning, had an equal chance of winning the next race and was debating which one to bet on. After he placed his money on Con Brio, however, he felt very confident that he had backed the winner. This example illustrates the effect of
   (a) cognitive dissonance.
   (b) the self-serving bias.
   (c) conformity.
   (d) social influence.

11. Jenny's score on her biology midterm exam was 90 percent, Jean's was 60 percent, and Jackie's was 75 percent. On the basis of these scores, Jackie thinks to herself that Jenny must be really intelligent and that Jean must be a little slow. Which of the following is true?

(a) Jackie has made an attribution.
(b) Jackie's assessment of her classmates' intelligence is accurate.
(c) Jackie's evaluation reflects the in-group bias.
(d) Jackie's assessment of her classmates' intelligence reflects her prejudice.

12. During a discussion about gun-control laws, Marylou said, "I believe it is every American's fundamental right to own a gun and that the government has no right to pass laws banning the ownership of guns under any circumstances." This statement reflects the _____ component of Marylou's attitude about guns and gun-control laws.

(a) cognitive   (c) behavioral
(b) affective   (d) dissonant

13. As part of a social psychology experiment, a group of male college students are asked to wear masks and clothes that hide their identities. Compared to a similar group wearing name tags and no masks, the anonymous group demonstrated more aggression. This example illustrates

(a) social facilitation.
(b) social striving.
(c) the rule of reciprocity.
(d) deindividuation.

14. Yoko was late for work because the traffic was particularly heavy. When she arrived at the office, she apologized to her boss, insisting that it was her fault for being late; if she were less lazy, it wouldn't have happened. According to Culture and Human Behavior (Explaining Failure and Murder), blaming an accidental occurrence on an internal, personal disposition rather than on situational factors is called the

(a) self-serving bias.
(b) self-effacing bias (modesty bias).
(c) actor–observer discrepancy.
(d) fundamental attribution error.

15. A number of persuasion techniques are used by professional marketers. According to the Application, which of the following is NOT one of those techniques?

(a) the door-in-the-face technique
(b) the that's-not-all technique
(c) the foot-in-the-mouth technique
(d) the low-ball technique
(e) the foot-in-the-door technique

Progress Test 3

After you have checked your understanding of the material in Progress Tests 1 and 2, and have done a complete chapter review with special focus on any areas of weakness, you are ready to further assess your knowledge with Progress Test 3. Check your answers. If you make a mistake, review your notes, the appropriate parts of the study guide, and, if necessary, the relevant sections of your textbook.

1. Dr. Saroya is a social psychologist whose research interests focus on how our behavior is affected by situational factors and other people, and in particular why we conform to group norms and why we help or don't help strangers. The basic area of social psychology that Dr. Saroya studies is called

(a) social cognition.
(b) social perception.
(c) social influence.
(d) social categorization.

2. When Ruby stepped into the subway car, she quickly looked around and decided it would be safer to sit next to the middle-aged, well-dressed woman than the man with bright orange hair and earrings. Ruby has engaged in the process of

(a) blaming the victim.
(b) person perception.
(c) ethnocentrism.
(d) cognitive dissonance.

3. When Mr. Denbridge was asked to donate to a fund to help people infected with hepatitis B and the HIV virus, he responded that he would not help these people because they caused their own misfortunes. It appears that Mr. Denbridge is

(a) blaming the victim.
(b) demonstrating the out-group homogeneity effect.
(c) responding to normative social influence.
(d) reducing his cognitive dissonance.

4. During a tour of a Latin American country, Susanne was surprised to find that almost everyone took a three-hour break in the middle of the day. She concluded that, compared with the United States, this country was not doing well economically because everyone was lazy, lacked motivation, and spent too much time sleeping. Susanne's conclusion reflects a form of in-group bias called

(a) ethnocentrism.
(b) the self-effacing bias.
(c) the self-serving bias.
(d) the actor–observer discrepancy.

5. In her fifth grade class, Miss Tausig uses a technique for improving cooperation that involves students working together in small, ethnically diverse groups on a mutual project. Miss Tausig is using the

(a) out-group homogeneity procedure.
(b) jigsaw classroom technique.
(c) normative social influence technique.
(d) actor–observer discrepancy technique.

6. Rita volunteers three or four evenings a week at a local shelter for the homeless because she believes in helping those less fortunate than herself. Richard also volunteers at the shelter because he believes the work experience will increase his chances of getting accepted in the master's degree program in social work. In this situation, Rita's motivation is guided by _____ and Richard's motivation reflects _____ .

(a) prosocial behavior; altruism
(b) normative social influence; informational social influence
(c) altruism; prosocial behavior
(d) informational social influence; normative social influence

7. Kyle is in sixth grade and, like most children in his school, believes that his school is better than all the other schools in town. This best illustrates

(a) in-group bias.
(b) ethnic stereotyping.
(c) cognitive dissonance.
(d) the fundamental attribution error.

8. Seeing a skier wipe out on a steep section of the run, Jenny comments, "A klutz like that shouldn't be allowed on the slopes!" Later, when Jenny wipes out in the same place, she blames the icy conditions. This is an example of

(a) the self-serving bias.
(b) the actor–observer discrepancy.
(c) social categorization.
(d) stereotyping.

9. Pietro notices that when there are empty seats on the bus, nobody ever sits beside a stranger; however, when the bus is crowded, people sit beside strangers all the time. He noticed that the same thing happens in movie theaters, the cafeteria, and even the classroom. Pietro's observation suggests that people's behavior in these situations is governed by

(a) prejudice.   (c) stereotypes.
(b) social categorization. (d) social norms.

10. Fraser loves wearing sandals or thongs and hates wearing shoes. However, when he went out to dinner with his girlfriend's family, he wore shoes because he did not want to evoke their disapproval. Fraser's behavior best illustrates the importance of

(a) informational social influence.
(b) normative social influence.
(c) diffusion of responsibility.
(d) obedience.

11. Lyle is studying alone late Friday night in the almost deserted library. His concentration is interrupted when he notices another student nearby slumped over his desk, making sounds that suggest he might be in pain. In this situation, it is very likely that Lyle will engage in _____ , because he is not constrained by _____ .

(a) prosocial behavior; the bystander effect
(b) social categorization; social norms
(c) blaming the victim; diffusion of responsibility
(d) altruism; self-serving bias

12. When Maryjane steps into the elevator, she quickly looks at the other passengers and decides that the gray-haired man with the beard must be a professor at the college. Maryjane has engaged in the process of

(a) prejudicial thinking.
(b) discrimination.
(c) social categorization.
(d) ethnocentrism.

13. During cross-examination, a witness repeatedly offers his opinion in answer to the lawyer's questions, so the judge orders him to confine his answers to a simple "yes" or "no." Following the judge's rebuke, the witness stops offering his opinions. This example best illustrates
    (a) obedience.
    (c) persuasion.
    (b) conformity.
    (d) prejudice.

14. According to Critical Thinking (Abuse at Abu Ghraib), the events of Abu Ghraib prison have the most parallels and similarities to two famous social psychology studies: _____ and _____ .
    (a) Latané and Darley's bystander studies; Asch's conformity research
    (b) Sherif's Robbers Cave prejudice experiments; Cialdini's persuasion studies
    (c) Lerner's just-world hypothesis research; Festinger's cognitive dissonance research
    (d) Milgram's obedience studies; Zimbardo's Stanford Prison Experiment

15. In the run-up to a fiercely contested local election, Birkley believes she can win if she can only get enough people to display her large poster on their front lawns. First, her supporters ask homeowners if they would be willing to put a very small poster in their window. Later, when they asked these same people if they could put a large poster on their front lawn, most agreed to the request. According to the Application, Birkley is using a technique called the _____ , which capitalizes on a powerful social norm, the _____ .
    (a) door-in-the-face technique; rule of reciprocity
    (b) foot-in-the-door-technique; rule of commitment
    (c) low-ball technique; rule of reciprocity
    (d) foot-in-the-mouth technique; rule of commitment

Answers

Introduction: What Is Social Psychology?

1. *Social psychology is* the branch of psychology that studies how people think, feel, and behave in social situations.

2. *Social cognition refers to* the mental processes people use to make sense out of their social environment.

3. *Social influence focuses on* the effects of situational factors and other people on an individual's social behavior.

Person Perception: Forming Impressions of Other People

1. *Person perception refers to* the mental processes we use to form judgments and draw conclusions about the characteristics and motives of others; it is an active and subjective process that always occurs in some interpersonal context.

2. *The four basic principles of person perception are (a)* Your reactions to others are determined by your perceptions of them, not by who or what they really are. *(b)* Your goals in a particular situation determine the amount and kind of information you collect about others. *(c)* In every situation, how you expect people to act in that situation partly determines how you evaluate them (you make reference to the social norms for the appropriate behavior in a particular social situation). *(d)* Your self-perception also influences how you perceive others and how you act on your perceptions.

3. *In combination, these four basic principles underscore that person perception is* not a one-way process in which we objectively survey other people, then logically evaluate their characteristics. Instead, the context, our self-perceptions, and the perception we have of others all interact.

4. *Social categorization is* the mental process of classifying people into groups (or social categories) on the basis of their shared characteristics. This is mostly automatic and spontaneous and occurs outside conscious awareness. *Its advantages and disadvantages are,* respectively, that it is cognitively efficient, natural, and adaptive, but that it ignores a person's unique qualities.

5. *An implicit personality theory is* a network of assumptions or beliefs about the relationships among various types of people, traits, and behaviors. *Like social categories, implicit personality theories are useful* as mental shortcuts in perceiving other people; however, they are not always accurate and in some instances can be dangerously misleading.

6. *Physical attractiveness is correlated with* being more popular, less lonely, and less anxious in social situations. *It is not correlated with* intelligence, mental health, or self-esteem.

Neuroscientists have shown that when people make direct eye contact with a physically attractive person, a brain area that predicts rewards (the ventral striatum) is activated; when the attractive person's gaze is averted away from the viewer, activity in this brain area decreases.

Attribution: Explaining Behavior

1. *Attribution is* the mental process of inferring the causes of people's behavior, including one's own (also refers to the explanation made for a particular behavior).

2. *The fundamental attribution error is the tendency to* attribute the behavior of others to internal, personal characteristics, while ignoring or underestimating the effects of external, situational factors.

3. *Blaming the victim is the tendency to* blame an innocent victim of misfortune for having somehow caused the problem or for not having taken steps to avoid or prevent it.

4. *The just-world hypothesis is* the assumption that the world is fair and that therefore people get what they deserve and deserve what they get.

5. *The actor–observer discrepancy is the tendency to* attribute one's own behavior to external, situational causes, while attributing the behavior of others to internal, personal causes, especially when the outcome is likely to be negative.

6. *The self-serving bias is the tendency to* attribute successful outcomes of our own behavior to internal causes and unsuccessful outcomes to external, situational causes.

Concept Check 1

1. self-serving bias
2. fundamental attribution error
3. actor–observer discrepancy
4. implicit personality theory
5. social norms
6. blaming the victim; just-world hypothesis
7. more intelligent, happier, better adjusted, and more socially competent
8. become activated; that activity in this area of the brain will decrease
9. not likely

Graphic Organizer 1

1. C; INT for own success; EXT for own failure

2. B; EXT for self; INT for other
3. A; INT for other

Matching Exercise 1

1. social norms
2. attribution
3. self-serving bias
4. social psychology
5. implicit personality theory
6. actor–observer discrepancy
7. blaming the victim
8. just-world hypothesis

True/False Test 1

1. F	3. T	5. F	7. T
2. T	4. T	6. T	8. T

The Social Psychology of Attitudes

1. *An attitude is defined as* a learned tendency to evaluate some object, person, or issue in a particular way; such evaluations may be positive, negative, or ambivalent.

2. *The three components of an attitude are (a)* cognitive (your thoughts and conclusions about the attitude object); *(b)* affective (your feelings or emotions about the object of your attitude); and *(c)* behavioral (your attitude is reflected in your actions).

3. *You are most likely to behave in accordance with your attitudes in any of five conditions: (a)* your attitudes are extreme or are frequently expressed; *(b)* your attitudes have been formed through direct experience; *(c)* you are very knowledgeable about the subject; *(d)* you have a vested interest in the subject; and *(e)* you anticipate a favorable outcome or response from others.

4. *Cognitive dissonance is* an unpleasant state of psychological tension or arousal (dissonance) that occurs when two thoughts or perceptions (cognitions) are inconsistent. *It commonly occurs in situations in which* you become uncomfortably aware that your behavior and your attitudes conflict with each other. If you can easily change your behavior to make it consistent with your attitude, then any dissonance can be quickly and easily resolved. When your behavior cannot be easily changed, you will tend to change your attitude to make it consistent with your behavior.

5. *Cognitive dissonance can also change* the strength of an attitude so that it is consistent with some behavior you've already performed.

6. *Cognitive dissonance also operates when you have to choose* between two basically equal alternatives; each choice has desirable and undesirable features, creating dissonance. Once a choice is made, however, attitudes are brought more closely in line with the commitment made, which reduces the dissonance. The negative features of the rejected option are emphasized ("sour grapes" rationalization), and the positive features of the chosen option are seen more favorably ("sweet lemons" rationalization).

Understanding Prejudice

1. *Prejudice is defined as* a negative attitude toward people who belong to a specific social group.

2. *A stereotype is* a cluster of characteristics that are associated with all members of a specific social group, often including qualities that are unrelated to the objective criteria that define the group.

3. *An in-group is* a social group to which one belongs. *An out-group is* a social group to which one does not belong.

4. *The out-group homogeneity effect refers to* the tendency to see members of out-groups as very similar to one another. *The in-group bias is* the tendency to judge the behavior of in-group members favorably and out-group members unfavorably.

5. *Ethnocentrism is the belief* that one's own culture or ethnic group is superior to all others and the related tendency to use one's own culture as a standard by which to judge other cultures.

6. *The emotional component of prejudice includes negative feelings such as* hatred, contempt, fear, and loathing. *Behaviorally, prejudice can result in* discrimination.

7. *In his classic study on overcoming prejudice, psychologist Muzafer Sherif demonstrated that* prejudice can be overcome when rival groups cooperate to achieve a common goal. *In the educational system,* cooperative learning, as used in the jigsaw classroom technique, is one way of reducing prejudice in the classroom.

Concept Check 2

1. stereotype
2. cognitive
3. out-group homogeneity
4. ethnocentrism
5. cognitive dissonance; reduce
6. jigsaw classroom technique
7. in-group; out-group
8. prejudice
9. stereotyping

Graphic Organizer 2

1. cognitive
2. behavioral
3. behavioral
4. affective
5. behavioral
6. affective
7. cognitive
8. affective
9. cognitive

Matching Exercise 2

1. Muzafer Sherif
2. ethnocentrism
3. attitude
4. in-group
5. cognitive dissonance
6. out-group
7. cognitive component
8. stereotype
9. Philip Zimbardo

True/False Test 2

1. T	3. F	5. F	7. T
2. T	4. T	6. T	8. T

Conformity: Following the Crowd

1. *Social influence is* the psychological study of the effects of situational factors and other people on an individual's behavior.

2. *Conformity is the tendency to* adjust one's behavior, attitudes, or beliefs to group norms in response to real or imagined group pressure.

3. *In studying the degree to which people would conform to the group even when the group opinion was clearly wrong, Asch found that* the vast majority conformed with the group judgment on at least one of the critical trials in the line judgment task.

4. *We conform to the larger group for two basic reasons: (a)* normative social influence (we want to be liked and accepted by the group); *(b)* informational social influence (we want to be right; when we're uncertain or doubt our own judgment, we may look to the group as a source of accurate information).

5. *In a cross-cultural meta-analysis, British psychologists found that* conformity is generally higher in collectivistic cultures than in individualistic cultures.

Obedience: Just Following Orders

1. *Obedience is defined as* the performance of an action in response to the direct orders of an authority or person of higher status.

2. *The basic design of Milgram's obedience experiment was as follows:* the subject (the teacher) thought he was delivering ever-increasing levels of electric shock to another person (the learner); if the teacher protested that he wished to stop, he was instructed by the experimenter to continue with the experiment.

3. *In contrast to predictions, the results of Milgram's original experiment showed that* most of the subjects (two-thirds) obeyed the experimenter and progressed to the maximum shock level.

4. *Aspects of the experimental situation that had a strong impact on the subjects' willingness to continue obeying the experimenter's orders were as follows:* the subjects had a previously well-established mental framework to obey; the context or situation influenced them (they believed the experiment would advance scientific knowledge and may have felt that defying the experimenter's orders would make them appear arrogant, rude, disrespectful, or uncooperative); the gradual, repetitive escalation of the task; the experimenter's behavior and reassurances (the experimenter took responsibility for the learner's well-being); and the physical and psychological separation from the learner.

5. *Some of the situational factors that made people less willing to obey were* when the buffers that separated the teacher from the learner were lessened or removed, such as when both of them were put in the same room; when subjects (teachers) were allowed to act as their own authority and freely choose the shock level, 95 percent of them did not go beyond 150 volts; and if the teacher observed two other teachers rebel and refuse to continue, then the obedience rate dropped to 10 percent.

Helping Behavior: Coming to the Aid of Strangers

1. *Altruism is* the act of helping another person with no expectation of personal reward or benefit, *whereas prosocial behavior is* any behavior that helps another person, whether the underlying motive is self-serving or selfless.

2. *According to Latané and Darley's general model, six factors increase the likelihood of bystander intervention: (a)* We tend to be more helpful when we're feeling good, successful, happy, or fortunate (the "feel good, do good" effect). *(b)* We tend to be more helpful when we're feeling guilty, such as after telling a lie or inadvertently causing an accident. *(c)* Seeing others who are willing to help increases the likelihood that we will help. *(d)* We're more likely to help people who are perceived as deserving, such as people who are in need through no fault of their own. *(e)* Knowing how to help contributes greatly to the decision to help someone else. *(f)* Any sort of personal relationship (even the most minimal social interaction, such as making eye contact or engaging in small talk) increases the likelihood that one person will help another.

3. *The bystander effect refers to* a phenomenon in which the greater the number of people present, the less likely each individual is to help someone in distress.

4. *There are two reasons for the bystander effect: (a)* The presence of other people creates a diffusion of responsibility, which means that the responsibility to intervene is shared (or diffused) among the other onlookers (because no one person feels all the pressure to respond, each bystander becomes less likely to help). *(b)* Each of us is motivated to some extent by the desire to behave in a socially acceptable way (normative social influence) and to appear correct (informational social influence), and consequently we often rely on the reactions of

others to help us define the situation and guide our responses.

5. *Other factors that decrease the likelihood of helping behavior are (a)* being in a big city or a very small town (people are less likely to help a stranger in very big cities [300,000 people or more] or in very small towns [5,000 people or less], but you are more likely to get help in towns with populations in between these two extremes); *(b)* when situations are vague or ambiguous and people are not certain that help is needed, such as in domestic disputes or a lovers' quarrel; and, *(c)* as a general rule, we tend to weigh the costs as well as the benefits in deciding whether to help others (when the cost of helping outweighs the benefit, we tend not to help).

The Influence of Groups on Individual Behavior

1. *Social loafing is* the tendency to expend less effort on a task when it is a group effort. *Social loafing is reduced or eliminated when* (a) the group is composed of people who know each other, (b) the members belong to a highly valued group, (c) the task is meaningful or unique, and (d) when the group members are female rather than male.

2. *Social striving is* a pattern where individuals work harder when they are part of a group compared to when they are alone. *Cross-cultural psychologists have found that social striving is very common* in many collectivistic cultures and social loafing is generally absent. Factors that influence this phenomenon are that group success is more highly valued than individual success and social norms in collectivistic cultures encourage a sense of social responsibility and hard work by individuals within groups.

3. *Social facilitation is* the tendency for the presence of other people to enhance individual performance, especially on a task that is relatively simple or well rehearsed.

4. *Deindividuation refers to* the reduction of self-awareness and inhibitions that can occur when a person is part of a group whose members feel anonymous.

Concept Check 3

1. normative

2. will

3. unlikely

4. is not

5. feel good, do good

6. diffusion of responsibility

7. prosocial behavior

8. informational social influence

9. door-in-the-face; reciprocity

10. social norms

11. social facilitation

12. social loafing; social striving

13. deindividuation

Graphic Organizer 3

1. Naive subjects yielded to group pressure in the line-judging task, even though the group opinion was wrong.

2. The Robbers Cave study helped clarify the conditions that produce intergroup conflict and harmony and led to the use of the jigsaw classroom technique to promote cooperative behavior.

3. Dramatic illustration of the pressure to obey an authority figure's request to shock another person in a mock learning experiment.

4. Showed the conditions under which people are more likely to help a stranger in distress as well as the factors that decrease helping behavior.

Matching Exercise 3

1. Stanley Milgram

2. conformity

3. Bibb Latané and John M. Darley

4. obedience

5. Solomon Asch

6. altruism

7. prosocial behavior

8. deindividuation

9. social facilitation

True/False Test 3

1. T	4. F	7. F
2. T	5. T	8. F
3. T	6. F	

Something to Think About

1. Why is it that people do not help others who are in obvious distress? What prevents bystanders from intervening? In some instances, such as in the Kitty Genovese case, people could easily help simply by making a phone call, but often they don't. Latané and Darley have conducted extensive research that addresses the question of why people don't intervene.

   Latané and Darley's final model identifies six specific factors that increase the likelihood that bystanders will help: (1) the "feel good, do good" effect, (2) feeling guilty, (3) seeing others who are willing to help, (4) perceiving others as deserving help, (5) knowing how to help, and (6) a personal relationship with the person who needs help.

   A number of factors decrease the likelihood of bystanders helping: (1) the presence of others, called the *bystander effect,* and the resulting diffusion of responsibility; (2) being in a big city or a very small town; (3) a vague or ambiguous situation; and (4) when the personal costs for helping outweigh the benefits. In a discussion of this issue it is important to be able to explain and give examples of each factor.

2. The summary in the Application (The Persuasion Game) provides the information you need to answer this question. First, define *persuasion,* then paraphrase the main strategies that professional persuaders use to manipulate people's attitudes and behaviors. These include the role of reciprocity, the door-in-the-face technique, the that's-not-all technique, the rule of commitment, the foot-in-the-door technique,

and the low-ball technique. You might also want to integrate material from the chapter, such as the role of cognitive dissonance in changing cognitions and behavior, and various aspects of conformity and obedience research. Finally, you should discuss the ways in which people can defend themselves against professional persuasion techniques—for example, sleeping on it, playing the devil's advocate, and paying attention to gut feelings.

Progress Test 1

1. a	6. b	11. d
2. b	7. b	12. b
3. c	8. d	13. c
4. d	9. a	14. e
5. a	10. d	15. a

Progress Test 2

1. d	6. c	11. a
2. c	7. d	12. a
3. b	8. c	13. d
4. b	9. c	14. b
5. c	10. a	15. c

Progress Test 3

1. c	6. c	11. a
2. b	7. a	12. c
3. a	8. b	13. a
4. a	9. d	14. d
5. b	10. b	15. b

CHAPTER 13

Stress, Health, and Coping

<table>
<tr>
<td>PREVIEW</td>
<td>Reading the section below first will give you a general sense of the chapter's contents and an initial introduction to some of the major concepts and terms. This will prime you for what you are about to read and help you to develop a "cognitive map" that will guide your study of the material in this chapter. Likewise, reading the preview questions at the beginning of each major section will improve your ability to understand, learn, and retain the information.</td>
</tr>
</table>

Chapter 13 . . . AT A GLANCE

Chapter 13 deals with the effects of stress on health and the ways that people cope with stress. Health psychologists, who study stress and other psychological factors that influence health, illness, and treatment, are guided by the biopsychosocial model. The life events approach to stress, first developed in the 1960s, is critically examined. More recently, researchers have focused on the importance of daily hassles, social and cultural factors, and conflict as sources of stress.

The physical effects of stress are discussed. Walter Cannon's fight-or-flight response and Hans Selye's three-stage general adaptation syndrome are described. Ader and Cohen's research on conditioning the immune system, and how this led to the establishment of psychoneuroimmunology, is presented along with research findings on the effects of stress on the immune system.

Psychological factors can also influence our response to stress. People's sense of personal control and their explanatory style—optimistic or pessimistic—are important in determining how a person responds to stress. The text notes that chronic negative emotions are related to the development of some chronic diseases and that the hostility component of the Type A behavior pattern can predict the development of heart disease. The role of social support in how people deal with stressful situations is explored.

The final section covers coping strategies. Depending on the situation, people use problem-focused or emotion-focused coping. Culture affects the choice of coping strategies; individualistic and collectivistic coping strategies are compared and contrasted. The Application offers some important advice for minimizing the effects of stress.

Introduction: What Is Stress?

Preview Questions

Consider the following questions as you study this section of the chapter.

- How is stress defined, and what is the main focus of health psychology?
- What is the biopsychosocial model?

Read the section "Introduction: What Is Stress?" and **write** *your answers to the following:*

1. Stress is defined as _____
   _____
   _____

2. Health psychologists focus on_____
   _____
   _____

3. The biopsychosocial model is _____
   _____
   _____

What Is Stress? Sources of Stress

Preview Questions

Consider the following questions as you study this section of the chapter.

- What are stressors, and what are some of the most important sources of stress?
- What is the life events approach, and what problems are associated with this approach?
- What are daily hassles, and how do they contribute to stress?
- How can social and cultural factors become sources of stress?
- What is conflict, and what are the three basic types of conflict?

Read the section "What Is Stress? Sources of Stress" and **write** *your answers to the following:*

1. Stressors are _____
   _____

2. Early stress researchers Holmes and Rahe
   believed that _____
   _____
   _____

3. Several problems with the life events approach have been pointed out:

   (a) _____
   _____
   _____
   _____
   _____

   (b) _____
   _____

   (c) _____
   _____

4. Daily hassles are _____
   _____
   _____

5. Social factors that are a source of stress include
   _____
   _____

6. In terms of culture, stress can result when
   _____
   _____

7. Conflict is _____
   _____

8. The three basic types of conflict are

   (a) _____
   _____

   (b) _____
   _____

   (c) _____

After you have carefully studied the preceding sections, complete the following exercises.

Concept Check 1

Read the following and write the correct term in the space provided.

1. Dr. Woodworth studies stress and how biological, behavioral, and social factors influence health, illness, medical treatment, and health-related behaviors. Dr. Woodworth is a _____ psychologist.

2. If Dr. Woodworth is like most psychologists in his specialty area, he adheres to the theory that health and illness are determined by the complex interaction of biological, psychological, and social factors. In other words, he is guided by the _____ model.

3. In the past year, Frank has been divorced, has moved twice, and has started a new relationship. He has also received a promotion and a big raise at work but now has many more responsibilities. His score on the Social Readjustment Rating Scale is likely to be _____ (high/low); according to the scale's developers, Holmes and Rahe, Frank has a(n) _____ (increased/decreased) likelihood of developing serious physical or psychological problems.

4. According to Richard Lazarus, Frank's major life events may create a ripple effect and generate a host of _____ (such as having to pack and repack all his belongings twice) that may accumulate to cause even greater stress.

5. Janet can take only one course this semester because of work commitments. She is torn between two courses she really wants to take, each of which fits her work schedule. Janet is probably experiencing an _____ conflict.

6. When Kailen got a speeding ticket, he complained bitterly about the unfairness of it all. When Kylie got a ticket, he perceived it as a lesson learned and decided that if he didn't want to waste his scarce resources, he should stop speeding. The two reactions to the same stressor were due, in part at least, to Kailen and Kylie's different _____ of the experience.

7. When Serena married Hiroyuki and went to live in Japan, she continued to value her North American customs and way of life, but she was also very determined to become part of her new culture. She now speaks fluent Japanese and moves comfortably between her new society and her original culture and feels almost equally at home in both countries. In terms of acculturation, Serena would be classified as _____ and her level of acculturative stress would be _____ (high/low).

8. Godfrey was very excited about an upcoming blind date. However, as the day of his dinner date approached, his level of anxiety and stress escalated and he vacillated between keeping and canceling the date. Godfrey could eliminate his _____ conflict by adopting a _____ strategy.

9. Pat has more daily hassles (mainly from family demands and interpersonal conflicts) and experiences higher levels of psychological stress than Les (whose main sources of stress are job-related and financial). It is very probable that Pat is _____ (male/female) and Les is _____ (male/female).

Graphic Organizer 1

*Read the following descriptions and decide which type of stress-producing conflict
is involved: approach–approach, avoidance–avoidance, or approach–avoidance.
In addition, label each one as producing either a high, medium, or low level of stress.*

Description	Type of Conflict/ Level of Stress (low/medium/high)
1. Lyndle wants to maintain a high grade-point average and needs to study hard before his exam tomorrow, but he has been asked by his girlfriend to go with her to a party this evening.	
2. A rat in the start box of a Y-shaped maze with two separate goal boxes at the end of each prong will receive an equally desirable food pellet in each one.	
3. Annalee is very happy to be doing well on her diet but now has to decide whether to go for lunch with her friends at her favorite Greek taverna or stay in the lunchroom and eat her low-calorie snack.	
4. In order to be allowed to borrow the family car for the evening, Jason has to decide between doing two equally unappealing chores: the family laundry or washing and waxing the bathroom and kitchen floors.	
5. Virginia entered her name in a contest and was overwhelmed when she won a seven-day Caribbean cruise. She has to decide between a seven-day eastern Caribbean cruise or a seven-day western Caribbean cruise.	
6. Melvin is overweight and out of shape and is given a choice of two daily exercise regimens by his doctor, one involving 40 minutes of running, riding an exercise bike, and weightlifting and the other involving 40 minutes of rowing machine, step-up machine, and weightlifting.	

Review of Terms, Concepts, and Names 1

*Use the terms in this list to complete the Matching
Test, then to help you answer the True/False items
correctly.*

stress
cognitive appraisal
health psychology
   (behavioral medicine)
biopsychosocial model
stressors
Social Readjustment
   Rating Scale
life change units
Richard Lazarus
daily hassles
Daily Hassles Scale

chronic stress
conflict
approach–approach
   conflict
avoidance–avoidance
   conflict
approach–avoidance
   conflict
partial-approach
   strategy
acculturative stress

Matching Exercise

*Match the appropriate term/name with its definition
or description.*

1. _____ American psychologist who
   helped promote the cognitive perspective in the
   study of stress and coping; emphasized the
   importance of cognitive appraisal in the stress
   response.

2. _____ Basic type of conflict in
   which you're faced with a choice between two
   equally appealing outcomes. As a rule, these
   conflicts are usually easy to resolve and don't
   produce much stress.

3. _____ Situation in which a person feels pulled between two or more opposing desires, motives, or goals.

4. _____ Everyday minor events that annoy and upset people.

5. _____ The branch of psychology that studies how biological, behavioral, and social factors influence health, illness, medical treatment, and health-related behaviors.

6. _____ Model that suggests that physical health and illness are determined by the complex interaction of biological, psychological, and social factors.

7. _____ On the Social Readjustment Rating Scale, the numerical rating assigned to each life event that estimates its relative impact on a person.

8. _____ Scale developed by Richard Lazarus that measures the occurrence of everyday annoyances and irritations.

9. _____ Type of stress that is persistent and ongoing.

True/False Test

Indicate whether each statement is true or false by placing T or F in the blank space next to each item.

1. ____ Stress refers to events or situations that are perceived as harmful, threatening, or challenging.

2. ____ The Social Readjustment Rating Scale was developed by Thomas Holmes and Richard Rahe in an attempt to measure the amount of stress people experienced as a function of life events that are likely to require some level of adaptation.

3. ____ An approach–avoidance conflict has a single goal with both desirable and undesirable aspects. When faced with this conflict, people often vacillate, or repeatedly go back and forth in their minds, unable to decide to approach or avoid the goal.

4. ____ Stressors refer to negative emotional states that occur in response to events that are perceived as taxing or exceeding a person's resources or ability to cope.

5. ____ An avoidance–avoidance conflict involves choosing between two unappealing or undesirable outcomes. People often delay making a decision when faced with this conflict, or they may bail out altogether.

6. ____ The stress that results from the pressure of adapting to a new culture is called acculturative stress.

7. ____ One way of dealing with the stress and anxiety of being stuck in an approach–avoidance conflict is to adopt a partial-approach strategy in which you test the waters but leave yourself a way out before making a final decision or commitment.

8. ____ Whether people experience stress depends largely on their perception of the event or situation, that is, on their *cognitive appraisal* of the event.

Check your answers and review any areas of weakness before going on to the next section.

Physical Effects of Stress: The Mind–Body Connection

Preview Questions

Consider the following questions as you study this section of the chapter.

- How can stress contribute to health problems both directly and indirectly?

- What is the fight-or-flight response, and what role do catecholamines play?

- What is the general adaptation syndrome, and what endocrine pathways are involved?

- What have neuroscientists demonstrated about the role of placebos in the perception of pain?

*Read the section "Physical Effects of Stress: The Mind–Body Connection" and **write** your answers to the following:*

1. Stress can indirectly affect a person's health by

_____

_____

2. High levels of stress can also interfere with

_____

_____

3. Stress can directly affect physical health by

_____

_____

4. The fight-or-flight response refers to _____

_____

_____

5. Catecholamines are _____

_____

_____

6. The general adaptation syndrome is _____

_____

_____

_____

7. Selye found that prolonged stress activates a

_____

_____

_____

8. Using positron emission tomography (PET), neuroscientists have shown that _____

_____

_____

_____

Physical Effects of Stress: Stress and the Immune System

Preview Questions

Consider the following questions as you study this section of the chapter.

- What is the immune system, and what is its function?
- What did the work of Ader and Cohen demonstrate, and what new interdisciplinary field did their research create?
- How does psychoneuroimmunology explain the interaction of the immune system with the nervous system?
- What kinds of stressors affect immune system functioning?

*Read the section "Physical Effects of Stress: Stress and the Immune System" and **write** your answers to the following:*

1. The immune system consists of _____

_____

_____

The function of this system is _____

_____

_____

2. Psychologist Robert Ader and immunologist Nicholas Cohen demonstrated that _____

_____

3. Their work helped establish a new interdisciplinary field called _____ which is _____

_____

_____

4. The three main findings of psychoneuroimmunological research are

(a) _____

_____

(b) _____

_____

(c) _____

_____

5. Extremely stressful events reduce _____

_____

_____

_____

6. Psychologist Janice Kiecolt-Glaser, immunologist Ronald Glaser, and others have found that

_____

_____

_____

After you have carefully studied the preceding sections, complete the following exercises.

Concept Check 2

Read the following and write the correct term in the space provided.

1. When Hans was hiking on a trail in the wilderness, he unexpectedly encountered a large brown bear and her two cubs. Hans froze in his tracks, and his heartbeat, blood pressure, and pulse increased dramatically. Fortunately, the bear and the cubs took off into the bush. The rapidly occurring chain of internal physical

reactions that Hans experienced was described by Walter Cannon as the

_____ response.

2. The physiological changes that Hans experienced when he was startled resulted from his sympathetic nervous system stimulating the _____ to secrete hormones called _____ .

3. After overcoming the initial shock of finding her new car badly damaged by a hit-and-run driver, Wilma phones the police and becomes actively involved in seeking witnesses to the incident. At this point, it is most likely that Wilma is in the _____ stage of the general adaptation syndrome.

4. Dr. Laslo believes that there is an interaction among psychological processes, the nervous and endocrine systems, and the immune system and that each system influences and is influenced by the other systems. It is very likely that Dr. Laslo works in the new interdisciplinary field called _____ .

5. When Georgia was under a lot of stress, she became ill from a viral infection. In response to this infection, the most important elements in her immune system, called

_____ , will try to defend against the foreign invader.

6. Dr. Batisic gave a painkilling drug to half the group of participants who were exposed to a

painful stimulus and a placebo to the other half. A PET scan of their brains is likely to reveal that _____ (a different/the same) area of the brain was activated in each group.

7. In a replication of Selye's work on the effects of prolonged stress, researchers confirmed the existence of a second endocrine pathway that involves the hypothalamus, the pituitary gland, and the adrenal cortex. Like Selye, they found that in response to a stressor the hypothalamus signals the pituitary gland to secrete a hormone called _____ , which in turn stimulates the adrenal cortex to release stress-related hormones called _____ , the most important of which is

_____ .

8. Eng-Seng had a tooth extracted just before going on summer vacation. Yihong had his tooth removed just before taking stressful final exams. Research by Kiecolt-Glaser and her colleagues suggests that Eng-Seng's gum will heal (faster/slower) than Yihong's.

9. Researchers investigating factors that are linked to susceptibility to respiratory infections, the common cold, and influenza, for example, are likely to discover that _____

_____

is (are) related to becoming ill.

Review of Terms, Concepts, and Names 2

Use the terms in this list to complete the Matching Test, then to help you answer the True/False items correctly.

fight-or-flight response
Walter Cannon
catecholamines
Hans Selye
general adaptation
  syndrome
alarm stage
resistance stage
exhaustion stage

adrenocorticotropic
  hormone (ACTH)
corticosteroids
cortisol
immune system
lymphocytes
Robert Ader
psychoneuroimmunology
Janice Kiecolt-Glaser

Matching Exercise

Match the appropriate term/name with its definition or description.

1. _____ American psychologist who made several important contributions to psychology, especially in the study of emotions; he described the fight-or-flight response, which involves the sympathetic nervous system and the endocrine system.

2. _____ Specialized white blood cells that are responsible for immune defenses.

3. _____ Hormones, including adrenaline and noradrenaline, secreted by the adrenal medulla that cause rapid physiological arousal.

4. _____ Canadian endocrinologist who was a pioneer in stress research; described a three-stage response to prolonged stress that he called the general adaptation syndrome.

5. _____ Hormones released by the adrenal cortex that play a key role in the body's response to long-term stressors.

6. _____ The first stage of the general adaptation syndrome, during which intense arousal occurs as the body mobilizes internal physical resources to meet the demands of the stress-producing event.

7. _____ Body system that produces specialized white blood cells that protect the body from viruses, bacteria, and tumor cells.

8. _____ The most important of the stress-related hormones called corticosteroids.

True/False Test

Indicate whether each statement is true or false by placing T or F in the blank space next to each item.

1. ____ Robert Ader is the American psychologist who, with immunologist Nicholas Cohen, first demonstrated that immune system responses could be classically conditioned; helped establish the new interdisciplinary field of psychoneuroimmunology.

2. ____ The rapidly occurring chain of internal physical reactions that prepare people to either fight or take flight from an immediate threat is called the general adaptation syndrome.

3. ____ In the resistance stage of the general adaptation syndrome, the body actively tries to resist or adjust to the continuing stressful situation.

4. ____ Janice Kiecolt-Glaser is the American psychologist who, with immunologist Ronald Glaser, conducted extensive research on the effect of stress on the immune system.

5. ____ The fight-or-flight response is Hans Selye's term for the three-stage progression of physical changes that occur when an organism is exposed to intense and prolonged stress.

6. ____ Psychoneuroimmunology is an interdisciplinary field that studies the interconnections among psychological processes, nervous and endocrine system functions, and the immune system.

7. ____ In the exhaustion stage of the general adaptation syndrome, the symptoms of the alarm stage reappear, only this time irreversibly; as the body's energy reserves become depleted, adaptation begins to break down, leading to exhaustion, physical disorders, and, potentially, death.

8. ____ In response to stress, a hormone called adrenocorticotropic hormone (ACTH) is released by the pituitary gland after it receives a signal from the hypothalamus.

Check your answers and review any areas of weakness before going on to the next section.

Individual Factors That Influence the Response to Stress: Psychological Factors

Preview Questions

Consider the following questions as you study this section of the chapter.

- What psychological factors can affect our response to stress?
- How do feelings of control, explanatory style, and negative emotions influence stress and health?
- What is Type A behavior, and what role does hostility play in its relationship to health?

Read the section "Individual Factors That Influence the Response to Stress" (up to "Social Factors") and **write** *your answers to the following:*

1. Psychological factors that influence responses to stressful events include _____

   _____

   _____

   Feeling a lack of control over events produces

   _____

   _____

2. According to psychologist Martin Seligman, how people characteristically explain _____

   _____

   _____

   _____

3. Explanatory style is related to health consequences in that _____

   _____

   _____

4. Two effects of chronic negative emotions on health are that_____

   _____

   _____

   _____

5. The Type A behavior pattern refers to _____

   _____

   _____

   _____

The critical component (and the strongest predictor of cardiac disease) in this type of behavior pattern is _____

_____

6. High levels of hostility are associated with

   _____

   _____

   _____

   _____

Individual Factors That Influence the Response to Stress: Social Factors

Preview Questions

Consider the following questions as you study this section of the chapter.

- What is meant by social support, and how does it benefit health?
- How can social support sometimes increase stress?
- What gender differences have been found in the effects of social support?

Read the section "Individual Factors That Influence the Reaction to Stress: Social Factors" and **write** *your answers to the following:*

1. Social support refers to _____

   _____

2. Social support may benefit our health and improve our ability to cope with stressors by

   (a) _____

   _____

   (b) _____

   _____

   (c) _____

   _____

3. Conversely, relationships with others can also be a significant source of stress for four reasons:

   (a) _____

   _____

   (b) _____

   _____

(c) _____

_____

(d) _____

_____

4. Some of the main gender differences in social support are

(a) _____

_____

(b) _____

_____

(c) _____

_____

(d) _____

_____

Coping: How People Deal with Stress

Preview Questions

Consider the following questions as you study this section of the chapter.

- How is *coping* defined?
- What are the two basic forms of coping, and when is each typically used?
- What are some of the most common coping strategies, and how does culture affect coping style?

*Read the section "Coping: How People Deal with Stress" and **write** your answers to the following:*

1. Coping refers to _____

_____

2. The two basic types of coping (and their uses) are _____

_____

_____

_____

3. Problem-focused coping strategies include

(a) _____

_____

(b) _____

_____

4. Emotion-focused coping strategies include

(a) _____

_____

(b) _____

_____

_____

(c) _____

_____

(d) _____

_____

(e) _____

_____

5. In terms of coping strategy, members of individualistic cultures tend to

_____

_____

_____

_____

Members of collectivistic cultures tend to

_____

_____

_____

_____

_____

After you have carefully studied the preceding sections, complete the following exercises.

Concept Check 3

Read the following and write the correct term in the space provided.

1. When Marie turned down Massimo's offer to go out for dinner on Friday night, he was disappointed. Upon reflection, however, he decided that Marie was really not his type anyway, and he'd be better off going out with someone else. Massimo's rationalization of the situation reflects a(n) _____ explanatory style.

2. When asked by her therapist to describe her husband, Cheryl said that he was very competitive and ambitious, he was always very busy, and any demands made on his time angered and irritated him. Cheryl's description suggests that her husband may have a(n) _____ behavior pattern.

3. In the case of Cheryl's husband, the critical component and the strongest predictor that he will suffer cardiac disease in his particular type of behavior pattern is _____ .

4. Irene constantly complains about her health, her job, and in general everything about her life. She tends to dislike most of the people she meets and always seems to be in a grouchy mood. It appears that Irene suffers from _____ emotions.

5. Masayuki is an engineer in a large industrial plant in Tokyo. When things get stressful, Masayuki tries to control the outward expression of his emotions and endeavors to accept the situation with maturity, serenity, and flexibility. Masayuki is using a(n) _____ coping strategy, which is more characteristic of collectivistic cultures than of individualistic cultures.

6. Shortly after he lost his job and his relationship with his girlfriend ended, Jim went to visit his family. Unfortunately, being with his family made him feel worse. He felt better only when he was with the family dog. It is possible that Jim perceived his family as being _____ and the dog as being _____ and unconditionally supportive.

7. Although Lambert was very disappointed when he didn't even come close to winning his first mountain bike race, he concluded that all his training and the knowledge he gained from the experience were beneficial. Lambert is using a very constructive emotion-focused strategy called _____ .

8. Researchers have found some gender differences in the stress response. The evolutionary perspective suggests that women have developed a "_____" behavioral response to stress, because this response is more likely to promote the survival of both the individual and the individual's offspring. The researchers have speculated that the effects of the hormone _____ , which is higher in females than in males, may be a factor.

9. Most evenings after work—especially if she has had a stressful day—Laureena deals with her high level of tension by swimming and exercising in the pool. Laureena is using a(n) _____-focused coping strategy called _____ .

10. The Bickersons have been married for five difficult years. When asked about his marriage, Mr. Bickerson admits that he and his wife have some "disagreements," but he thinks the fights are "no big deal." He also jokes about the relationship, saying about women: "You can't live with them but you can't live without them." On the other hand, Mrs. Bickerson thinks their marriage is not going well and openly discusses her problems with friends and family. Mr. Bickerson appears to be using a coping strategy called _____ , and his wife deals with her marital problems by _____ .

Graphic Organizer 2

Read the following statements and decide which researcher(s) is (are) most likely to have expressed these views. These statements cover material throughout the chapter.

Statement	Researcher(s)
1. I believe that when we are faced with danger or any threatening or stress-producing situation, we have an immediate physical reaction that involves the sympathetic nervous system and the endocrine system and the release of catecholamines. I call these internal physical changes the fight-or-flight response.	
2. When we published the results of our research, we realized that we were challenging the prevailing scientific view that the immune system operates independently of the brain and psychological processes. However, our results, which demonstrated that the immune response in rats could be classically conditioned, have been replicated by many other researchers.	
3. We were two of the earliest researchers to study stress. In an attempt to measure the amount of stress people experienced, we developed the Social Readjustment Rating Scale. Our view at the time was that any changes, either positive or negative, would cause stress and that high levels of stress, as measured by life change units, would lead to the development of serious physical and psychological problems.	
4. My research on stress led me to postulate a three-stage model to prolonged stress, called the general adaptation syndrome. I believe that the stress response involves the hypothalamus, pituitary gland, adrenal cortex, and release of hormones such as ACTH and corticosteroids.	
5. My view is that what causes us problems in the long run is not so much the major life events, which do cause stress, but the cumulative effect of daily hassles that annoy, irritate, and upset people. I have developed a scale to measure these hassles. The number of daily hassles is a better predictor of physical illness and symptoms than the number of major life events experienced.	
6. In my view, the way people characteristically explain their failures and defeats determines who will persist and who will not. I think there are two basic types of explanatory style, an optimistic explanatory style and a pessimistic explanatory style. Those who use a pessimistic explanatory style experience more stress than those who use an optimistic explanatory style.	
7. We are a husband-and-wife team who collected immunological and psychological data from medical students, who face three-day exam periods several times each academic year. We have consistently found that even the rather commonplace stress of exams adversely affects the immune system.	

Review of Terms, Concepts, and Names 3

Use the terms in this list to complete the Matching Test, then to help you answer the True/False items correctly.

Martin Seligman
optimistic explanatory
    style
pessimistic explanatory
    style
Type A behavior pattern
Type B behavior pattern
hostility
social support
stress contagion effect

coping
problem-focused coping
emotion-focused coping
confrontive coping
planful problem solving
escape–avoidance
seeking social support
distancing
denial
positive reappraisal

Matching Exercise

Match the appropriate term/name with its definition or description.

1. _____ Behavioral and cognitive responses used to contend with stressors; involves our efforts to change circumstances, or our interpretation of circumstances, to make them more favorable and less threatening.

2. _____ Problem-focused coping strategy in which the person relies on aggressive or risky efforts to change the situation.

3. _____ American psychologist who conducted research on explanatory style and the role it plays in stress, health, and illness.

4. _____ Emotion-focused coping strategy in which the person shifts his or her attention away from the stressor and toward other activities.

5. _____ Behavioral and emotional style characterized by a sense of time urgency, hostility, and competitiveness.

6. _____ The tendency of women to become upset about negative life events that happen to other people whom they care about.

7. _____ Resources provided by other people in times of need.

8. _____ Emotion-focused coping strategy that involves turning to friends, relatives, or other people for emotional, tangible, or informational support.

9. _____ Emotion-focused coping strategy that involves the refusal to acknowledge that the problem exists.

True/False Test

Indicate whether each item is true or false by placing T or F in the space next to each item.

1. ____ An optimistic explanatory style involves accounting for negative events or situations with internal, stable, and global explanations.

2. ____ The Type B behavior pattern is a behavioral and emotional style characterized by a relatively relaxed and laid-back approach to situations and problems.

3. ____ Emotion-focused coping efforts are aimed primarily at relieving or regulating the emotional impact of a stressful situation.

4. ____ The most constructive emotion-focused coping strategy is positive reappraisal, which involves not only minimizing the negative emotional aspects of the situation but also trying to create positive meaning by focusing on personal growth.

5. ____ A pessimistic explanatory style involves accounting for negative events or situations with external, unstable, and specific explanations.

6. ____ An emotion-focused coping strategy in which the individual acknowledges the stressor but attempts to minimize or eliminate its emotional impact is called distancing.

7. ____ Problem-focused coping efforts are aimed primarily at directly changing or managing a threatening or harmful stressor.

8. ____ A problem-focused coping strategy that involves efforts to rationally analyze the situation, identify potential solutions, and then implement them is called planful problem solving.

9. ____ The critical component of the type A behavior pattern that is the strongest predictor of cardiac disease and other health problems is hostility.

Check your answers and review any areas of weakness before going on to the next section.

Something to Think About

It sometimes seems that everyone you meet is stressed out. There are things to be done, deadlines to be met, social and family obligations, financial pressures, work-related problems, and so on. How can people cope with all this stress? Is there anything that can be done? Fortunately, there are several strategies for coping with stress. What advice would you give someone who is experiencing stress?

Check your answers and review any areas of weakness before completing the progress tests.

Progress Test 1

Review the complete chapter (including all boxed inserts), review all your study notes, and then test yourself on the following progress test. Check your answers. If you make a mistake, review your notes, check the appropriate section in the study guide, and if necessary, go back and read the relevant part of the chapter in your textbook.

1. Natasha experienced a great deal of anxiety when she had three exams on the same day. In this situation, the exams are _____ and her response is called _____.
   (a) stress; stressor
   (b) the biological component; the cognitive component
   (c) stressors; stress
   (d) the social component; the biological component

2. Dr. Turnbull uses the biopsychosocial model to guide his research into how psychological factors influence health, illness, and treatment. Dr. Turnbull is most likely a
   (a) developmental psychologist.
   (b) health psychologist.
   (c) psychoneuroimmunologist.
   (d) psychiatrist.

3. Donald scored 300 points on the Social Readjustment Rating Scale. According to the current view of the meaning of scores on the SRRS, which of the following is true?
   (a) It is absolutely certain that Donald will develop physical and psychological problems.
   (b) It is impossible to accurately predict whether Donald will develop physical and psychological problems.

   (c) Donald has probably experienced very few daily hassles during the past year.
   (d) Donald's subjective appraisal of the events in his life during the previous year will have no bearing on his health and well-being.

4. Del got up late and nicked himself three times while shaving. Later, he poured a cup of coffee but he couldn't drink it because there was no cream in the fridge. Then, as he was tying his shoe laces, one of them broke. Richard Lazarus would call these incidents
   (a) major life events.   (c) minor life events.
   (b) daily hassles.   (d) life change units.

5. To earn money so that he can buy a ticket to a rock concert, Ken has to either wash and wax the two family cars or wash and wax the kitchen and bathroom floors. In trying to decide between these two equally unappealing choices, Ken is likely to experience an _____ conflict.
   (a) approach–avoidance
   (b) approach–approach
   (c) avoidance–avoidance
   (d) escape–avoidance

6. Carmen is leaving Bogota, Colombia, to work and live in the United States and is very excited about the move. When Carmen arrives and starts work in the United States, she is likely to
   (a) be much more relaxed and laid back than she was in Colombia.
   (b) experience increased levels of stress due to the acculturation process.
   (c) become physically and psychologically ill within weeks.
   (d) adapt to the new environment without experiencing any stress whatsoever.

7. When Nibras was chased and attacked by a dog during his regular morning run, he experienced the classic symptoms of the fight-or-flight response. According to Walter Cannon, it is likely that his sympathetic nervous system stimulated his adrenal medulla to secrete hormones called
   (a) catecholamines.   (c) corticosteroids.
   (b) ACTH.   (d) lymphocytes.

8. After overcoming the initial shock of having his house broken into and many of his personal possessions stolen, Vincent calls the police for help and starts thinking of ways to help catch the burglar and retrieve his belongings. At this point, Vincent is most likely in the _____ stage of the general adaptation syndrome.

   (a) alarm
   (b) resistance
   (c) exhaustion
   (d) denial

9. When Claudia became ill because of a viral infection, the _____ of her immune system kicked into high gear to defend her against the virus.

   (a) lymphocytes.
   (b) corticosteroids.
   (c) catecholamines.
   (d) noradrenaline.

10. Dr. Blackman studies the interconnections among psychological processes, the nervous and endocrine systems, and the immune system. Like other specialists in the field of psychoneuroimmunology, Dr. Blackman is aware that researchers have discovered that

    (a) the central nervous system and the immune system are directly linked.
    (b) the surfaces of lymphocytes contain receptor sites for neurotransmitters and hormones, including catecholamines and cortisol.
    (c) lymphocytes themselves produce neurotransmitters and hormones.
    (d) all of these statements are true.

11. When Darcy was taking his statistics exam, he was very anxious and nervous. According to researchers such as Janice Kiecolt-Glaser, the stress of exams

    (a) adversely affects the immune system.
    (b) has no effect on the immune system.
    (c) has a beneficial effect on the immune system.
    (d) has none of these effects.

12. Whenever anything goes wrong in his life, Dean typically feels that it must be something about him that causes the problem. He also believes that no amount of personal effort will improve his situation. Martin Seligman would say that Dean has

    (a) a Type A behavior pattern.
    (b) an optimistic explanatory style.
    (c) a Type B behavior pattern.
    (d) a pessimistic explanatory style.

13. After his third month of low sales, Allen is called into the sales manager's office and told that he had better start meeting his quota or he will be laid off. The manager appears to be coping with the problem of low sales by using a(n) _____ strategy called _____ .

    (a) problem-focused; confrontive coping
    (b) emotion-focused; escape–avoidance
    (c) problem-focused; planful problem solving
    (d) emotion-focused; distancing

14. According to In Focus (Gender Differences in Responding to Stress), males tend to adopt the _____ response, and females typically engage in the _____ behavioral pattern of responding.

    (a) fight-or-flight; escape–avoidance
    (b) tend-and-befriend; fight-or-flight
    (c) fight-or-flight; tend-and-befriend
    (d) escape–avoidance; fight-or-flight

15. Critical Thinking (Do Personality Factors Cause Disease?) points out that psychologists and other scientists are cautious in the statements they make about the connection between personality and health. Which of the following reasons is (are) cited for this caution?

    (a) Many studies investigating the role of psychological factors in disease are correlational, which does not indicate causality.
    (b) Personality factors might indirectly lead to disease via poor health habits.
    (c) It may be that the disease influences a person's emotions, rather than the other way around.
    (d) All of these factors are cited as reasons.

Progress Test 2

After you have checked your understanding of the material in Progress Test 1 and have done a complete chapter review with special focus on any areas of weakness, you are ready to assess your knowledge on Progress Test 2. Check your answers. If you make a mistake, review your notes, the relevant section of the study guide, and, if necessary, the appropriate part of your textbook.

1. When Janeen was caught in a large traffic jam, she experienced a severe headache. In this case, the traffic jam is to _____ as her headache is to _____ .
   - (a) fight; flight
   - (b) stressor; stress
   - (c) flight; fight
   - (d) stress; stressor

2. For his birthday, Liam has to decide between a snowboard and a mountain bike. In trying to decide between these two equally attractive alternatives, Liam is likely to experience an _____ conflict.
   - (a) approach–avoidance
   - (b) approach–approach
   - (c) avoidance–avoidance
   - (d) escape–avoidance

3. Fifty-five-year-old Maxwell is a very impatient and competitive defense lawyer who feels that he must be the best in his field. In addition, he has a reputation for being hostile toward judges and prosecuting attorneys. Maxwell's behavior is likely to be classified as a(n)
   - (a) Type A behavior pattern.
   - (b) pessimistic explanatory style.
   - (c) Type B behavior pattern.
   - (d) optimistic explanatory style.

4. Donald exhibits all the characteristics of a Type A behavior pattern. The component of his behavior that is most likely to contribute to health problems is his
   - (a) impatience.
   - (b) competitiveness.
   - (c) achievement orientation.
   - (d) hostility.

5. Heloise is an emergency room nurse. Whenever she has a particularly hectic and stressful shift, she and some of the other nurses find themselves making fun of the patients and the doctors. Heloise is using an emotion-focused coping strategy called
   - (a) confrontive coping.
   - (b) denial.
   - (c) distancing.
   - (d) positive reappraisal.

6. Madge wants advice on how to cope with the stress of returning to college after being out of school for a number of years. She would be best advised to approach her classes
   - (a) with a sense of personal control and optimism.
   - (b) with a realistic but pessimistic attitude.
   - (c) using an emotion-focused coping strategy called distancing.
   - (d) using an emotion-focused coping strategy called denial.

7. Whenever Beth experiences problems in her relationship with her fiancée, she typically talks to her family about her troubles. Beth is using a(n) _____ strategy called _____ .
   - (a) problem-focused; confrontive coping
   - (b) emotion-focused; distancing
   - (c) problem-focused; planful problem solving
   - (d) emotion-focused; seeking social support

8. While researching a paper for her psychology class, Joyce came across the research of Ader and Cohen on conditioning and immune system functioning. She is likely to conclude that their work was important for which of the following reasons?
   - (a) It challenged the prevailing scientific view that the immune system operates independently of the brain and psychological processes.
   - (b) It demonstrated that humans could be conditioned to salivate just like Pavlov's dogs.
   - (c) Before their research was published, everyone believed that there was a strong interconnectedness among psychological processes, nervous and endocrine system functions, and the immune system.
   - (d) It proved conclusively that the immune system could not be classically conditioned.

9. After a bank was robbed, the bank tellers and the customers got up off the floor, where they had been held at gunpoint. Because it was such a frightening experience, they are likely to have experienced a rapidly occurring chain of internal physical reactions called

   (a) daily hassles.
   (b) the fight-or-flight response.
   (c) the general adaptation syndrome.
   (d) the stress contagion effect.

10. Following a bank robbery, the customers and tellers who were very frightened probably experienced increased activation of the sympathetic nervous system, stimulation of the adrenal medulla, and the release of hormones called

    (a) lymphocytes.   (c) testosterone.
    (b) catecholamines.   (d) estrogen.

11. During her final year of medical training, Lissette was under constant pressure; she never seemed to get enough sleep, was anxious and nervous most of the time, and experienced many physical symptoms and disorders. As a result of this prolonged stress, it is likely that her hypothalamus, pituitary gland, and adrenal cortex will work together to release stress-related hormones called

    (a) lymphocytes.   (c) corticosteroids.
    (b) catecholamines.   (d) acetylcholine.

12. Gregory was very disappointed when he wasn't accepted to the graduate program at State University. Upon reflection, however, he decided that the preparations he made in putting his application together and the knowledge he gained from the interview were beneficial experiences. Gregory is using a(n) _____ strategy called _____ .

    (a) problem-focused; confrontive coping
    (b) emotion-focused; positive reappraisal
    (c) problem-focused; planful problem solving
    (d) emotion-focused; escape–avoidance

13. Focus on Neuroscience discusses a research project in which the experimental group underwent a painful procedure followed by an injection of an actual opioid painkiller; the control group was injected with a saline solution placebo after the procedure. A PET scan revealed that in one participant an area of the brain, called the anterior cingulate cortex, became very active. It is likely that the person, who reported that the injection provided pain relief

    (a) was definitely in the experimental group.
    (b) was definitely in the control group.
    (c) was faking and was, in reality, experiencing extreme pain.
    (d) could have been in either the experimental group or the control group.

14. According to In Focus (Providing Effective Social Support), which of the following is NOT recommended for helping someone in distress?

    (a) Express affection for the person, whether by a warm hug or simply a pat on the arm.
    (b) Be a good listener and show concern and interest.
    (c) Ask questions that encourage the person under stress to express his or her feelings and emotions.
    (d) Give advice that the person has not asked for.

15. When Sanjeev went to Britain to attend one of the top universities in the country, he was enthralled by all things English and decided that he would like to live there permanently. He took up cricket, lawn bowling, and polo, preferred to be called Sandy rather than Sanjeev, and enthusiastically embraced the "pub" culture of his adopted home. According to Culture and Human Behavior (The Stress of Adapting to a New Culture), Sanjeev has adopted a pattern of acculturation called _____ and has probably experienced a _____ degree of stress as a result of abandoning his old cultural identity.

    (a) integration; low
    (b) separation; high
    (c) assimilation; moderate
    (d) marginalization; high

Progress Test 3

After you have checked your understanding of the material in Progress Tests 1 and 2, and have done a complete chapter review with special focus on any areas of weakness, you are ready to further assess your knowledge with Progress Test 3. Check your answers. If you make a mistake, review your notes, the appropriate parts of the study guide, and, if necessary, the relevant sections of your textbook.

1. Following a bitter divorce and a long-fought custody battle over her two children, Luzmilda is in the exhaustion stage of the general adaptation syndrome. According to Selye, this prolonged stress is likely to activate an endocrine pathway that involves _____ and the release of _____ .
   (a) the hypothalamus, the pituitary gland, the adrenal cortex; corticosteroids
   (b) the hypothalamus, the sympathetic nervous system, the adrenal medulla; catecholamines
   (c) the sympathetic nervous system, the adrenal medulla, the immune system; oxytocin
   (d) classical conditioning, the adrenal cortex, the immune system; lymphocytes

2. When Argento encountered a wild cougar on the hiking trail, he experienced acute stress. Which of the following would Walter Cannon consider the correct sequence of Argento's fight-or-flight response?
   (a) pituitary, hypothalamus, ACTH release, sympathetic nervous system.
   (b) secretion of corticosteroids, ACTH release, perspiration, cognitive appraisal.
   (c) hypothalamus, sympathetic nervous system, adrenal medulla, secretion of catecholamines
   (d) perspiration, ACTH release, respiration, parasympathetic nervous system, secretion of catecholamines

3. If Dr. Penman is like most researchers in the field of psychoneuroimmunology, he probably holds the view that
   (a) it is impossible to classically condition the immune system.
   (b) the immune system works independently of other body systems.
   (c) the endocrine system and the immune system are interconnected, but psychological processes operate independently.

   (d) there are interconnections among psychological processes, nervous and endocrine system functions, and the immune system.

4. Rita and Richard both have a large network of social relationships, including close friends and family members. Compared with Richard, Rita may be potentially vulnerable to some of the problematic aspects of social support because
   (a) women are less likely than men to serve as providers of support.
   (b) women, in general, are more likely than men to suffer from the stress contagion effect.
   (c) women tend to rely on a close personal relationship with their spouse and place less importance on relationships with other people.
   (d) women are less likely than men to become upset about what happens to their friends and relatives.

5. Reena has a successful accounting practice and frequently works 60 hours or more a week. She has to manage her time efficiently in order to keep up with the demands of her career and family life. Despite all the pressure, Reena loves her job, is always kind and considerate to her employees, and has a cheerful personality. Which of the following is most likely to be true of Reena?
   (a) Because of her stressful lifestyle, she probably has high levels of corticosteroids.
   (b) She is at a high risk for coronary disease and other health problems.
   (c) She is likely to develop coronary disease because of her Type A behavior pattern.
   (d) Because she is low in hostility, her risk of developing coronary disease is no higher than that of anyone else.

6. Forty-year-old Lannie is a widow, lives alone, has very few friends, and rarely interacts with other people except at work. Research suggests that compared with people who have many social contacts and relationships, social isolation such as Lannie's is correlated with
   (a) higher-than-normal levels of catecholamines.
   (b) poor health and higher death rates.
   (c) lower-than-normal levels of corticosteroids.
   (d) good health and lower death rates.

7. In replicating Ader and Cohen's original research, Dr. Andrews and his colleagues also found that the suppression of the immune system was influenced by
   (a) Type A behavior.
   (b) the general adaptation syndrome.
   (c) classical conditioning.
   (d) aerobic exercise.

8. Kari is a very laid-back, easygoing mail carrier. She loves her job because it allows her to meet people and get daily exercise. Kari would be classified as having a
   (a) Type A behavior pattern.
   (b) high risk of heart disease.
   (c) Type B behavior pattern.
   (d) stress contagion syndrome.

9. Jacob was naturally disappointed when he didn't get the job he applied for. However, in his usual way, he thought that he would have better luck next time, especially if he took some courses to make himself more qualified for the position. Martin Seligman would say that Jacob has a(n)
   (a) Type A behavior pattern.
   (b) optimistic explanatory style.
   (c) problem-focused coping style.
   (d) pessimistic explanatory style.

10. Helga, a college student, has been offered a new job. On the plus side, the higher salary and increased benefits are appealing; on the down side, she will have to work longer hours, take on extra responsibilities, and have a longer commute to work. She needs the extra money but she also needs to keep her high GPA at college. Helga is likely experiencing a type of conflict called _____ conflict.
    (a) approach–approach
    (b) avoidance–avoidance
    (c) escape–avoidance
    (d) approach–avoidance

11. Anders, a 52-year-old insurance salesperson, is unexpectedly called into the sales manager's office and told that he is going to be laid off because the company is downsizing. Which stage of the general adaptation syndrome is Anders likely experiencing?
    (a) alarm stage   (c) exhaustion stage
    (b) resistance stage   (d) denial stage

12. Dr. Chambers has a very busy clinical practice. To clear his mind of all the problems he faces each day and to cope with the high level of stress, he goes to the gym for a workout four or five times a week. Dr. Chambers is using a(n) _____ coping strategy called _____ .
    (a) emotion-focused; escape–avoidance
    (b) problem-focused; denial
    (c) emotion-focused; wishful thinking
    (d) problem-focused; confrontive coping

13. Toward the end of the semester, Reza was under a lot of stress; he had three term papers to write and four final exams to prepare for, and he was called into work much more often than he had anticipated. In contrast, his roommate Erik finished all his term papers and had only two final exams to prepare for. If both people are exposed to the same common cold virus, it is very probable that
    (a) Erik will contract a respiratory infection but Reza will not.
    (b) both Erik and Reza will contract a respiratory infection; exposure to the virus is sufficient, and infection rates are independent of levels of psychological stress.
    (c) neither one will contract a respiratory infection; there is no relationship between psychological stress and rates of respiratory infection.
    (d) Reza will contract a respiratory infection but Erik will not.

14. When Lester was having personal and academic problems in college, he went to see a guidance counselor. The counselor provided some helpful suggestions for improving his study habits and advised him to enroll in a remedial reading course. According to In Focus (Providing Effective Social Support), the type of social support that Lester received is called _____ support.
    (a) emotional   (c) informational
    (b) tangible   (d) confrontive

15. Despite all Chikako's efforts to resolve numerous stressful situations in her life, her problems persist. In order to minimize the adverse impact of stress on her physical and psychological well-being, which of the following should Chikako AVOID doing (according to the Application)?

(a) Exercise regularly; do a brisk 20-minute walk four or five times a week.

(b) Use stimulants such as caffeine or nicotine; they will help induce relaxation by lowering blood pressure and heart rate.

(c) Get sufficient sleep, which promotes resistance to health problems and helps buffer the effects of stress.

(d) Practice a relaxation technique: try progressive muscle relaxation or meditation to reduce stress-related symptoms.

Answers

Introduction: What Is Stress?

1. *Stress is defined as* a negative emotional state occurring in response to events that are perceived as taxing or exceeding a person's resources or ability to cope.

2. *Health psychologists focus on* how biological, behavioral, and social factors influence health, illness, medical treatment, and health-related behaviors (health psychology is also sometimes referred to as behavioral medicine).

3. *The biopsychosocial model is* the belief that physical health and illness are determined by the complex interaction of biological factors, psychological and behavioral factors, and social conditions.

What Is Stress? Sources of Stress

1. *Stressors are* events or situations that are perceived as harmful, threatening, or challenging.

2. *Early stress researchers Holmes and Rahe believed that* any change, whether positive or negative, that required you to adjust your behavior or lifestyle would cause stress (they developed the Social Readjustment Rating Scale in an attempt to measure the amount of stress people experienced).

3. *Several problems with the life events approach have been pointed out:* (a) The link between scores on the Social Readjustment Rating Scale and the development of physical and psychological problems is relatively weak. Most people don't develop physical or mental problems as a result of major life events. (b) The Social Readjustment Rating Scale does not take into account a person's subjective appraisal of an event, response to that event, or ability to cope with the event (it assumes that a given life event will have the same impact on virtually everyone). (c) The life events approach assumes change in itself, whether good or bad, produces stress (research has shown that health is most adversely affected by negative life events, especially when they are unexpected or uncontrollable, whereas positive or desirable events are much less likely to affect health adversely). Efforts have been made to revise and update the SRRS in an attempt to take into account the influences of gender, age, marital status, and other characteristics.

4. *Daily hassles are* everyday minor events that annoy and upset people. The frequency of daily hassles is linked to psychological distress and physical symptoms: The number of daily hassles people experience is a better predictor of physical illness and symptoms than is the number of major life events experienced.

5. *Social factors that are a source of stress include* crowding, crime, unemployment, poverty, racism and discrimination (real or suspected), inadequate health care, and substandard housing (people in the lowest socioeconomic levels of society tend to have the highest levels of psychological distress, illness, and death).

6. *In terms of culture, stress can result when* cultures clash; for refugees, immigrants, and their children, adapting to a new culture can be extremely stress-producing.

7. *Conflict is* a situation in which a person feels pulled between two or more opposing desires, motives, or goals.

8. *The three basic types of conflict are* (a) approach–approach conflict (a win-win situation in which the choice is between two equally appealing outcomes); (b) avoidance–avoidance conflict (in which the choice is between two unappealing or undesirable outcomes); and (c) approach–avoidance conflict (a very stressful situation in which the goal has both desirable and undesirable aspects).

Concept Check 1

1. health
2. biopsychosocial
3. high; increased

4. daily hassles
5. approach–approach
6. cognitive appraisals
7. integrated; low
8. approach–avoidance; partial-approach
9. female; male

Graphic Organizer 1

1. approach–avoidance; high
2. approach–approach; low
3. approach–avoidance; high
4. avoidance–avoidance; medium
5. approach–approach; low
6. avoidance–avoidance; medium

Matching Exercise 1

1. Richard Lazarus
2. approach–approach conflict
3. conflict
4. daily hassles
5. health psychology
6. biopsychosocial model
7. life change units
8. Daily Hassles Scale
9. chronic stress

True/False Test 1

1. F	3. T	5. T	7. T
2. T	4. F	6. T	8. T

Physical Effects of Stress: The Mind–Body Connection

1. *Stress can indirectly affect a person's health by* prompting behaviors that jeopardize physical well-being, such as not eating or sleeping properly.

2. *High levels of stress can also interfere with* cognitive abilities, such as attention, concentration, and memory; in turn, such disruptions can increase the likelihood of accidents and injuries.

3. *Stress can directly affect physical health by* altering body functions, leading to symptoms, illness, or disease (for example, stress can cause neck and head muscles to contract and tighten, resulting in stress-induced tension headaches).

4. *The fight-or-flight response refers to* a rapidly occurring chain of internal physical reactions that prepare people to either fight or take flight from an immediate threat (involves both the sympathetic nervous system and the endocrine system).

5. *Catecholamines are* hormones secreted by the adrenal medulla that cause rapid physiological arousal (they include adrenaline and noradrenaline).

6. *The general adaptation syndrome is* Selye's term for the three-stage progression of physical changes that occur when an organism is exposed to intense and prolonged stress; the three stages are alarm, resistance, and exhaustion.

7. *Selye found that prolonged stress activates a* second endocrine pathway that involves the hypothalamus, the pituitary gland, and the adrenal cortex, which secretes a hormone called adrenocorticotropic hormone (ACTH), which in turn stimulates the adrenal cortex to release stress-related hormones called corticosteroids, the most important of which is cortisol.

8. *Using positron emission tomography (PET), neuroscientists have shown that* both a genuine painkilling drug and a placebo activated the same brain area, the anterior cingulate cortex, which is known to contain many opioid receptors. Although exactly how placebos produce their results is not clear, these researchers concluded that this substantiated the mind–body connection, and that higher mental processes (expectations, learned associations, and emotional responses) can have a profound effect on the perception of pain.

Physical Effects of Stress: Stress and the Immune System

1. *The immune system consists of* the bone marrow, the spleen, the thymus, and lymph nodes. Most important are the lymphocytes, which are manufactured in the bone marrow. *The function of this system is* to detect and battle foreign invaders, such as bacteria, viruses, and tumor cells.

2. *Psychologist Robert Ader and immunologist Nicholas Cohen demonstrated that* the immune system response in rats could be classically conditioned.

3. *Their research helped establish a new interdisciplinary field called* psychoneuroimmunology, *which is* the scientific study of the interconnections among psychological processes (psycho-), the nervous system (-neuro-), and the immune system (-immunology).

4. *The three main findings of psychoneuroimmunological research are (a)* The central nervous system and the immune system are directly linked via sympathetic nervous system fibers, which influence the production and functioning of lymphocytes. *(b)* The surfaces of lymphocytes contain receptor sites for neurotransmitters and hormones, including catecholamines and cortisol. *(c)* Lymphocytes themselves produce neurotransmitters and hormones, which, in turn, influence the nervous and endocrine systems.

5. *Extremely stressful events reduce* immune-system functioning. Thus, common negative life events, such as the end or disruption of important interpersonal relationships and chronic stressors that continue for years, can diminish immune-system functioning.

6. *Psychologist Janice Kiecolt-Glaser, immunologist Ronald Glaser, and others have found that* even the rather commonplace stress of exams adversely affects the immune system and that reduced immune system functioning as a result of stress puts us at greater risk for health problems, with slower recovery times for illnesses and injuries.

Concept Check 2

1. fight-or-flight
2. adrenal medulla; catecholamines
3. resistance
4. psychoneuroimmunology
5. lymphocytes
6. the same
7. adrenocorticotropic hormone (ACTH); corticosteroids; cortisol
8. faster
9. high levels of stress and chronic stress

Matching Exercise 2

1. Walter Cannon
2. lymphocytes
3. catecholamines
4. Hans Selye

5. corticosteroids
6. alarm stage
7. immune system
8. cortisol

True/False Test 2

1. T
2. F
3. T
4. T
5. F
6. T
7. T
8. T

Individual Factors That Influence the Response to Stress: Psychological Factors

1. *Psychological factors that influence responses to stressful events include* people's appraisal of the event and their resources for coping with it; whether they have a sense of control over the stressful situation; and being able to take steps to minimize or avoid the stressor. *Feeling a lack of control over events produces* all the hallmarks of the stress response: levels of catecholamines and corticosteroids increase, and the effectiveness of the immune system functioning decreases.

2. *According to psychologist Martin Seligman, how people characteristically explain their failures and defeats makes the difference:* People who have an optimistic explanatory style tend to use external, unstable, and specific explanations for negative events; people who have a pessimistic explanatory style use internal, stable, and global explanations for negative events.

3. *Explanatory style is related to health consequences in that* explanatory style in early adulthood predicts physical health status decades later; those with optimistic explanatory styles have significantly better health than those with pessimistic explanatory styles and are more likely to cope effectively with stressful situations.

4. *Two effects of chronic negative emotions on health are that* people who are habitually anxious, depressed, angry, and hostile are more likely to develop chronic diseases such as arthritis or heart disease, and people who are tense, angry, and unhappy experience more stress than happier people (they also report more frequent and intense daily hassles and react much more intensely to the stressful events they encounter).

5. *The Type A behavior pattern refers to* a behavioral and emotional style characterized by a sense of time urgency, hostility, and intense ambition and competitiveness. *The critical component (and the strongest predictor of cardiac disease) in this type of behavior pattern is* hostility, which refers to the tendency to feel anger, annoyance, resentment, and contempt and to hold cynical and negative beliefs about human nature in general.

6. *High levels of hostility are associated with* suspiciousness, mistrust, cynicism, and pessimism; an increased likelihood of dying from all natural causes, including cancer; increased blood pressure, heart rate, and the production of stress-related hormones; more intense reactions to stressors and a tendency to create more stress; and more severe, negative life events and daily hassles than other people.

Individual Factors That Influence the Response to Stress: Social Factors

1. *Social support refers to* the resources provided by other people in times of need.

2. *Social support may benefit our health and improve our ability to cope with stressors by* (a) modifying our appraisal of a stressor's significance, including the degree to which we perceive it as threatening or harmful (simply knowing that support and assistance are readily available may make the situation seem less threatening); (b) decreasing the intensity of physical reactions to a stressor; and (c) making us less likely to experience negative emotions (in contrast, loneliness and depression are unpleasant emotional states that increase levels of stress hormones and adversely affect immune system functioning).

3. *Conversely, relationships with others can also be a significant source of stress for four reasons:* (a) Negative interactions with other people are more effective in creating psychological distress than positive interactions are in improving well-being. (b) Marital conflict has been shown to have adverse effects on health, especially for women. (c) When people are perceived as being judgmental, their presence may increase the individual's physical reaction to a stressor. (d) Well-meaning friends or family members may offer unwanted or inappropriate social support.

4. *Some of the main gender differences in social support are* (a) Women are more likely than men to serve as providers of support, which can be a very stressful role. (b) Women may be

more likely to suffer from the stress contagion effect, becoming upset about negative life events that happen to other people whom they care about. (c) Men are more likely to be distressed only by negative events that happen to their immediate family—their wives and children. (d) Men generally tend to rely heavily on a close relationship with their spouse, placing less importance on relationships with other people (women, in contrast, are more likely to list close friends along with their spouses as confidants).

Coping: How People Deal with Stress

1. *Coping refers to* behavioral and cognitive responses used to deal with stressors; it involves our efforts to change circumstances, or our interpretations of circumstances, to make them more favorable and less threatening.

2. *The two basic types of coping (and their uses) are* problem-focused coping (aimed at managing or changing a threatening or harmful stressor) and emotion-focused coping (aimed at relieving or regulating the emotional impact of the stressful situation).

3. *Problem-focused coping strategies include* (a) confrontive coping (relying on aggressive or risky efforts to change the situation) and (b) planful problem solving (rationally analyzing the situation, identifying potential solutions, and then implementing them).

4. *Emotion-focused coping strategies include* (a) escape–avoidance (shifting attention away from the stressor and toward other activities, with the basic goal of escaping or avoiding the stressor and neutralizing distressing emotions), (b) seeking social support (turning to friends, relatives, or other people for emotional, tangible, or informational support), (c) distancing (acknowledging the stressor while attempting to minimize or eliminate its emotional impact), (d) denial (the refusal to acknowledge that the problem even exists), and (e) positive reappraisal (minimizing the negative emotional aspects of the situation but also trying to create positive meaning by focusing on personal growth).

5. *In terms of coping strategies, members of individualistic cultures tend to* emphasize personal autonomy and personal responsibility in dealing with problems (they are less likely to seek social support in stressful situations than are members of collectivistic cultures) and to favor problem-focused strategies, such as confrontive

coping and planful problem solving. *Members of collectivistic cultures tend to* be more oriented toward their social group, family, or community and to seek help with their problems; they also place greater emphasis on controlling personal reactions to a stressful situation rather than trying to control the situation itself.

Concept Check 3

1. optimistic
2. Type A
3. hostility
4. chronic negative
5. emotion-focused
6. judgmental; nonjudgmental
7. positive reappraisal
8. "tend-and-befriend"; oxytocin
9. emotion; escape–avoidance
10. distancing; seeking social support

Graphic Organizer 2

1. Walter Cannon
2. Robert Ader and Nicholas Cohen
3. Thomas Holmes and Richard Rahe
4. Hans Selye
5. Richard Lazarus
6. Martin Seligman
7. Janice Kiecolt-Glaser and Ronald Glaser

Matching Exercise 3

1. coping
2. confrontive coping
3. Martin Seligman
4. escape–avoidance
5. Type A behavior pattern
6. stress contagion effect
7. social support
8. seeking social support
9. denial

True/False Test 3

1. F	5. F	9. T
2. T	6. T	
3. T	7. T	
4. T	8. T	

Something to Think About

A good place to start in giving advice to someone is to explain what stressors are and what the stress reaction is. Identifying potential sources of stress, from major life events to daily hassles, is useful, and noting how our subjective cognitive appraisal of stressors influences our reactions is also important. It is also helpful to know about physical reactions and psychological and social factors that influence our response to stress.

People vary a great deal in the way they respond to distressing events. Psychologists have identified several different factors that influence an individual's response to stressful events. Having a sense of control reduces the impact of stressors and decreases feelings of anxiety and depression. The type of explanatory style we use—optimistic, pessimistic, or, as in most cases, somewhere in between—can also have an effect on our health. People with a pessimistic explanatory style tend to have poorer physical health, whereas people with an optimistic, confident, and generally positive outlook have better immune system responses and better physical health. Furthermore, chronically grouchy people experience more stress, have more frequent and intense daily hassles, and generally react with far greater distress to stressful events.

Many different strategies can be used to deal with stress, some of which are more adaptive than others. Having good social support is beneficial, but so too are the types of strategies that we adopt to cope with distressing events. Problem-focused and emotion-focused coping strategies are two that the text discusses in detail. In addition, we can minimize the impact of stressors by exercising regularly, avoiding or minimizing stimulants such as coffee, tea, or cigarettes, and by regularly practicing a relaxation technique such as meditation or progressive muscle relaxation. Stress is an unavoidable part of life and can influence both our physical and psychological well-being. How we choose to cope with stress can reduce and minimize its destructive effects.

Progress Test 1

1. c	6. b	11. a
2. b	7. a	12. d
3. b	8. b	13. a
4. b	9. a	14. c
5. c	10. d	15. d

Progress Test 2

1. b	6. a	11. c
2. b	7. d	12. b
3. a	8. a	13. d
4. d	9. b	14. d
5. c	10. b	15. c

Progress Test 3

1. a	6. b	11. a
2. c	7. c	12. a
3. d	8. c	13. d
4. b	9. b	14. c
5. d	10. d	15. b

CHAPTER 14

Psychological Disorders

PREVIEW	Reading the section below first will give you a general sense of the chapter's contents and an initial introduction to some of the major concepts and terms. This will prime you for what you are about to read and help you to develop a "cognitive map" that will guide your study of the material in this chapter. Likewise, reading the **preview questions** at the beginning of each major section will improve your ability to understand, learn, and retain the information.

Chapter 14 . . . AT A GLANCE

Chapter 14 begins by addressing the distinction between normal and abnormal behavior, the criteria for diagnosing psychological disorders, according to DSM-IV-TR, and the prevalence of psychological disorders.

Although most people experience anxiety, only when it becomes maladaptive is it considered a disorder. The prevalence, course, and possible causes of anxiety disorders, including generalized anxiety disorder (GAD), panic disorder, phobias, posttraumatic stress disorder (PTSD), and obsessive–compulsive disorder (OCD), are discussed.

Mood disorders (also called affective disorders) involve serious, persistent disturbances in emotions that cause psychological discomfort and/or impair the ability to function. The symptoms of major depression, dysthymic disorder, and bipolar disorder are identified, and the course and potential causes of these mood disorders are discussed.

Eating disorders are covered next. The defining characteristic of anorexia nervosa and bulimia nervosa are outlined, and the causes of eating disorders are examined.

Personality disorders are characterized by inflexible and maladaptive personality traits. The symptoms and causes of paranoid, antisocial, and borderline personality disorders are discussed.

Dissociative experiences involve a disruption in awareness, memory, and personal identity. The symptoms and possible causes of dissociative amnesia, dissociative fugue, and dissociative identity disorder (DID) are examined.

The main symptoms and subtypes of schizophrenia are identified, and the prevalence and course of the disorder are presented. Various theories of the causes of schizophrenia are explored, and the conclusion is reached that no single factor has emerged as causing this psychological disorder. The Application suggests ways of helping to prevent suicide.

Introduction: Understanding Psychological Disorders

Preview Questions

Consider the following questions as you study this section of the chapter.

- What is psychopathology, and what characterizes psychological disorders?
- What is DSM-IV-TR, and how was it developed?
- How prevalent are psychological disorders?

*Read the section "Introduction: Understanding Psychological Disorders" and **write** your answers to the following:*

1. Psychopathology is _____

    _____

2. A psychological, or mental, disorder can be

    defined as _____

    _____

    _____

3. DSM-IV-TR stands for _____

    _____

    This manual describes _____

    _____

    _____

4. The National Comorbidity Survey found that psychological disorders were more common than previously thought, which can be interpreted to mean _____

    _____

    _____

    _____

Anxiety Disorders

Preview Questions

Consider the following questions as you study this section of the chapter.

- What are the main symptoms of anxiety disorder, and how does pathological anxiety differ from normal anxiety?

- What characterizes generalized anxiety disorder (GAD) and panic disorder?
- What are the phobias, and how have they been explained?

*Read the section "Anxiety Disorders" (up to "Posttraumatic Stress Disorder") and **write** your answers to the following:*

1. Anxiety is defined as _____

    _____

    It is often adaptive and normal because _____

    _____

    _____

2. In the anxiety disorders, the anxiety is _____

    _____

3. The three features that distinguish normal anxiety from pathological anxiety are

    (a) _____

    _____

    (b) _____

    _____

    (c) _____

4. Generalized anxiety disorder (GAD) is characterized by _____

    _____

    _____

5. A panic attack is _____

    _____

6. A panic disorder is _____

    Its cause is thought to be _____

    _____

    _____

7. A phobia is _____

    _____

    A specific phobia is _____

    _____

8. Phobias are assumed by some to involve various forms of learning such as _____

_____

_____

_____

_____

Anxiety Disorders: Posttraumatic Stress Disorder and Obsessive–Compulsive Disorder

Preview Questions

Consider the following questions as you study these sections of the chapter.

- How is *posttraumatic stress disorder (PTSD)* defined?
- What are the main characteristics of PTSD, and what causes the disorder?
- What is obsessive–compulsive disorder (OCD), and what causes it?

Read the sections "Anxiety Disorders: Posttraumatic Stress Disorder" and "Obsessive–Compulsive Disorders" and **write** *your answers to the following:*

1. Posttraumatic stress disorder (PTSD) is _____

_____

2. The three core symptoms that characterize PTSD are

    (a) _____

    _____

    (b) _____

    _____

    (c) _____

    _____

3. Factors that influence the likelihood of developing posttraumatic stress disorder are

    (a) _____

    _____

    (b) _____

    _____

    (c) _____

    _____

4. Obsessive–compulsive disorder (OCD) is

_____

_____

Obsessions are _____

_____

_____

Compulsions are _____

_____

_____

5. People with obsessive–compulsive disorder commonly experience _____

_____

_____

6. Two biological factors that seem to be involved in obsessive–compulsive disorder are _____

_____

_____

_____

After you have carefully studied the preceding sections, complete the following exercises.

Concept Check 1

Read the following and write the correct term in the space provided.

1. Dr. Janz is a psychiatrist who assesses and treats patients in a mental institution. Dr. Sloane is a clinical psychologist who works with a similar population of patients in a mental health clinic. Dr. Janz is likely to describe his patients as suffering from _____ disorders, whereas Dr. Sloane is more likely to use the term _____ disorder when referring to his patients' problems.

2. Seventeen-year-old Brad has a shaved head, and he has rings in his nose, ears, and navel. Shortly after purchasing a new pair of jeans, he cut and tore horizontal slits across the thigh and knee areas of each leg. In our present culture, Brad would be classified as

_____ .

3. Mr. and Mrs. Jefferson want to hire a new housekeeper. Mr. Jefferson suggests that the best person would be someone who has an excessive dislike and fear of dirt, germs, and insects and who deals with anxiety about contamination by using a very thorough cleaning, washing, and disinfecting routine. Mrs. Jefferson thinks that any person fitting that description might have a problem called

_____ disorder.

4. Mr. Alviro suffers from intense anxiety most of the time. He is nervous and worried and is overly concerned about a wide range of life circumstances with little or no justification. Mr. Alviro probably suffers from

_____ disorder.

5. Maurice is very quiet and introverted. He is painfully shy in the presence of other people and has dropped many courses at college simply because they involved oral presentations. He can't get a job because he is intensely afraid and anxious about being interviewed. Maurice would probably be classified as having

_____ .

6. Mr. Shenasi frequently recalls the horrors he and his family experienced in his native Iraq. He suffers from sleep disturbances and is often awakened by terrifying nightmares. Mr. Shenasi is experiencing _____ disorder.

7. Ever since the sudden death of her husband, Mrs. Baxter has experienced a number of terrifying and unexpected episodes in which her heart suddenly starts to pound hard for no apparent reason; she typically feels a choking sensation, has trouble breathing, and starts to sweat and tremble. Mrs. Baxter is probably experiencing _____ .

8. Dr. Felkar believes that some phobias can be explained in terms of basic learning principles. For example, Tina's irrational fear of cats may have developed because of _____ conditioning, _____ conditioning, or _____ learning.

9. Thea has been diagnosed with obsessive–compulsive disorder. Although its cause is not fully understood, biological factors such as a deficiency in the neurotransmitter

_____ and dysfunctions in brain areas such as the _____ lobes and the _____ may all be implicated in obsessive–compulsive disorder.

Graphic Organizer 1

List the main symptoms of each of the following anxiety disorders:

Generalized Anxiety Disorder	Panic Disorder	Phobias

Posttraumatic Stress Disorder	Obsessive–Compulsive Disorder

Review of Terms and Concepts 1

Use the terms in this list to complete the Matching Test, then to help you answer the True/False items correctly.

psychopathology
psychological disorder (mental disorder)
DSM-IV-TR
anxiety
anxiety disorders
generalized anxiety disorder (GAD)
panic attack
panic disorder
cognitive-behavioral theory of panic disorder
ataque de nervios (attack of nerves)
phobia
specific phobia (simple phobia)
agoraphobia
social phobia (social anxiety disorder)
taijin kyofusho
posttraumatic stress disorder (PTSD)
obsessive–compulsive disorder (OCD)
obsessions
compulsions
caudate nucleus

Matching Exercise

Match the appropriate term with its definition or description.

1. _____ The scientific study of the origins, symptoms, and development of psychological disorders.

2. _____ Abbreviation for the *Diagnostic and Statistical Manual of Mental Disorders, Fourth Edition, Text Revision,* the book published by the American Psychiatric Association that describes the specific symptoms and diagnostic guidelines for different psychological disorders.

3. _____ Anxiety disorder in which the symptoms of anxiety are triggered by intrusive, repetitive thoughts and urges to perform certain actions.

4. _____ Unpleasant emotional state characterized by physical arousal and feelings of tension, apprehension, and worry.

5. _____ Strong or irrational fear of something, usually a specific object or situation, that does not necessarily interfere with the ability to function in daily life.

6. _____ Anxiety disorder in which chronic and persistent symptoms of anxiety develop in response to an extreme physical or psychological trauma.

7. _____ Anxiety disorder involving the extreme and irrational fear of experiencing a panic attack in a public situation and being unable to escape or get help.

8. _____ Anxiety disorder characterized by an extreme or irrational fear of a specific object or situation that interferes with the ability to function in daily life.

9. _____ Disorder that usually affects young Japanese males and is characterized by extreme social anxiety, avoidance of social situations, and a fear that his appearance or smell, facial expression, or body language will offend, insult, or embarrass other people.

10. _____ Theory that people with panic disorder tend to misinterpret the physical signs of arousal as catastrophic and dangerous.

True/False Test

Indicate whether each statement is true or false by placing T or F in the blank space next to each item.

1. ___ Compulsions refer to repeated, intrusive, and uncontrollable irrational thoughts or mental images that cause extreme anxiety and distress.

2. ___ A psychological (or mental) disorder is a pattern of behavioral and psychological symptoms that cause significant personal distress, impair the ability to function in one or more important areas of daily life, or both.

3. ___ Generalized anxiety disorder (GAD) is characterized by excessive, global, and persistent symptoms of anxiety; also called free-floating anxiety.

4. ___ Panic disorder is an anxiety disorder in which the person experiences frequent and unexpected panic attacks.

5. ___ Obsessions refer to repetitive behaviors or mental acts that are performed to prevent or reduce anxiety.

6. ___ Social phobia (social anxiety disorder) is an anxiety disorder involving the extreme and irrational fear of being embarrassed, judged, or scrutinized by others in social situations.

7. ___ Anxiety disorders are a category of psychological disorders in which extreme anxiety, the main diagnostic feature, causes significant disruptions in the person's cognitive, behavioral, and interpersonal functioning.

8. ___ A panic attack is a sudden episode of extreme anxiety that rapidly escalates in intensity.

9. ___ In addition to the many symptoms common to panic disorder, the person with ataque de nervios (attack of nerves) exhibits such symptoms as hysterical screaming, swearing, striking others, and breaking things.

10. ___ The caudate nucleus, which is involved in regulating movements, is a brain area that has been implicated in obsessive–compulsive disorder.

Check your answers and review any areas of weakness before going on to the next section.

Mood Disorders: Emotions Gone Awry

Preview Questions

Consider the following questions as you study this section of the chapter.

- What are mood (or affective) disorders?
- What characterizes major depression, and what is dysthymic disorder?
- What is seasonal affective disorder (SAD)?
- How is *bipolar disorder* defined?
- What characterizes a manic episode, and what is cyclothymic disorder?
- What factors contribute to mood disorders?

*Read the section "Mood Disorders: Emotions Gone Awry" and **write** your answers to the following:*

1. Mood disorders (also called affective disorders) are _____

_____

_____

_____

2. Major depression is characterized by _____

_____

_____

3. Dysthymic disorder is _____

_____

_____

4. Seasonal affective disorder is a mood disorder in which _____

_____

5. Bipolar disorder is defined as _____

_____

_____

6. A manic episode is a _____

_____

_____

7. Cyclothymic disorder is a mood disorder characterized by _____

_____

8. Multiple factors appear to be involved in the development of mood disorders. These include

_____

_____

_____

Eating Disorders: Anorexia and Bulimia

Preview Questions

Consider the following questions as you study this section of the chapter.

- What is an eating disorder?
- What behaviors and symptoms are associated with anorexia nervosa and bulimia nervosa?
- What factors have been implicated in the development of eating disorders?

Read the section "Eating Disorders: Anorexia and Bulimia" and write your answers to the following:

1. Eating disorders involve _____

_____

_____

_____

2. Anorexia nervosa is an eating disorder characterized by _____

_____

_____

3. Bulimia nervosa is an eating disorder characterized by _____

_____

Bulimia shares many of the characteristics of anorexia, with the main differences being that

_____

_____

_____

4. People with anorexia tend to suffer from

_____

_____

5. The main factors implicated in the development of eating disorders are _____

_____

_____

Personality Disorders: Maladaptive Traits

Preview Questions

Consider the following questions as you study this section of the chapter.

- What are the main characteristics of personality disorders, and how are personality disorders categorized into clusters?
- What characterizes the behavior of someone with a paranoid, antisocial, or borderline personality disorder?

*Read the section "Personality Disorders: Maladaptive Traits" and **write** your answers to the following:*

1. Personality disorder is defined as _____

_____

The basic clusters that the 10 personality disorders are grouped into are _____

_____

_____

_____

2. The paranoid personality disorder is characterized by _____

_____

_____

3. The antisocial personality disorder is characterized by _____

_____

_____

4. Borderline personality disorder is characterized by _____

_____

_____

The Dissociative Disorders: Fragmentation of the Self

Preview Questions

Consider the following questions as you study this section of the chapter.

- How is a *dissociative experience* defined, and what are dissociative disorders?
- What are dissociative amnesia and dissociative fugue?
- What is dissociative identity disorder (DID), and what is thought to cause it?

Read the section "The Dissociative Disorders: Fragmentation of the Self" and **write** *your answers to the following:*

1. The dissociative experience is _____

_____

2. Dissociative disorders are _____

_____

3. Dissociative amnesia is a disorder involving

_____

Dissociative fugue is _____

_____

4. Dissociative identity disorder (DID) involves

_____

_____

_____

5. According to one theory, DID is caused by _____

_____

_____

After you have carefully studied the preceding sections, complete the following exercises.

Concept Check 2

Read the following and write the correct term in the space provided.

1. Ursula is generally happy about her move to northern Canada six years ago, but at regular intervals since then she has suffered episodes of depression during the fall and winter months. Ursula is probably suffering from _____ disorder.

2. Laura suffers from a mood disorder. Her therapist has taken a family history and found that Laura's mother and two sisters also suffer from the same problem. Although her therapist is aware that multiple factors may be involved in her problem, he is most likely to conclude that Laura may have a(n) _____ predisposition for the disorder.

3. Dr. Markoff has prescribed lithium for Sandro's mood disorder. It is most likely that Sandro suffers from _____ disorder.

4. Nedzad has a chronic disorder involving moderate but frequent mood swings that are not severe enough to qualify as bipolar disorder or major depression. He is perceived as being very moody, unpredictable, and inconsistent; taken together, these symptoms may indicate _____ disorder.

5. Marion Einer, a fifth-grade schoolteacher in Jersey City, disappeared a few days after her husband left her. One year later, she was discovered working as a waitress in a cocktail lounge in San Diego. Calling herself Faye Bartell, she claimed to have no recollection of her past life and insisted that she had never been married. This example illustrates

_____ .

6. When Vanessa goes to a movie, she tends to become totally absorbed in the plot and loses all track of time and place; she is also often momentarily disoriented when she leaves the theater. These episodes represent

   _____ .

7. Karlson recently survived an airplane crash. Although he escaped from the burning plane with very few injuries, three of his friends were killed in the crash. Karlson is unable to recall any details from the time of the accident until a week later. Karlson has experienced

   _____ .

8. Dr. Rendell studies people who typically disregard and violate the rights of others and who appear to have no remorse or conscience about their destructive behaviors. Her colleague Dr. Gideon studies people who have a personality disorder characterized by instability of interpersonal relationships, self-image, and emotions and marked impulsivity. Dr. Rendell studies

   _____ personality disorder, and Dr. Gideon studies _____ personality disorder.

9. Without any valid evidence or logical reason, Bruce has an all-consuming distrust and suspiciousness of his co-workers, supervisor, friends, and family members. He is constantly on guard because he is convinced that other people, even family members, are out to harm, exploit, or trick him. Bruce is displaying symptoms of

   _____ .

10. Although Claire is of average height and weighs only 85 pounds, she has an irrational fear of gaining weight and has a distorted body-self perception. She has lost 30 pounds over the past eight or nine months by eating very little and going to aerobics classes twice a day. Claire probably suffers from

    _____ .

Graphic Organizer 2

List the main symptoms of the mood disorders:

Major Depression	Bipolar Disorder
1.	1.
2.	2.
3.	3.
4.	
5.	
6.	
Dysthymic Disorder	**Cyclothymic Disorder**
1.	1.

Review of Terms and Concepts 2

Use the terms in this list to complete the Matching Test, then to help you answer the True/False items correctly.

mood (or affective) disorders
major depression
dysthymic disorder
double depression
seasonal affective disorder (SAD)
bipolar disorder
manic episode
flight of ideas
cyclothymic disorder
rapid cycling
lithium
glutamate
eating disorder
anorexia nervosa
lanugo
bulimia nervosa

personality
personality traits
personality disorder
paranoid personality disorder
antisocial personality disorder (psychopath or sociopath)
conduct disorder
borderline personality disorder
dissociative experience
dissociative disorders
dissociative amnesia
dissociative fugue
dissociative identity disorder (DID)
alters (alter egos)

Matching Exercise

Match the appropriate term with its definition or description.

1. _____ Personality disorder characterized by a pervasive pattern of disregarding and violating the rights of others; such individuals are also referred to as psychopaths or sociopaths.

2. _____ Once called manic depression, this mood disorder involves periods of incapacitating depression alternating with periods of extreme euphoria and excitement.

3. _____ Mood disorder in which episodes of depression typically occur during fall and winter and subside during spring and summer.

4. _____ Mood disorder characterized by extreme and persistent feelings of despondency, worthlessness, and hopelessness, causing impaired emotional, cognitive, behavioral, and physical functioning.

5. _____ Sudden, rapidly escalating emotional state characterized by extreme euphoria, excitement, physical energy, and rapid thoughts and speech.

6. _____ Break or disruption in consciousness during which awareness, memory, and personal identity become separated or divided.

7. _____ Inflexible, maladaptive patterns of thoughts, emotions, behavior, and interpersonal functioning that are stable over time and across situations and deviate from the expectations of the individual's culture.

8. _____ Consistent and enduring patterns of thinking, feeling, and behaving that characterize a person as an individual.

9. _____ A dissociative disorder involving extensive memory disruptions along with the presence of two or more distinct identities, or "personalities"; *formerly called multiple personality disorder.*

10. _____ A personality disorder characterized by a pervasive distrust and suspiciousness of the motives of others without sufficient basis.

11. _____ Medication that helps control bipolar disorder.

12. _____ Term used to describe the distinct identities or personalities of a person with dissociative identity disorder.

13. _____ A diagnostic term for a pattern of behavior during childhood and adolescence that draws the attention of authorities, such as being cruel to animals, attacking or harming adults or other children, stealing, setting fires, and destroying property.

14. _____ A category of mental disorders characterized by severe disturbances in eating behavior.

15. _____ The soft, downy, fine body hair that normally occurs during the later stages of human fetal development but can also develop in severe cases of anorexia nervosa or starvation.

True/False Test

Indicate whether each statement is true or false by placing T or F in the blank space next to each item.

1. ____ Mood (or affective) disorders are a category of mental disorders in which significant and persistent disruptions in mood or emotion cause impaired cognitive, behavioral, and physical functioning.

2. ___ Dissociative fugue involves the partial or total inability to recall important personal information but does not involve sudden, unexpected travel from home.

3. ___ Dissociative amnesia involves sudden and unexpected travel away from home, extensive amnesia, and identity confusion.

4. ___ Cyclothymic disorder involves chronic, low-grade feelings of depression that produce subjective discomfort but do not seriously impair the ability to function and are not severe enough to qualify as major depression.

5. ___ Dissociative disorders are a category of psychological disorders in which extreme and frequent disruptions of awareness, memory, and personal identity impair the ability to function.

6. ___ Borderline personality disorder is characterized by instability of interpersonal relationships, self-image, and emotions, as well as by marked impulsivity.

7. ___ Dysthymic disorder is a mood disorder characterized by moderate but frequent mood swings that are not severe enough to qualify as either bipolar disorder or major depression.

8. ___ Personality traits are relatively stable predispositions to behave or react in certain ways and reflect different dimensions of a person's personality.

9. ___ Flight of ideas refers to thoughts that rapidly and loosely shift from topic to topic during a manic episode when attention is very easily distracted.

10. ___ A small percentage of people with bipolar disorder display rapid cycling, experiencing four or more manic or depressive episodes every year.

11. ___ Lithium regulates the availability of the neurotransmitter *glutamate,* which acts as an excitatory neurotransmitter in many brain areas.

12. ___ Some people with dysthymic disorder experience *double depression,* in which one or more episodes of major depression occur on top of their ongoing dysthymic disorder.

13. ___ Anorexia nervosa is an eating disorder characterized by binges of extreme overeating followed by self-induced vomiting, misuse of laxatives, or other inappropriate methods to purge the excessive food and prevent weight gain.

14. ___ Bulimia nervosa is an eating disorder characterized by excessive weight loss, an irrational fear of gaining weight, and distorted body self-perception.

Check your answers and review any areas of weakness before going on to the next section.

Schizophrenia: A Different Reality

Preview Questions

Consider the following questions as you study this section of the chapter.

- How is schizophrenia characterized?
- How do positive and negative symptoms differ?
- What are the main subtypes of schizophrenia?
- What evidence points to the involvement of genetic factors and brain abnormalities in the development of schizophrenia?
- How do environmental factors affect the development of schizophrenia?

Read the section "Schizophrenia: A Different Reality" and **write** *your answers to the following:*

1. Schizophrenia is a psychological disorder that involves _____

   _____

2. Positive symptoms include _____

   _____

   _____

   _____

   _____

   Negative symptoms reflect _____

   _____

   _____

3. The three basic subtypes of schizophrenia are

   (a) _____

   _____

   (b) _____

   _____

   (c) _____

   _____

A fourth label, _____ ,
is used to describe individuals who _____

_____

_____

4. Evidence that genetic factors are involved in
   the development of schizophrenia comes from

   _____

5. Research on paternal age and the risk of schizophrenia indicates that _____

   _____

   _____

   _____

6. One environmental factor implicated in the
   development of schizophrenia is that _____

   _____

   _____

7. Neurological evidence from research examining
   abnormal brain structures indicates that

   _____

   _____

8. The idea that schizophrenia is the result of
   abnormal brain chemistry is supported largely
   by two pieces of indirect evidence:
   (a) _____

   _____

   (b) _____

   _____

9. Research into psychological factors, such as
   unhealthy families, has found _____

   _____

   _____

**After you have carefully studied the preceding
section, complete the following exercises.**

Concept Check 3

*Read the following and write the correct term in the
space provided.*

1. Franko and Alberto are identical twins. Franko
   has developed schizophrenia. The probability
   that Alberto will also develop schizophrenia is
   about _____ percent.

2. Dr. Hansen is conducting research on the viral
   infection theory. He is likely to find that people
   born in the winter and spring months, when
   upper respiratory infections are most common,
   are _____ (more/less) likely to suffer from schizophrenia than those born at other
   times of the year.

3. Derrick hears voices that tell him to be careful
   because he is being watched by aliens. Kirk
   believes that he is a famous rock star. Both suffer from the positive symptoms of schizophrenia. Derrick is experiencing _____ ,
   and Kirk is having _____ .

4. Quincy falsely believes that others are plotting
   against him and are trying to kill him. He
   believes that these agents are putting poison in
   the hospital's coffee supply and will attack him
   if he ever tries to leave the ward. This example
   illustrates a positive symptom of schizophrenia
   called _____ .

5. Neuroscientists researching changes in the
   brain structures of normal adolescents and
   adolescents with schizophrenia took high-
   resolution brain scans of the participants over a
   five-year period. Normal teens showed about 1
   percent loss of gray matter, while teens with
   schizophrenia lost more than 5 percent; the
   amount of loss was directly correlated with clinical symptoms of schizophrenia. More rapid
   gray matter losses in the temporal lobe were
   associated with _____ (positive/
   negative) symptoms; more rapid losses in the
   frontal lobes were associated with _____
   (positive/negative) symptoms.

6. Mrs. Perez usually sits passively in a motionless stupor, but if the nurse moves her arms to
   a new position, she will stay in that position for
   a very long time. This symptom of catatonic
   schizophrenia is called _____ .

7. When Darcy was examined by his psychologist, she noted that he displayed some combination of positive and negative symptoms that did not clearly fit the criteria for _____ , _____ , or _____ types of schizophrenia, so she diagnosed him as having an undifferentiated type of schizophrenia.

Graphic Organizer 3

Write the main positive and negative symptoms of schizophrenia in the spaces provided.

Positive Symptoms	Negative Symptoms
1.	1.
2.	2.
3.	3.

Review of Terms and Concepts 3

Use the terms in this list to complete the Matching Test, then to help you answer the True/False items correctly.

schizophrenia
positive symptoms
negative symptoms
delusion
delusions of reference
delusions of grandeur
delusions of persecution
hallucination
flat affect
alogia (poverty of
  speech)
avolition
paranoid type of
  schizophrenia

catatonic type of
  schizophrenia
waxy flexibility
disorganized type of
  schizophrenia
  (hebephrenic
  schizophrenia)
undifferentiated type of
  schizophrenia
ventricles
gray matter
dopamine hypothesis

Matching Exercise

Match the appropriate term with its definition or description.

1. _____ View that schizophrenia is related to, and may be caused by, excess activity of the neurotransmitter dopamine in the brain.

2. _____ Psychological disorder in which the ability to function is impaired by severely distorted beliefs, perceptions, and thought processes.

3. _____ Subtype of schizophrenia that is characterized by the presence of delusions, hallucinations, or both; the person shows virtually no cognitive impairment, disorganized behavior, or negative symptoms; instead, well-organized delusions of persecution or grandeur are operating, and auditory hallucinations are often evident.

4. _____ Unusual symptom of catatonic schizophrenia in which the person can be molded into any position and will hold that position indefinitely.

5. _____ Commonly seen negative symptom of schizophrenia in which an individual consistently shows a dramatic reduction in emotional responsiveness and a lack of normal facial expression; few expressive gestures are made, and the person's speech is slow and monotonous, lacking normal vocal inflections.

6. _____ Falsely held belief that persists in spite of compelling contradictory evidence.

7. _____ Delusion in which the person believes that other people are constantly talking about her or that everything that happens is somehow related to her.

8. _____ False or distorted perception that seems vividly real to the person experiencing it.

9. _____ Subtype of schizophrenia in which an individual displays some combination of positive and negative symptoms that does not clearly fit the criteria for the paranoid, catatonic, or disorganized type.

10. _____ Fluid-filled cavities located deep within the brain.

True/False Test

Indicate whether each item is true or false by placing T or F in the space next to each item.

1. ____ In schizophrenia, positive symptoms reflect defects or deficits in normal functioning and include flat affect, alogia, and avolition.

2. ____ Avolition refers to the inability to initiate or persist in even simple forms of goal-directed behaviors, such as dressing, bathing, or engaging in social activities.

3. ____ The catatonic type of schizophrenia is marked by highly disturbed movements or actions and may include bizarre postures or grimaces, waxy flexibility, extremely agitated behavior, complete immobility, echoing words spoken by others, and assuming rigid postures that resist being moved.

4. ____ Alogia, which is also referred to as poverty of speech, is used to describe the symptom in which speech production is greatly reduced.

5. ____ The basic theme of delusions of grandeur is that the person is extremely important, powerful, or wealthy.

6. ____ In schizophrenia, negative symptoms reflect excesses or distortions of normal functioning and include delusions, hallucinations, and disorganized thoughts and behaviors.

7. ____ In delusions of persecution, the person believes that others are plotting against him or trying to harm him or someone close to him.

8. ____ The prominent features of the disorganized type of schizophrenia are extremely disorganized behavior, disorganized speech, and flat affect; this subtype is sometimes called hebephrenic schizophrenia.

9. ____ Gray matter is made up of glial cells, neuron cell bodies, and unmyelinated axons that comprise the quarter-inch-thick cerebral cortex.

Check your answers and review any areas of weakness before going on to the next section.

Something to Think About

1. One of the most common misconceptions about mental, or psychological, disorders is that schizophrenia and dissociative identity disorder are the same thing. This myth is fostered by inaccurate portrayals and misinformation in the media. What are the important distinctions between these two disorders, and what would you say to someone who thought they were the same thing?

2. Most people are curious about mental, or psychological, disorders. Students frequently recognize aspects of themselves in the descriptions they read and wonder if they could one day suffer from some form of psychological disorder. What is normal, and what is abnormal? What are the chances of developing symptoms of psychopathology, and what causes such disorders? How would you answer these questions?

3. Suppose a friend says that he read somewhere that cigarette smoking causes psychological disorders. Based on what you know from reading the text, how would you respond to this claim?

Check your answers and review any areas of weakness before completing the progress tests.

Progress Test 1

Review the complete chapter (including all boxed inserts), review all your study notes, and then test yourself on the following progress test. Check your answers. If you make a mistake, review your notes, check the appropriate section in the study guide, and if necessary, go back and read the relevant part of the chapter in your textbook.

1. Phoebe believes that she is the president of the United States and thinks that her indecipherable scribblings are actually top secret memos. Phoebe is most clearly suffering from a(n)
   (a) delusion.   (c) hallucination.
   (b) panic attack.   (d) obsession.

2. Shayna has very erratic, unstable relationships, emotions, and self-image. She is extremely impulsive and goes to great lengths to avoid real or imagined abandonment. It is most probable that Shayna has a disorder called
   (a) agoraphobia.
   (b) borderline personality disorder.
   (c) antisocial personality disorder.
   (d) cyclothymic disorder.

3. Dr. Koopman deals with people who suffer from a variety of problems that cause them significant personal distress and impair their ability to function in one or more important areas of their lives. Like most people in his profession, Dr. Koopman uses the term *mental disorder* to describe these symptoms. Dr. Koopman is most likely a

   (a) clinical psychologist.
   (b) psychiatrist.
   (c) social psychologist.
   (d) developmental psychologist.

4. Kaila often appears nervous and agitated. She frequently talks in a loud voice and giggles at almost everything she hears. Her behavior is most likely to be diagnosed as a psychological disorder if it

   (a) is not caused by some biological dysfunction.
   (b) is the result of a genetic predisposition.
   (c) represents a significant departure from the prevailing social and cultural norms.
   (d) is caused by drugs or medication.

5. Sidney, a college student, complains that he feels nervous and fearful most of the time but doesn't know why. He worries constantly about everything, and if he manages to deal with one problem, he starts worrying about a dozen others. Sidney most likely suffers from _____ disorder.

   (a) generalized anxiety (c) dissociative
   (b) bipolar   (d) cyclothymic

6. Imogene, a third-grade teacher, sometimes experiences a pounding heart, rapid breathing, breathlessness, and a choking sensation. She breaks out in a sweat, starts to tremble, and experiences light-headedness and chills. These symptoms last for about 10 minutes and are characteristic of

   (a) posttraumatic stress disorder (PTSD).
   (b) dysthymic disorder.
   (c) cyclothymic disorder.
   (d) panic attack.

7. Paula has been diagnosed with agoraphobia. Her symptoms include which of the following?

   (a) an extreme and irrational fear of experiencing a panic attack in a public place and being unable to escape or get help
   (b) a sudden, rapidly escalating emotional state characterized by extreme euphoria, excitement, physical energy, and rapid thoughts and speech

   (c) partial or total inability to recall important personal information
   (d) all of these symptoms

8. Erin has been diagnosed with bulimia nervosa. The main symptoms of her eating disorder are

   (a) binges of extreme overeating and purging by self-induced vomiting and misuse of laxatives or other methods to purge the excessive food and prevent weight gain.
   (b) an increase in brain activity of the neurotransmitter serotonin.
   (c) being 15 to 20 percent below the ideal body weight and having an irrational fear of gaining weight.
   (d) severe food restriction, maladaptive dieting, and the development of lanugo.

9. Kevin was working in a building when an explosion occurred; although he escaped with relatively minor injuries, he can't stop thinking about all the dead and seriously injured people he saw. He has frequent nightmares about the event and feels guilty that he survived when many of his co-workers did not. Kevin's symptoms are indicative of

   (a) dissociative fugue.
   (b) dysthymic disorder.
   (c) cyclothymic disorder.
   (d) posttraumatic stress disorder (PTSD).

10. Mrs. Landon has been diagnosed as suffering from major depression. Which of the following symptoms is she most likely to be experiencing?

    (a) feelings of guilt, worthlessness, inadequacy, emptiness, and hopelessness
    (b) awkward and slower than usual speech, movement, and gestures and frequent crying spells for no apparent reason
    (c) dull and sluggish thought processes and problems concentrating
    (d) loss of physical energy and vague aches and pains
    (e) all of these symptoms

11. Karla suffers from a chronic, low-grade depression characterized by many of the symptoms of major depression but less intense; these problems started many years ago when both her parents were killed in a car accident. Karla is likely to be diagnosed as suffering from

    (a) dysthymic disorder.
    (b) agoraphobia.
    (c) cyclothymic disorder.
    (d) dissociative amnesia.

12. About six months ago, 15-year-old Kirsten went on a drastic weight-loss diet that caused her to drop from 115 to 85 pounds. Although she is dangerously underweight and undernourished, she continues to think she looks fat. Kirsten probably suffers from
    (a) ataque de nervios.
    (b) anorexia nervosa.
    (c) bulimia nervosa.
    (d) cyclothymic disorder.

13. Twenty-five-year-old Daisuke suffers from a disorder, similar to social phobia, called *taijin kyofusho*. In addition to extreme social anxiety and avoidance of social situations, Daisuke is likely
    (a) to have a preoccupation with imagined diseases based on his misinterpretation of bodily symptoms or function.
    (b) to be very concerned with being embarrassed in public.
    (c) to worry about being overcome with an irresistible urge to set fire to people and things.
    (d) to fear that his appearance or smell, facial expressions, or body language will offend, insult, or embarrass others.

14. According to Critical Thinking (Are People with Mental Illness as Violent as the Media Portray Them?), which of the following is true?
    (a) People with mental disorders are generally portrayed with great accuracy in the media.
    (b) Twenty percent of "normal" television characters are murderers, but only 5 percent of "mentally ill" characters are killers.
    (c) The incidence of violent behavior among current or former mental patients is grossly exaggerated in media portrayals.
    (d) Seventy percent of "normal" television characters are violent, but only 40 percent of television characters labeled mentally ill are violent.

15. According to Critical Thinking (Does Smoking Cause Depression and Other Psychological Disorders?), which of the following is true?
    (a) Smoking cigarettes is a major cause of mental illness and psychological disorders.
    (b) Mental illness is a major cause of cigarette smoking behavior in both adolescents and adults.
    (c) Although there is a positive correlation between cigarette smoking and the prevalence of mental illness, the exact causal connection has not been clearly established.
    (d) One of the main active ingredients in cigarettes, nicotine, has no known psychoactive properties, nor does it have any effect on brain structures or on the release of various neurotransmitters.

Progress Test 2

After you have checked your understanding of the material in Progress Test 1 and have done a complete chapter review with special focus on any areas of weakness, you are ready to assess your knowledge on Progress Test 2. Check your answers. If you make a mistake, review your notes, the relevant section of the study guide, and, if necessary, the appropriate part of your textbook.

1. Dr. Moretti believes that schizophrenia is the result of abnormal brain chemistry. Her views are consistent with the
    (a) viral infection theory.
    (b) dopamine hypothesis.
    (c) genetic predisposition theory.
    (d) cognitive-behavioral theory.

2. Researchers scan the brains of normal adolescents and adolescents with early-onset schizophrenia. If their results are consistent with the findings of other neuroscientists, they are likely to discover that
    (a) teenagers with schizophrenia have a severe loss of gray matter (5 percent), compared to normal teens (1 percent).
    (b) the amount of gray matter lost is directly correlated with patients' clinical symptoms; the more gray matter lost the greater the increase in psychotic symptoms.
    (c) more rapid loss of gray matter in the temporal lobes is associated with positive symptoms of schizophrenia
    (d) more rapid loss of gray matter in the frontal lobes is correlated with negative symptoms of schizophrenia.
    (e) all of these statements are true.

3. Dr. Crewe believes that people with panic disorder tend to misinterpret the physical signs of arousal as catastrophic and dangerous, and this misinterpretation only adds to the problem by causing even more physiological arousal. Eventually, they become conditioned to respond with fear to the physical symptoms of arousal, and repeated panic attacks lead to panic disorder. Dr. Crewe's explanation is most consistent with the _____ of panic disorder.

   (a) social-cultural explanation
   (b) biological theory
   (c) cognitive-behavioral theory
   (d) genetic predisposition explanation

4. Nima suffers from a type of schizophrenia that is characterized by hallucinations and delusions of grandeur, but she shows virtually no cognitive impairment, disorganized behavior, or negative symptoms. Nima suffers from _____-type schizophrenia.

   (a) paranoid
   (b) catatonic
   (c) disorganized
   (d) undifferentiated

5. Tara, a young married woman, has wandered from her home to a distant city where she has completely forgotten her family and her identity. This example illustrates

   (a) undifferentiated-type schizophrenia.
   (b) dissociative fugue.
   (c) disorganized-type schizophrenia.
   (d) dissociative amnesia.

6. Maury repeatedly checks to see if the stove is turned off and frequently turns around on his way to work to go back home to double check. This is an example of a(n)

   (a) delusion.
   (b) obsession.
   (c) hallucination.
   (d) compulsion.

7. Otis turned down a very high-paying job because it meant he would have to fly to the head office in Tokyo two or three times a year. He doesn't know why, but the thought of flying absolutely terrifies him. Otis may have

   (a) undifferentiated-type schizophrenia.
   (b) a phobia.
   (c) bipolar disorder.
   (d) posttraumatic stress disorder (PTSD).

8. Every semester just before midterm exams, Lilly gets very anxious and worries about how she is going to do. To reduce her apprehension, she studies very hard. Lilly suffers from

   (a) anxiety disorder.
   (b) free-floating disorder.

   (c) panic disorder.
   (d) obsessive–compulsive disorder (OCD).
   (e) none of these disorders; her symptoms are quite normal.

9. Jessica rarely leaves her home. She doesn't go shopping because she is frightened of having a panic attack and getting lost or trapped in a crowd. Jessica has symptoms that indicate she may have

   (a) agoraphobia.
   (b) cyclothymic disorder.
   (c) posttraumatic stress disorder (PTSD).
   (d) seasonal affective disorder (SAD).

10. Yvette usually stands motionless and will echo words just spoken to her. She resists directions from others and sometimes assumes a rigid posture to prevent people from moving her. These symptoms suggest that Yvette has a type of _____ called _____ type.

    (a) schizophrenia; catatonic
    (b) mood disorder; cyclothymic
    (c) schizophrenia; disorganized
    (d) mood disorder; dysthymic

11. Brandy's doctor prescribed lithium for her symptoms; as long as she keeps taking the medication, she feels fine. It is very likely that Brandy suffers from

    (a) schizophrenia.
    (b) generalized anxiety disorder (GAD).
    (c) bipolar disorder.
    (d) dissociative identity disorder (DID).

12. Regardless of the situation, Philip responds in an emotionally flat manner and consistently shows greatly reduced emotional responsiveness. His speech is slow and monotonous, and he is unable to initiate even simple forms of goal-directed behavior, such as dressing, bathing, or engaging in social activities. Philip is suffering from _____ , and his symptoms are _____ .

    (a) schizophrenia; positive
    (b) anxiety disorder; positive
    (c) schizophrenia; negative
    (d) anxiety disorder; negative

13. Perry has dropped out of college because of the extreme distress that being in social situations causes him. He is unemployed because he is unable to bring himself to go for a job interview. Perry has

    (a) disorganized-type schizophrenia.
    (b) a dissociative disorder.
    (c) a generalized anxiety disorder (GAD).
    (d) social phobia (social anxiety disorder).

14. Within the last two years, John has been fired from four different jobs for stealing money and goods from his employers. He feels no remorse and thinks his bosses were stupid for making it so easy to steal from them. John has a long history of problems with the law, which started in his early teens when he was diagnosed with a conduct disorder. It is most likely that John has

    (a) an antisocial personality disorder.
    (b) an obsessive–compulsive disorder (OCD).
    (c) paranoid-type schizophrenia.
    (d) dissociative identity disorder (DID).

15. According to Culture and Human Behavior (Travel Advisory: The Jerusalem Syndrome), which of the following is true?

    (a) The content of schizophrenic hallucinations and delusions is virtually identical across cultures.
    (b) People who suffer from the Jerusalem syndrome are typically people who have a long history of dissociative identity disorder (DID).
    (c) The content of schizophrenic hallucinations and delusions can vary from one culture to another and may be influenced by a particular culture's religious beliefs.
    (d) The Jerusalem syndrome is a personality disorder caused by inherited genetic factors.

Progress Test 3

After you have checked your understanding of the material in Progress Tests 1 and 2, and have done a complete chapter review with special focus on any areas of weakness, you are ready to further assess your knowledge with Progress Test 3. Check your answers. If you make a mistake, review your notes, the appropriate parts of the study guide, and, if necessary, the relevant sections of your textbook.

1. Wendell repeatedly steals small items that he doesn't need and could easily pay for if he wanted to. Harman frequently sets fire to property for no obvious reason other than the pleasure he derives from seeing buildings on fire.

    According to Table 13.1 (Some Key Diagnostic Categories in DSM IV-TR), Wendell suffers from _____ and Harman has a disorder called _____ .

    (a) kleptomania; pyromania
    (b) Tourette's disorder; hypochondriasis
    (c) autistic disorder; fetishism
    (d) agoraphobia; pyrophobia

2. Fear of having a panic attack in a public situation is to _____ as an extreme and irrational fear of being embarrassed, judged, or scrutinized by others in social situations is to

    _____ .

    (a) social phobia (social anxiety disorder); agoraphobia
    (b) bibliophobia; phonophobia
    (c) agoraphobia; social phobia
    (d) phobophobia; ergophobia

3. Shayne suffers from posttraumatic stress disorder (PTSD). If he is similar to most people who have this disorder, he is likely to exhibit which of the following symptoms?

    (a) frequent, intrusive recollections of a traumatic event, numbing of emotional responsiveness, and avoidance of particular situations
    (b) recurrent episodes of unintended sleep in inappropriate situations, such as during a meeting or while driving a car
    (c) repetitive behaviors or mental acts that are performed to prevent or reduce anxiety
    (d) the urge to set fires for pleasure, gratification, or relief of tension
    (e) all of these symptoms

4. Mandy is a 45-year-old administrative assistant. Based on the National Comorbidity Survey (NCS), the chance that Mandy may have experienced the symptoms of a psychological disorder at some point in her life is about _____ percent.

    (a) 10   (c) 80
    (b) 50   (d) 100

5. Dr. Burstein explains the development of phobias in terms of basic learning principles. Which of the following are likely to be included in his explanation?

    (a) classical conditioning
    (b) operant conditioning
    (c) observational learning
    (d) All of these types of learning may be involved in his explanation.

6. After several weeks of feeling very apathetic and dissatisfied with his life, Elmiro has suddenly become extremely euphoric and full of energy. He talks so rapidly that he is hard to understand, he sleeps very little, and he has gone on a number of very expensive shopping sprees. He gets very irritated when anyone tells him to take it easy and slow down. Elmiro is exhibiting all the signs of
   (a) obsessive–compulsive disorder (OCD).
   (b) catatonic schizophrenia.
   (c) dissociative identity disorder (DID).
   (d) bipolar disorder.

7. Lucille suffers from dissociative identity disorder (DID). If she is like most people diagnosed with this disorder, she is likely to have experienced
   (a) extreme physical or sexual abuse in childhood.
   (b) episodes when she believed she was the reincarnation of some famous and powerful person.
   (c) exposure to a viral infection during prenatal development or early infancy.
   (d) excess dopamine in her brain during childhood.
   (e) all of these events.

8. When Christy was young she was badly scratched and bitten by a cat she tried to pet. She now has an extreme fear of all cats in general and has learned to reduce her anxiety by avoiding cats whenever possible. Christy's phobia and avoidance behavior can best be explained by
   (a) the dopamine hypothesis.
   (b) learning theory, specifically classical and operant conditioning.
   (c) the viral infection theory.
   (d) the catatonic hypothesis.

9. Dr. Arnkoff and his colleagues found that people born in the winter and spring months were more likely to suffer from schizophrenia than those born at other times of the year. This correlational research provides support for the _____ and the influence of _____ factors.
   (a) viral infection theory; environmental
   (b) dopamine hypothesis; genetic
   (c) paternal age hypothesis; environmental
   (d) unhealthy families theory; genetic

10. Vera has been diagnosed with cyclothymic disorder. Her symptoms are likely to include
    (a) moderate but frequent mood swings for two years or longer.
    (b) chronic low-grade feelings of depression that produce subjective discomfort but do not seriously impair her ability to function.
    (c) partial or total inability to recall important personal information.
    (d) irrational fears of a specific object or situation.
    (e) all of these symptoms.

11. Nester's sense of self-esteem is wildly inflated, and he exudes supreme self-confidence. He has delusional, grandiose plans for obtaining wealth, power, and fame and is engaged in a frenzy of goal-directed activities that could cost thousands of dollars. This is an example of a(n)
    (a) manic episode.
    (b) obsession.
    (c) social phobia (social anxiety disorder).
    (d) hallucination.

12. Deidre suffers from frequent and unexpected panic attacks. Despite her apprehension about these episodes, Deidre functions fairly well in her job and has a relatively normal social life. Deidre is likely to be diagnosed with
    (a) panic disorder.
    (b) social phobia (social anxiety disorder).
    (c) bipolar disorder.
    (d) dissociative fugue.

13. Scott repeatedly thinks that he might get a gun and kill all his colleagues at work. These thoughts are very disturbing, intrusive, and uncontrollable and cause Scott great distress and anxiety. Scott is experiencing a(n)
    (a) delusion.   (c) hallucination.
    (b) obsession.   (d) compulsion.

14. Konrad has experienced numerous psychiatric and physical symptoms and memory loss, and he has a chaotic personal history. During a session with his therapist, Konrad suddenly began speaking in a very childlike voice and claimed that his name was Arnold and that he was only 10 years old. A short time later he reverted to his normal adult voice and claimed to have no recollection of the incident. Konrad is likely to be diagnosed as suffering from
    (a) paranoid-type schizophrenia.
    (b) dissociative identity disorder (DID).
    (c) paranoid personality disorder.
    (d) posttraumatic stress disorder.

15. According to the Application, the best way to help prevent someone from committing suicide is to
    (a) use some well-known platitudes like "every cloud has a silver lining."
    (b) not let the person talk too much about what is bothering him because it will only make him more depressed.
    (c) suggest that seeking professional help would be a total waste of time and money in the present situation.
    (d) ask the person to delay his decision and encourage him to seek professional help.

Answers

Introduction: Understanding Psychological Disorders

1. *Psychopathology is* the scientific study of the origins, symptoms, and development of psychological disorders.

2. *A psychological, or mental, disorder can be defined as* a pattern of behavioral and psychological symptoms that causes significant personal distress, impairs the ability to function in one or more important areas of daily life, or both. These symptoms must represent a serious departure from prevailing social and cultural norms.

3. *DSM-IV-TR stands for* the *Diagnostic and Statistical Manual of Mental Disorders, Fourth Edition, Text Revision;* it was published by the American Psychiatric Association in 2000 and represents the consensus of a wide range of mental health professionals and organizations. *This manual describes* approximately 250 specific psychological disorders (including the symptoms, the exact criteria that must be met to make a diagnosis, and the typical course for each mental disorder) and provides mental health professionals with a common language for labeling mental disorders and comprehensive guidelines for diagnosing mental disorders.

4. *The National Comorbidity Survey found that psychological disorders were more common than previously thought, which can be interpreted to mean* that many people who could benefit from treatment do not seek it. However, it seems that most of these people weather the symptoms without becoming completely debilitated.

Anxiety Disorders

1. *Anxiety is defined as* an unpleasant emotional state characterized by physical arousal and feelings of tension, apprehension, and worry that often hits during personal crises and everyday conflicts. *It is often adaptive and normal because* it puts you on physical and mental alert and helps you focus attention on the threatening situation.

2. *In the anxiety disorders, the anxiety is* maladaptive, disrupting everyday activities, moods, and thought processes.

3. *The three features that distinguish normal anxiety from pathological anxiety are (a)* Pathological anxiety is irrational (it is provoked by perceived threats that are exaggerated or nonexistent, and the anxiety response is out of proportion to the actual importance of the situation). *(b)* Pathological anxiety is uncontrollable (the person can't shut off the alarm reaction, even when he or she knows it's unrealistic). *(c)* Pathological anxiety is disruptive (it interferes with relationships, job or academic performance, or everyday activities).

4. *Generalized anxiety disorder (GAD) is characterized by* excessive, global, and persistent symptoms of anxiety (also called free-floating anxiety).

5. *A panic attack is* a sudden episode of extreme anxiety that rapidly escalates in intensity. The most common symptoms are a pounding heart, rapid breathing, breathlessness, and a choking sensation, often accompanied by sweating, trembling, lightheadedness, chills, or hot flashes.

6. *A panic disorder is* an anxiety disorder in which the person experiences frequent and unexpected panic attacks. *Its cause is thought to be* both biological and psychological. The cognitive-behavioral theory proposes that

people with panic disorder tend to misinterpret physical symptoms of arousal as catastrophic and dangerous.

7. *A phobia is* a strong or irrational fear of something, usually a specific object or situation, that does not necessarily interfere with the ability to function in daily life. *A specific phobia is* characterized by an extreme and irrational fear of a specific object or situation that interferes with the ability to function in daily life (e.g., agoraphobia, and social phobia).

8. *Phobias are assumed by some to involve various forms of learning such as* classical conditioning (the feared object is the conditioned stimulus, and the learned fear is the conditioned response, which can generalize to other similar stimuli); operant conditioning, which can also be involved in the avoidance behavior that characterizes phobias (the conditioned response of avoiding the feared object is negatively reinforced by the relief from anxiety and fear that the behavior brings about); observational learning (people can learn to be phobic of certain objects or situations by observing the fearful reactions of someone else who acts as a model in the situation or through seeing media accounts of disasters and catastrophes); and biological preparedness (humans are predisposed through our evolutionary history to acquire fears of certain animals or situations).

Anxiety Disorders: Posttraumatic Stress Disorder and Obsessive–Compulsive Disorder

1. *Posttraumatic stress disorder (PTSD) is* a long-lasting anxiety disorder in which chronic and persistent symptoms of anxiety develop in response to an extreme physical or psychological trauma (extreme traumas are events that produce intense feelings of horror and helplessness, such as a serious physical injury or threat of injury to yourself or to loved ones).

2. *The three core symptoms that characterize PTSD are (a)* The person frequently recalls the event, replaying it in his or her mind (it is often unwanted or intrusive and interferes with normal thought processes). *(b)* The person avoids stimuli or situations that tend to trigger memories of the experience and undergoes a general numbing of emotional responsiveness. *(c)* The person experiences the increased physical arousal associated with anxiety (he or she may be easily startled, experience sleep disturbances, have problems concentrating and

remembering, and be prone to irritability or angry outbursts).

3. *Factors that influence the likelihood of developing posttraumatic stress disorder are (a)* People with a personal or family history of psychological disorders are more likely to develop PTSD when exposed to extreme trauma. *(b)* The magnitude of the trauma plays an important role—more extreme stressors are more likely to produce PTSD. *(c)* When people undergo multiple traumas, the incidence of PTSD can be quite high.

4. *Obsessive–compulsive disorder (OCD) is* an anxiety disorder in which the symptoms of anxiety are triggered by intrusive, repetitive thoughts and urges to perform certain actions. *Obsessions are* repeated, intrusive, and uncontrollable irrational thoughts or mental images that cause extreme anxiety and distress (they have little or no basis in reality and are often extremely farfetched). *Compulsions are* repetitive behaviors that are performed to prevent or reduce anxiety and are typically ritual behaviors (overtly physical or covertly mental) that must be carried out in a certain pattern or sequence.

5. *People with obsessive–compulsive disorder commonly experience* both obsessions and compulsions, which are often linked in some way, even if the behaviors bear little logical relationship to the feared consequences (in all cases, people with obsessive–compulsive disorder feel that something terrible will happen if the compulsive action is left undone).

6. *Two biological factors that seem to be involved in obsessive–compulsive disorder are* a deficiency in the neurotransmitter serotonin (drugs that increase the availability of serotonin in the brain decrease symptoms), and dysfunctions in specific brain areas, such as the frontal lobes (which play a key role in our ability to think and plan ahead) or the caudate nucleus (which is involved in regulating movements).

Concept Check 1

1. mental; psychological
2. normal
3. obsessive–compulsive
4. generalized anxiety
5. social phobia (social anxiety disorder)
6. posttraumatic stress

7. panic attacks

8. classical; operant; observational

9. serotonin; frontal; caudate nucleus

Graphic Organizer 1

Generalized Anxiety Disorder
Persistent, chronic, unreasonable worry and anxiety, characterized by general symptoms of anxiety, including persistent physical arousal.

Panic Disorder
Frequent and unexpected panic attacks, with no specific or identifiable trigger.

Phobias
A strong or irrational fear of something, usually a specific object or situation that does not necessarily interfere with the ability to function in daily life. Phobias include specific phobia, social phobia, and agoraphobia (fear of having a panic attack in a public or inescapable situation).

Posttraumatic Stress Disorder
Anxiety triggered by memories of an extreme physical or psychological traumatic experience.

Obsessive–Compulsive Disorder
Anxiety caused by uncontrollable, persistent, recurring, and intrusive thoughts (obsessions) and/or urges to perform certain actions (compulsions).

Matching Exercise 1

1. psychopathology

2. DSM-IV-TR

3. obsessive–compulsive disorder (OCD)

4. anxiety

5. phobia

6. posttraumatic stress disorder (PTSD)

7. agoraphobia

8. specific phobia

9. taijin kyofusho

10. cognitive-behavioral theory of panic disorder

True/False Test 1

1. F	5. F	8. T
2. T	6. T	9. T
3. T	7. T	10. T
4. T		

Mood Disorders: Emotions Gone Awry

1. *Mood disorders (also called affective disorders) are* a category of mental disorders in which significant and persistent disruptions in mood or emotions cause impaired cognitive, behavioral, and physical functioning.

2. *Major depression is characterized by* extreme and persistent feelings of despondency, worthlessness, and hopelessness, causing impaired emotional, cognitive, behavioral, and physical functioning.

3. *Dysthymic disorder* is a mood disorder involving chronic, low-grade feelings of depression that produce subjective discomfort but do not seriously impair the ability to function.

4. *Seasonal affective disorder is a mood disorder in which* episodes of depression typically occur during the fall and winter and subside during the spring and summer.

5. *Bipolar disorder is defined as* a mood disorder involving periods of incapacitating depression alternating with periods of extreme euphoria and excitement (formerly called manic depression).

6. *A manic episode is a* sudden, rapidly escalating emotional state characterized by extreme euphoria, excitement, physical energy, and rapid thoughts and speech.

7. *Cyclothymic disorder is a mood disorder characterized by* moderate but frequent mood swings that are not severe enough to qualify as bipolar disorder or major depression.

8. *Multiple factors appear to be involved in the development of mood disorders. These include* genetic predispositions, stress, and disruptions in brain chemistry (the neurotransmitters serotonin and norepinephrine have been implicated in depression, and glutamate may be involved in bipolar disorder).

Eating Disorders: Anorexia and Bulimia

1. *Eating disorders involve* serious and maladaptive disturbances in eating behavior and can include extreme reduction of food intake, severe bouts of overeating, and obsessive concerns about body shape and weight.

2. *Anorexia nervosa is an eating disorder characterized by* excessive weight loss, an irrational

fear of gaining weight, and distorted body self-perception.

3. *Bulimia nervosa is an eating disorder characterized by* binges of extreme overeating followed by self-induced vomiting, misuse of laxatives, or other inappropriate methods to purge excessive food and prevent weight gain. *Bulimia shares many of the characteristics of anorexia, with the main differences being that* people with bulimia stay within a normal weight range, or may be slightly overweight, and they usually recognize that they have an eating disorder.

4. *People with anorexia tend to suffer from* perfectionism, rigid thinking, poor peer relations, social isolation, and low self-esteem.

5. The main factors implicated in the development of eating disorders are genetics, decreases in brain activity of serotonin, disruptions in chemical signals that normally regulate eating behavior, and contemporary Western cultural attitudes about thinness and dieting.

Personality Disorders: Maladaptive Traits

1. *Personality disorder is defined as* inflexible, maladaptive patterns of thought, emotions, behavior, and interpersonal functioning that are stable over time and across situations and deviate from the expectations of the individual's culture. *The basic clusters that the 10 personality disorders are grouped into are* the odd, eccentric cluster; the dramatic, emotional, erratic cluster; and the anxious, fearful cluster.

2. *Paranoid personality disorder is characterized by* a pervasive distrust and suspiciousness of the motives of others without sufficient basis.

3. *The antisocial personality disorder is characterized by* a pervasive pattern of disregarding and violating the rights of others (such individuals are often referred to as psychopaths or sociopaths).

4. *Borderline personality disorder is characterized by* instability of interpersonal relationships, self-image, and emotions and marked impulsivity.

The Dissociative Disorders: Fragmentation of the Self

1. *The dissociative experience is* a break or disruption in consciousness during which awareness, memory, and personal identity become separated or divided.

2. *Dissociative disorders are* a category of psychological disorders in which extreme and frequent disruptions of awareness, memory, and personal identity impair the ability to function.

3. *Dissociative amnesia is a disorder involving* the partial or total inability to recall important personal information. *Dissociative fugue is* a disorder involving sudden and unexpected travel away from home, extensive amnesia, and identity confusion.

4. *Dissociative identity disorder (DID) involves* extensive memory disruptions along with the presence of two or more distinct identities, or "personalities"; formerly called *multiple personality disorder.*

5. *According to one theory, DID is caused by* trauma in childhood and represents an extreme form of coping through dissociation.

Concept Check 2

1. seasonal affective
2. genetic
3. bipolar
4. cyclothymic
5. dissociative fugue
6. dissociative experiences
7. dissociative amnesia
8. antisocial; borderline
9. paranoid personality disorder
10. anorexia nervosa

Graphic Organizer 2

Major Depression

1. Loss of interest or pleasure in almost all activities
2. Despondent mood, feelings of emptiness or worthlessness, or excessive guilt
3. Preoccupation with death or suicidal thoughts
4. Difficulty sleeping or excessive sleeping
5. Diminished ability to think, concentrate, or make decisions
6. Diminished appetite and significant weight loss or excessive eating and weight gain

Bipolar Disorder

1. One or more manic episodes characterized by euphoria, high energy, grandiose ideas, flight of ideas, inappropriate self-confidence, and decreased need for sleep

2. Usually also has one or more episodes of major depression

3. May alternate rapidly between symptoms of mania and major depression

Dysthymic Disorder

1. Chronic, low-grade depressed feelings that are not severe enough to qualify as major depression

Cyclothymic Disorder

1. Moderate, recurring, up-and-down mood swings that are not severe enough to qualify as major depression or bipolar disorder

Matching Exercise 2

1. antisocial personality disorder

2. bipolar disorder

3. seasonal affective disorder (SAD)

4. major depression

5. manic episode

6. dissociative experience

7. personality disorder

8. personality

9. dissociative identity disorder (DID)

10. paranoid personality disorder

11. lithium

12. alters (alter egos)

13. conduct disorder

14. eating disorder

15. lanugo

True/False Test 2

1. T	6. T	11. T
2. F	7. F	12. T
3. F	8. T	13. F
4. F	9. T	14. F
5. T	10. T	

Schizophrenia: A Different Reality

1. *Schizophrenia is a psychological disorder that involves* severely distorted beliefs, perceptions, and thought processes that impair an individual's ability to function.

2. *Positive symptoms include* delusions (false beliefs that persist in spite of compelling contradictory evidence), hallucinations (false perceptions that seem vividly real to the person experiencing them), and severely disorganized thought processes, speech, and behavior. *Negative symptoms reflect* defects or deficits in normal functioning, including flat affect, alogia, and avolition.

3. *The three basic subtypes of schizophrenia are (a)* paranoid type (presence of delusions, hallucinations, or both, but no cognitive impairment, disorganized behavior, or negative symptoms); *(b)* catatonic type (highly disturbed movements or actions, such as bizarre postures or grimaces, extremely agitated behavior, complete immobility, echoing words spoken by others or imitating their movements); and *(c)* disorganized type (extremely disorganized behavior, disorganized speech, flat affect, and sometimes disorganized delusions and hallucinations; formerly called hebephrenic schizophrenia). *A fourth label,* undifferentiated, *is used to describe individuals who* display some combination of positive and negative symptoms but who do not fit the criteria for the other three types.

4. *Evidence that genetic factors are involved in the development of schizophrenia comes from* family, twin, adoption, and gene studies, but studies of identical twins demonstrate that nongenetic factors play at least an equal role.

5. *Research on paternal age and the risk of schizophrenia indicates that* the risk of schizophrenia is higher in the offspring of older fathers, but older paternal age failed to account for the majority (75%) of cases of schizophrenia in these studies.

6. *One environmental factor implicated in the development of schizophrenia is that* schizophrenia might be caused by exposure to an influenza virus or other viral infection during prenatal development or shortly after birth.

7. *Neurological evidence from research examining abnormal brain structures indicates that* about half the people with schizophrenia show some type of brain structure abnormality, such as enlargement of the fluid-filled ventricles, and significant loss of gray matter in the brain. Note, however, that the evidence is correlational and does not indicate causality. Research continues in this area to determine whether differences in brain structure are the cause or consequence of schizophrenia.

8. *The idea that schizophrenia is the result of abnormal brain chemistry is supported largely by two pieces of indirect evidence: (a)* Antipsychotic drugs that reduce schizophrenic symptoms in many people reduce or block dopamine activity in the brain. *(b)* Drugs such as amphetamines or cocaine enhance dopamine activity in the brain (use of these drugs can produce schizophrenia-like symptoms in normal adults or increase symptoms in people who already suffer from schizophrenia). This indirect evidence provides some support for the dopamine hypothesis, but the exact role this neurotransmitter plays in schizophrenia is not clear.

9. *Research into psychological factors, such as unhealthy families, has found that* while there is a complex interaction of genetic and environmental factors involved in the development of schizophrenia, adopted children who are genetically at risk for the disorder benefit from being raised in a healthy psychological environment, and conversely, a psychologically unhealthy family environment can act as a catalyst for the onset of schizophrenia in individuals, especially for those with a genetic history of schizophrenia.

Concept Check 3

1. 50
2. more
3. hallucinations; delusions
4. delusions of persecution
5. positive; negative
6. waxy flexibility
7. paranoid, catatonic; disorganized

Graphic Organizer 3

Positive Symptoms
1. delusions
2. hallucinations
3. disorganized thoughts and behavior

Negative Symptoms
1. flat effect
2. alogia (poverty of speech)
3. avolition

Matching Exercise 3

1. dopamine hypothesis
2. schizophrenia
3. paranoid type of schizophrenia

4. waxy flexibility
5. flat affect (affective flattening)
6. delusion
7. delusions of reference
8. hallucination
9. undifferentiated type of schizophrenia
10. ventricles

True/False Test 3

1.	F	4.	T	7.	T
2.	T	5.	T	8.	T
3.	T	6.	F	9.	T

Something to Think About

1. Dissociative identity disorder (DID), formerly called multiple personality disorder, involves extensive memory disruptions for personal information along with the presence of two or more distinct identities or personalities. Typically, each personality has its own name and each will be experienced as if it has its own personal history and self-image. These alternate personalities, or alters, may be of widely varying ages and of different genders. Typically, the primary personality is unaware of the existence of the alternate personalities. However, the alters may have knowledge of each other's existence and share memories. Sometimes the experiences of one alter are accessible to another alter but not vice versa. From this description of the disorder, it is clear that symptoms of amnesia and memory problems are a central part of DID. In addition, people with DID have numerous psychiatric and physical symptoms as well as a chaotic personal history.

   Contrast DID with a description of schizophrenia and the differences between the two disorders become apparent. Schizophrenia is a psychological disorder that involves severely distorted beliefs, perceptions, and thought processes. During a schizophrenic episode, people lose their grip on reality. The positive symptoms of schizophrenia reflect an excess or distortion of normal functioning and include hallucinations, delusions, and severely disorganized thought processes, speech, and behavior. The negative symptoms reflect a restriction or reduction of normal functions and include flat affect, alogia (poverty of speech), and avolition, or the inability to initiate or persist in even simple forms of goal-directed behavior. There are three different subtypes of schizophrenia: paranoid, catatonic, and disorganized, plus an undifferentiated type, which does not fit any single category. In addition, as noted in the text, the prevalence, course, and cause of schizophrenia are markedly different from those of DID.

2. The first thing to note is that the line that divides normal and abnormal behavior is not clearly defined. In addition, it is affected by the social and cultural context in which the behavior occurs. Psychopathology is the scientific study of the origins, symptoms, and development of psychological disorders. As you learned in this chapter, DSM-IV-TR is the book that describes about 250 specific disorders, including their symptoms, the exact criteria that must be met to make a diagnosis, and the typical course of each psychological disorder. The main categories of psychological disorders are the anxiety disorders, mood disorders, personality disorders, dissociative disorders, and schizophrenia.

   According to the text, the chance that someone will experience symptoms of psychological disorder some time in his or her lifetime is about 50–50. About one in three people will have experienced the symptoms of psychological disorder during the last year. However, about 80 percent of those people will not have sought professional help. The good news is that most people seem to weather the symptoms without becoming completely debilitated and without professional intervention. It is estimated that 3 to 5 percent of people have really serious symptoms that demand immediate treatment, and these people usually have developed several mental disorders over time, not just one disorder that suddenly appears. Women tend to have a higher prevalence of anxiety and depression, whereas men tend to have a higher prevalence of substance abuse disorders and antisocial personality disorder.

   Nobody knows for sure what causes psychological disorders. There is no shortage of theories, however. Biological and genetic factors have been implicated, as have abnormalities in brain structure and chemical imbalances. Various environmental and social explanations have also been suggested. Research continues, and someday we may be closer to finding the cause or causes of these abnormalities.

3. The first thing to note about the studies on the relationship between cigarette smoking and the incidence of mental illness is that these studies are correlational in nature. Causality (cause-effect relationships) cannot be inferred on the basis of correlations; properly conducted experimental research is required in order to conclude anything about causality. While there is a positive correlation between cigarette smoking and the prevalence of psychological disorders, it is not clear what the causal factors are. Does smoking cigarettes cause mental illness, does being mentally ill cause people to smoke more, or are other unknown causal factors at work here? Correlational research does not answer these questions.

   To make the point even clearer consider the following example. Suppose researchers found that there was a positive correlation between the consumption of chicken soup and the incidence of cold and flu symptoms. Obviously, you would not conclude that chicken soup consumption causes flu or cold symptoms or that having a cold or the flu causes people to eat chicken soup. Other variables, such as cultural factors, traditions, beliefs about natural remedies, and so on could be involved.

   However, correlational research does allow predictions to be made. For example, you could predict that when the prevalence of cold and flu symptoms diminish, the consumption of chicken soup should also decrease, and vice versa. Likewise, with cigarette smoking and the level of mental illness. You could predict that if the rate of cigarette smoking declined over a period of a decade or two, then the prevalence of mental illness should also decrease. This, however, has not happened. The level of cigarette smoking has decreased quite dramatically over the last couple of decades but the incidence of mental illness in the population has not. This further illustrates the complex nature of the relationship between these two variables. Further research may shed light on these intriguing correlational research findings.

Progress Test 1

1. a	6. d	11. a
2. b	7. a	12. b
3. b	8. a	13. d
4. c	9. d	14. c
5. a	10. e	15. c

Progress Test 2

1. b	6. d	11. c
2. e	7. b	12. c
3. c	8. e	13. d
4. a	9. a	14. a
5. b	10. a	15. c

Progress Test 3

1. a	6. d	11. a
2. c	7. a	12. a
3. a	8. b	13. b
4. b	9. a	14. b
5. d	10. a	15. d

CHAPTER 15

Therapies

<table>
<tr>
<td>PREVIEW</td>
<td>Reading the section below first will give you a general sense of the chapter's contents and an initial introduction to some of the major concepts and terms. This will prime you for what you are about to read and help you to develop a "cognitive map" that will guide your study of the material in this chapter. Likewise, reading the preview questions at the beginning of each major section will improve your ability to understand, learn, and retain the information.</td>
</tr>
</table>

Chapter 15 . . . AT A GLANCE

Chapter 15 discusses the use of psychotherapies and biomedical therapies to treat psychological disorders. Psychoanalysis, which is based on Freud's theory of personality, is described, including its basic assumptions and techniques. Contemporary short-term dynamic psychotherapies are based on psychoanalytic theory but differ in that they are typically time-limited and have specific goals, and the therapist's role is active rather than neutral.

Client-centered therapy is discussed as the prime example of the humanistic approach to psychotherapy. A recent application of humanistic therapy, designed to help people commit to change, is motivational interviewing. Behavior therapy is based on learning principles and assumes that maladaptive behaviors are learned. Techniques based on classical conditioning and operant conditioning are examined. The cognitive therapies, which assume that psychological problems are caused by maladaptive patterns of thinking, are explored next. Cognitive-behavioral therapy combines cognitive and behavioral techniques in an integrated but flexible treatment plan. Group and family therapies are contrasted with individual therapy, and the advantages and benefits of each are examined.

The effectiveness of psychotherapy is explored. The conclusion is that psychotherapy is generally better than no treatment at all; also no particular form of psychotherapy is superior to any other. Certain factors contribute to the effectiveness of all forms of therapy, however.

The most common biomedical therapy is psychotropic medication. The discussion includes the nature of these drugs, their effects on the brain, their side effects, and the disorders for which they are prescribed. Electroconvulsive therapy (ECT), a different type of biomedical therapy, is used for treating severe depression. The Application provides useful information about what to expect in psychotherapy.

Introduction: Psychotherapy and Biomedical Therapy

Preview Questions

Consider the following questions as you study this section of the chapter.

- How is *psychotherapy* defined, and what types of problems are treated using psychotherapy?
- What is the basic assumption common to all forms of psychotherapy?
- What is biomedical therapy, and what is its basic assumption?

Read the section "Introduction: Psychotherapy and Biomedical Therapy" and **write** *your answers to the following:*

1. Psychotherapy refers to _____ _____ _____

2. A basic assumption of all psychotherapies is that _____ _____

3. Biomedical therapies involve _____ _____ _____

4. The biomedical therapies are based on the assumption that _____ _____

Psychoanalytic Therapy

Preview Questions

Consider the following questions as you study this section of the chapter.

- What is psychoanalysis, and who developed this form of therapy?
- What techniques are used in psychoanalysis, and what is their purpose?
- What role does insight play in psychoanalytic techniques?
- What are short-term dynamic therapies?
- What is interpersonal therapy (IPT), and what four categories of personal problems does it deal with?

Read the section "Psychoanalytic Therapy" and **write** *your answers to the following:*

1. Psychoanalysis is a _____ _____ _____

2. The main psychoanalytic techniques (and their purpose) are

    (a) _____ _____

    (b) _____ _____

    (c) _____ _____

    (d) _____

    (e) _____

3. Together, these psychoanalytic techniques are designed to _____ _____

4. The various forms of short-term dynamic therapies (all based on traditional psychoanalytic notions) have four features in common:

    (a) _____ _____

    (b) _____ _____

    (c) _____ _____

    (d) _____

5. Interpersonal therapy (IPT) is _____ _____ _____

    The four categories of personal problems dealt with are

    (a) _____ _____

(b) _____

_____

(c) _____

_____

(d) _____

_____

_____

After you have carefully studied the preceding sections, complete the following exercises.

Concept Check 1

Read the following and write the correct term in the space provided.

1. During a session with her psychoanalyst, Felicity was asked to elaborate on her negative feelings about her husband. She responded by making a few wisecracks about men and then abruptly changed the subject. Her therapist would say she is engaging in

   _____ .

2. When Felicity's therapist urges her to report all her spontaneous thoughts, mental images, and feelings, he is using the technique called

   _____ .

3. Felicity's therapist offers a carefully timed explanation of her free associations, hoping to facilitate the recognition of her unconscious conflicts or motivations. This technique is called _____ .

4. Although her therapist has remained neutral and nonjudgmental throughout their sessions, Felicity is beginning to express feelings of hostility and anger toward him. This part of the psychoanalytic process is called

   _____ .

5. When Felicity describes a dream she had the previous night, her therapist explores the content and analyzes it for disguised or symbolic wishes and motivations. Her therapist is using

   _____ .

6. Rabia's therapist uses medication and other medical treatments to deal with the symptoms associated with her psychological disorder. On the other hand, Dean's therapist uses psychological techniques to help him modify his troubling behavior and to encourage him to understand the basis of his emotional problems. This example illustrates the difference between two broad forms of therapy, _____ and _____ .

7. Dr. Keller believes that symptoms of depression and other psychological problems are caused and maintained by interpersonal problems; thus, his therapy focuses on the person's current relationships and social interactions rather than on his history. Dr. Keller practices a type of psychotherapy called

   _____ .

8. When Ethan first started therapy, his therapist made a relatively quick assessment and both she and Ethan agreed on specific, concrete, realistic goals. Now, after only a couple of months of sessions that included free associations, interpretations, and active dialogue with the therapist, Ethan is feeling much better. It is probable that Ethan has experienced

   _____ therapy.

9. Vanja is referred to a therapist who uses a short-term psychodynamic therapy called interpersonal therapy (IPT). Her therapist is likely to try to identify the interpersonal problems that are causing difficulties in her overall psychological functioning. The four categories of personal problems he will be concerned with are _____ ,

   _____ , _____ ,

   or _____ .

Review of Terms, Concepts, and Names 1

Use the terms in this list to complete the Matching Test, then to help you answer the True/False items correctly.

psychotherapy
biomedical therapies
psychotropic
  medications
psychoanalysis
Sigmund Freud
repressed
insight
free association
resistance
dream interpretation

interpretation
transference
short-term dynamic
  therapies
interpersonal therapy
  (IPT)
unresolved grief
role disputes
role transitions
interpersonal deficits

Matching Exercise

Match the appropriate term/name with its definition or description.

1. _____ In interpersonal therapy, absent or faulty social skills that limit the ability to start or maintain healthy relationships with others.

2. _____ The treatment of emotional, behavioral, and interpersonal problems through the use of psychological techniques designed to encourage understanding of problems and modify troubling feelings, behaviors, or relationships.

3. _____ Psychoanalytic technique in which the psychoanalyst offers a carefully timed explanation of the patient's dreams, free associations, or behavior to facilitate the recognition of unconscious conflicts or motivations.

4. _____ Type of psychotherapy originated by Sigmund Freud in which free association, dream interpretation, and analysis of resistance and transference are used to explore repressed or unconscious impulses, anxieties, and internal conflicts.

5. _____ The use of medications, electroconvulsive therapy, or other medical treatment to treat the symptoms associated with psychological disorders.

6. _____ Psychotherapies that are based on traditional psychoanalytic notions in which therapeutic contact typically lasts for no more than a few months rather than years.

7. _____ Drugs used to treat psychological or mental disorders.

8. _____ In interpersonal therapy, the repetitive conflicts with significant others, such as the person's partner, family members, co-workers, or friends.

9. _____ Founder of psychoanalysis who theorized that psychological symptoms are the result of unconscious and unresolved conflicts stemming from early childhood.

True/False Test

Indicate whether each statement is true or false by placing T or F in the blank space next to each item.

1. ____ Psychoanalysts believe that it is essential to move conflicts from the patient's unconscious to his or her conscious awareness. The process of recognizing and ultimately resolving these long-standing repressed conflicts is called insight.

2. ____ Interpersonal therapy (IPT) is a brief, psychodynamic psychotherapy that focuses on current relationships and assumes that symptoms are caused and maintained by interpersonal problems.

3. ____ In psychoanalysis, the patient's unconscious attempts to block the revelation of repressed memories and conflicts is called resistance.

4. ____ Dream interpretation is a technique used in psychoanalysis in which the content of dreams is analyzed for disguised or symbolic wishes, meanings, and motivations.

5. ____ Free association is a technique used in psychoanalysis in which the patient spontaneously reports all thoughts, feelings, and mental images as they come to mind as a way of revealing unconscious thoughts and emotions.

6. ____ Transference is the process by which emotions and desires originally associated with a significant person in the patient's life, such as a parent, are unconsciously transferred to the psychoanalyst.

7. ____ In interpersonal therapy, problems dealing with the death of significant others is called unresolved grief.

8. ____ In interpersonal therapy, role transitions refer to problems with major life changes such as going away to college, parenthood, marriage, divorce, or retirement.

9. ____ When early experiences result in unresolved conflicts and frustrated urges, these

emotionally charged memories are *repressed,* or pushed out of conscious awareness.

Check your answers and review any areas of weakness before going on to the next section.

Humanistic Therapy

Preview Questions

Consider the following questions as you study this section of the chapter.

- What is the most influential humanistic therapy, and who developed it?
- What therapeutic conditions and techniques are important in client-centered therapy?
- How do client-centered therapy and psychoanalysis differ as insight-oriented therapies?
- What is motivational interviewing (MI)?

*Read the section "Humanistic Therapy" and **write** your answers to the following:*

1. The most influential humanistic therapy is
   _____ ; it was developed by
   _____ , who deliberately used the word
   client rather than *patient* because
   _____
   _____
   _____
   _____

2. In client-centered therapy, the main conditions
   are that _____
   _____
   _____

3. Unlike psychoanalysis, humanistic therapy
   does not offer _____
   _____
   _____

4. Motivational interviewing is designed to
   _____
   _____

Behavior Therapy

Preview Questions

Consider the following questions as you study this section of the chapter.

- What is the goal of behavior therapy?
- What is the basic assumption of behavior therapy?
- How are classical and operant conditioning principles used to treat and modify problem behaviors?

*Read the section "Behavior Therapy" and **write** your answers to the following:*

1. The goal of behavior therapy is to _____
   _____
   _____

2. Behavior therapists assume that maladaptive
   behaviors are _____
   _____
   Therefore, the basic strategy in behavior
   therapy involves _____
   _____

3. Behavior therapists employ techniques that are
   based on the learning principles of _____
   _____
   _____

4. Mary Cover Jones's procedure, called counterconditioning, involved _____
   _____
   _____
   _____

5. Along with counterconditioning, Jones used
   _____
   _____

6. Based on the same premise as counterconditioning, systematic desensitization involves
   _____
   _____

7. The three basic steps of systematic desensitization are
   (a) _____
   _____

(b) _____

_____

(c) _____

_____

8. Virtual reality (VR) therapy combines _____

_____

_____

_____

9. The bell and pad treatment uses classical conditioning techniques to help bedwetters by _____

_____

_____

_____

10. Aversive conditioning involves _____

_____

_____

11. B. F. Skinner's operant conditioning model of learning is based on the simple principle that behavior is _____

_____

12. The token economy is a form of behavior therapy in which _____

_____

A modified version of the token economy is called _____

_____

After you have carefully studied the preceding sections, complete the following exercises.

Concept Check 2

Read the following and write the correct term in the space provided.

1. Dr. Soos does not analyze or interpret his clients' motives or problems. Instead, he believes that the client is in the best position to discover his or her own ways of effectively dealing with problems and that the role of the therapist is to provide the right conditions that foster self-awareness, psychological growth, and self-directed change. Dr. Soos is obviously a(n) _____ psychologist who uses _____ therapy.

2. In an attempt to help her husband overcome his deep fear of traveling by sea, Mrs. Bowman brings home travel brochures showing exotic destinations reached by cruise ships. She asks her husband to imagine both of them sitting in their deck chairs enjoying the warm sunshine and cool beverages. At the same time, she reassures him that these big ships are totally safe and comfortable and that he has nothing to worry about. Mrs. Bowman's efforts to reduce her husband's fear most closely resemble techniques used in _____ .

3. To help Trevor overcome his addiction to nicotine, Dr. Clarke asks him to smoke some cigarettes and at the same time administers electric shock to his arm. Dr. Clarke is using a technique called _____ conditioning.

4. Children in a group home for the mentally handicapped are given plastic chips for making their beds, brushing their teeth, washing their hands, and being on time for meals. They are allowed to exchange these chips for candy, cookies, or additional TV time. The group home is using a behavioral technique called the _____ .

5. Eight-year-old Darryl has problems with bedwetting. His mother takes him to a behavior therapist, who recommends a procedure that fixes the problem in a matter of weeks. The therapist most likely is using the _____ .

6. Desiree told her therapist, "I feel so inadequate and useless; I can't seem to cope with even the smallest things in my life. What should I do?" Her therapist answered, "You are feeling very helpless about things in your life, and sometimes you feel unable to cope. Can you think where these feelings come from?" The therapist is using _____ therapy and appears to be communicating with _____ .

7. Three-year old Graham cries and screams whenever he is put in his bed at night; he stops only when his parents allow him to sleep in their bed. To deal with this problem, Graham's parents implement a program that involves consistently ignoring the screaming and crying and abundantly praising and encouraging good behaviors. They are using _____ to decrease undesirable behaviors and _____ to increase desirable behaviors.

8. Rosalynn, who is in an institution for people with psychological disorders, refuses to leave her room and go to the dining room for her meals. To help her overcome this problem, therapists first give her a reward for leaving her room, then for walking part way down the hallway, then for venturing the whole way, then for going to the staircase, and so on. Eventually, she is rewarded only when she sits at the table. This example illustrates a behavioral technique called _____ .

Review of Terms, Concepts, and Names 2

Use the terms in this list to complete the Matching Test, then to help you answer the True/False items correctly.

humanistic perspective
client- (or person-)
  centered therapy
Carl Rogers
genuineness
unconditional positive
  regard
conditional acceptance
empathic understanding
self-actualization
motivational
  interviewing (MI)
behavior therapy
  (behavior modification)
Mary Cover Jones
counterconditioning
observational learning

systematic
  desensitization
progressive relaxation
anxiety hierarchy
control scene
bell and pad treatment
aversive conditioning
Antabuse
shaping
reinforcement (positive
  and negative)
extinction
baseline rate
token economy
contingency
  management
  interventions

Matching Exercise

Match the appropriate term/name with its definition or description.

1. _____ American psychologist who conducted the first clinical demonstrations of behavior therapy.

2. _____ Psychological perspective that emphasizes human potential, self-awareness, and freedom of choice.

3. _____ Form of behavior therapy in which the therapeutic environment is structured to reward desired behaviors with tokens or points that may eventually be exchanged for tangible rewards.

4. _____ In client-centered therapy, the critical quality of the therapist that involves honestly and openly sharing his or her thoughts and feelings with the client.

5. _____ Type of psychotherapy that focuses on directly changing maladaptive behavior patterns by using basic learning principles and techniques.

6. _____ American psychologist who helped found humanistic psychology and developed client-centered therapy.

7. _____ The first step in systematic desensitization, which involves successively relaxing one muscle group after another until a deep state of relaxation is achieved.

8. _____ Behavior therapy technique used to treat nighttime bedwetting by conditioning arousal from sleep in response to bodily signals of a full bladder.

9. _____ Type of psychotherapy developed by humanist Carl Rogers in which the therapist is nondirective and reflective, and the client directs the focus of each therapy session.

10. _____ Medication that causes extreme nausea if alcohol is consumed after it is taken; used as a form of aversive conditioning in the treatment of alcohol abuse.

11. _____ In behavior therapy, the rate of occurrence of a problem behavior before treatment begins; more generally, data or condition used as a reference with which to compare future observations or results.

12. _____ A technique used to help people overcome fears and phobias by encouraging them to watch others modeling nonfearful behavior while interacting with the feared stimulus.

13. _____ List of anxiety-provoking images associated with the feared situation, arranged in order from least to most anxiety-producing, that the therapist helps the patient construct as part of systematic desensitization.

True/False Test

Indicate whether each statement is true or false by placing T or F in the blank space next to each item.

1. ___ Aversive conditioning is a behavior therapy technique based on classical conditioning that involves modifying behavior by conditioning a new response that is incompatible with a previously learned response.

2. ___ In client-centered therapy, *empathic understanding* involves active listening and reflecting the content and personal meaning of feelings being experienced by the client.

3. ___ Systematic desensitization is a type of behavior therapy in which phobic responses are reduced by pairing relaxation with a series of mental images or real-life situations that the person finds progressively more fear provoking; it is based on the principle of counterconditioning.

4. ___ In behavior therapy, when a behavior decreases because it no longer leads to a reinforcer, *extinction* has occurred.

5. ___ In systematic desensitization, the therapist may have the client create a very relaxing scene, unrelated to the hierarchy of anxiety-provoking images, called a control scene.

6. ___ In client-centered therapy, unconditional positive regard is created when the therapist values, accepts, and cares for the client, whatever her problems or behaviors.

7. ___ In behavior therapy, the process by which a desired behavior is increased as the result of its consequences is called reinforcement.

8. ___ When a person has received acceptance by significant others only if she conforms to their expectations, she is said to have experienced conditional acceptance.

9. ___ Counterconditioning, a relatively ineffective type of behavior therapy, involves repeatedly pairing an aversive stimulus with the occurrence of undesirable behaviors or thoughts.

10. ___ One application of the token economy, in which a group of clients receives vouchers or other conditioned reinforcers that can be exchanged for prizes to reinforce carefully specified behaviors or behavioral goals, is called contingency management interventions.

11. ___ Self-actualization is the realization of a person's unique potential and talents.

12. ___ Shaping involves reinforcing successive approximations of a desired behavior and can be used with extremely impaired patients in whom the desired responses do not normally occur.

13. ___ Motivational interviewing is designed to help clients overcome the mixed feelings or reluctance they might have about committing to change; it is more directive than traditional client-centered therapy, and its main goal is to encourage or strengthen the client's self-motivated statements or "change talk."

Check your answers and review any areas of weakness before going on to the next section.

Cognitive Therapies

Preview Questions

Consider the following questions as you study this section of the chapter.

- On what assumption are cognitive therapies based?

- What is rational-emotive therapy (RET), and who developed it?

- What is Beck's cognitive therapy (CT), and how does it differ from rational-emotive therapy?

- What is cognitive-behavioral therapy (CBT)?

*Read the section "Cognitive Therapies" and **write** your answers to the following:*

1. Cognitive therapies assume that _____ _____ _____

2. The goal of cognitive therapy is to _____ _____ _____

3. Rational-emotive therapy (RET) was developed by_____ , and it focuses on _____ _____ _____

4. Beck's cognitive therapy (CT) focuses on _____ _____

5. Like Ellis, Beck believes that_____ _____ _____ _____

6. In contrast with RET's emphasis on "irrational" thinking, Beck believes that _____ _____ _____ _____

7. Cognitive-behavioral therapy (CBT) refers to _____ _____

   They are based on the assumption that _____ _____ _____ _____

Group and Family Therapy

Preview Questions

Consider the following questions as you study this section of the chapter.

- What is group therapy, and what are some of the advantages of this approach?
- What are family therapy and couple therapy?

*Read the section "Group and Family Therapy" and **write** your answers to the following:*

1. Group therapy involves _____ _____

2. Some of the key advantages of group therapy are that _____ _____ _____ _____

3. Family therapy is based on the assumption that _____ _____ _____

4. Couple therapy focuses on _____ _____

Evaluating the Effectiveness of Psychotherapy

Preview Questions

Consider the following questions as you study this section of the chapter.

- What is meta-analysis, and what has it demonstrated about the general effectiveness of psychotherapy?
- Is one form of psychotherapy superior to another?
- What common factors contribute to effective psychotherapy, and what is eclecticism?

*Read the section "Evaluating the Effectiveness of Psychotherapy" and **write** your answers to the following:*

1. When meta-analysis is used to summarize studies, the researchers consistently arrive at the same conclusion: _____ _____

2. Researchers have identified a number of factors that are related to a positive therapy outcome:
   (a) _____ _____

(b) 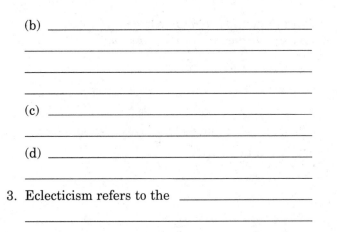 _____

_____

_____

(c) _____

_____

(d) _____

_____

3. Eclecticism refers to the _____

_____

_____

*After you have carefully studied the preceding
sections, complete the following exercises.*

Concept Check 3

*Read the following and write the correct term in the
space provided.*

1. Dr. McGilvery wants to determine whether psychotherapy is effective for particular psychological disorders. In attempting to analyze the results of numerous published studies on the issue, he should use a technique called

    _____ .

2. Mike, a mental health professional, tries to tailor his therapeutic approach to the problems and characteristics of the person seeking help. Mike's pragmatic and integrated use of diverse psychotherapeutic techniques would classify him as a(n) _____ therapist.

3. Dr. Samson believes that a key aspect of resolving some psychological problems is getting individuals to realize that others have problems similar to their own. To achieve this goal, _____ therapy would be useful.

4. Jay's therapist attacks and openly criticizes Jay's irrational and self-defeating ways of thinking. Jay's therapist is most likely a _____ therapist.

5. Dr. Beaven tries to help her clients learn to recognize and monitor the automatic thoughts that occur without conscious effort or control; she then encourages them to test the reality of these thoughts empirically. Dr. Beaven's approach is most consistent with _____ therapy.

6. Dr. Sidhu believes that in order to understand psychological problems, it is important to investigate interactions among family members within the context of the dynamic family system in which each member plays a unique role. Dr. Sidhu is most likely a _____ therapist.

7. Ivana's therapist believes that thoughts affect behavior and moods, and that behavior, in turn, can affect cognitions and emotional states. His approach to treating her depression involves a flexible, integrated use of diverse behavioral and cognitive techniques tailored to her unique problem. Ivana's therapist is most likely a _____ therapist.

8. Draco has been attending Alcoholics Anonymous meetings and learning about their 12-step program ever since he was cited for DUI (driving under the influence) and his driver's license was suspended. Draco is seeking help from a(n) _____ .

9. Judd's therapist asks him to focus on the mental image of the traumatic aftermath of the explosion that destroyed his place of work. While Judd is doing this, the therapist moves his finger back and forth in front of Judd's eyes and asks him to visually track the movement. Judd's therapist is using a technique called

    _____ ,

    a therapeutic approach that is _____ (significantly better/no better) than other forms of psychotherapy.

10. When Fernandez started experiencing a number of psychological problems, he decided that he needed professional help. Before talking with a therapist, however, he discussed his plan with his extended family, including his grandparents and his in-laws, and with some of his closest friends. This tendency of Latinos to stress interdependence over independence and the importance of the extended family network is called _____ .

Graphic Organizer 1

Fill in each of the following with the correct information.

Type of Therapy	Founder	Source of Problems	Treatment Techniques	Goals of Therapy
Psychoanalysis				
Client-Centered Therapy				
Behavior Therapy				
Rational-Emotive Therapy				
Cognitive Therapy				
Cognitive-Behavioral Therapy				

Review of Terms, Concepts, and Names 3

Use the terms in this list to complete the Matching Test, then to help you answer the True/False items correctly.

cognitive therapies
Albert Ellis
rational-emotive therapy (RET)
ABC model
Aaron T. Beck
cognitive therapy (CT)
cognitive-behavioral therapy (CBT)
group therapy
self-help groups and support groups
family therapy
couple therapy
behavioral couple therapy
spontaneous remission
meta-analysis
empirically supported treatments
eye movement desensitization reprocessing (EMDR) therapy
exposure therapy
eclecticism

Matching Exercise

Match the appropriate term/name with its definition or description.

1. _____ Form of psychotherapy that is based on the assumption that the family is a system and that treats the family as a unit.

2. _____ Group of psychotherapies that are based on the assumption that psychological problems are due to maladaptive patterns of thinking; treatment techniques focus on recognizing and altering these unhealthy thinking patterns.

3. _____ Type of therapy, developed by psychiatrist Aaron Beck, that focuses on changing the client's unrealistic beliefs.

4. _____ Form of psychotherapy that involves one or more therapists working simultaneously with a small group of clients.

5. _____ Type of psychotherapy, developed by psychologist Albert Ellis, that focuses on changing the client's irrational beliefs.

6. _____ Therapy that integrates cognitive and behavioral techniques and is based on the assumption that thoughts, moods, and behaviors are interrelated.

7. _____ Therapy technique in which the client holds a vivid mental image of a troubling event or situation while rapidly moving his eyes back and forth in response to the therapist's waving finger, or while the therapist administers some other form of bilateral stimulation such as sounding tones in alternate ears.

8. _____ A statistical technique that involves pooling or combining the results of many studies into a single analysis that essentially creates one large study that can reveal overall trends in the data.

9. _____ A form of couple therapy, based on the assumption that couples are satisfied when they experience more reinforcement than punishment in their relationships, that focuses on increasing caring behaviors and teaching couples how to constructively resolve conflict and problems.

True/False Test

Indicate whether each item is true or false by placing T or F in the space next to each item.

1. ____ Albert Ellis founded cognitive therapy (CT), a psychotherapy based on the assumption that depression and other psychological problems are caused by biased perceptions, distorted thinking, and inaccurate beliefs.

2. ____ Eclecticism is the pragmatic and integrated use of techniques from different psychotherapies.

3. ____ Spontaneous remission is the phenomenon in which people eventually improve or recover from psychological symptoms simply with the passage of time.

4. ____ Self-help groups and support groups deal with a wide array of psychological, medical, and behavioral problems through group processes and interactions that are typically organized and led by nonprofessionals.

5. ____ Aaron T. Beck founded the cognitive therapy called rational-emotive therapy (RET), which emphasizes recognizing and changing irrational beliefs.

6. ____ Empirically supported treatments are psychotherapies whose effectiveness has been validated by empirical research.

7. ____ A behavioral therapy, used for phobias, panic disorder, posttraumatic stress disorder, or related anxiety disorders, and in which the person is repeatedly exposed to the disturbing object or situation under controlled conditions, is called exposure therapy.

8. ____ Couple therapy attempts to improve communication and problem-solving skills as well as increase the intimacy between two people in a relationship.

9. ___ According to the ABC model, when an activating event (A) occurs, it is the person's belief (B) about the event that causes emotional consequences (C).

Check your answers and review any areas of weakness before going on to the next section.

Biomedical Therapies

Preview Questions

Consider the following questions as you study this section of the chapter.

- What is biomedical therapy?
- What are the most important antipsychotic, atypical antipsychotic, antianxiety, and antidepressant medications, how do they achieve their effects, and what are their advantages?
- What is lithium used to treat, and how is electroconvulsive therapy used?

*Read the section "Biomedical Therapies" and **write** your answers to the following:*

1. The biomedical therapies are _____

2. Antipsychotic medications (neuroleptics) are

   The most common antipsychotic medications include _____

3. The atypical antipsychotic drugs include

   and they act by_____

   A third generation of antipsychotic medications includes _____ which regulates _____

4. Antianxiety medications are _____

   The most common antianxiety medications include _____

5. Lithium is _____

6. The antidepressant medications are _____

   The most common antidepressant medications include _____

   New antidepressants, including _____

   tend to _____

7. Electroconvulsive therapy (ECT) is a biomedical therapy used primarily_____

After you have carefully studied the preceding section, complete the following exercises.

Concept Check 4

Read the following and write the correct term in the space provided.

1. For no apparent reason, Mrs. Bell has constant and persistent feelings of anxiety, nervousness, and apprehension that interfere with her ability to eat, sleep, and perform daily activities. Her psychiatrist is most likely to prescribe a type of psychoactive medication called an _____ medication.

2. Mr. Millis still experiences intense feelings of despondency, hopelessness, and dejection, and has suicidal thoughts, despite extensive psychotherapy and months of psychotropic medication. Because of this lack of responsiveness, his doctor is likely to consider using _____ therapy.

3. After being on antipsychotic medications for many years, Florence has developed a number of serious symptoms, such as severe, uncontrollable facial tics and grimaces, chewing movements, and other involuntary movements of the lips, jaw, and tongue. Florence suffers from _____ .

4. Dwayne has been diagnosed with bipolar disorder. His doctor is most likely to prescribe _____ .

5. To treat Debra's schizophrenic symptoms, which included apathy, social withdrawal, and flat emotions, the psychiatrist prescribed a psychotropic medication that selectively affected the levels of the neurotransmitters serotonin and dopamine in her brain. To minimize the potential side effects of the first atypical antipsychotics, he is likely to have prescribed an atypical antipsychotic such as _____ , _____ , or _____ , or a third generation antipsychotic called _____ .

6. After 12 weeks of interpersonal therapy (IPT) or 12 weeks of antidepressant medication (Paxil), depressed patients underwent PET scans. It is very likely that there will be _____ (a higher/a lower/the same) level of normalization of brain activity in the drug group compared to the therapy group.

7. Mari has been given a prescription for the benzodiazepine drug called Xanax. It is very probable that Mari suffers from _____ .

8. Virgil has been diagnosed with major depression. To avoid the side effects associated with the earlier medications, his doctor prescribes a drug from the third generation of antidepressants, which primarily affect the availability of the neurotransmitter serotonin. These drugs are called _____ , the most popular of which are _____ ,

_____ , and _____ . If Virgil does experience side effects, his doctor may prescribe one of the new dual-action antidepressants, such as _____ , _____ , or _____ .

Review of Terms and Concepts 4

Use the terms in this list to complete the Matching Test, then to help you answer the True/False items correctly.

psychotropic
  medications
antipsychotic
  medications
  (neuroleptics)
tardive dyskinesia
atypical antipsychotic
  medications
aripiprazole (Abilify)
antianxiety medications
benzodiazepines
GABA
Buspar

lithium
glutamate
antidepressant
  medications
tricyclics and MAO
  inhibitors
selective serotonin
  reuptake inhibitors
  (SSRIs)
dual-action
  antidepressants
electroconvulsive
  therapy (ECT)

Matching Exercise

Match the appropriate term with its definition or description.

1. _____ A naturally occurring substance that is used in the treatment of bipolar disorder.

2. _____ Drugs that alter mental functions, alleviate psychological symptoms, and are used to treat psychological or mental disorders.

3. _____ Biomedical therapy used primarily in the treatment of depression that involves electrically inducing a brief brain seizure; also called *shock therapy* and *electric shock therapy*.

4. _____ Prescription drugs used to alleviate the symptoms of anxiety.

5. _____ Prescription drugs used to reduce the symptoms associated with depression.

6. _____ Potentially irreversible motor disorder that results from the long-term use of antipsychotic medications and is characterized by severe, uncontrollable facial tics and grimaces, chewing movements, and other involuntary movements of the lips, jaw, and tongue.

7. _____ New antidepressants (such as Serzone, Remeron, and Celexa) that affect serotonin levels, are as effective as SSRIs but with a somewhat different mechanism, and have different side effects.

8. _____ A neurotransmitter that inhibits the transmission of nerve impulses in the brain and slows brain activity.

True/False Test

Indicate whether each item is true or false by placing T or F in the space next to each item.

1. ___ Antipsychotic medications (also called neuroleptics) are prescription drugs that are used to reduce psychotic symptoms; frequently used in the treatment of schizophrenia.

2. ___ A third generation of antipsychotic medications includes aripiprazole (Abilify), which regulates the availability of dopamine by blocking the dopamine receptors when levels are too high and mimicking dopamine when levels are too low.

3. ___ Benzodiazepines are a group of addictive antianxiety drugs that increase levels of the neurotransmitter GABA throughout the brain.

4. ___ Atypical antipsychotic medications are antipsychotic medications which, in contrast to the early antipsychotic drugs, block dopamine receptors in brain regions associated with psychotic symptoms rather than more globally throughout the brain, resulting in fewer side effects.

5. ___ Selective serotonin reuptake inhibitors (SSRIs) are a class of antidepressant medication, which includes Prozac, Paxil, and Zoloft, that increase the availability of serotonin in the brain and cause fewer side effects than earlier antidepressants.

6. ___ Tricyclics and MAO inhibitors are first-generation antidepressants that affect multiple neurotransmitter pathways and increase the availability of norepinephrine and serotonin.

7. ___ An antianxiety drug that is not a benzodiazepine and does not affect the neurotransmitter GABA but may affect dopamine and serotonin levels is called Buspar.

8. ___ Lithium stabilizes the availability of *glutamate*, which is an excitatory neurotransmitter found in many areas of the brain.

Check your answers and review any areas of weakness before going on to the next section.

Something to Think About

1. Many people become fearful and anxious if they have to take an exam or go to the dentist or doctor or on a job interview, for example. These kinds of fears are normal, and most people manage to cope with such anxiety-provoking situations. Other fears are more serious and may cause the person intense distress and somehow interfere with his or her normal functioning. Imagine a situation in which a friend or family member comes to you seeking help about how to overcome his fear of flying. Based on what you know about the behavior therapy technique of systematic desensitization, what might you say to this person?

2. Many people with psychological problems do not seek help from mental health professionals. There are many reasons for this. One reason may have to do with a lack of understanding about what to expect in psychotherapy. What are some of the important things a person should know about psychotherapy?

Check your answers and review any areas of weakness before completing the progress tests.

Progress Test 1

Review the complete chapter (including all boxed inserts), review all your study notes, and then test yourself on the following progress test. Check your answers. If you make a mistake, review your notes, check the appropriate section in the study guide, and if necessary, go back and read the relevant part of the chapter in your textbook.

1. Jacqueline's therapist uses dream interpretation and free association to help her to become more aware of unresolved conflicts in her childhood. The therapist's techniques and goals best reflect the primary aim of
   (a) psychoanalysis.
   (b) client-centered therapy.
   (c) behavior therapy.
   (d) cognitive therapy.

2. Mrs. Alverz gives her third-grade students a silver sticker every time they get a perfect score on their weekly spelling test. At the end of the term, students can exchange their stickers for prizes. Mrs. Alverz is using a strategy based on _____ conditioning called the _____ .

   (a) classical; bell and pad method
   (b) classical; token economy
   (c) operant; bell and pad method
   (d) operant; token economy

3. Laurel's therapist uses rational-emotive therapy (RET). After identifying Laurel's core irrational beliefs, her therapist is likely to

   (a) help her formulate an anxiety hierarchy.
   (b) encourage her to use free association so that she can get insight into her unconscious motivations and feelings.
   (c) provide her with a warm, supportive atmosphere, unconditional positive regard, and empathic understanding.
   (d) vigorously dispute and challenge her irrational beliefs.

4. Dr. Whorley offers a number of explanations for his patient's dreams and free associations in order to help the patient recognize unconscious conflicts and motivations. Dr. Whorley is using a psychoanalytic technique called

   (a) interpretation.   (c) resistance.
   (b) transference.   (d) conditional acceptance.

5. Twenty-five-year-old Melissa told her therapist that she felt worthless and unattractive because she didn't have a boyfriend; she was sure she was going to end up single and unloved. Her therapist said, "Your way of thinking is not only irrational but also totally stupid and absurd! You are worthless only if you *think* you are!" Her therapist is most likely

   (a) a behavior therapist.
   (b) a client-centered therapist.
   (c) a rational-emotive therapist.
   (d) a psychoanalyst.
   (e) none of these therapists; no therapist would talk like that to a client.

6. Once a week, Gardner attends a local health clinic, where he attempts to deal with some of his psychological problems by discussing them with five or six other people and two psychologists. Gardner is involved in

   (a) individual therapy.
   (b) group therapy.
   (c) a biomedical treatment program.
   (d) interpersonal therapy (IPT).

7. Mr. Lansdon's intense feelings of despondency and helplessness are periodically interrupted by episodes in which he experiences excessive feelings of personal power and a grandiose optimism that he can change the world to fit his strange ideological beliefs. A biomedical therapist would most likely prescribe

   (a) electroconvulsive therapy.
   (b) lithium.
   (c) antipsychotic medications.
   (d) antidepressant medications.

8. Gabrielle's feelings of unhappiness, despondency, dejection, and hopelessness have become so extreme that she has attempted suicide. Which of the following treatments is likely to provide her with the quickest relief from her misery?

   (a) systematic desensitization
   (b) the bell and pad treatment
   (c) psychoanalysis
   (d) electroconvulsive therapy (ECT)

9. Because of his persistent psychological problems, Werner has been prescribed a benzodiazepine drug called Valium. It is most likely that Werner suffers from

   (a) bipolar disorder.   (c) anxiety.
   (b) schizophrenia.   (d) depression.

10. When Christos was younger, he experienced a very painful tooth extraction. He now has an extreme fear of going to the dentist and has not been for a dental checkup in years. To help Christos overcome his irrational fear, a behavioral therapist is likely to use

    (a) rational-emotive therapy.
    (b) systematic desensitization.
    (c) the bell and pad treatment.
    (d) antianxiety medication.

11. Kathleen is on a committee at a community health-care facility that has the task of determining which of the major forms of psychotherapy is most effective. After she reviews studies that used meta-analysis to assess the results of treatment outcomes, she is most likely to conclude that

    (a) behavior therapy is the single most effective therapy available.
    (b) client-centered therapy has been consistently more effective than all the other forms of therapy.
    (c) in general, there is little or no difference in the effectiveness of the different forms of psychotherapy.
    (d) psychoanalysis works best for schizophrenia, and cognitive therapy works best for phobias.

12. Tyler has been diagnosed with schizophrenia. His doctor is most likely to prescribe

    (a) electroconvulsive therapy.
    (b) lithium.
    (c) antipsychotic medication.
    (d) antianxiety medication.

13. According to the Application, which of the following is true?

    (a) Therapy is a collaborative effort.
    (b) Expect therapy to challenge how you think and act.
    (c) Your therapist will not become a substitute friend.
    (d) Your therapist will not make decisions for you.
    (e) All of these statements are true.

14. Mr. Keiko, a middle-aged Japanese American, has been referred to a Western-style psychologist because he is displaying the classic symptoms of anxiety and depression. According to Culture and Human Behavior (Cultural Values and Psychotherapy), Mr. Keiko

    (a) may be reluctant to discuss personal, intimate details of his life with a stranger.
    (b) might try to avoid focusing on upsetting thoughts and resist exploring painful thoughts and feelings that could help resolve his psychological problems.
    (c) may not agree that becoming more assertive, more self-sufficient, less dependent on others, and caring for his own needs first is a good idea.
    (d) might do all of these things.

15. After a session with her therapist, in which she finally expressed all the anger and hostility she felt toward her parents and described the terrible guilt she felt about it, Charlene felt an enormous reduction in and relief from her emotional and physical tension. According to the Application, Charlene has probably experienced

    (a) resistance.
    (b) catharsis.
    (c) transference.
    (d) extinction.

Progress Test 2

After you have checked your understanding of the material in Progress Test 1 and have done a complete chapter review with special focus on any areas of weakness, you are ready to assess your knowledge of Progress Test 2. Check your answers. If you make a mistake, review your notes, the relevant section of the study guide, and, if necessary, the appropriate part of your textbook.

1. Dr. Rassmunsen uses medication and other medical procedures, including electroconvulsive therapy, to treat the symptoms of psychological disorders. Dr. Rassmunsen's approach would most likely be classified as

   (a) cognitive therapy.
   (b) behavioral therapy.
   (c) humanistic therapy.
   (d) biomedical therapy.

2. Mr. Damson suffers from auditory hallucinations and falsely believes that his co-workers are not only trying to steal his "secret inventions" but are also plotting to kill him. A biomedical therapist would most likely prescribe

   (a) electroconvulsive therapy.
   (b) lithium.
   (c) antipsychotic medications.
   (d) antidepressant medications.

3. Mervyn's therapist prescribed a medication that is classified as a selective serotonin reuptake inhibitor (SSRI) for his psychological symptoms. It is most likely that Mervyn suffers from

   (a) schizophrenia.   (c) anxiety disorder.
   (b) bipolar disorder.   (d) depression.

4. When Freda told her therapist that she wanted his advice on what she should do about her relationship problems, he replied, "It sounds to me like you are experiencing some difficulties with your relationship. Is that right?" The therapist's response reflects the technique of
   (a) transference.
   (b) free association.
   (c) empathic understanding.
   (d) counterconditioning.

5. It is very probable that Freda's therapist is a _____ therapist.
   (a) cognitive   (c) behavior
   (b) psychoanalytic   (d) humanistic

6. When Greta's psychoanalyst asked her to elaborate on certain aspects of her dream, she couldn't think of anything to say. Her lack of responsiveness is likely to be interpreted as
   (a) resistance.
   (b) extinction.
   (c) transference.
   (d) spontaneous remission.

7. Dr. Whelan believes that people can overcome their problems if they learn to recognize and monitor their automatic thoughts and then try to test the reality of those thoughts empirically. Her approach is most consistent with
   (a) behavior therapy.
   (b) biomedical therapy.
   (c) cognitive therapy.
   (d) psychoanalysis.

8. A behavior therapist trains a child, who has a problem with bedwetting, to awaken and use the bathroom. This is accomplished by arranging for an alarm to sound every time the child wets the bed. This technique is called _____ and illustrates the use of _____ conditioning principles.
   (a) aversive therapy; operant
   (b) the bell and pad treatment; classical
   (c) aversive therapy; classical
   (d) the bell and pad treatment; operant

9. For which patient is Dr. Kelly most likely to prescribe the atypical antipsychotic medication olanzapine, which affects both serotonin and dopamine levels in the brain?
   (a) Celia, who smokes three packs of cigarettes a day

   (b) Garth, who irrationally believes that aliens are trying to steal his thoughts
   (c) Manuel, who fluctuates between extreme moods of euphoria and depression
   (d) Rachel, who suffers from nervous apprehension, intense anxiety, and an inability to relax

10. Quentin has an irrational fear of riding in elevators. His therapist first teaches him to relax completely, then he asks him to come up with a list of anxiety-provoking images associated with elevators. Finally, the therapist asks Quentin to close his eyes and imagine very clearly the least fearful scene on the list. Quentin's therapist is a _____ therapist using _____ .
    (a) behavior; systematic desensitization
    (b) cognitive; rational-emotive techniques
    (c) humanistic; empathic understanding
    (d) psychoanalytic; free association

11. Jeneen is taking a prescription drug that is a naturally occurring substance called lithium. It is most probable that she is suffering from
    (a) schizophrenia.   (c) chronic depression.
    (b) bipolar disorder.   (d) anxiety disorder.

12. Ursula, who lives in a home for children with behavior problems, is able to earn points for getting dressed, maintaining personal hygiene, and engaging in appropriate social interactions. These points can be exchanged for access to desirable items or special privileges. This example illustrates the use of
    (a) aversive conditioning.
    (b) counterconditioning.
    (c) systematic desensitization.
    (d) a token economy.

13. Seven-year-old Niall chews the ends of all his pens and pencils, so his mother paints them with a foul-tasting, but harmless, substance. After a few days of this treatment, Niall stops chewing his pens and pencils. Niall's mother has used a form of
    (a) transference.
    (b) counterconditioning.
    (c) aversive therapy.
    (d) electroconvulsive therapy.

14. To overcome his fear of heights, Gaetan is fitted with special motion-sensitive goggles that expose him to a computer-generated, three-dimensional environment that appears very real. He is progressively exposed to views from different heights as he practices relaxation. According to In Focus (Using Virtual Reality to Conquer Phobias), this approach

    (a) is very likely to make his phobia worse.
    (b) is considered to be a pseudoscience by most psychologists.
    (c) is one form of Naikan therapy.
    (d) is very likely to reduce his fear of heights.

15. According to Science Versus Pseudoscience (EMDR), eye movement desensitization reprocessing (EMDR)

    (a) has been used to treat posttraumatic stress disorder (PTSD), panic disorder, addiction, substance abuse, sleep disorders, and other psychological disorders.
    (b) is very popular and lucrative; more than 40,000 trained practitioners have treated close to a million patients since 1990.
    (c) is no more effective than standard approaches, such as exposure therapy, in the treatment of anxiety disorders, including PTSD.
    (d) displays the fundamental characteristics of a pseudoscience, according to some psychologists.
    (e) has all of these characteristics.

Progress Test 3

After you have checked your understanding of the material in Progress Tests 1 and 2, and have done a complete chapter review with special focus on any areas of weakness, you are ready to further assess your knowledge with Progress Test 3. Check your answers. If you make a mistake, review your notes, the appropriate parts of the study guide, and, if necessary, the relevant sections of your textbook.

1. After reviewing the literature on the use of lithium and the mechanism involved in its effectiveness in treating bipolar disorder, Richelle is likely to conclude that lithium

    (a) stabilizes the availability of glutamate, an excitatory neurotransmitter, preventing both abnormal highs and lows.
    (b) boosts the levels of dopamine in the brain.
    (c) selectively inhibits the reuptake of serotonin.

    (d) stabilizes the levels of both dopamine and serotonin in the brain.

2. Aaron Beck is to _____ as Carl Rogers is to _____ .

    (a) cognitive therapy; rational-emotive therapy
    (b) behavior therapy; client-centered therapy
    (c) biomedical therapy; psychoanalysis
    (d) cognitive therapy; client-centered therapy

3. Because of Rhian's persistent feelings of hopelessness, dejection, and guilt, and her suicidal thoughts, her doctor prescribes an antidepressant drug. Rhian is most likely to be taking a(n)

    (a) selective serotonin reuptake inhibitor (SSRI) called Prozac.
    (b) benzodiazepine drug called Valium.
    (c) neuroleptic medication called Thorazine.
    (d) anticonvulsant medicine called Depakote.

4. When Clifford decided to pursue a career as an artist instead of complying with his father's wish for him to become a lawyer, both parents were angry, critical, and rejecting. Carl Rogers would say that Clifford's parents are demonstrating

    (a) conditional acceptance.
    (b) empathic understanding.
    (c) unconditional positive regard.
    (d) unconscious motivations and feelings.

5. Mrs. Blonska has been diagnosed with generalized anxiety disorder. Because her doctor is concerned with the long-term treatment of her global and persistent feelings of anxiety, he is likely to prescribe

    (a) Buspar.   (c) Depakote.
    (b) Prozac.   (d) Clozapine.

6. Mr. MacKaskill has a serious drinking problem. To reduce his intake of alcohol, a behavior therapist might give Mr. MacKaskill a medication called Antabuse, which induces nausea whenever it is taken with alcohol. This behavioral technique is called

    (a) counterconditioning.
    (b) systematic desensitization.
    (c) aversive conditioning.
    (d) the token economy.

7. For no obvious reason, Mr. Henderson has recently begun to express feelings of annoyance, irritability, and anger toward his therapist, who has been consistently patient, concerned, and supportive. Freud would most likely consider Mr. Henderson's hostility toward his therapist to be an example of
   (a) insight. (c) aversion.
   (b) counterconditioning. (d) transference.

8. Dr. Elson uses a therapeutic technique that involves modifying behavior by conditioning a new response that is incompatible with a previously learned undesired response. Dr. Elson is most likely a _____ therapist who is using _____ .
   (a) behavior; counterconditioning
   (b) cognitive; rational-emotive techniques
   (c) psychoanalytic; free association
   (d) biomedical; ECT

9. Nelson's therapist believes that a therapist should be nondirective, providing unconditional positive regard in an open, honest way. Nelson's therapist is most likely a _____ therapist.
   (a) psychoanalytic (c) cognitive
   (b) behavioral (d) humanistic

10. During a lecture to students interested in graduate work in clinical psychology, Dr. Barton is asked what factors contribute most to effective psychotherapy. He is most likely to respond that
    (a) mutual respect, trust, and hope in the therapeutic situation are important factors.
    (b) therapists who have warmth, sensitivity, sincerity, and genuineness are usually effective.
    (c) clients who are motivated, expressive, and actively committed to therapy enhance the success of therapy.
    (d) all of these factors contribute to effective psychotherapy.

11. Brian's therapist attempts to tailor her approach to his particular problems and characteristics and, in doing so, uses techniques from different psychotherapies. Brian's therapist would most likely be classified as a(n) _____ therapist.
    (a) humanistic (c) behavior
    (b) eclectic (d) cognitive

12. Which of the following individuals is most likely to benefit from a psychoactive drug that affects the level of the neurotransmitter dopamine in the brain?
    (a) Herman, who hears imaginary voices telling him that he is going to be abducted by aliens
    (b) Marcel, who is very nervous and anxious all the time
    (c) Carla, who feels sad, despondent, dejected, and worthless most of the time
    (d) Faith, who drinks at least a six-pack of beer every day

13. Harriet has asked her psychology professor whether psychotherapy is more effective than no therapy at all. If her professor is familiar with the meta-analytic studies on the topic, he is most likely to answer that
    (a) psychotherapy is no more effective than talking to a friend.
    (b) it is not possible to measure the effectiveness of psychotherapy.
    (c) psychotherapy harms more people than it helps.
    (d) psychotherapy is significantly more effective than no treatment.

14. According to In Focus (Self-Help Groups), which of the following is true about self-help groups?
    (a) Compared with therapy provided by mental health professionals, self-help groups are generally ineffective for the vast majority of psychological problems.
    (b) All self-help groups are organized and led by nonprofessionals.
    (c) Compared with professional mental health services, self-help groups are much more likely to cause harm to the people involved.
    (d) To operate legally, self-help groups must employ at least one registered professional, such as a clinical psychologist, or a licensed physician, such as a psychiatrist.

15. Masahara goes to a therapist who specializes in a Japanese psychotherapy called Naikan therapy. According to Culture and Human Behavior (Cultural Values and Psychotherapy), it is very probable that he will be advised to
    (a) avoid being self-absorbed because it is the surest path to psychological suffering.
    (b) focus on developing a sense of gratitude and obligation toward significant others.

(c) meditate on how much his parents and others have done for him and how he may have failed to meet their needs.

(d) reflect on the trouble and problems he may have caused significant others.

(e) do all of these things.

Answers

Introduction: Psychotherapy and Biomedical Therapy

1. *Psychotherapy refers to* the treatment of emotional, behavioral, and interpersonal problems through the use of psychological techniques designed to encourage understanding of problems and to modify troubling feelings, behaviors, or relationships.

2. *A basic assumption of all psychotherapies is that* psychological factors play a significant role in a person's troubling feelings, behaviors, or relationships.

3. *Biomedical therapies involve* the use of medications, electroconvulsive therapy, or other medical treatments to treat the symptoms associated with psychological disorders.

4. *The biomedical therapies are based on the assumption that* the symptoms of many psychological disorders involve biological factors, such as abnormal brain chemistry.

Psychoanalytic Therapy

1. *Psychoanalysis is a* type of psychotherapy originated by Sigmund Freud in which free association, dream interpretation, and analysis of resistance and transference are used to explore repressed or unconscious impulses, anxieties, and internal conflicts.

2. *The main psychoanalytic techniques (and their purpose) are (a)* free association, in which the patient spontaneously reports all her thoughts, mental images, and feelings while lying on a couch; *(b)* resistance, the patient's unconscious attempts to block the process of revealing repressed memories and conflicts; *(c)* dream interpretation, the analysis of dream content for disguised or symbolic wishes, meanings, and motivations; *(d)* interpretation, in which the psychoanalyst offers a carefully timed explanation of the patient's dreams, free associations, or behavior to facilitate the recognition of unconscious conflicts or motivations; and

(e) transference, the process by which emotions and desires originally associated with a significant person in the patient's life, such as a parent, are unconsciously transferred to the psychoanalyst.

3. *Together, these psychoanalytic techniques are designed to* help uncover unconscious conflicts so the patient attains insight as to the real source of her problems.

4. *The various forms of short-term dynamic therapies (all based on traditional psychoanalytic notions) have four features in common:* (a) Contact lasts for no more than a few months. (b) The patient's problems are quickly assessed at the beginning of therapy. (c) The therapist and patient agree on specific, concrete, and attainable goals. (d) In the actual sessions, most psychodynamic therapists are more directive than traditional psychoanalysts, actively engaging the patient in a dialogue.

5. *Interpersonal therapy (IPT) is* a brief, psychodynamic psychotherapy that focuses on current relationships and social interactions and is based on the assumption that symptoms are caused and maintained by interpersonal problems. *The four categories of personal problems dealt with are (a)* unresolved grief (problems dealing with the death of significant others); *(b)* role disputes (repetitive conflicts with others, such as a person's partner, family members, friends, or co-workers); *(c)* role transitions (problems involving major life changes such as going away to college, becoming a parent, marriage, divorce, or retirement); and *(d)* interpersonal deficits (absent or faulty social skills that limit the ability to start or maintain healthy relationships with others).

Concept Check 1

1. resistance
2. free association
3. interpretation
4. transference
5. dream interpretation
6. biomedical therapies; psychotherapy
7. interpersonal therapy (IPT)
8. short-term dynamic
9. unresolved grief; role disputes; role transitions; interpersonal deficits

Matching Exercise 1

1. interpersonal deficits
2. psychotherapy
3. interpretation
4. psychoanalysis
5. biomedical therapies
6. short-term dynamic therapies
7. psychotropic medications
8. role disputes
9. Sigmund Freud

True/False Test 1

1. T	4. T	7. T
2. T	5. T	8. T
3. T	6. T	9. T

Humanistic Therapy

1. *The most influential humanistic therapy is* client- (or person-) centered therapy; *it was developed by* Carl Rogers *who deliberately used the word* client *rather than* patient *because* he wanted to get away from the idea that the person was sick and was seeking treatment from an all-knowing authority figure. He also wanted to emphasize the client's subjective perception of himself and his environment.

2. *In client-centered therapy, the main conditions are that* the therapist should be nondirective; the client should direct the focus of therapy sessions; and the therapist should be genuine, demonstrate unconditional positive regard, and communicate empathic understanding.

3. *Unlike psychoanalysis, humanistic therapy does not offer* solutions or interpretations about the client's unconscious feelings and motivations, but instead is nondirective and reflective.

4. *Motivational interviewing is designed to* help clients overcome the mixed feelings or reluctance they might have about committing to change; it is more directive than traditional client-centered therapy, and its main goal is to encourage or strengthen the client's self-motivated statements or "change talk."

Behavior Therapy

1. *The goal of behavior therapy is to* modify specific problem behaviors, not to change the entire personality.

2. *Behavior therapists assume that maladaptive behaviors are* learned, just as adaptive behaviors are. *Therefore, the basic strategy in behavior therapy involves* unlearning maladaptive behaviors and learning more adaptive behaviors in their place.

3. *Behavior therapists employ techniques that are based on the learning principles of* classical conditioning, operant conditioning, and observational learning.

4. *Mary Cover Jones's procedure, called counterconditioning, involved* gradually introducing the feared stimulus and pairing it with a pleasant stimulus, such as food, which elicits a positive response that is incompatible with the original conditioned response (this procedure also eliminated fear of objects that were similar to the original feared stimulus).

5. *Along with counterconditioning, Jones used* social imitation, or observational learning, techniques and demonstrated that seeing others acting in a fearless manner encourages the fearful individual to imitate the fearless behavior.

6. *Based on the same premise as counterconditioning, systematic desensitization involves* learning a new conditioned response (relaxation) that is incompatible with or inhibits the old conditioned response (fear and anxiety).

7. *The three basic steps involved in systematic desensitization are (a)* The patient learns progressive relaxation. *(b)* The therapist helps the client construct a hierarchy of anxiety-provoking images and develop a relaxing control scene. *(c)* The process of desensitization begins by getting the deeply relaxed patient to imagine the least threatening scene in the anxiety hierarchy (over several sessions the client gradually works his way up the anxiety hierarchy).

8. *Virtual reality (VR) therapy combines* systematic desensitization techniques with exposure to a computer-generated, three-dimensional environment, which the viewer experiences as if it were real.

9. *The bell and pad treatment uses classical conditioning techniques to help bedwetters by* pairing the sensation of a full bladder (conditioned stimulus) with a loud bell (the unconditioned stimulus, which is triggered by a wet bed), which wakens the child (the unconditioned response). Eventually, the sensation of a full bladder by itself (conditioned stimulus) will cause the child to waken (conditioned response) before he wets the bed.

10. *Aversive conditioning involves* repeatedly pairing an aversive stimulus with the occurrence of undesirable behaviors or thoughts (a relatively ineffective type of behavior therapy).

11. *B. F. Skinner's operant conditioning model of learning is based on the simple principle that behavior is* shaped and maintained by its consequences. This model uses positive reinforcement for desired behaviors and extinction (or nonreinforcement) for undesired behaviors.

12. *The token economy is a form of behavior therapy in which* the therapeutic environment is structured to reward desired behaviors with tokens or points that may eventually be exchanged for tangible rewards. *A modified version of the token economy is called* contingency management intervention.

Concept Check 2

1. humanistic; client-centered
2. behavior therapy (systematic desensitization)
3. aversive
4. token economy
5. bell and pad treatment
6. client-centered; empathic understanding
7. extinction; positive reinforcement
8. shaping

Matching Exercise 2

1. Mary Cover Jones
2. humanistic perspective
3. token economy
4. genuineness
5. behavior therapy (behavior modification)
6. Carl Rogers
7. progressive relaxation
8. bell and pad treatment
9. client-centered therapy
10. Antabuse
11. baseline rate
12. observational learning
13. anxiety hierarchy

True/False 2

1. F	4. T	7. T	10. T	13. T
2. T	5. T	8. T	11. T	
3. T	6. T	9. F	12. T	

Cognitive Therapies

1. *Cognitive therapies assume that* most people blame unhappiness and problems on external events and situations, but the real cause of unhappiness is the way the person thinks about the events, not the events themselves.

2. *The goal of cognitive therapy is to* identify the maladaptive patterns of thinking and then to change them to more adaptive, healthy patterns.

3. *Rational-emotive therapy (RET) was developed by* Albert Ellis, *and it focuses on* identifying, disputing, and changing the client's irrational beliefs (explained by the ABC model [an Activating event triggers Beliefs that cause Consequences]).

4. *Beck's cognitive therapy (CT) focuses on* changing the client's unrealistic and distorted beliefs, and on correcting the cognitive biases that underlie depression and other psychological disorders.

5. *Like Ellis, Beck believes that* what people think creates their moods and emotions; like RET, CT involves helping clients identify faulty thinking and replace unhealthy patterns of thinking with healthier ones.

6. *In contrast with RET's emphasis on "irrational" thinking, Beck believes that* depression and other psychological problems are caused by distorted thinking and unrealistic beliefs, and the cognitive therapist encourages the client to empirically test the accuracy of his or her assumptions and beliefs.

7. *Cognitive-behavioral therapy (CBT) refers to* a group of psychotherapies that integrate cognitive and behavioral techniques. *They are based on the assumption that* thoughts, moods, and behaviors are interrelated; changes in thought patterns affect moods and behaviors, and changes in behavior affect cognitions and emotional states.

Group and Family Therapy

1. *Group therapy involves* one or more therapists working simultaneously with a small group of clients (the group may be as small as 3 or 4 people or as large as 10 or more people).

2. *Some of the key advantages of group therapy are that* it is cost-effective; therapists can observe clients interacting with other group members; clients can benefit from the support, encouragement, and practical suggestions provided by

other group members; and people can try out new behaviors in a safe, supportive environment.

3. *Family therapy is based on the assumption that* the family is an interdependent system; it focuses on treating the family as a unit, rather than on treating the individual.

4. *Couple therapy focuses on* improving communication, problem-solving skills, and intimacy between members of any couple in a committed relationship.

Evaluating the Effectiveness of Psychotherapy

1. *When meta-analysis is used to summarize studies, the researchers consistently arrive at the same conclusion:* psychotherapy is significantly more effective than no treatment and no particular form of therapy is superior to any other.

2. *Researchers have identified a number of factors that are related to a positive therapy outcome: (a)* The most important factors are those associated with the therapeutic relationship, such as mutual respect, trust, and hope; *(b)* certain characteristics of the therapist, such as warmth, sensitivity, responsiveness, being perceived as sincere and genuine, and actively helping people to understand and face their problems and the therapists' sensitivity to the cultural differences that may exist between themselves and their clients; *(c)* client characteristics, such as level of motivation, commitment to therapy, active involvement in the process, along with emotional and social maturity and the ability to express thoughts and feelings; *(d)* external circumstances, such as supportive family members and a stable living situation.

3. *Eclecticism refers to the* pragmatic and integrated use of techniques from different psychotherapies (eclectic psychotherapists carefully tailor their approach to the problems and characteristics of the person seeking help).

Concept Check 3

1. meta-analysis
2. eclectic
3. group
4. rational-emotive
5. cognitive
6. family
7. cognitive-behavioral
8. self-help group

9. eye movement desensitization reprocessing (EMDR); no better
10. familismo

Graphic Organizer 1

Psychoanalysis:
Founder: Sigmund Freud
Source of Problems: Repressed, unconscious conflicts stemming from early childhood experiences
Treatment Techniques: Free association, analysis of dream content, interpretation, and transference
Goals of Therapy: To recognize, work through, and resolve long-standing conflicts

Client-Centered Therapy:
Founder: Carl Rogers
Source of Problems: Conditional acceptance and dependence that cause a person to develop a distorted self-concept and worldview
Treatment Techniques: Nondirective therapy, with therapist displaying unconditional positive regard, genuineness, and empathic understanding
Goals of Therapy: To develop self-awareness, self-acceptance, and self-determination

Behavior Therapy:
Founder: Various; derived from the fundamental principles of learning
Source of Problems: Learned maladaptive behavior patterns
Treatment Techniques: Counterconditioning, systematic desensitization, bell and pad treatment, aversive conditioning, reinforcement and extinction, token economy, and observational learning
Goals of Therapy: To unlearn maladaptive behaviors and learn adaptive behaviors in their place

Rational-Emotive Therapy:
Founder: Albert Ellis
Source of Problems: Irrational beliefs
Treatment Techniques: Very directive therapy: identifying, logically disputing, and challenging irrational beliefs
Goals of Therapy: To surrender irrational beliefs and absolutist demands

Cognitive Therapy:
Founder: Aaron T. Beck
Source of Problems: Unrealistic, distorted perceptions and interpretations of events due to cognitive biases
Treatment Techniques: Directive collaboration: teaching client to monitor automatic thoughts; testing accuracy of conclusions; correcting distorted thinking and perception

Goals of Therapy: To accurately and realistically perceive self, others, and external events

Cognitive-Behavioral Therapy:
Founder: Various (derived from both cognitive and behavioral traditions)
Source of Problems: Cognitions, behaviors, and emotional responses are functionally interrelated; negative thoughts affect moods and behaviors, and maladaptive behaviors affect thoughts and moods
Treatment Techniques: Pragmatic approach that integrates the most appropriate cognitive and behavioral therapeutic approaches for each individual's needs and problems
Goals of Therapy: To replace maladaptive behaviors and irrational, distorted, unrealistic perceptions and cognitions with more adaptive healthier ones

Matching Exercise 3

1. family therapy
2. cognitive therapies
3. cognitive therapy
4. group therapy
5. rational-emotive therapy
6. cognitive-behavioral therapy (CBT)
7. eye movement desensitization reprocessing (EMDR)
8. meta-analysis
9. behavioral couple therapy

True/False Test 3

1. F	4. T	7. T
2. T	5. F	8. T
3. T	6. T	9. T

Biomedical Therapies

1. *The biomedical therapies are* medical treatments for the symptoms of psychological disorders.

2. *Antipsychotic medications (neuroleptics) are* prescription drugs that are used to reduce psychotic symptoms (frequently used in the treatment of schizophrenia). *The most common antipsychotic medications include* reserpine and chlorpromazine, which alter dopamine levels in the brain; while the early antipychotics reduced the positive symptoms of schizophrenia, they were not very effective in eliminating the negative symptoms (serious side effects can include tardive dyskinesia after long-term use).

3. *The atypical antipsychotic medications include* clozapine, risperidone, olanzapine, sertindole, and quietapine, *and they act by* selectively affecting both serotonin and dopamine levels in the brain (the atypical antipsychotics have fewer side effects than the older antipsychotics and are more effective in treating both positive and negative symptoms of schizophrenia). *A third generation of antipsychotic medications includes* aripiprazole (Abilify), *which regulates* the availability of dopamine by blocking the dopamine receptors when levels are too high and mimicking dopamine when levels are too low.

4. *Antianxiety medications are* prescription drugs that are used to alleviate the symptoms of anxiety. *The most common antianxiety medications include* the benzodiazepines, which are effective in the treatment of anxiety but are potentially addictive and have many side effects (Buspar is a newer antianxiety drug that has a very low risk of physical addiction).

5. *Lithium is* a naturally occurring substance that is used in the treatment of bipolar disorder; it appears to work by stabilizing the availability of glutamate, an excitatory neurotransmitter, preventing both abnormal highs and lows. (Depakote has also been introduced as a drug treatment for those who don't respond to lithium and for those who cycle rapidly.)

6. *The antidepressant medications are* prescription drugs that are used to reduce the symptoms associated with depression. *The most common antidepressant medications include* the first-generation tricyclics and MAO inhibitors, and the second-generation antidepressants trazodone and bupropion. *New antidepressants, including* the selective serotonin reuptake inhibitors (SSRIs) Prozac, Paxil, and Zoloft; the dual-action antidepressants Serzone, Remeron, and Celexa; and the dual-reuptake inhibitors Effexor and Cymbalta, *tend to* produce fewer side effects than the first and second generation antidepressants.

7. *Electroconvulsive therapy (ECT) is a biomedical therapy used primarily* in the treatment of severe depression; it involves electrically inducing brief brain seizures (also called shock therapy and electric shock therapy).

Concept Check 4

1. antianxiety
2. electroconvulsive

3. tardive dyskinesia

4. lithium

5. olanzapine; sertindole; quietapine; aripiprazole (Abilify)

6. the same

7. anxiety disorder

8. selective serotonin reuptake inhibitors (SSRIs); Prozac; Zoloft; Paxil; Serzone; Remeron; Celexa

Matching Exercise 4

1. lithium

2. psychotropic medications

3. electroconvulsive therapy (ECT)

4. antianxiety medications

5. antidepressant medications

6. tardive dyskinesia

7. dual-action antidepressants

8. GABA

True/False Test 4

1. T	3. T	5. T	7. T
2. T	4. T	6. T	8. T

Something to Think About

1. The first thing to tell someone with a phobia is that there are many different therapeutic approaches in psychology, such as psychoanalysis, client-centered therapy, cognitive therapy, and behavior therapy. It would be appropriate to briefly explain the differences between each of these approaches and to advise the person to seek professional help if he feels that his problem is severe. Having said that, you can then go on to describe an approach that has been relatively effective in dealing with phobias—systematic desensitization.

   The first step in systematic desensitization is for the person to learn how to relax completely. This is because a state of complete relaxation is incompatible with being tense and anxious. The second step is to have the person generate a hierarchy of feared situations associated with flying. For example, the most feared situation the person can imagine might be sitting on the plane during takeoff and the least fearful might be hearing someone talking about flying. Once the person is totally relaxed, he can start imagining the least fearful situation in the hierarchy. When he can do that for a number of times without tensing up, he can move to the next situation in the hierarchy, and so on. It is also helpful for the person to create an unrelated, relaxing control scene, such as lying on the beach watching the waves roll in, which can be used to help him relax. Over a number of sessions, the person works his way up the hierarchy while relaxing completely, until eventually he can approach the real situation.

   In practice, systematic desensitization is often combined with other techniques, such as counterconditioning (pairing pleasant associations, such as being able to travel to exotic islands, with the feared situation) and observational learning (using the real situation or a video), which involves watching other people being calm and relaxed in the anxiety-provoking situation. A newer technology-based therapy combines systematic desensitization techniques with exposure to a computer-generated, three-dimensional environment, which the viewer experiences as if it were real. Virtual reality therapy has been effective in treating a variety of phobias, including fear of flying.

2. First, people seek help from mental health professionals not only for psychological problems but also for dealing with troubled relationships, coping with transitions in life, and other troubling situations. Second, there should be no stigma attached to getting help when it is needed. The prevalence of psychological disorders and similar types of problems is much higher than most people realize, so we all probably know someone who is or has been in therapy or perhaps needs to be. So, what should we expect from psychotherapy? The Application gives some important guidelines about the therapist–client relationship and the psychotherapy process.

   The cornerstone of psychotherapy is the relationship between the therapist and the person seeking help. This relationship is a collaborative endeavor in which the client is actively involved in the therapeutic process. Therapy requires work not only during the therapy sessions but also outside them. So people should expect to be involved and active. In addition, people should not expect the therapist to make decisions for them. Virtually all forms of therapy are designed to increase a person's sense of responsibility, confidence, and mastery in dealing with life's problems. The therapist is there to help.

   A therapist is not a substitute friend. Rather, he or she is more of a consultant, responding objectively and honestly to issues and problems. In addition, ethically and legally, everything that goes on in therapy is totally confidential. And, under no circumstances does therapeutic intimacy include sexual intimacy.

A person should also expect therapy to challenge how he or she thinks and acts, which sometimes can be a painful process. But becoming aware that changes are needed is a necessary step toward developing healthier forms of thinking and behavior. It is important, however, not to confuse insight with change. Just because people gain an understanding of the sources and nature of their psychological problems does not mean that they will automatically resolve these problems. Likewise, the catharsis that often results from therapy is not synonymous with change. With some effort and the help of the therapeutic process, people can move toward changing how they think, behave, and react to other people, but this will not happen overnight.

Progress Test 1

1. a	6. b	11. c
2. d	7. b	12. c
3. d	8. d	13. e
4. a	9. c	14. d
5. c	10. b	15. b

Progress Test 2

1. d	6. a	11. b
2. c	7. c	12. d
3. d	8. b	13. c
4. c	9. b	14. d
5. d	10. a	15. e

Progress Test 3

1. a	6. c	11. b
2. d	7. d	12. a
3. a	8. a	13. d
4. a	9. d	14. b
5. a	10. d	15. e

APPENDIX A

Statistics: Understanding Data

PREVIEW	Reading the section below first will give you a general sense of the chapter's contents and an initial introduction to some of the major concepts and terms. This will prime you for what you are about to read and help you to develop a "cognitive map" that will guide your study of the material in this chapter. Likewise, reading the **preview questions** at the beginning of each major section will improve your ability to understand, learn, and retain the information.

APPENDIX A . . . AT A GLANCE

Appendix A explains how and when various statistical techniques are used. Descriptive statistics are used to organize and summarize data in a meaningful way. Examples discussed include frequency distributions, which can be presented as a table, histogram, or frequency polygon; measures of central tendency (mode, median, and mean); and measures of variability (range and standard deviation). z scores are explained, and the concept of the normal distribution is presented.

Correlation, which is introduced in Chapter 1, is described, and how to calculate the correlation coefficient is explained. Both positive and negative correlations are discussed. The relationship between two variables may be presented visually in a scatter diagram. The point is made that correlational research is restricted to prediction and cannot be used to identify cause-and-effect relationships.

Inferential statistics are used to determine whether outcomes of a study can be generalized to a larger population, and they provide information about the probability of a particular result if only random factors are operating. An example of an inferential test is the t-test which can be used to compare the means of two groups to see if any differences are statistically real or simply due to random factors. To compare the means of more than two groups, researchers use the analysis of variance (ANOVA) technique. If the probability of the outcome resulting from chance factors is small, the findings are said to be statistically significant. However, researchers could erroneously conclude that results are significant (a Type I error,), or fail to find a significant effect when it really exists (a Type II error). Use of inferential statistics allows researchers to have confidence that the results from a sample are statically significant and can be generalized to the population that the sample represents.

Descriptive Statistics

Preview Questions

Consider the following questions as you study this section of the chapter.

- What are descriptive statistics, and what are they used for?
- What are frequency distributions, histograms, and frequency polygons?
- What is a skewed distribution, and what is a symmetrical distribution?
- What are the three measures of central tendency?
- What are the two measures of variability, and what are *z* scores?
- What is the standard normal curve (standard normal distribution)?

*Read the section "Descriptive Statistics" and **write** your answers to the following:*

1. Descriptive statistics are mathematical methods used to _____

   _____

2. A frequency distribution is _____

   _____

   _____

3. A histogram is _____

   _____

   _____

4. A frequency polygon is _____

   _____

   _____

5. A skewed distribution is _____

   _____

   _____

6. A symmetrical distribution is _____

   _____

   _____

7. Measures of central tendency are _____

   The mode is _____

   The median is _____

   _____

The mean is _____

_____

8. Measures of variability are _____

   _____

   The range is _____

   _____

   The standard deviation is _____

   _____

9. A *z* score is _____

   _____

10. The standard normal curve (standard normal distribution) is _____

    _____

    _____

    A person with a *z* score of +1 on a normal distribution (1 SD above the mean) has _____

    _____

    _____

After you have carefully studied the preceding section, complete the following exercises.

Concept Check 1

Read the following and write the correct term in the space provided.

1. Professor Wilson calculated the mode, median, and mean of the scores from the midterm exam. These descriptive statistics are referred to as

   _____ .

2. Professor Wilson noticed that the most frequently occurring score was 73; this score is called the _____ .

3. To determine the spread of the scores, Professor Wilson subtracted the lowest score in the distribution from the highest. In this instance, he has calculated a measure of _____ called the _____ .

4. Next, he subtracted the mean from each score in the distribution, squared each of these deviations, added them, divided by the number of scores in the distribution, and took the square root of the number just calculated. Professor Wilson has calculated a measure of _____ called the

_____ .

5. Finally, Professor Wilson graphically represented the frequency distribution by placing a mark above each score at the point representing its frequency and then connecting these points with straight lines. This type of graph is called a _____ .

Review of Terms and Concepts 1

Use the terms in this list to complete the Matching Test, then to help you answer the True/False items correctly.

statistics	measure of central
descriptive statistics	tendency
frequency distribution	mode
histogram	median
frequency polygon	mean
skewed distribution	measure of variability
positively skewed	range
distribution	standard deviation
negatively skewed	z score
distribution	standard normal curve
symmetrical distribution	(standard normal
	distribution)

Matching Exercise

Match the appropriate term with its definition or description.

1. _____ A number, expressed in standard deviation units, that shows a score's deviation from the mean.

2. _____ Mathematical methods used to organize and summarize data.

3. _____ A symmetrical distribution forming a bell-shaped curve in which the mean, median, and mode are all equal and fall in the exact middle.

4. _____ A summary of how often various scores occur in a sample of scores. Score values are arranged in order of magnitude, and the number of times each score occurs is recorded.

5. _____ Measure of variability; expressed as the square root of the sum of the squared deviations around the mean divided by the number of scores in the distribution.

6. _____ An asymmetrical distribution; more scores pile up on one side of the distribution than on the other.

7. _____ A single number that presents information about the spread of scores in a frequency distribution.

8. _____ Distribution in which the scores fall equally on both sides of the graph. The normal curve is an example.

9. _____ Measure of variability; the highest score in a distribution minus the lowest score.

True/False Test

Indicate whether each statement is true or false by placing T or F in the blank space next to each item.

1. ____ In a positively skewed distribution, most people have high scores.

2. ____ The mode is the most frequently occurring score in a distribution.

3. ____ A measure of central tendency is a single number that presents some information about the "center" of a frequency distribution.

4. ____ In a negatively skewed distribution, most people have low scores.

5. ____ A histogram is a way of graphically representing a frequency distribution where frequency is marked above each score category on the graph's horizontal axis and the marks are connected by straight lines.

6. ____ The mean is the sum of a set of scores in a distribution divided by the number of scores; it is usually the most representative measure of central tendency.

7. ____ A frequency polygon is a way of graphically representing a frequency distribution and is a type of bar chart using vertical bars that touch.

8. ____ The median is the score that divides a frequency distribution exactly in half, so that the same number of scores lies on each side of it.

9. ____ The branch of mathematics used by researchers to organize, summarize, and interpret data is called statistics.

Check your answers and review any areas of weakness before going on to the next section.

Correlation and Inferential Statistics

Preview Questions

Consider the following questions as you study these sections of the chapter.

- How is *correlation* defined, and what is the correlation coefficient?
- What is the difference between a positive and a negative correlation?
- How are correlations depicted graphically?
- What are inferential statistics?
- What are *t*-tests and the analysis of variance (ANOVA) technique used for?
- What are Type I and Type II errors, and how can researchers deal with the problem of these errors?
- What is meant by statistical significance?
- What is meant by the terms *population* and *sample*?

*Read the sections "Correlation" and "Inferential Statistics" and **write** your answers to the following:*

1. Correlation is the _____
   _____

2. The correlation coefficient is a numerical indication of _____
   _____
   _____

3. A positive correlation is a finding that _____
   _____
   _____

4. A negative correlation is a finding that _____
   _____
   _____

5. A correlation coefficient close to 1.00 (whether positive or negative) indicates _____
   _____
   while a number close to zero indicates _____
   _____

6. Correlations are depicted graphically _____
   _____
   A positive correlation is indicated by _____
   _____
   _____

A negative correlation is indicated by _____
_____
_____

7. Inferential statistics are _____
   _____
   _____

8. A *t*-test is used to _____
   _____
   analysis of variance (ANOVA) is used to _____
   _____
   _____

9. Statistical significance refers to the fact that if the results of a study are _____
   _____
   _____

10. A Type I error occurs when _____
    _____
    _____
    A Type II error occurs when _____
    _____
    _____
    Because of the possibility of a Type I error, it is important that _____
    _____
    _____
    _____
    One way to avoid a Type II error is to _____
    _____
    _____
    _____

11. A population is _____
    _____
    Because the entire population of interest usually cannot be studied, researchers use _____
    _____

After you have carefully studied the preceding section, complete the following exercises.

Concept Check 2

Read the following and write the correct term in the space provided.

1. Dr. Jabul discovers that the more education people have, the more money they tend to earn. Dr. Jabul has discovered a _____ correlation.

2. Based on his research, Dr. Jabul can use one variable to _____ the other, but he cannot say that one variable _____ the other.

3. When Professor Alphonse plotted his data on a scatter diagram (scatter plot), he noticed that they clustered in a pattern that extends from the upper left of the graph to the lower right. This pattern suggests that the two variables are _____ correlated.

4. When Kayla analyzed the correlational data for her psychology project, the correlation coefficient was +.07. Kayla can conclude that the two variables _____ (are/are not) correlated.

5. When researchers analyzed the data from their experiment, they found large differences between the control group and the experimental group that were not due to chance. They can conclude that the results are

   _____ .

6. In order to discover how people feel about the level of service provided, ABC Company asks a randomly selected subset of their customers to fill out a brief questionnaire. ABC's customers represent the _____ , and the subset surveyed is a _____ .

7. The means of the two groups being studied were different. To increase confidence that this difference was not simply due to chance alone the researchers should use a test called

   _____ .

8. In her research, Dr. Quinn compared the means from four different groups to determine if the observed differences between the means were statistically significant. Dr. Quinn has used an inferential technique called

   _____ .

9. After the data had been collected and analyzed, the researchers erroneously concluded that the study results were significant, a mistake called a _____ .

10. Dr. Kaslo was disappointed that the results of his study failed to reach statistical significance, so he replicated the study using a better research design and twice as many participants. Dr. Kaslo has increased the _____ of the study in an attempt to avoid a

    _____ .

Review of Terms and Concepts 2

Use the terms in this list to complete the Matching Test, then to help you answer the True/False items correctly.

correlation	analysis of variance
correlation coefficient	(ANOVA)
positive correlation	statistically significant
negative correlation	Type I error
scatter diagram (scatter	Type II error
plot)	power
experimental method	population
inferential statistics	sample
t-test	

Matching Exercise

Match the appropriate term with its definition or description.

1. _____ Graph that represents the relationship between two variables.

2. _____ Numerical indication of the magnitude and direction of the relationship (the correlation) between two variables.

3. _____ Mathematical methods used to determine how likely it is that a study's outcome is due to chance and whether the outcome can be legitimately generalized to a larger population.

4. _____ A complete set of something —people, nonhuman animals, objects, or events.

5. _____ The relationship between two variables.

6. _____ Test used to establish whether the means of two groups are statistically different from each other.

7. _____ A mistake that occurs when researchers erroneously conclude that the results of the study are significant—that is, they reject the null hypothesis.

8. _____ A technique used in inferential statistics to compare the means of more than two groups for statistical significance.

True/False Test

Indicate whether each statement is true or false by placing T or F in the blank space next to each item.

1. ____ Results can be considered statistically significant when the probability of obtaining them, if chance, or random, factors alone are operating, is less than .05 (5 chances out of 100).

2. ____ A positive correlation is a finding that two factors vary systematically in opposite directions, one increasing in size as the other decreases.

3. ____ A sample is a subset of a population.

4. ____ A negative correlation is a finding that two factors vary systematically in the same direction, increasing or decreasing in size together.

5. ____ The experimental method is the only research method that can provide scientific evidence of a cause-and-effect relationship between two or more variables.

6. ____ A Type II error occurs when researchers fail to find a significant effect when the significant effect actually exists, that is, when they fail to reject the null hypothesis when they should.

7. ____ Higher *power* can be achieved in a study by improving the research design and measuring instruments, or by increasing the number of participants or subjects being studied.

Check your answers and review any areas of weakness before completing the progress tests.

Progress Test 1

Review the complete appendix, review all your study notes, and then test yourself on the following progress test. Check your answers. If you make a mistake, review your notes, review the relevant section of the study guide, and, if necessary, go back and read the appropriate part of your textbook.

1. Professor Admunson used a scatter diagram to depict the relationship between her students' high school GPA and their first-year grade point average (GPA) in college. She noticed that the data points clustered in a pattern that extends from the lower left corner of the graph to the upper right corner. This pattern suggests that the two variables
   (a) are negatively correlated.
   (b) have no relationship.
   (c) are positively correlated.
   (d) have a cause-and-effect relationship.

2. A measure of variability is to _____ as a measure of central tendency is to _____ .
   (a) mode; median
   (b) correlation; scatter plot
   (c) standard deviation; mean
   (d) histogram; frequency polygon

3. One student in the class got an extremely low score of 10 out of 100 on a test. Which measure of central tendency is most affected by this low score?
   (a) mode   (c) median
   (b) mean   (d) range

4. Following the final exam, Professor Farrar calculated a number of statistics and noticed that the standard deviation was extremely small. This indicates that
   (a) the scores on the exam were clustered around the mean and not spread out.
   (b) the distribution was skewed.
   (c) the scores had a great deal of variability and were not clustered around the mean.
   (d) there were very few students in her class.

5. Mrs. Kodiak has seven children aged 3, 5, 8, 9, 12, 15, and 15. The median age of her children is
   (a) 9.   (c) 12.
   (b) 15.   (d) 67.

6. When the results of an experiment were examined and the appropriate statistics calculated, the researchers concluded that the probability of obtaining these results, if random factors alone were operating, was less than .01. The results are
   (a) probably due to chance.
   (b) not statistically significant.
   (c) skewed.
   (d) statistically significant.

7. For his class presentation, Liam prepared a graph that depicted a frequency distribution with vertical bars that touched each other. Liam has constructed a
   (a) scatter diagram.
   (b) frequency polygon.
   (c) histogram.
   (d) standard deviation.

8. Liam's graph is a symmetrical distribution with an equal number of scores on each side of the graph. It is very likely that the
   (a) mean is larger than the median.
   (b) mode is larger than the mean.
   (c) mean, mode, and median have the same value.
   (d) median is larger than the mode.

9. When researchers calculated the correlation coefficients for two different sets of data, they discovered that set A had a negative correlation of −.85 and set B had a positive correlation of +.62. They can conclude that
   (a) set A has a stronger correlation than set B.
   (b) set A has a weaker correlation than set B.
   (c) set B has a stronger correlation than set A.
   (d) both (b) and (c) are true.

10. Students in a methodology class conducted individual experiments. After completing his statistical analysis Peter failed to find a significant effect even though the significant effect actually existed. On the other hand, Tanya erroneously concluded that her results were significant. Peter's conclusion reflects a _____ and Tanya's conclusion reflects a _____ .
   (a) failure to use the correct inferential statistic; failure to use the correct descriptive statistic.
   (b) Type II error; Type I error
   (c) failure to replicate his findings; lack of power in her study
   (d) Type I error; Type II error

Progress Test 2

After you have checked your understanding of the material in Progress Test 1 and have done a complete chapter review with special focus on any areas of weakness, you are ready to assess your knowledge on Progress Test 2. Check your answers. If you make a mistake, review your notes, the relevant section of the study guide, and, if necessary, the appropriate part of your textbook.

1. In addition to calculating the range, Matthew also calculated the standard deviation for his frequency distribution of scores. Matthew is using
   (a) measures of variability.
   (b) inferential statistics.
   (c) measures of central tendency.
   (d) correlational statistics.

2. When Professor Kitahara finished marking the final exams, he plotted the results on a graph by marking the frequency above each score category on the horizontal axis and then connecting the marks using straight lines. Professor Kitahara has constructed a
   (a) frequency distribution.
   (b) histogram.
   (c) frequency polygon.
   (d) scatter diagram.

3. Professor Kitahara observed that the graph was a symmetrical distribution that resembled a bell-shaped curve and that the mean, median, and mode were all equal. A student who scored better than 84 percent of the other students in this distribution would have a z score of
   (a) +1.   (c) +.84.
   (b) −1.   (d) −.84.

4. Hanna has a grade point average of 3.5. What measure of central tendency was used to calculate this statistic?
   (a) median
   (b) standard deviation
   (c) mode
   (d) mean

5. In her research, Dr. Simiak found that the more credit cards people have, the less money they have in their savings accounts. Dr. Simiak has found a _____ correlation between the number of credit cards owned and savings.
   (a) positive   (c) negative
   (b) zero   (d) skewed

6. Range is to mode as _____ is to

   _____ .

   (a) correlation; scatter diagram
   (b) median; mode
   (c) correlation coefficient; z score
   (d) variability; central tendency

7. In comparing two frequency distributions, Fydor noticed that in the first distribution most people had low scores and in the second distribution most people had high scores. The first distribution is _____ , and the second distribution is _____ .

   (a) positively skewed; negatively skewed
   (b) symmetrical; normal
   (c) negatively skewed; positively skewed
   (d) a polygon; a histogram

8. When Tyborg calculated the mean and standard deviation for a set of scores, he found that the mean was 55 out of 100, and the standard deviation was 15. If the scores are normally distributed, Tyborg can conclude that approximately 68 percent of the scores are between

   (a) 40 and 70.   (c) 55 and 70.
   (b) 25 and 85.   (d) 40 and 55.

9. Dr. Hadley found a difference in the means between his experimental group and control group. He then used a t-test to establish whether the difference was statistically significant. Dr. Hadley is using

   (a) descriptive statistics.
   (b) inferential statistics
   (c) correlational statistics.
   (d) the analysis of variance (ANOVA) technique.

10. During the past month Karianne read 8 books, Kyle read 2 books, Phyllis read 4 books, and Philip read 6 books. The mean number of books read by this group is

    (a) 5.   (c) 8.
    (b) 20.   (d) 6.

Progress Test 3

After you have checked your understanding of the material in Progress Tests 1 and 2, and have done a complete chapter review with special focus on any areas of weakness, you are ready to further assess your knowledge with Progress Test 3. Check your answers. If you make a mistake, review your notes, the appropriate parts of the study guide, and, if necessary, the relevant sections of your textbook.

1. A complete set of something (people, objects, events, etc.) is to a _____ as a representative subset is to a _____ .
   (a) descriptive statistics; inferential statistics
   (b) sample; population
   (c) inferential statistics; descriptive statistics
   (d) population; sample

2. Dr. Soryun carried out the appropriate calculations on her data and noticed that results were more extreme than would be expected by chance. She concluded that the probability of obtaining these results if random factors alone were operating was less than 1 chance out of 100. Dr. Soryun has used _____ statistics, and the results can be called

   _____ .

   (a) descriptive statistics; statistically significant
   (b) inferential statistics; positively skewed
   (c) descriptive statistics; positively skewed
   (d) inferential statistics; statistically significant

3. Organizing and summarizing data is to _____ as making inferences and drawing conclusions is to _____ .
   (a) descriptive statistics; inferential statistics
   (b) correlational research; experimental research
   (c) inferential statistics; descriptive statistics
   (d) experimental research; correlational research

4. Researchers at State University are interested in determining the extent to which personality variables such as impatience, aggressiveness, and hostility could be used to predict the risk of cardiovascular disease. These researchers are most likely to use _____ in their research.
   (a) a measure of variability
   (b) the correlation coefficient
   (c) the standard normal distribution
   (d) the standard deviation

5. After analyzing his data, Jamie decided to depict his results in a graph. He noticed that the data points clustered in a pattern that extended from the upper left to the lower right on his graph. Jamie has constructed a _____ that shows a _____ .

   (a) polygon; skewed distribution
   (b) scatter diagram; positive correlation
   (c) histogram; symmetrical distribution
   (d) scatter diagram; negative correlation

6. In his survey research, Dr. Khrod discovered that the more education people have, the less television they watch. Dr. Khrod has discovered a(n) _____ between television watching and level of education.

   (a) negative correlation
   (b) illusory correlation
   (c) positive correlation
   (d) cause-and-effect relationship

7. When Harpinder plotted his data, his graph closely resembled the normal curve and had a mean of 50 and a standard deviation of 5. Harpinder can be confident that approximately 68 percent of the scores are between

   (a) +1 and –1 SDs.
   (b) +2 and –2 SDs.
   (c) +3 and –3 SDs.
   (d) correlation coefficients of +1.00 and –1.00.

8. Raphael's z-score on the midterm was +1. If the class scores are normally distributed, Raphael has

   (a) scored better than 34.13 percent of the class.
   (b) scored worse than 34.13 percent of the class.
   (c) scored better than 84 percent of the class.
   (d) scored worse than 84 percent of the class.

9. When Professor Exman compared the statistics from her two introductory biology classes, she noticed that the standard deviation was 8.24 in class A and 3.76 in class B. She can conclude that

   (a) the students in class A studied much harder than those in class B.
   (b) the scores in class A had much more variability than those in class B.
   (c) the range for both classes is likely to be identical.
   (d) one very extreme score probably distorted the standard deviation for class A.

10. As a first step in analyzing her data, Tracianne calculated the mean, the mode, and the median. Tracianne has

    (a) used inferential statistics.
    (b) determined the statistical significance of her results.
    (c) used descriptive statistics.
    (d) calculated measures of variability.

Answers

Descriptive Statistics

1. *Descriptive statistics are mathematical methods used to* organize and summarize data.

2. *A frequency distribution is* a summary of how often various scores occur in a sample of scores. Score values are arranged in order of magnitude, and the number of times each score occurs is recorded.

3. *A histogram is* a way of graphically representing a frequency distribution. It is like a bar chart with two special features: the bars are always vertical, and they always touch.

4. *A frequency polygon is* another way of graphically representing a frequency distribution. In contrast to a histogram, or a frequency distribution, a mark is made above each category at the point representing its frequency, and these marks are then connected by straight lines.

5. *A skewed distribution is* an asymmetrical distribution with more scores piled up on one side of the distribution than on the other. If most people have low scores, the distribution is positively skewed; if most people have high scores, the distribution is negatively skewed.

6. *A symmetrical distribution is* a distribution in which scores fall equally on both halves of the graph (an example of a symmetrical distribution is the normal curve).

7. *Measures of central tendency are* single numbers that present some information about the "center" of a frequency distribution. *The mode is* the score or category that occurs most frequently in a set of raw scores or in a frequency distribution. *The median is* the score that divides a frequency distribution exactly in half, so that the same number of scores lie on each side of it. *The mean is* the sum of a set of scores in a distribution divided by the number of scores, and is usually the most representative measure of central tendency.

8. *Measures of variability are* single numbers that present information about the spread of scores in a distribution. *The range is* the highest score in a distribution minus the lowest score. *The standard deviation is* expressed as the square root of the sum of the squared deviations around the mean divided by the number of scores in the distribution.

9. *A z score is* a number, expressed in standard deviation units, that shows a score's deviation from the mean.

10. *The standard normal curve (standard normal distribution) is* a symmetrical distribution forming a bell-shaped curve in which the mean, median, and mode are all equal and fall in the exact middle. *A person with a z score of +1 on a normal distribution (1 SD above the mean) has* scored better than 84 percent of the other people in the distribution (34.13 percent between 0 and +1, plus the 50 percent that falls below 0).

Concept Check 1

1. measures of central tendency

2. mode

3. variability; range

4. variability; standard deviation

5. frequency polygon

Matching Exercise 1

1. *z* score

2. descriptive statistics

3. standard normal curve (standard normal distribution)

4. frequency distribution

5. standard deviation

6. skewed distribution

7. measure of variability

8. symmetrical distribution

9. range

True/False Test 1

1. F		4. F		7. F	
2. T		5. F		8. T	
3. T		6. T		9. T	

Correlation and Inferential Statistics

1. *Correlation is the* relationship between two variables; it does not indicate causality between the two variables.

2. *The correlation coefficient is a* numerical indication of the magnitude and direction of the relationship (the correlation) between two variables.

3. *A positive correlation is a finding that* two factors vary systematically in the same direction, increasing or decreasing in size together.

4. *A negative correlation is a finding that* two factors vary systematically in opposite directions, one increasing in size as the other decreases.

5. *A correlation coefficient close to 1.00 (whether positive or negative) indicates* a strong relationship, *while a number close to zero indicates* a weak relationship.

6. *Correlations are depicted graphically* on a scatter diagram (scatter plot), which is a graph that represents the relationship between two variables. *A positive correlation is indicated by* the upward-sloping pattern of dots, from lower left to upper right (when one variable is high, the other also tends to be high, and vice versa). *A negative correlation is indicated by* the downward-sloping pattern of dots, from upper left to lower right (when one variable is high, the other tends to be low, and vice versa).

7. *Inferential statistics are* mathematical methods used to determine how likely it is that a study's outcome is due to chance and whether the outcome can be legitimately generalized to a larger population.

8. *A t-test is used to* establish whether the means of two groups are statistically different from each other; *analysis of variance (ANOVA) is used to* compare the means of more than two groups for statistical significance.

9. *Statistical significance refers to the fact that if the results of a study are* more extreme than would be expected by chance alone, we reject the idea that no real effect has occurred and conclude that the manipulation of the independent variable is the reason for the obtained results; when this happens, the results are statistically significant, and the probability of getting these results, if random factors alone are operating, is less than .05 (5 chances in 100) or .01 (1 chance in 100).

10. *A Type I error occurs when* researchers erroneously conclude that the results of the study are significant—that is, they reject the null hypothesis (see page 417 for an explanation of the null hypothesis). *A Type II error occurs when* they fail to find a significant effect even though a significant effect actually exists, that

is, when they fail to reject the null hypothesis when they should. *Because of the possibility of a Type I error, it is important that* the study be repeated or replicated; if the same results are found, it can be assumed that a Type 1 error was not likely to have occurred, and we can have more confidence that the results were, in fact, statistically significant. *One way to avoid a Type II error is to* increase the power of a study by improving the research design and measuring instruments, or by increasing the number of participants or subjects in the study.

11. *A population is* a complete set of something—people, nonhuman animals, objects, or events. *Because the entire population of interest usually cannot be studied, researchers use* a sample, which is a subset of a population.

Concept Check 2

1. positive
2. predict; causes
3. negatively
4. are not
5. statistically significant
6. population; sample
7. *t*-test
8. analysis of variance (ANOVA)
9. Type I error
10. power; Type II error

Matching Exercise 2

1. scatter diagram (scatter plot)
2. correlation coefficient
3. inferential statistics
4. population
5. correlation
6. *t*-test
7. Type I error
8. analysis of variance (ANOVA)

True/False Test 2

1. T	4. F	7. T
2. F	5. T	
3. T	6. T	

Progress Test 1

1. c	5. a	9. a
2. c	6. d	10. b
3. b	7. c	
4. a	8. c	

Progress Test 2

1. a	5. c	9. b
2. c	6. d	10. a
3. a	7. a	
4. d	8. a	

Progress Test 3

1. d	5. d	9. b
2. d	6. a	10. c
3. a	7. a	
4. b	8. c	

NOTE: The null hypothesis concept is not covered in your textbook but is part of the traditional definitions of Type I and Type II errors. Simply put, the idea is that at the start of their research, investigators have to assume that there will be no real difference between the groups or conditions in their experiments. This assumption of "no difference" is called the *null hypothesis.*

Of course, they hope that there will be a statistically significant difference between groups or conditions, and that is what their hypotheses usually state. If a real difference is found, they can reject the null hypothesis (which predicted "no difference") and claim support for their predicted difference.

When this happens, researchers can potentially make two types of errors. A Type 1 error occurs when they think they have a real difference but they don't actually have one (so they mistakenly reject the null hypothesis, which would have correctly predicted "no difference"). A Type II error occurs when they have a real effect or difference but do not detect that difference, so they reject their own hypothesized or predicted difference and accept the null hypothesis, which states "no difference" (i.e., they fail to reject the null hypothesis when they should have done so).

APPENDIX B

Industrial/Organizational Psychology

PREVIEW

Reading the section below first will give you a general sense of the chapter's contents and an initial introduction to some of the major concepts and terms. This will prime you for what you are about to read and help you to develop a "cognitive map" that will guide your study of the material in this chapter. Likewise, reading the **preview questions** at the beginning of each major section will improve your ability to understand, learn, and retain the information.

APPENDIX B . . . AT A GLANCE

Appendix B first identifies and briefly describes the nine content areas of industrial/organizational (I/O) psychology. Next, a brief history of industrial/organization (I/O) psychology is provided, and the two main specialty areas of I/O are identified and explored in depth. Personnel psychology is the "I," or industrial, side of I/O psychology and organizational behavior is the "O," or organizational, side of I/O psychology.

Job analysis, personnel selection, effective job training programs, and accurate evaluation of job performance are all part of the work carried out in personnel psychology. Personnel psychologists use many devices to help with the goal of selecting the best applicants for jobs and are concerned with the validity of these selection devices.

The discussion of organizational behavior begins with the topic of job satisfaction. Researchers have tried to explain different levels of job satisfaction by using the discrepancy hypothesis, which focuses on gaps between what a person wants from a job and what he or she actually experiences. A number of approaches used to explain leader effectiveness are explored, including the trait, the behavioral, and the situational, or contingency, theories of leader effectiveness. Blake and Mouton's Managerial Grid identifies five different leadership styles. The leader–member exchange model examines how supervisors and subordinates interact and identifies two types of relationships that can develop (positive leader–member and negative leader–member). A discussion of narcissistic leaders and servant leaders is included in this section. Finally, workplace trends and issues within I/O psychology are presented, and for those interested in pursuing a career in I/O psychology, information on work settings, type of training, earnings, and employment outlook is provided.

What Is Industrial/Organizational Psychology?

Preview Questions

Consider the following questions as you study this section of the chapter.

- What is industrial/organizational psychology?
- What are the nine content areas of industrial/organizational psychology, and what is the main focus of each?
- What two psychologists played a role in the development of I/O psychology, and what were their contributions?

Read the section "What Is Industrial/Organizational Psychology?" and **write** *your answers to the following:*

1. Industrial/organizational psychology is

   _____

   _____

   The "I" side of I/O psychology is called

   _____ and is

   concerned with _____

   _____

   It helps companies _____

   The "O" side of I/O psychology is called

   _____ and is concerned

   with _____

   _____

   It helps companies _____

2. The nine content areas of I/O psychology (and the focus of each) are

   (a) _____

   _____

   _____

   (b) _____

   _____

   _____

   (c) _____

   _____

   _____

   (d) _____

   _____

   _____

   (e) _____

   _____

   _____

   (f) _____

   _____

   _____

   (g) _____

   _____

   _____

   (h) _____

   _____

   _____

   (i) _____

   _____

   _____

3. Wundt's first research assistant was

   _____ , and his contributions

   to I/O psychology were _____

   _____

   _____

   Another one of Wundt's students was

   _____ , and he is considered by many to be _____

   _____

   His book, _____

   _____

Personnel Psychology

Preview Questions

Consider the following questions as you study this section of the chapter.

- What are the three major goals of personnel psychology?
- What is job analysis, and how is it important for designing training programs and performance appraisal systems?
- What is selection device validity?
- What are the most common types of psychological tests and personnel selection devices used in personnel psychology?

*Read the section "Personnel Psychology" and **write** your answers to the following:*

1. The three major goals of personnel psychologists are (a) _____
   (b) _____
   (c) _____

2. Job analysis is a technique in which _____
   _____
   _____
   _____

   It is also important for designing _____
   _____
   _____

   Finally, it is useful in designing _____
   _____
   _____

3. Selection device validity refers to _____
   _____
   _____

4. The six most common psychological tests are
   (a) _____
   (b) _____
   (c) _____
   (d) _____
   (e) _____
   (f) _____

   Assessment of abnormal personality characteristics might be appropriate for _____
   _____

   More common for the selection of employees are
   _____

5. The three most common types of personnel selection devices are
   (a) Work samples, which are typically used for
   _____
   _____

   (b) Situation exercises, which are typically used for _____
   _____

(c) Unstructured selection interviews are
_____

structured behavioral interviews are
_____

The structured interview should be based on
_____
_____

Organizational Behavior

Preview Questions
Consider the following questions as you study these sections of the chapter.

- What is the focus of organizational behavior (OB)?
- How is the *discrepancy hypothesis* defined, what three ideas does it consist of, and what other factors have been identified as very important job satisfaction aspects for employees?
- What is leadership, and how do the trait, behavioral, and situational (or contingency) theories explain leader effectiveness?
- What is the Blake and Mouton Managerial Grid, and what five leadership styles have been identified?
- What is the leader–member exchange model and what are the consequences of positive versus negative leader–member relationships?
- What other topics has leadership research focused on recently?

*Read the section "Organizational Behavior" and **write** your answers to the following:*

1. Organizational behavior focuses on _____
   _____
   _____

2. The discrepancy hypothesis consists of three ideas:
   (a) _____
   _____
   (b) _____
   _____
   (c) _____
   _____

3. Other factors that have been identified as contributing to job satisfaction are _____

_____

_____

_____

4. The trait approach to leader effectiveness is based on _____

_____

_____

5. Behavioral theories of leader effectiveness focus on _____

_____

_____

Blake and Mouton's Managerial Grid has two dimensions: _____

_____

_____

This grid identifies five different leadership styles:

(a) _____

(b) _____

(c) _____

(d) _____

(e) _____

6. Situational (contingency) theories of leader effectiveness focus on _____

_____

_____

7. The leader–member exchange model of leadership suggests _____

_____

_____

Positive leader–member relationships are characterized by _____

_____

_____

They have many benefits, including _____

_____

Negative leader–member relationships show

_____

They lead to _____

_____

8. More recently, leadership research has focused on topics such as _____

_____

_____

Workplace Trends and Issues
Preview Questions

Consider the following questions as you study this section of the chapter.

- What are the six major challenges that companies face, and what does the workforce of the future need to focus on?
- How are companies addressing four of these issues?
- What role will I/O psychologists play in the future?

Read the section "Workplace Trends and Issues" and **write** *your answers to the following:*

1. The Society for Human Resource Management (SHRM, 2007) has identified six challenges facing companies today:

(a) _____

_____

(b) _____

_____

(c) _____

_____

(d) _____

_____

(e) _____

_____

(f) _____

_____

2. To face these challenges, the workplace of the future is expected to become _____

_____

_____

3. The four challenges discussed in detail (and how they are being met) are:

(a) _____

_____

_____

(b) _____

_____

(c) _____

_____

(d) _____

_____

4. In the future, I/O psychologists will _____

_____

_____

Work Settings, Type of Training, Earnings and Employment Outlook

Preview Questions

Consider the following questions as you study this section of the chapter.

- What are the requirements for working in the field of I/O psychology, and what are the principal employment settings of I/O psychologists?

- What jobs and careers are open to people with bachelor's degrees, and what are the earning potential for those with doctorate and master's degrees?

*Read the section "Work Settings, Type of Training, Earnings and Employment Outlook" and **write** your answers to the following:*

1. The principal employment settings for I/O psychologists are _____

(a) _____

(b) _____

(c) _____

(d) _____

2. To work in the field of I/O psychology you require _____

_____

_____

3. In terms of qualifications, the majority of SIOP (Society for Industrial and Organizational Psychologists) members hold _____

_____

4. To obtain a doctorate degree requires _____

_____

It qualifies you for _____

_____

5. Most master's degree programs require _____

A master's degree qualifies you to _____

_____

_____

6. People with bachelor's degrees may find work as _____

_____

7. The 2006 SIOP survey indicated that the median salary for I/O psychologists with doctorate degrees was _____ ; for those with master's degrees the median salary was

_____ .

After you have carefully studied the preceding sections, complete the following exercises.

Concept Check

Read the following and write the correct term in the space provided.

1. Dr. Lomburg works in an area of industrial/organizational psychology that is primarily concerned with the "I" side of I/O. This side of I/O psychology is often called

_____ .

2. Rather than focusing on the impact of leaders on followers, Dr. Hagan's research is concerned with the interaction between supervisors and subordinates and in particular with the unique relationships between leaders and their followers. Dr. Hagan is interested in the

_____ of leader effectiveness.

3. Gertrude has just graduated with a Ph.D. in I/O psychology and is seeking employment. According to text Figure B.5 (Work Settings of I/O Psychologists), if she is like most I/O psychologists, she will work _____ .

4. When Laleet applied for job as a mechanic, he was given a test in which he had to take apart the car's gearbox and locate and fix an engine problem. Laleet has experienced a _____ personnel selection test.

5. The management style of Snape Corporation was assessed by an independent I/O psychology consulting firm. The report indicated that the company leaders were low on both the X and Y dimensions of the Managerial Grid (1,1). The management style of Snape Corporation would therefore be _____ .

6. Ursula's job at ABC Company is to determine the duties of particular positions and the personal characteristics that best match those duties. As part of her job, she interviews employees, observes them at work, and asks them to complete surveys regarding major job duties and tasks. Ursula is most likely employed as _____ .

7. While studying the history of I/O psychology, Pete discovered that _____ is considered by many to be the founding father of I/O psychology and that his book, *Psychology of Industrial Efficiency* (1913), was the field's first textbook.

8. To deal with some of the challenges facing companies today, Extra Dimension Electronics Company hired an industrial/organization psychologist. One aspect of his job is to focus on factors that contribute to a productive and healthy workforce such as perk-packages and employee-centered policies. This content area of I/O psychology is called _____ .

9. In his consulting practice, Dr. Moreno specializes in finding the most appropriate candidates for sensitive jobs, such as nuclear plant operators and airline pilots. The selection device most likely to be used for this purpose is a _____ test, which is designed to measure _____ .

10. Dr. Harrison is an I/O psychologist who conducts research on job satisfaction. He believes that job satisfaction results from the difference between what a person desires from a job and how that person evaluates what is actually experienced. Dr. Harrison's view of job satisfaction is most consistent with the _____ .

Review of Terms and Concepts

Use the terms in this list to complete the Matching Test, then to help you answer the True/False items correctly.

industrial/organizational (I/O) psychology
personnel psychology
organizational behavior
job analysis
selection and placement
training and development
performance management and evaluation
organizational development
leadership development
team building
quality of work life
ergonomics
selection device validity
integrity tests

cognitive ability tests
mechanical ability tests
motor ability tests
sensory ability tests
personality tests
structured behavioral interviews
discrepancy hypothesis
trait approach to leader effectiveness
behavioral theories of leader effectiveness
situational (contingency) theories of leadership
leader–member exchange model
work-life balance (work-family conflict)

Matching Exercise

Match the appropriate term with its definition or description.

1. _____ Technique that identifies the major responsibilities of a job and the human characteristics needed to fill it.

2. _____ Content area of I/O psychology that focuses on bringing about positive change in an organization, through the assessment of the organizational social environment and culture.

3. _____ Model of leadership emphasizing that the quality of the interactions between supervisors and subordinates varies depending on the unique characteristics of both.

4. _____ Branch of psychology that focuses on the study of human behavior in the workplace.

5. _____ Leadership theories claiming that various situational factors influence a leader's effectiveness.

6. _____ Approach to explaining job satisfaction that focuses on the discrepancy, if any, between what a person wants from a job and how that person evaluates what is actually experienced at work.

7. _____ Tests that measure fine dexterity in fingers and hands, accuracy and speed of arm and hand movement, as well as eye–hand coordination.

8. _____ Content area of I/O psychology that strives to identify the traits, behaviors, and skills that great leaders have in common.

9. _____ Tests that measure visual acuity, color vision, and hearing.

10. _____ Content area of I/O psychology that focuses on the development of assessment techniques to help select job applicants most likely to be successful in a given job or organization.

11. _____ Tests that measure mechanical reasoning and that may be used to predict job performance for engineering, carpentry, and assembly work.

12. _____ Content area of I/O psychology that focuses on designing customized training programs and evaluating the effectiveness of these programs.

13. _____ Content area of I/O psychology that is concerned with ways to improve companies' performance evaluation systems; it includes teaching managers how to collect evaluation data, how to avoid evaluation errors, and how to communicate the results.

True/False Test

Indicate whether each statement is true or false by placing T or F in the blank space next to each item.

1. ____ Personality tests are designed to measure either abnormal or normal personality traits and characteristics.

2. ____ Personnel psychology is a subarea of I/O psychology that focuses on the workplace culture and its influence on employee behavior.

3. ____ Behavioral theories of leader effectiveness focus on differences in the behaviors of effective and ineffective leaders.

4. ____ Ergonomics is a content area of I/O psychology that focuses on the design of equipment and the development of work procedures in accordance with human capabilities and limitations.

5. ____ Selection device validity is the extent to which a personnel selection device is successful in distinguishing between those who will become high performers at a certain job and those who will not.

6. ____ Quality of work life, one content area of I/O psychology, focuses on factors that contribute to a productive and healthy workforce, such as perk-packages and employee-centered policies.

7. ____ An approach to determining what makes an effective leader that focuses on the personal characteristics displayed by successful leaders is called the trait approach to leader effectiveness.

8. ____ Organizational behavior is a subarea of I/O psychology that focuses on matching people's characteristics to job requirements, accurately measuring job performance, and assessing employee training needs.

9. ____ Work-life balance is a challenge facing companies today and refers to the struggle of trying to juggle the demands of a career with the demands of one's family (also called work-family conflict).

10. ____ Team building is a content area of I/O psychology that focuses on team membership and successful team design.

11. ____ Integrity tests attempt to assess an applicant's level of honesty.

12. ____ Cognitive ability tests measure general intelligence or specific cognitive skills, such as mathematical or verbal ability.

13. ____ The structured behavioral interview is based on job analysis, prepared in advance, standardized for all applicants, and evaluated by a panel of interviewers trained to record and rate the applicant's responses using a numeric scale.

Check your answers and review any areas of weakness before completing the progress tests.

Progress Test 1

Review the complete appendix, review all your study notes, and then test yourself on the following progress test. Check your answers. If you make a mistake, review your notes, review the relevant section of the study guide, and, if necessary, go back and read the appropriate part of your textbook.

1. Dr. Garcia is an I/O psychologist who is concerned with developing assessment techniques to help select from a pool of job applicants those who are most likely to be successful in a given job or organization. Dr. Darton, on the other hand, focuses on identifying criteria or standards that determine the degree to which employees are performing their jobs well, accurately measuring their job performance, and honestly conveying performance results to these employees. Dr. Garcia works in the content area called _____ , and Dr. Darton works in _____ .
   (a) training and development; quality of work life
   (b) selection and placement; performance management and evaluation
   (c) ergonomics; organizational development
   (d) performance management and evaluation; ergonomics

2. Dr. Foggerty focuses on the design of equipment and the development of work procedures in accordance with human capabilities and limitations. Dr. Foggerty's area of interest is called
   (a) ergonomics.
   (b) personnel psychology.
   (c) performance management and evaluation.
   (d) organizational behavior.

3. When Kamal goes to graduate school, she plans to specialize in matching people's characteristics to job requirements, accurately measuring job performance, and assessing employee training needs. Kamal is interested in
   (a) personnel psychology.
   (b) organizational psychology.
   (c) organizational development.
   (d) ergonomics.

4. Helmut has a bachelor's degree and is interested in working in the field of I/O psychology. Which of the following statements about Helmut's prospects is true?
   (a) It will be very easy for him to find employment as an I/O psychologist, either at a university or as a consultant.
   (b) Some areas related to I/O, such as personnel, training, and labor relations specialists, are open to him.
   (c) There are no employment opportunities for people with bachelor's degrees in the field of I/O psychology.
   (d) His earning potential for work within the field of I/O psychology is $72,000 to $98,000.

5. Olivia's research focuses on how the organization and the social environment in which people work affect their attitudes and behaviors. Olivia works in a subarea of I/O psychology called
   (a) personnel psychology.
   (b) selection and placement.
   (c) ergonomics.
   (d) organizational behavior.

6. Gulbinder is the chief personnel officer for a large corporation. She is very concerned that the methods and techniques used in personnel selection are successful in distinguishing between applicants who will become high performers and those who will not. Gulbinder's concerns are related to
   (a) quality of work life.
   (b) ergonomics.
   (c) selection device validity.
   (d) organizational development.

7. Bradford believes that leaders are born, not made, and he cites many examples of people who possess certain qualities or characteristics that make them natural leaders. Bradford's views are most consistent with the
   (a) situational (or contingency) theories of leader effectiveness.
   (b) behavioral theories of leader effectiveness.
   (c) leader–member exchange model of leadership.
   (d) trait approach to leader effectiveness.

8. Surveys have shown that although most Americans report that they are satisfied with their jobs, they appear less satisfied with some aspects than with others. In order to explain differences in job satisfaction, researchers are likely to use an approach based on the
   (a) managerial grid concept of job satisfaction.
   (b) behavioral theory of job satisfaction.
   (c) contingency hypothesis of job satisfaction
   (d) discrepancy hypothesis of job satisfaction.

9. Mrs. Afyia uses a technique to determine the major responsibilities of a job and the personal characteristics needed to fill it. Her goal is to select appropriate people for a particular position. Mrs. Afyia is using a technique called
   (a) ergonomics.
   (b) job analysis.
   (c) selection device validity.
   (d) the managerial grid approach.

10. In Focus notes that some leaders take an employee-centered approach. They recognize and encourage emerging employee leaders and create organizational support for them to reach their potential. According to In Focus, this style of leadership exemplifies the _____ leader.
    (a) servant
    (b) team
    (c) transactional
    (d) charismatic

Progress Test 2

After you have checked your understanding of the material in Progress Test 1 and have done a complete chapter review with special focus on any areas of weakness, you are ready to assess your knowledge on Progress Test 2. Check your answers. If you make a mistake, review your notes, the relevant section of the study guide, and, if necessary, the appropriate part of your textbook.

1. Dr. Daviduk has just completed a report identifying major workplace trends and issues. Which of the following is not likely to appear in her report?
   (a) telecommuting or telework
   (b) Internet recruiting
   (c) workforce diversity
   (d) the issue of work–life balance
   (e) All of these issues are likely to be included in the report.

2. Before building their new factory, ABC Manufacturing Company hired an I/O psychologist to help in the design of new equipment, work procedures, and safety standards. This consultant is involved in which content area of I/O psychology?
   (a) quality of work life
   (b) ergonomics
   (c) organizational development
   (d) performance management and evaluation

3. In his research on leader effectiveness, Dr. Grether focuses on differences in the behavior of effective and ineffective leaders. Dr. Grether's work is most consistent with the _____ of leader effectiveness.
   (a) trait theories
   (b) behavioral theories
   (c) situational theories
   (d) leader–member exchange model

4. Lance wants to become an I/O psychologist but he is not sure what the future holds for this profession. Research on this topic is likely to reveal that
   (a) I/O psychologists will continue to have a significant impact on the workplace.
   (b) most I/O psychologists will become redundant in the near future due to technological advances.
   (c) increased diversity of the workforce, technological advances, and a global economy will mean a gradual decline in the need for I/O psychologists.
   (d) it will be extremely difficult for people with bachelor's degrees to find employment in the field of I/O psychology.

5. Mr. Wentworth wants to bring about positive change in his organization through assessment of the organizational social environment and culture. The content area of I/O psychology most concerned with this issue is
   (a) personnel psychology.
   (b) ergonomics.
   (c) organizational development.
   (d) performance management and evaluation.

6. Gladys believes that job satisfaction results from the difference between what a person wants from a job and how that person evaluates what is experienced. Gladys's view supports the _____ hypothesis of job satisfaction.
   (a) trait
   (b) behavioral
   (c) discrepancy
   (d) contingency

7. At a party, Justina was asked what she does for a living. She replied that she focuses on the study of human behavior in the workforce. Justina is most likely a(n)
   (a) behavioral psychologist.
   (b) social psychologist.
   (c) industrial/organizational psychologist.
   (d) clinical psychologist.

8. When asked to elaborate on the type of work she does as an I/O psychologist, Stacey said that she is primarily interested in research on factors that contribute to a productive and healthy workforce, such as perk-packages and employee-centered policies. Stacey works in the content area of I/O psychology called
   (a) quality of work life.
   (b) training and development.
   (c) selection and placement.
   (d) performance management and evaluation.

9. In her work, Dr. Tahler uses a variety of psychological tests that measure cognitive ability, mechanical aptitude, motor and sensory ability, and normal and abnormal personality traits. It is most likely that Dr. Tahler is a(n)
   (a) behavioral psychologist.
   (b) personnel psychologist.
   (c) organizational psychologist.
   (d) ergonomics psychologist.

10. In Focus discusses the way different generations of workers respond to feedback. Which one of the following people is most likely to respond to the issue of feedback with the statement "Once a year, with lots of documentation"?
   (a) Kerri who was born in 1985
   (b) Dwayne who was born in 1950
   (c) Polly who was born in 1944
   (d) Quentin who was born in 1970

Progress Test 3

After you have checked your understanding of the material in Progress Tests 1 and 2, and have done a complete chapter review with special focus on any areas of weakness, you are ready to further assess your knowledge with Progress Test 3. Check your answers. If you make a mistake, review your notes, the appropriate parts of the study guide, and if necessary, the relevant sections of your textbook.

1. The employees of a small but very successful company are committed people with a "common stake" in the company's goals. The owner, Harvey, encourages interdependence and is well respected and trusted by those who work for him. According to the managerial grid concept, which of the following leadership styles best describes Harvey?
   (a) country-club management
   (b) impoverished management
   (c) team management
   (d) organization man management

2. Researchers interested in leader effectiveness believe that the quality of the interactions among supervisors and subordinates varies depending on the unique characteristics of both. Their approach to the topic of leadership is most consistent with
   (a) the trait approach to leader effectiveness.
   (b) the leader–member exchange model.
   (c) the behavioral theories of leader effectiveness.
   (d) the situational (contingency) theories of leadership.

3. Gregory believes that a leader's effectiveness most likely results from a particular combination of personality characteristics, rather than from situational factors. Gregory's views are most consistent with _____ theories of leader effectiveness.
   (a) behavioral
   (b) contingency
   (c) team management
   (d) trait

4. Professor Kress focuses on the design of equipment and the development of work procedures in light of human capabilities and limitations. Professor Fergus focuses on bringing about positive change in organizations through the assessment of the organizational social environment and culture. Professor Kress works in an area of I/O called _____ , and Professor Fergus works in _____ .
   (a) ergonomics; organizational development
   (b) training and development; performance management
   (c) organizational development; ergonomics
   (d) performance management and evaluation; selection and placement

5. The personnel psychologist at El Gourdo Corporation uses a number of different psychological tests for employee selection purposes. Which of the following is he NOT likely to use in the selection process?
   (a) personality tests
   (b) cognitive ability tests
   (c) the polygraph test
   (d) mechanical, motor, and sensory ability tests

6. Zander Corporation is concerned about selecting the appropriate person for the job of production manager. Mrs. Juarez, the personnel manager, assesses and records the position's responsibilities and the personal characteristics required by the job. Mrs. Juarez is using a technique called
   (a) quality of work analysis.
   (b) job analysis.
   (c) ergonomic analysis.
   (d) discrepancy analysis.

7. In a report for the personnel department of Utopia Corporation, Dr. Raimundo makes recommendations regarding the validity and reliability of the company's various selection devices. Which of the following is Dr. Raimundo likely to suggest has the lowest validity?
   (a) work samples
   (b) unstructured selection interviews
   (c) psychological testing
   (d) situational exercises

8. The job application process as we know it today was influenced by advances in the field of mental testing and, in particular, by the contributions of _____ who founded the Psychological Corporation, one of the largest publishers of psychological tests.
   (a) Michael Scott
   (b) Robert Blake and Jane Mouton
   (c) Hugo Munsterberg
   (d) James McKeen Cattell

9. Hannalee is interested in improving the performance evaluation systems in her rapidly expanding company. She would like her managers to learn how to collect evaluation data, to avoid evaluation errors, and to effectively communicate the results. Hannalee should probably consult an I/O psychologist who specializes in a subarea called
   (a) leadership development.
   (b) ergonomics.
   (c) job analysis.
   (d) performance management and evaluation.

10. Mrs. Addersly is considered by most of her employees to be a servant leader. According to In Focus, her most prominent trait is likely to be her
    (a) conscientiousness.
    (b) humility.
    (c) efficiency.
    (d) sense of humor.

Answers

What Is Industrial/Organizational Psychology?

1. *Industrial/organizational psychology is* the branch of psychology that focuses on the study of human behavior in the workplace. *The "I" side of I/O psychology is called* personnel psychology *and is concerned with* matching human characteristics to job requirements, accurately measuring job performance, and assessing

employee training needs. *It helps companies attract, recruit, select, and train the best employees for the organization. The "O" side of I/O psychology is called* organizational behavior (OB) *and is concerned with* the workplace culture and its influence on employee behavior. *It helps companies* develop a culture that fulfills organizational goals while addressing employee needs and applies psychological findings to areas such as leadership development, team building, motivation, ethics training, and wellness planning.

2. *The nine content areas of I/O psychology (and the focus of each) are (a)* Job analysis, which focuses on matching personal characteristics with the duties of a particular position. *(b)* Selection and placement, which focuses on the development of assessment techniques to help select job applicants most likely to be successful in a given job or organization. *(c)* Training and development, which focuses on designing and evaluating customized training programs. *(d)* Performance management and evaluation is concerned with ways to improve a company's performance evaluation system. *(e)* Organizational development, whose goal is to bring about positive change in an organization. *(f)* Leadership development, which strives to identify the traits, behaviors, and skills of great leaders. *(g)* Team building, which focuses on team membership and successful team design. *(h)* Quality of work life, which focuses on factors that contribute to a productive and healthy workforce. *(i)* Ergonomics, which focuses on the design of equipment and the development of work procedures based on human capabilities and limitations.

3. *Wundt's first research assistant was* James McKeen Cattell *and his contributions to I/O psychology were* the concept of mental testing, which influenced the job application process as we know it today, and founding the Psychological Corporation, one of the largest publishers of psychological tests. *Another one of Wundt's students was* Hugo Munsterberg, *and he is considered by many to be* the founding father of I/O psychology. *His book, Psychology of Industrial Efficiency* (1913) *was* the field's first textbook.

Personnel Psychology

1. *The three major goals of personnel psychologists are (a)* selecting the best applicants for jobs, *(b)* training employees so that they perform their jobs effectively, and *(c)* accurately evaluating employee performance.

2. *Job analysis is a technique in which* the major responsibilities of a job, along with the human characteristics needed to fill it, are determined. Information about the job is usually collected from employees who currently hold the job or from their supervisors and this may be done through interviews, observations, or surveys. *It is also important for designing* effective training programs that integrate job analysis data with organizational goals. To maximize success, modern training programs should include collaborative and on-demand delivery methods, such as e-learning, virtual classrooms, and podcasts and training objectives should be linked to performance measures for best results. *Finally, it is useful in designing* performance appraisal systems where job competencies are clarified in order that performance appraisal instruments can be developed and training results assessed. This process helps managers make their expectations and ratings clear and easier for the employees to understand.

3. *Selection device validity refers to* the extent to which a selection device is successful in distinguishing between those applicants who will become high performers at a certain job and those who will not.

4. *The six most common psychological tests are (a)* Integrity tests *(b)* Cognitive ability tests *(c)* Mechanical ability tests *(d)* Motor ability tests *(e)* Sensory ability tests *(f)* Personality tests. *Assessment of abnormal personality characteristics might be appropriate for* selecting people for sensitive jobs, such as nuclear plant operator, police officer, and airline pilot. *More common for the selection of employees* are tests designed to measure the Big Five personality traits.

5. *The three most common types of personnel selection devices are (a) Work samples, which are typically used for* positions involving the manipulation of objects. *(b) Situational exercises, which are typically used for* jobs involving managerial or professional skills. *(c) Unstructured selection interviews are* subjective, outdated, and non-research based; nevertheless, they continue to be used (40 percent of companies responding to the SHRM survey used them). *Structured behavioral interviews are* adequate

predictors of job performance if they are developed and conducted properly. *The structured behavioral interview should be based on* job analysis, prepared in advance, standardized for all applicants, and evaluated by a panel of interviewers trained to record and rate the applicant's responses using a numeric scale.

Organizational Behavior

1. *Organizational behavior focuses on* how the organization and the social environment in which people work affect their attitudes (especially regarding job satisfaction) and behaviors.

2. *The discrepancy hypothesis consists of three ideas (a)* that people differ in what they want from a job; *(b)* that people differ in how they evaluate what they experience at work; and *(c)* that job satisfaction is based on the difference between what is desired and what is experienced.

3. *Other factors that have been identified as contributing to job satisfaction are* compensation, benefits, job security, work/life balance, and communication between employees and senior management.

4. *The trait approach to leader effectiveness is based on* the idea that leaders are born, not made, and focuses on the personal characteristics displayed by successful leaders.

5. *Behavioral theories of leader effectiveness focus on* differences in the behaviors of effective and ineffective leaders. *Blake and Mouton's Managerial Grid has two dimensions:* concern for production (X axis) and concern for people (Y axis), each having a 1 (low) to 9 (high) scale. *The grid identifies five different leadership styles: (a)* country-club management (1,9), *(b)* impoverished management (1,1), *(c)* team management (9,9), *(d)* authority obedience (9,1), and *(e)* organization man management (5,5).

6. *Situational (contingency) theories of leader effectiveness focus on* how a particular situation influences a leader's effectiveness.

7. *The leader–member exchange model of leadership suggests* that the quality of the interactions between supervisors and subordinates varies depending on the unique characteristics of both. *Positive leader–member relationships are characterized by* mutual trust, respect, and liking. *They have many benefits, including* higher job satisfaction, goal commitment, improved work climate, and lower turnover rates. *Negative leader–member relationships show* a lack of trust, respect, and liking. *They lead to* decreased job satisfaction and job performance, among other consequences.

8. *More recently, leadership research has focused on topics such as* transformational versus transactional leadership, charismatic leadership, shared leadership, and servant leadership.

Workplace Trends and Issues

1. *The Society for Human Resource Management (SHRM, 2007) has identified six challenges facing companies today:*
   (a) succession planning (replacement of retiring leaders)
   (b) recruitment and selection of talented employees
   (c) engaging and retaining talented employees
   (d) providing leaders with the skills to be successful
   (e) rising health care costs
   (f) creating/maintaining a performance-based culture (rewarding exceptional job performance)

2. *To face these challenges, the workplace of the future is expected to become* more dynamic, diversified, flexible, and responsive, with a need for organizations and employees to adapt to the ever-changing world of work, complete with resource limitations and technological innovations.

3. *The four challenges discussed in detail (and how they are being met) are*
   (a) The challenge of workforce diversity (recruiting and retaining diverse talent) has been addressed by creating perk-packages, offering telecommuting, and other benefits, such as compressed workweeks, on-site gyms, and on-site child care.
   (b) The challenge of telework and telecommuting is being met by companies offering more telework options to employees (up from 30 percent in 2007 to 42 percent in 2008). Research has shown that telecommuting has predominately positive effects for both employees and employers, including higher job satisfaction, employee morale, autonomy, and improved supervisor–employee relations.
   (c) Internet recruiting (using the Web to recruit top talent) has changed the way in which employees are recruited: Research has found that 73 percent of job seekers used the Internet to find information about prospective employers, to post résumés on job boards, and to gain career advice. This has posed new challenges for employers, such as compliance with new

legal requirements for online applicant tracking, or simply how to narrow down the large number of résumé submissions.

(d) The work/life balance (engaging and retaining employees with families) challenge is not been met very successfully; paid maternity leave, paid sick days, alternative work schedules, and other family-friendly polices are lacking in many U.S. companies. More employers must begin to adopt family-friendly policies and build pro-family cultures to attract and retain this large sector of the workforce.

4. *In the future, I/O psychologists will continue* to have a significant role in the workplace, and in order to keep pace with the changing needs of employees and rapid technological advances, I/O psychologists will constantly need to adjust the focus of their research and its applications to improve the experiences of people at work.

Work Settings, Type of Training, Earnings and Employment Outlook

1. *The principal employment settings for I/O psychologists are (a)* academic settings, primarily universities and colleges, *(b)* consulting for organizations, (c) working in private organizations, *(d)* working for public organizations.

2. *To work in the field of I/O psychology you require* a doctorate (Ph.D.) or master's degree (M.A.) (some areas that are closely related to I/O are open to those with bachelor's degrees).

3. *In terms of qualifications, the majority of SIOP (Society for Industrial and Organizational Psychologists) members hold* doctorate degrees (87 percent) as opposed to master's degrees (13 percent).

4. *To obtain a doctorate degree requires* attending graduate school full time for 5 to 6 years, conducting a detailed research project, and writing a dissertation. *It qualifies you for* I/O positions at major corporations, research and teaching positions at universities and colleges, and it provides the most credibility to conduct consulting work.

5. *Most master's degree programs require* 2 to 3 years of graduate coursework and the completion of a research project. *A master's degree qualifies you to* work as an I/O psychologist carrying out I/O duties for private or public organizations, teach at two-year colleges, and take on consulting work.

6. *People with bachelor's degrees may find work as* personnel, training, and labor-relations specialists, and as managers and employment interviewers.

7. *The 2006 SIOP survey indicated that the median salary for I/O psychologists with doctorate degrees was $98,500; for those with master's degrees the median salary was $72,000.*

Concept Check 1

1. personnel psychology
2. leader–member exchange model
3. in an academic setting (college or university)
4. work sample
5. impoverished management
6. a job analyst
7. Hugo Munsterberg
8. quality of work life
9. personality; either abnormal or normal personality characteristics.
10. discrepancy hypothesis

Matching Exercise

1. job analysis
2. organizational development
3. leader–member exchange model
4. industrial/organizational (I/O) psychology
5. situational (or contingency) theories of leader effectiveness
6. discrepancy hypothesis
7. motor ability tests
8. leadership development
9. sensory ability tests
10. selection and placement
11. mechanical ability tests
12. training and development
13. performance management and evaluation

True/False Test

1. T	6. T	11. T
2. F	7. T	12. T
3. T	8. F	13. T
4. T	9. T	
5. T	10. T	

Progress Test 1

1. b	5. d	9. b
2. a	6. c	10. a
3. a	7. d	
4. b	8. d	

Progress Test 2

1. e	5. c	9. b
2. b	6. c	10. b
3. b	7. c	
4. a	8. a	

Progress Test 3

1. d	5. c	9. d
2. b	6. b	10. b
3. d	7. b	
4. a	8. d